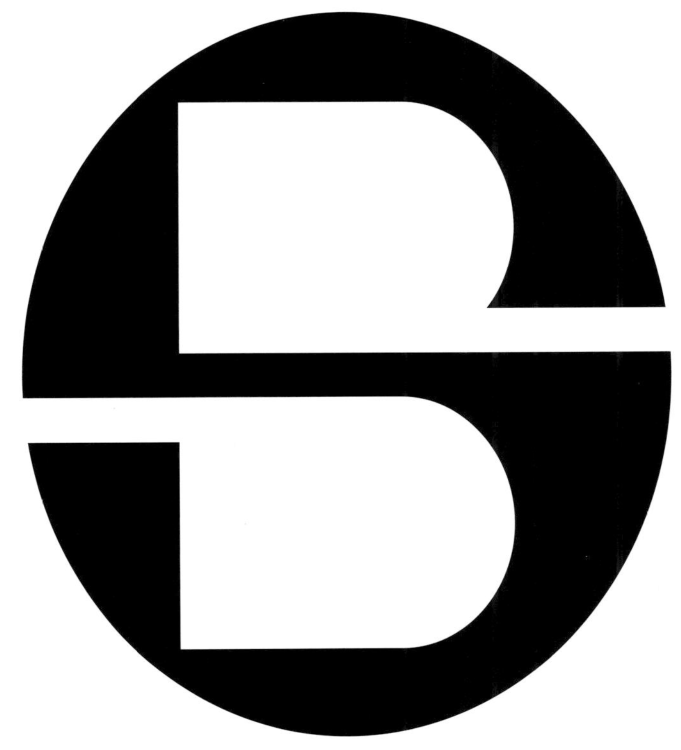

SEEING BLACK

Black Photography In New Orleans 1840 & Beyond

Shana M. griffin | Kalamu ya Salaam | Eric Waters

SEEING BLACK Black Photography in New Orleans 1840 & Beyond

Design & Layout by Lidya Araya for Vizual I Alex Dimeff for UNO Press

ISBN: 978-1-60801-302-9

SEEING BLACK: Black Photography in New Orleans 1840 & Beyond has been made possible in part by a major grant from the National Endowment for the Humanities: Democracy demands wisdom.

Any views, findings, conclusions, or recommendations expressed in this book do not necessarily represent those of the National Endowment for the Humanities.

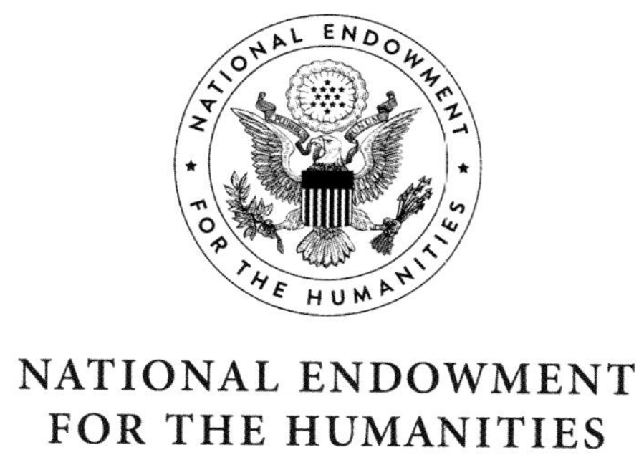

NATIONAL ENDOWMENT
FOR THE HUMANITIES

THE UNIVERSITY OF NEW ORLEANS PRESS

SEEING BLACK

Black Photography In New Orleans 1840 & Beyond

Shana M. griffin | Kalamu ya Salaam | Eric Waters

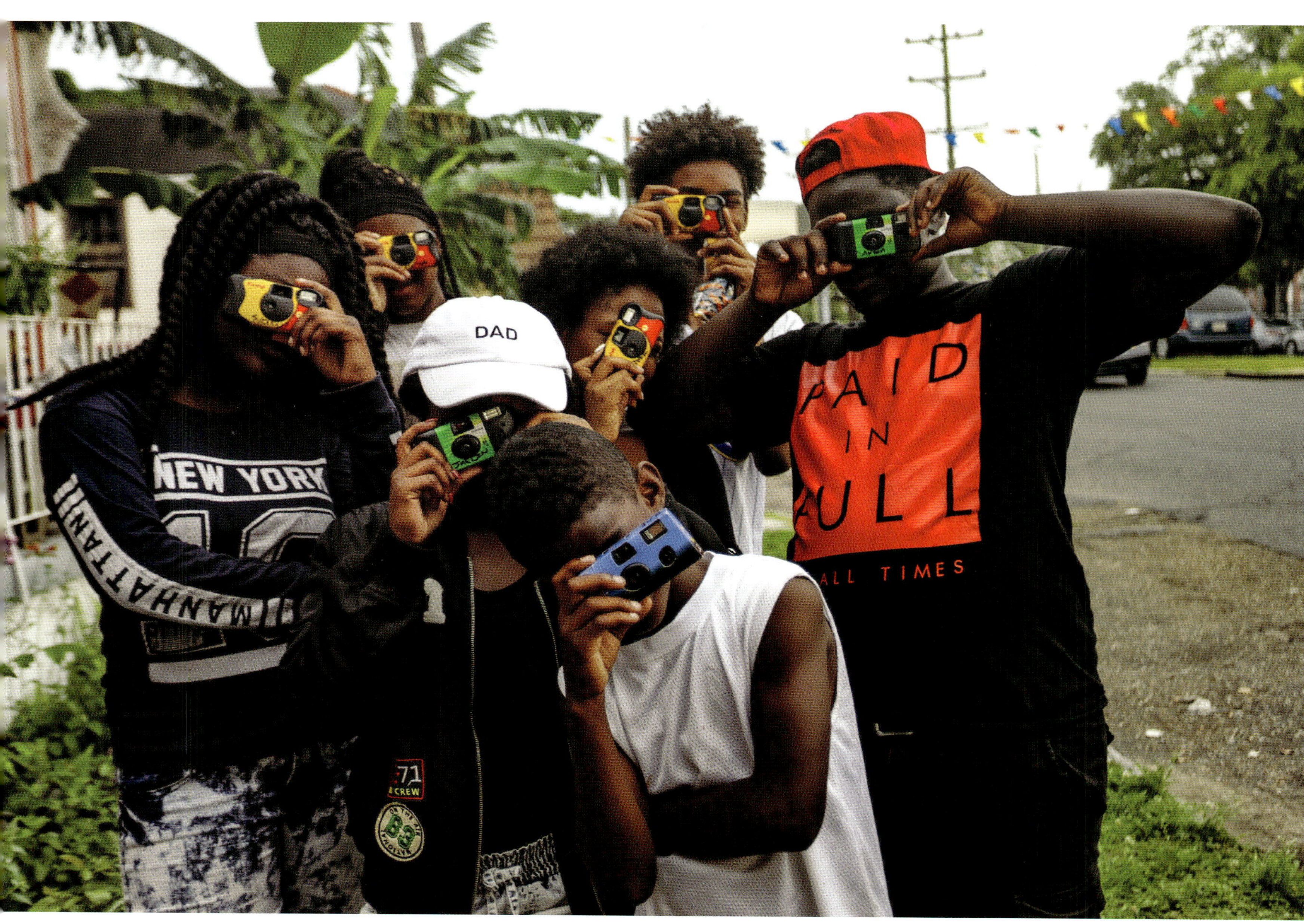

"Proof of Our Exposure," 2017. Photo: Christine "Cfreedom" Brown. Courtesy of the Artist.

"I have said that man is a picture-making and a picture-appreciating animal and have pointed out that fact as an important line of distinction between man and all other animals."

— Frederick Douglass
"Lecture On Pictures," 1861

"I am unapologetically enthralled by the everyday photographs created by Black communities. Photographs speak in unique ways to our circumstances."

— Tina M. Campt
A Black Gaze: Artists Changing How We See, 2023

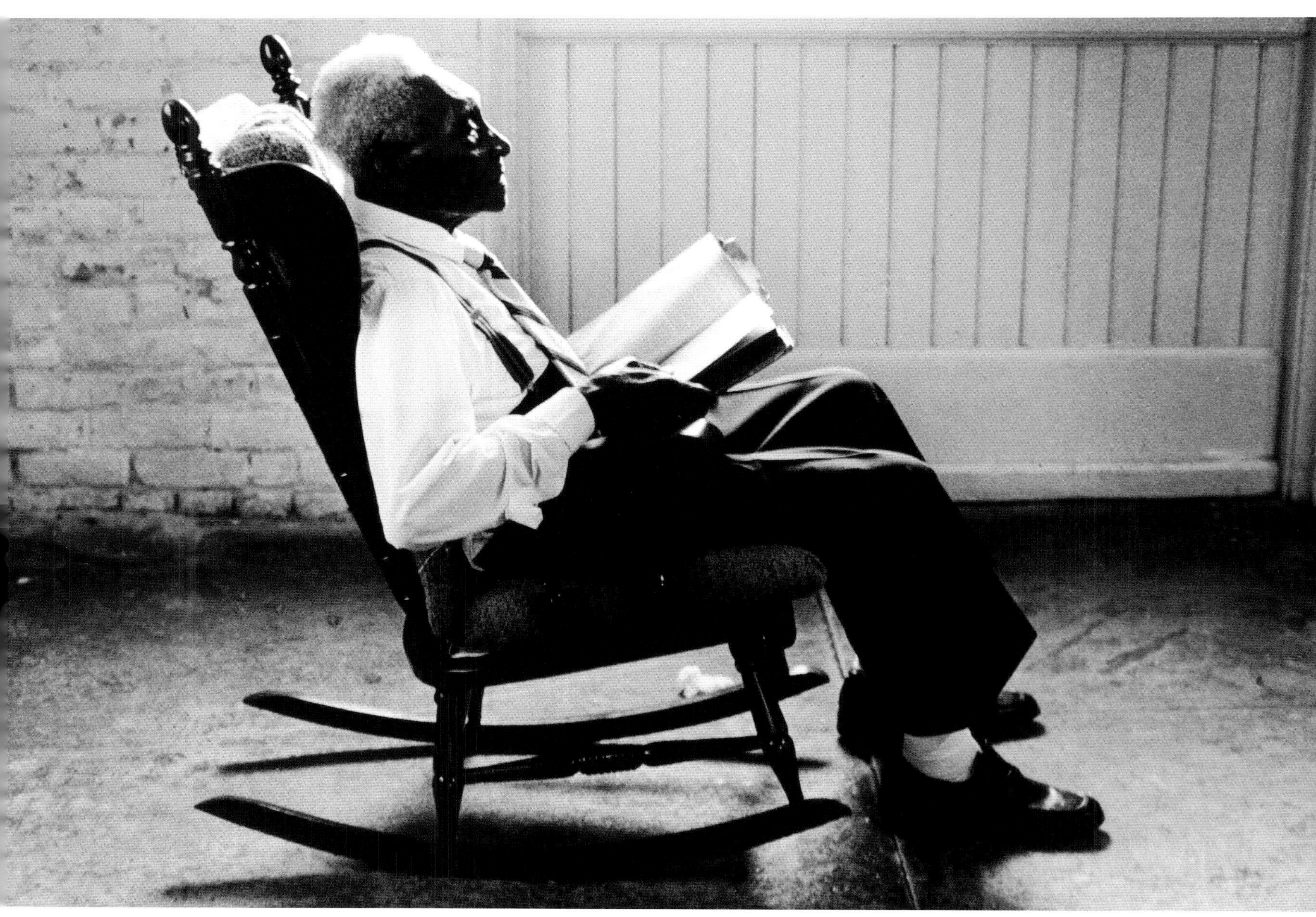

"Reverend Brown, Lower 9th Ward," 1980. Photo: Keith Calhoun. Courtesy of the Artist.

CONTENTS

ESSAYS

END MATTER

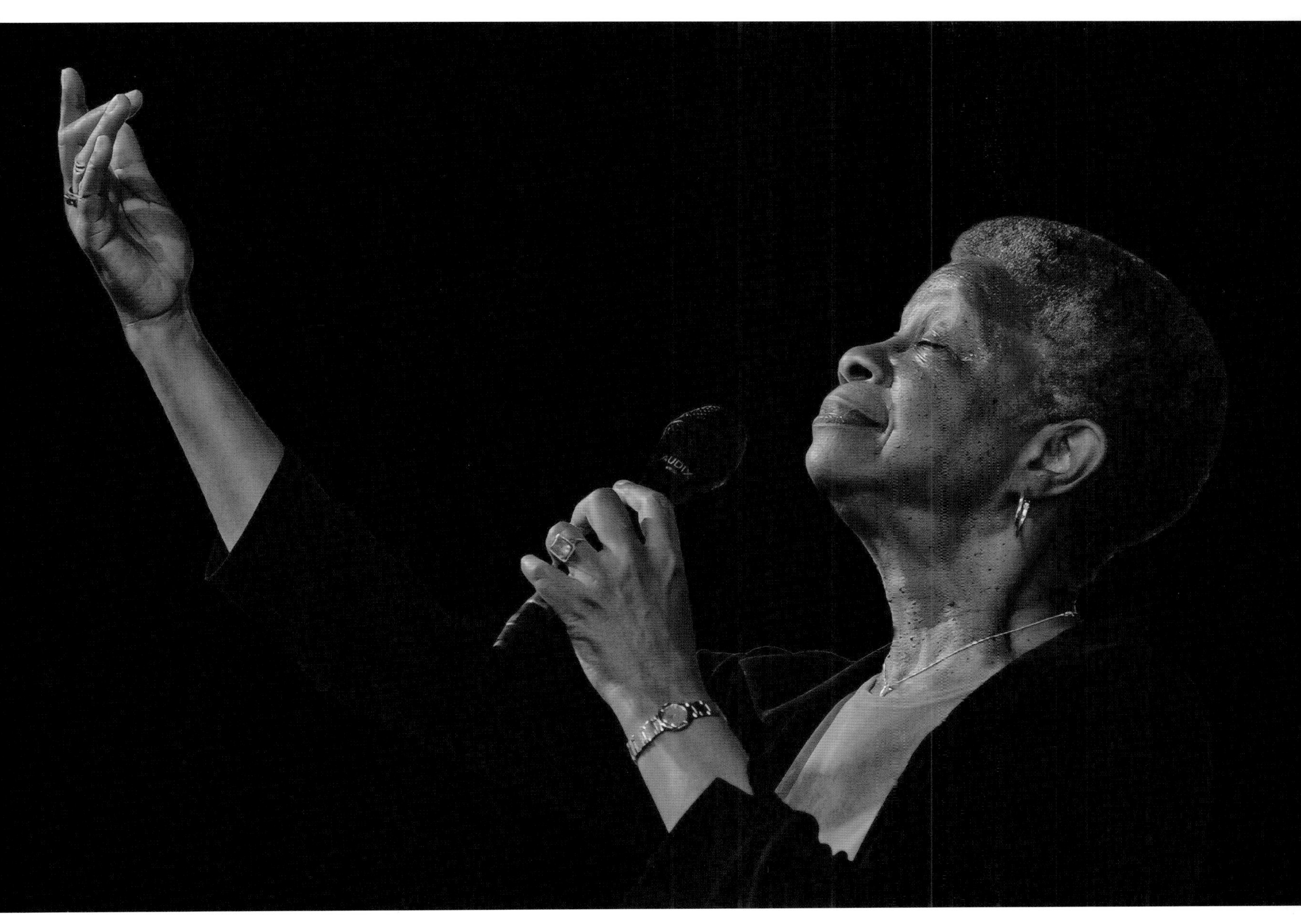

"Germaine Bazzle," 2006. Photo: Eric Waters. Courtesy of the Artist.

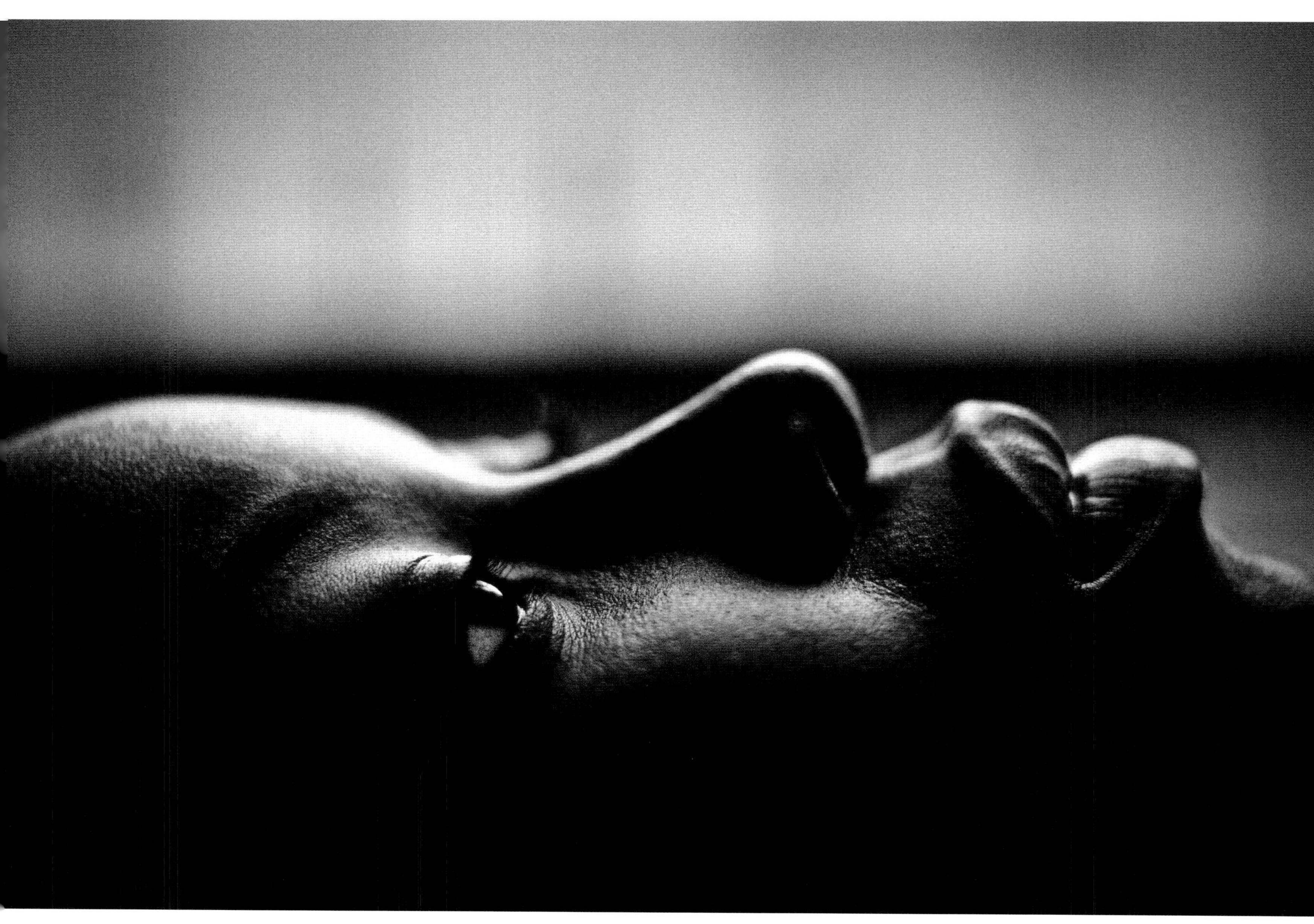

"Things Are Looking Up," 2011. Photo: Saddi Khali. Courtesy of the Artist.

The Origins of

SEEING BLACK

The Origins of *SEEING BLACK*

Kalamu ya Salaam

I woke up one morning with an idea: put together a team to produce a major book on photography in New Orleans.

I have made my mark as a writer and activist. I got into writing as a result of my English teacher, Mrs. O. E. Nelson, turning me on to Langston Hughes during my eighth grade year at Rivers Frederick Junior High School in New Orleans. She said, "Put your books away, I want you to hear something." On a small portable record player, she dropped a recording of Langston Hughes reciting poetry accompanied by a jazz band. That was the moment when I began a life long dedication to writing.

Earlier in my education, however, I had been taught photography by my seventh grade industrial arts teacher, Mr. Conrad. He had converted a closet into a darkroom and taught photography after school. I was enthralled and soon was known as "the picture man" to my classmates.

I describe my half-century long creative writing career as simply an extension of adolescent dreams: I kissed photography but I married writing.

I have owned a camera (my first was a Yashica twin-lens reflex) all my life since that introduction and not withstanding that my adult life has revolved around creative writing and activism, I have never entirely abandoned photography, which eventually included making movies (check out my online presence as a cinematographer at kalamu.com). Hence, I was not totally surprised that I had a dream: do a major book on photography.

I called on Eric Waters, who is a professional photographer whom I first met as my high school classmate in 1961 at Saint Augustine High School. I next called on another professional photographer Girard Mouton,III. The fourth member of our team was Shana M. griffin, whom I knew through her work as an activist and organizer.

That was the core group who constituted the project SEEING BLACK. Although I didn't know the history when I initially had the idea, I've learned that photography was introduced into the United States immediately after its 1839 founding in France. Professional painter and lithographer Jules Lion, who was born in France but domiciled in New Orleans, held an 1840 display of his daguerreotypes, the first documented exhibition of photography in Louisiana, approximately three or four months after an exhibition was held in New York City.

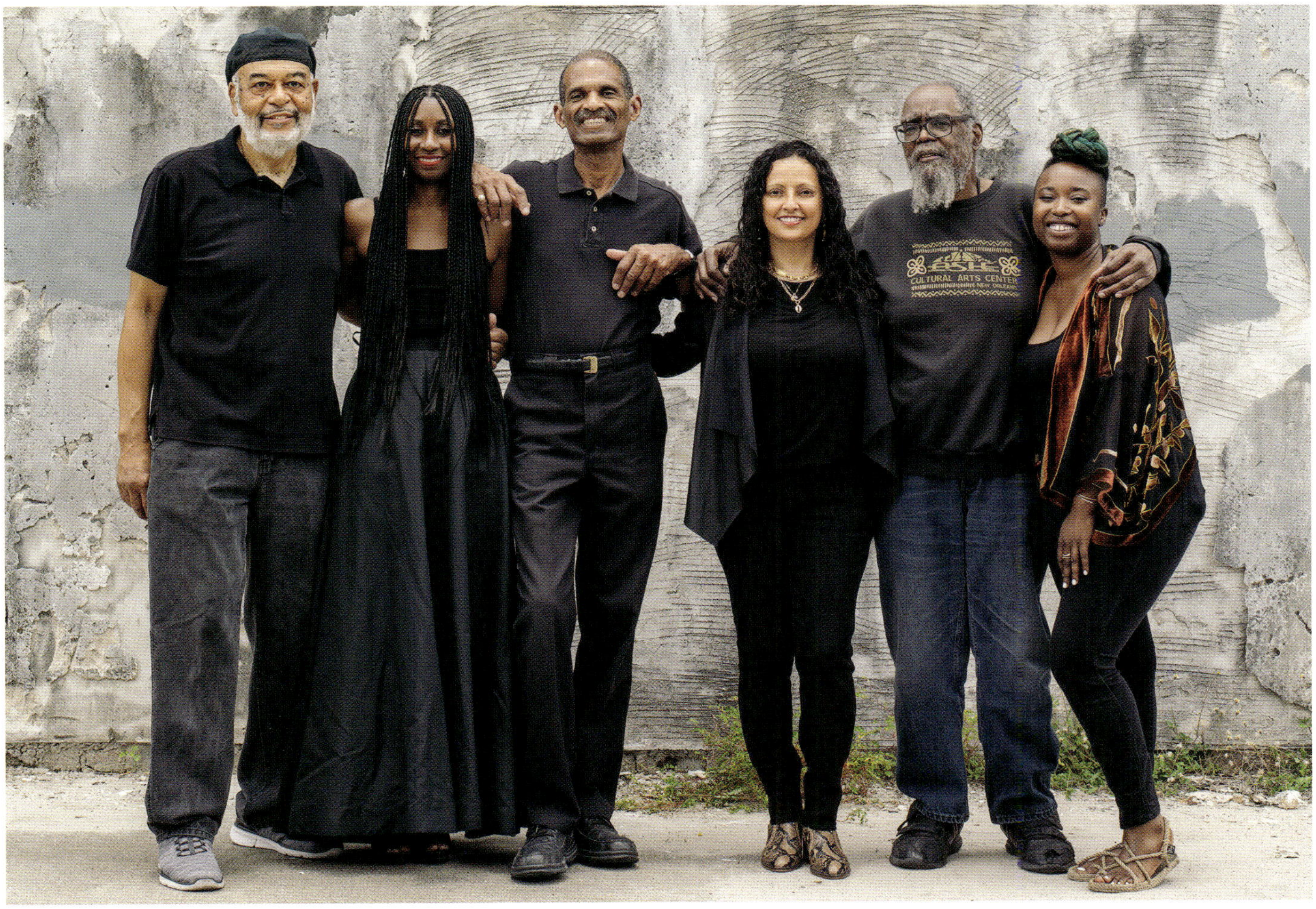

Left to right: Eric Waters, Shana M. griffin, Girard Mouton,III, Lidya Araya, Kalamu ya Salaam, and Renee Royale, 2023. New Orleans. Photo: Eric Waters. Courtesy of the Artist.

Eric Waters and Girard Mouton,III both deepened and broadened my appreciation of photography as an art form but, more than that, they had a working knowledge of photographers in New Orleans.

Shana M. griffin is an expert researcher and curator, among many things. She took the lead in mounting major exhibitions at the New Orleans African American Museum in the historic Tremé section of New Orleans, and at Ashé Cultural Arts Center and Ashé Powerhouse Theater on Oretha Castle Haley Blvd., culminating in a two-story exhibition at the Contemporary Arts Center, New Orleans in the Warehouse/Arts District. Artist and writer Renee Royale served as an assistant to Shana M. griffin. Lidya Araya took on the task of designing both the logo and the SEEING BLACK book.

Although widely celebrated for food and music, and to a lesser extent for early architecture in the United States, New Orleans also has a long history of photography. However, few people know about photography beginning in New Orleans in 1840 and even fewer think of our city as a major focus of photography.

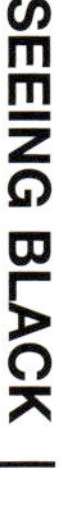

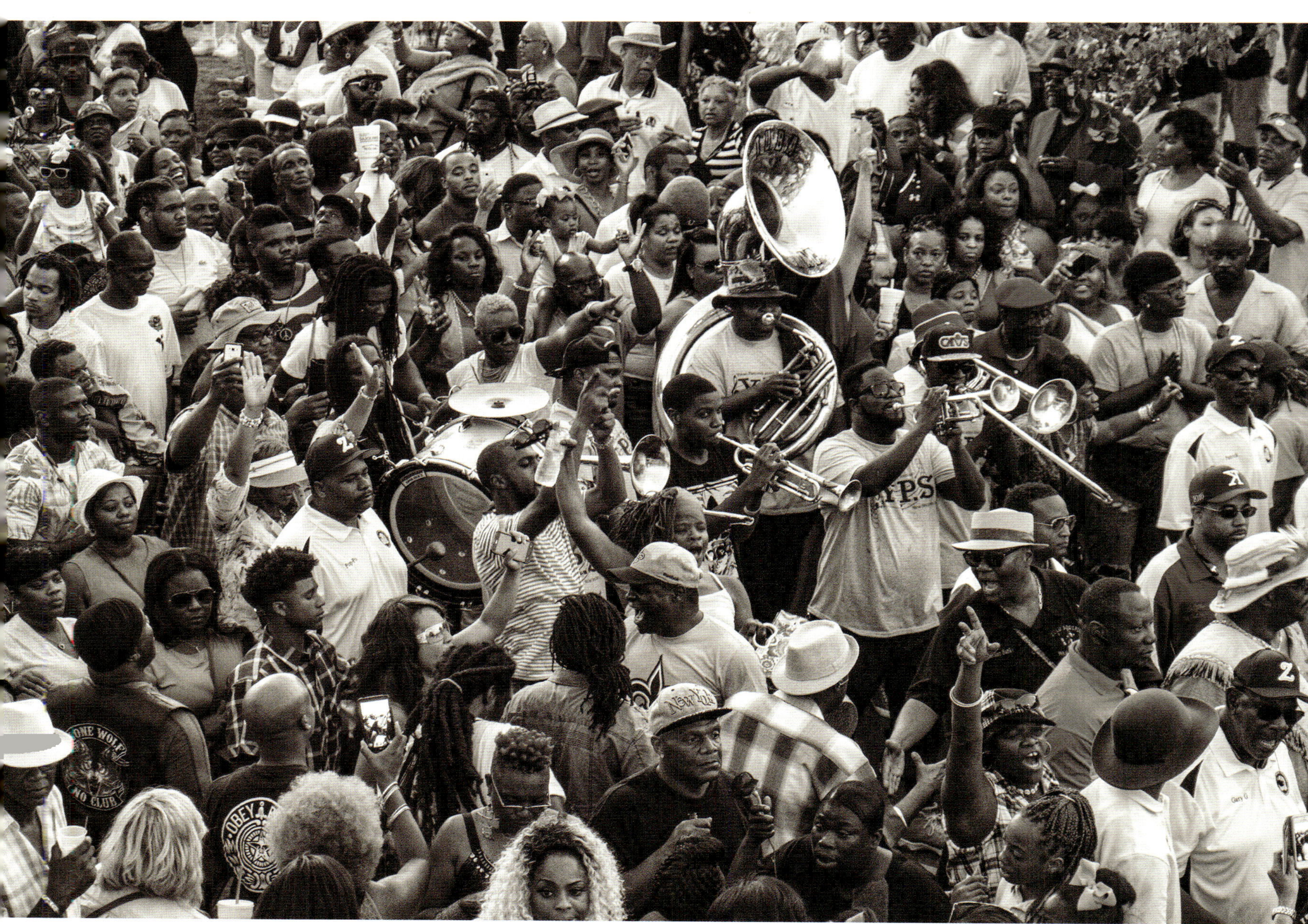

"Sunday in the 504," 2016. Photo: Tod Smith. Courtesy of the Artist.

Race Men, Race Women

VISUAL CULTURE THAT SPEAKS TO THE STREETS

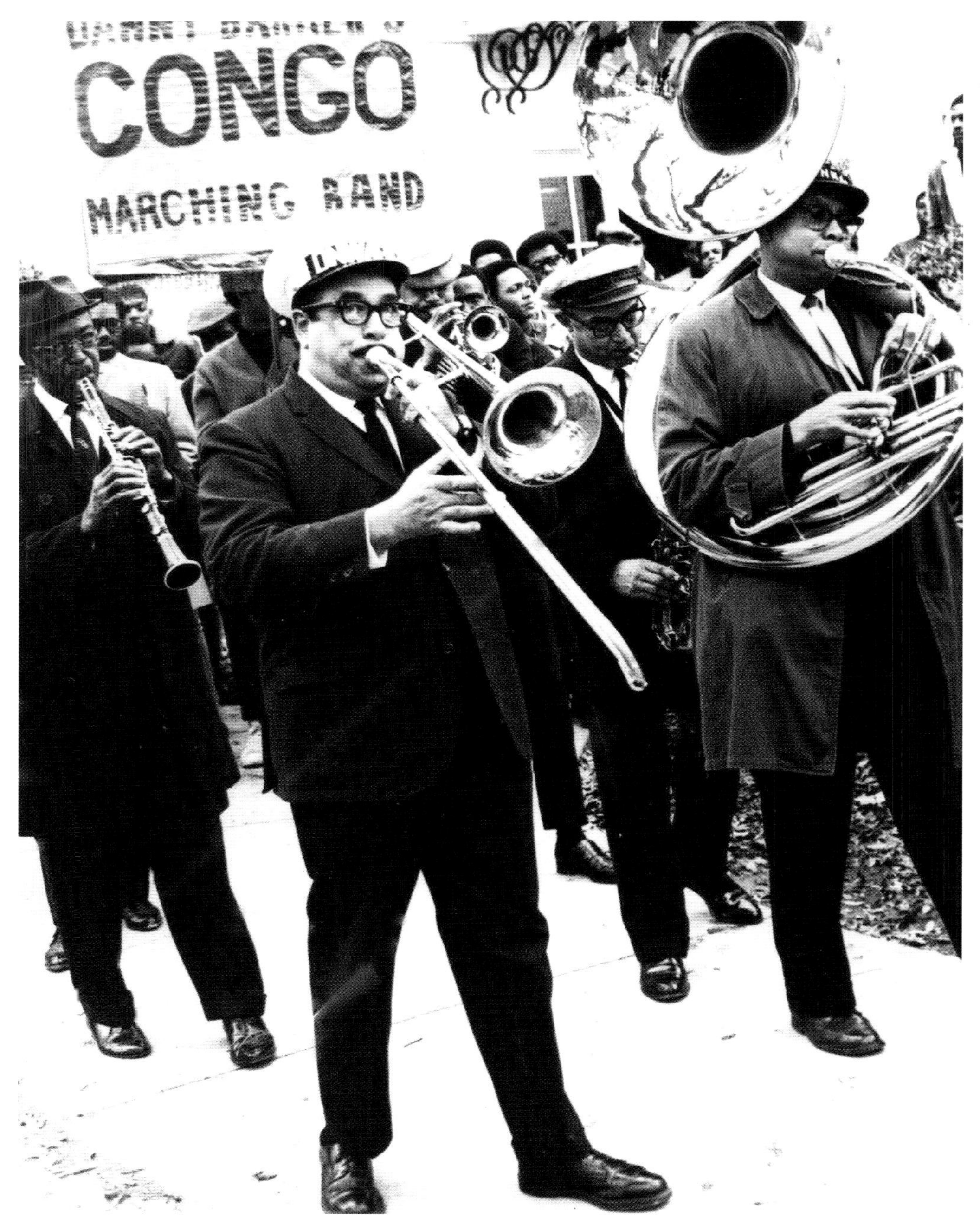

"Onward Brass Band," 1968. Photo: Sekou Fela. Courtesy of the Artist.

Race Men, Race Women

Visual Culture That Speaks to the Streets

Joyce Marie Jackson

As a native New Orleanian, growing up in Baton Rouge, I loved both Mississippi River cities. Early on I noticed a difference in my New Orleans relatives and my Baton Rouge relatives. Like my New Orleans relatives, I had a love for music, food, people and a joie de vivre imparted to me at an early age as if by osmosis. New Orleans is a very unique place and as a child and adult I returned as much as possible and had several extended yearly stays. The Crescent City is mystical, often maligned, bizarre, revolutionary, celebratory, complicated, backwards, forward, and quite unlike any other American city. The photographers featured in *Seeing Black: Black Photography in New Orleans 1840 & Beyond* capture all of this amalgam of flavors. Although most have not received the recognition they deserve, some have attained a measure of renown in their lifetime, both in New Orleans and other cities.

New Orleans has been home to a vibrant and diverse community of photographers throughout its history. Among them, Black photographers have made significant contributions to the field of photography, documenting the city's rich culture and history from their unique perspectives. In this book, we will explore the work of Black photographers in New Orleans, highlighting them and their influence on the city's visual culture.

Seeing Black is more than an eclectic collection of photographs from bygone and current days. It is a visual and subjective interpretation of a particular period of time in New Orleans history. In one sense the collection may appear as a random assemblage, in another it constitutes a partial cultural inventory, a clue to aesthetics, attitudes, and values and to the range of contrasts a people can embody. The collection is also important because many vintage images of African Americans have been irretrievably lost in various environmental and man-made disasters including Hurricanes Betsy and Katrina. This collection cannot make up for what has been lost but makes accessible the rich and varied glimpses of people and places past and present. Obviously, the photographs do not present a total picture of a culture, but they do provide intriguing clues and the possibility for insight for years to come.

Another reason why this work is so important is because not only this generation, but future generations will be enriched by the knowledge and experience of the photographers in this collection, each one unique, yet all united by a common struggle and culture. Many of the artists have shared history and traditions that shape their works and their ability to navigate certain arenas—public, academic, critical, popular, commercial, local, national, and international—in which they operate.

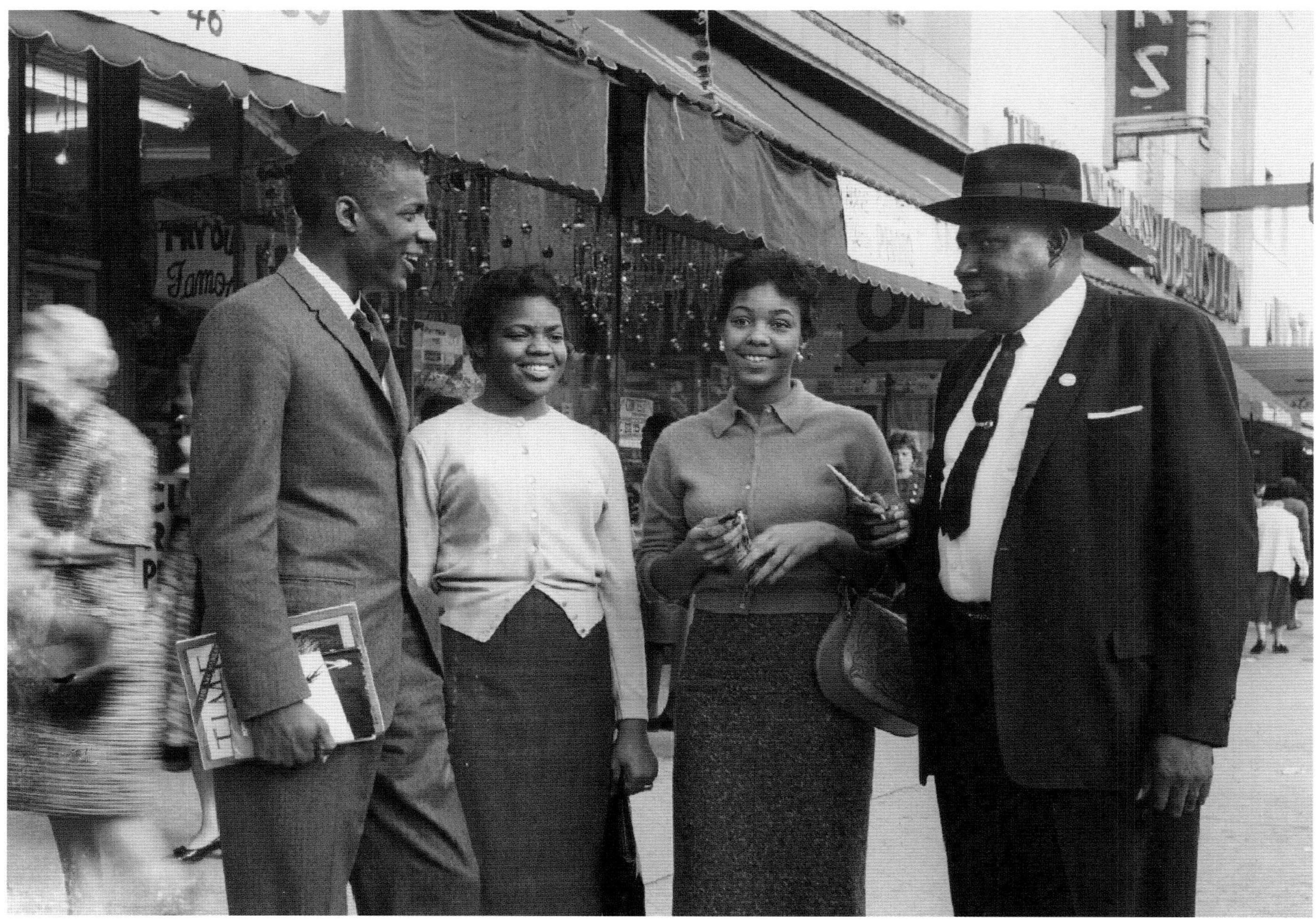

Left to right: Jerome Smith, Julie Aaron, Doris Jean Castle, and Reverend Avery Alexander, ca. 1960–1964. Canal Street, New Orleans. Photo: Marion J. Porter. Courtesy of The City Archives & Special Collections, New Orleans Public Library.

Lastly, this book and subsequent exhibitions are so significant because they will stimulate interest in the larger subject of African American photography, which remains underrepresented and not well known. For while there is no one monolithic African American photography, within the work of individual artists one finds the embodiment of what it means to be an African American, in all its complexity and distinctions. Whether one sees the prevalence of legendary musical faces, bands and instruments with amazing silhouettes in J. R. Thomason's work or the haunting, but beautiful portraits of Jourdan Barnes or the historical and political themes of Sekou Fela and Sorena Briley, they all have something to tell us about influences, opportunities, training, and visions of a specific photographer. Each of them has a distinctive voice and a unique set of experiences that led them into photography as a profession or pastime. They possess a common vision of the significance of photography in African American community life, a vision articulated by the images they share.

In order to understand the context of this work, it is important to briefly speak of some of the photographers and their work—and I interchange the words photographer and artist as they are one and the same. The medium was invented by 19th-century artists for their own purposes. These artists were searching for a lasting visual record of themselves and their environment and they found it. However, other artists were not so pleased with this discovery and did not see such a scientific (chemical) means of capturing a visual record as art. This dissent aside, a new art form had been found, and thus a new mode of expression and communication that was immediate, literal, and an expression of reality.

This new medium of expression and communication was used readily for activism and, combined with art, quickly had a heavy role to play in cultural expressions, revolutionary struggles, black political empowerment and social justice issues. Many African American photographer-activists wore both hats.

In New Orleans as in other areas of the South, the Black Arts Movement was shaped by the region's large population of historically Black colleges and universities. New Orleans alone has three. It was the students enrolled at these schools who took on leadership positions in the civil rights struggle through involvement in SNCC and CORE. The Black Power Movement and Black Arts Movement coalesced due to the artists (mostly literary and visual) also being activists. Their artistic and political grassroots circuits were often the same. The photographers were chronicling both movements and often making special efforts to be at sites of contention. In New Orleans the grassroots cultural work was led by BLKARTSOUTH, founded by Tom Dent and Kalamu ya Salaam (Val Ferdinand), both playwrights. The majority of the group members were living in New Orleans and were also involved in practical political work in addition to touring and performing theatrical and poetic works. Photographers also chronicled this work.

One of the most prominent Black photographers in New Orleans was Arthur Paul Bedou. Born in New Orleans in 1882, Bedou became a prolific photographer, capturing the daily life of the city's African American community. His photographs were often published in newspapers, including *The New Orleans Tribune* and *The Louisiana Weekly*, the city's Black newspapers and *The Times-Picayune*, the city's daily paper. Bedou's images documented everything from jazz funerals to Black Masking Indians, providing a rare glimpse into the cultural practices of New Orleans' Black community. He also captured the images of countless "race men,"[1] including Booker T. Washington, Marcus Garvey, Walter Cohen, and Emmett Scott.

In a recent conversation I had with A. P. Tureaud Jr. while viewing family images from his collection, Tureaud recalled some memories of Bedou:

> I have many original family portraits taken by Bedou. Copies are at Amistad. I remember him as a very serious man who was totally committed to his art–photography. He had the classic box camera on a tripod which he covered with a large black cloth and got under it to do the shoot. He gave

1 Race men or race women are loyal members of the Black community who dedicate their lives to directly contributing to the betterment of Black people. As defined by Assata Shakur, race men and race women remain confrontational with the ideas, people, institutions, and/or nations that threaten the well-being of Black people.

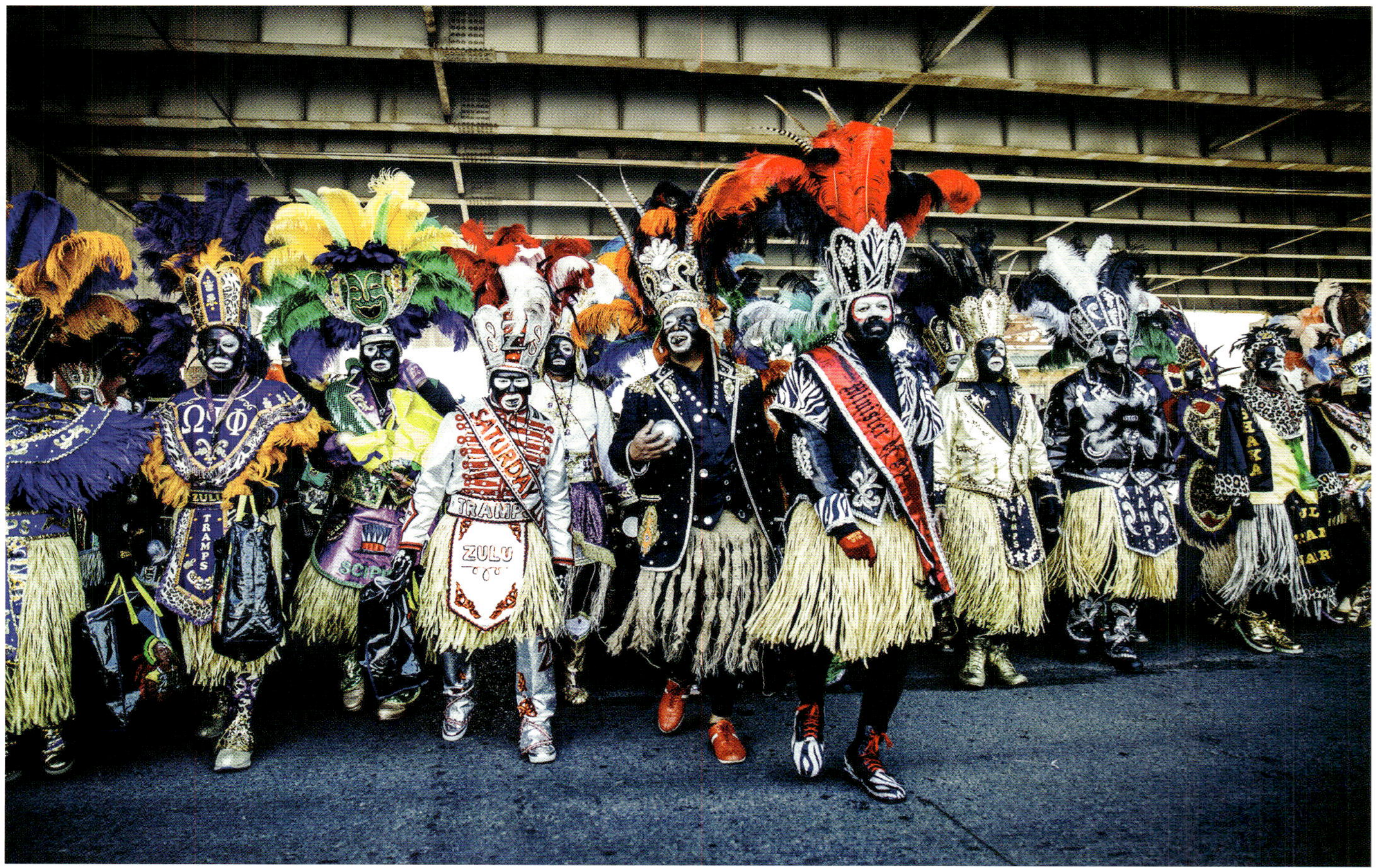

"Zulu Tramps, Orleans & Claiborne, Mardi Gras Day," 2020. Photo: Ashley Lorraine. Courtesy of the Artist.

> commands to his subjects and staged each position until he thought it was perfect. His subjects often grew weary during the shoot. "Hurry up Bedou" became a quote often heard in the New Orleans Creole community. The camera was his muse (Tureaud 4/28/23).

Bedou's work is now housed at Xavier University and in The Historic New Orleans Collection, where it serves as a valuable record of the city's visual history.

Another important Black photographer in New Orleans was Marion James Porter (1908–1983) who was also a civil rights activist with a passion for photographic storytelling. His images of New Orleans' Black community in the 1950s and 1960s document the changing social landscape of the city during the civil rights movement. Porter's images captured important moments in the struggle for civil rights, including the integration of schools and the desegregation of public spaces. He was also well known as a portrait photographer. Images of New Orleans residents, both Black and white, captured the unique personalities of his subjects. Porter was also a photojournalist who documented the daily life of the city's Black community in the 1940s and 1950s. He had his own business, Porter's Photo News, and worked for several publications including the *Louisiana Weekly*, *Black Data Weekly*, *Ebony*, *Jet*, *Black Enterprise* and *Sepia*. His photographs of musicians, race men and race women, and other residents who either lived in or visited New Orleans, including A. P. Tureaud Sr., Reverend Avery Alexander,

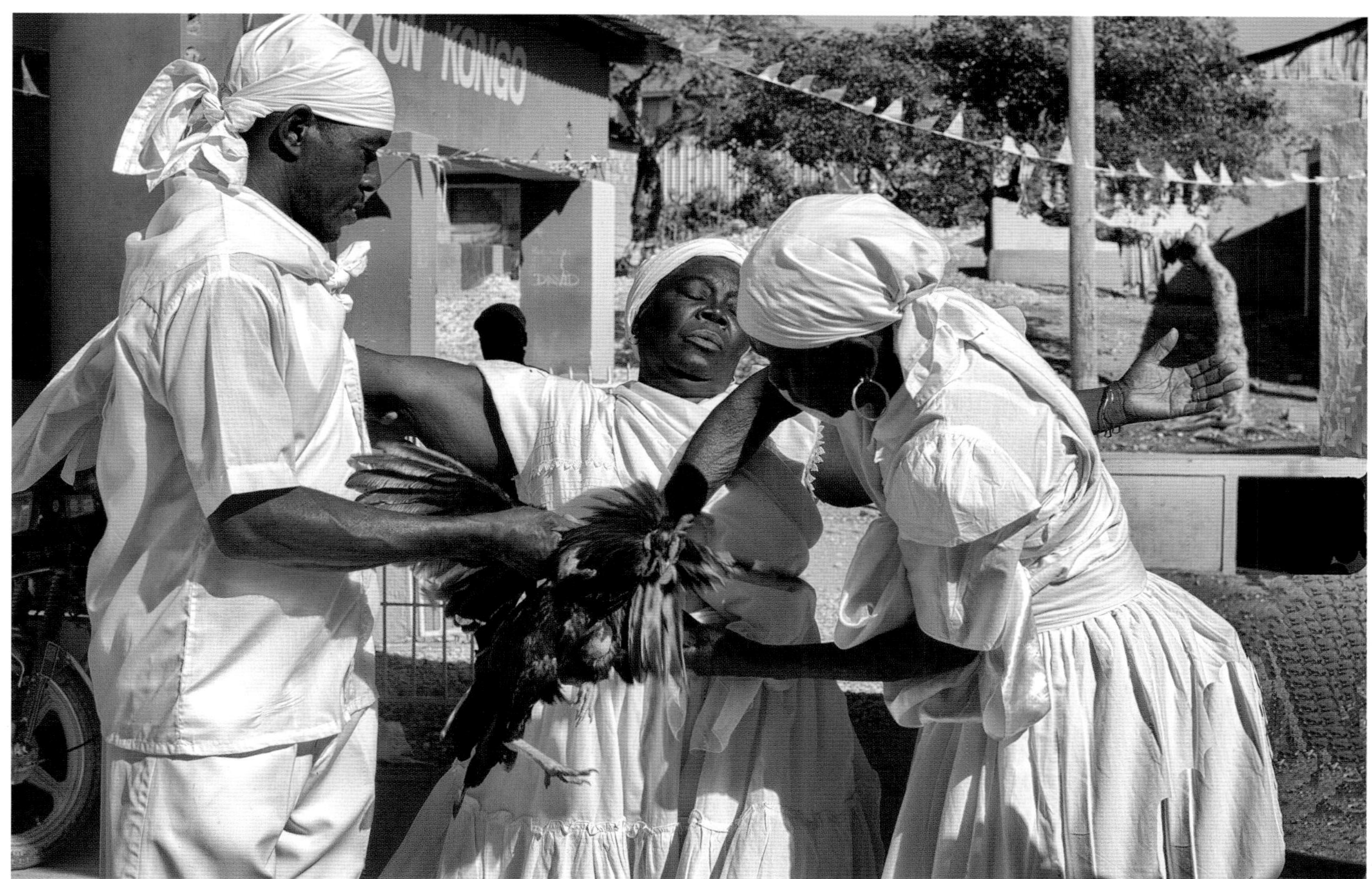

"Lakou Soukri," 2014. Gonaives, Haiti. Photo: Sokari Ekine. Courtesy of the Artist.

Dr. Martin Luther King Jr., Thurgood Marshall, Haile Selassie, Duke Ellington, Louis Armstrong, Jesse Owens, and Jackie Robinson provide a vivid snapshot of life in the city during this time.

In addition to these early prominent photographers, there were and are many others who contribute to the city's visual culture. Today these younger Black photographers continue to play an important role in New Orleans' visual culture. Contemporary photographers like Ashley Lorraine, Sokari Ekine, and Selwhyn Sthaddeus "Polo Silk" Terrell have gained recognition for their work documenting the city's diverse communities as well as others.

Ashley Lorraine brings on the New Orleans traditional, celebratory kaleidoscope of colorful and animated images. Her work depicts the Zulu Tramps en masse in a strikingly vibrant image, Buck Jumpers, Prince of Wales, and roof dancers—all a part of the city's repertoire of Social Aid and Pleasure Clubs (SAPCs). I am not sure of the dates for all of these images, but they remind me of the energy of people coming back out to the streets after a long hiatus of being inside. Coming back to the streets again after the COVID pandemic was similar to coming back after Katrina—folks experienced joy and pain—joy for the reunion of family and friends and pain for the loss of family and friends. Also joy from experiencing the tradition again and what some refer to as the "forward-moving dance party" accompanied by the infectious beat of a New Orleans brass band. This is quintessential New Orleans.

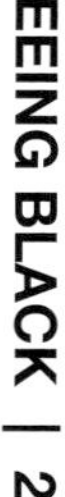

In Sokari Ekine's work in this collection, it is difficult to discern the geographical location. These images are of traditional sacred rituals, including black-and-white images that depict women participants in Afrocentric sacred rituals. These rituals could easily be conducted in New Orleans, but I speculate that the location is Haiti, since the writing on the building is in French. For the two color images, one is of a funeral procession with a brass band consisting of all men moving through a wooded rural pathway; the other is of a vibrant altar. The altar is laid on top of a colorful African textile piece, setting the stage backdrop for candles, fruits, nuts, cowry shells, water, flowers, tree leaves, and other assorted food items.

Selwhyn Sthaddeus "Polo Silk" Terrell's images of New Orleans residents, particularly those in the city's new generation hip-hop and bounce music scenes, capture the energy and vibrancy of the city's youth culture. For example, consider images of women pallbearers holding up a pink casket in a street funeral procession; a young couple with mouth grills and blinged jewelry around neck, wrists and fingers; "Who Dat Called Da Police," mural art; New Look Kids Second Line Parade; and Marc Morial showing off, his hands throwing the victory symbol, while he stands in front of a mural that reads "Lets Go to the Second Line."

These images capture the vibrancy of the neighborhoods while depicting the changing of gender roles, as with the women pallbearers, while another photographer depicts a women's motorcycle club, with most of the women wearing colorful and blinged-out platform stiletto heels in traditionally male-dominated cultural arenas. In this same vein, Black liberation has always been the greater cause for a large number of Black Americans, with some men even today reacting negatively to women's liberation and to those Black women whom they consider too forward or aggressive or too educated, thereby intimidating men. Yet the history of Black liberation in the United States is deeply intertwined with the experiences of Black women. From the era of slavery, where Black women endured the double oppression of racism and sexism, to the Civil Rights Movement, where their contributions were often overshadowed, Black women have been central to the struggle for liberation.

The African American community has a rich history shaped by resilience, cultural heritage, and a constant quest for equality. One notable aspect of this cultural evolution is the changing landscape of gender roles within the community. From historical challenges rooted in slavery to the present-day pursuit of empowerment and equality, the roles of men and women in Black society have undergone a profound transformation. The rise of strong, empowered Black women in various fields, including politics, entertainment, and business, has shattered stereotypes and inspired younger generations, as is evident in images taken by younger photographers. Obviously, the women in these images are not concerned about the supposed tension between racial and gender liberation.

Black Americans have long defied stereotypes and pushed the boundaries of traditional gender norms. The ongoing journey towards equality and empowerment underscores the

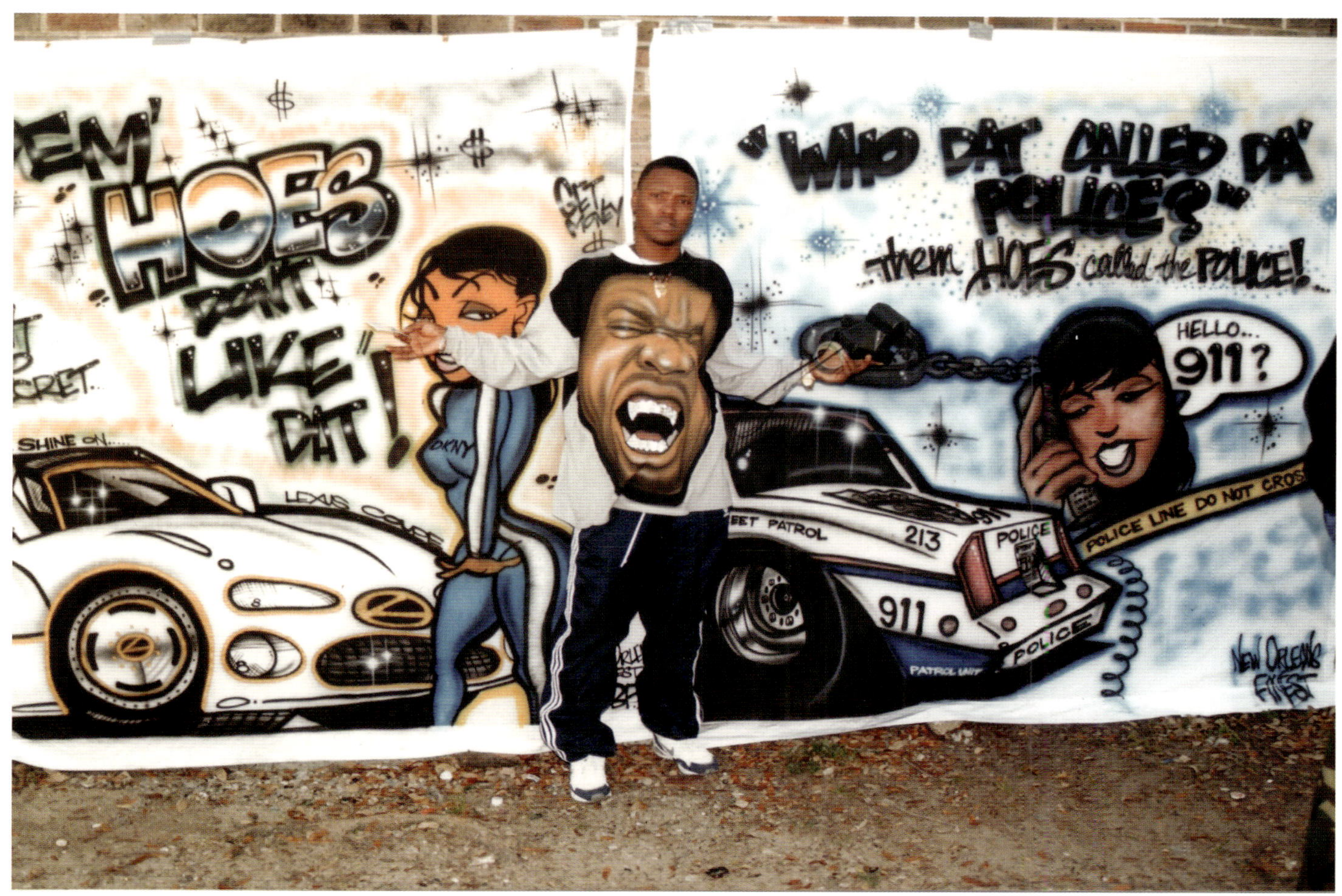

"Buddy," 1998. Photo: Selwhyn Sthaddeus "Polo Silk" Terrell. Courtesy of the Artist.

importance of recognizing the diverse experiences within the community and building a future that embraces the strengths and contributions of all its members.

Children are also prominent in the changing street scenes, especially with the SAPCs. Many clubs include children in the parades and some even have dedicated youth divisions. The New Look, Kids Second Line Parade, is a newer addition to the large celebratory roster of neighborhood clubs. Just like other traditions including the Black Masking Indians, children are brought into the scene early to learn and be trained to carry the traditions on for future generations. In recognition of their essential role in preserving and passing on the culture, youth are depicted in many images in this book.

In conclusion, Black photographers have made significant contributions to New Orleans' visual culture throughout the city's history. From Arthur P. Bedou to contemporary photographers like Sokari Ekine and Selwhyn Sthaddeus "Polo Silk" Terrell, these artists have documented the city's cultural practices, social movements, and everyday life. Their work serves as a valuable record of New Orleans' past and present, providing unique perspectives on the city's rich history and diverse communities.

Seeing Black includes poignant and exhilarating images and many more await our attention. We have selected two to four images from the photographers in the collection for inclusion here, a sampler meant to whet rather than satisfy the appetite for this important work. Out first goal is the spread the word about these remarkable artists to all those who care about our art and history.

As we look to the future of African American photography this publication's role comes into focus. For it is in the effort to reach educators and young people and their parents that the real power and impact of this undertaking lies. Hopefully, this book will spark both knowledge and further inquiry in younger readers, and possibly an urge to pick up a camera.

We urge everyone to challenge the prevailing wisdom about American arts and culture and open their eyes to the experience all of our artists. To the artists and to all those who respond to them, we dedicate this book.

Seeing Black is a priceless legacy for future generations of New Orleanians. It captures a moment in our collective past. These photographers not only document but validate the African American experience. Although that moment is gone, it is forever frozen by the photographers' artistry and etched permanently in the minds and hearts of those who love and live in this profoundly complicated and compelling place called New Orleans.

Aché
Joyce Marie Jackson, Ph.D.

References

Beaumont, Newhall. 1982. *The History of Photography*. New York: Museum of Modern Art.

Smethurst, James Edward. 2005. *The Black Arts Movement: Literary Nationalism in the 1960s and 1970s*. Chapel Hill, NC: University of North Carolina Press.

The Ties That Bind: Making Family New Orleans Style. 2000. New Orleans: Annie E. Casey Foundation.

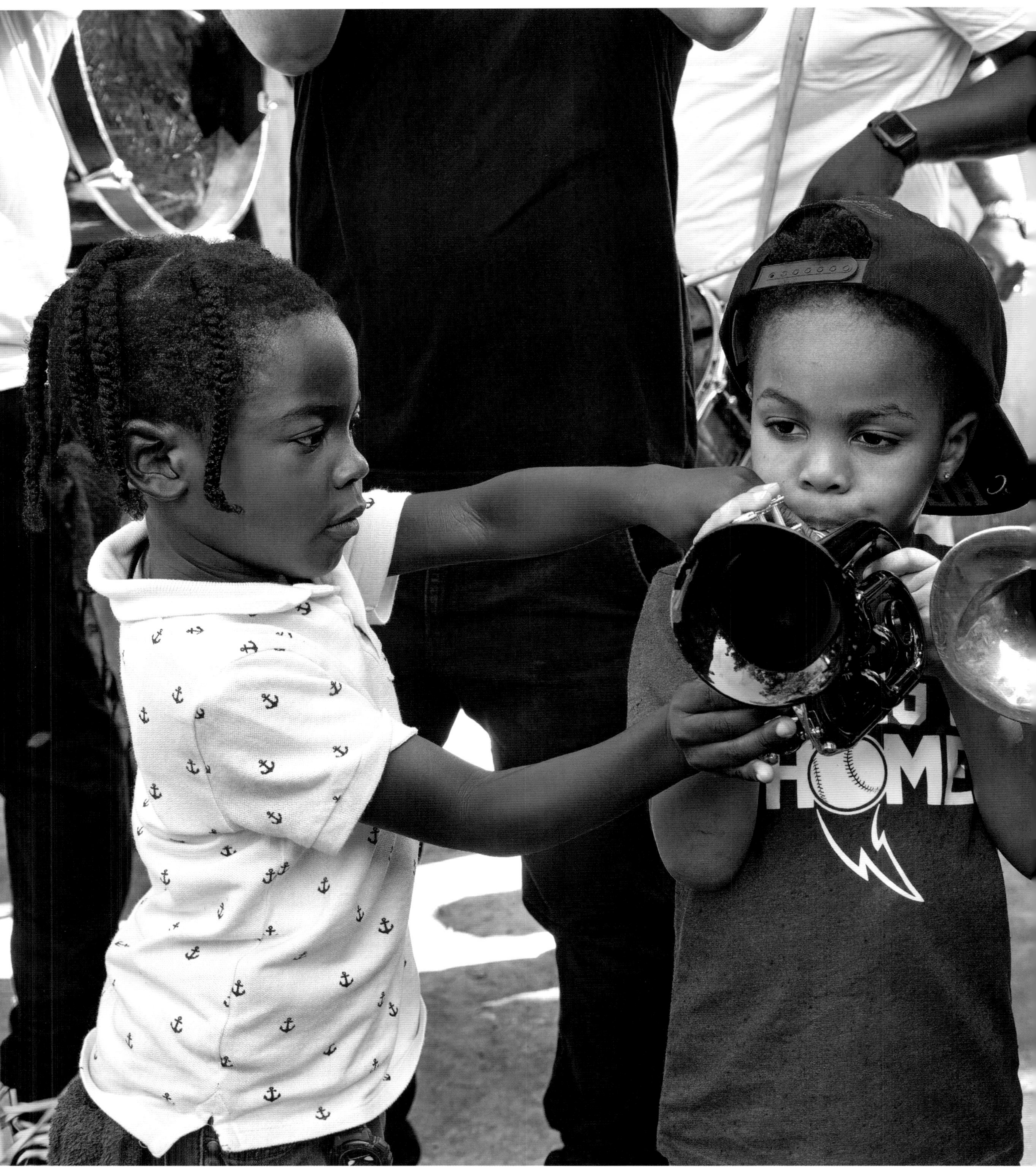

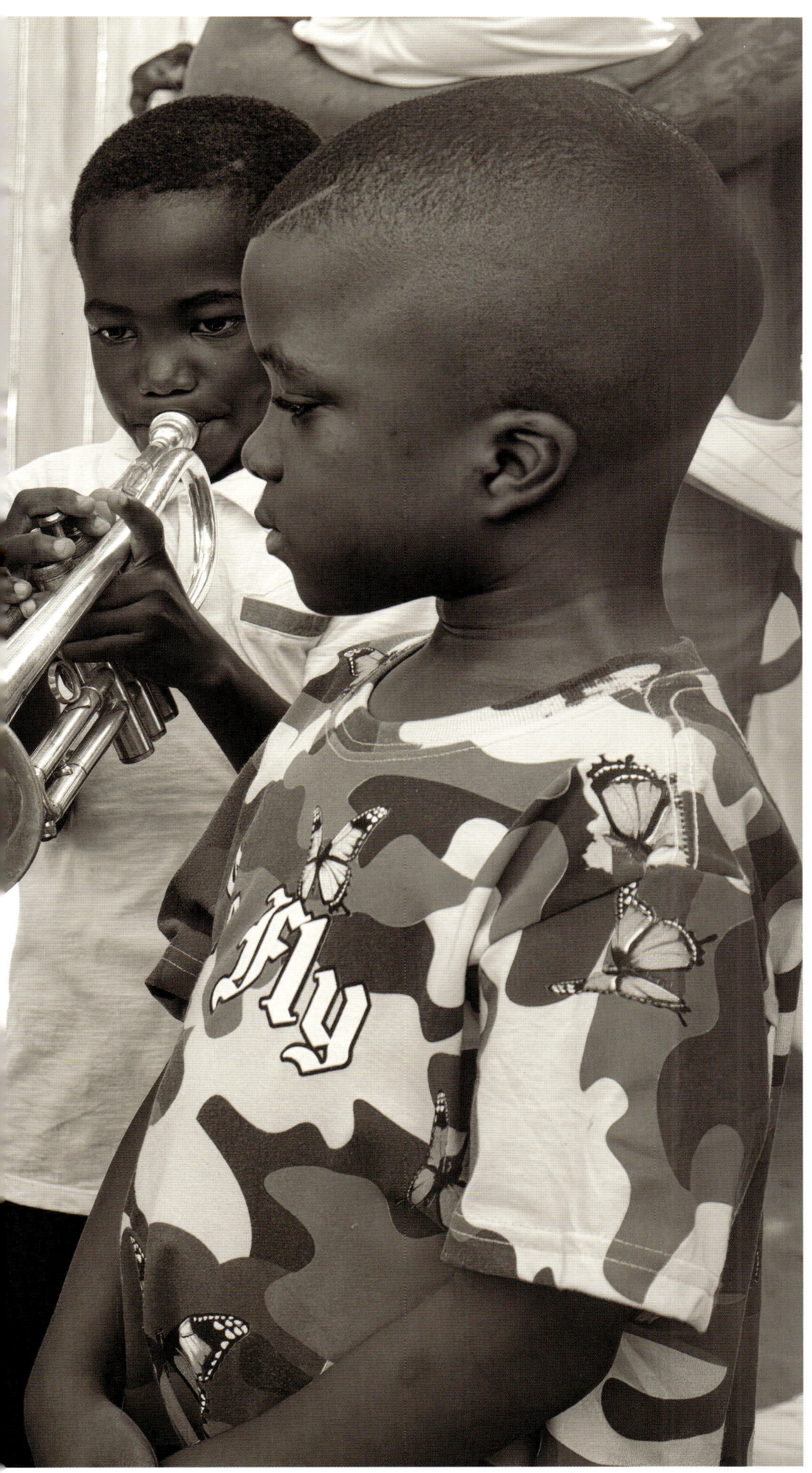

"It Goes Like This (Four Boys with Two Trumpets)," 2021.
Photo: Eric Waters. Courtesy of the Artist.

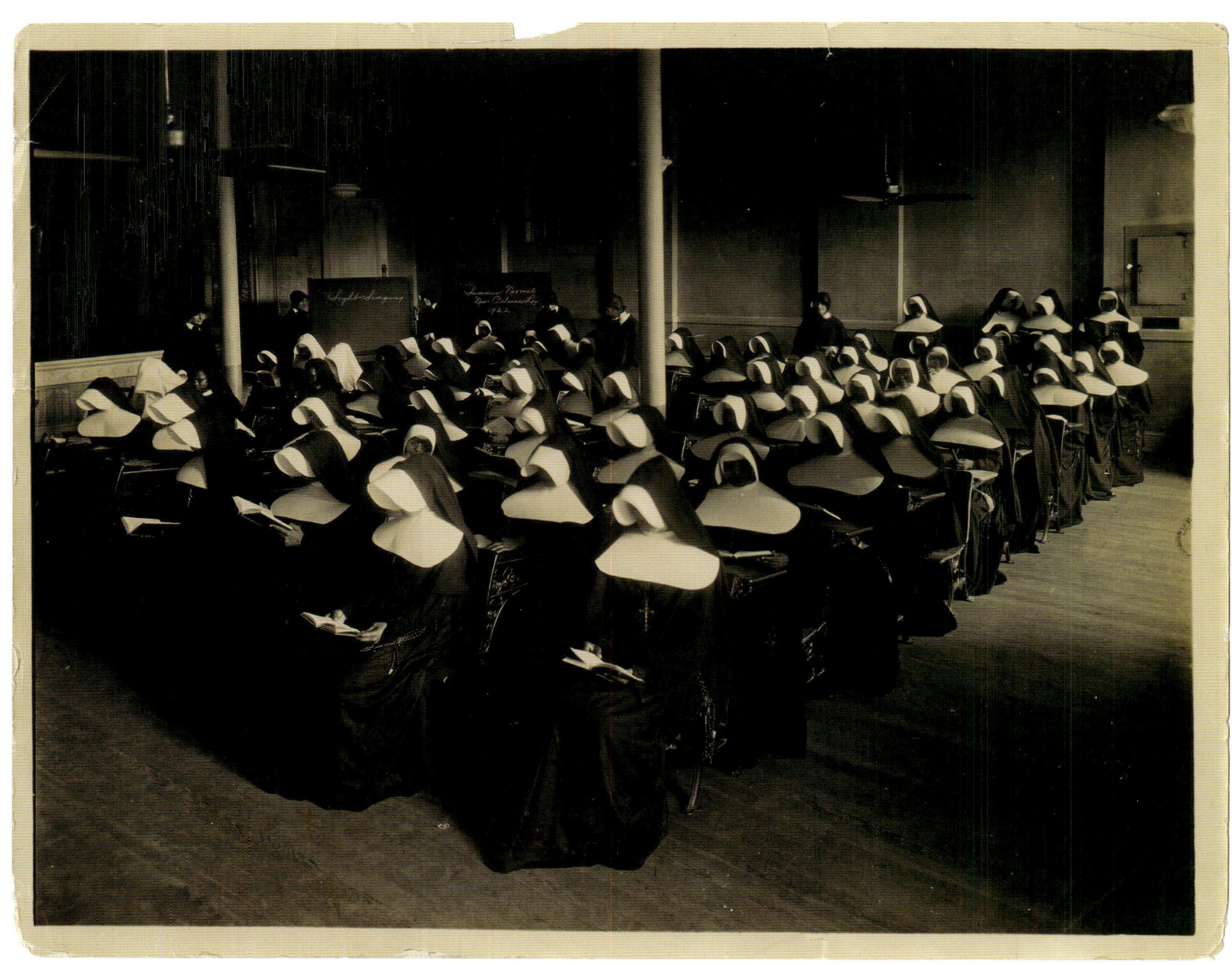

Sisters of the Holy Family Classroom portrait, 1922. Photo: A. P. Bedou. Courtesy of Xavier University of Louisiana, Archives & Special Collections.

historical photographers

1900s–1940s

A. P. Bedou

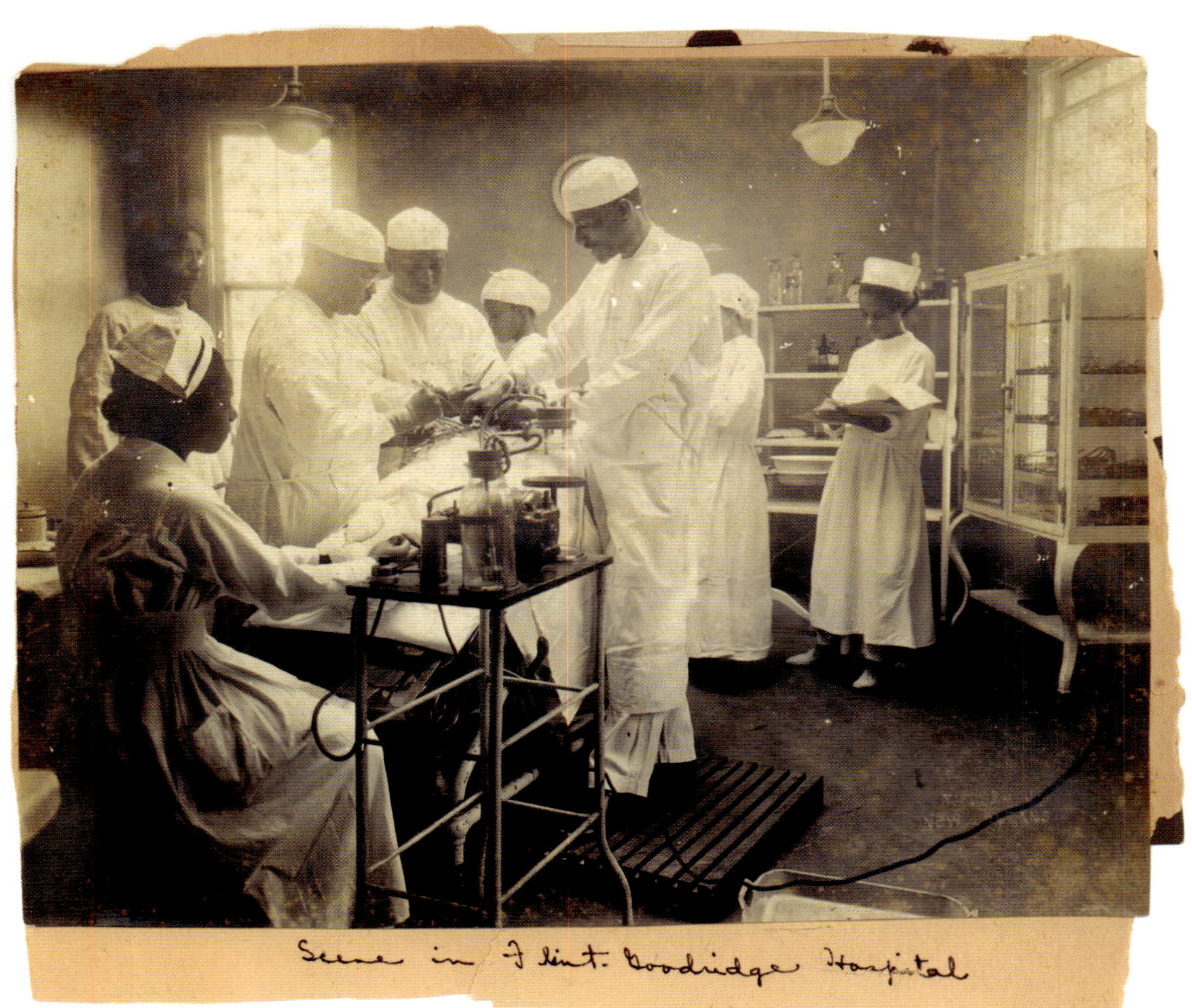

A. R. Dela Houssaye

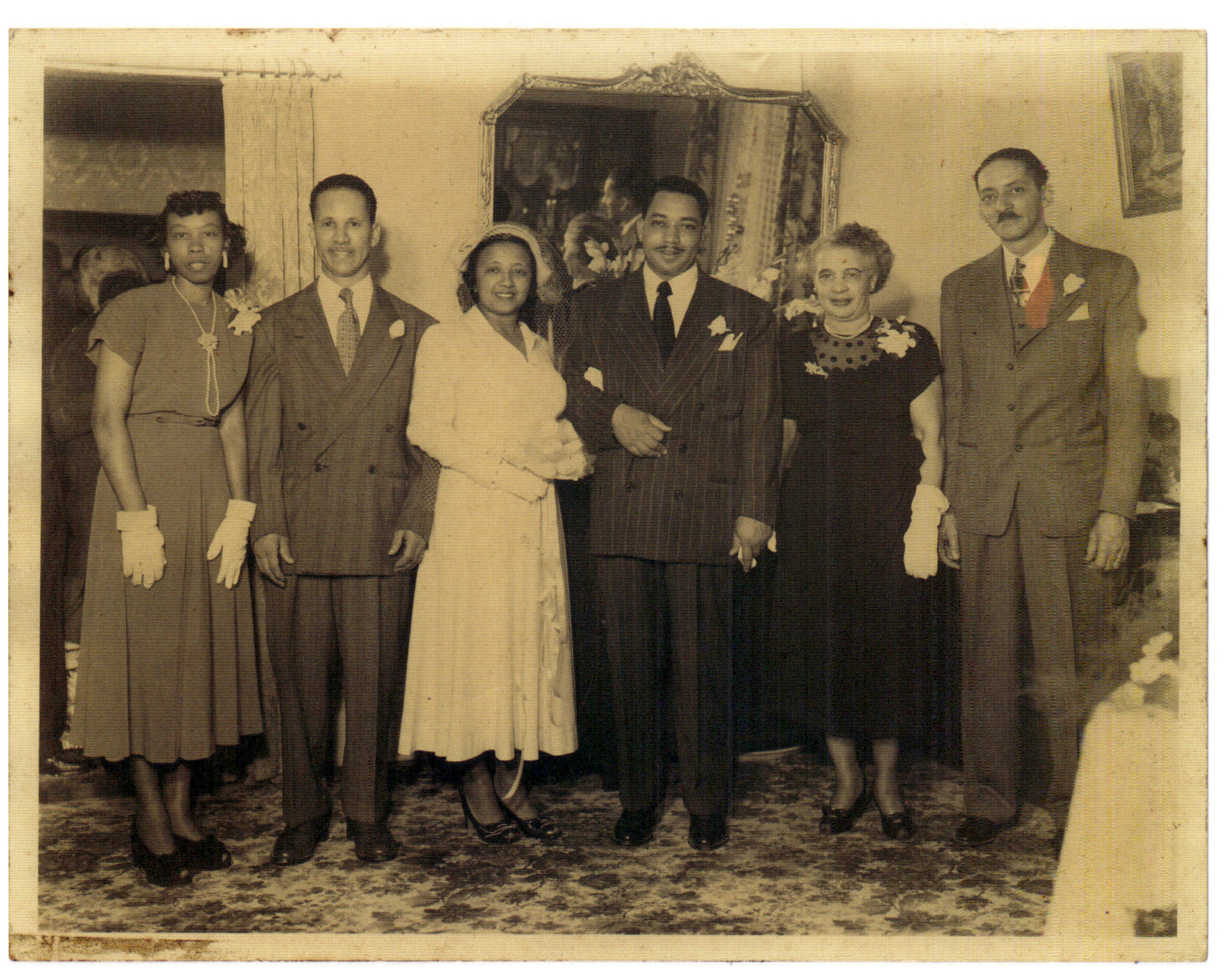

Arthur J. Perrault

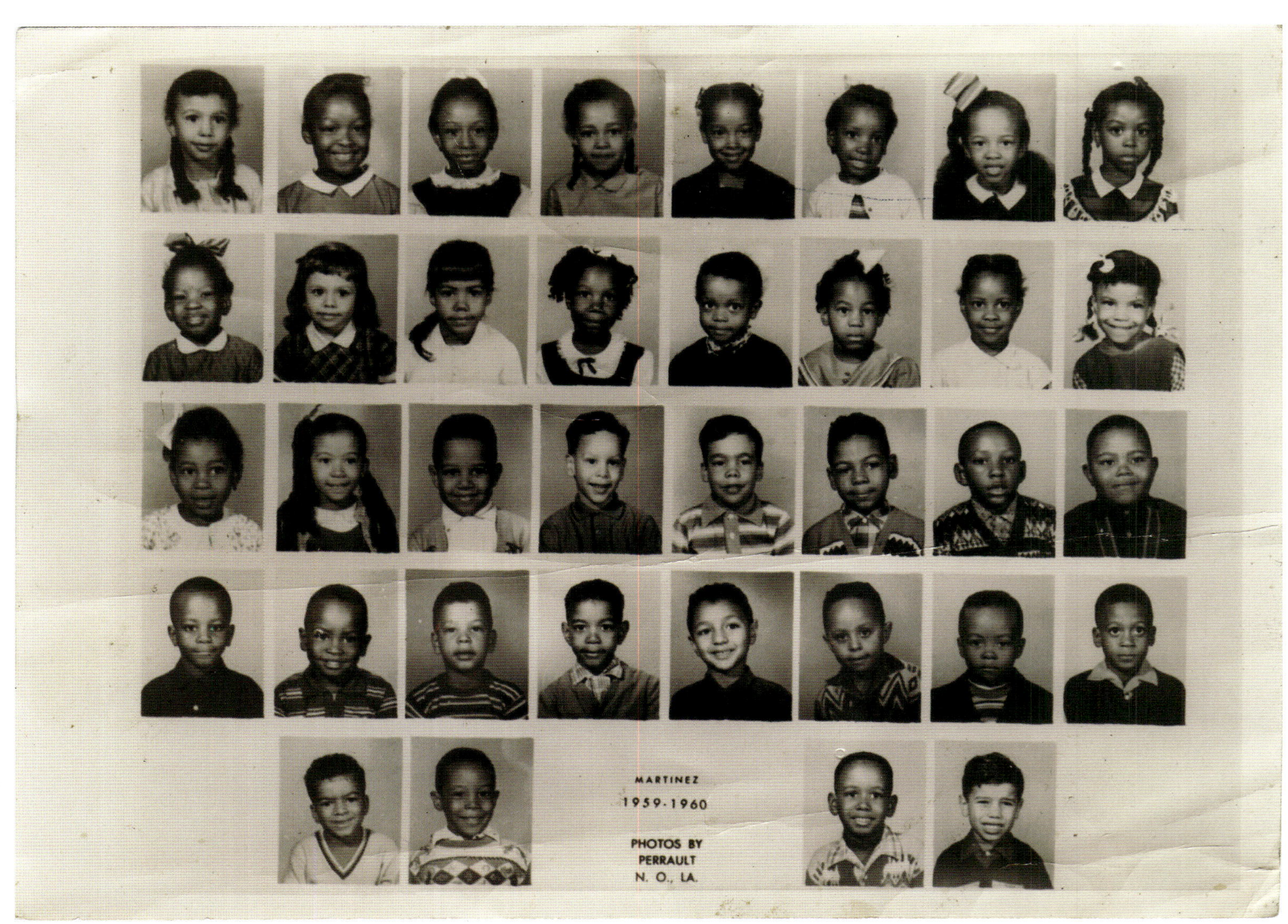

Celeste T. Broadway

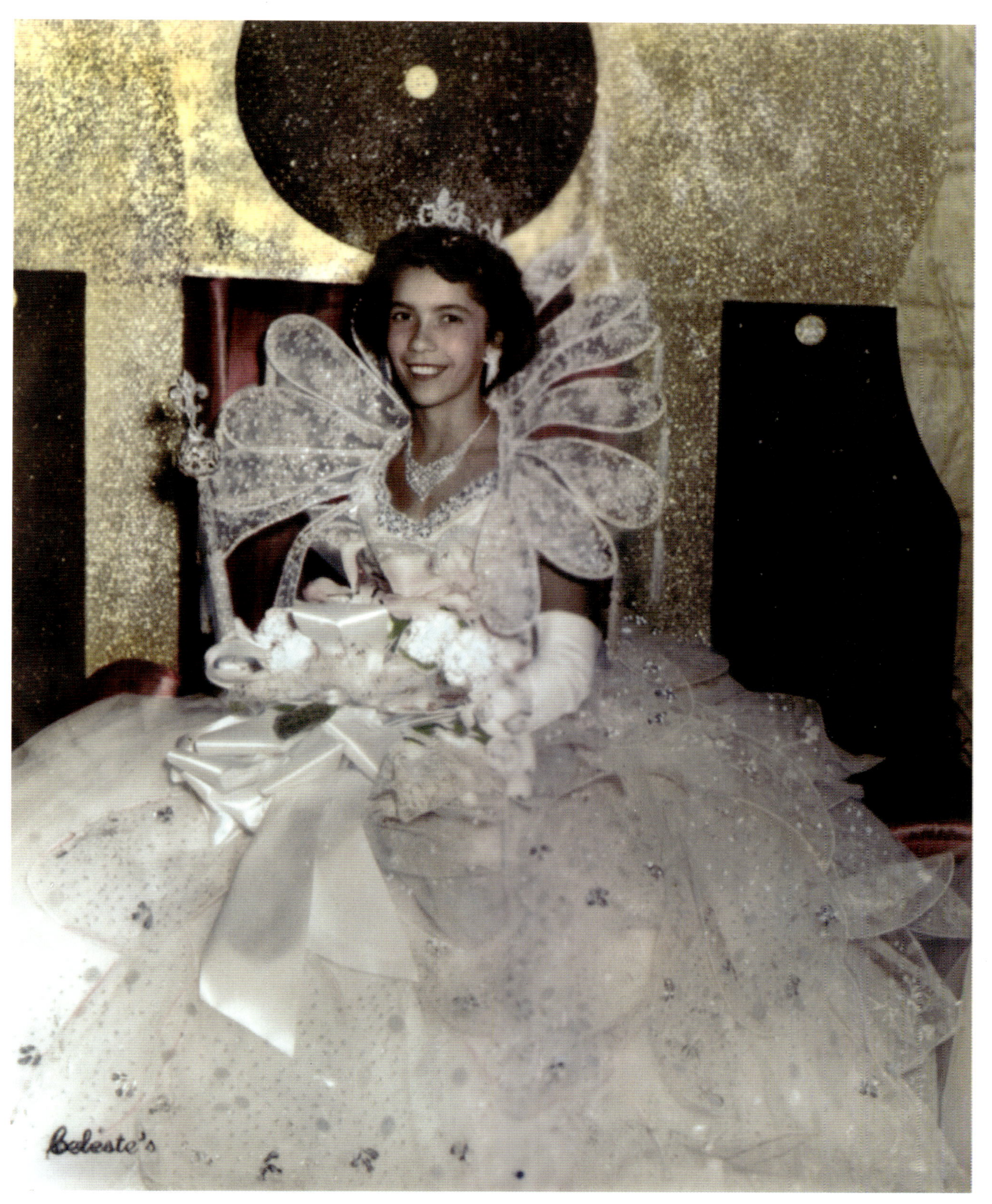

Florestine Collins

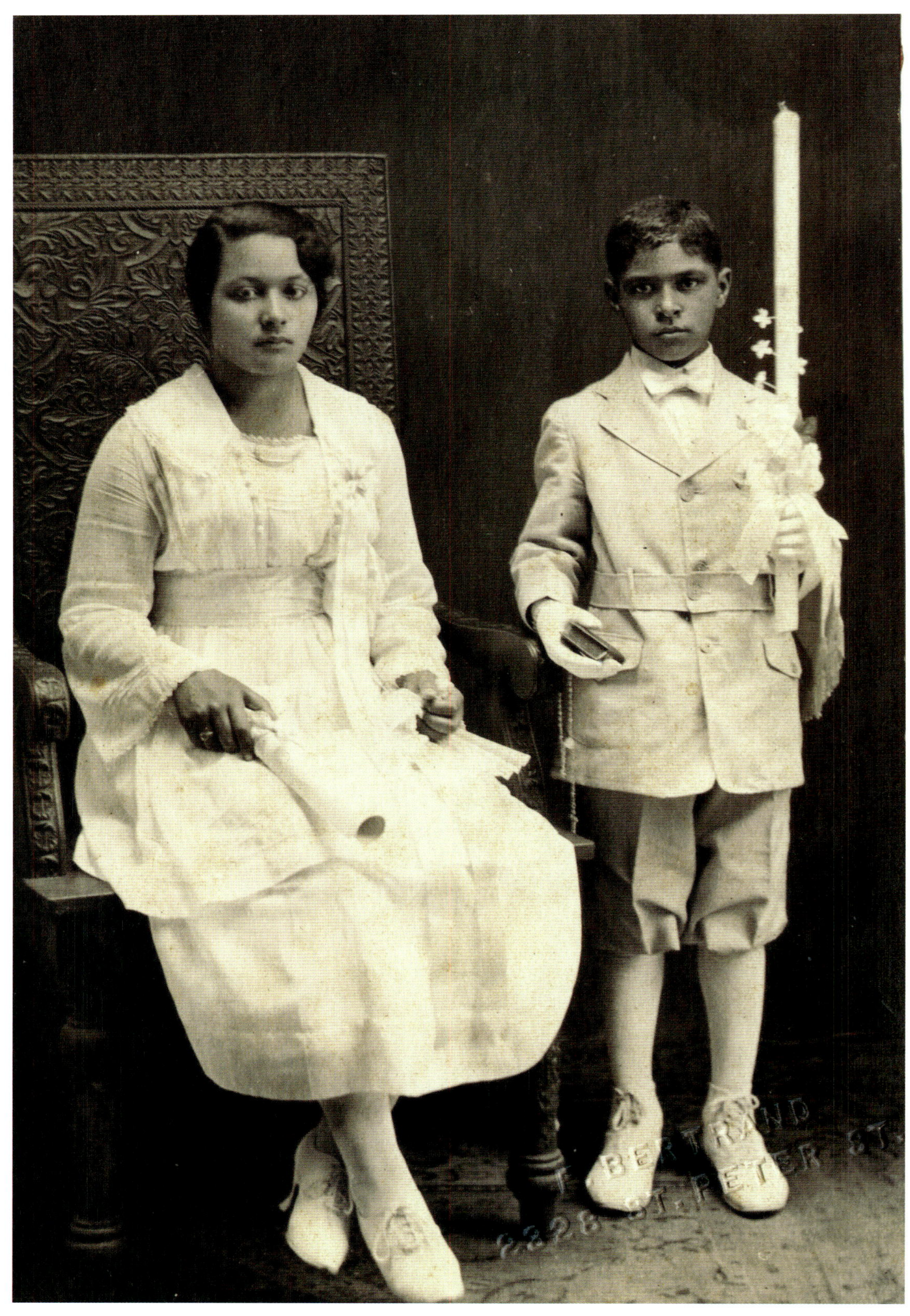

For a Beautiful Complexion, Use PRESTO FACE CREAM.

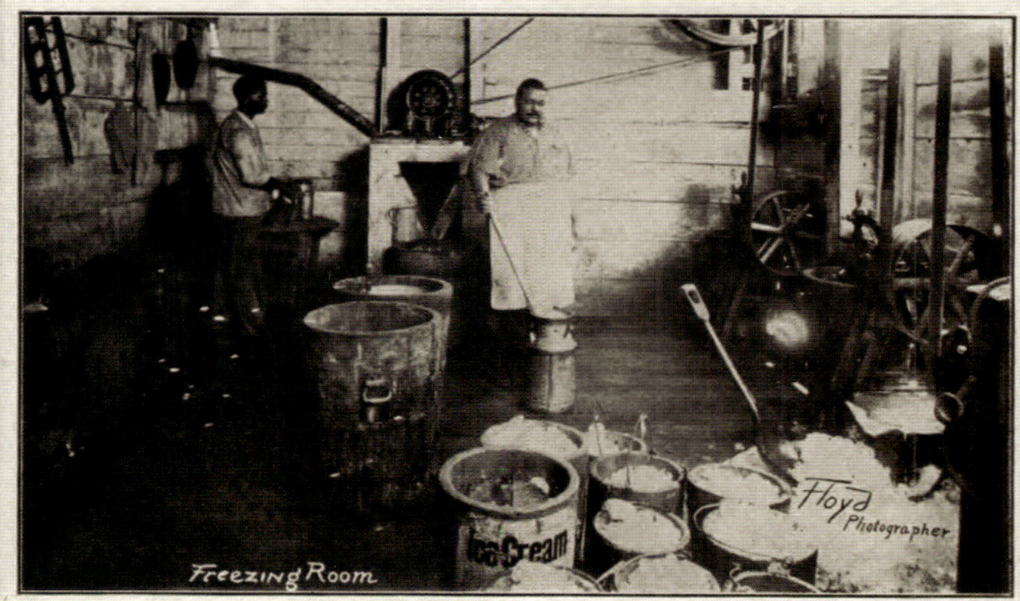

Orleans Ice Cream Works

MRS. KATIE ROBINSON and WILLIAM MORRIS,
Proprietors.

Ice Cream, Ices, Charlotte Russe and Biscuit Furnished for all Occasions.

We deliver to all parts of the city — Country orders Solicited

2217 DRYADES STREET, — Phone Jackson 842.

NEW ORLEANS, LA.

Read THE CRISIS. (See Ad. on Back Cover.)

—28—

Joseph "Scoop" Jones

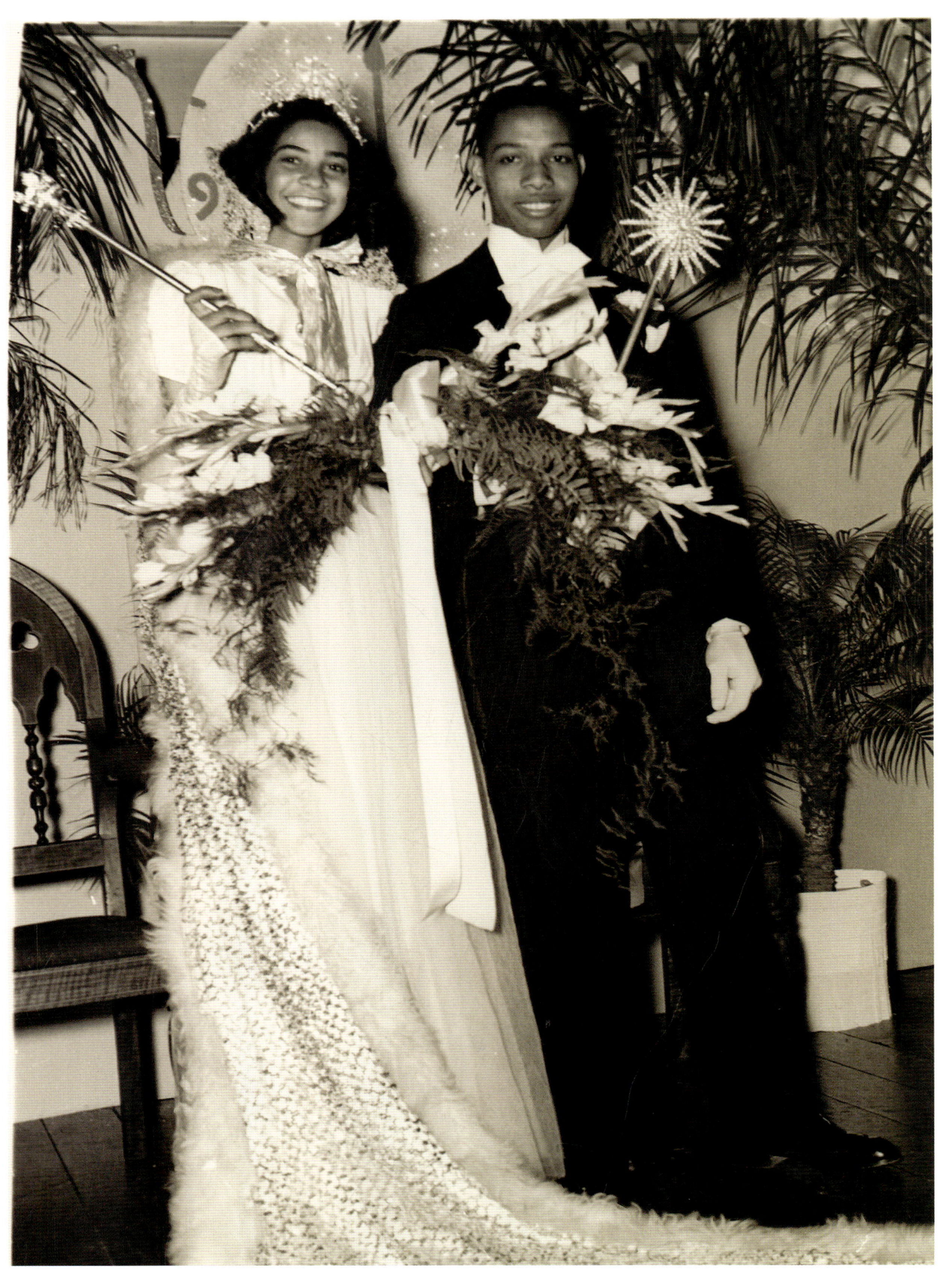

Magnolia Studio

ISOM M. MCCORMICK & WALTER ABADIE SR.

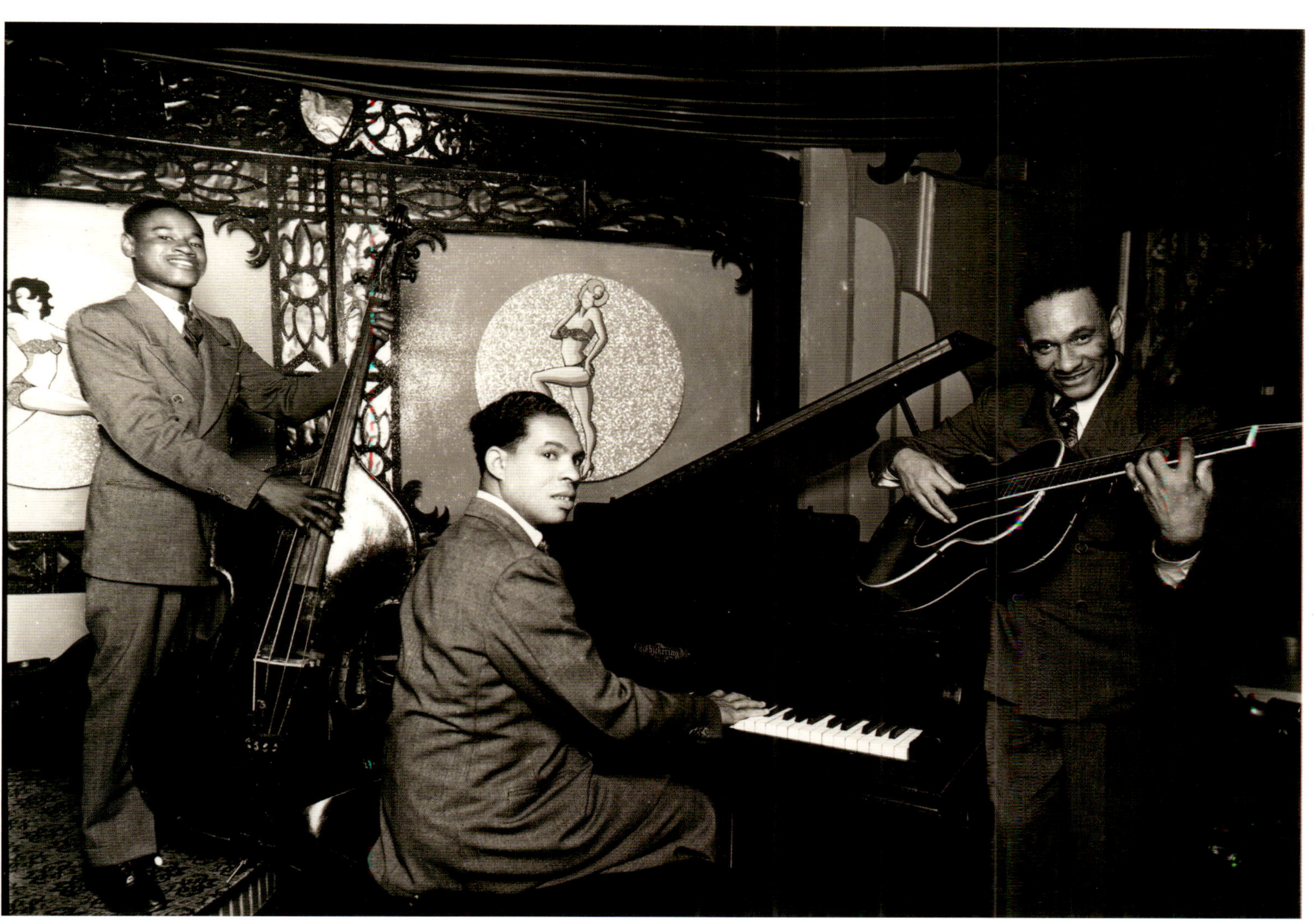

Nolan A. Marshall

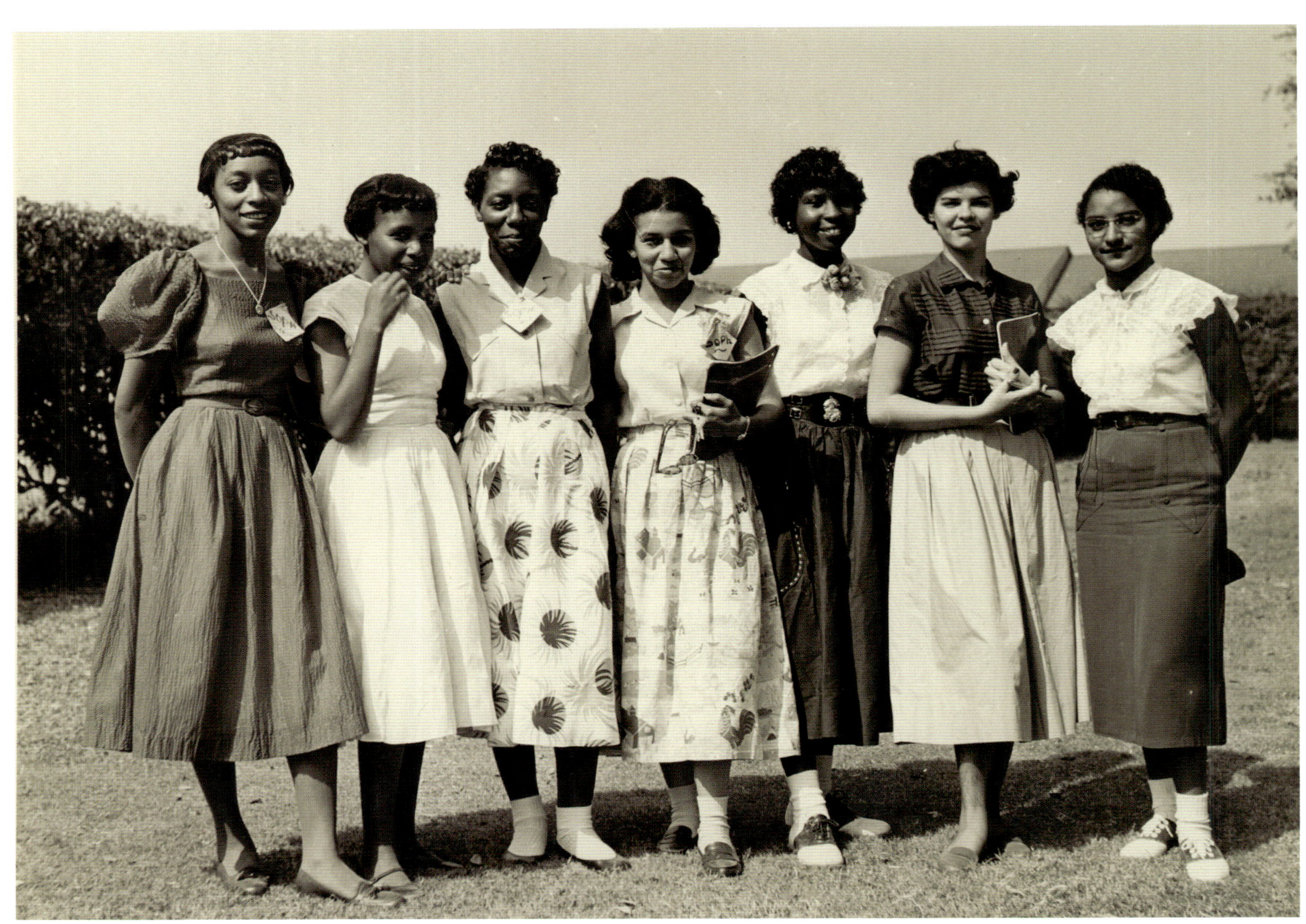

Rene Jacques Roussève

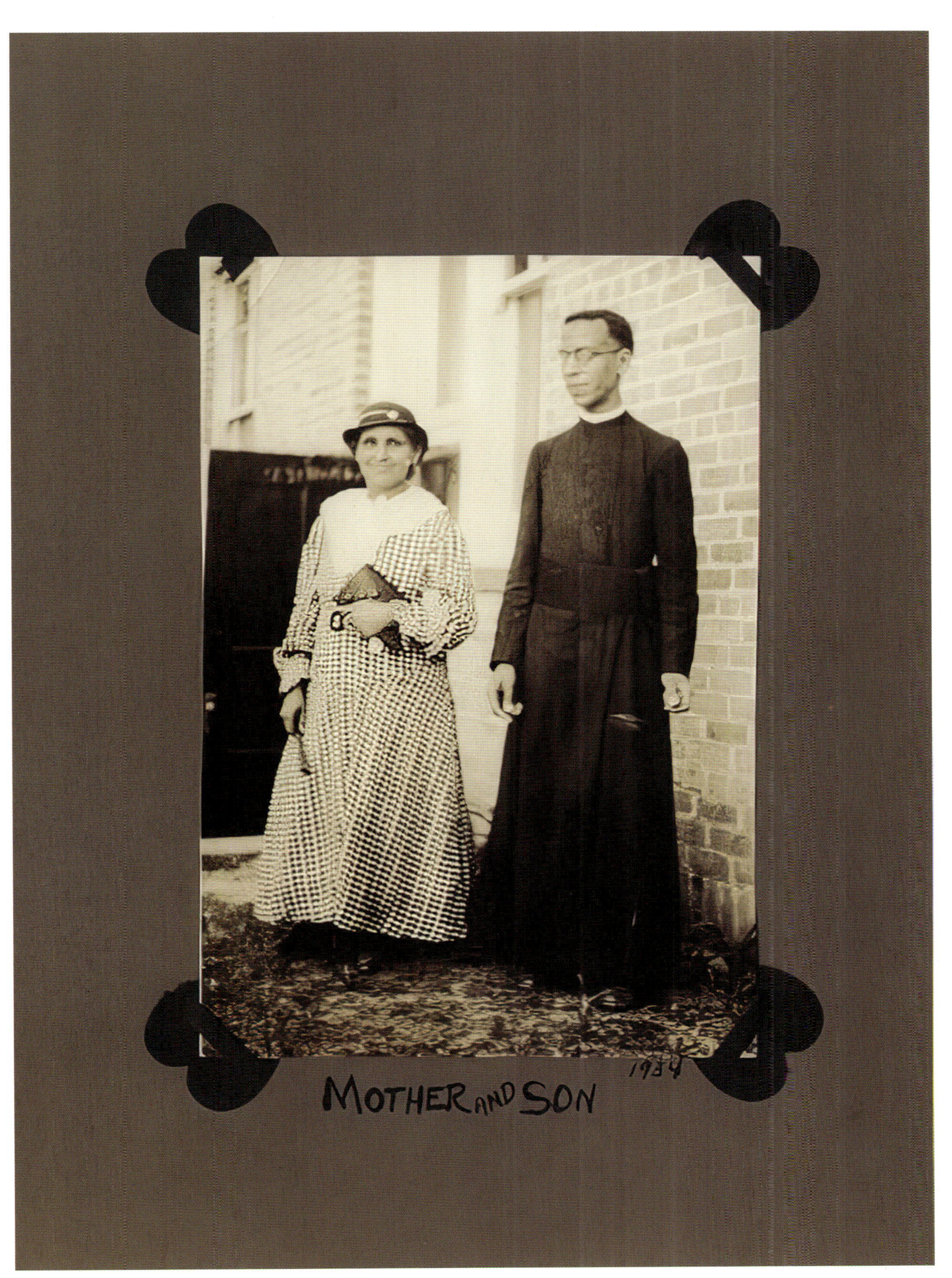

Villard Paddio

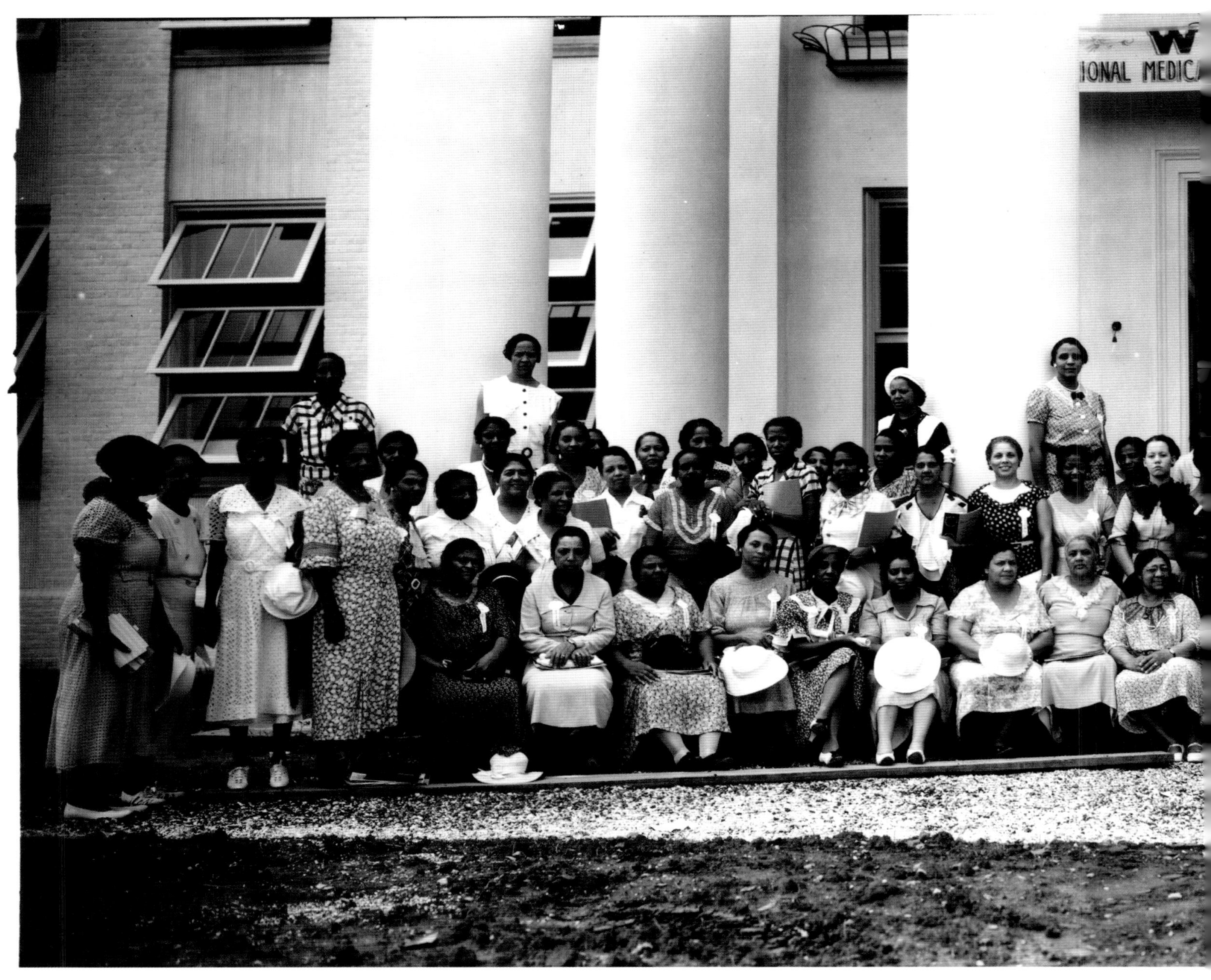

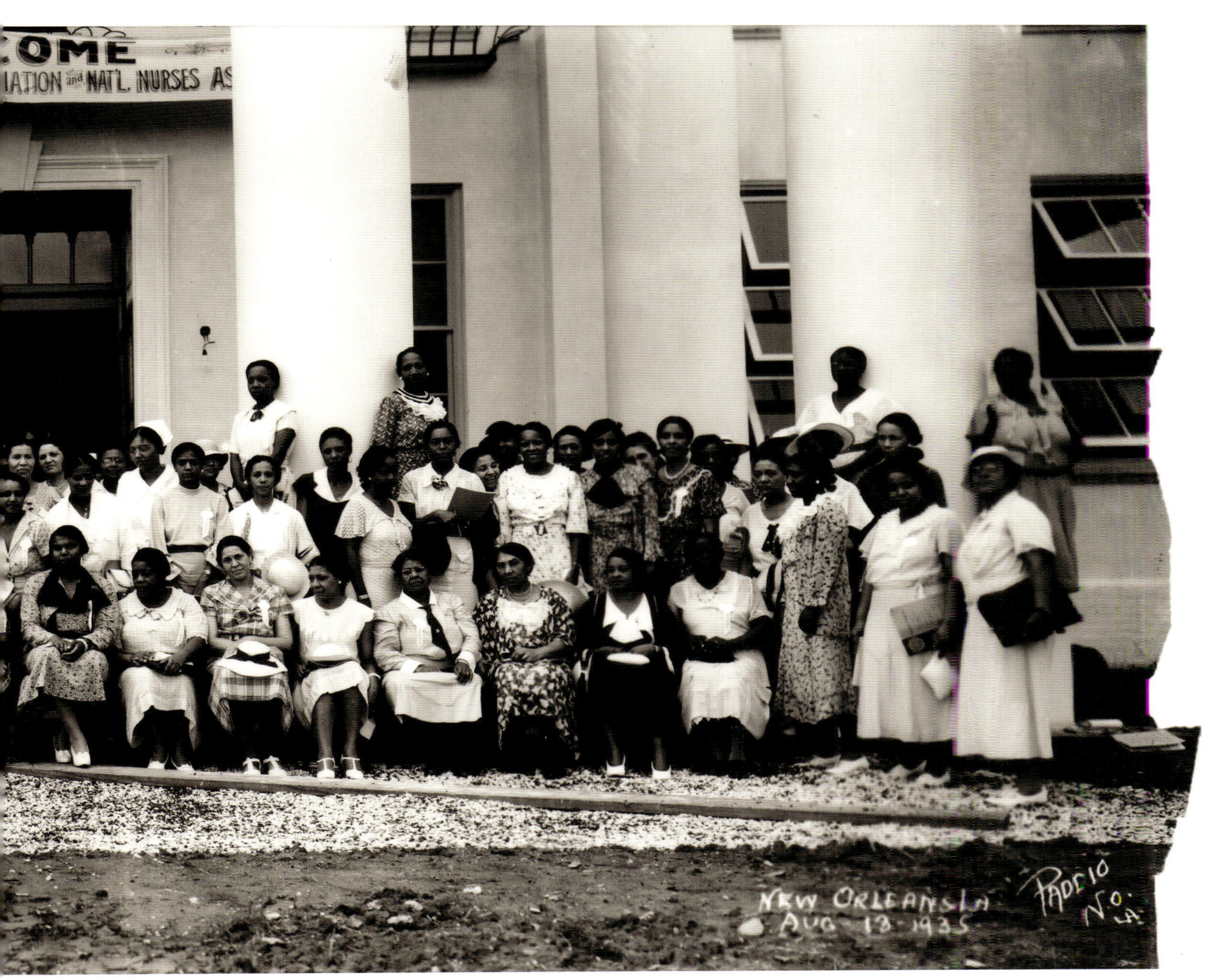
COME
IATION and NAT'L. NURSES AS
NEW ORLEANS LA
AUG 13 1935
PADEIO
NO. LA

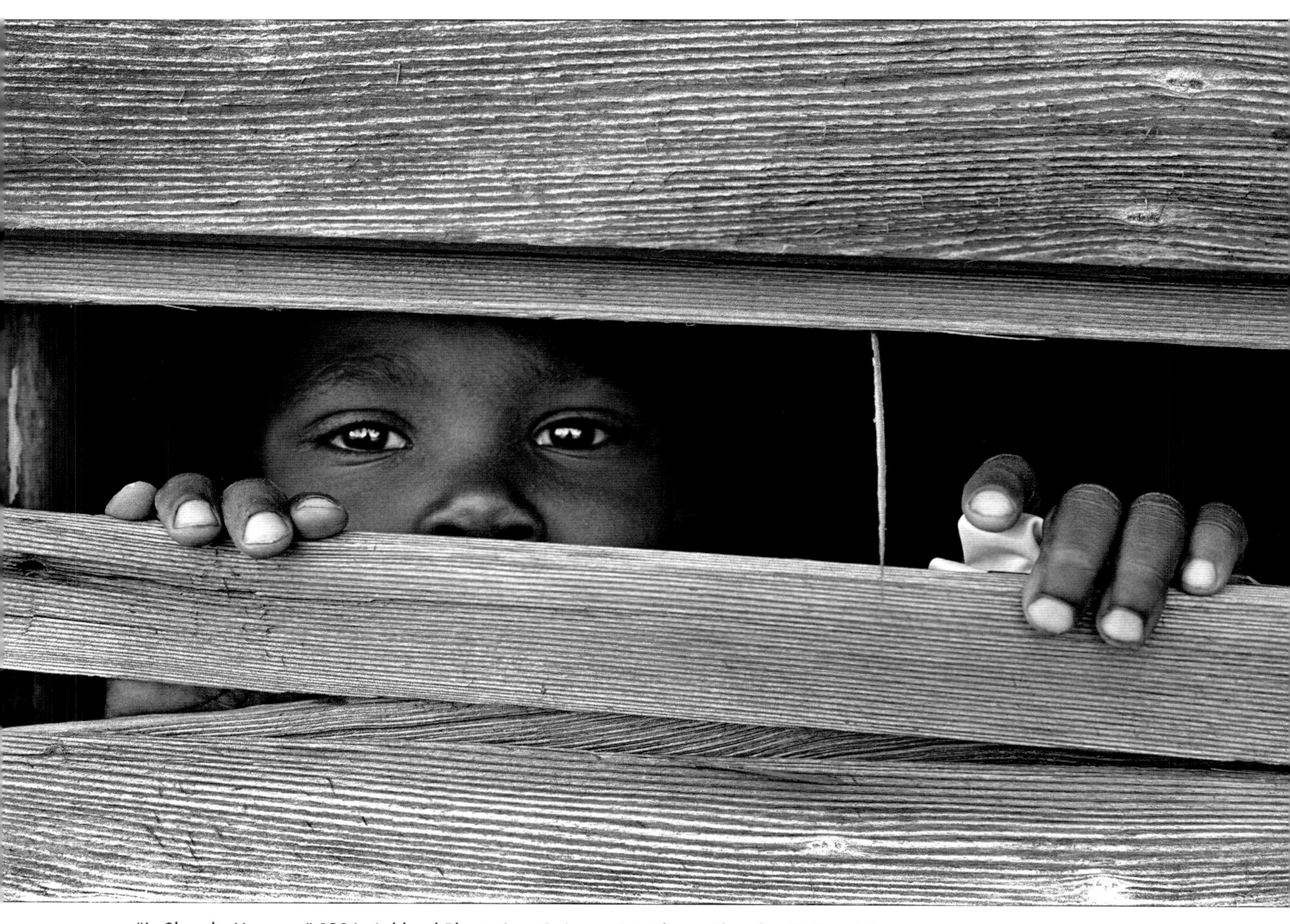

"LaShonda Morgan," 1986. Ashland Plantation, Geismar, LA. Photo: Chandra McCormick. Courtesy of the Artist.

contemporary photographers

1950 & beyond

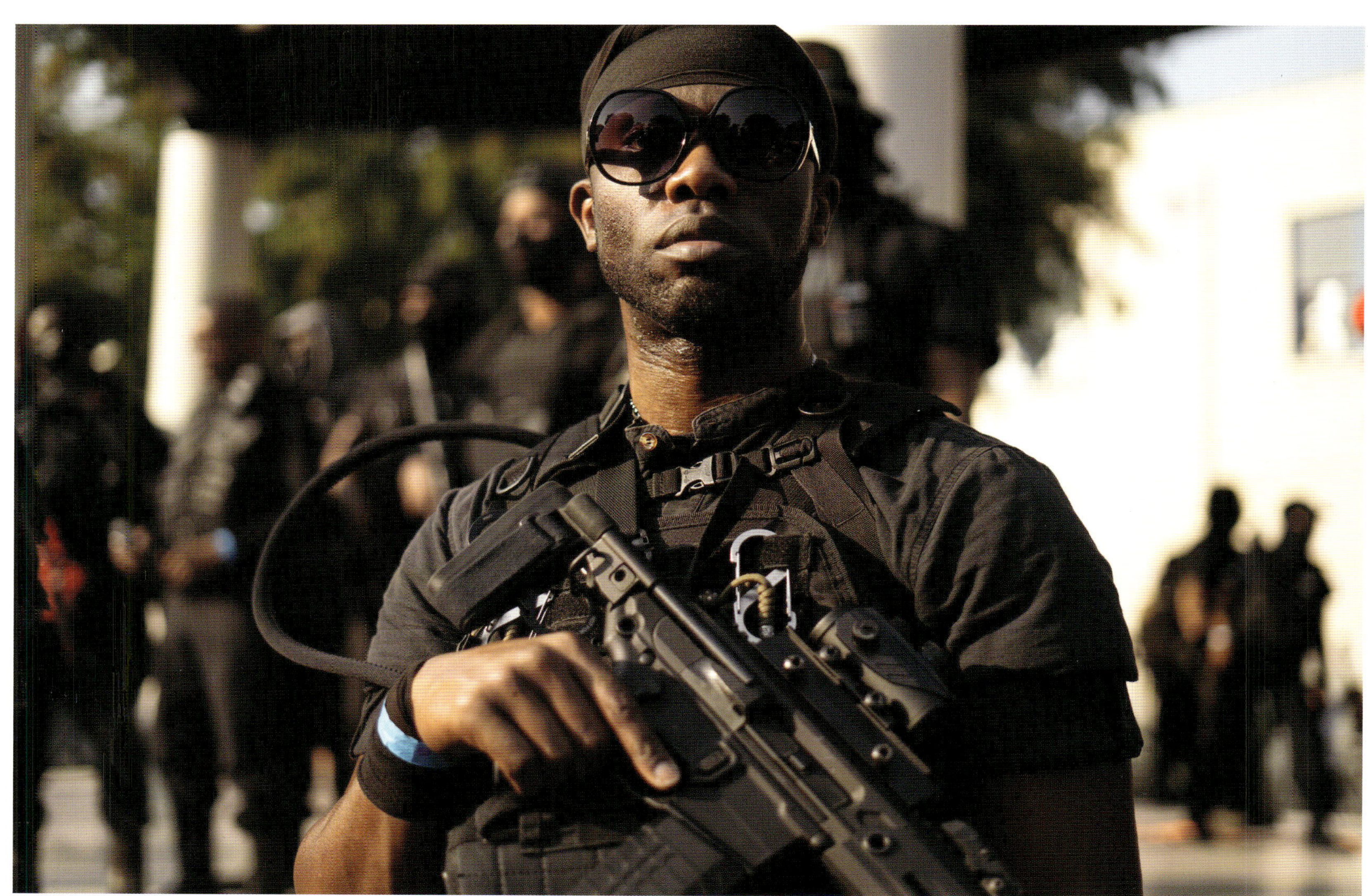

Abdul Aziz

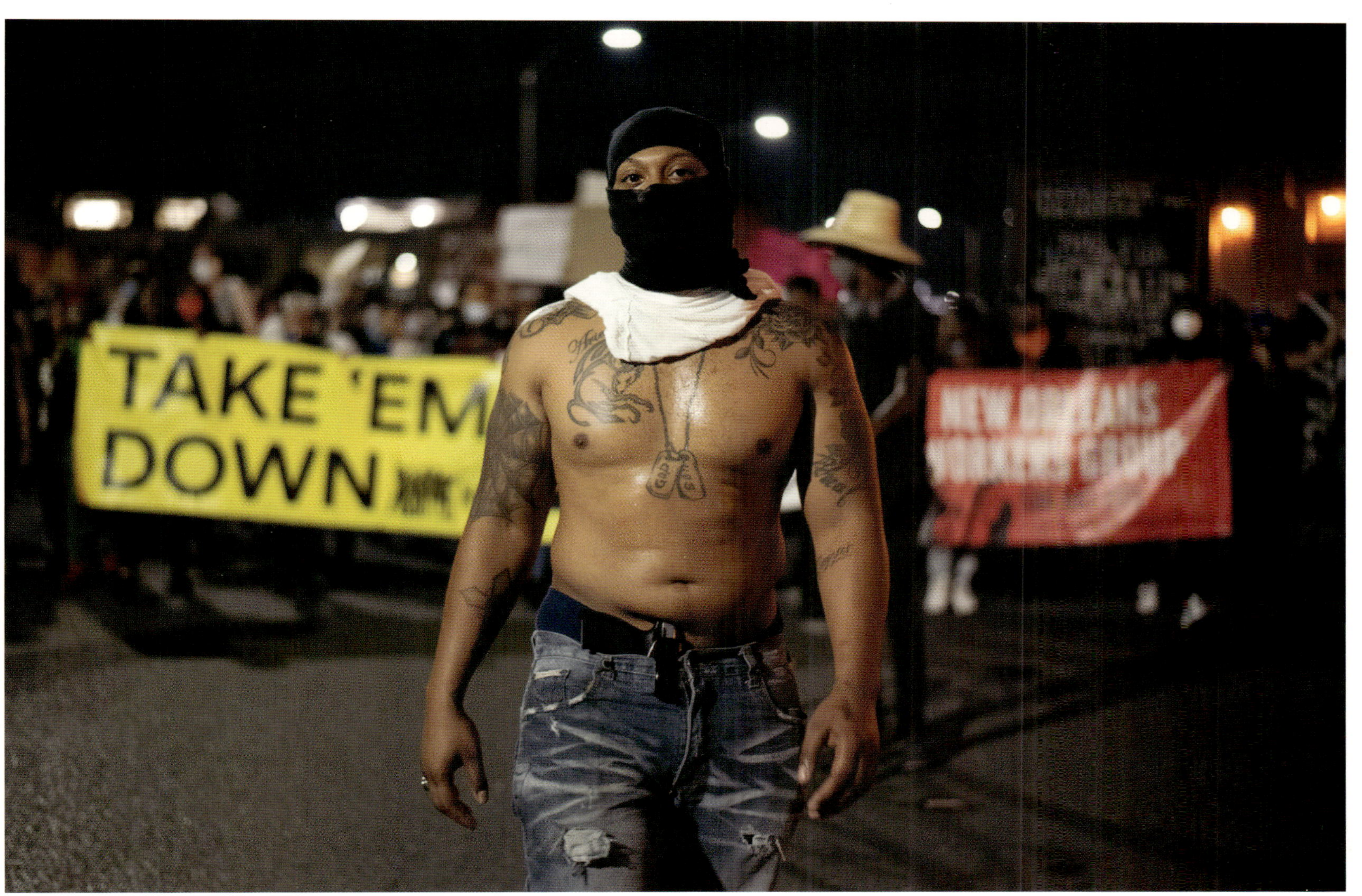

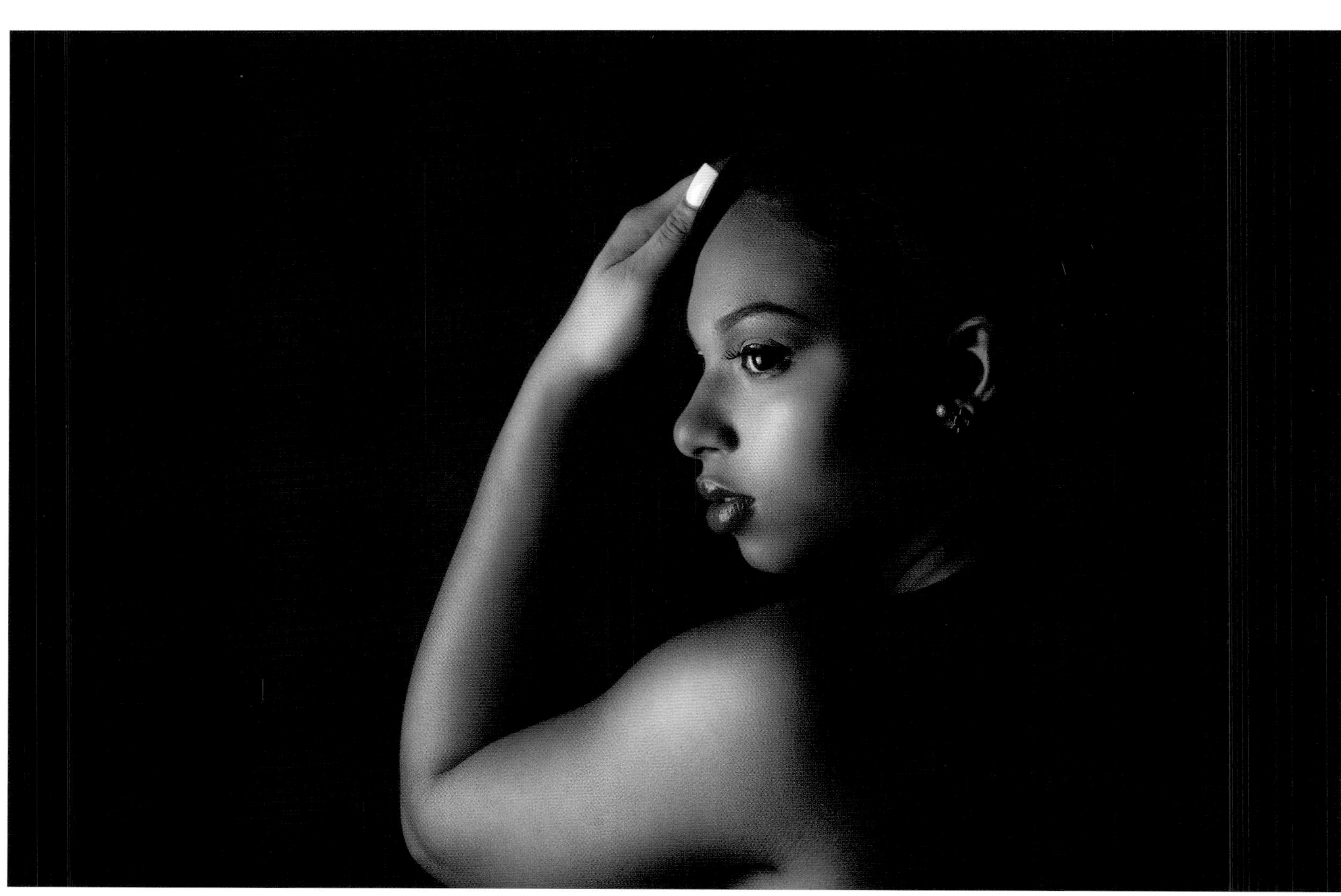

Adrien Broussard III

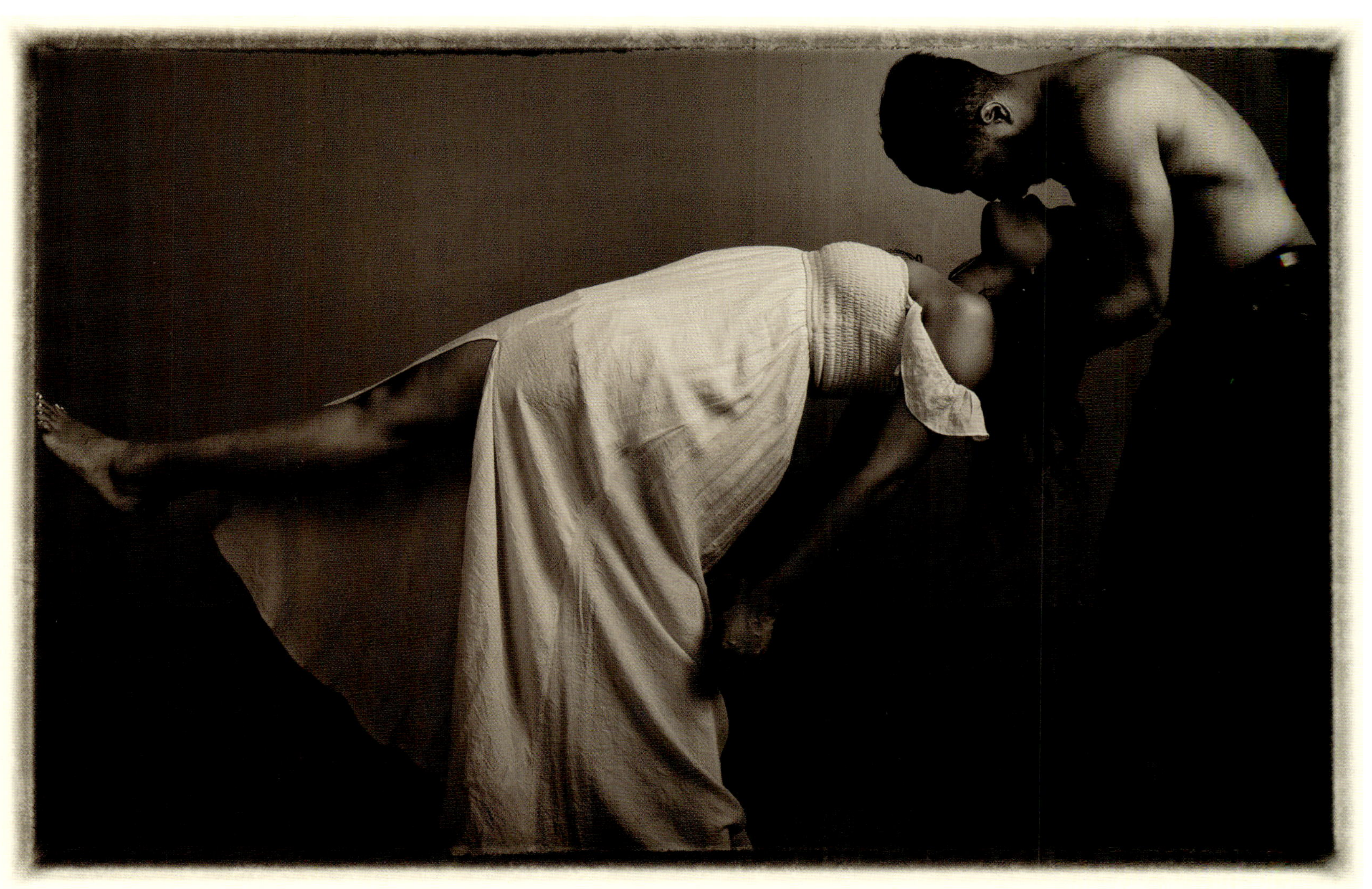

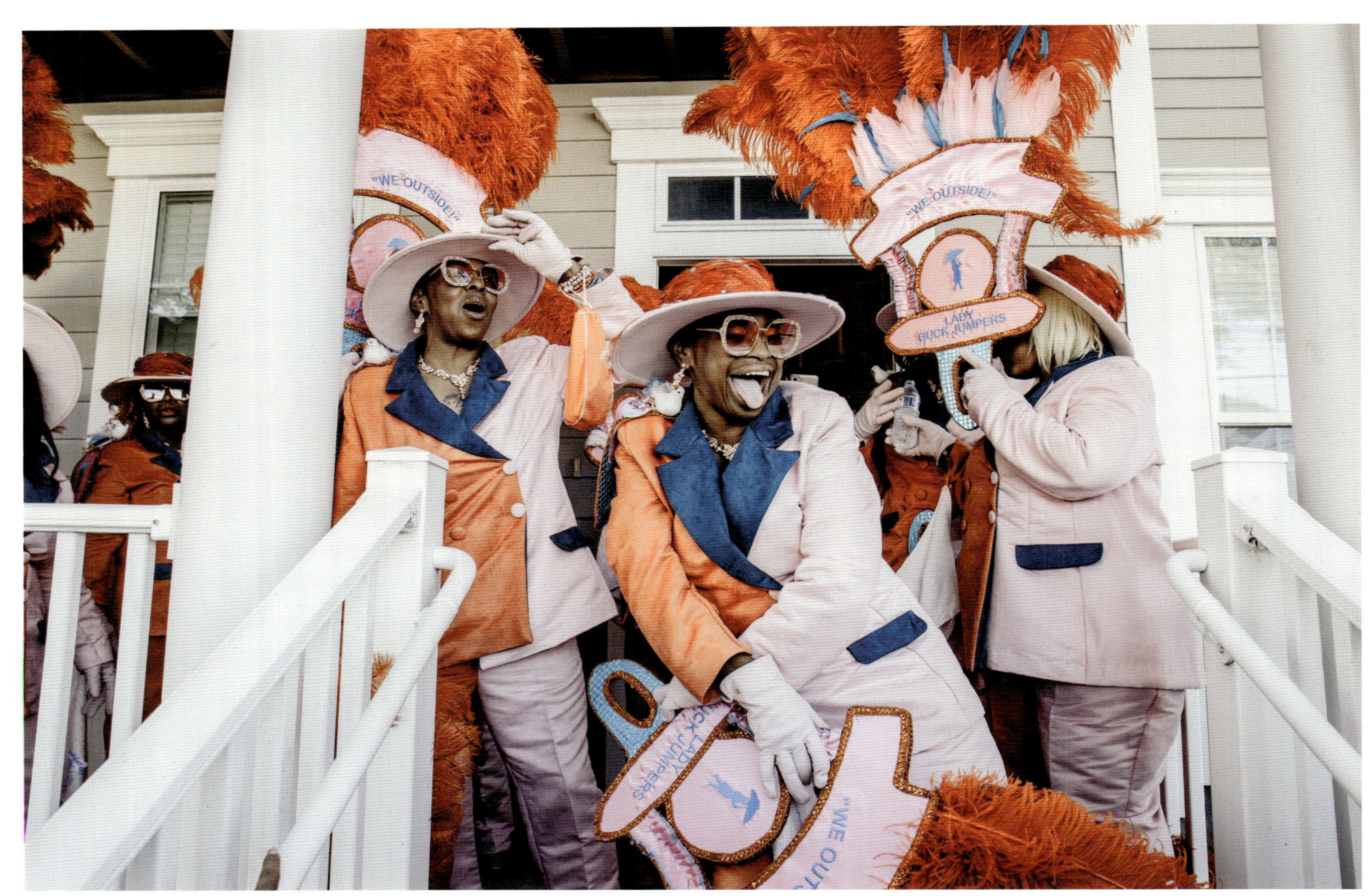
"WE OUTSIDE!"
"WE OUTSIDE!"
LADY
BUCK JUMPERS

Ashley Lorraine

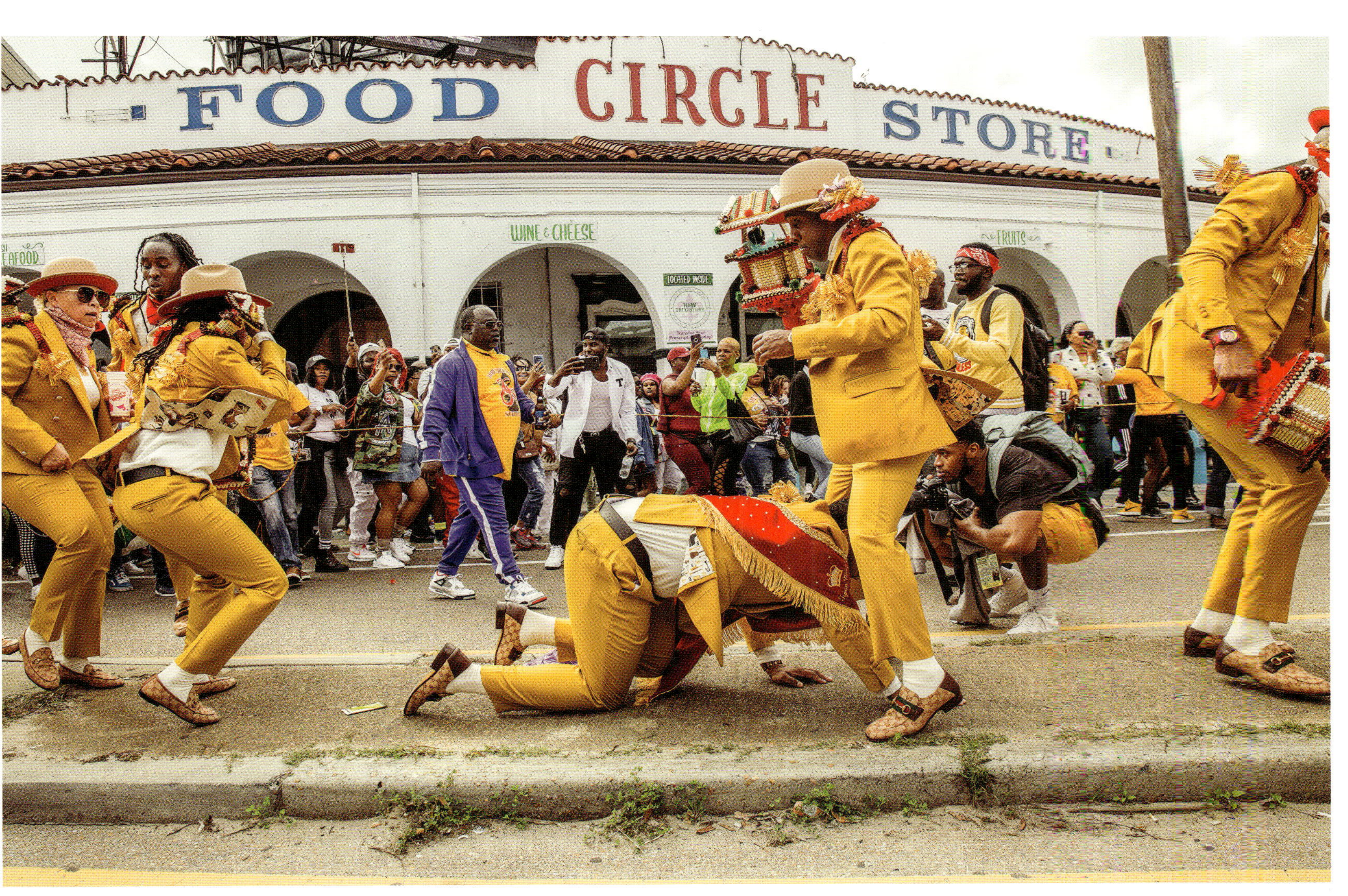

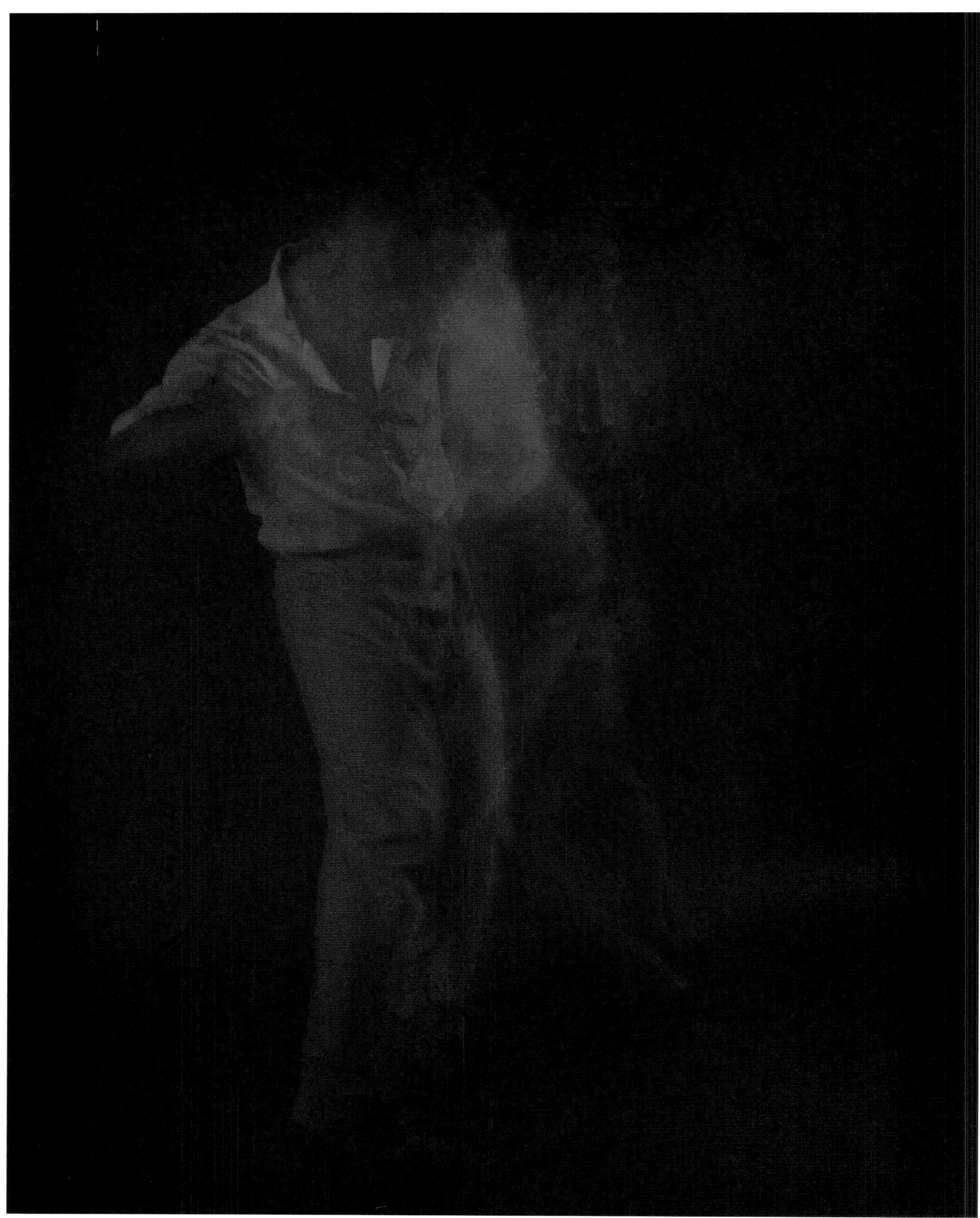

Benicia King

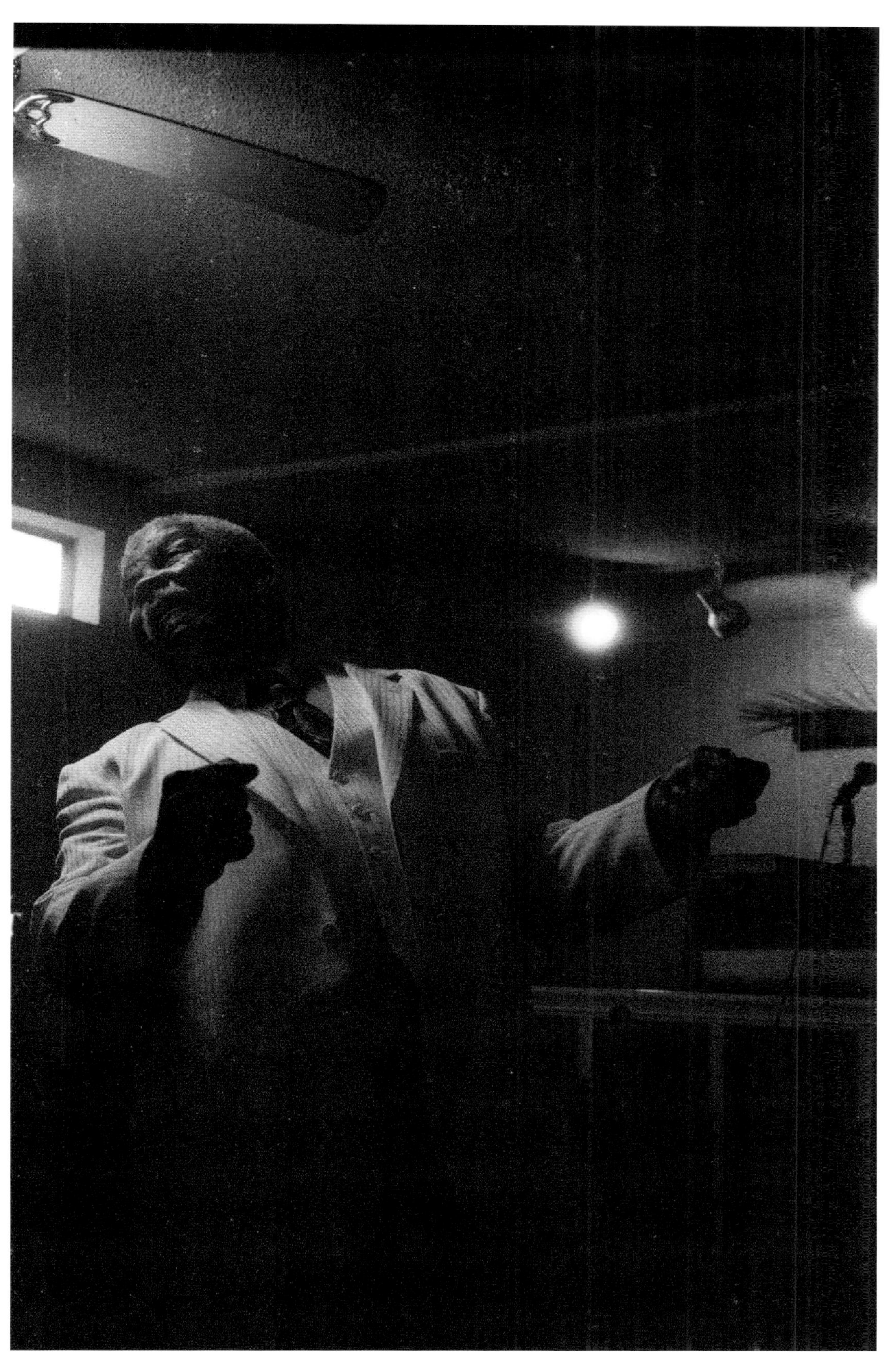

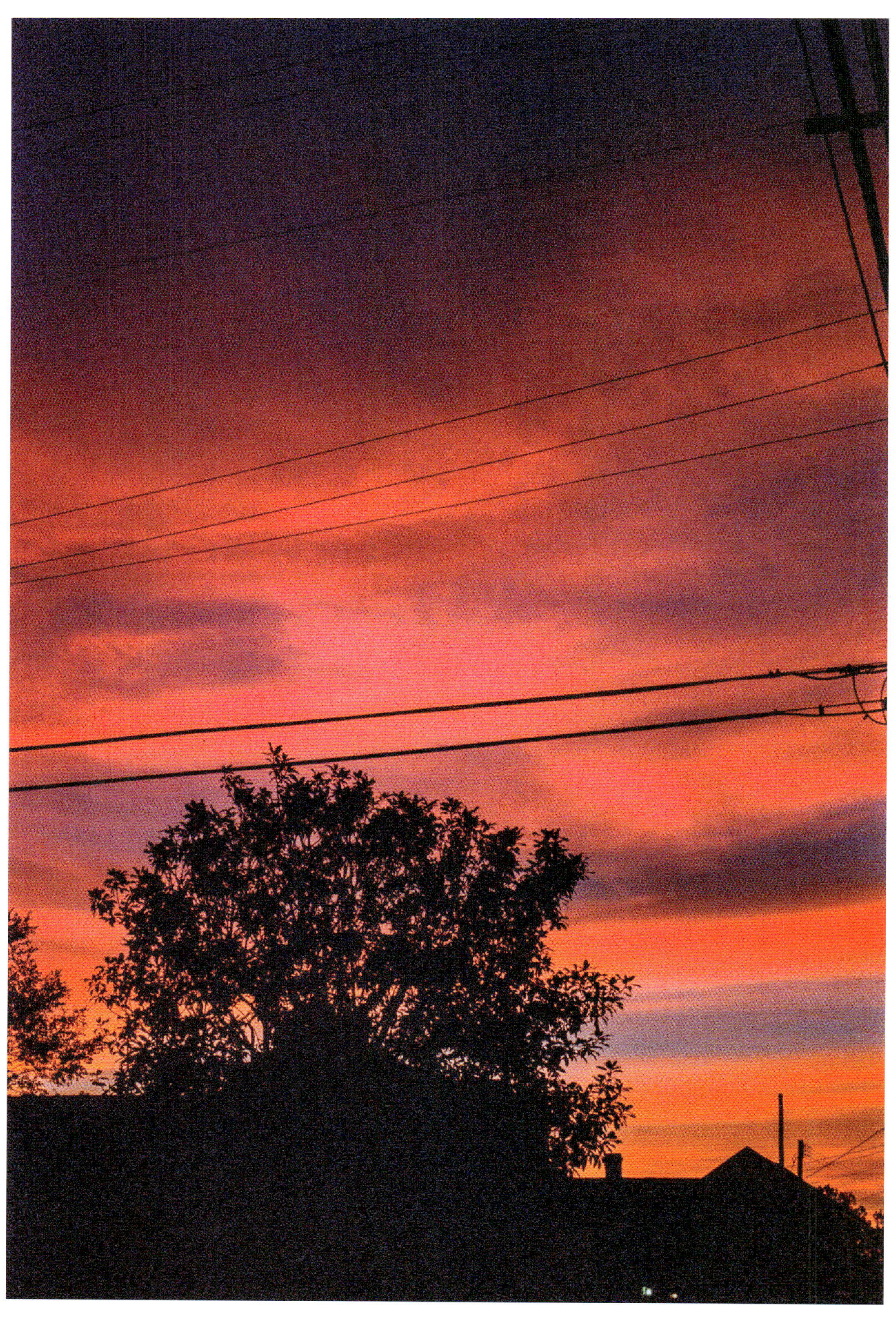

Bruce Q. Williams

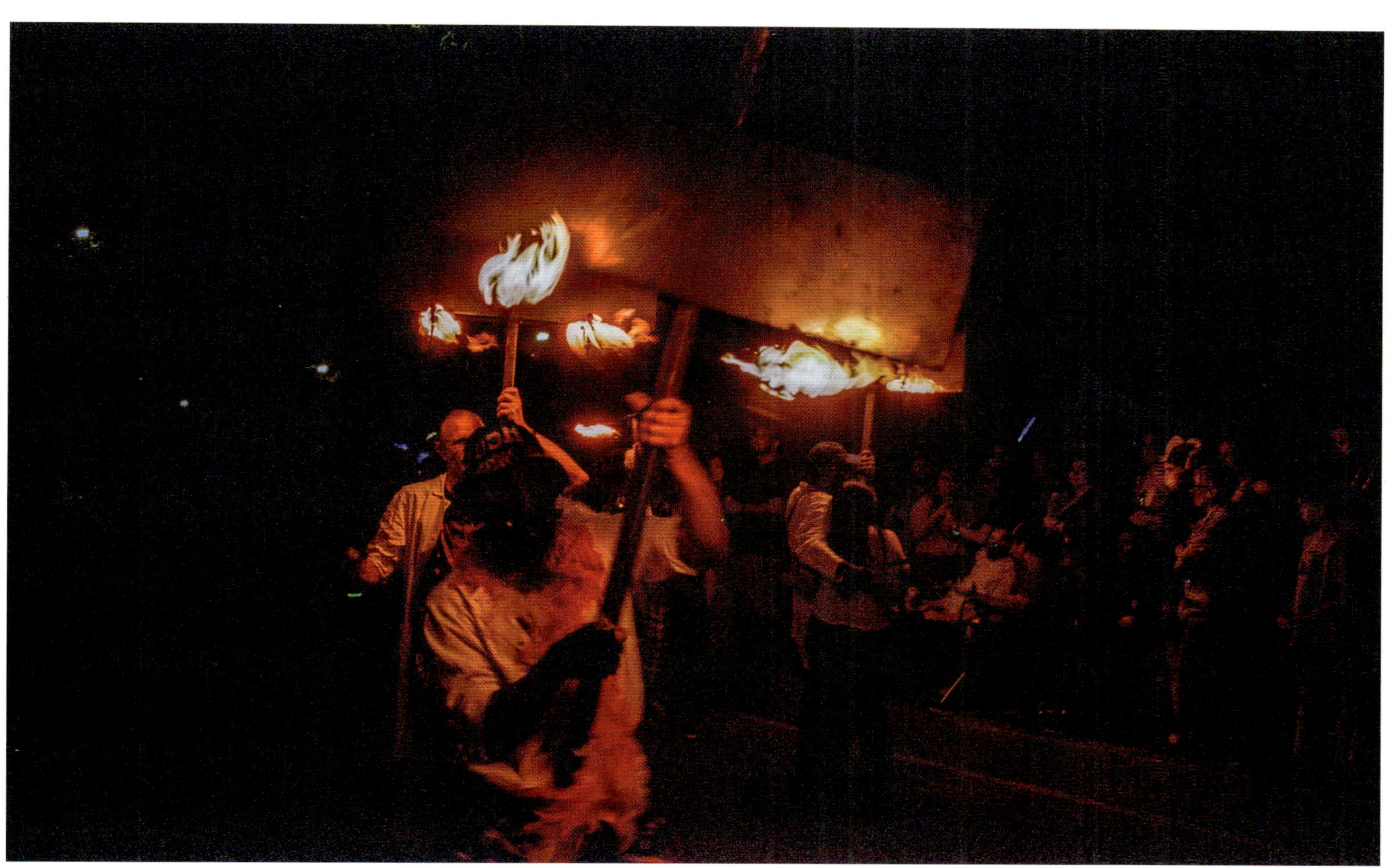

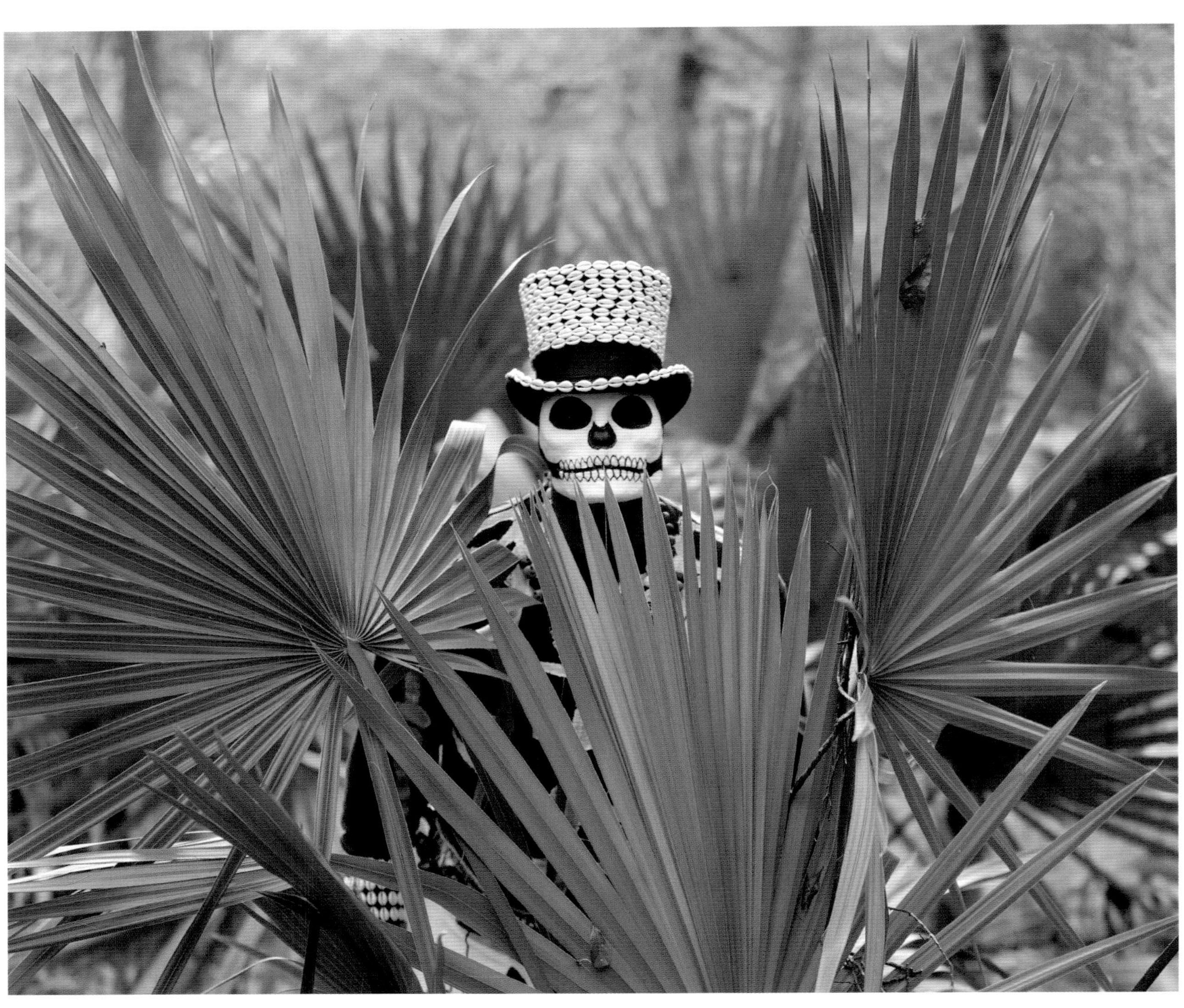

Bruce "Sunpie" Barnes

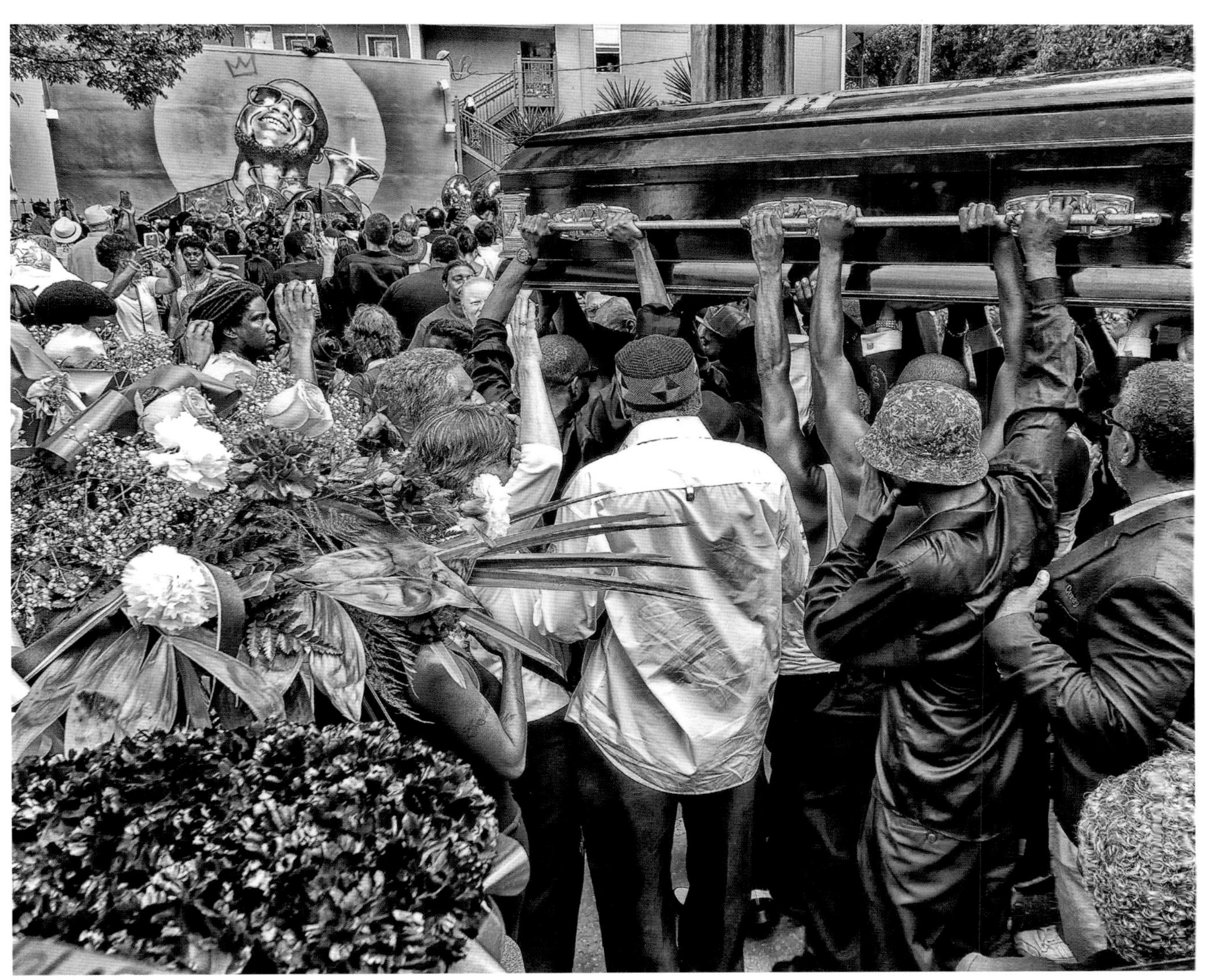

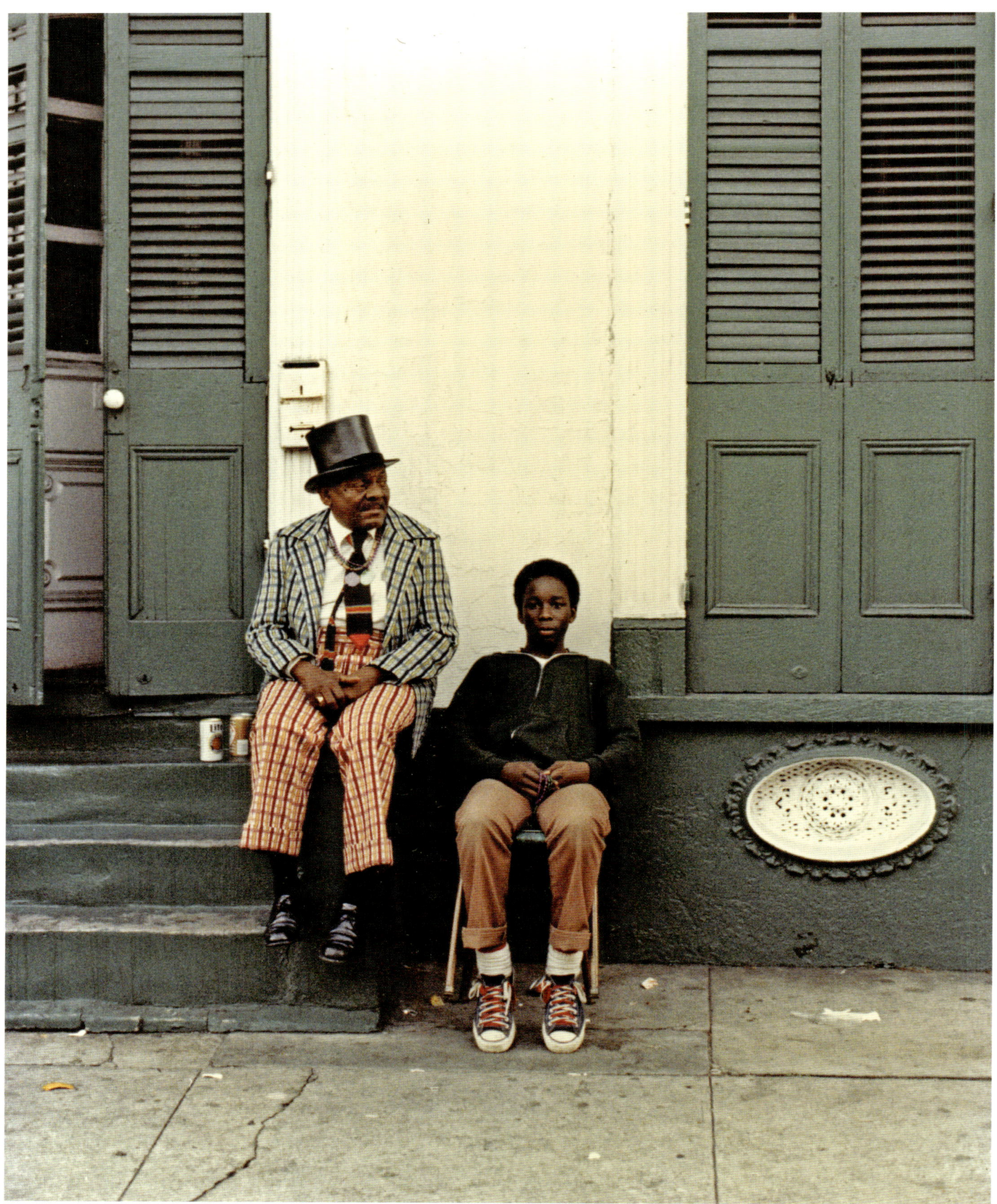

Bryan Hithe

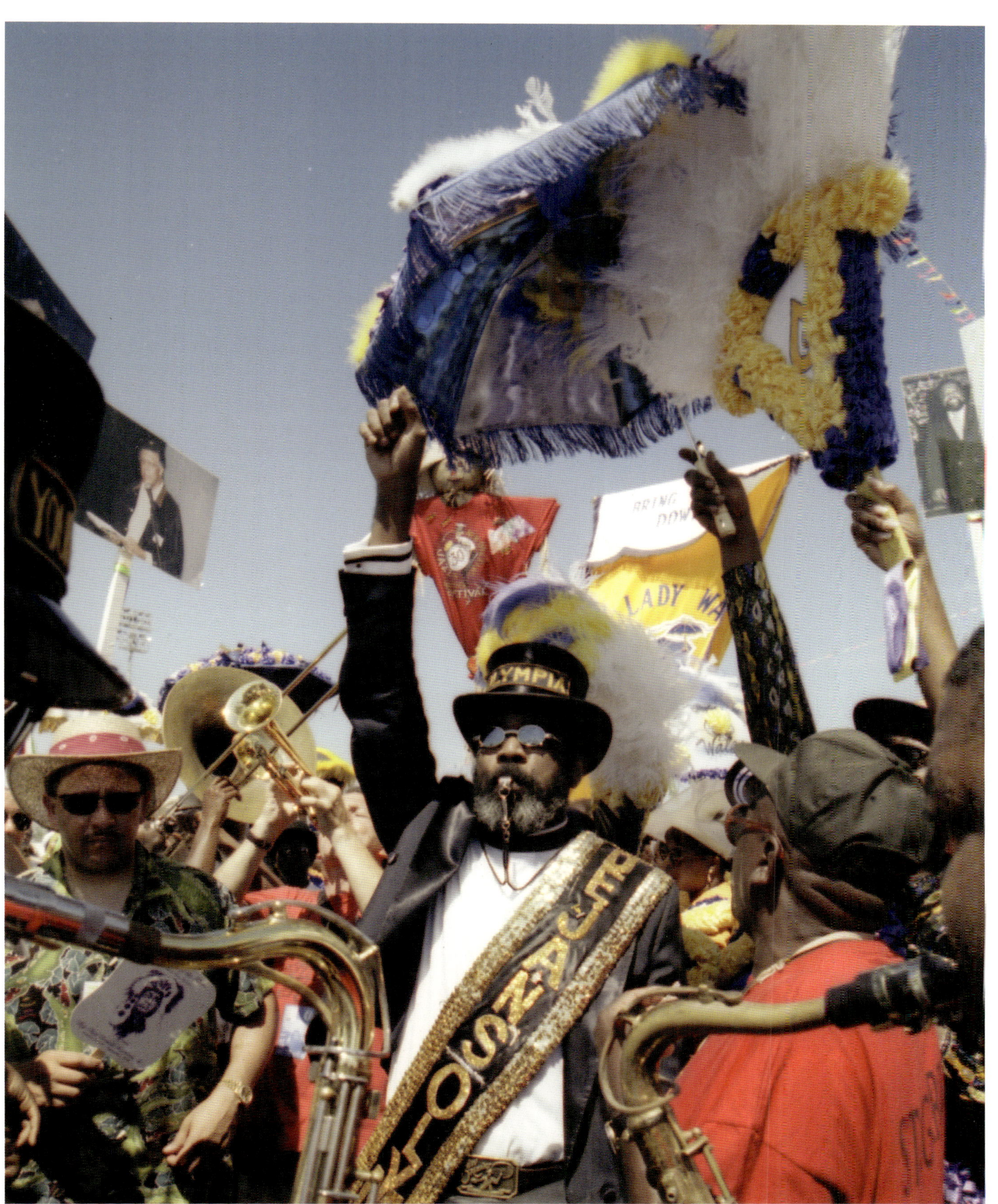

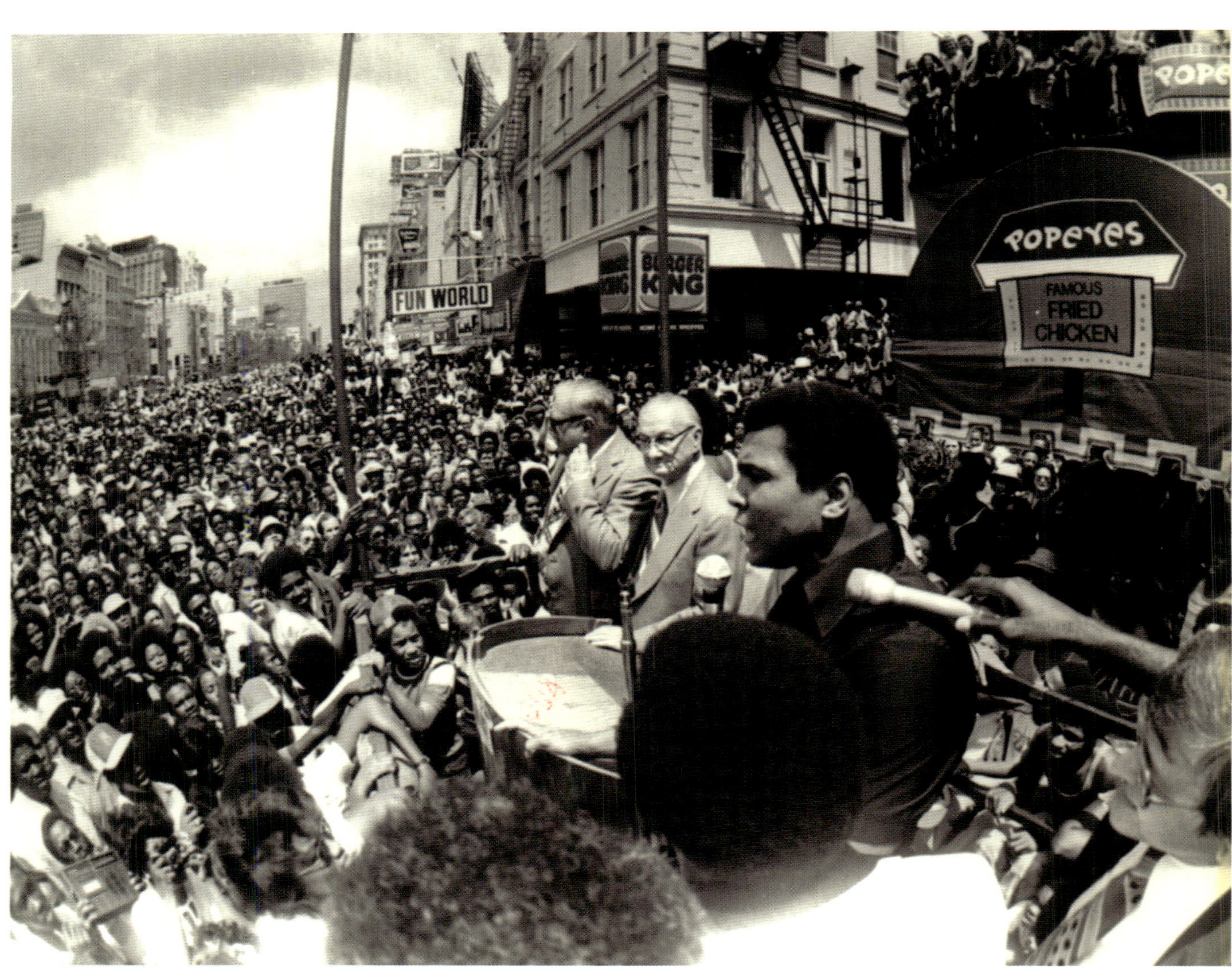
FUN WORLD
BURGER KING
BURGER KING
POPEYES
FAMOUS
FRIED
CHICKEN

Bryan S. Berteaux Sr.

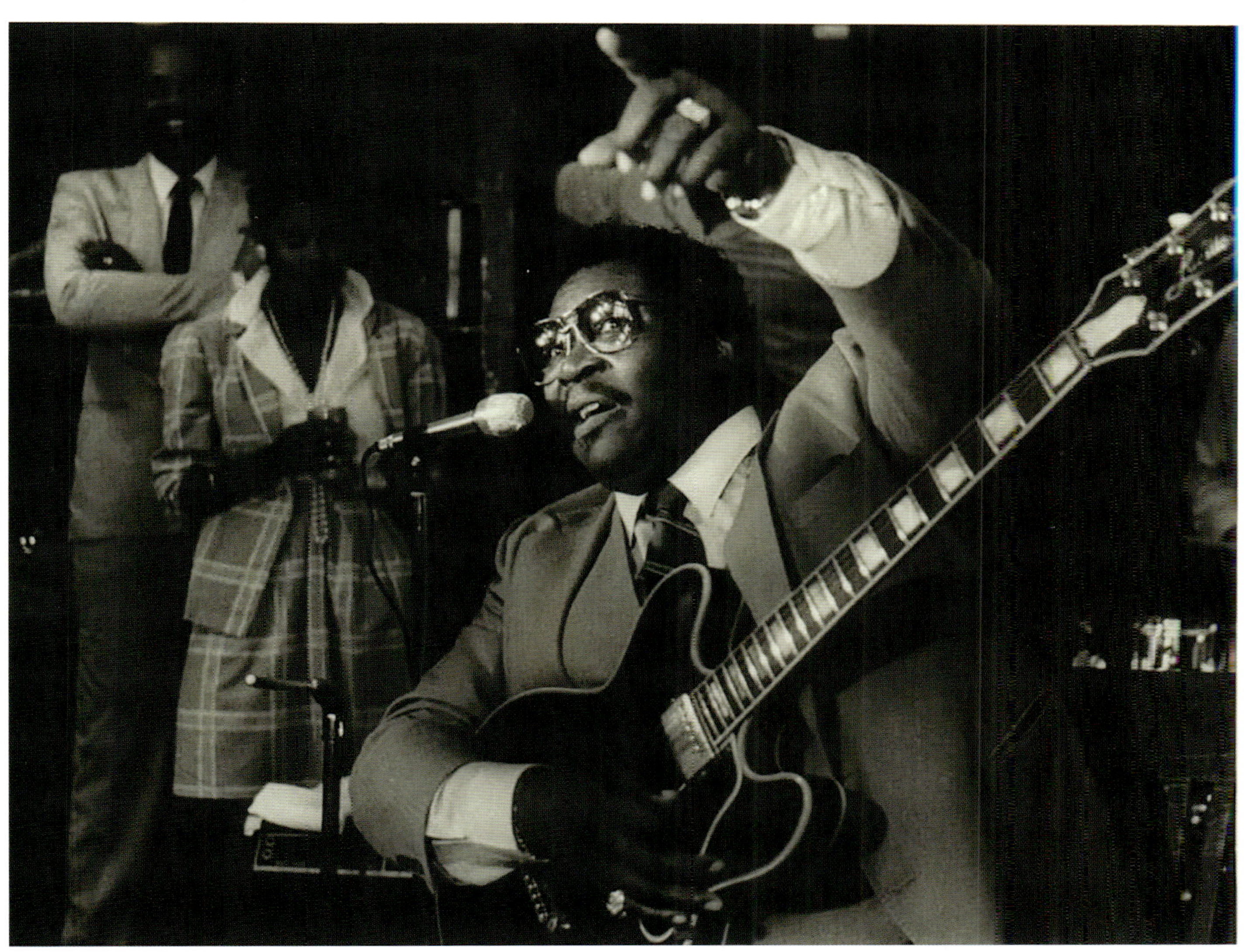

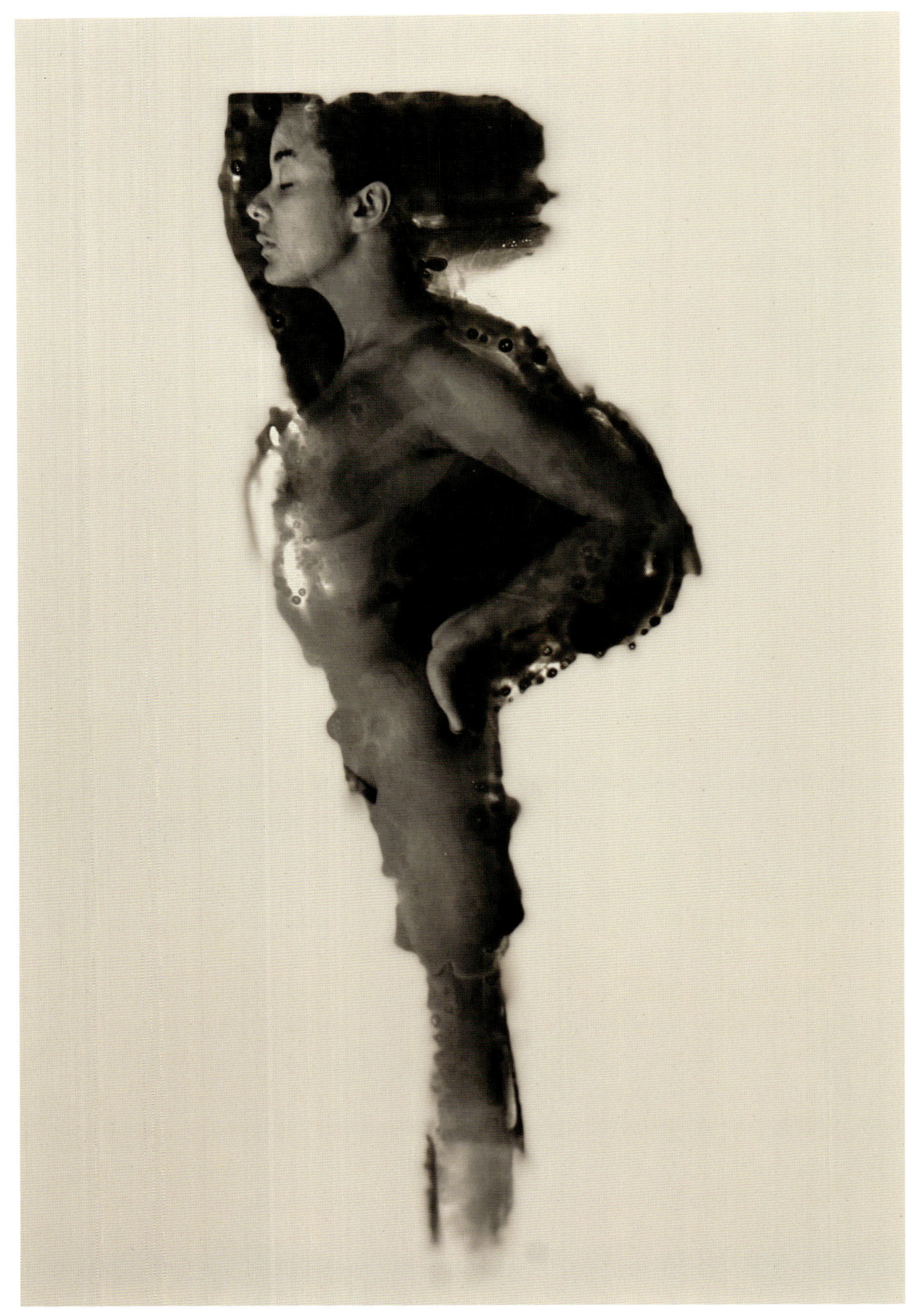

Carla Williams

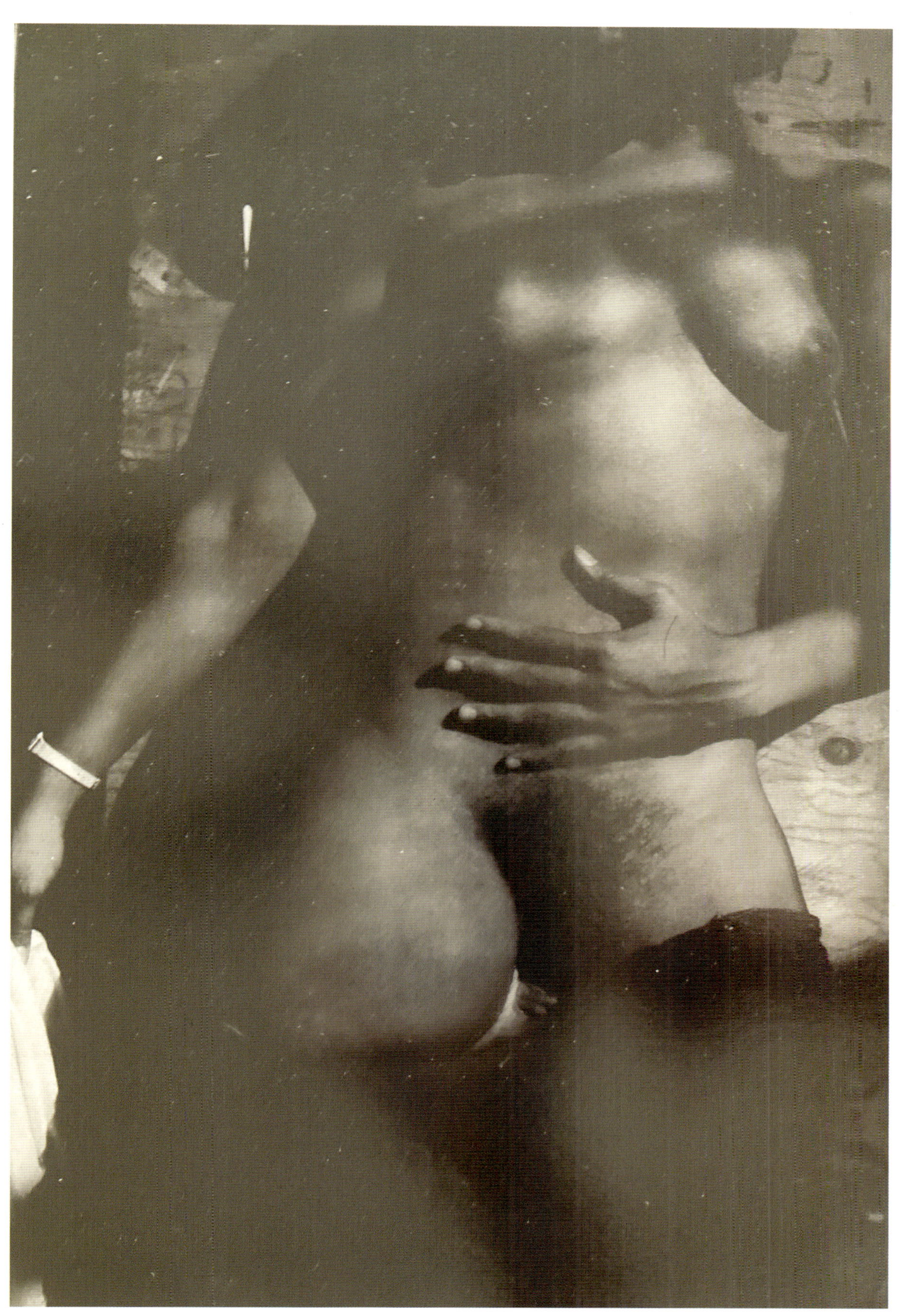

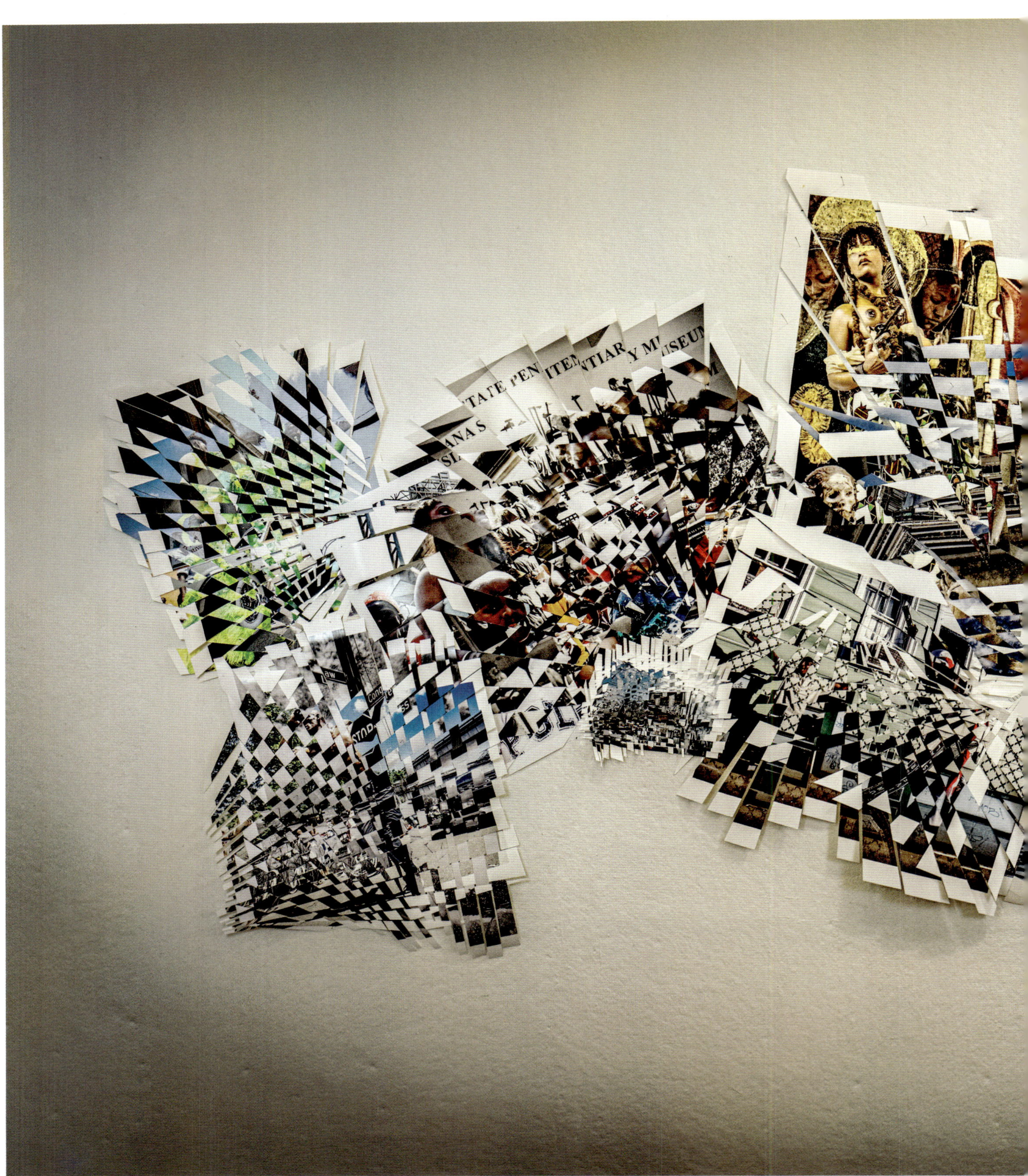

Cecelia Fernandes

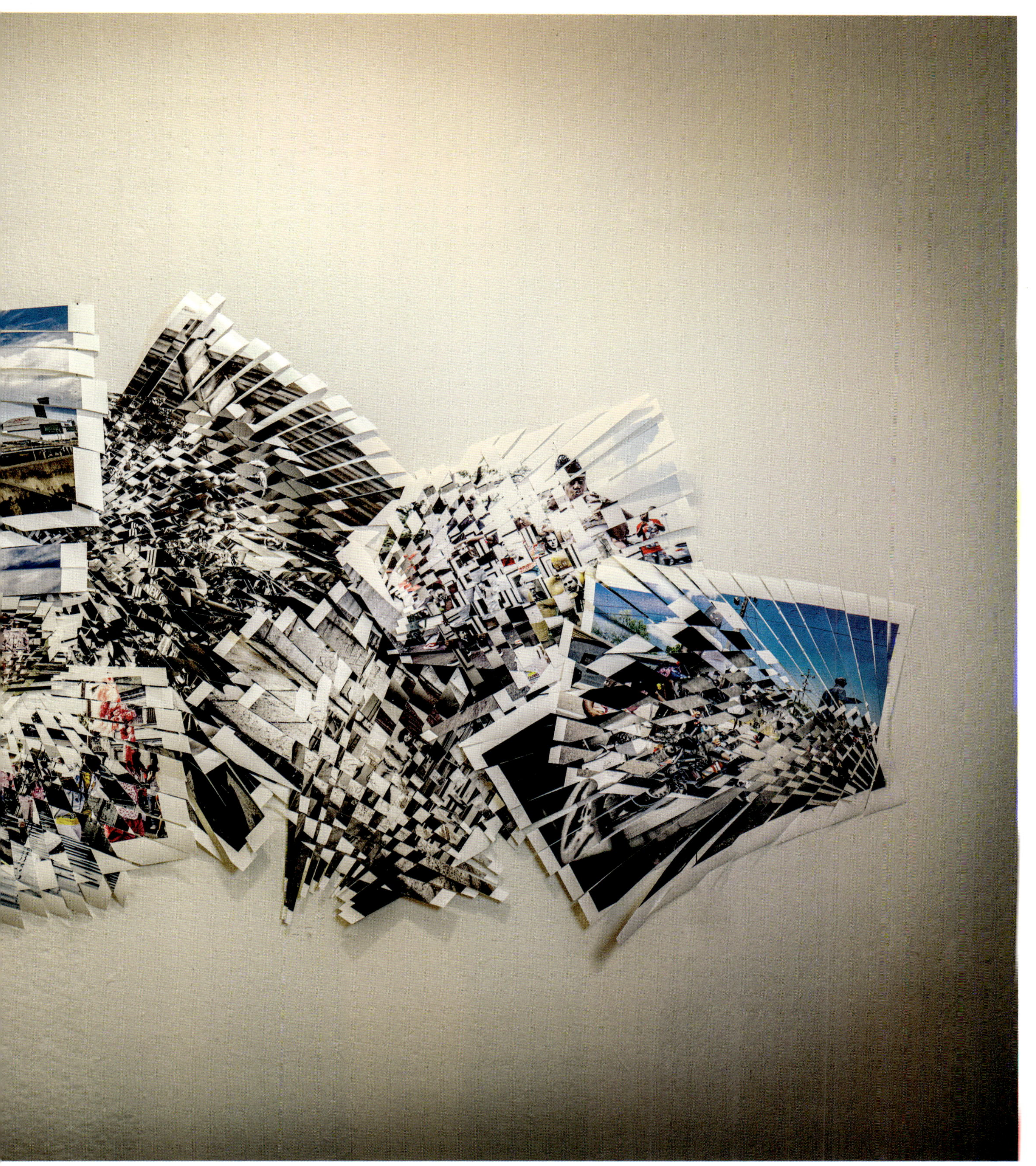

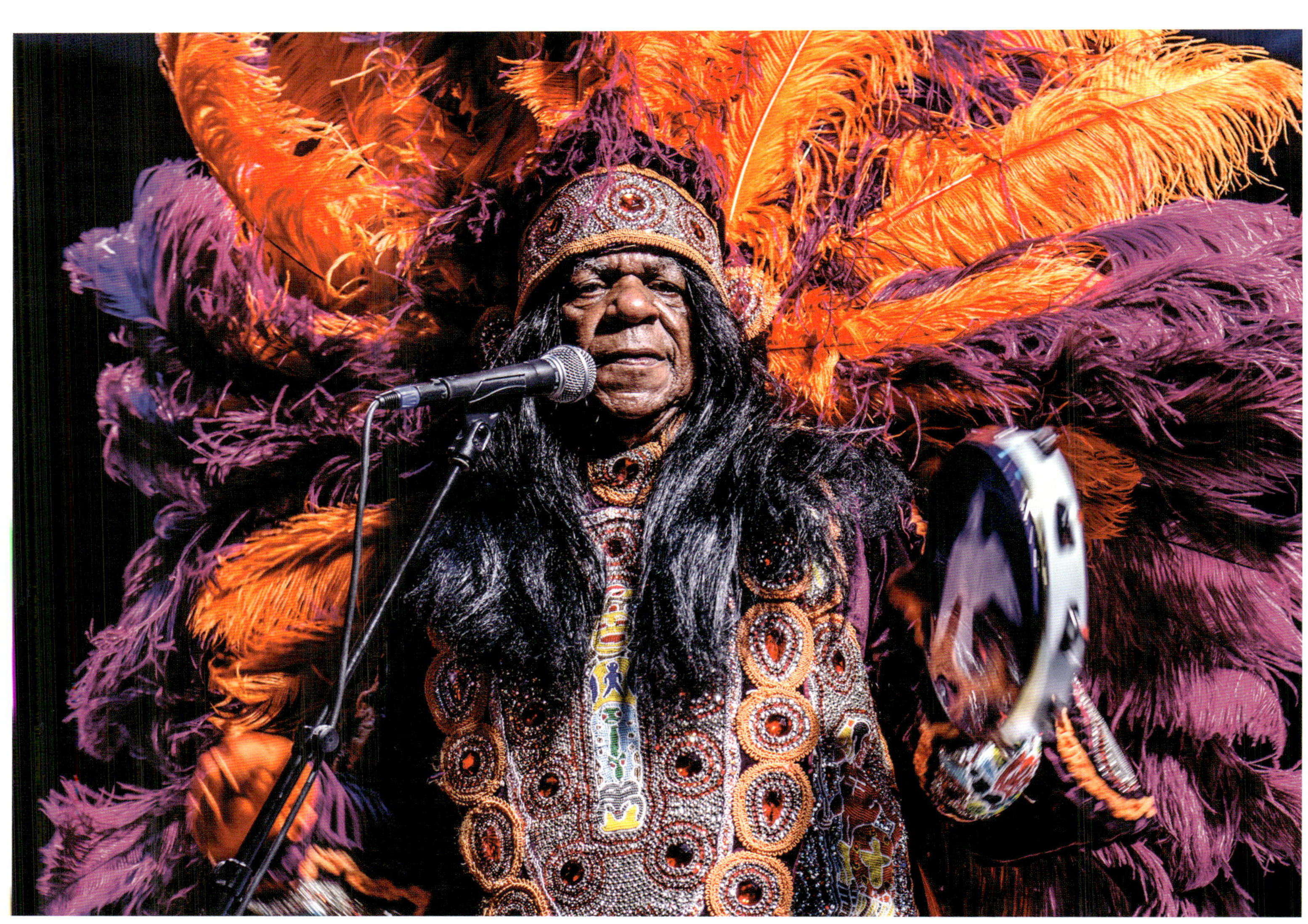

Cedric A. Ellsworth

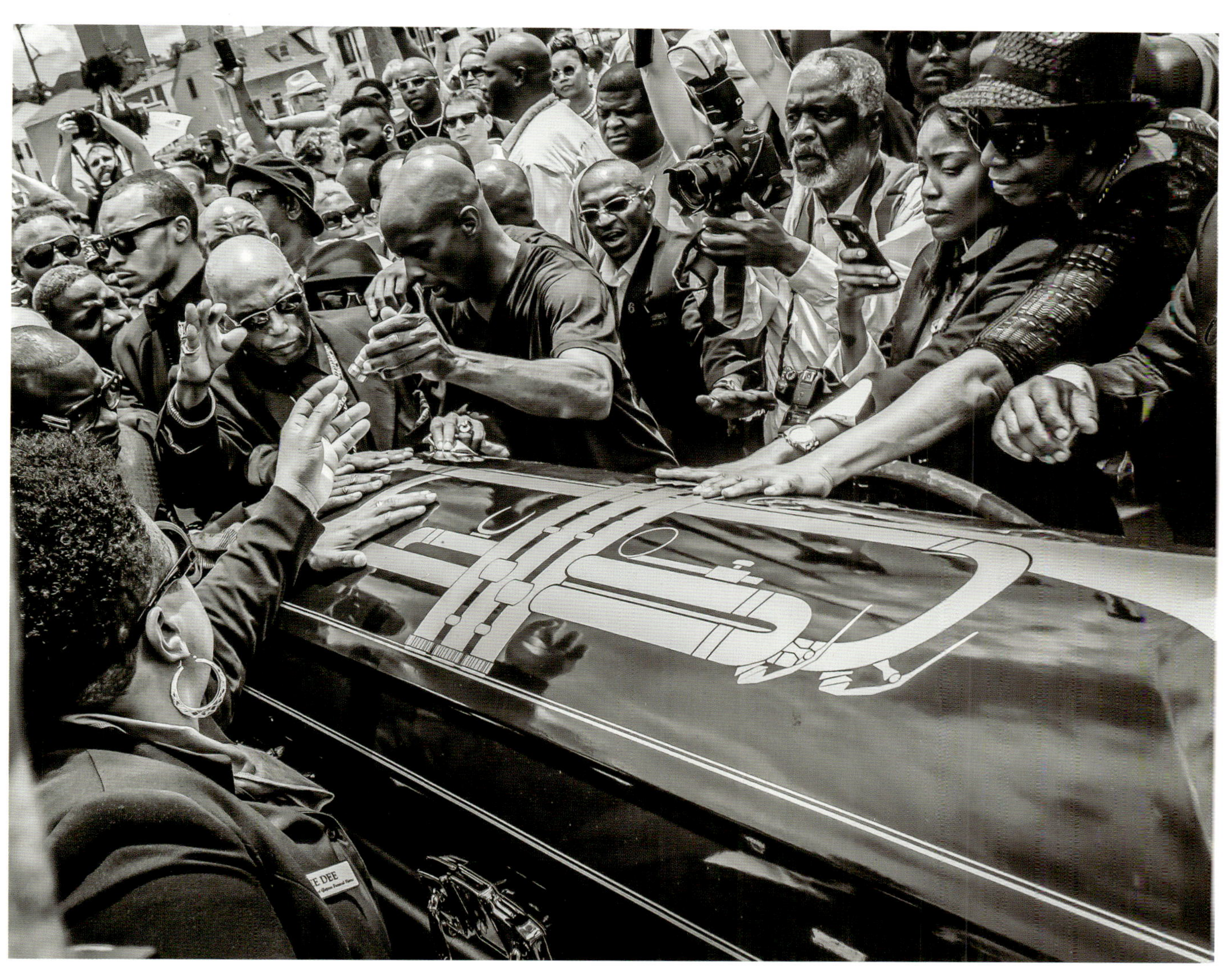

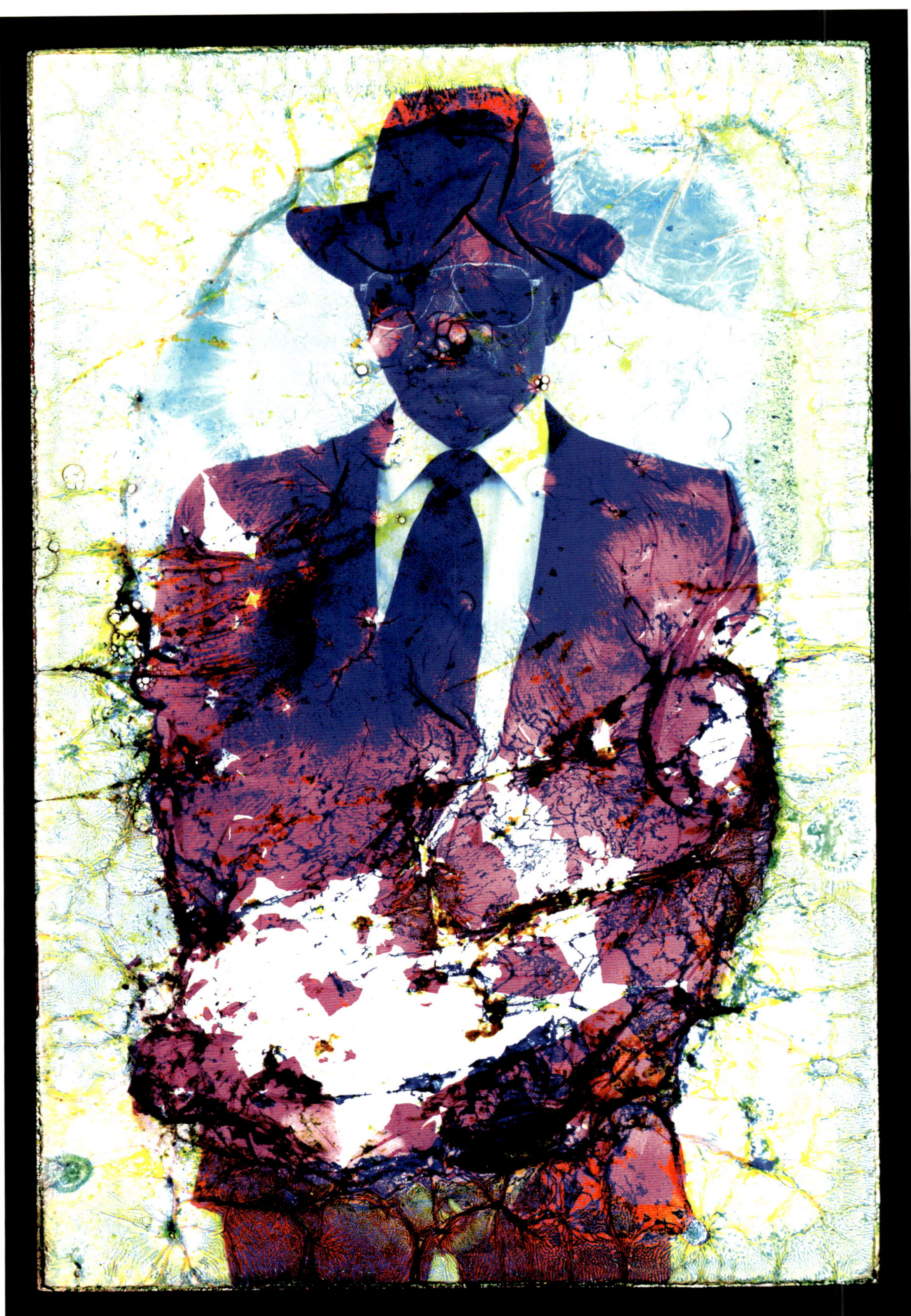

Chandra McCormick

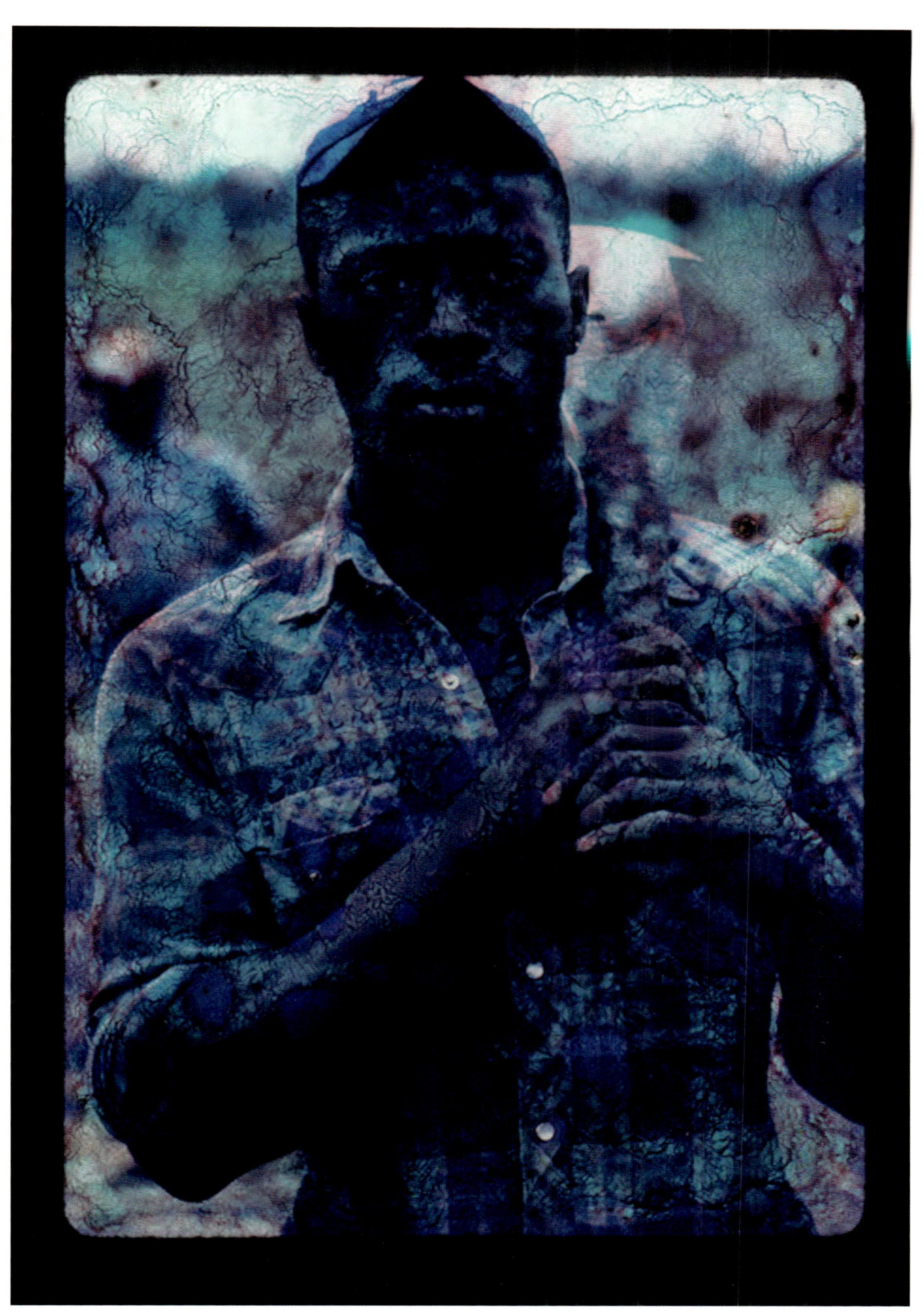

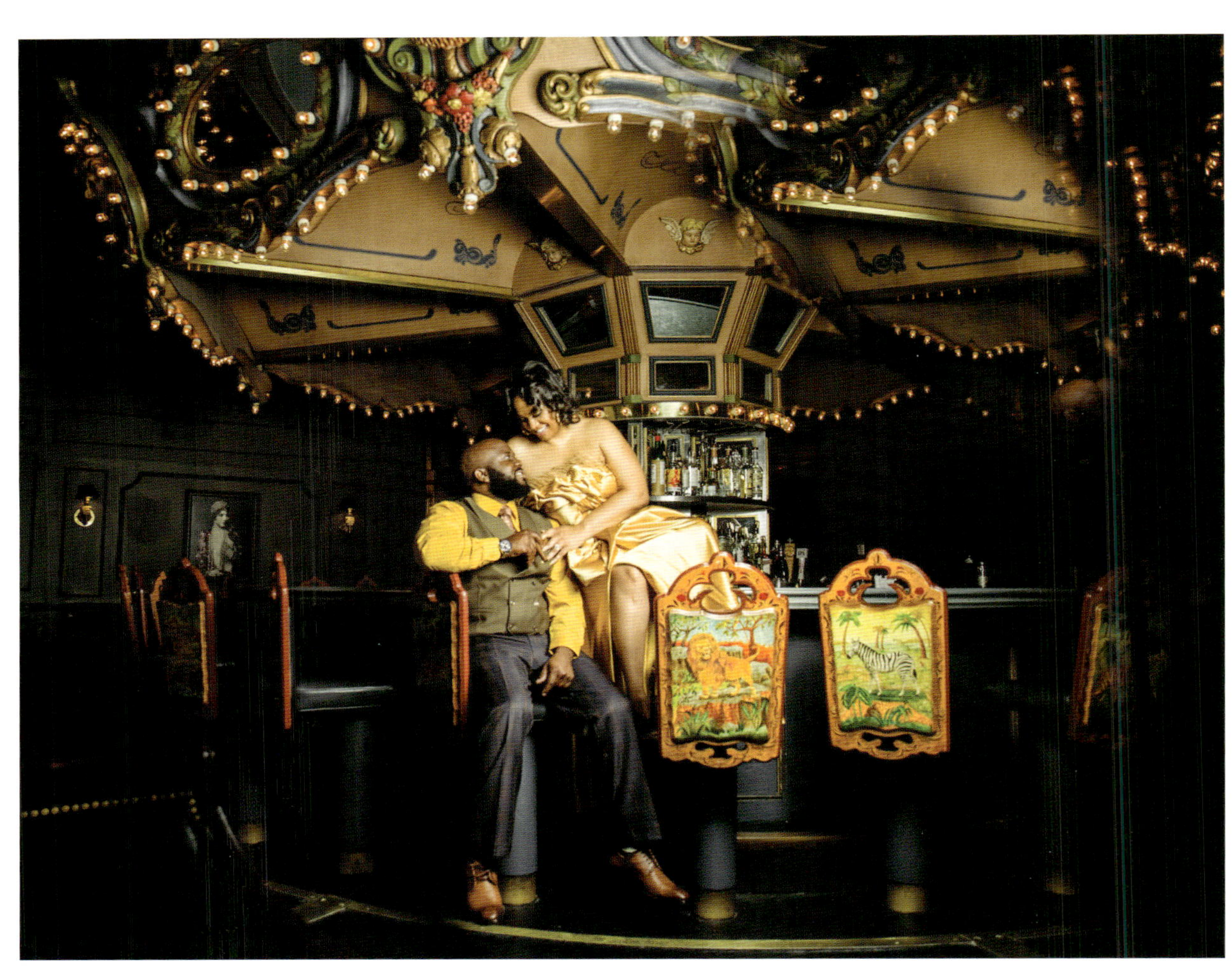

Chanelle Harris

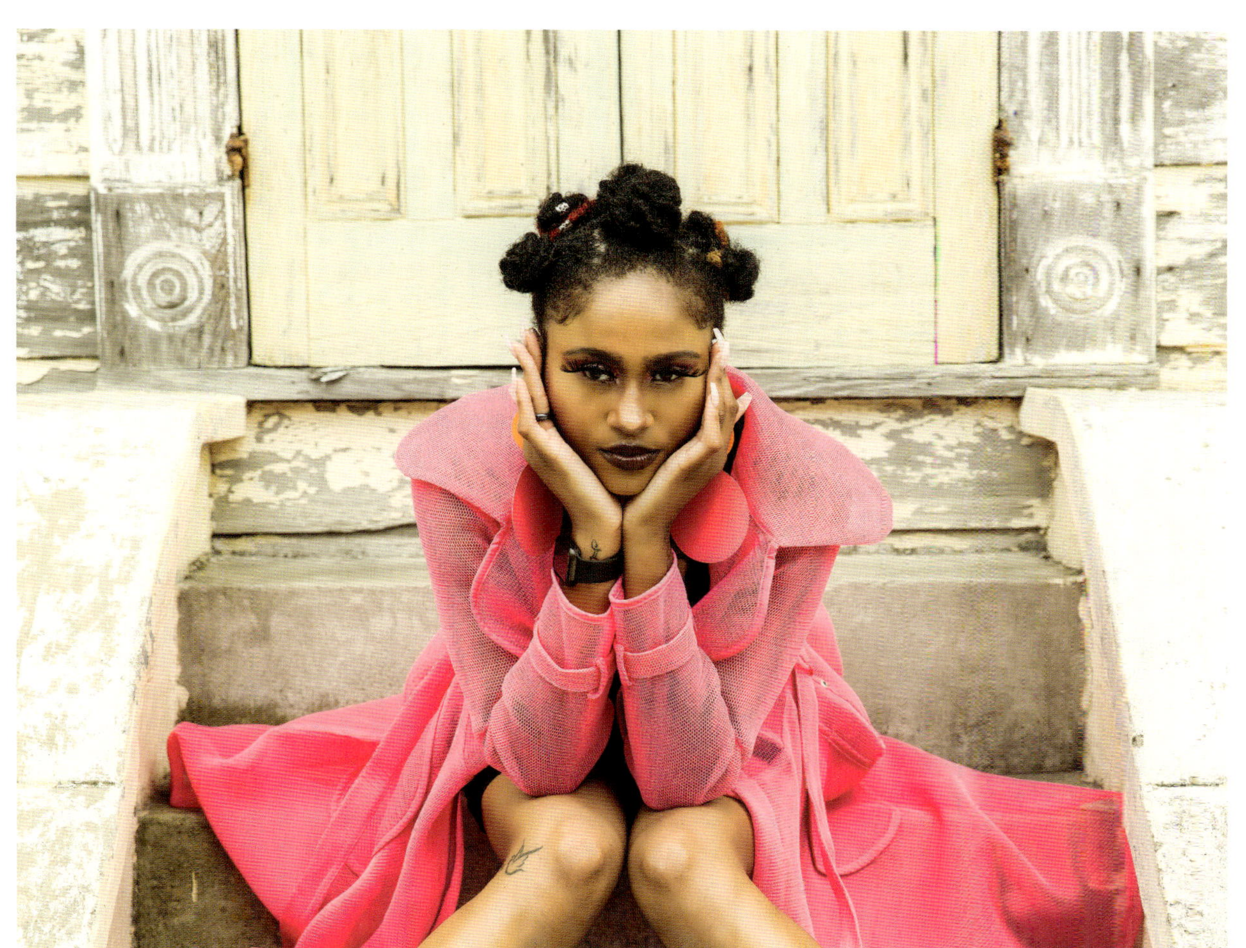

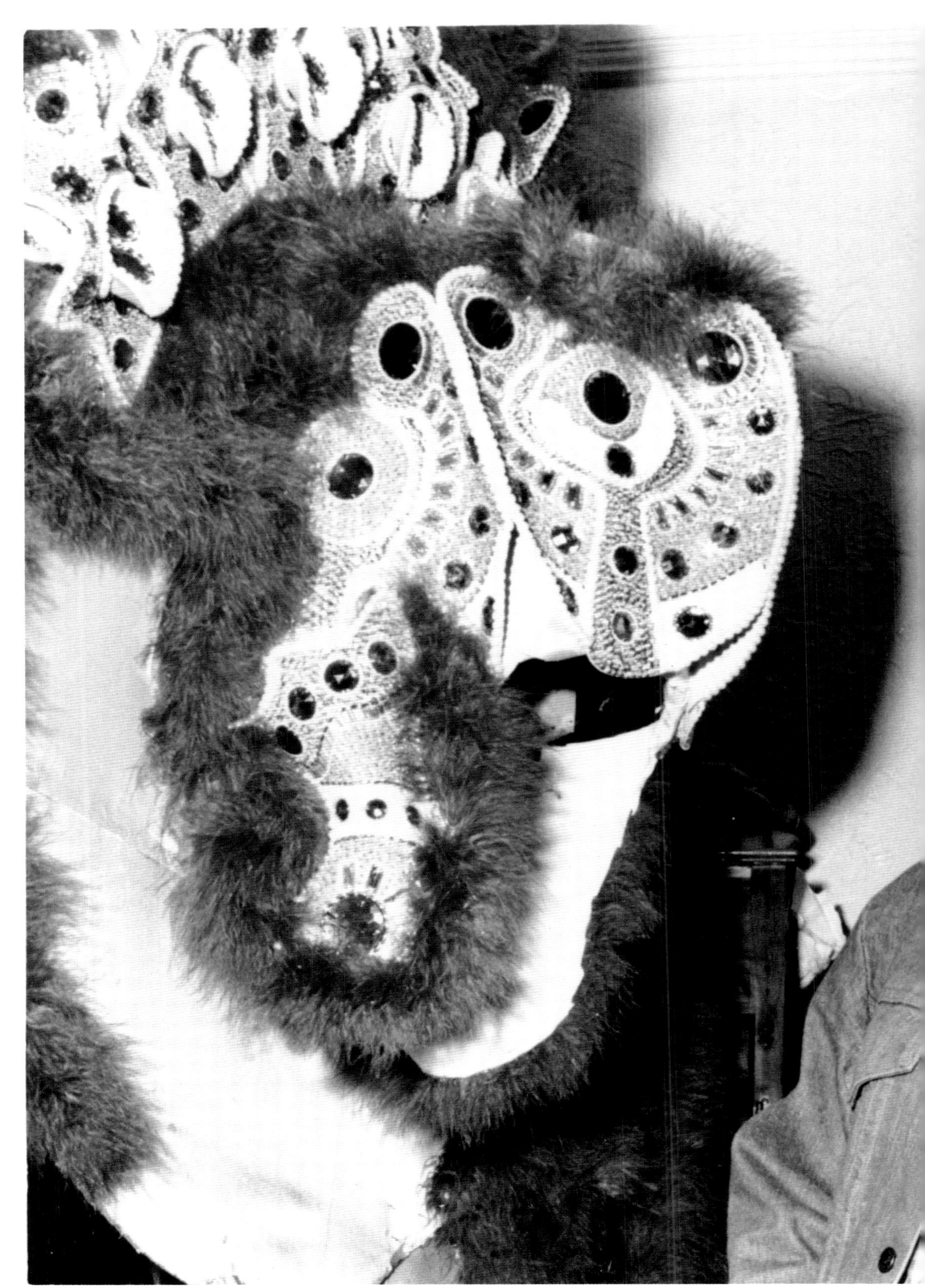

Charlene Legaux Richard

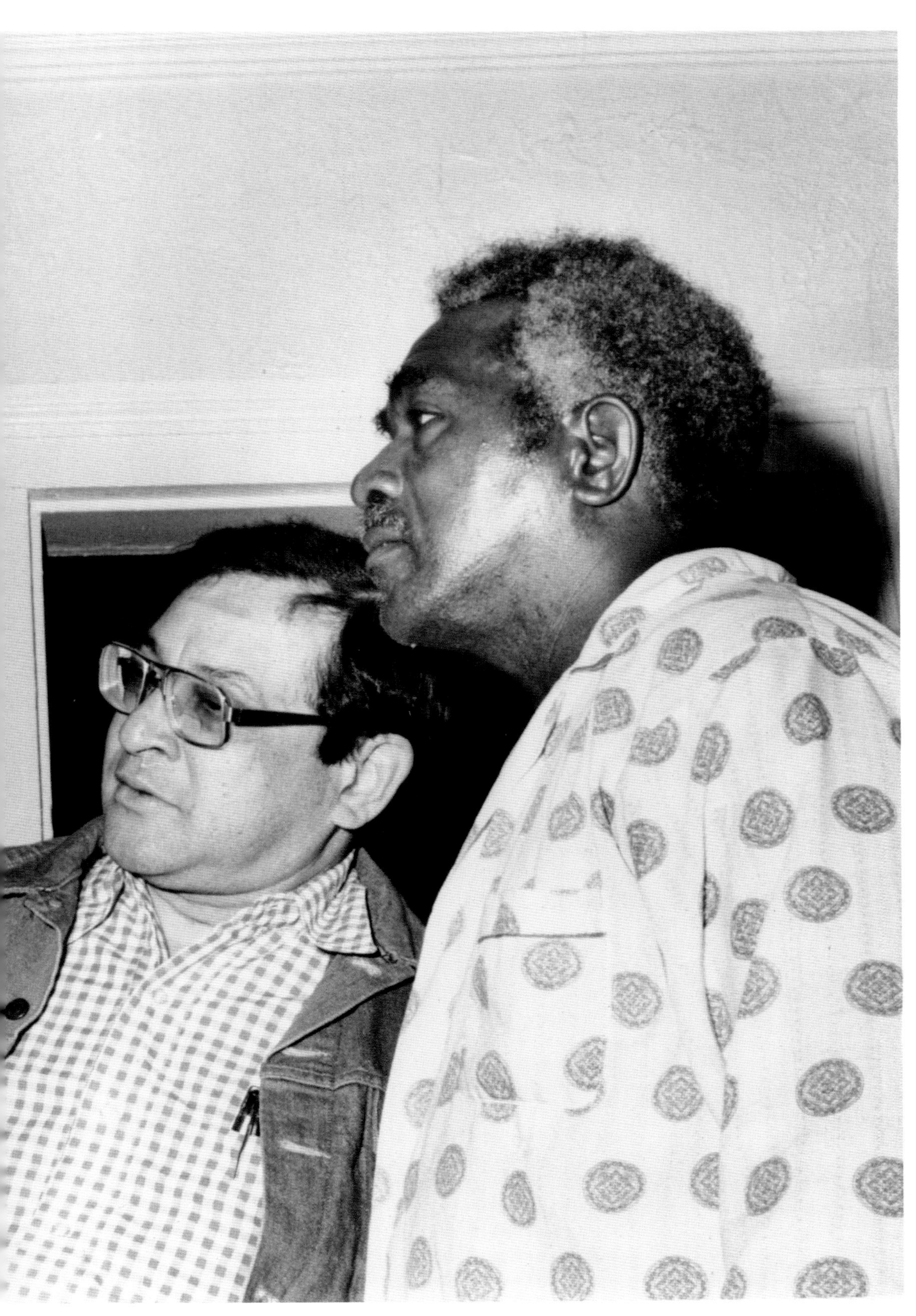

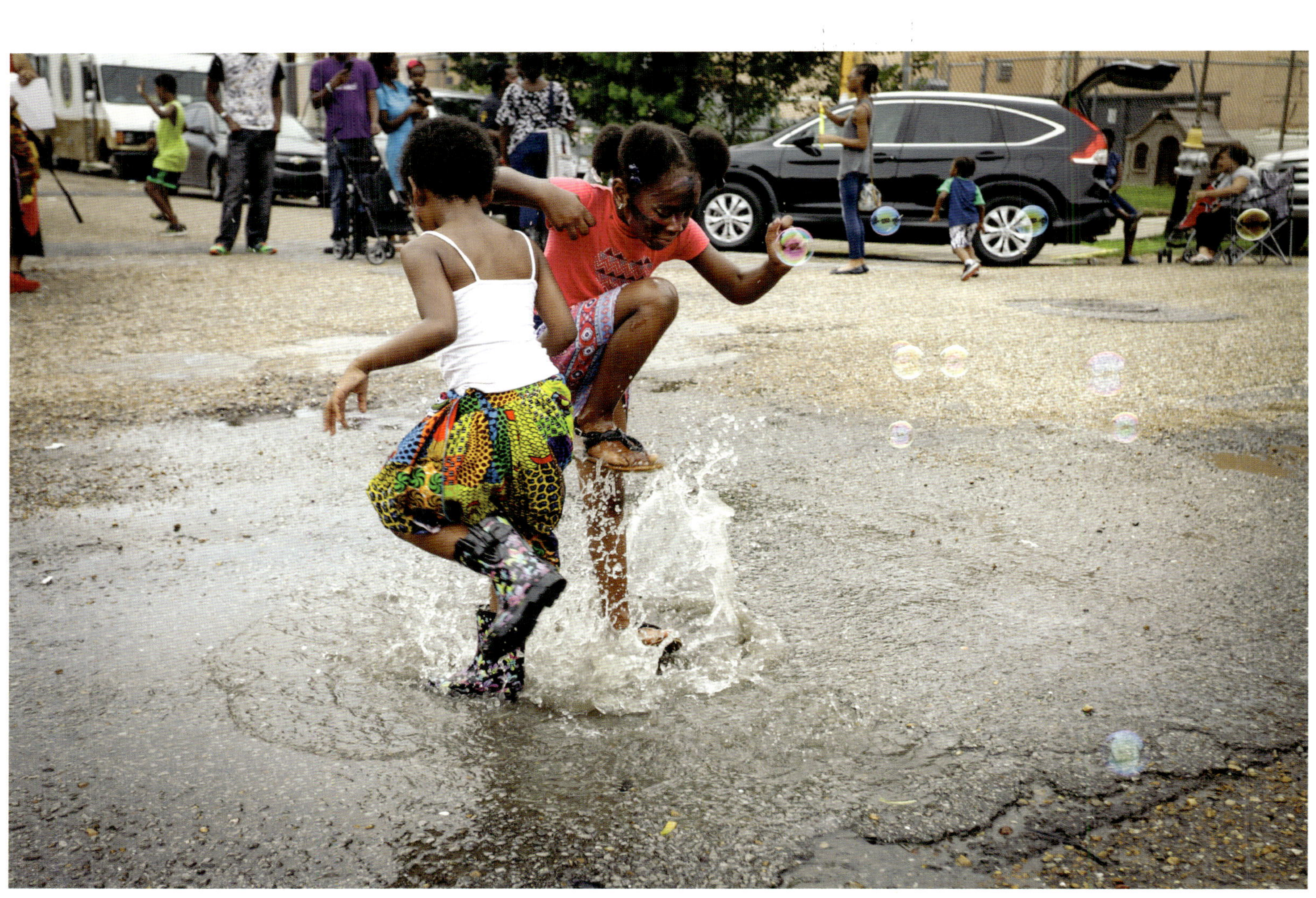

Christine "Cfreedom" Brown

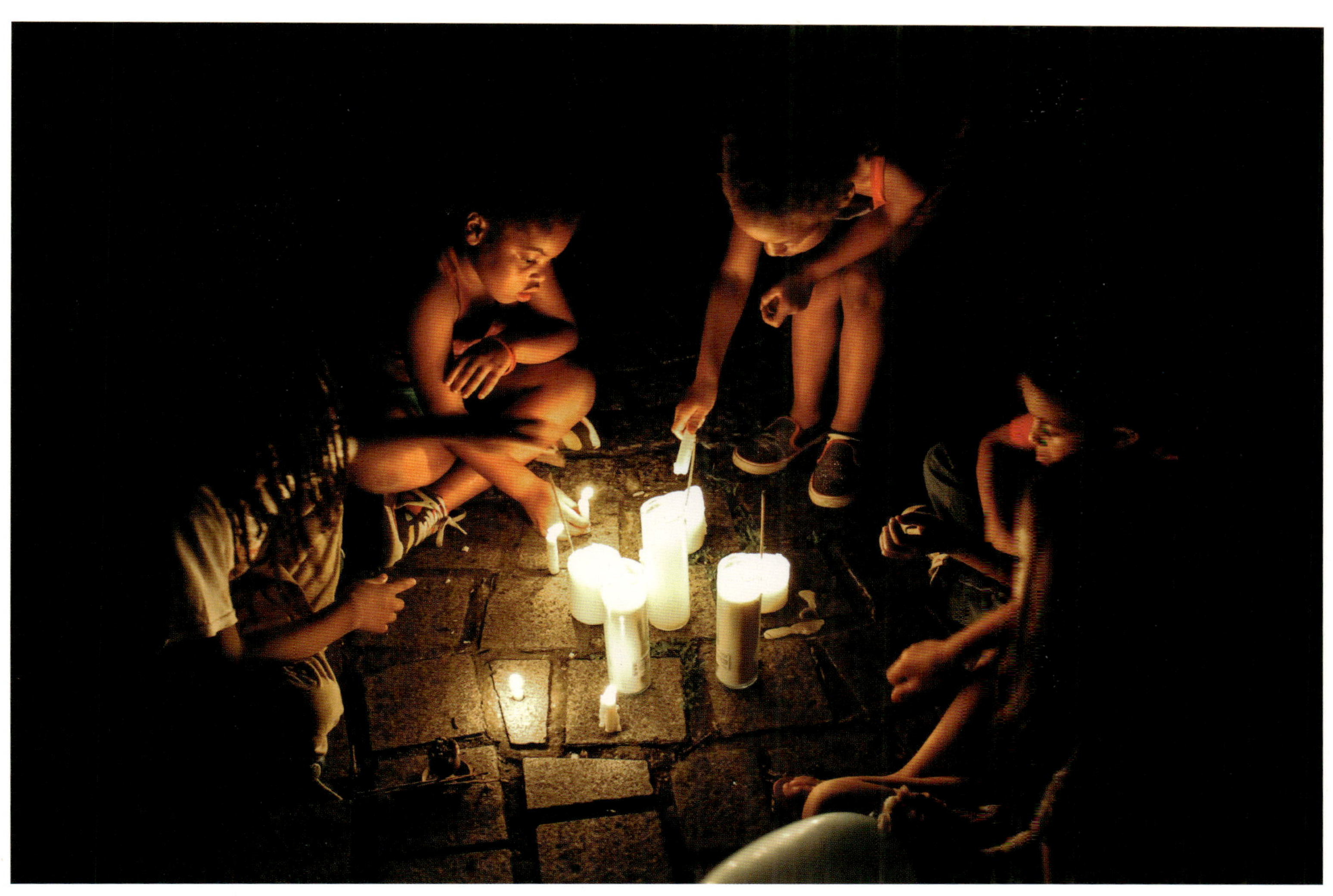

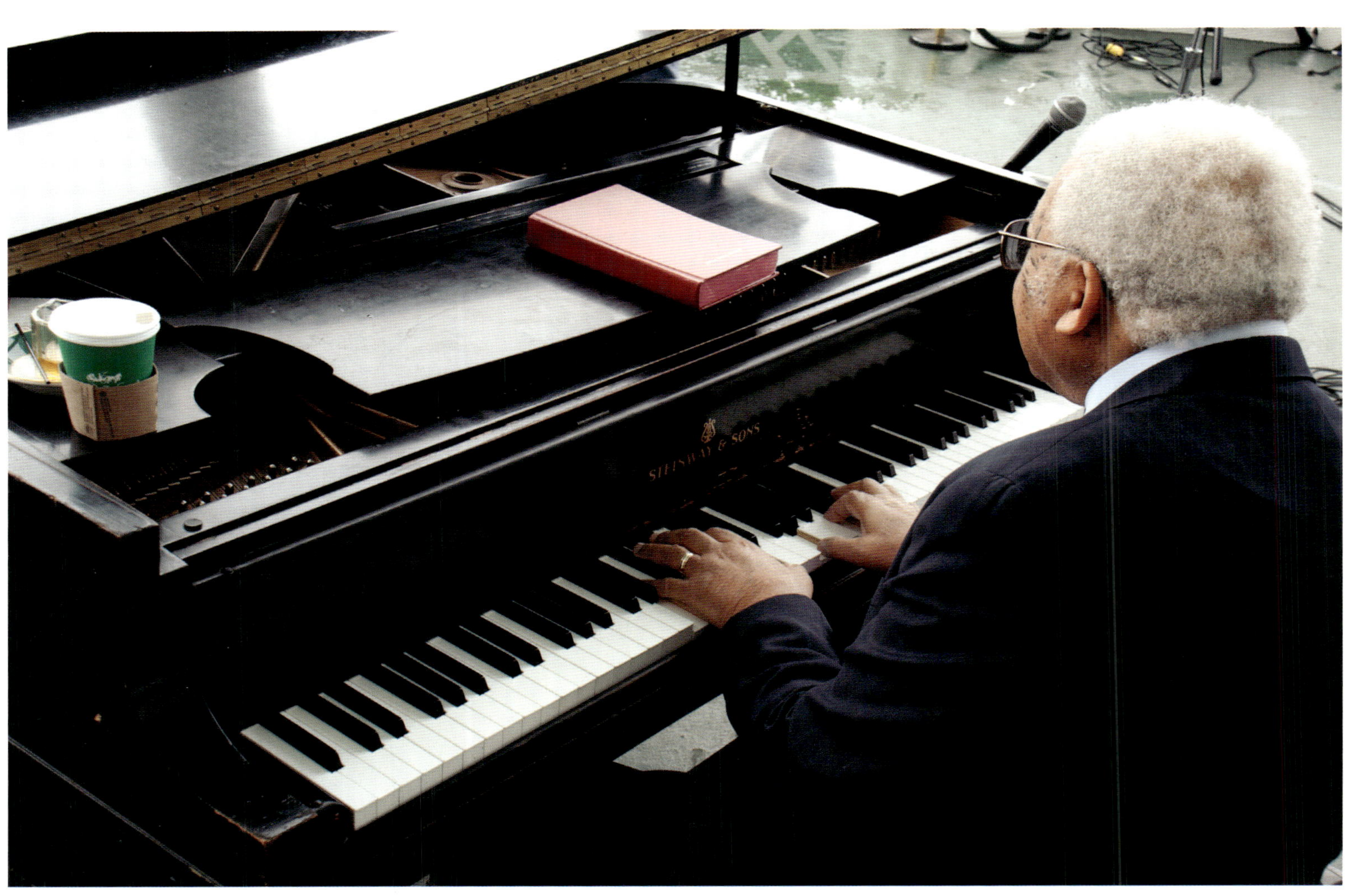
STEINWAY & SONS

Clifton J. Faust

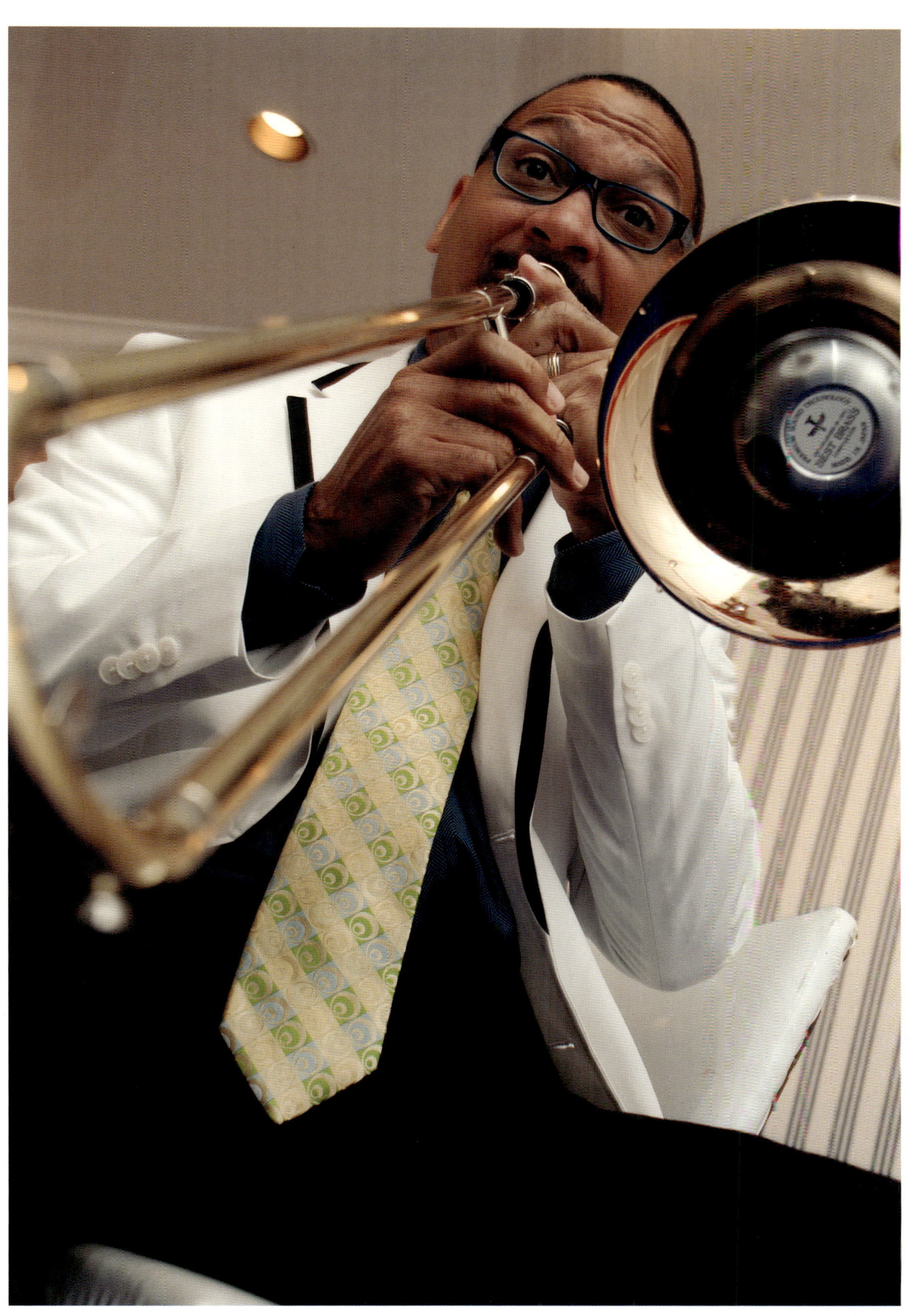

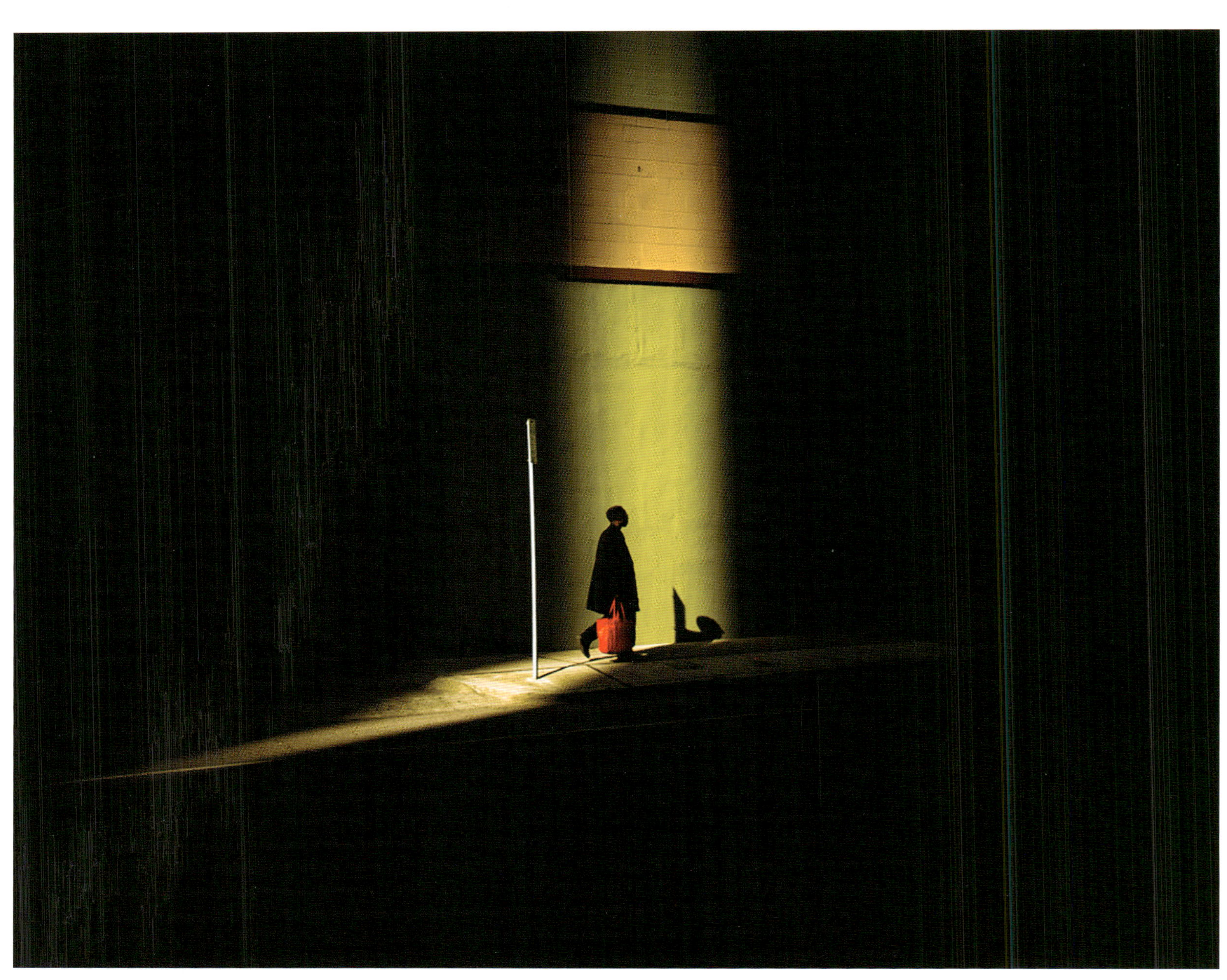

Corey Anthony

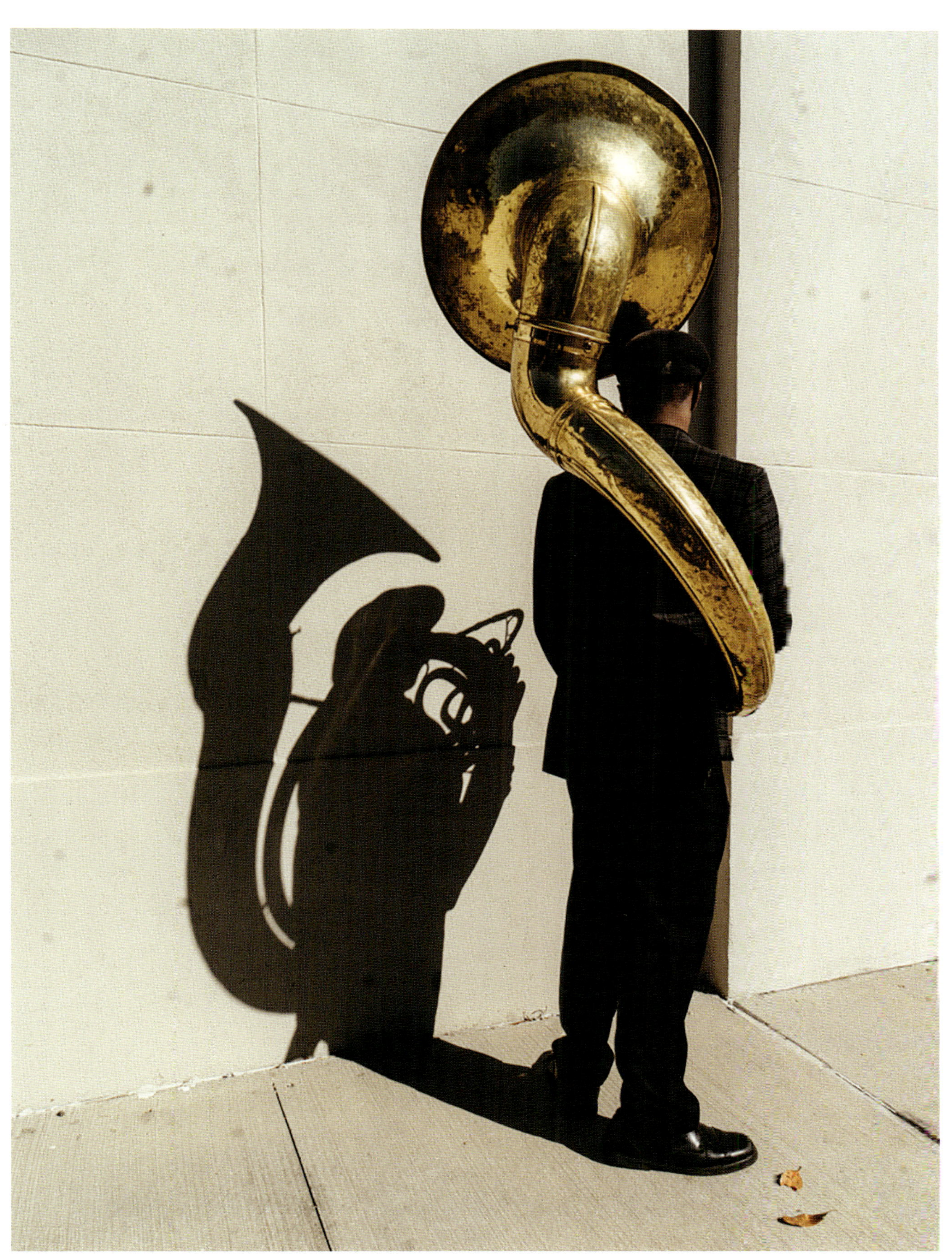

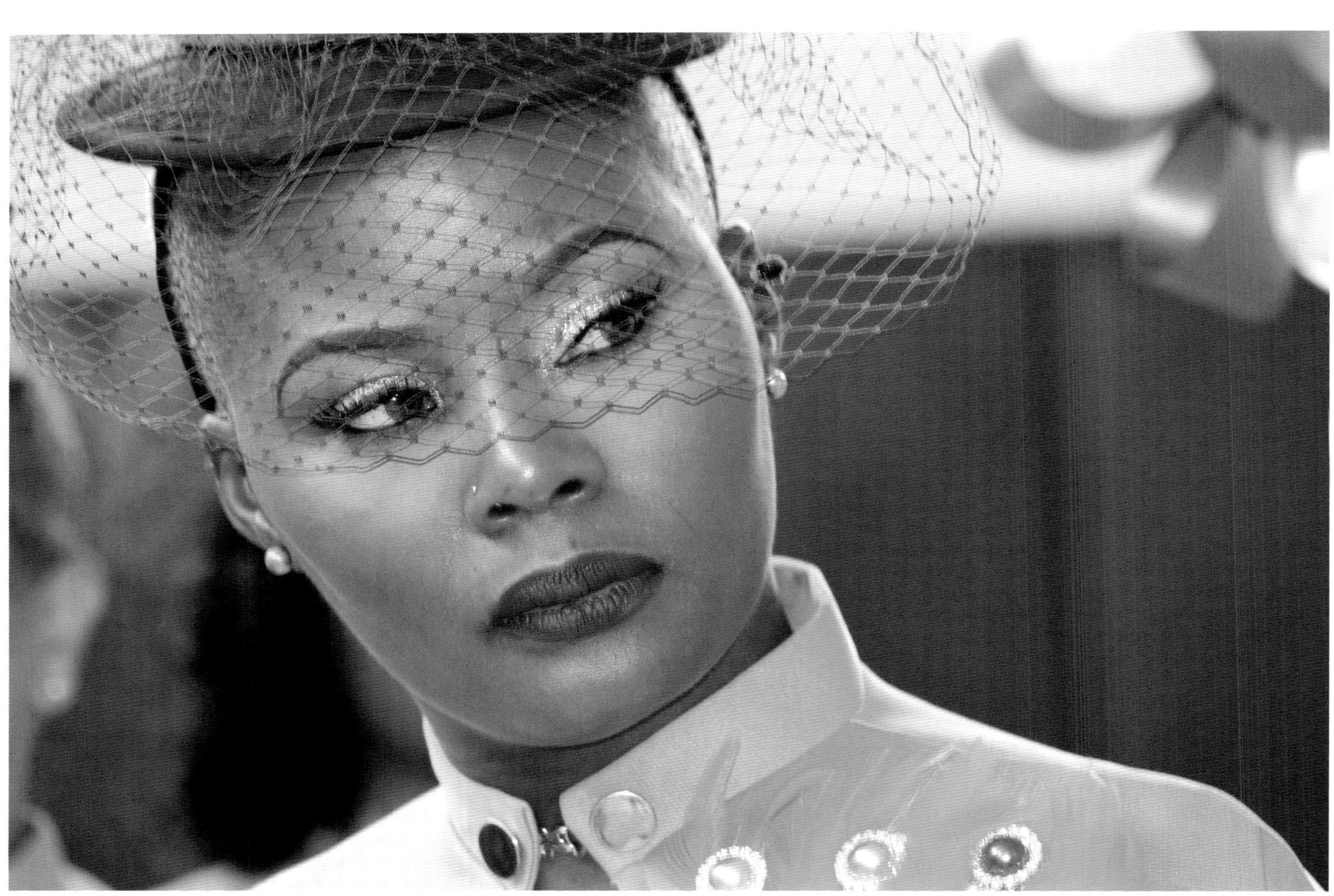

Danette M. Vincent

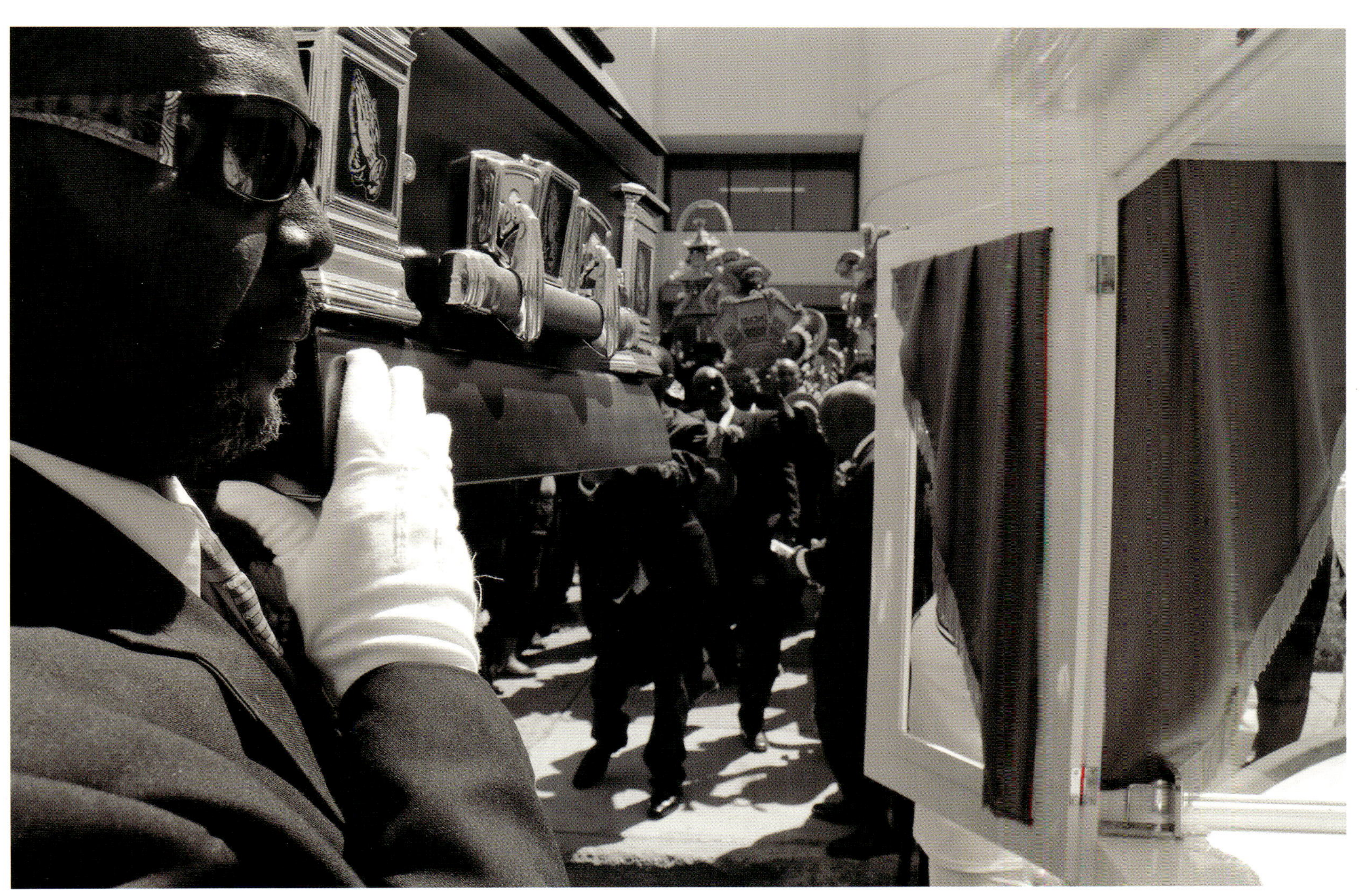

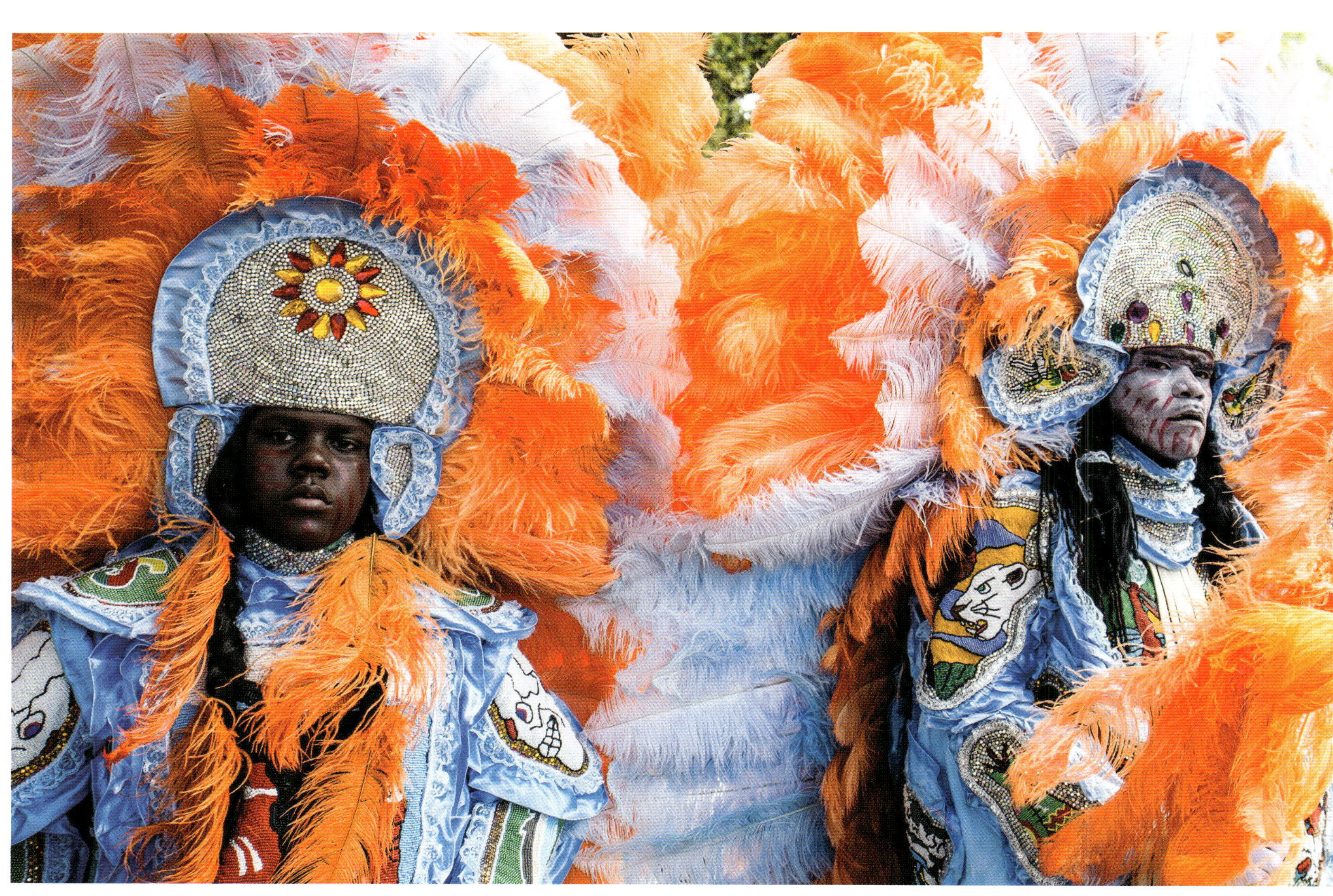

danielle c. miles

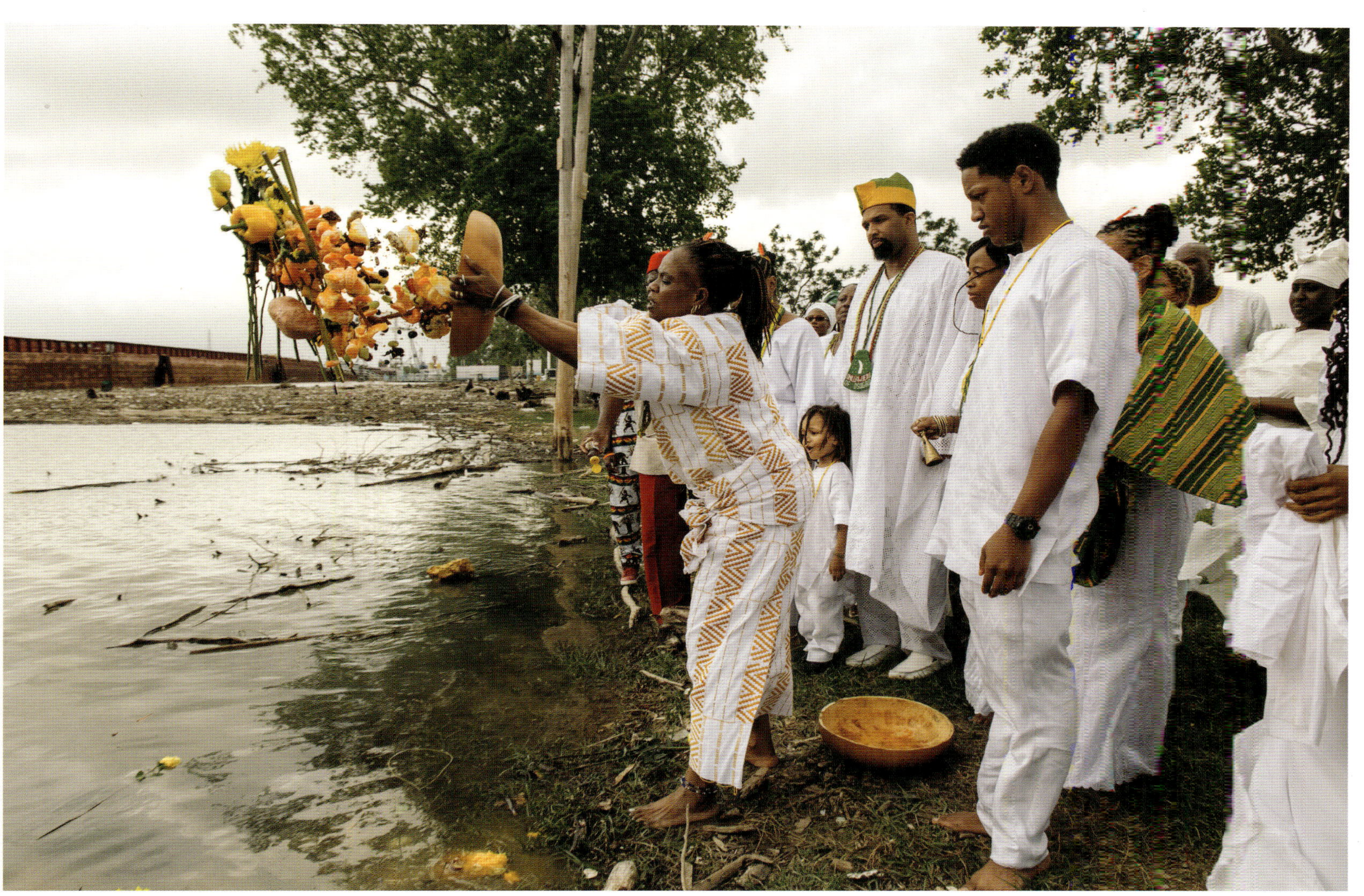

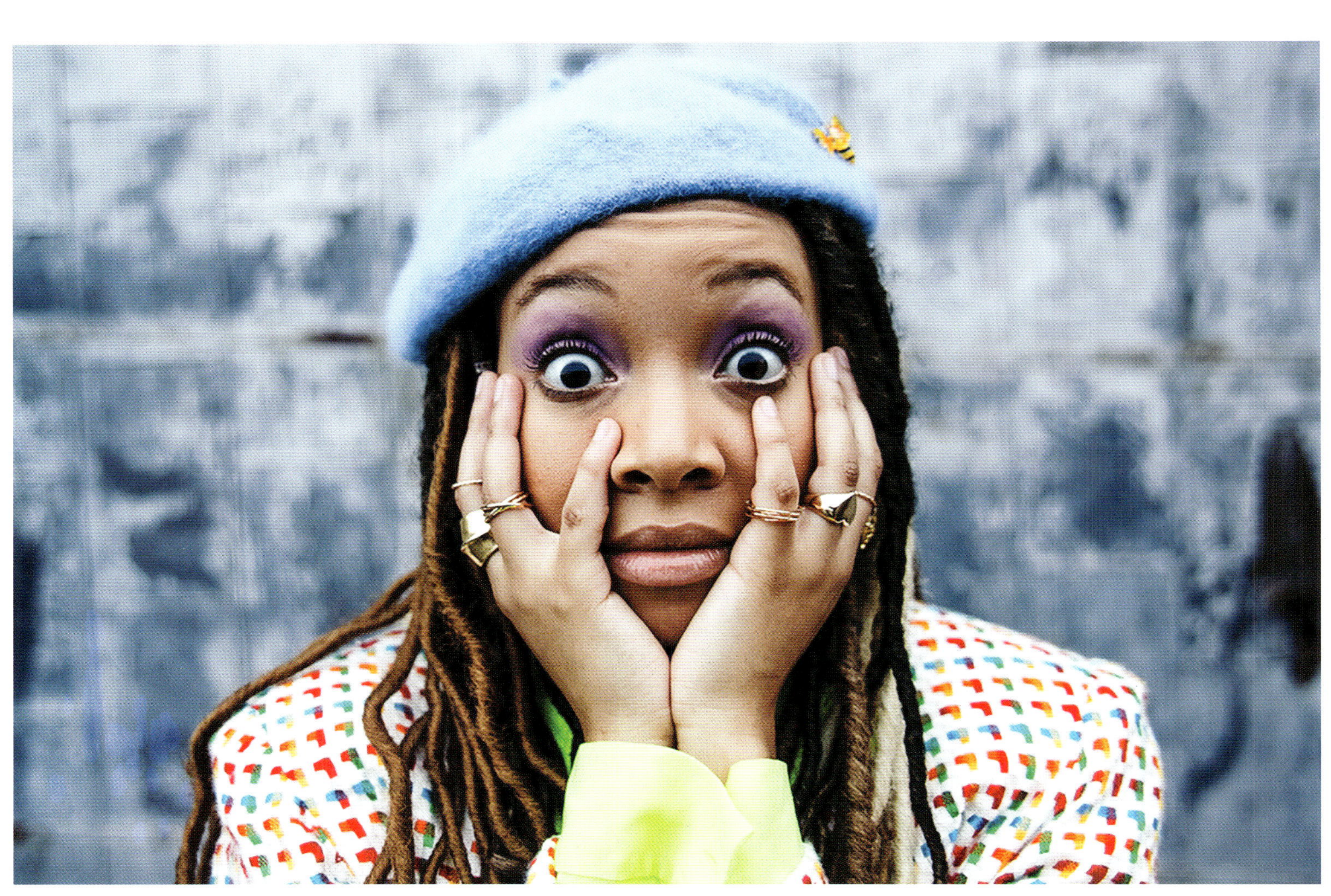

Dawnie Marie

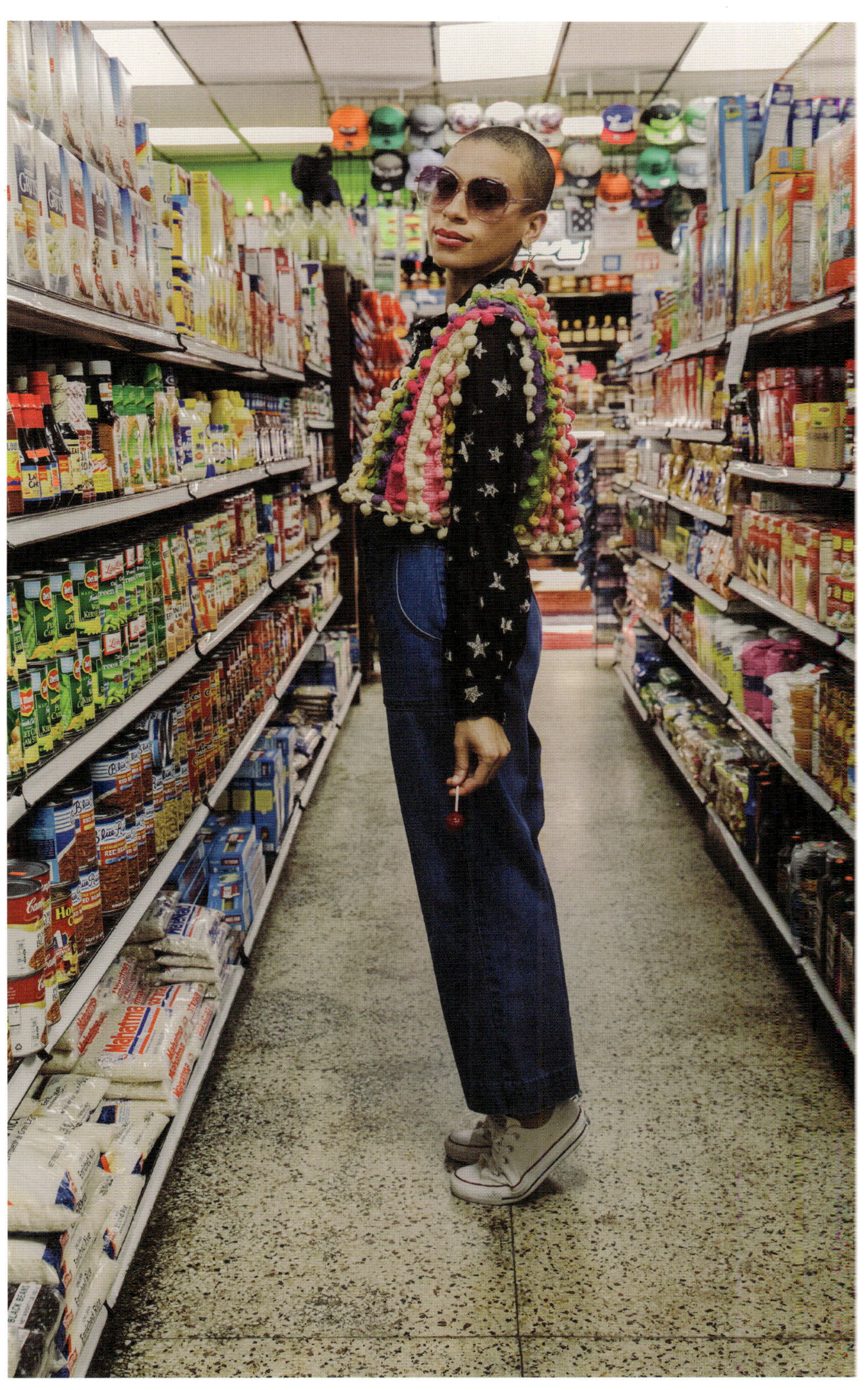

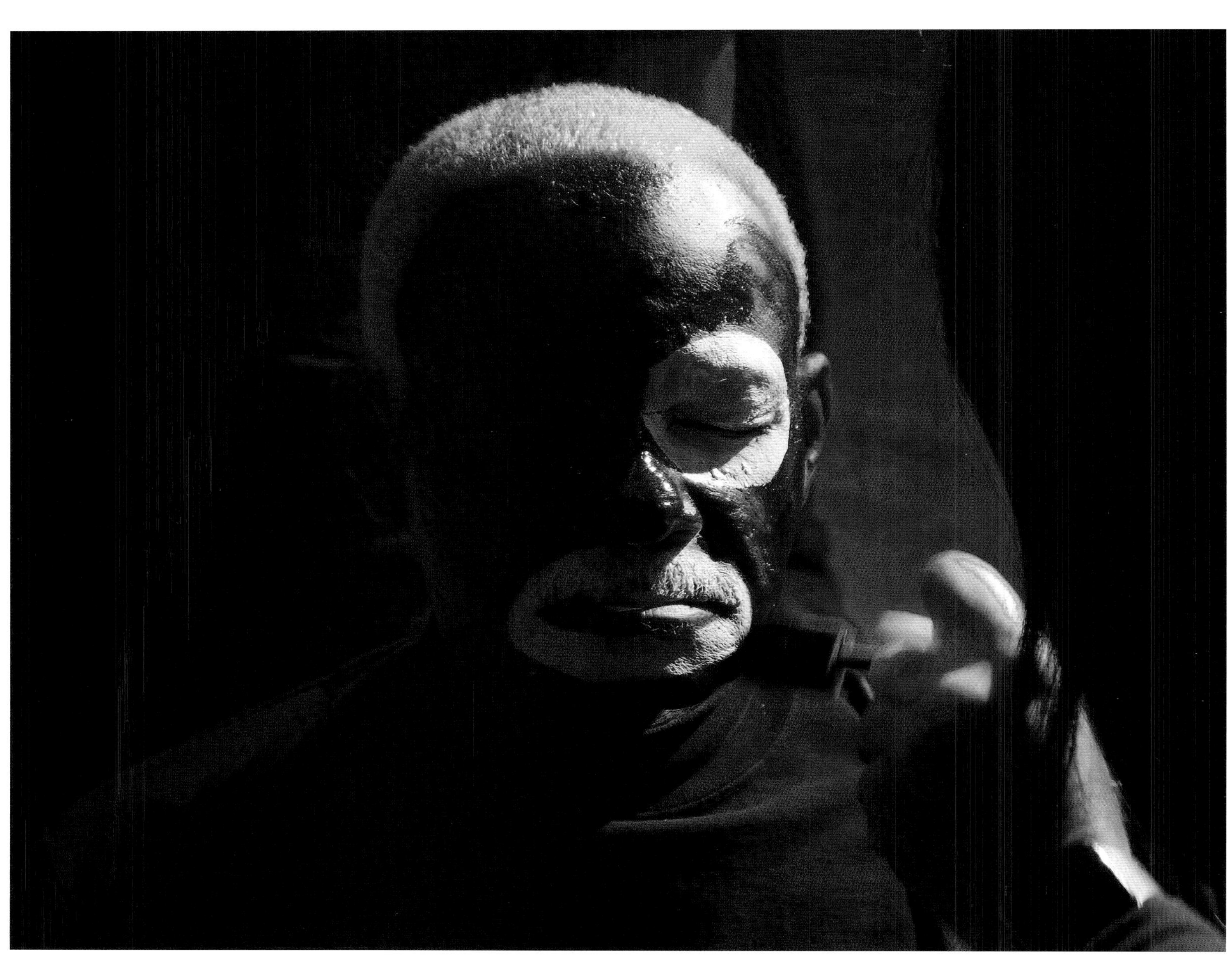

Dean Gagé

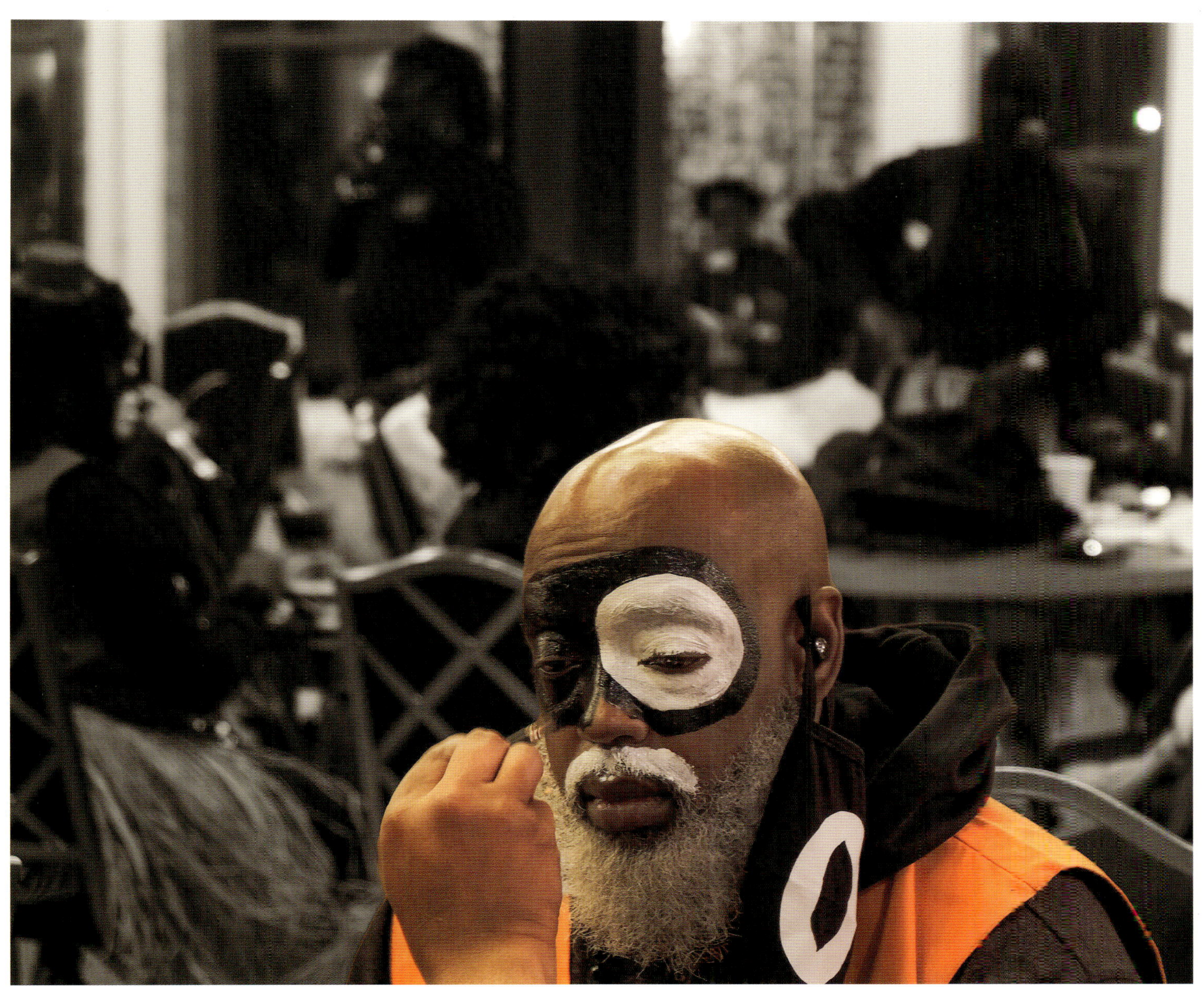

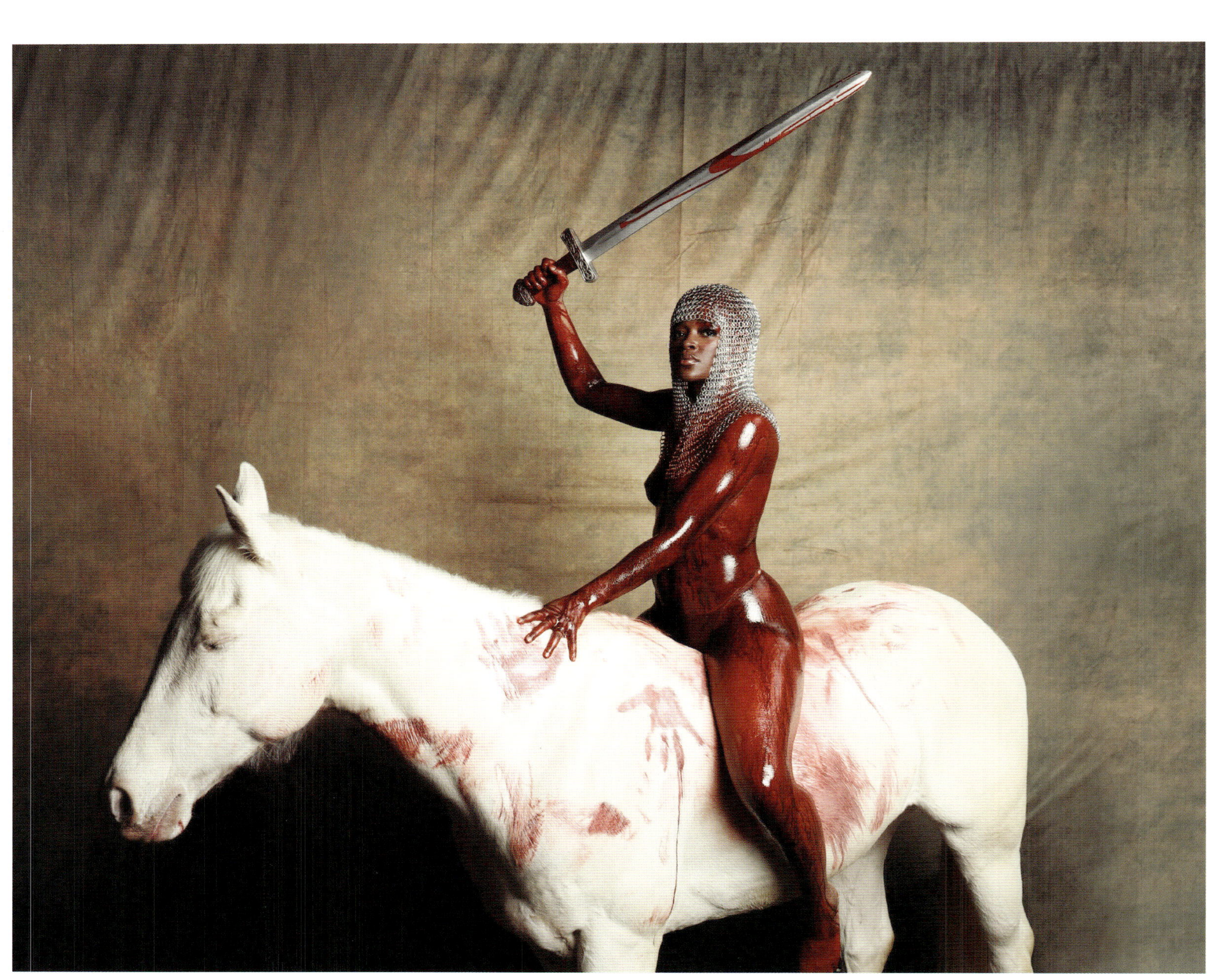

Delaney George

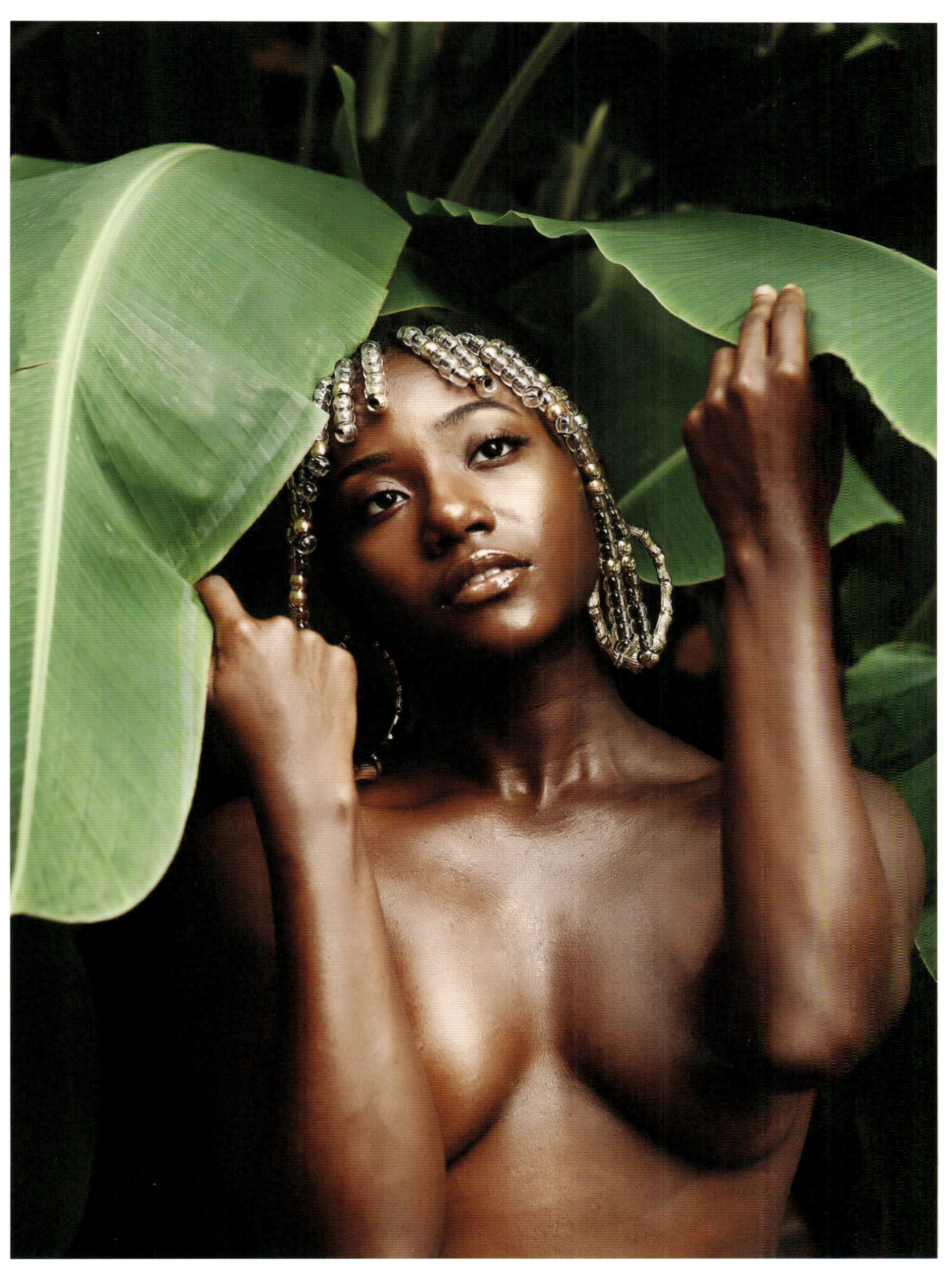

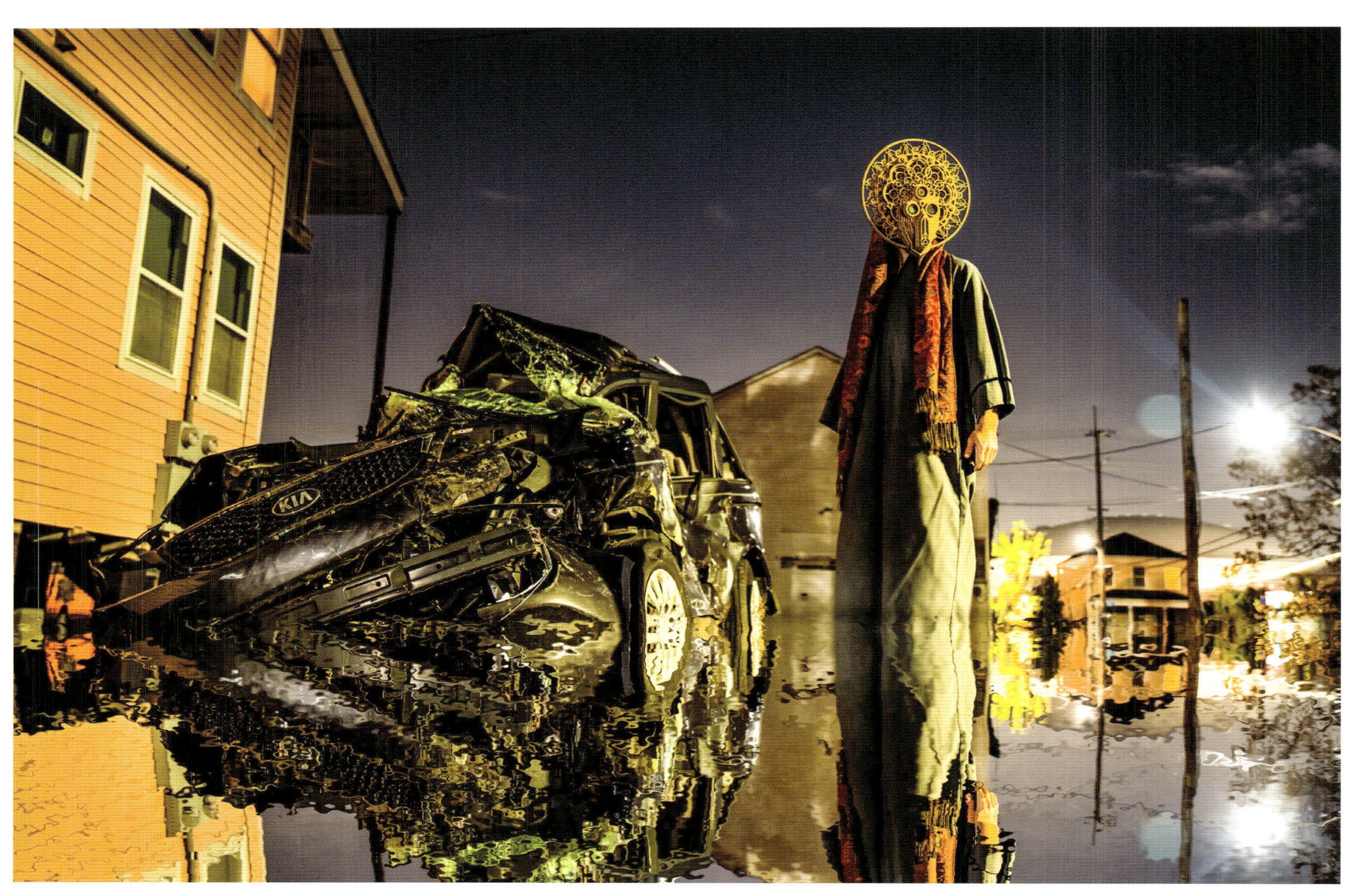
KIA

Durado Brooks

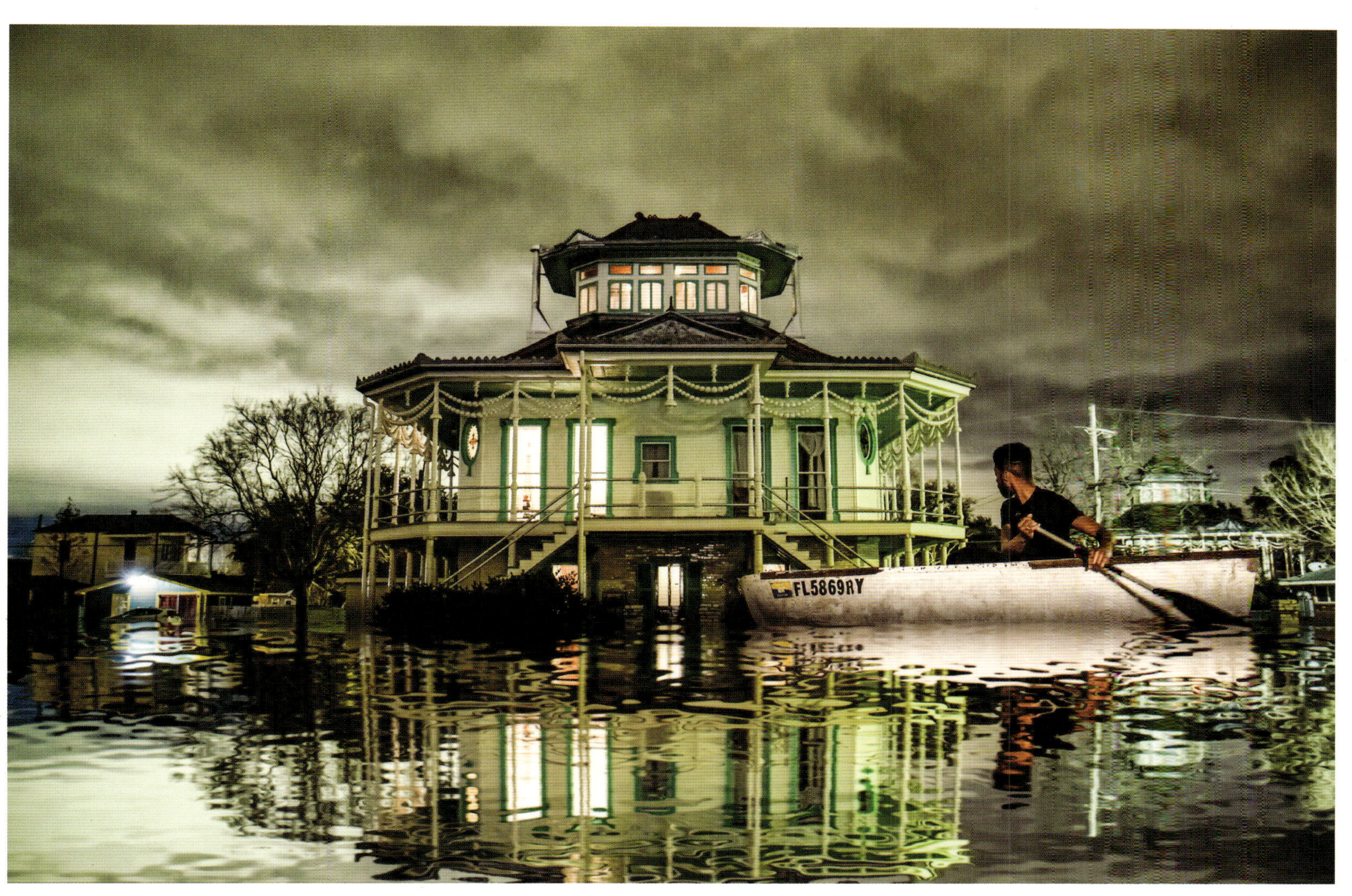

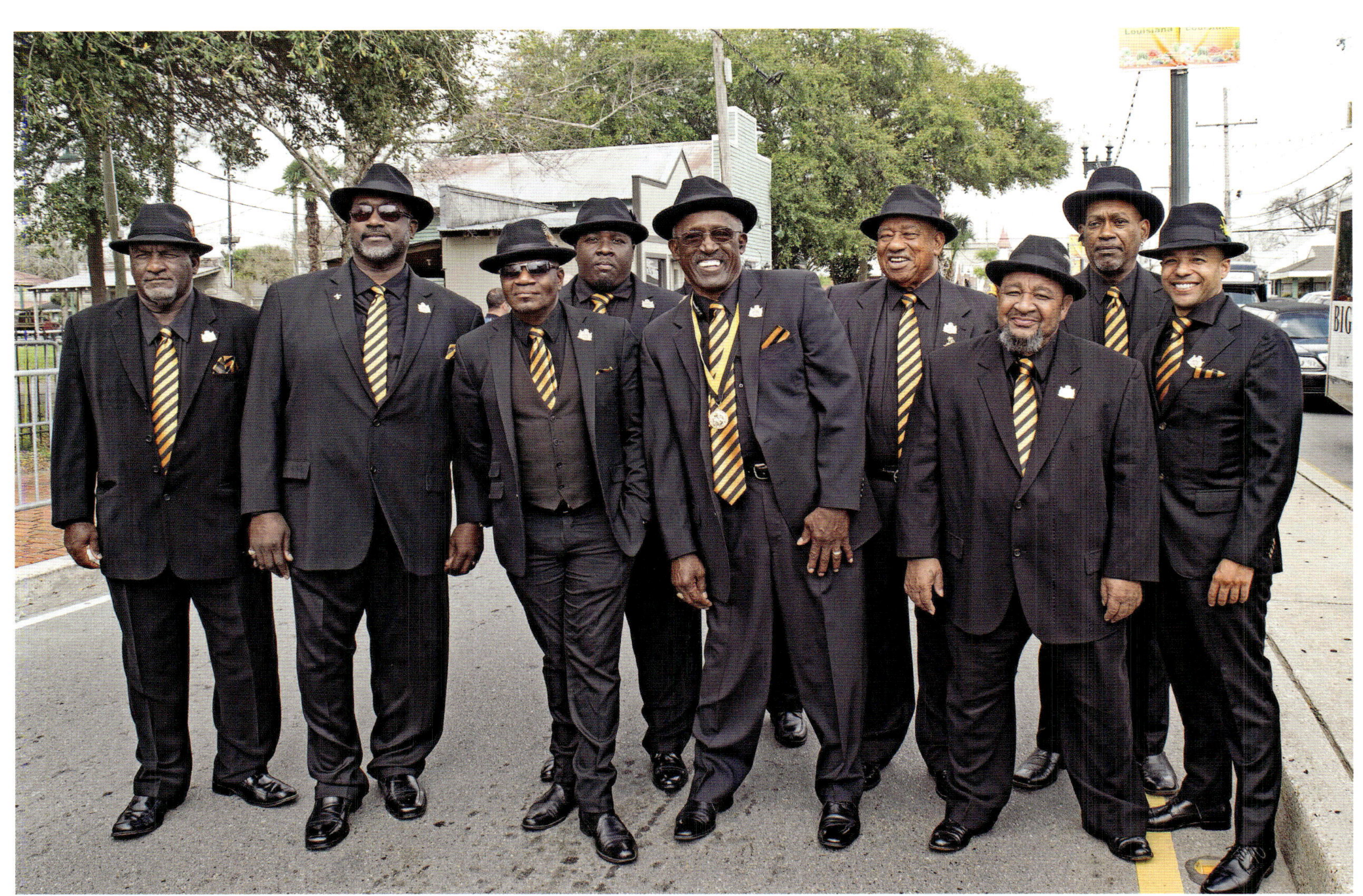
Louisiana

Dwight A. Harris

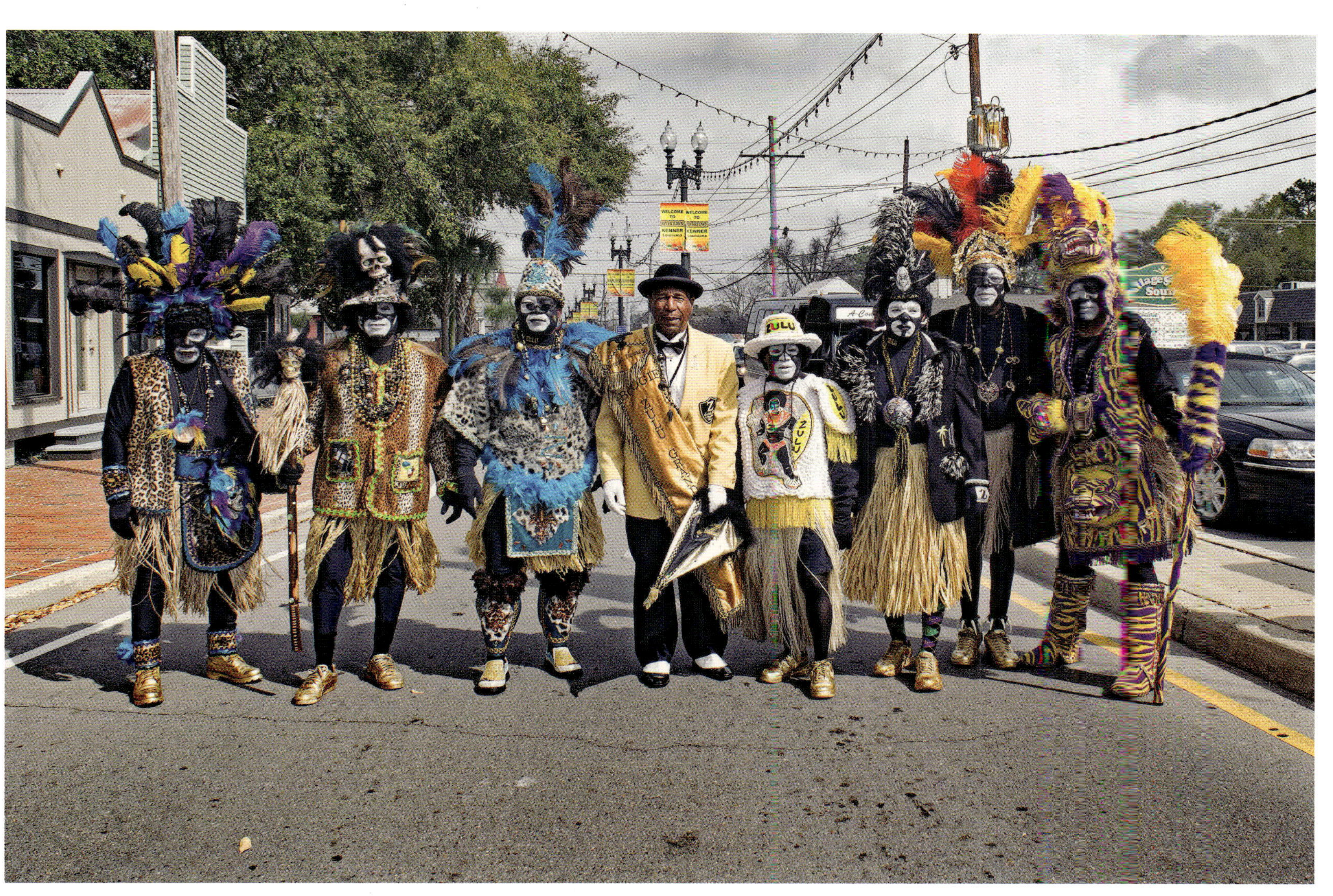

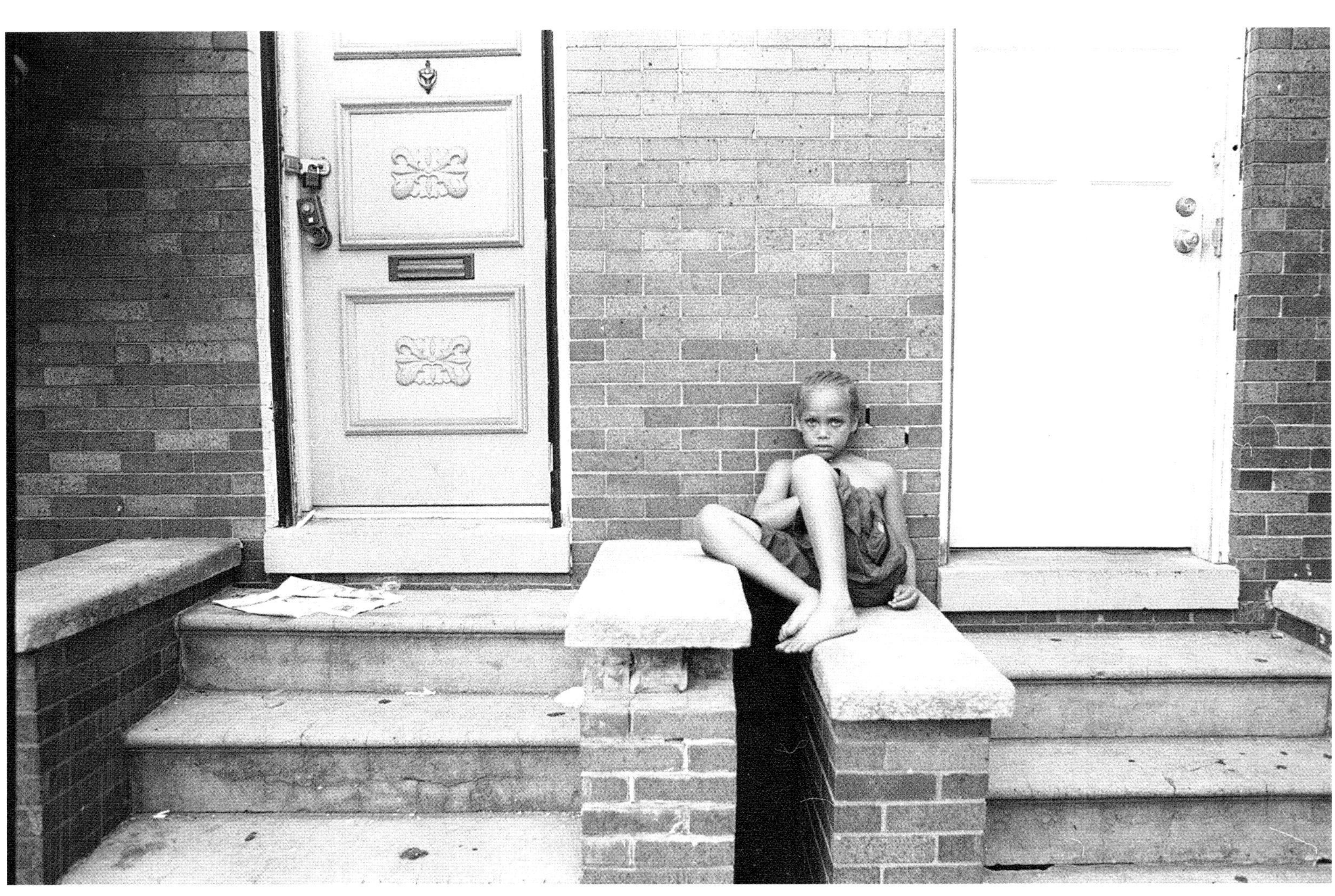

Ellis Marsalis III

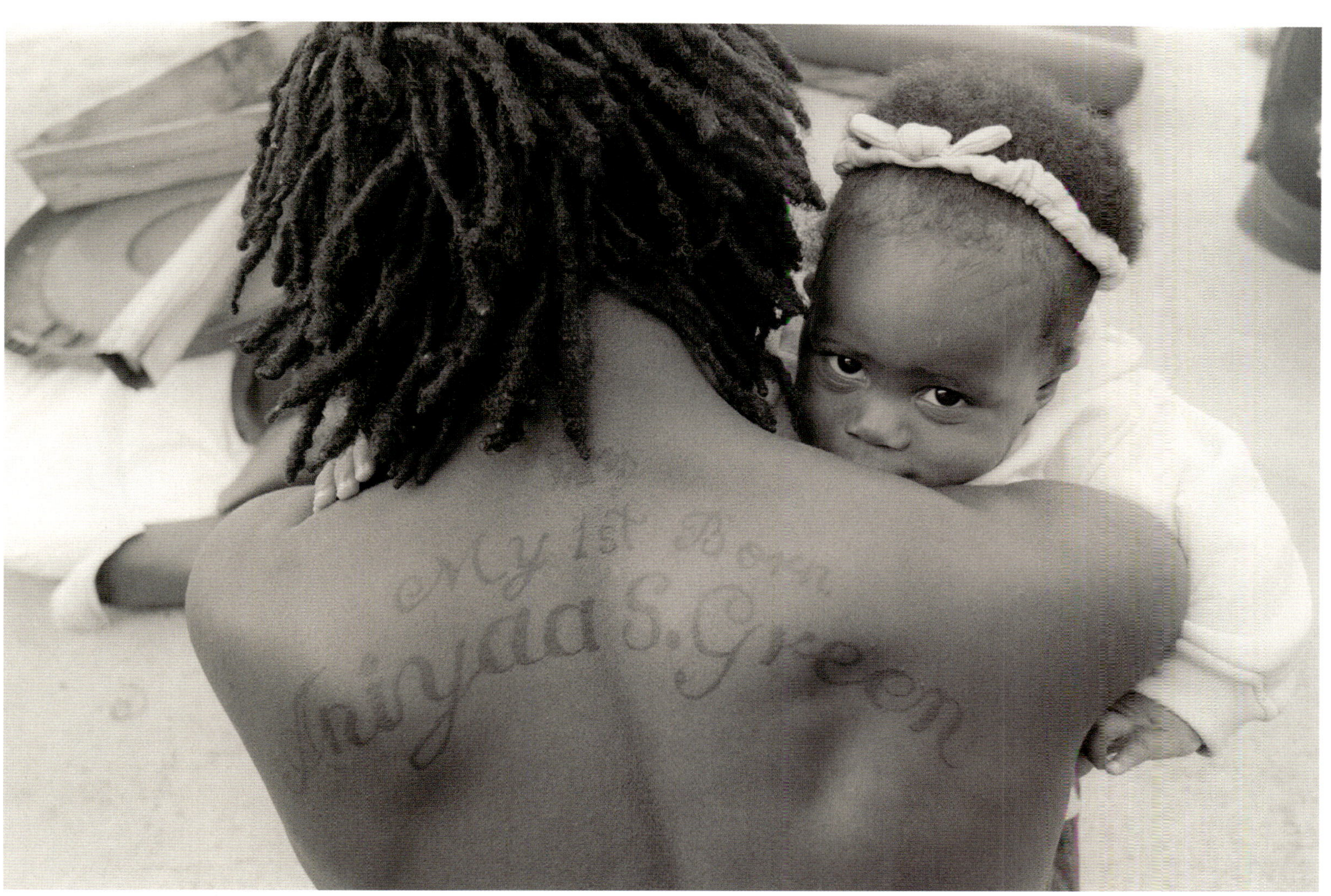

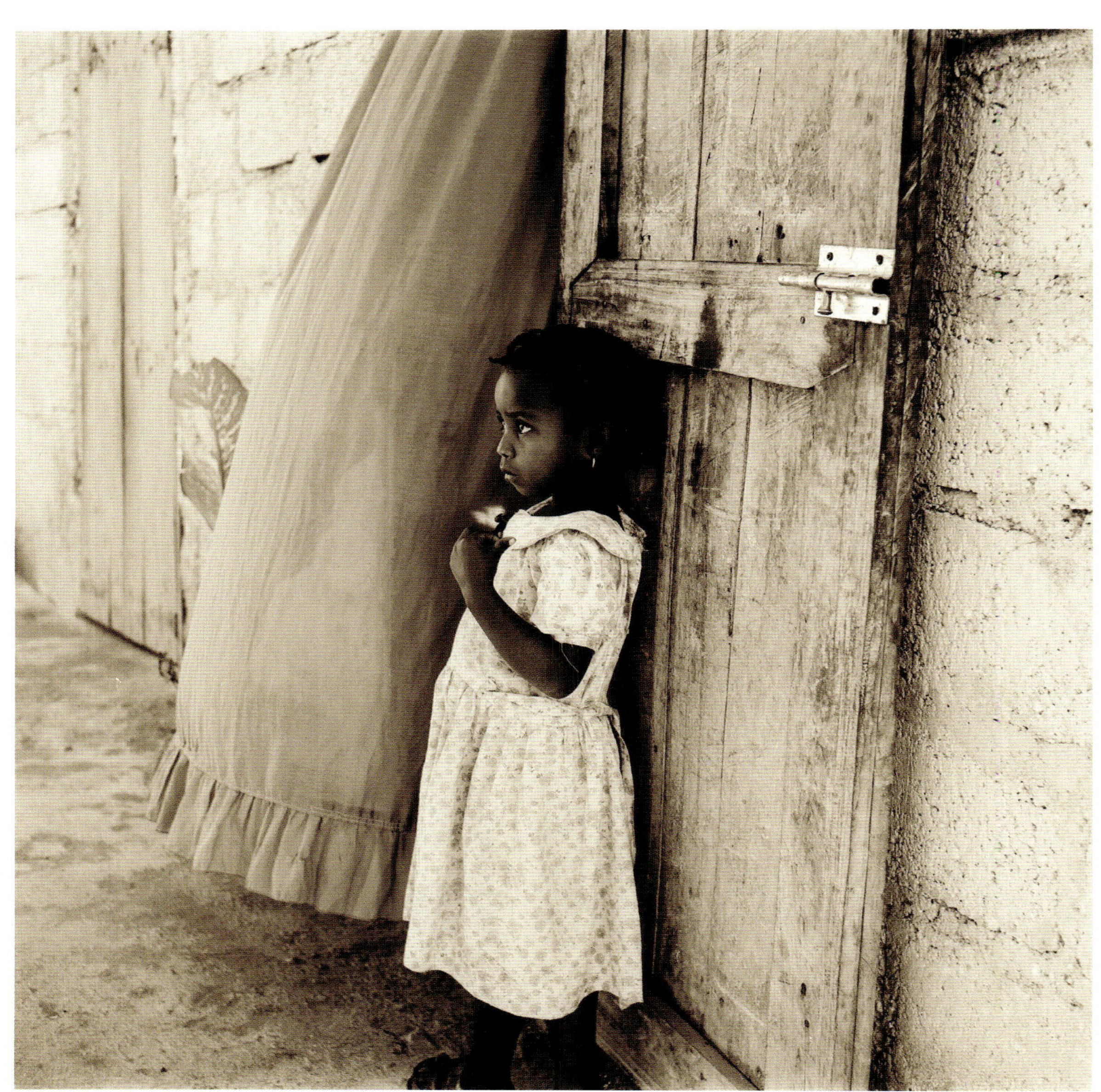

Epaul Julien

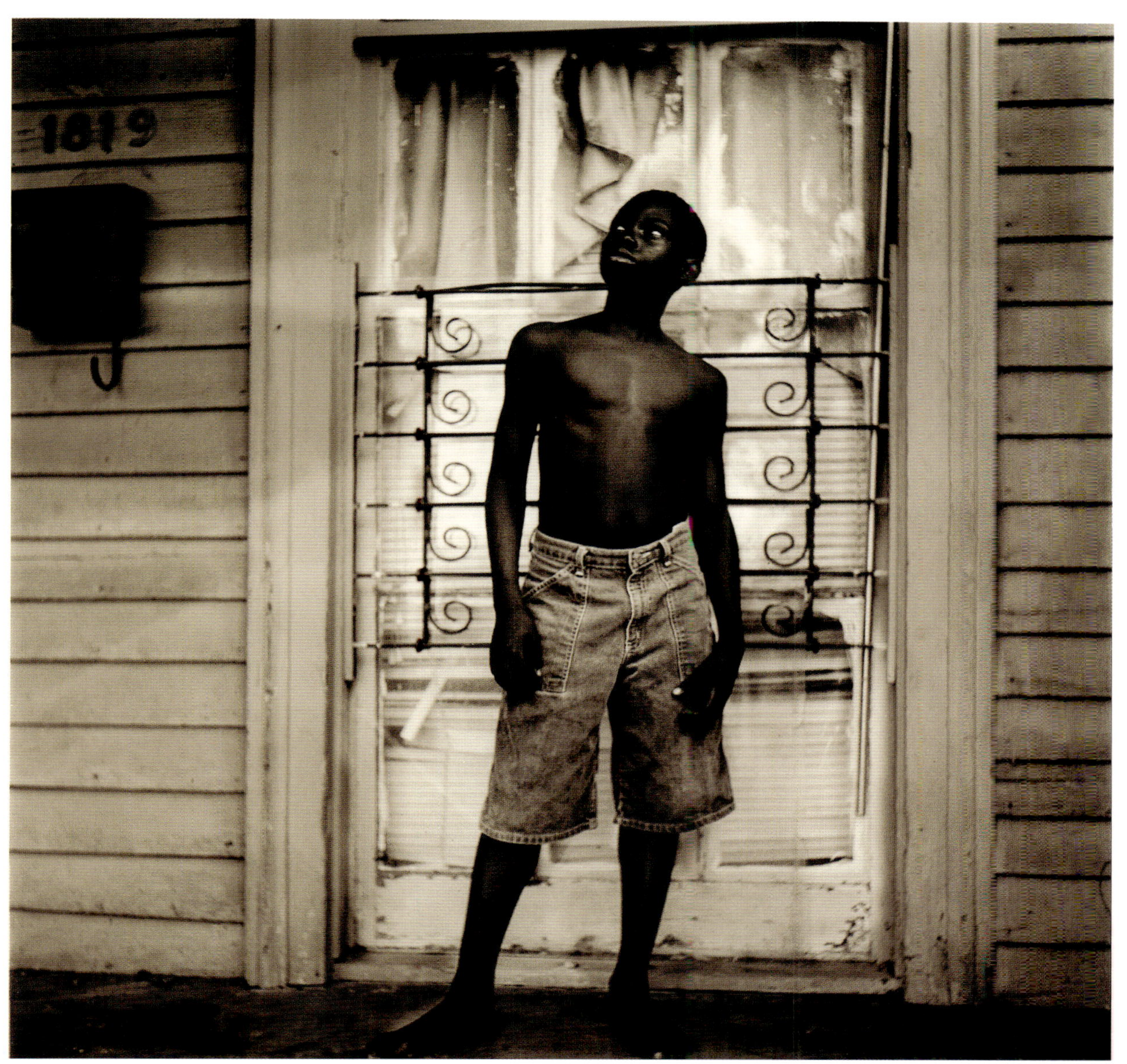

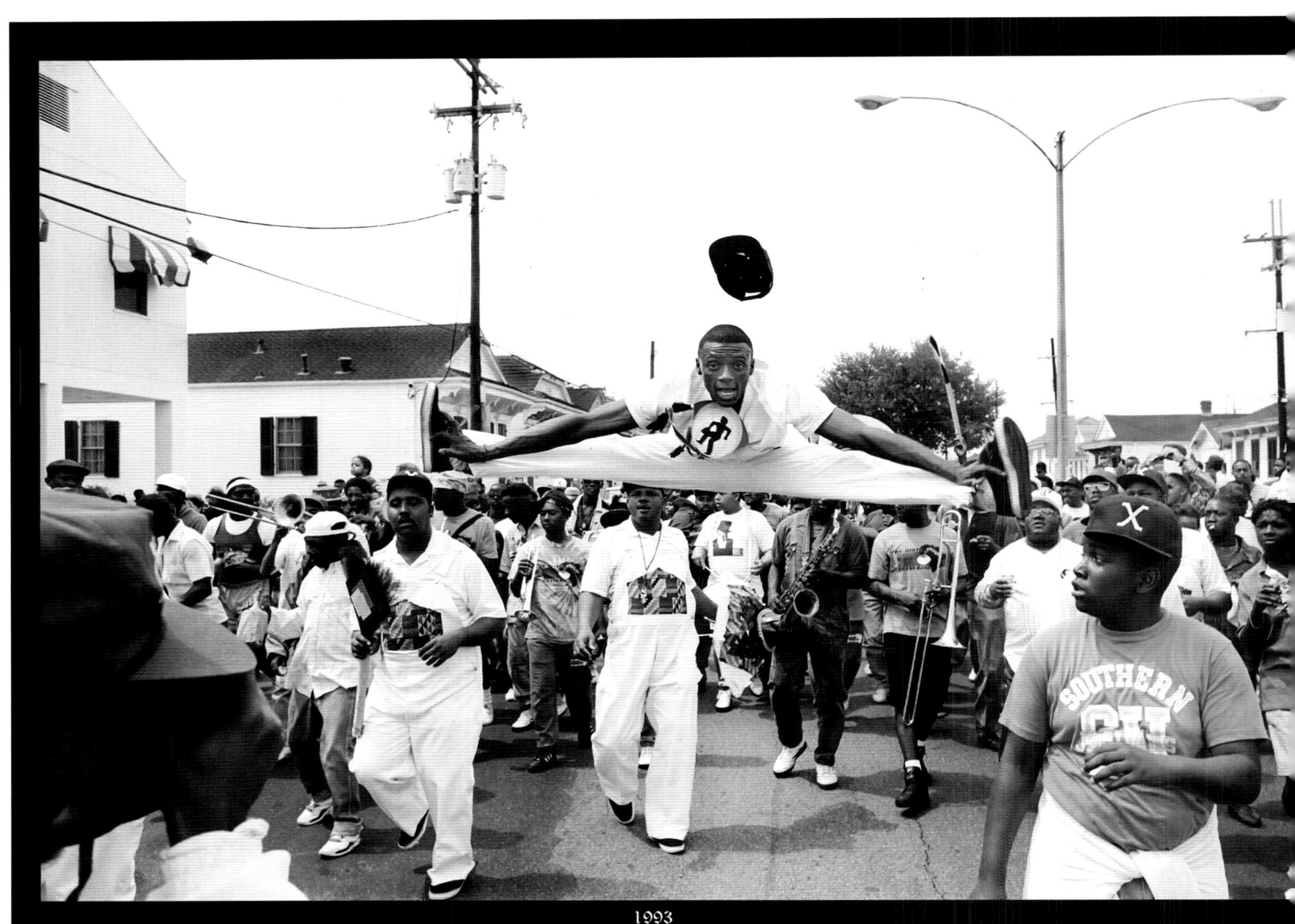

1993

Eric Waters

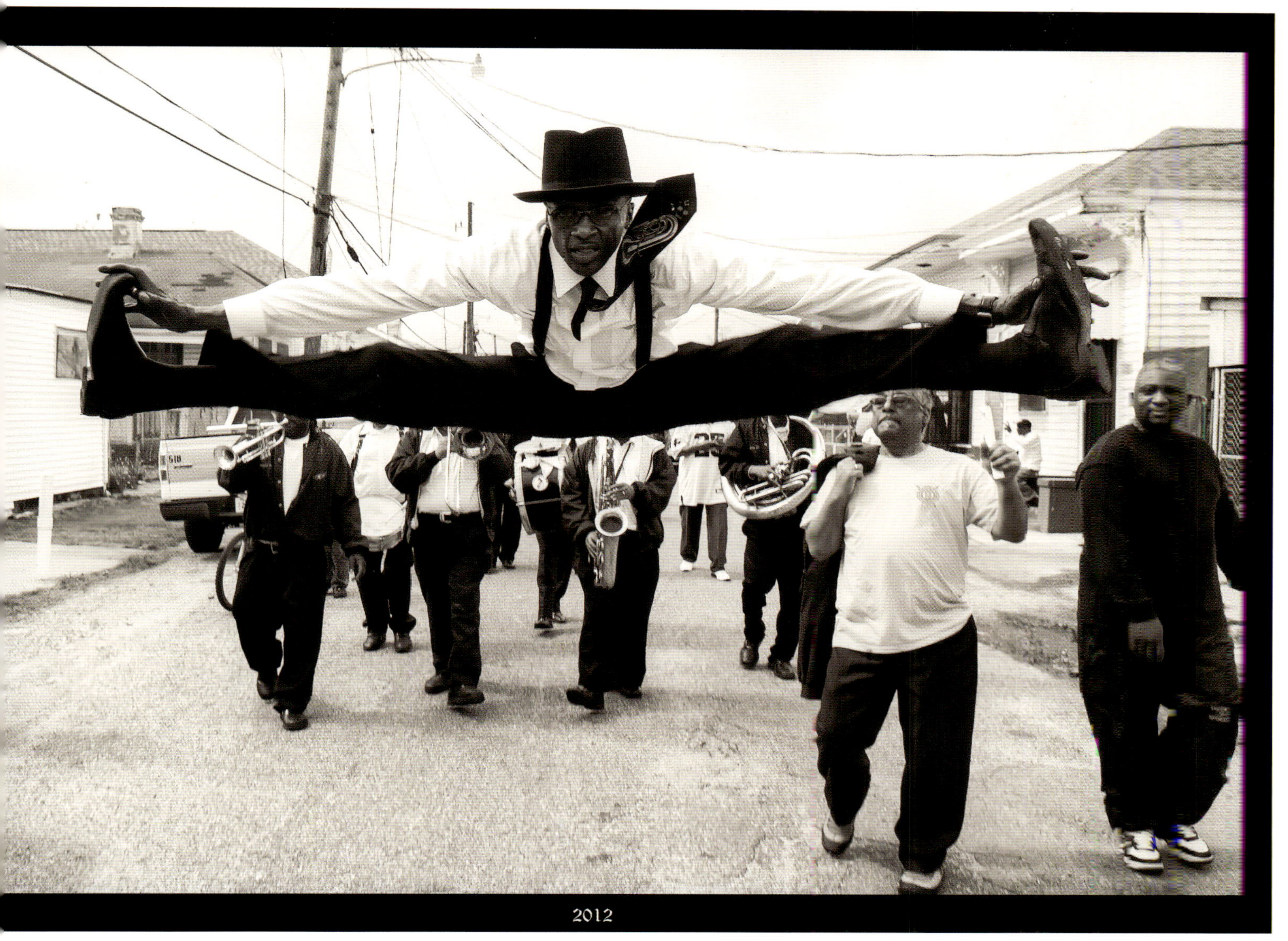

2012

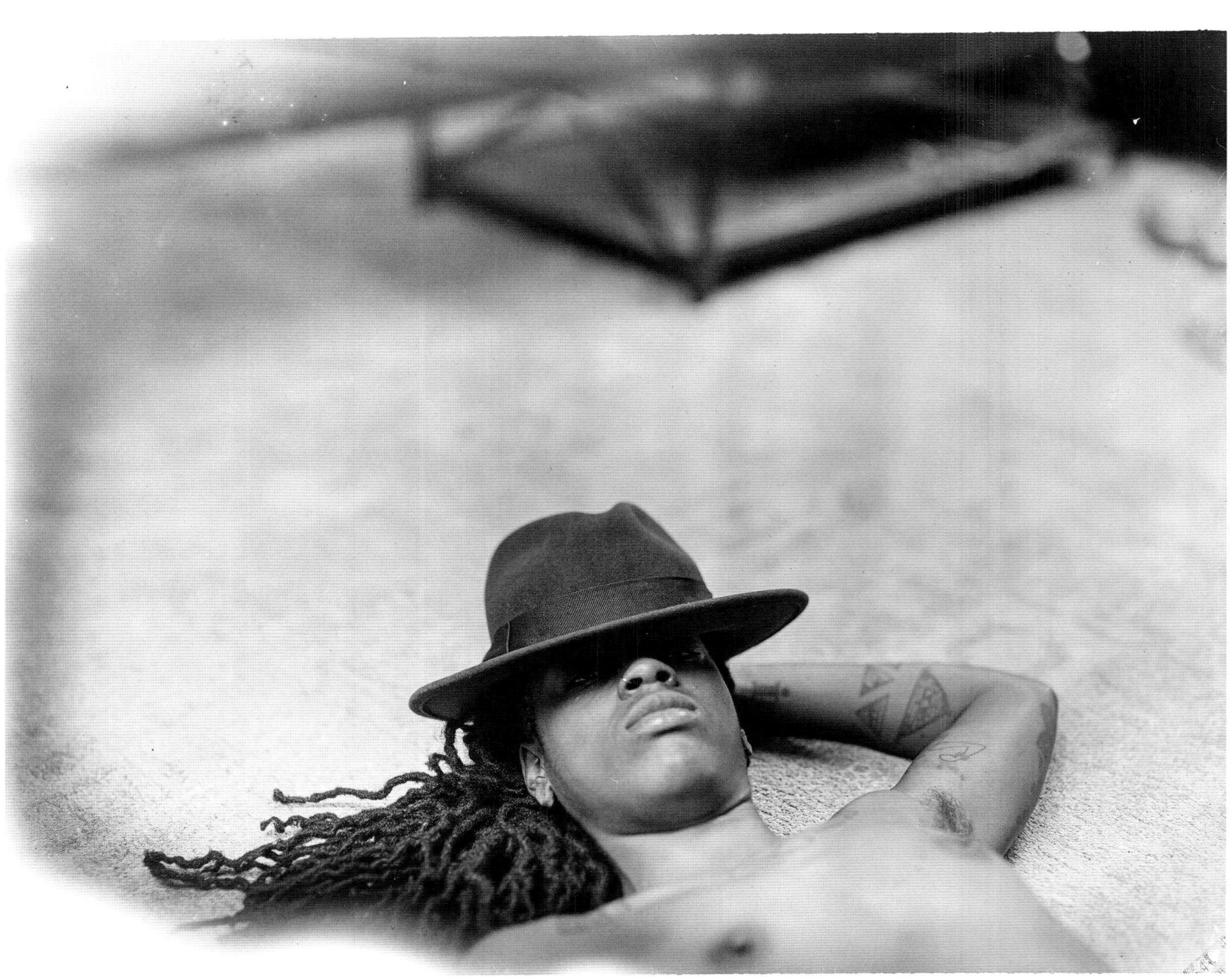

Felicita Felli Maynard

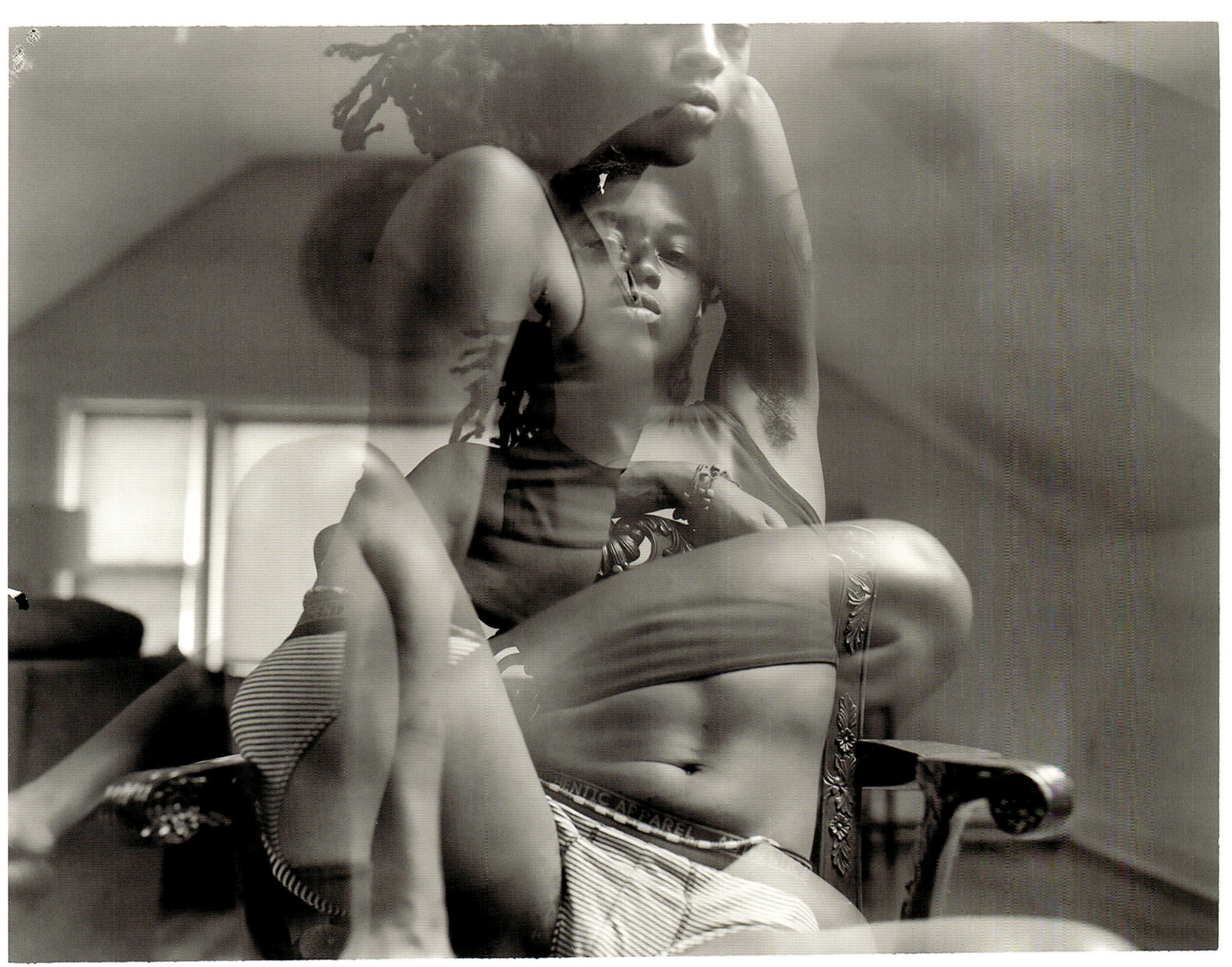

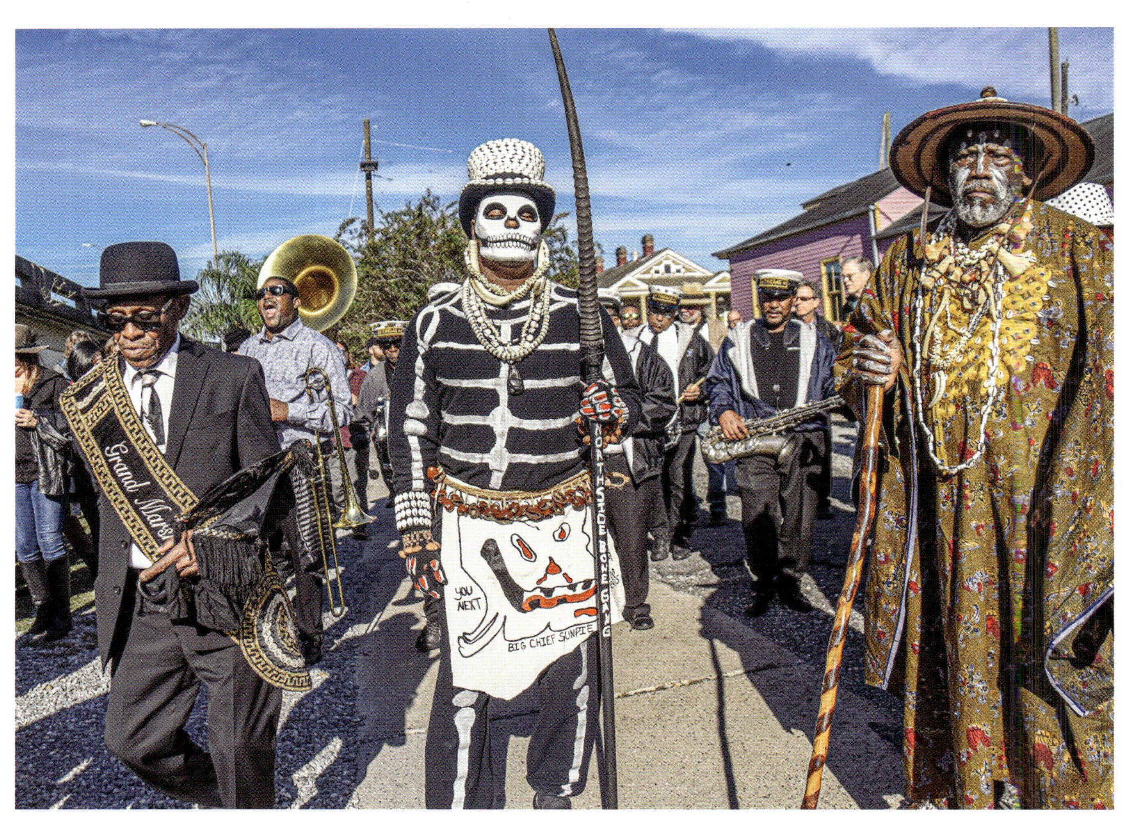
Grand Mars
NORTHSIDE BONE GANG
YOU NEXT
BIG CHIEF SUNPIE

Freddye Hill

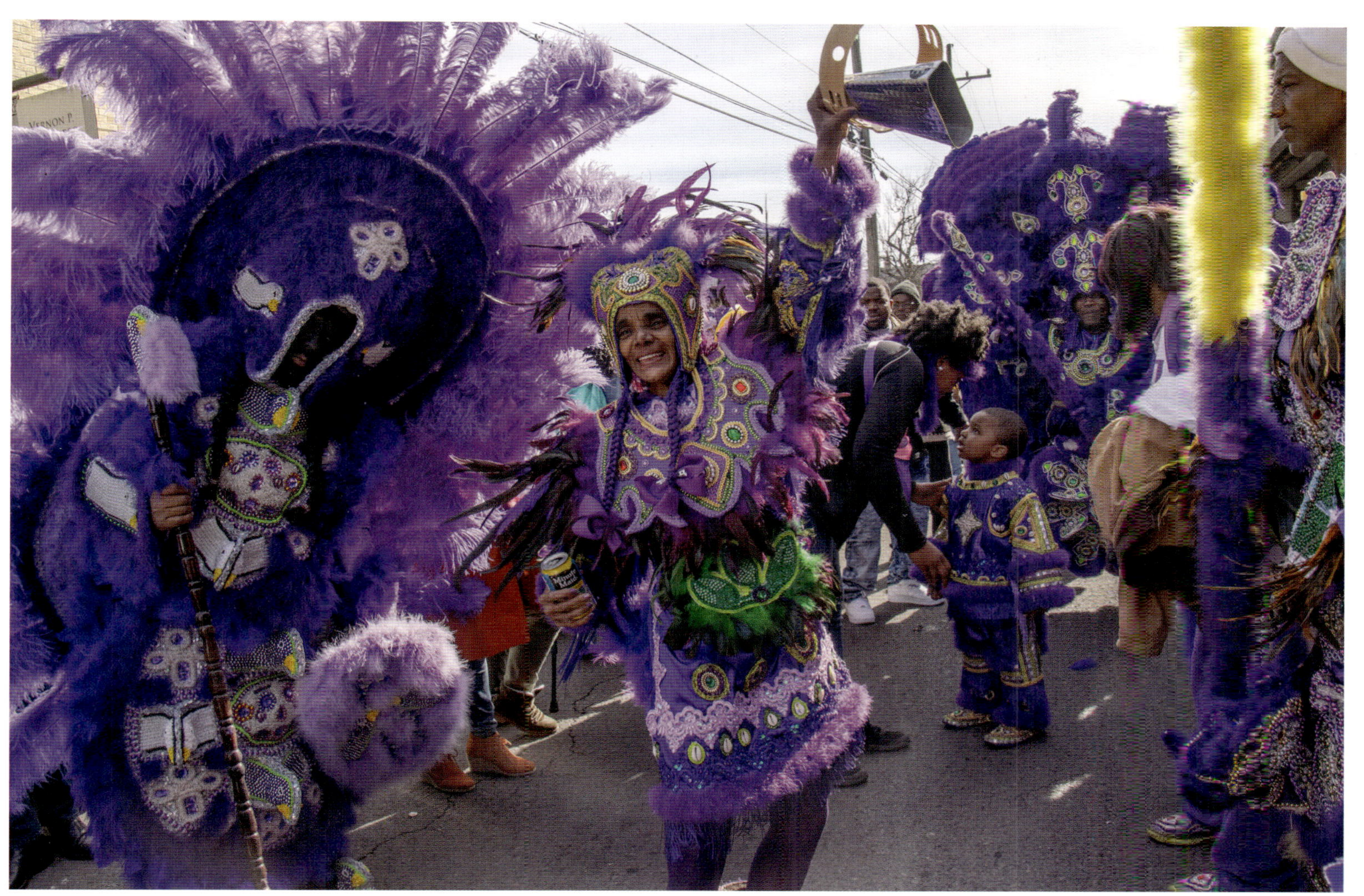

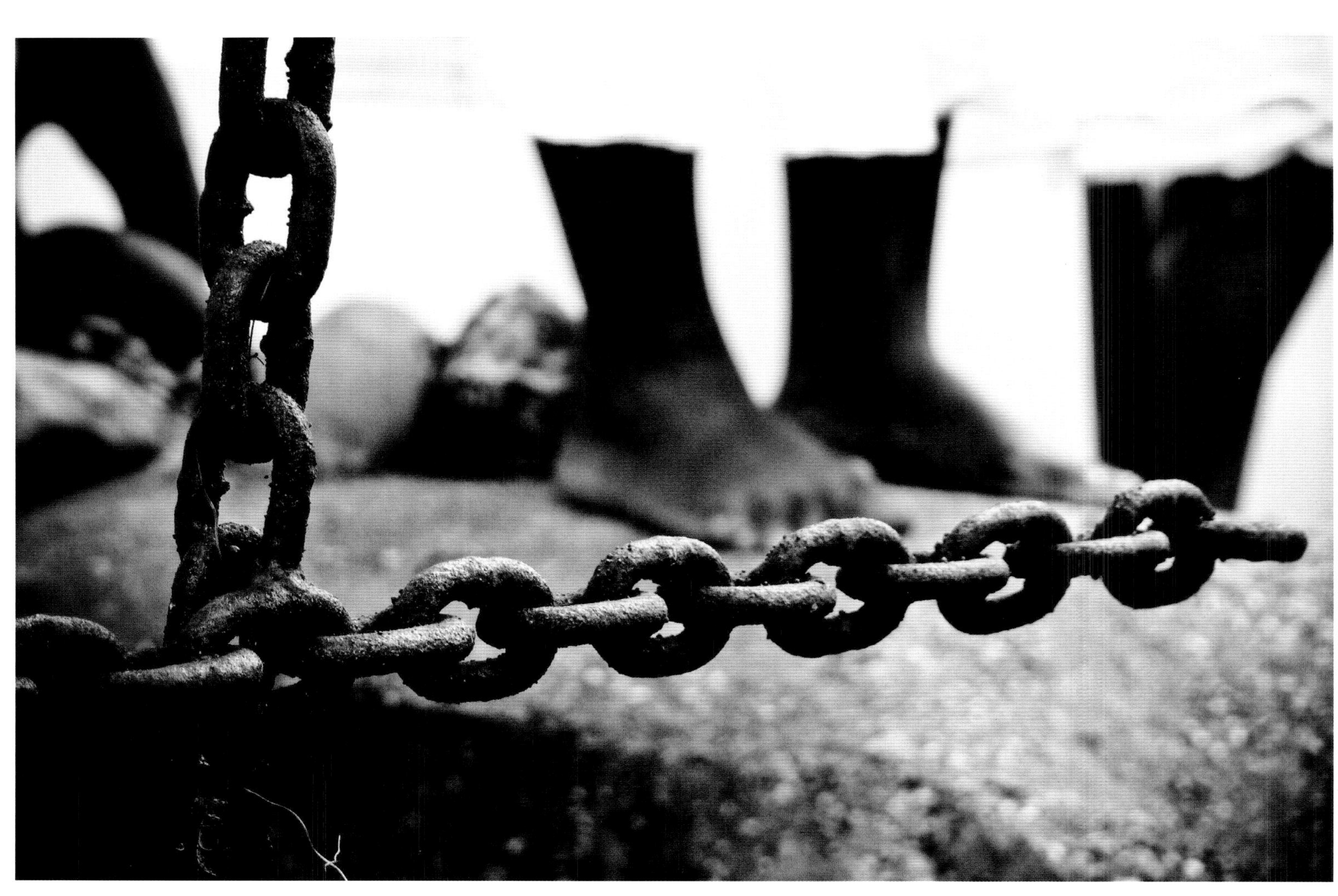

Gason Ayisyin

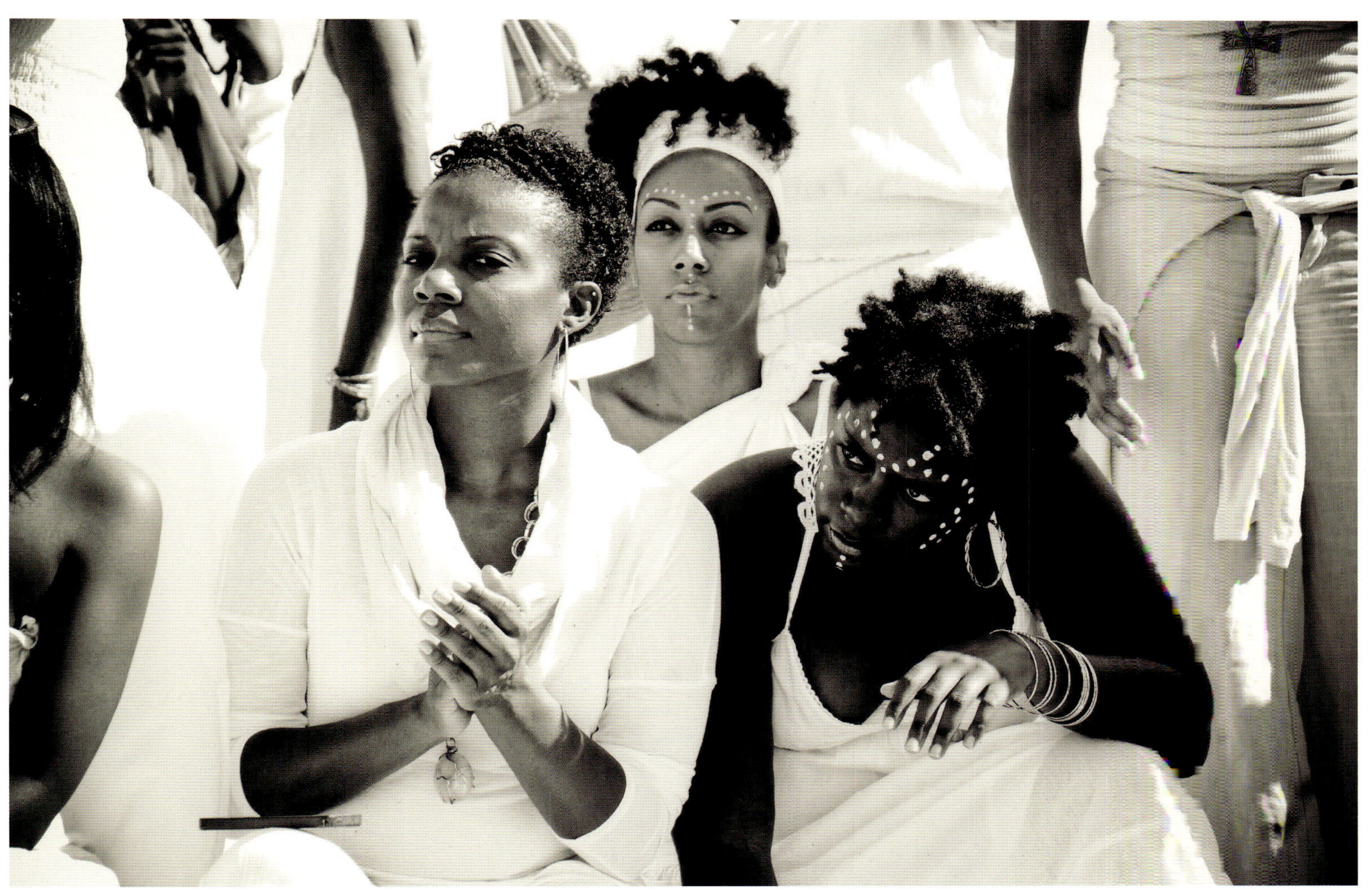

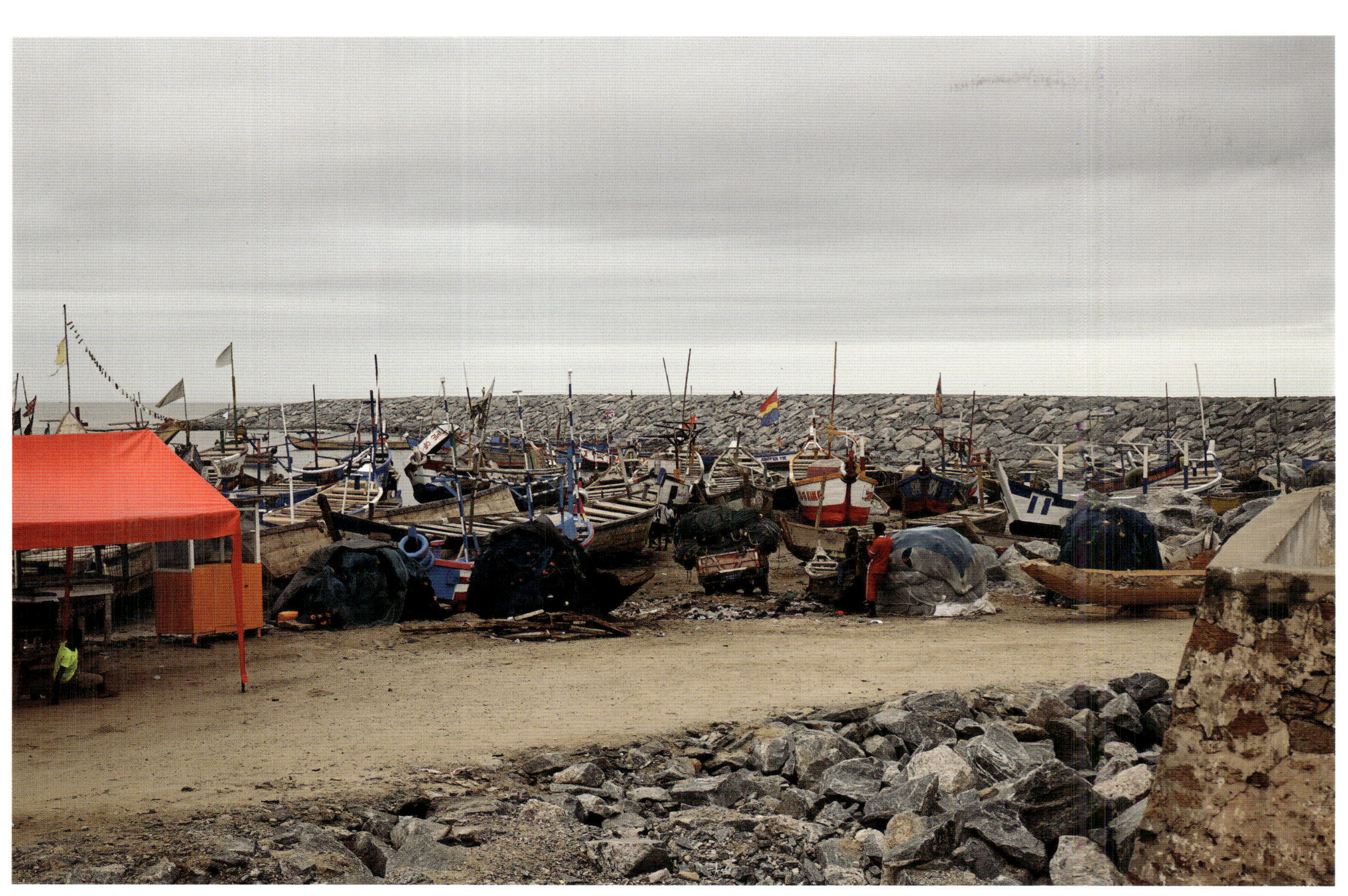

Giani M. Jones

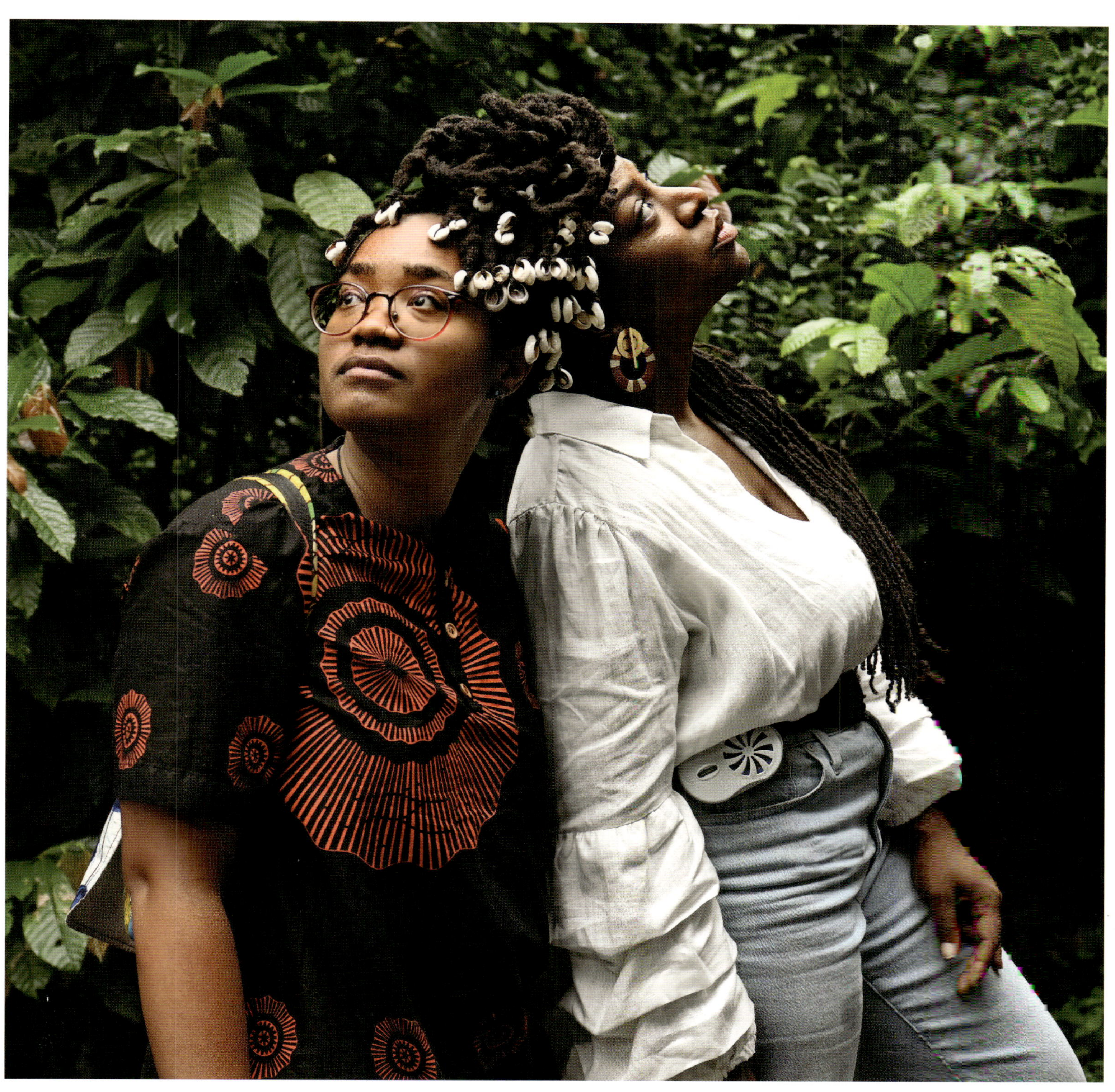

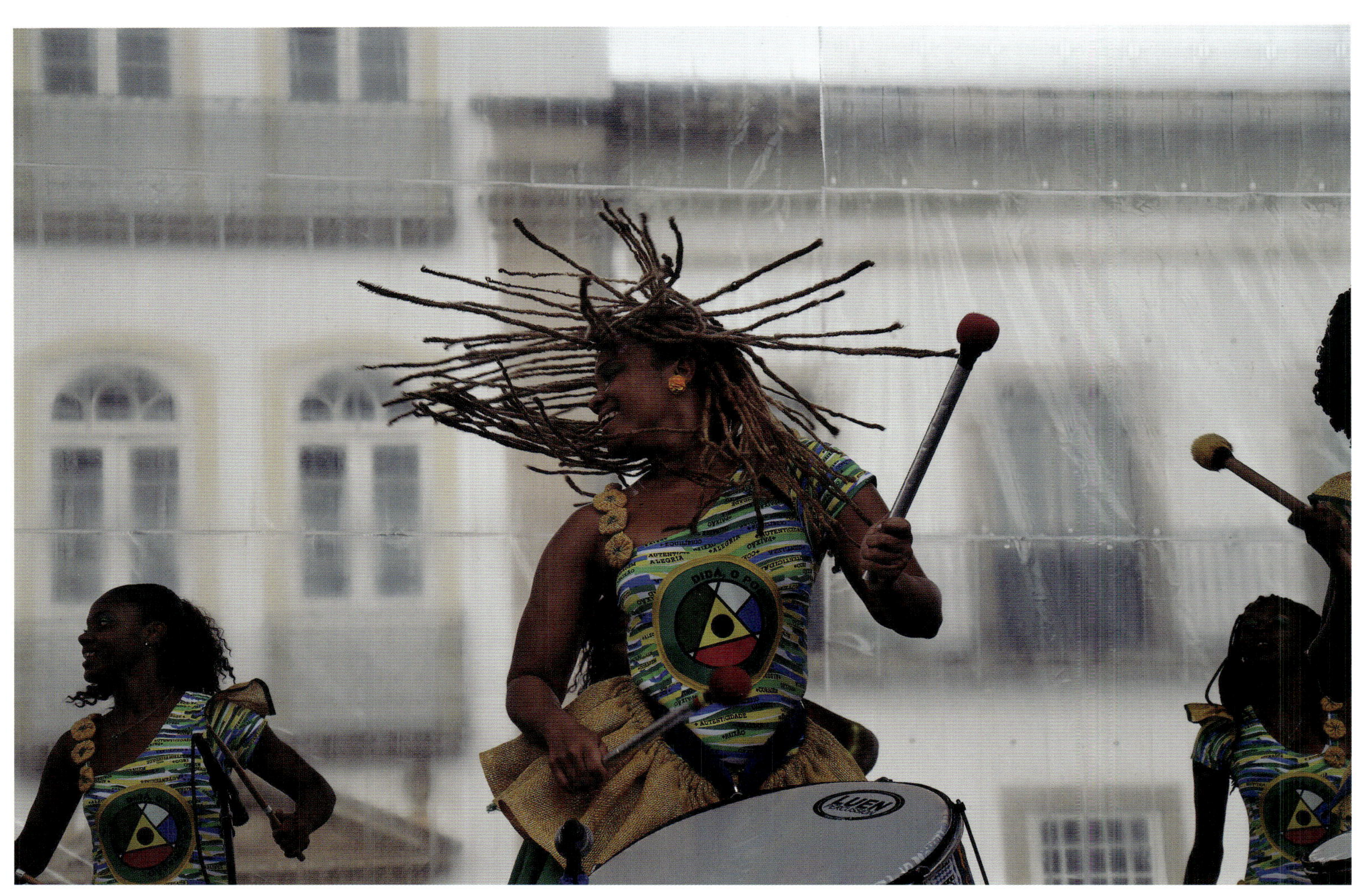
LUEN

Gillian Maris Jones

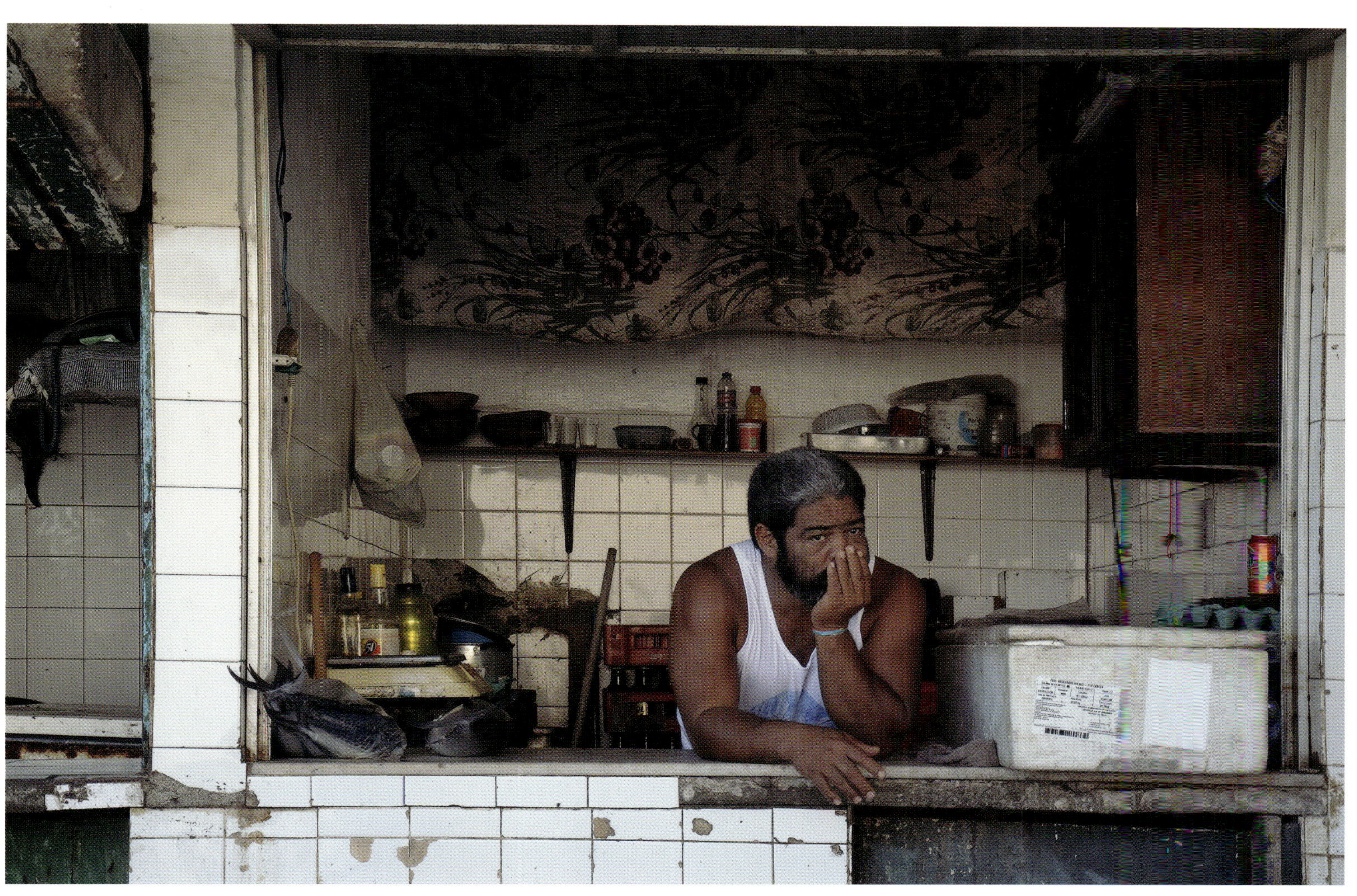

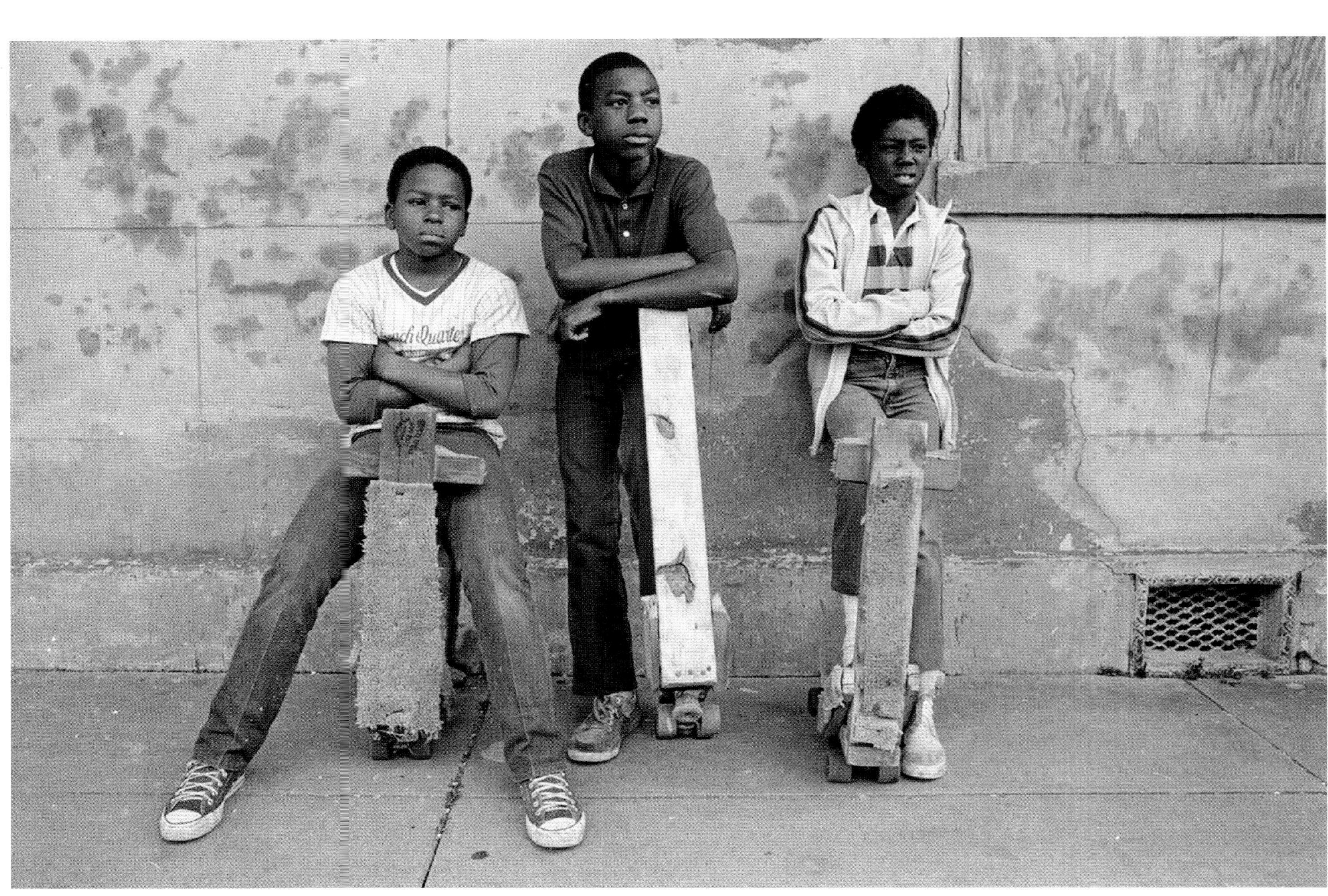

Girard Mouton, III

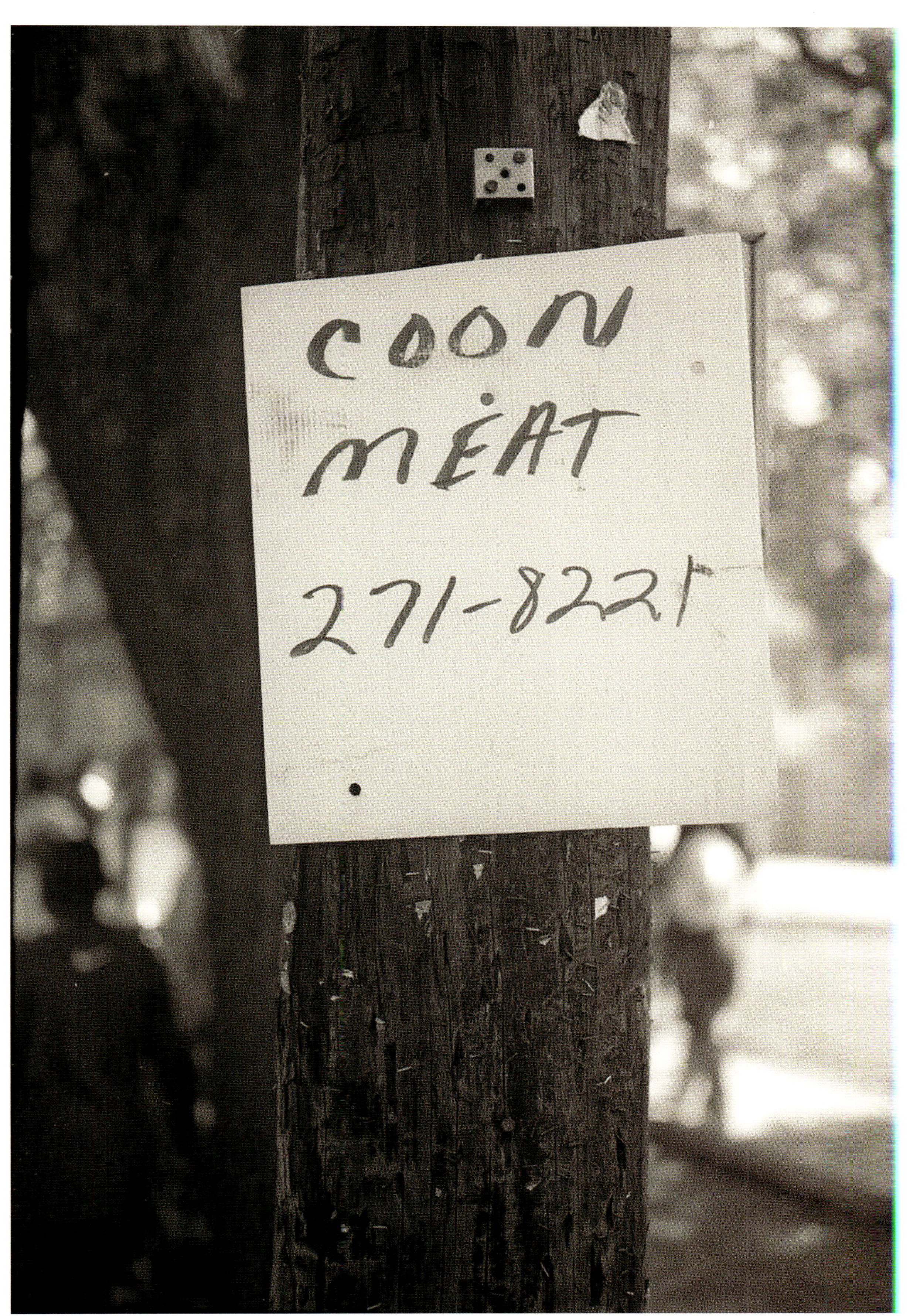

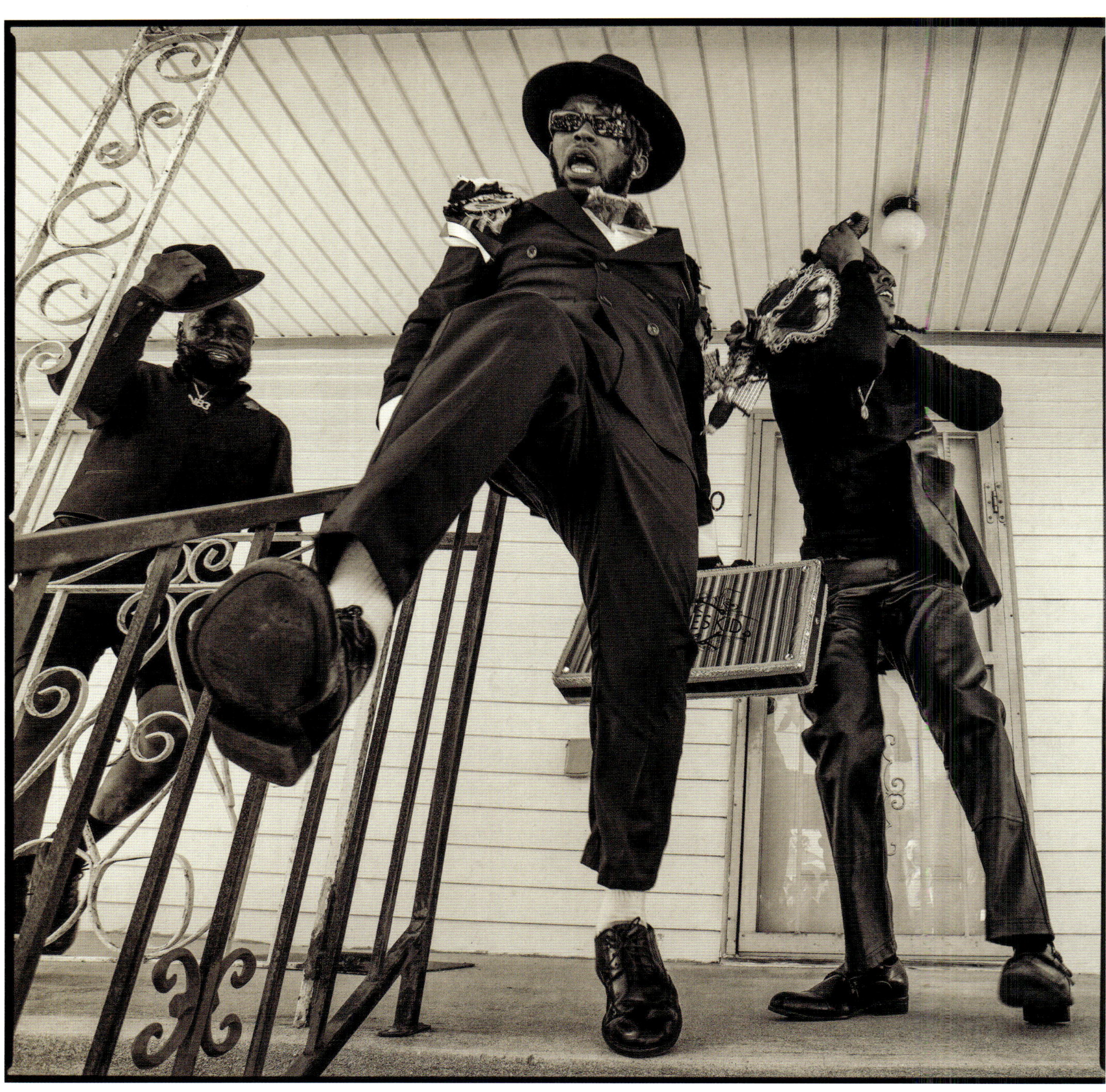

Gus Bennett

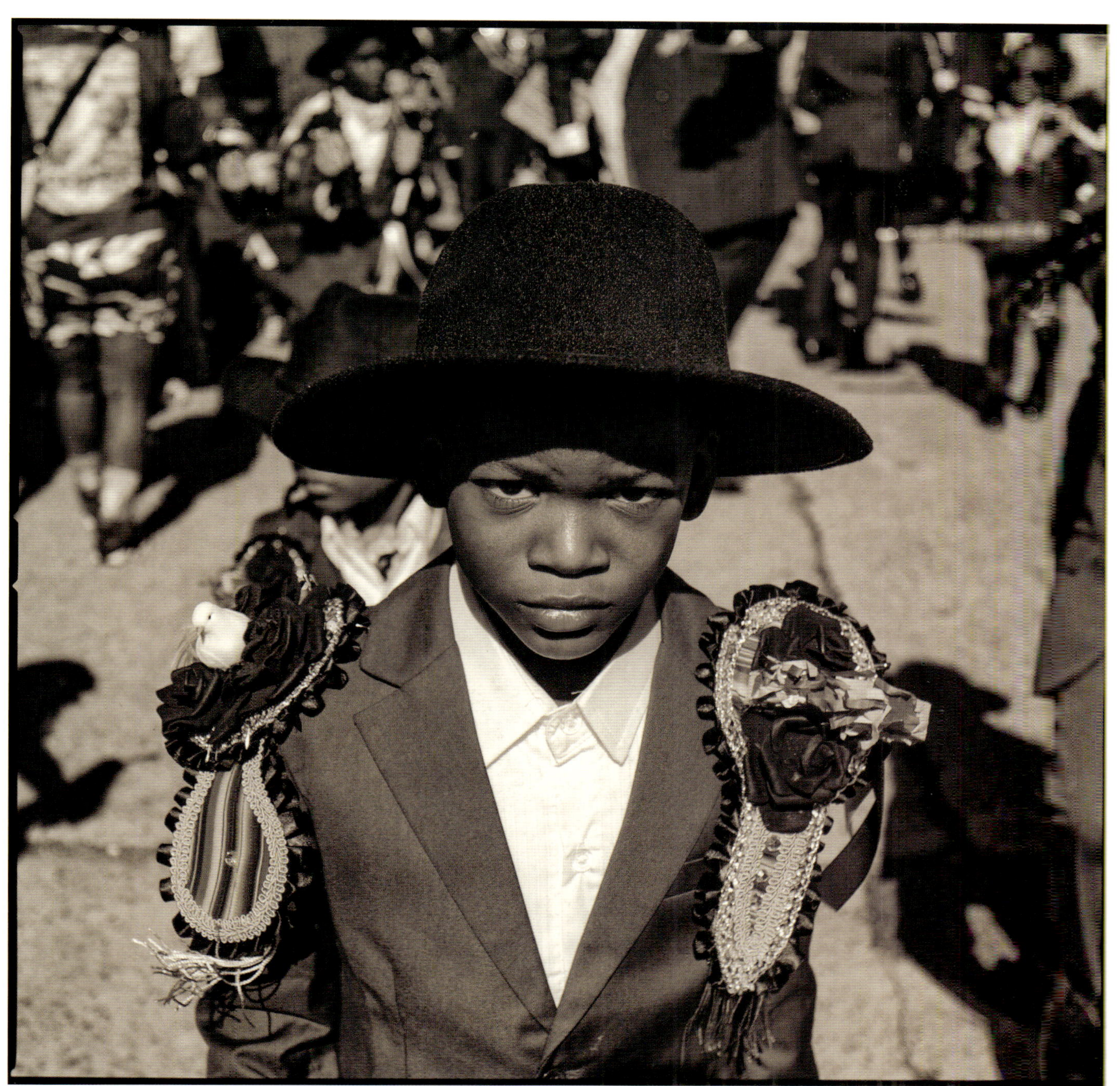

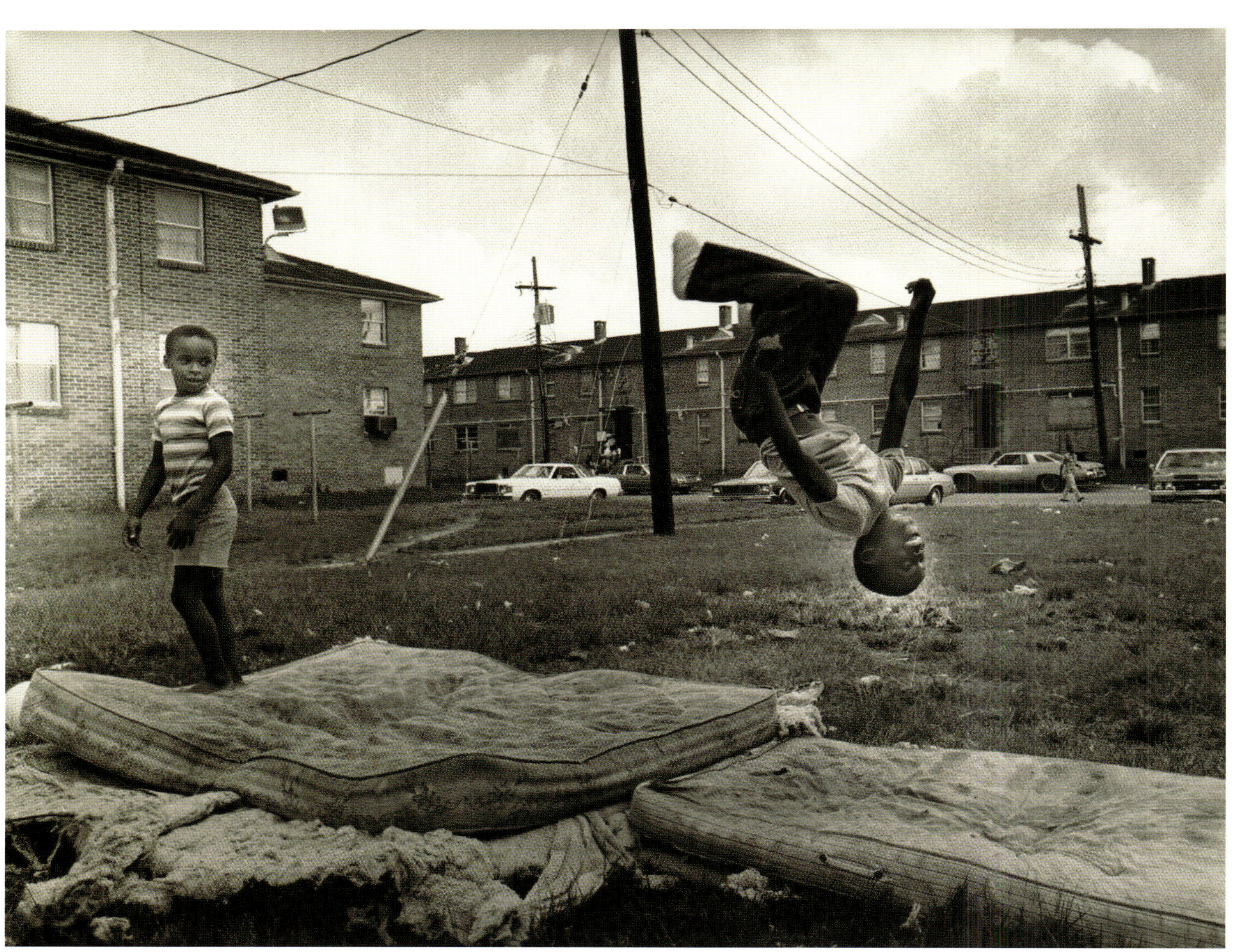

Harold Baquet

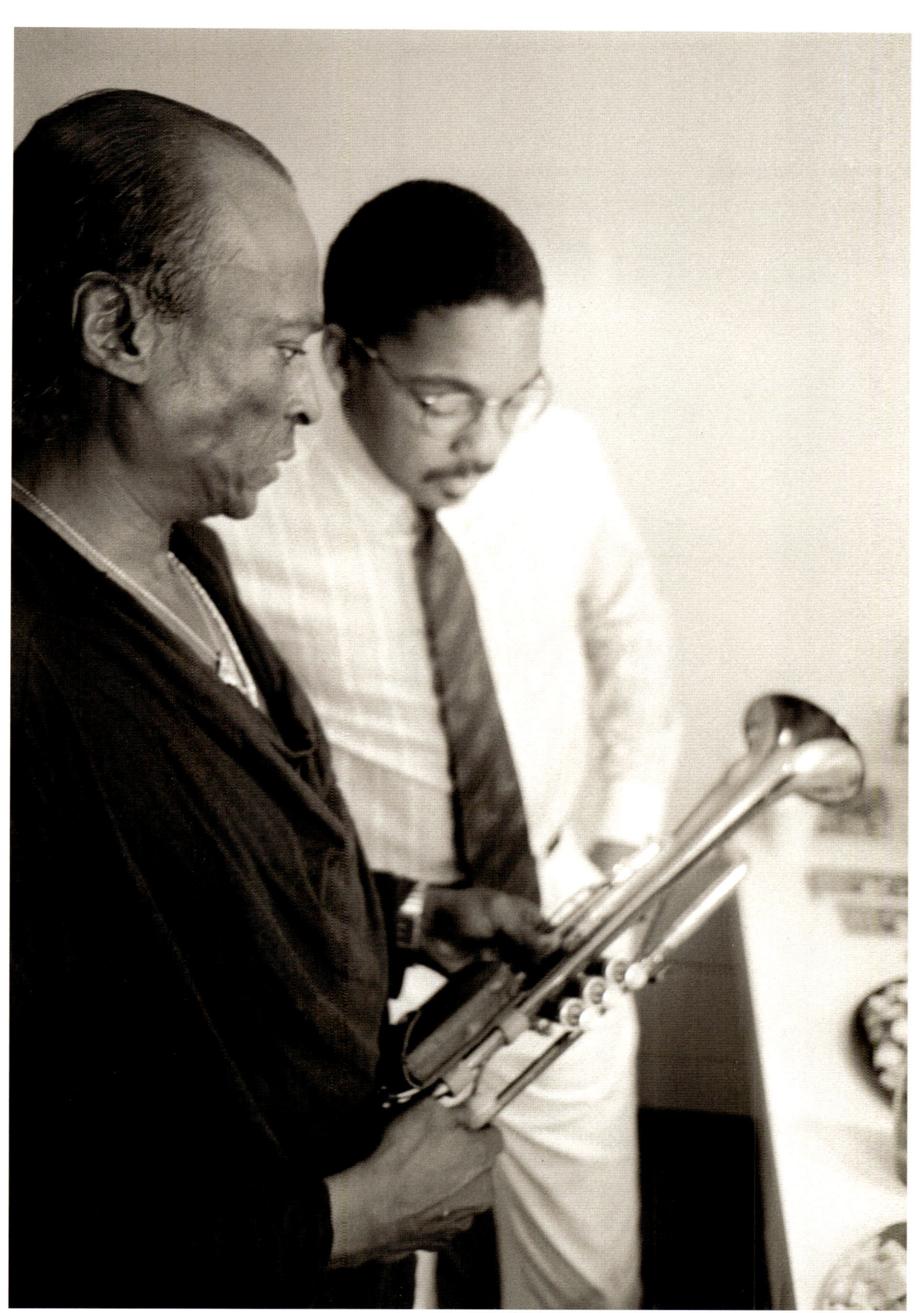

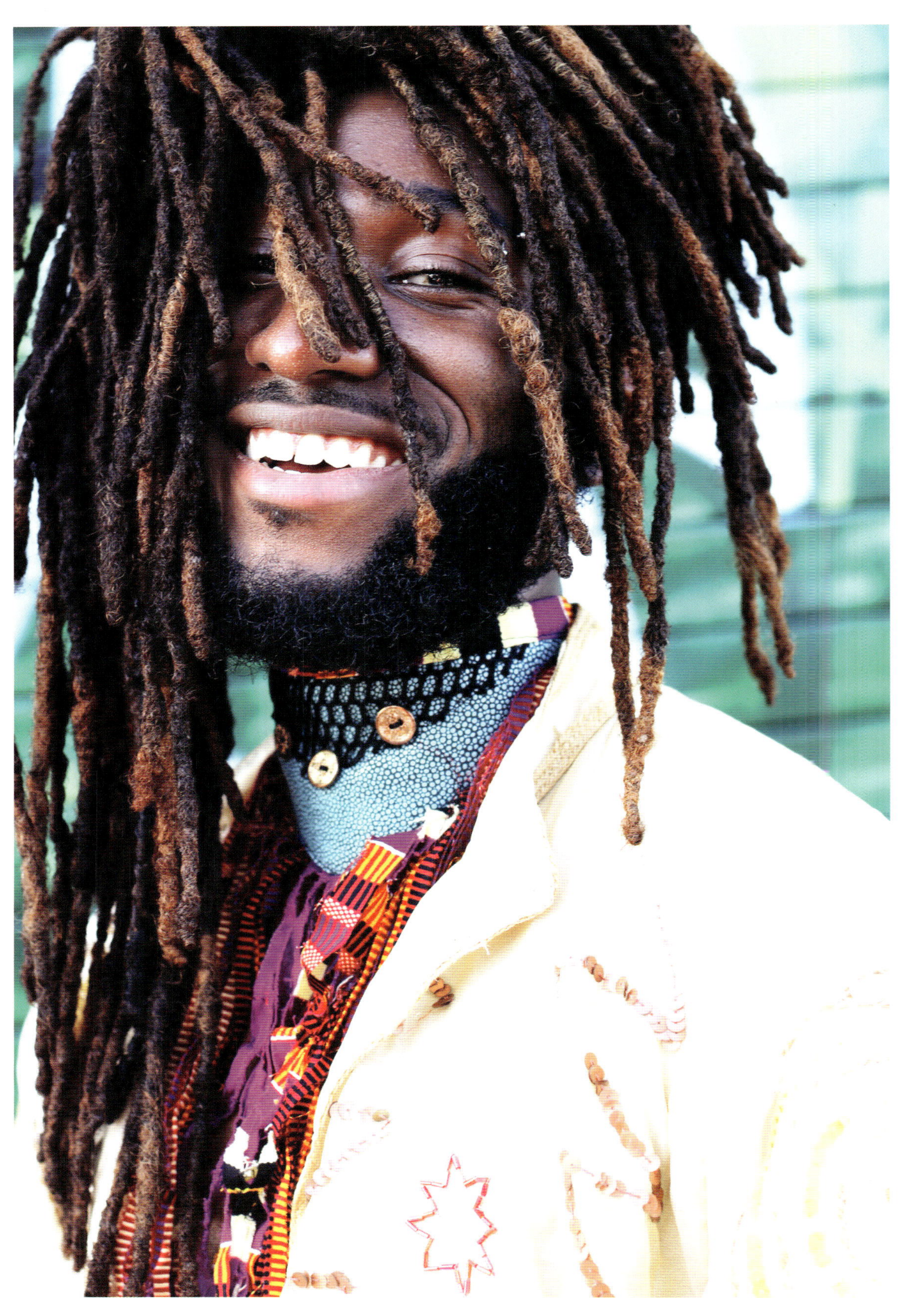

Heidi Hickman

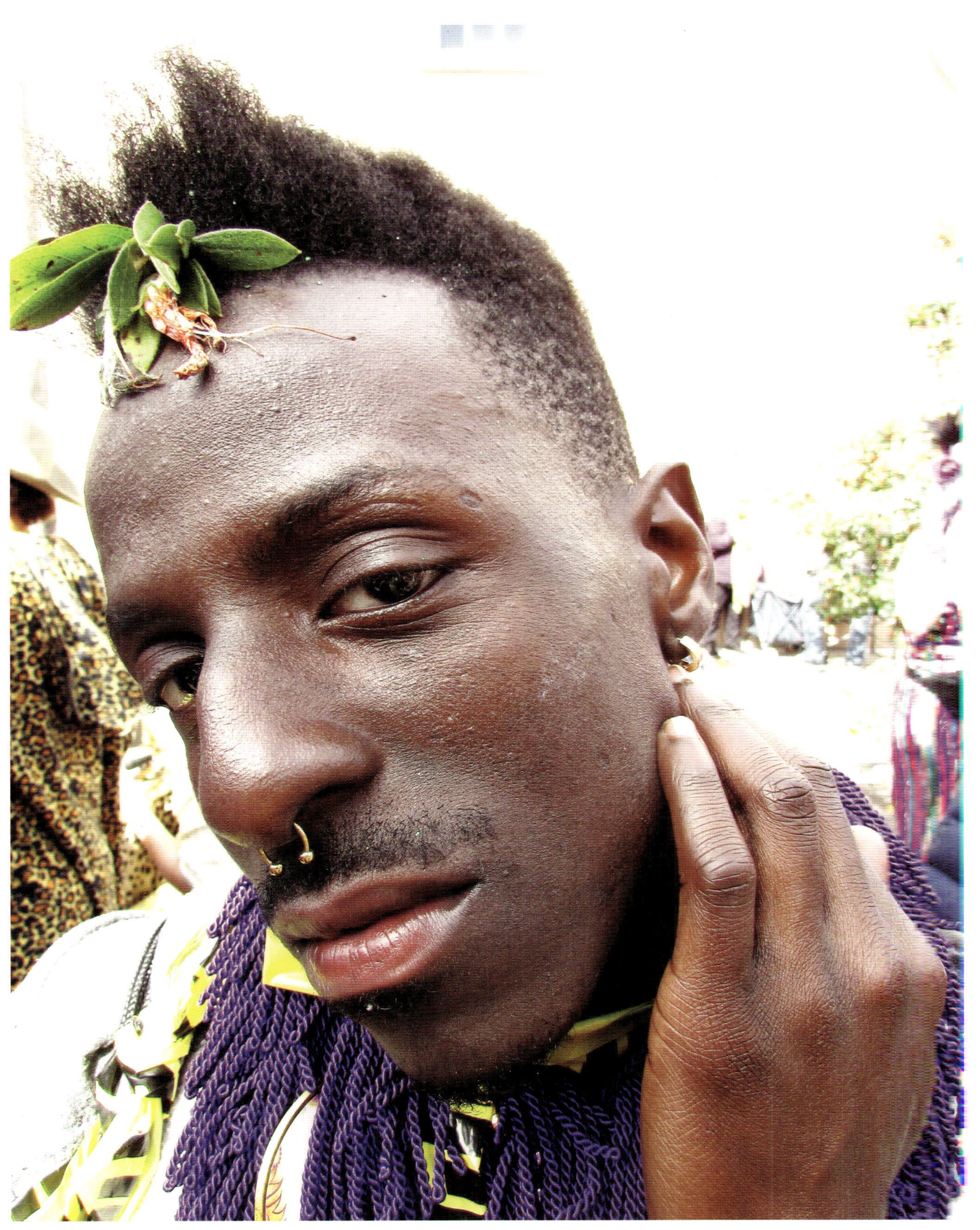

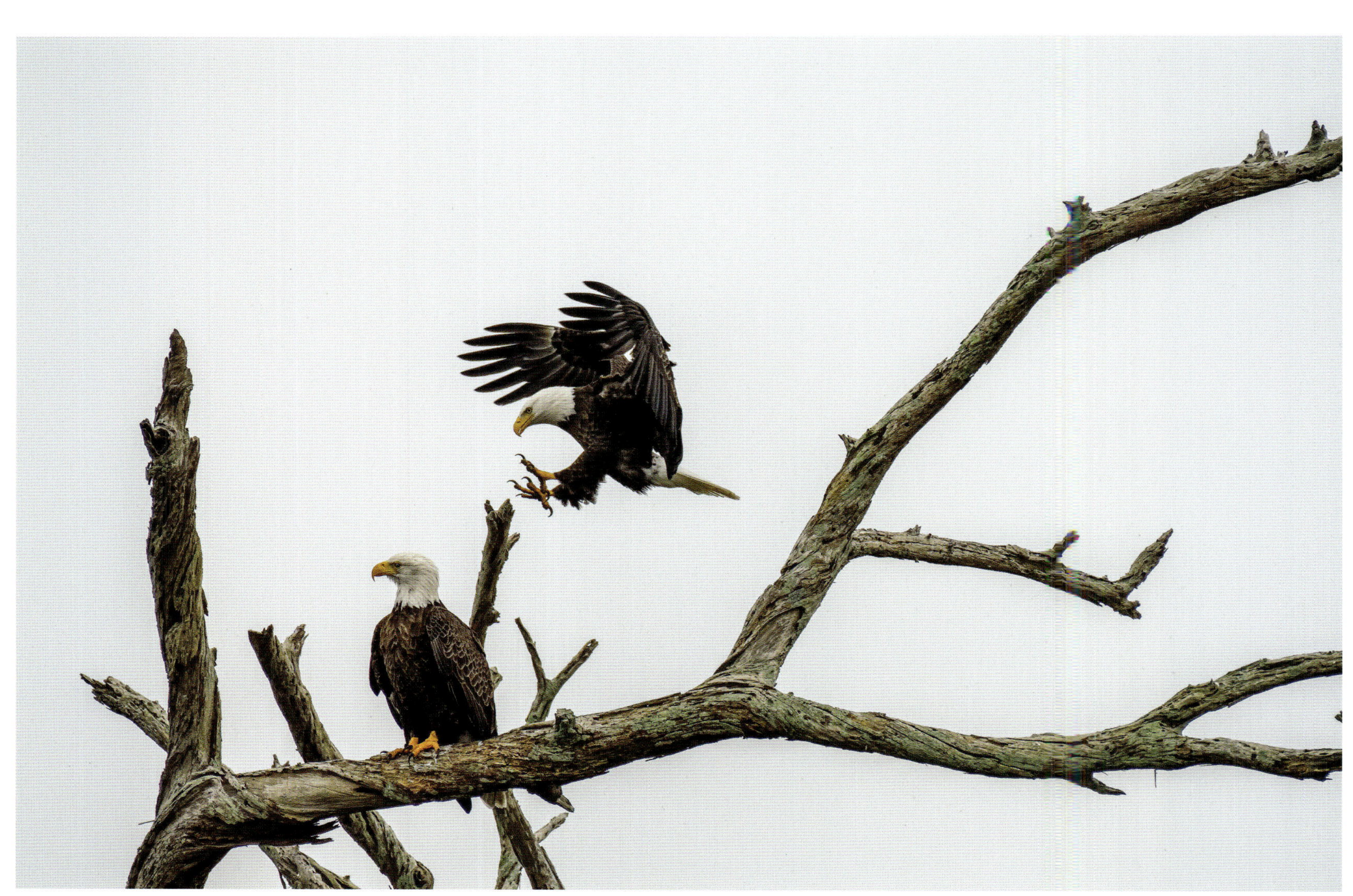

Irving Johnson III

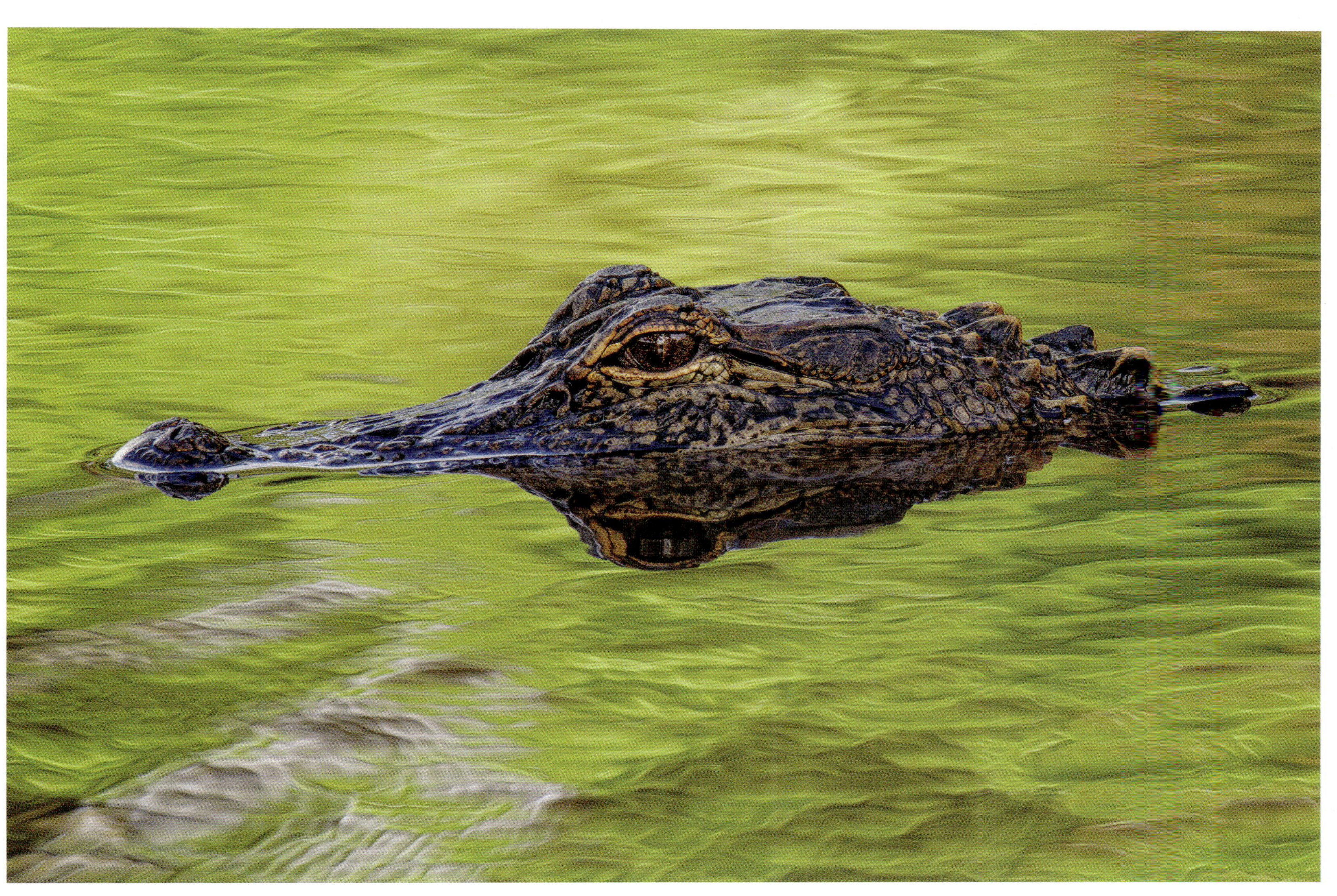

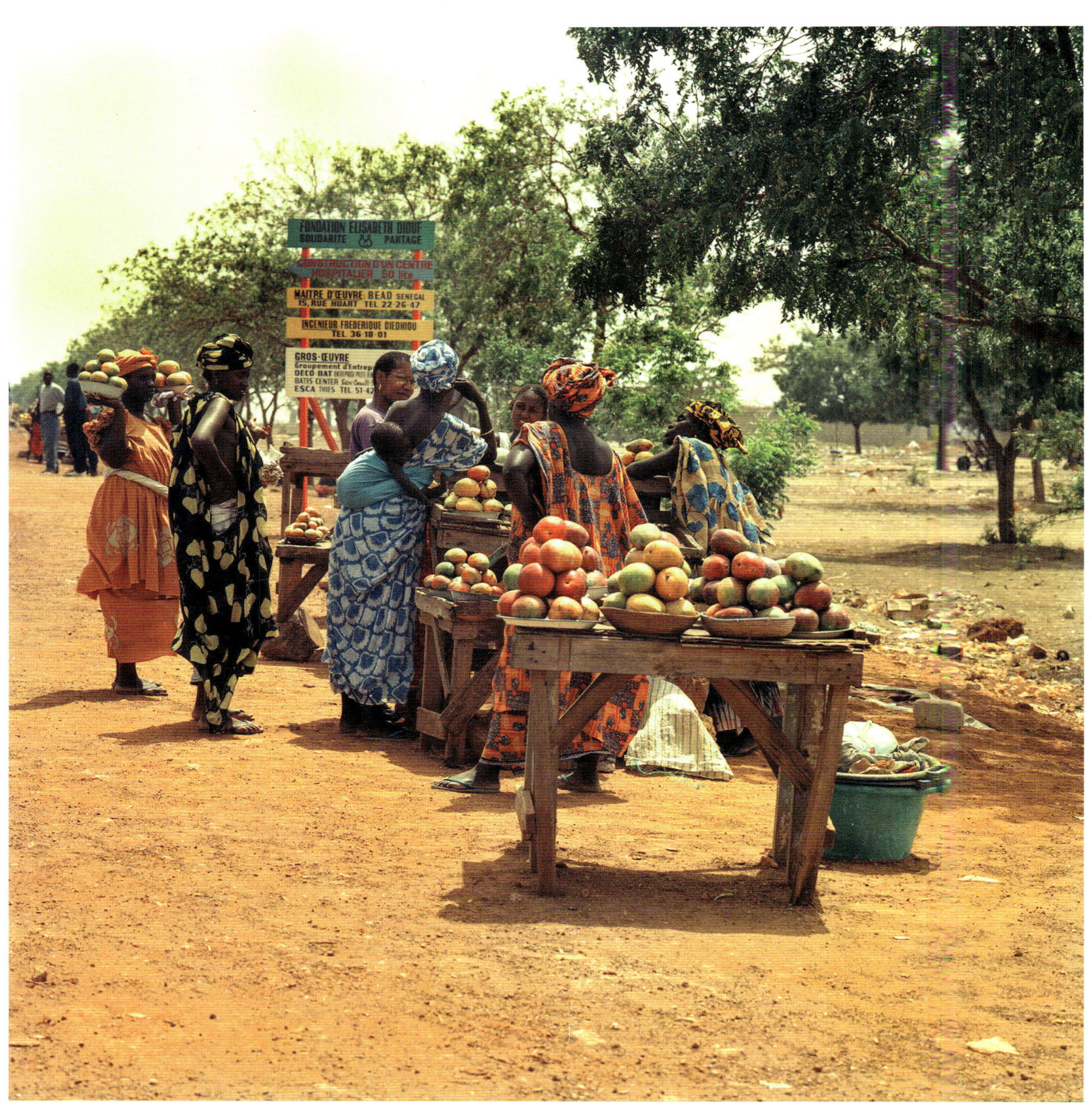
FONDATION ELISABETH DIOUF
SOLIDARITE PARTAGE
CONSTRUCTION D'UN CENTRE
HOSPITALIER 50 lits
MAITRE D'ŒUVRE BEAD SENEGAL
15, RUE HUART TEL 22-26-47
INGENIEUR FREDERIQUE DIEDHIOU
TEL 36-18-01
GROS-ŒUVRE

J Nash Porter

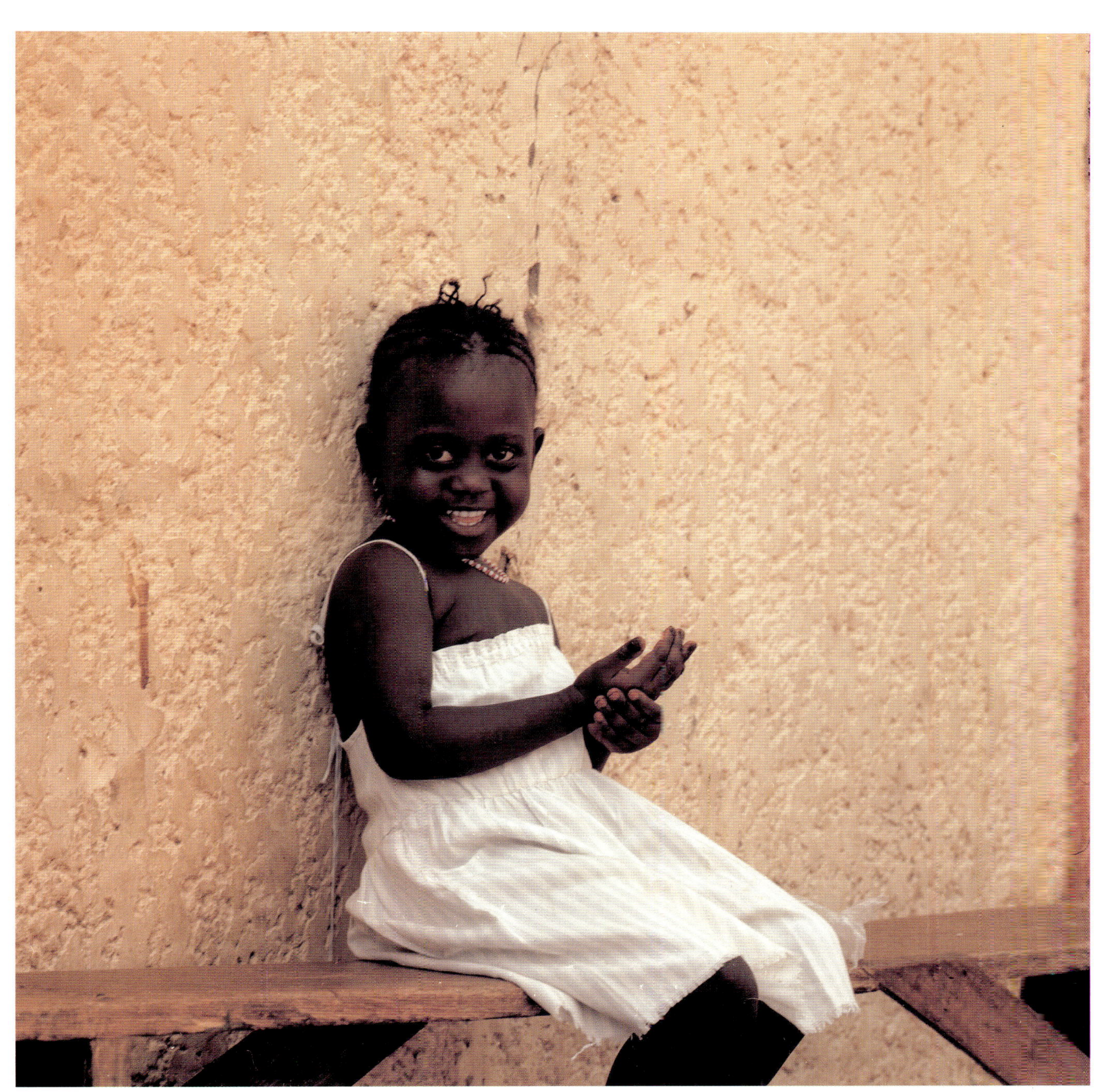

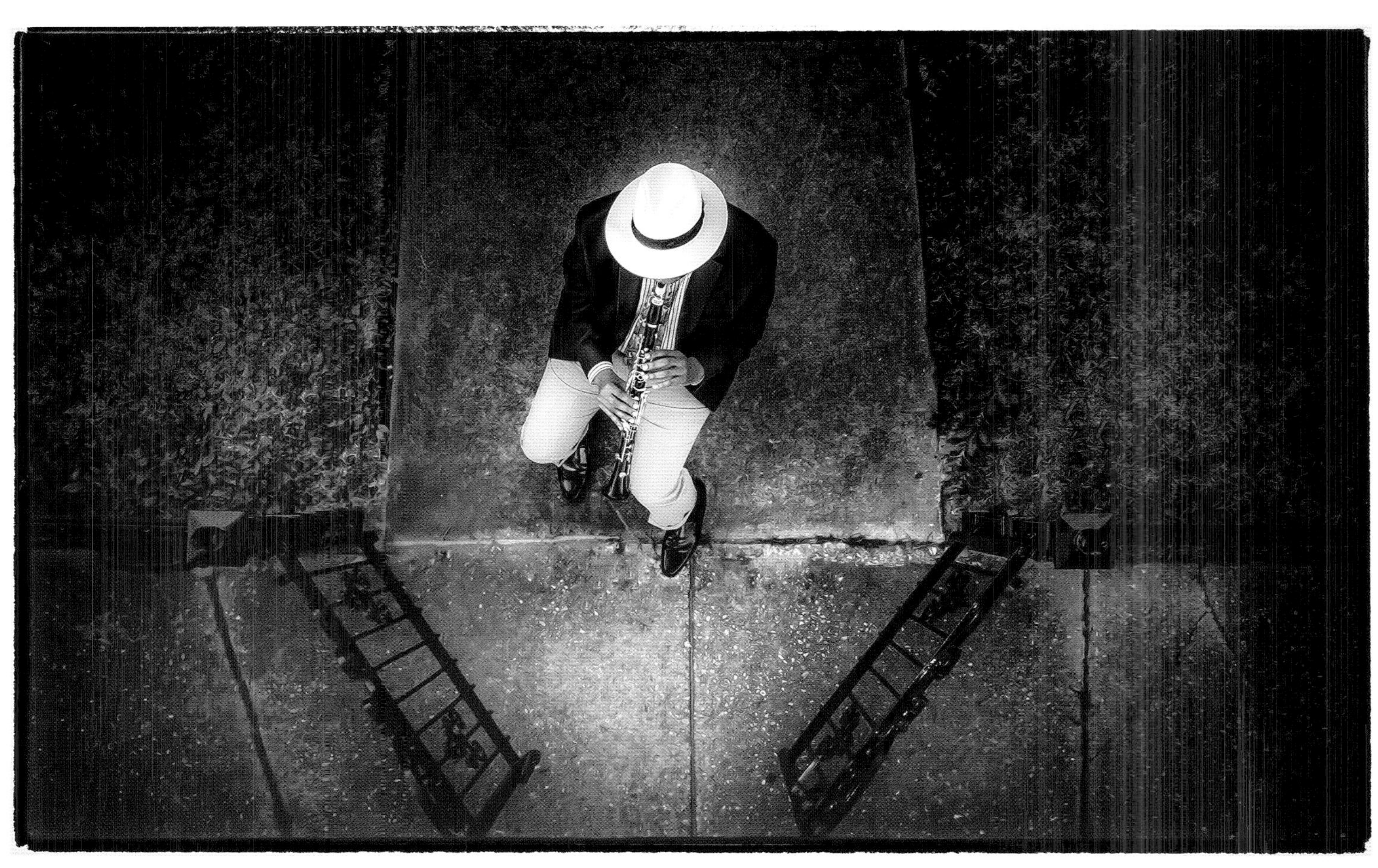

J. R. Thomason

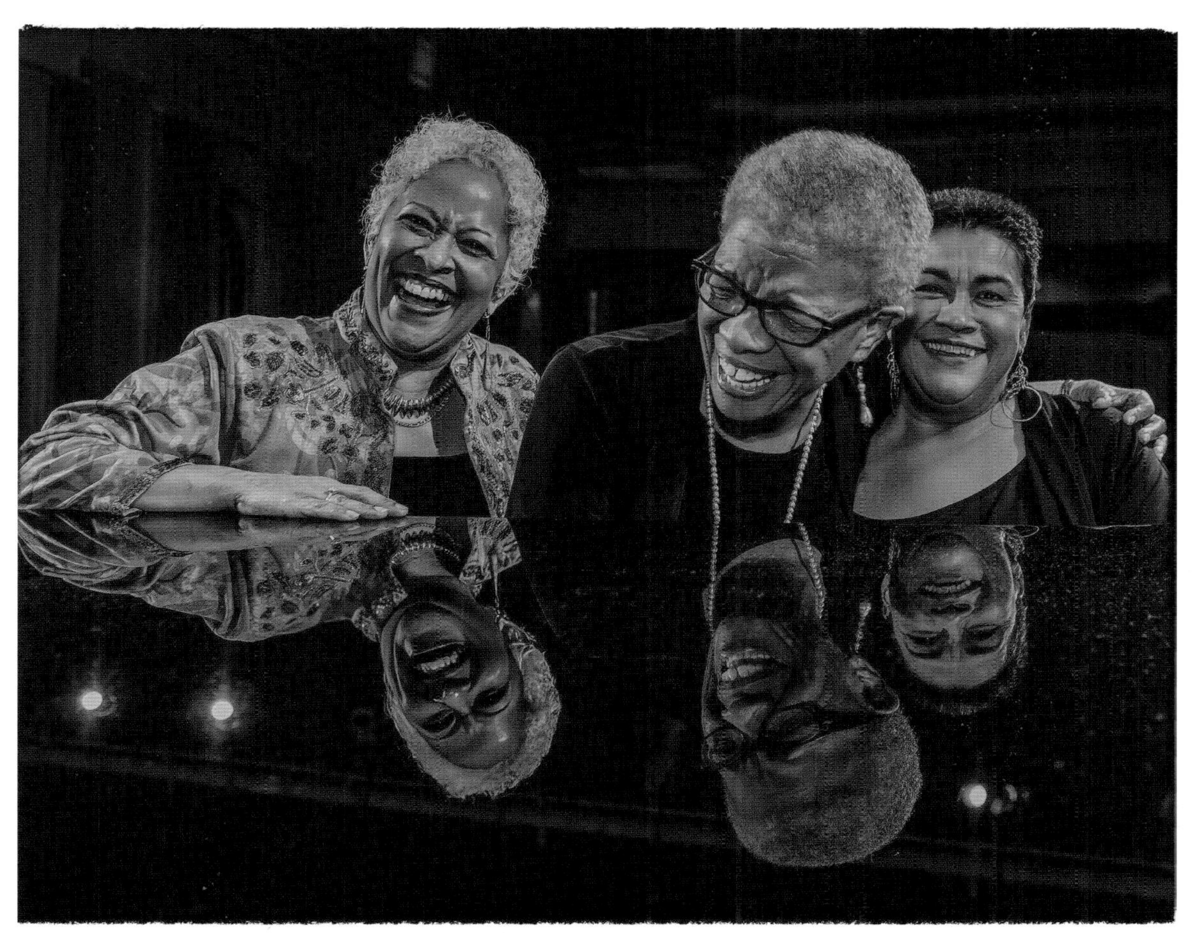

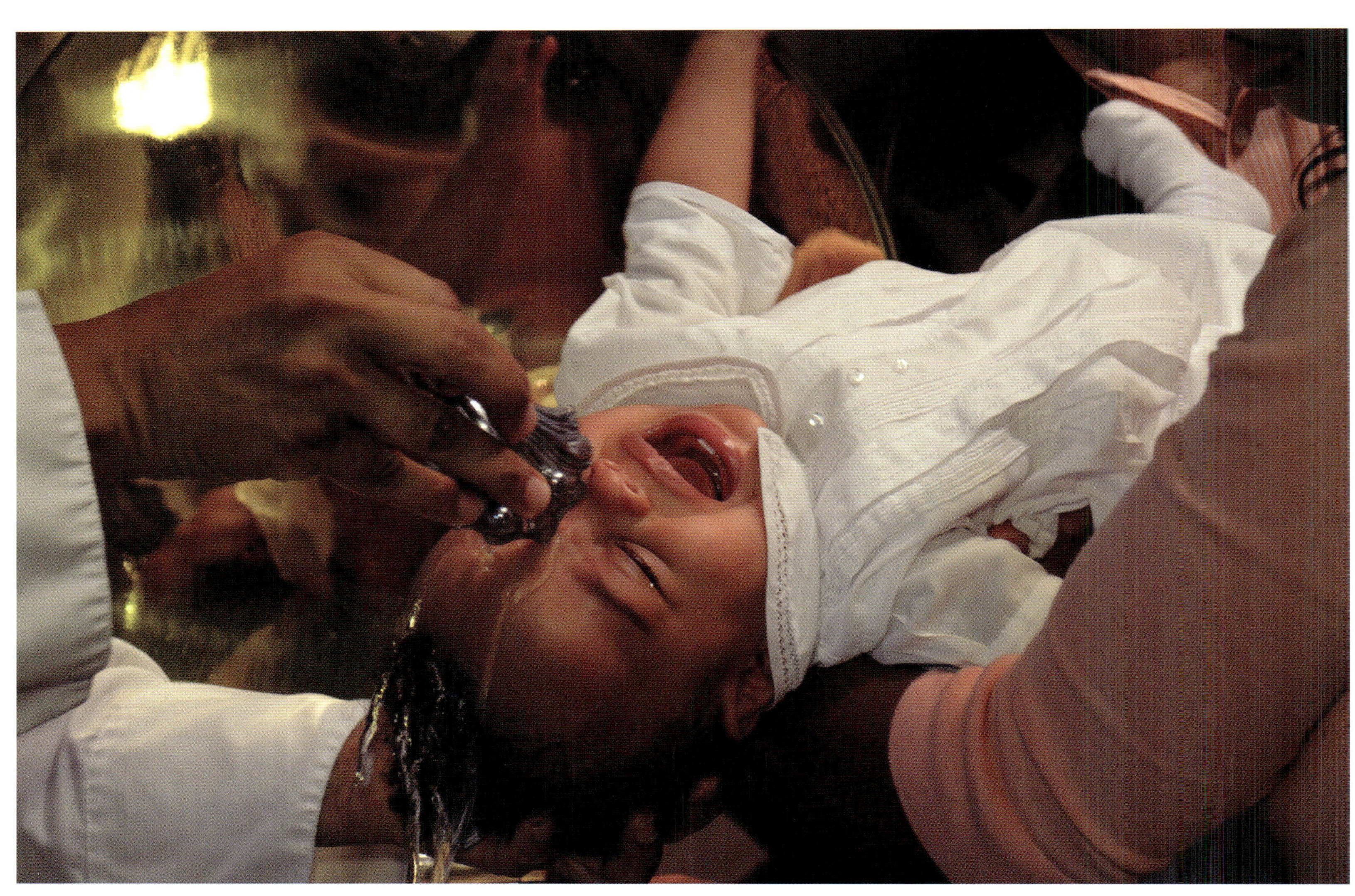

Jacques Detiege

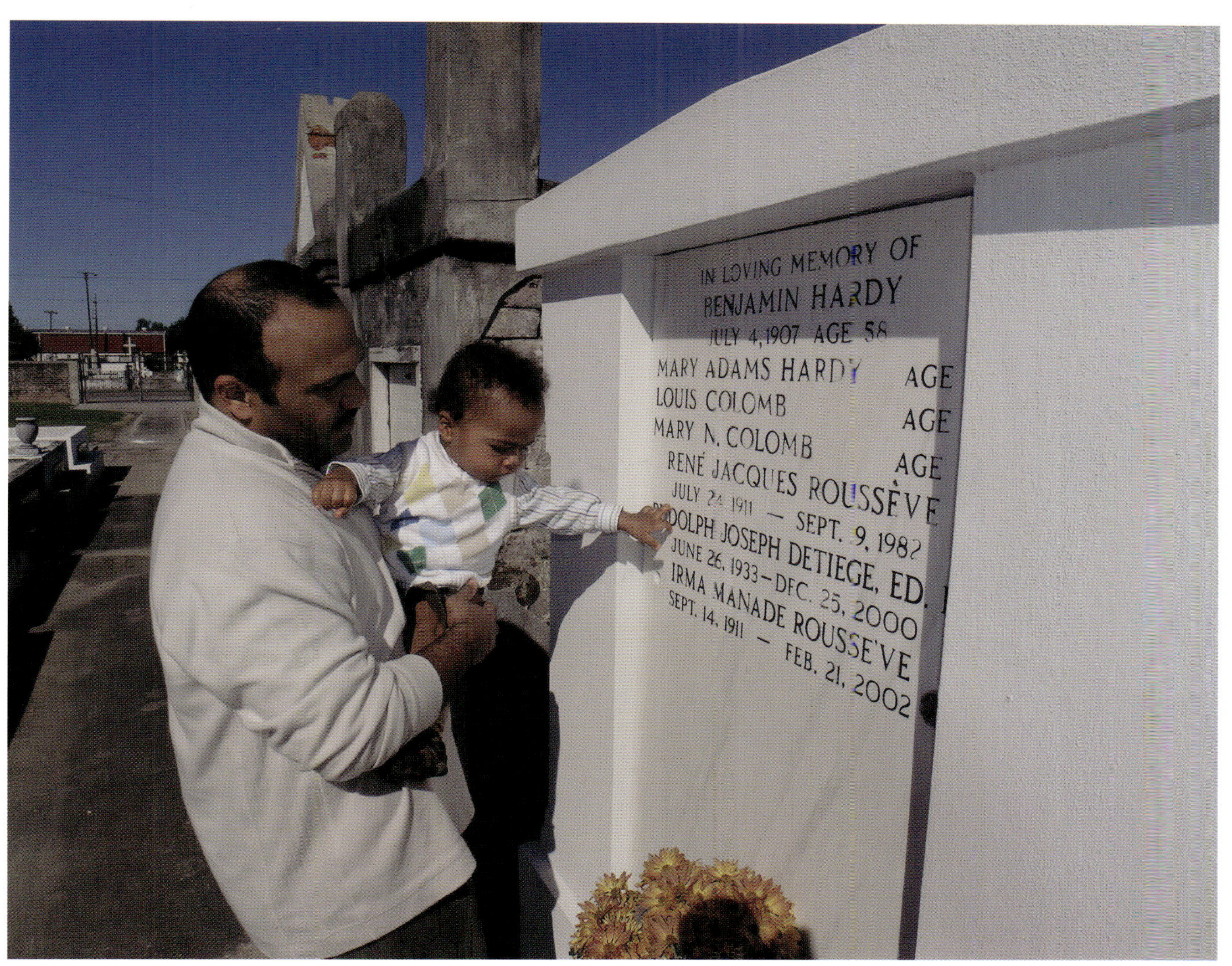

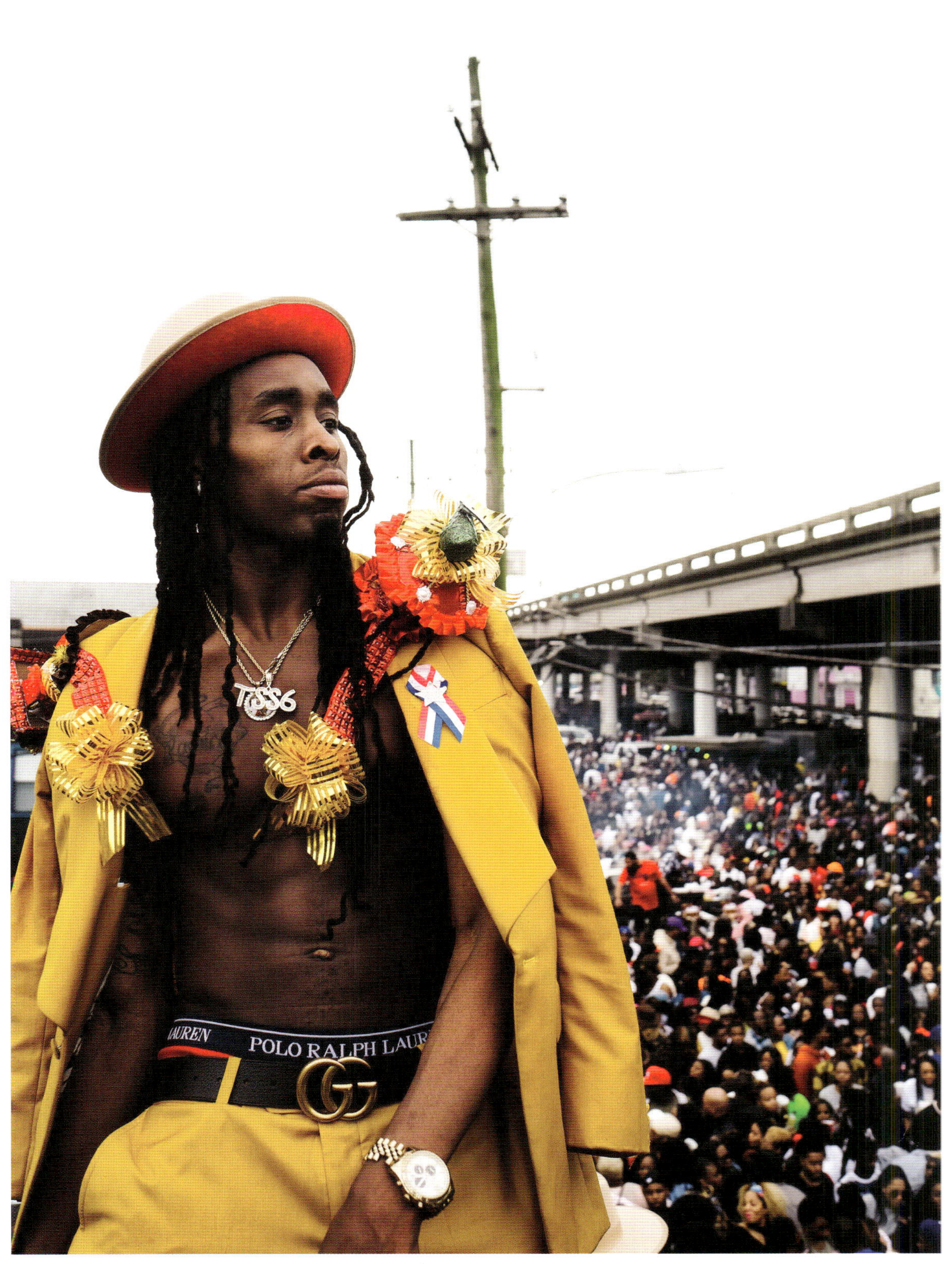
TSS6
LAUREN
POLO RALPH LAUR

Jamal Denzel Barnes

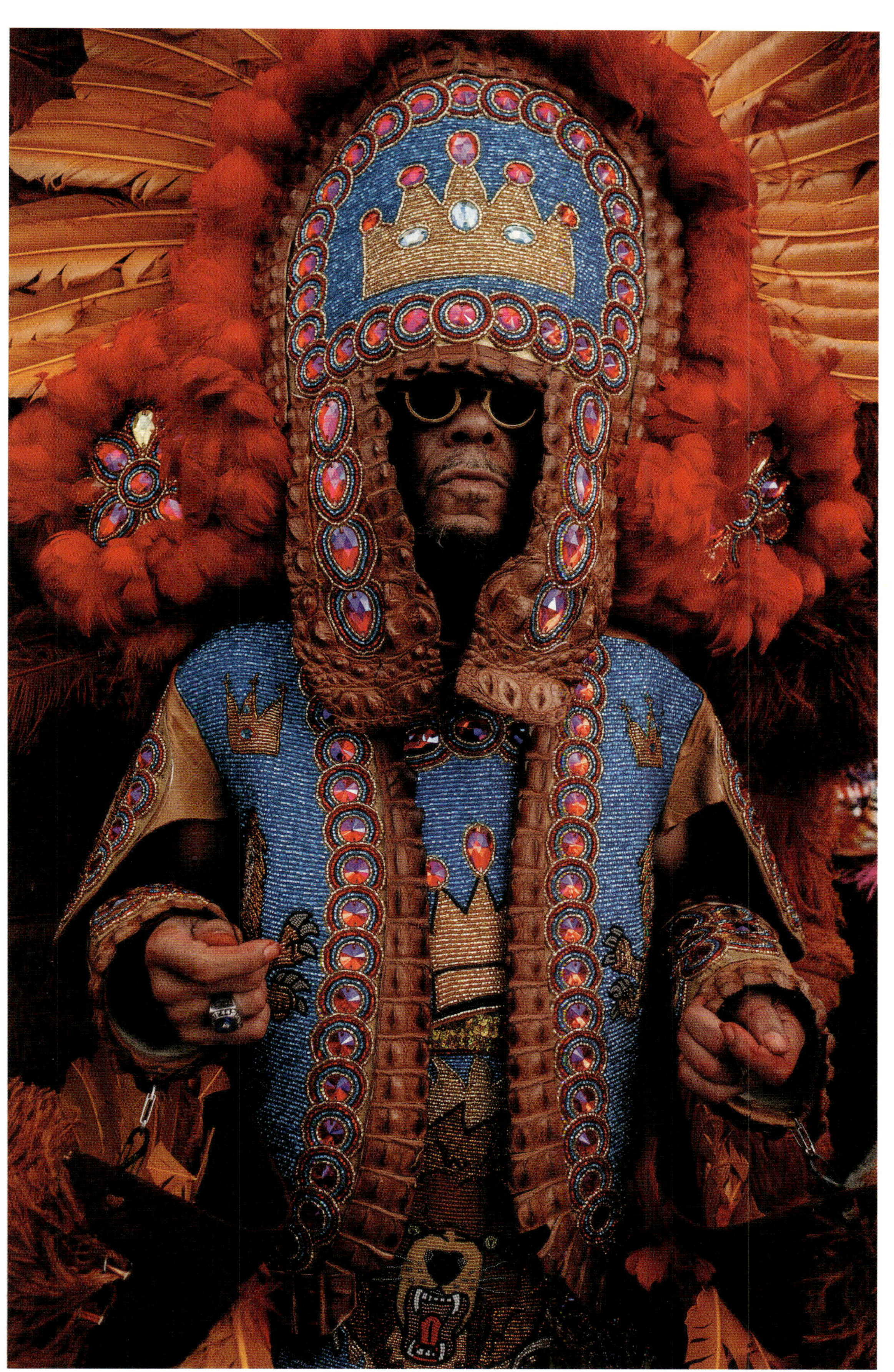

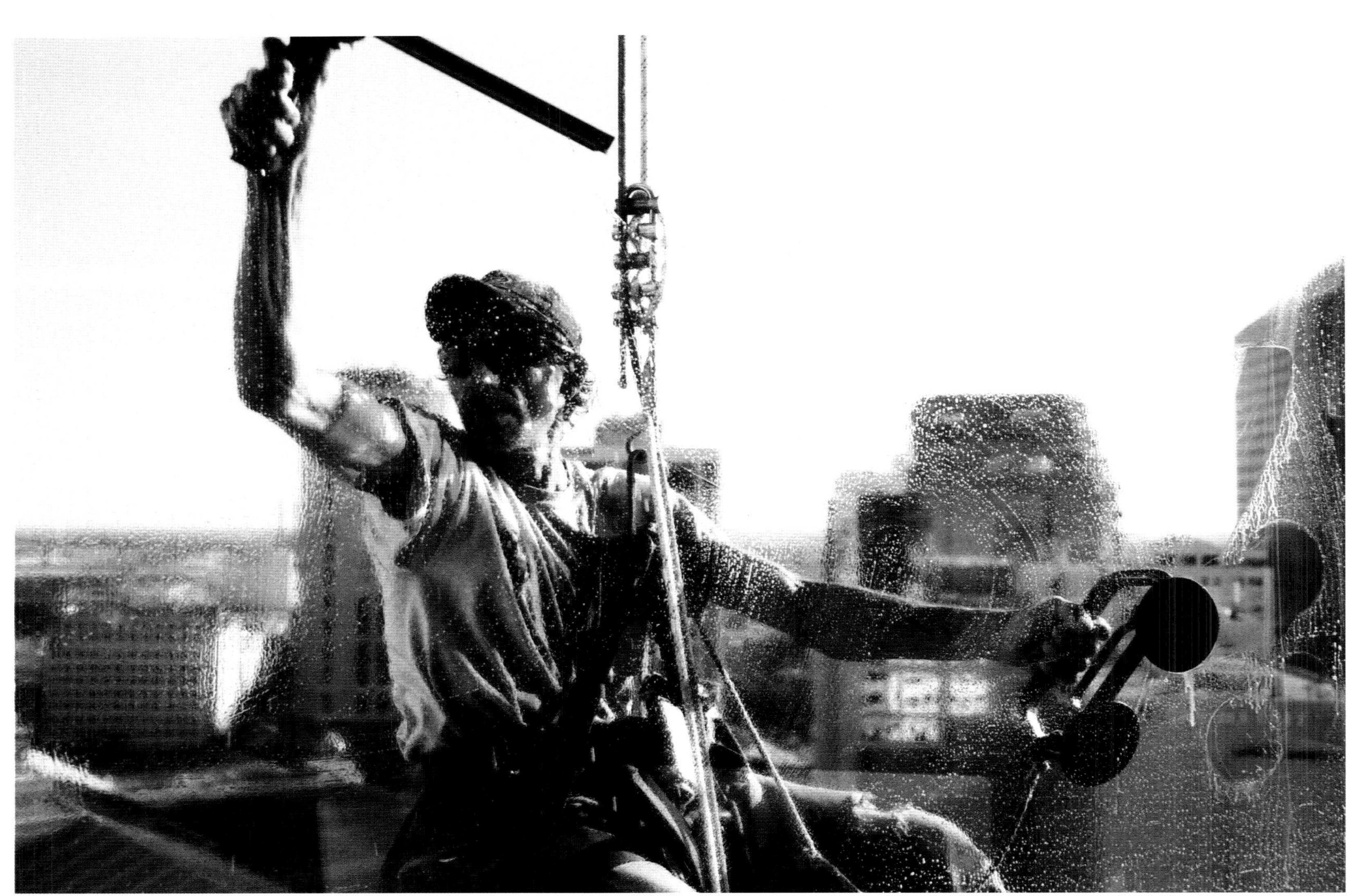

Jason R. A. Foster

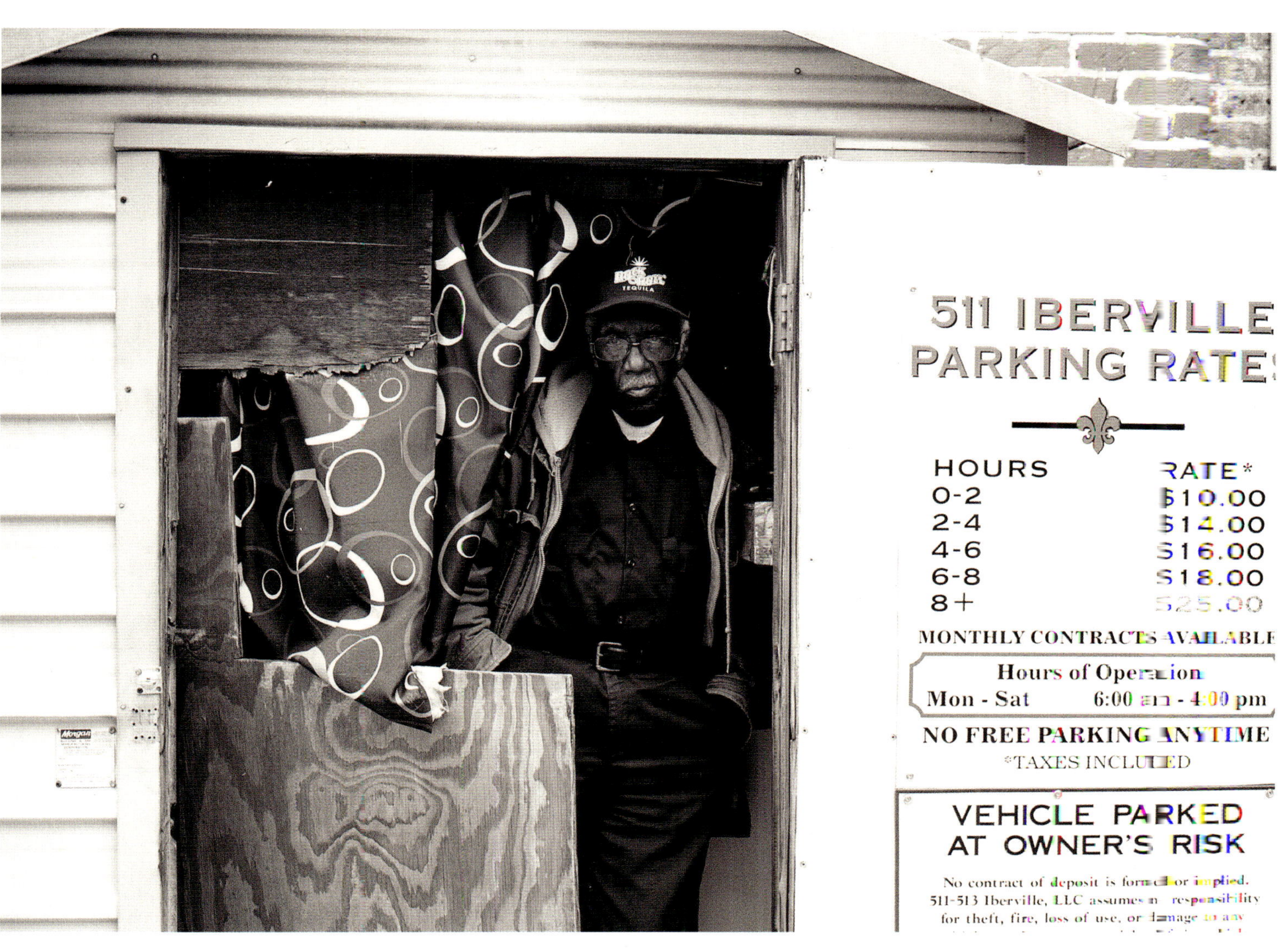

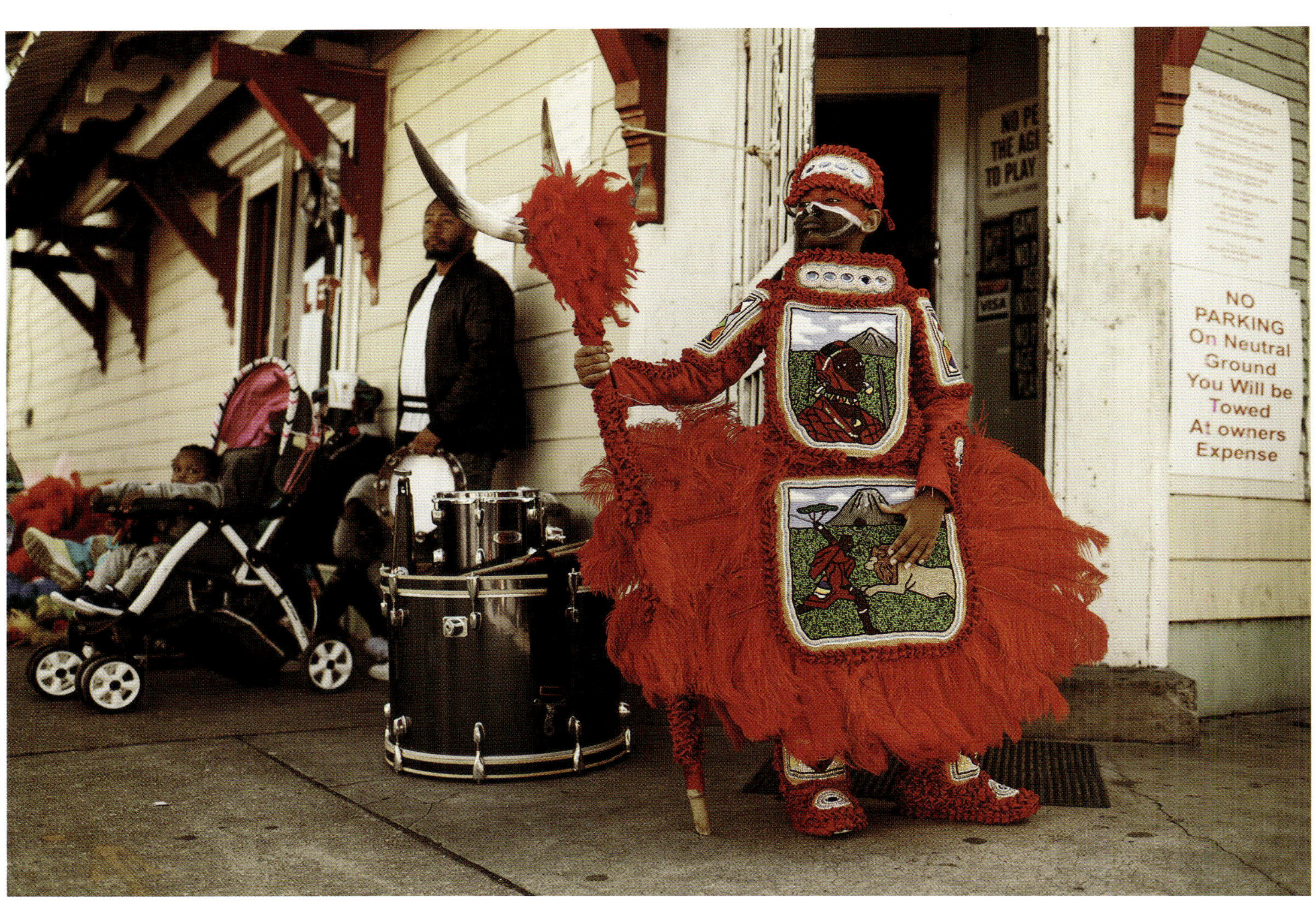
NO
PARKING
On Neutral
Ground
You Will be
Towed
At owners
Expense

Jeremy Tauriac

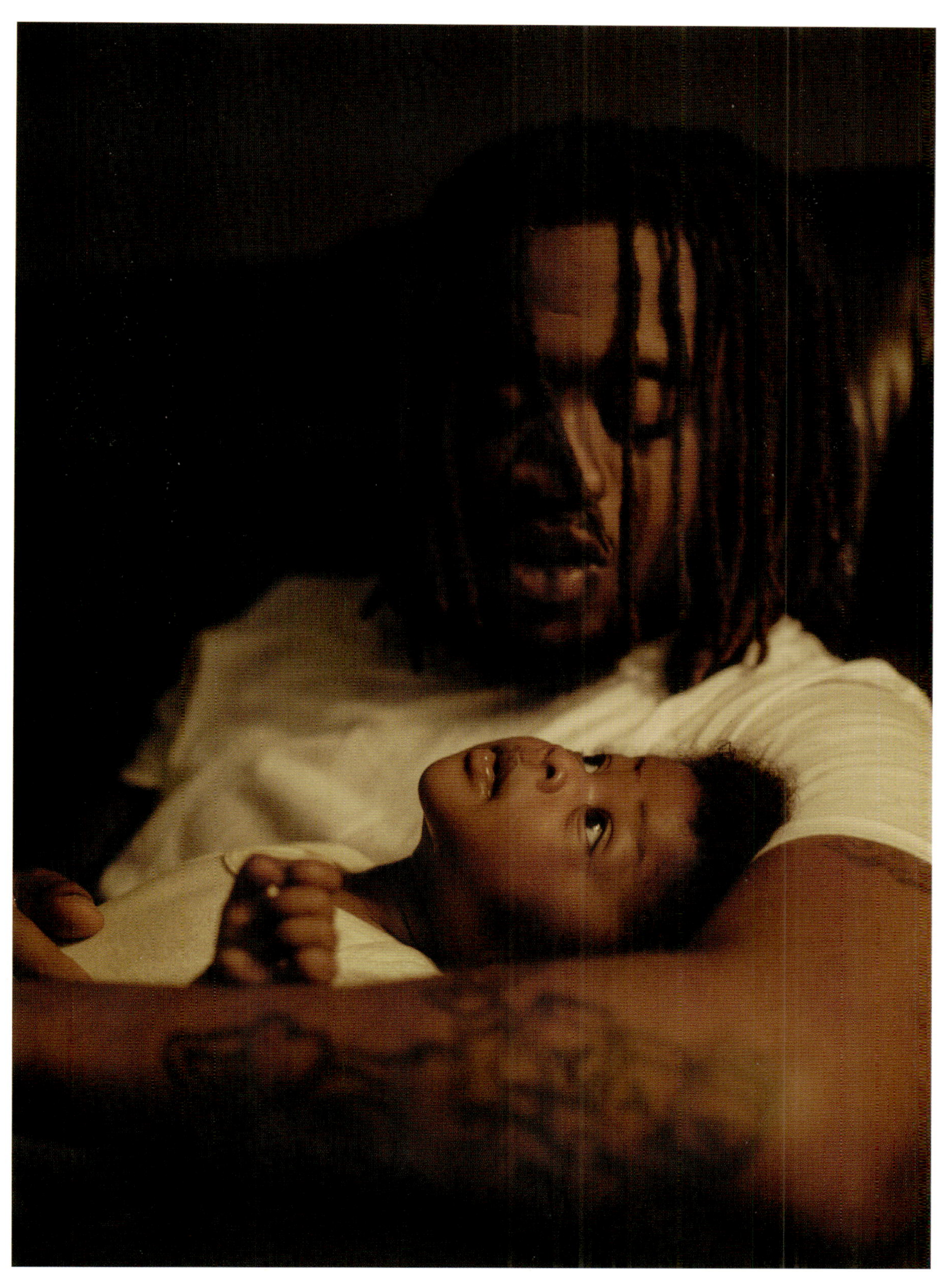

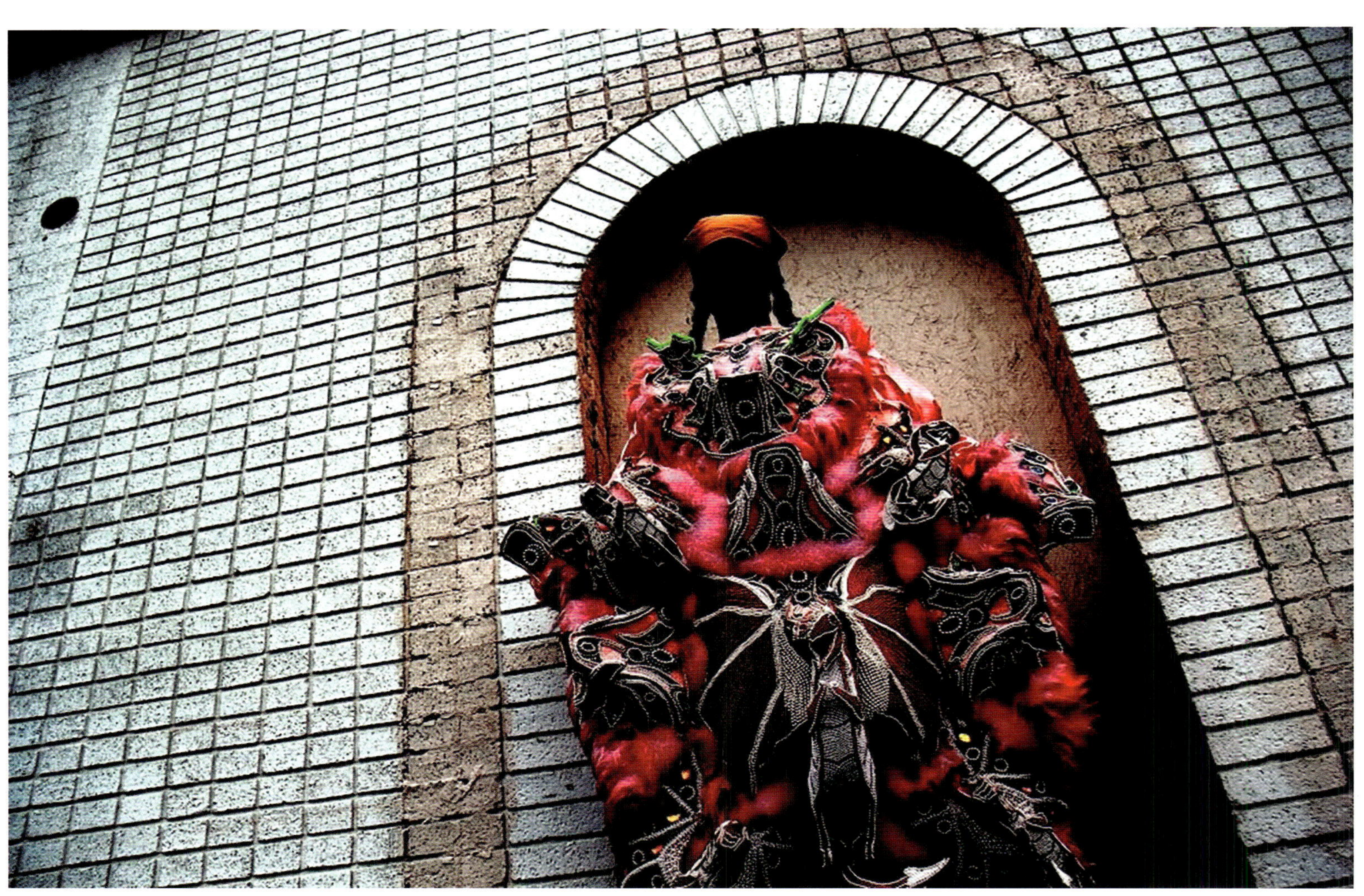

Jeri Hilt

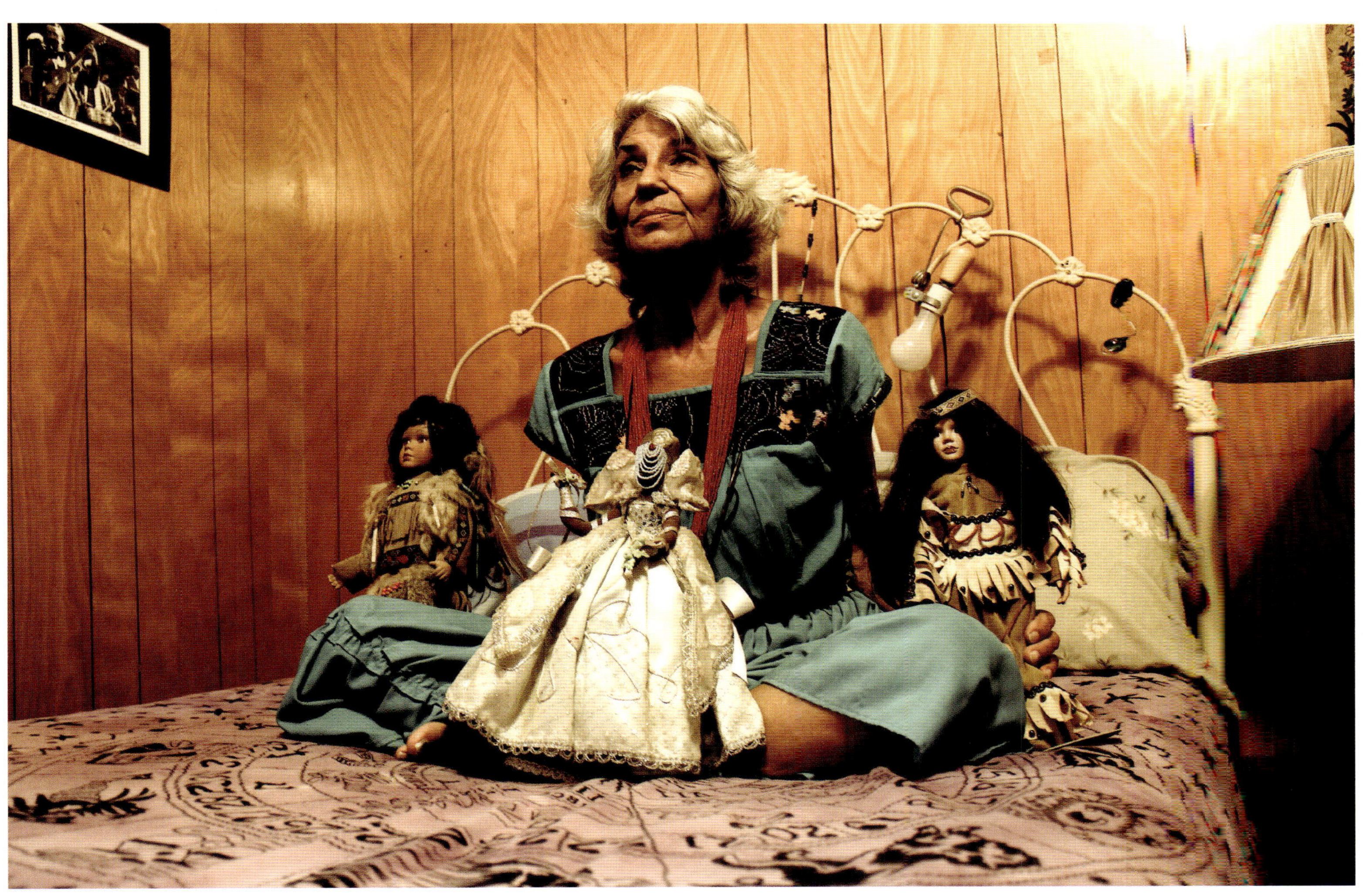

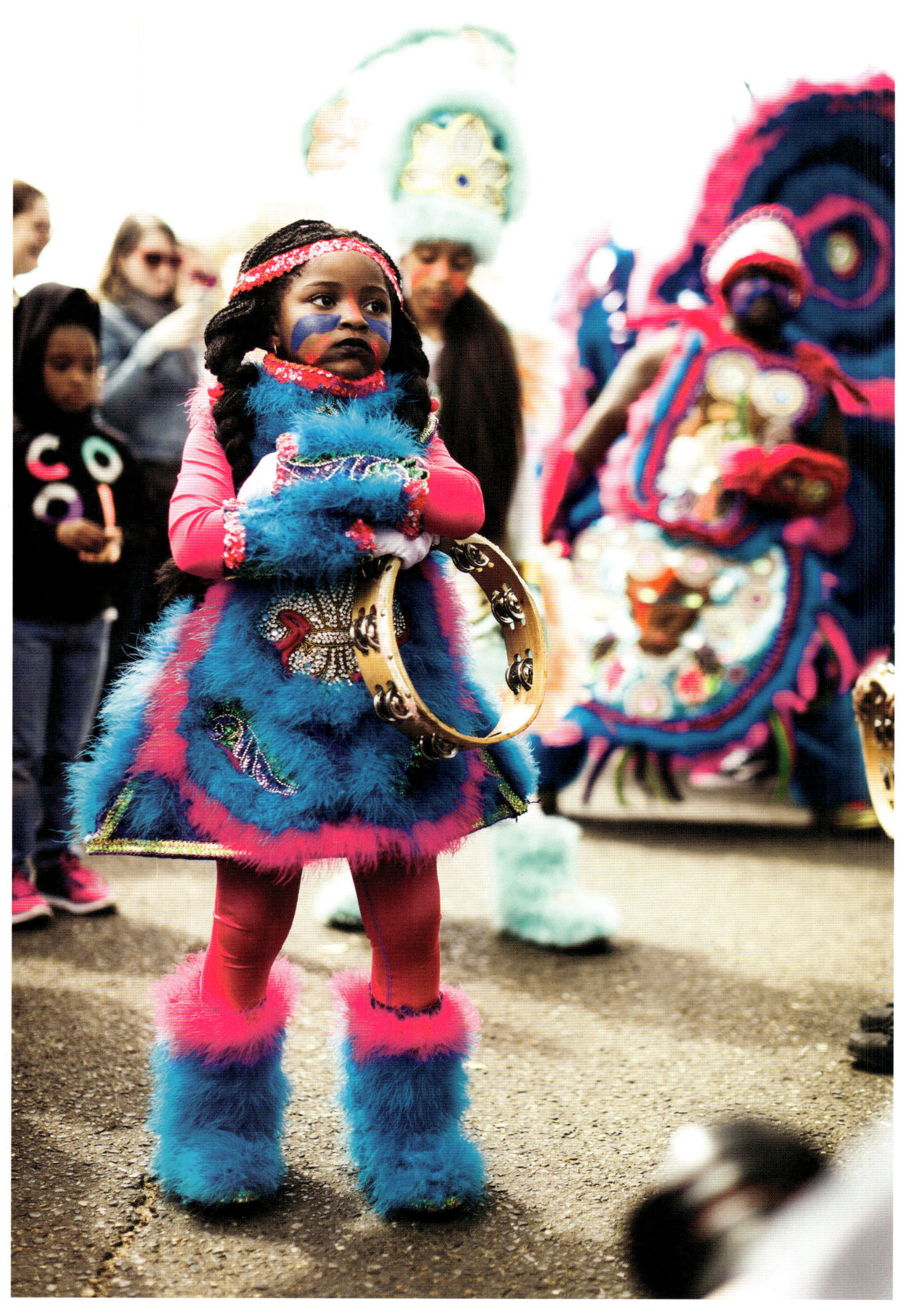

Jose Cotto

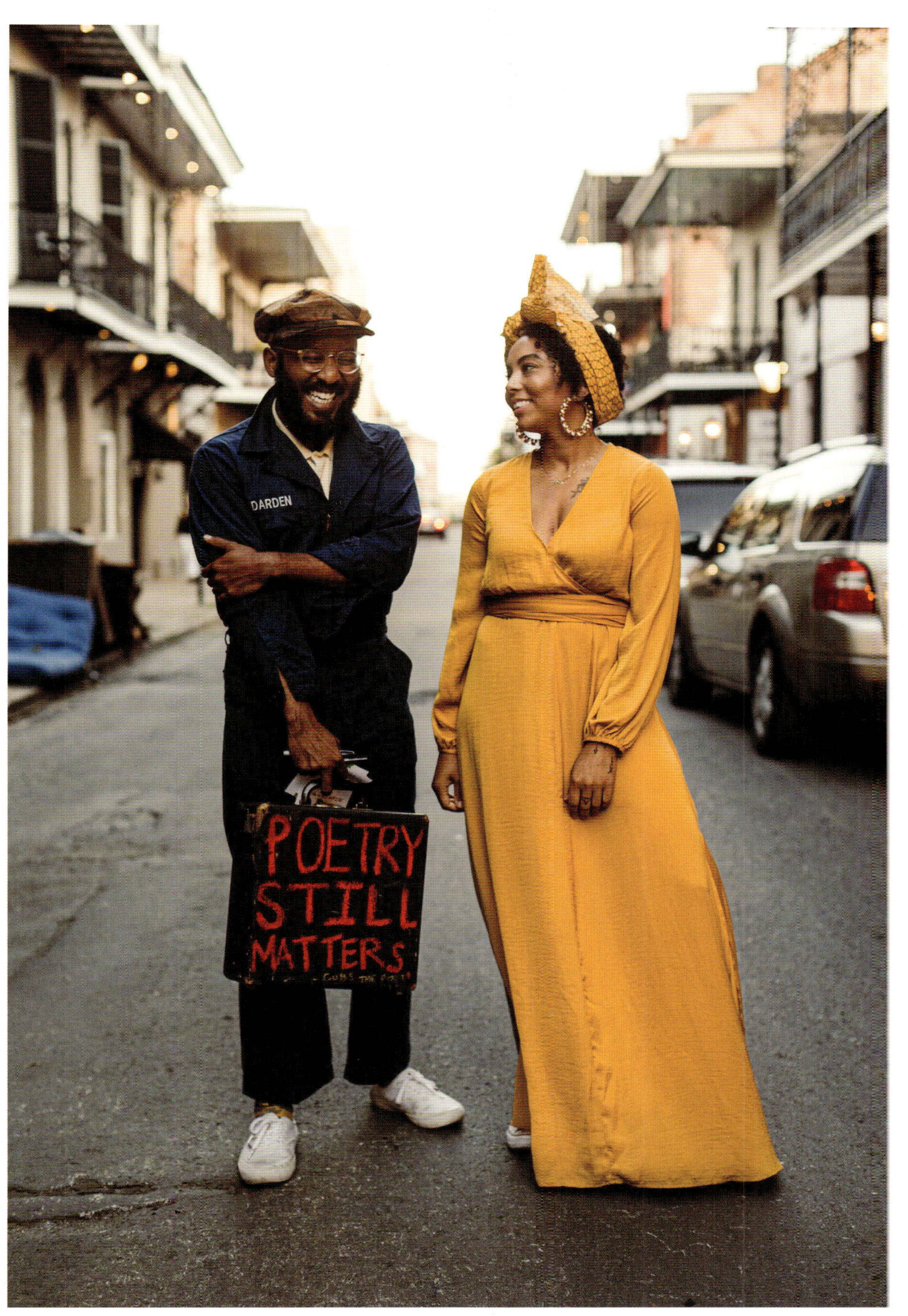

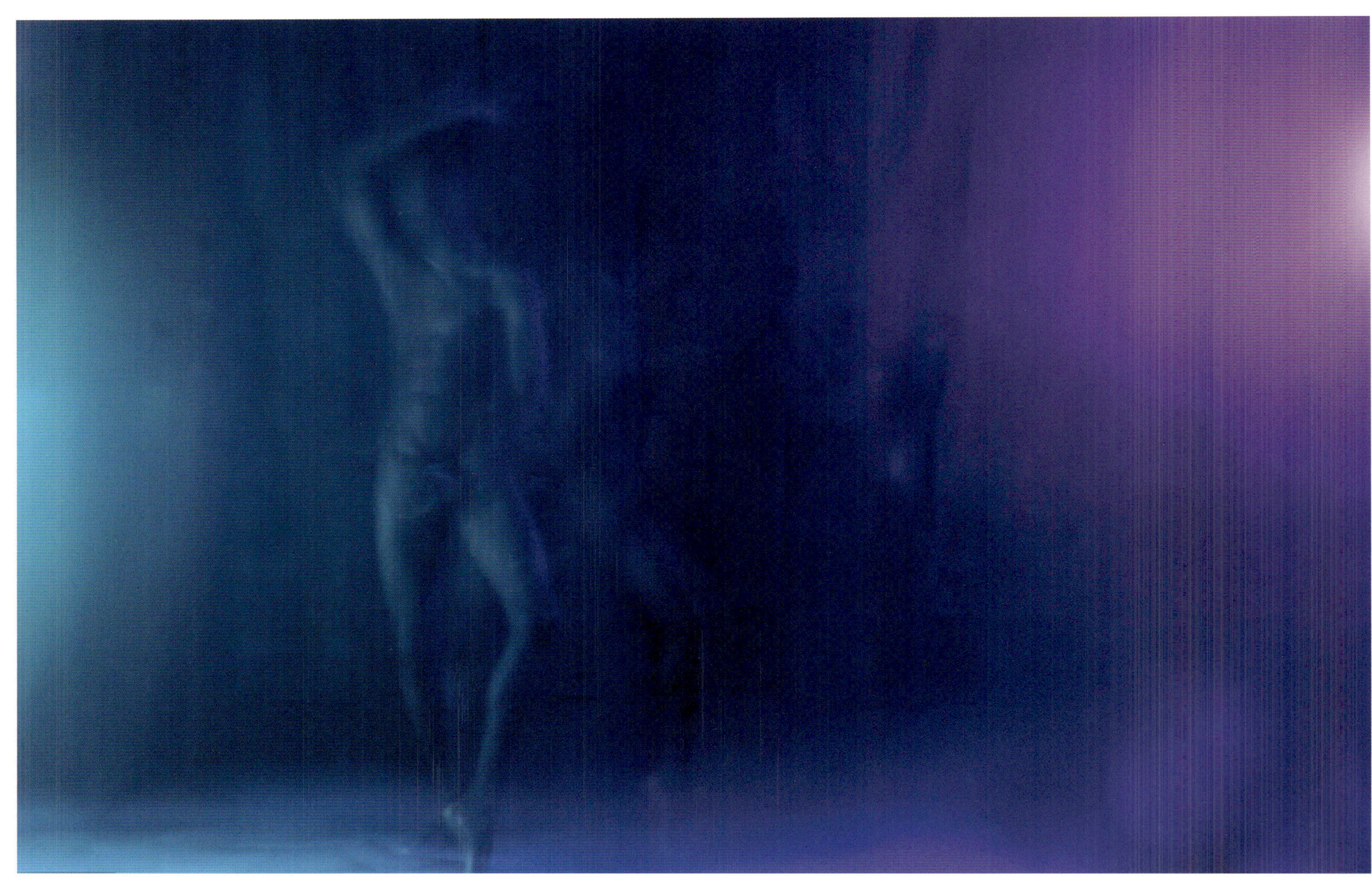

Jourdan Barnes

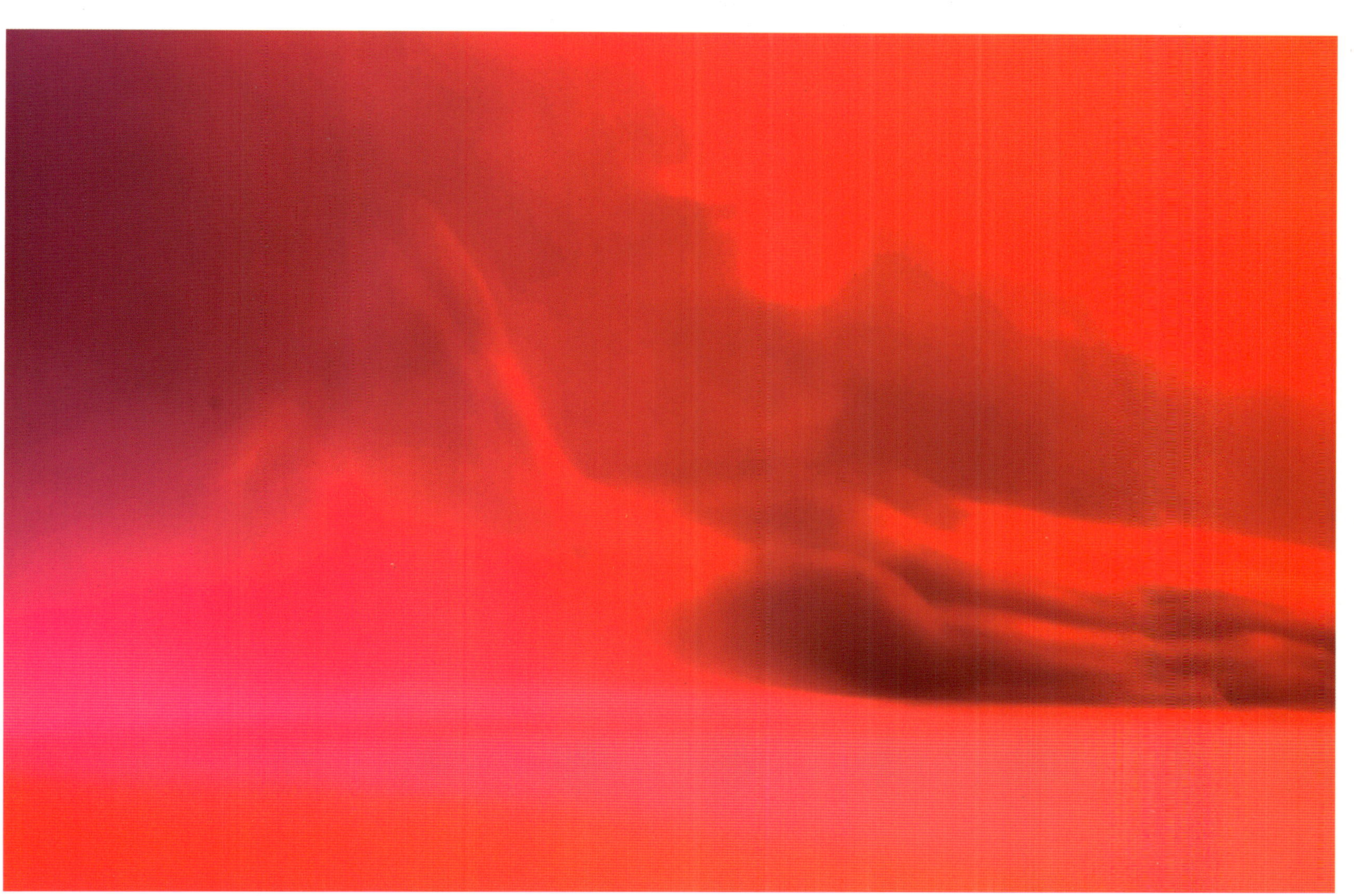

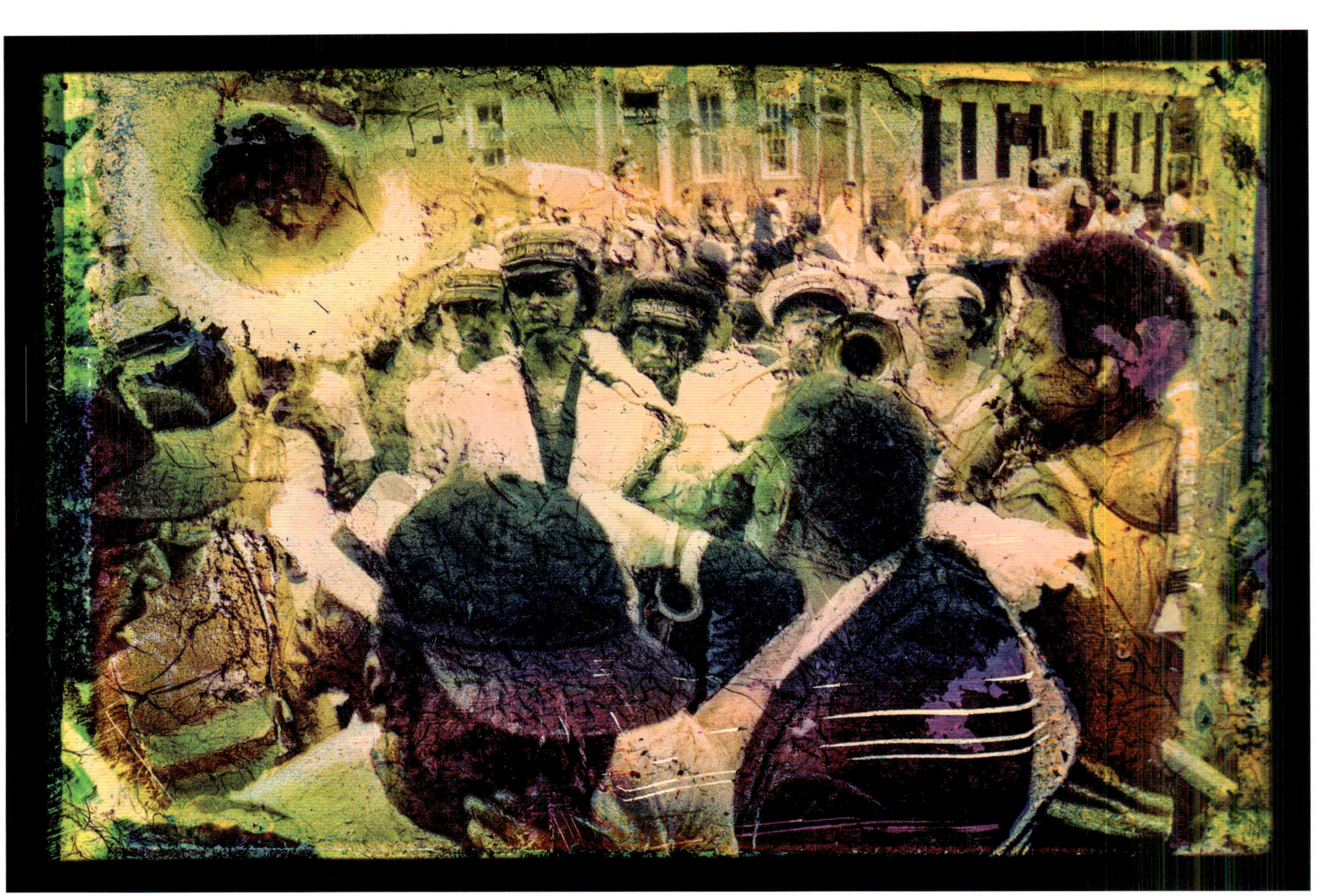

Keith Calhoun

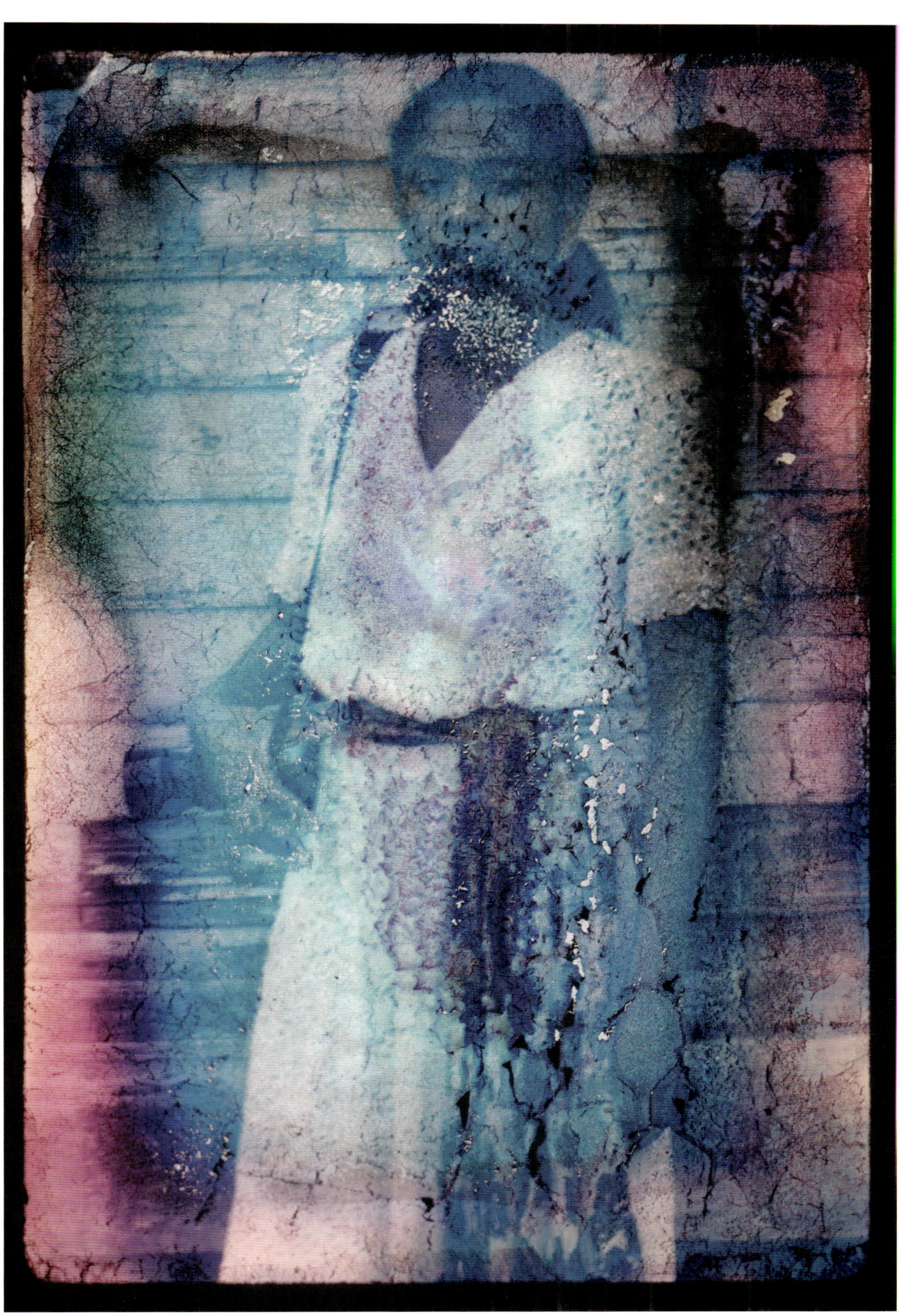

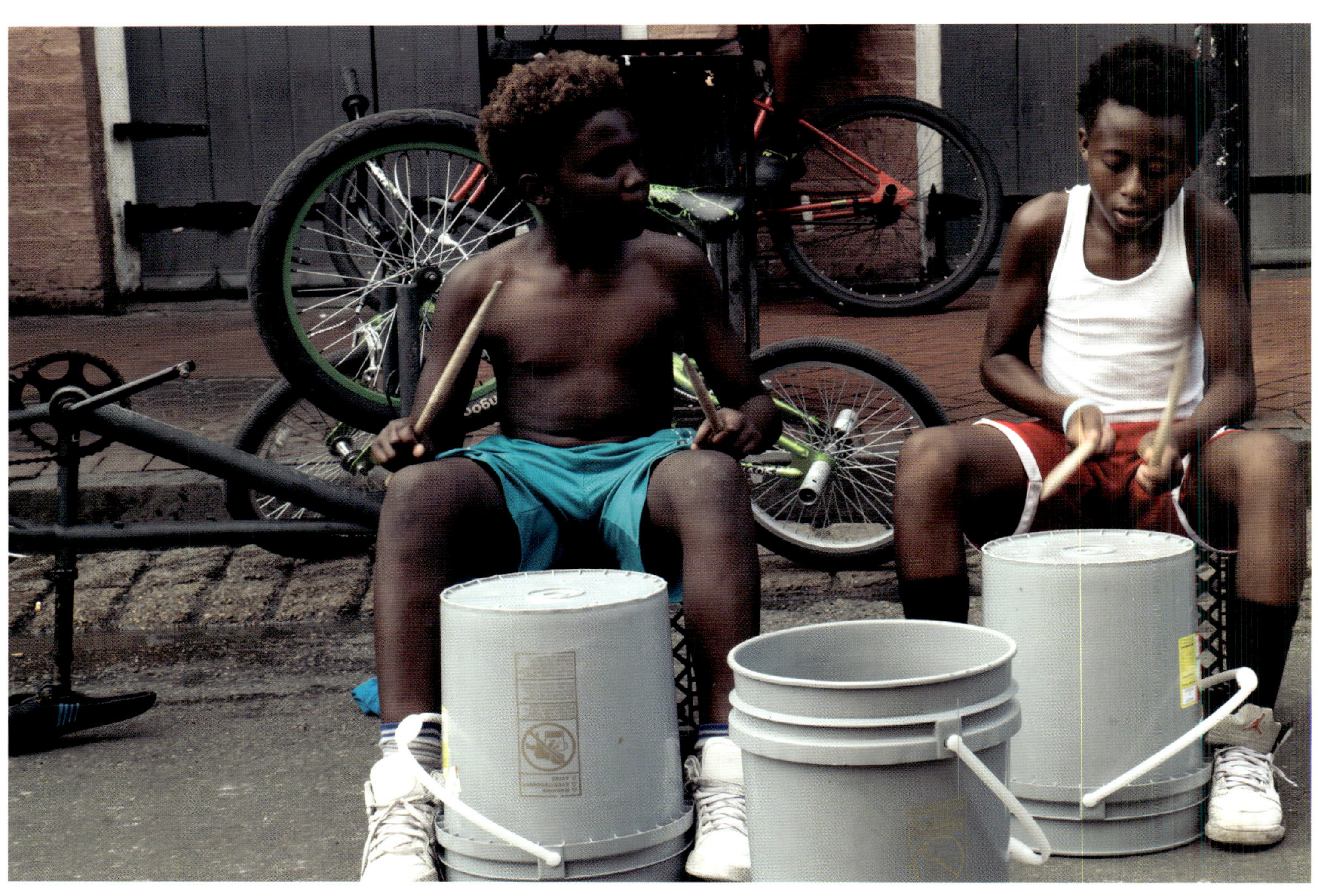

Kevin Jones

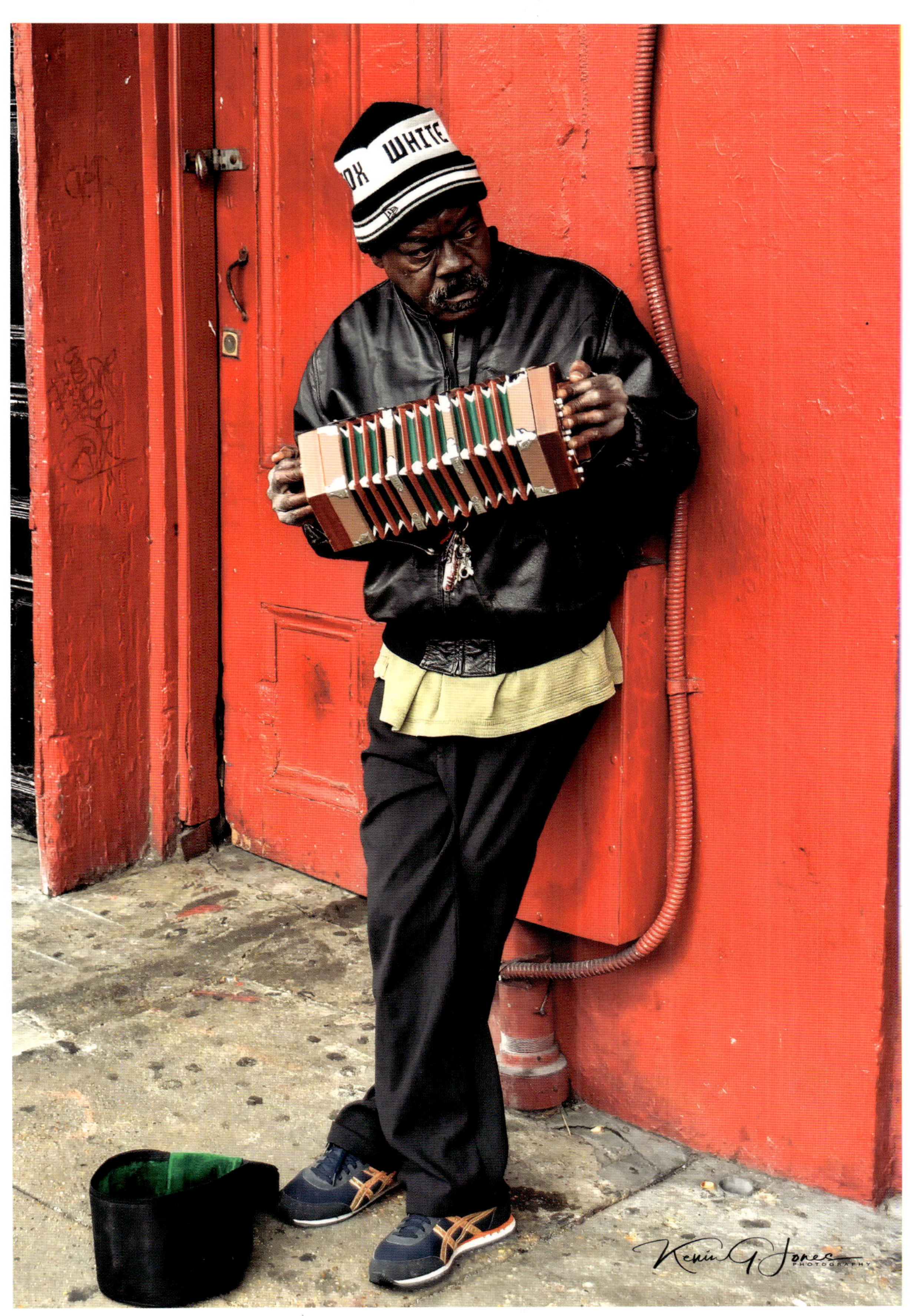

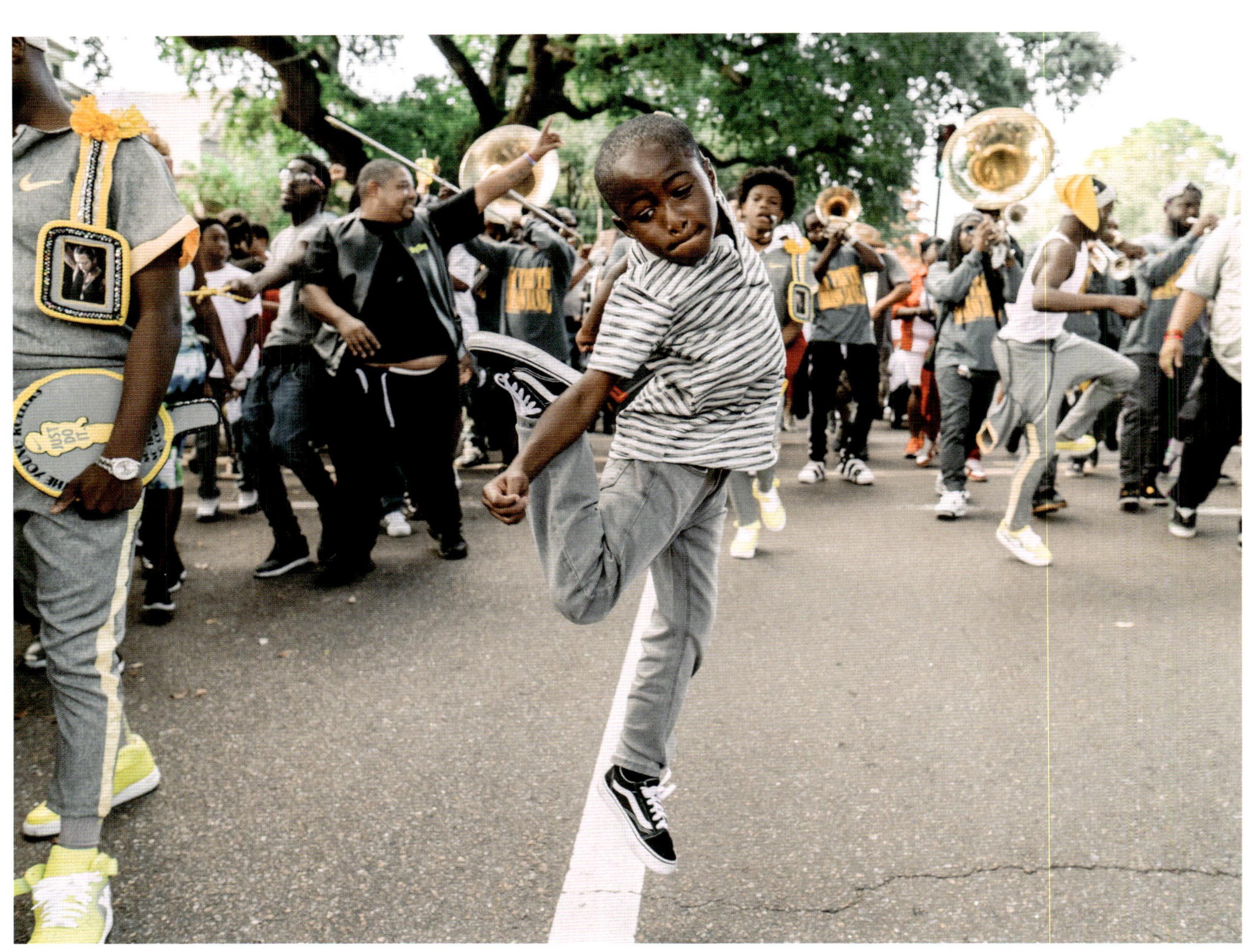

Kewon Hunter

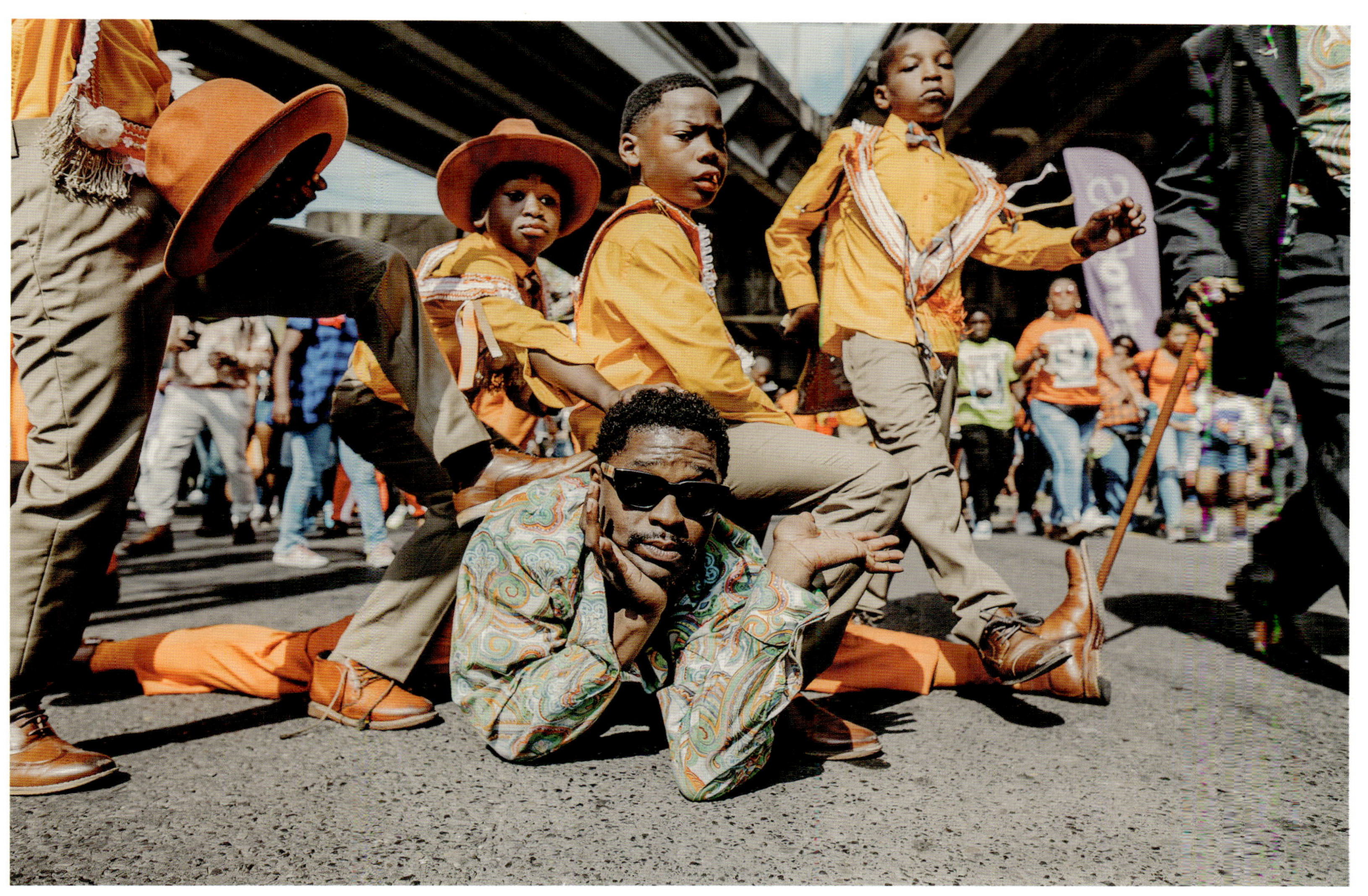

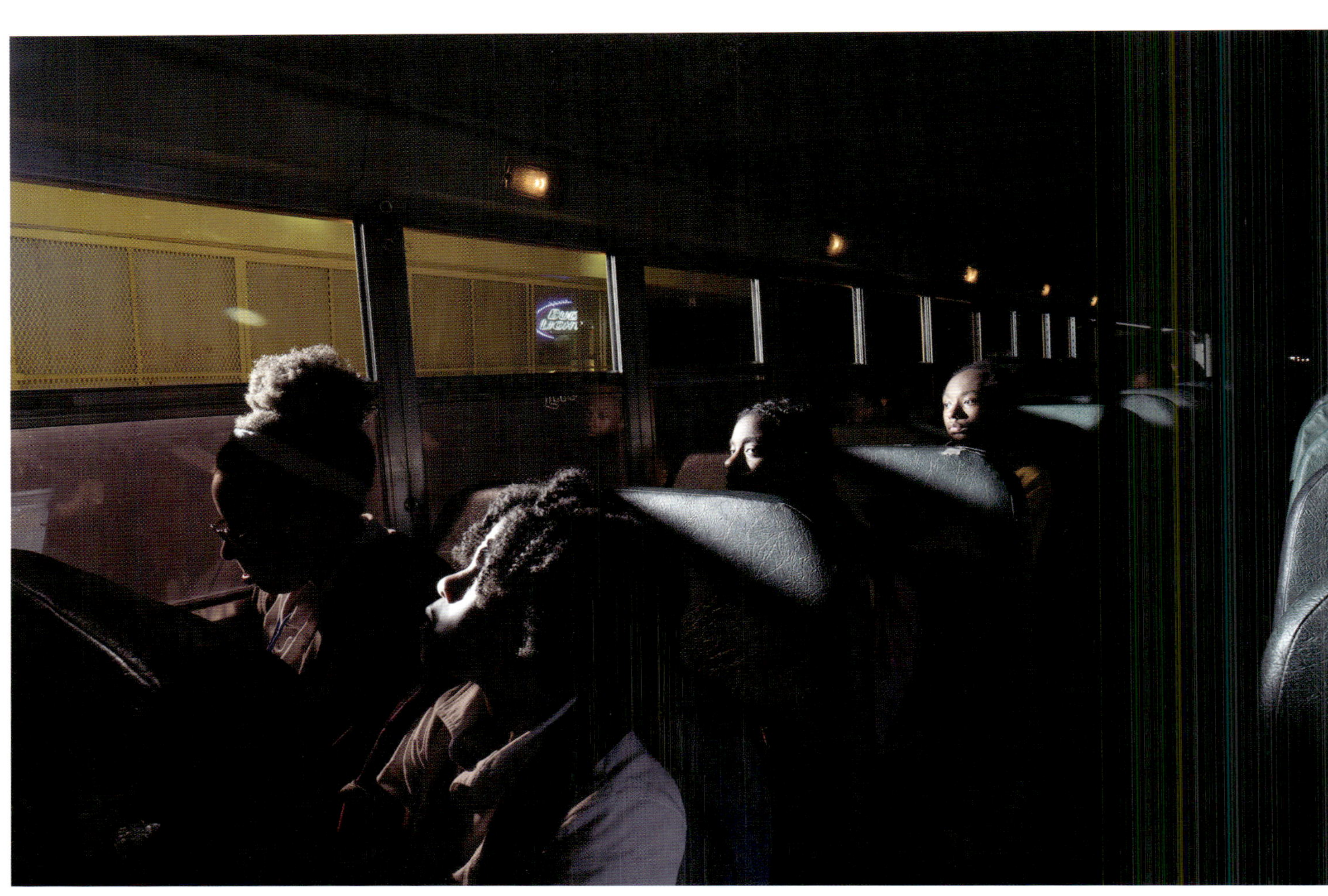

L. Kasimu Harris

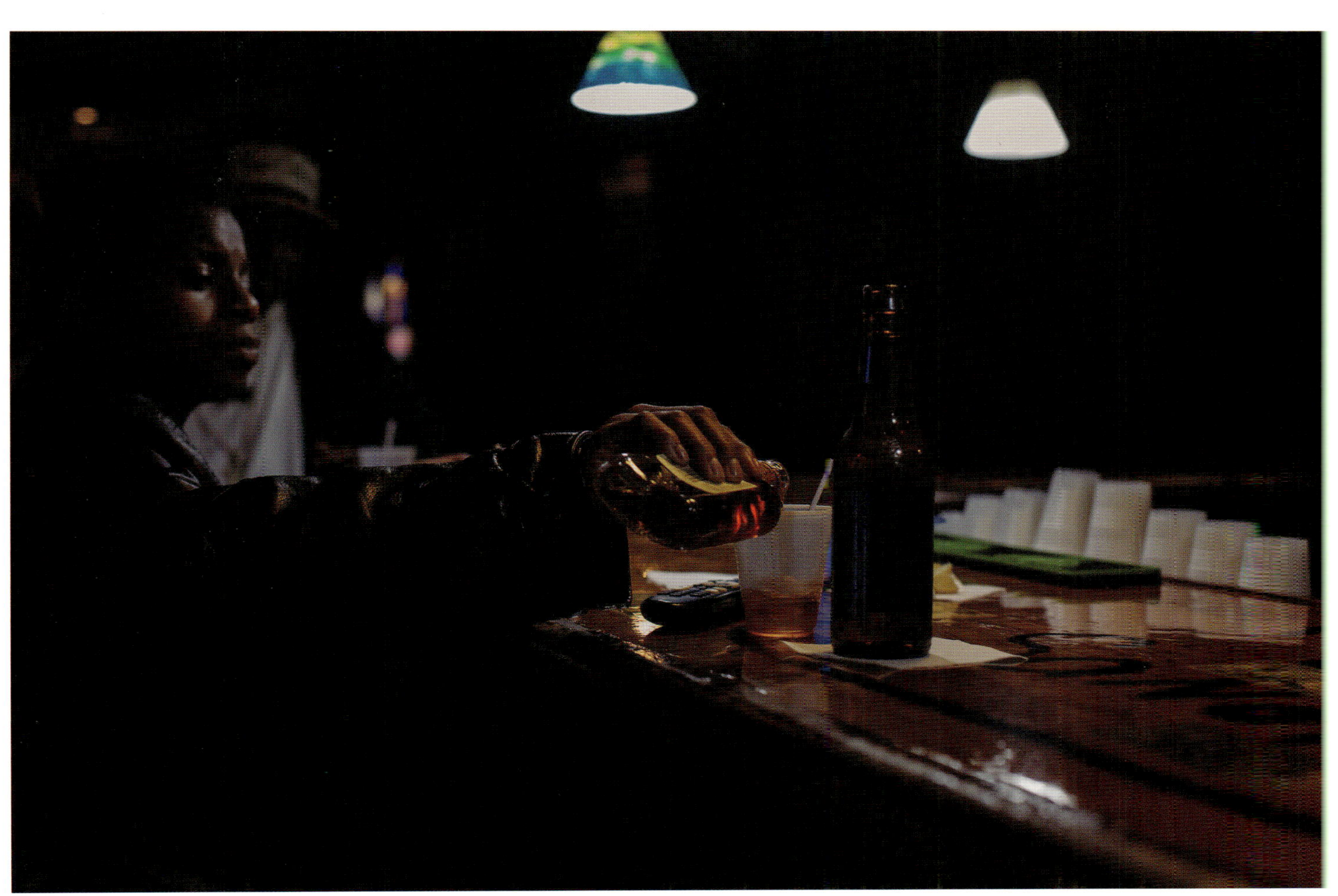

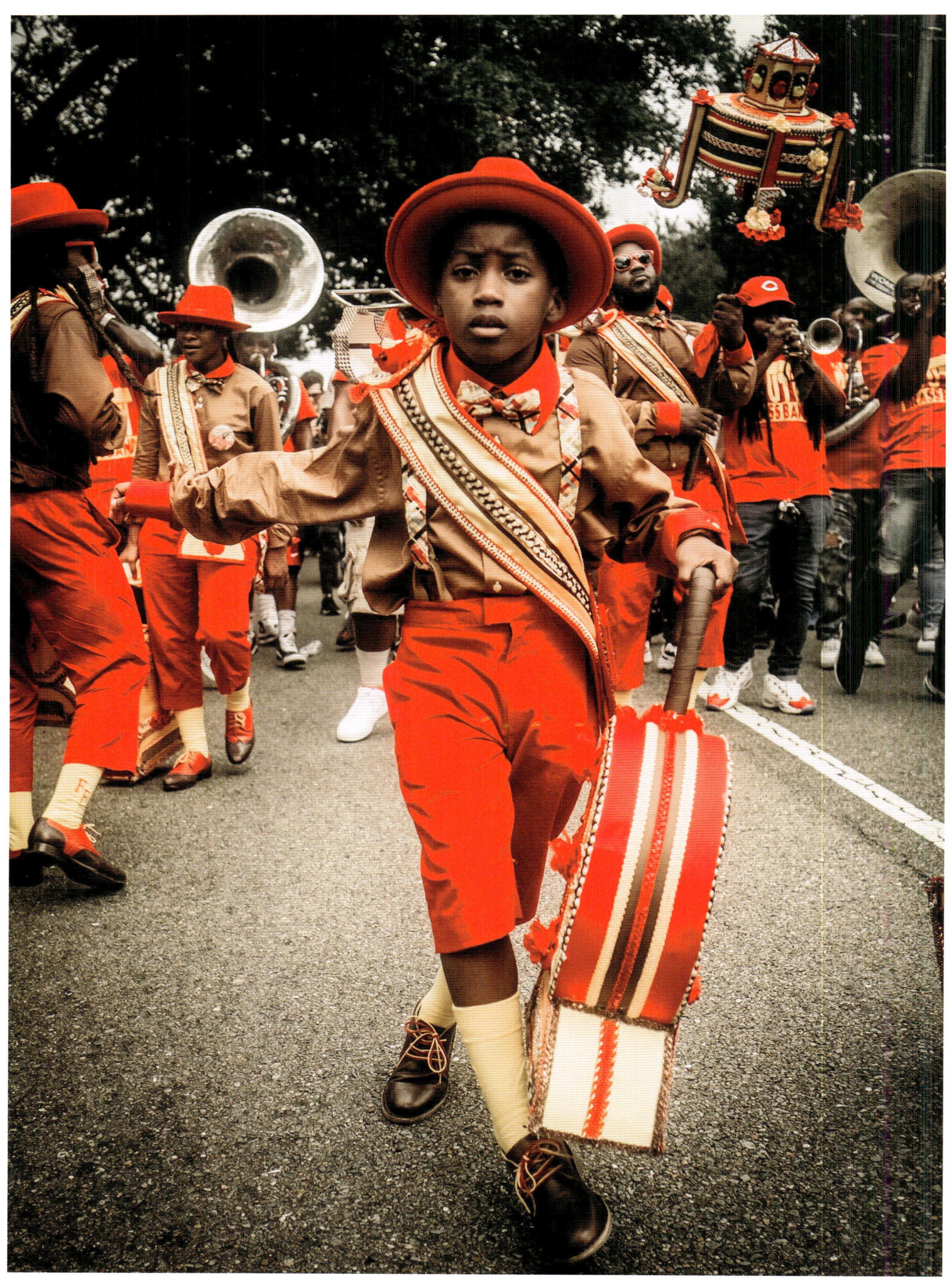

Larry Everage

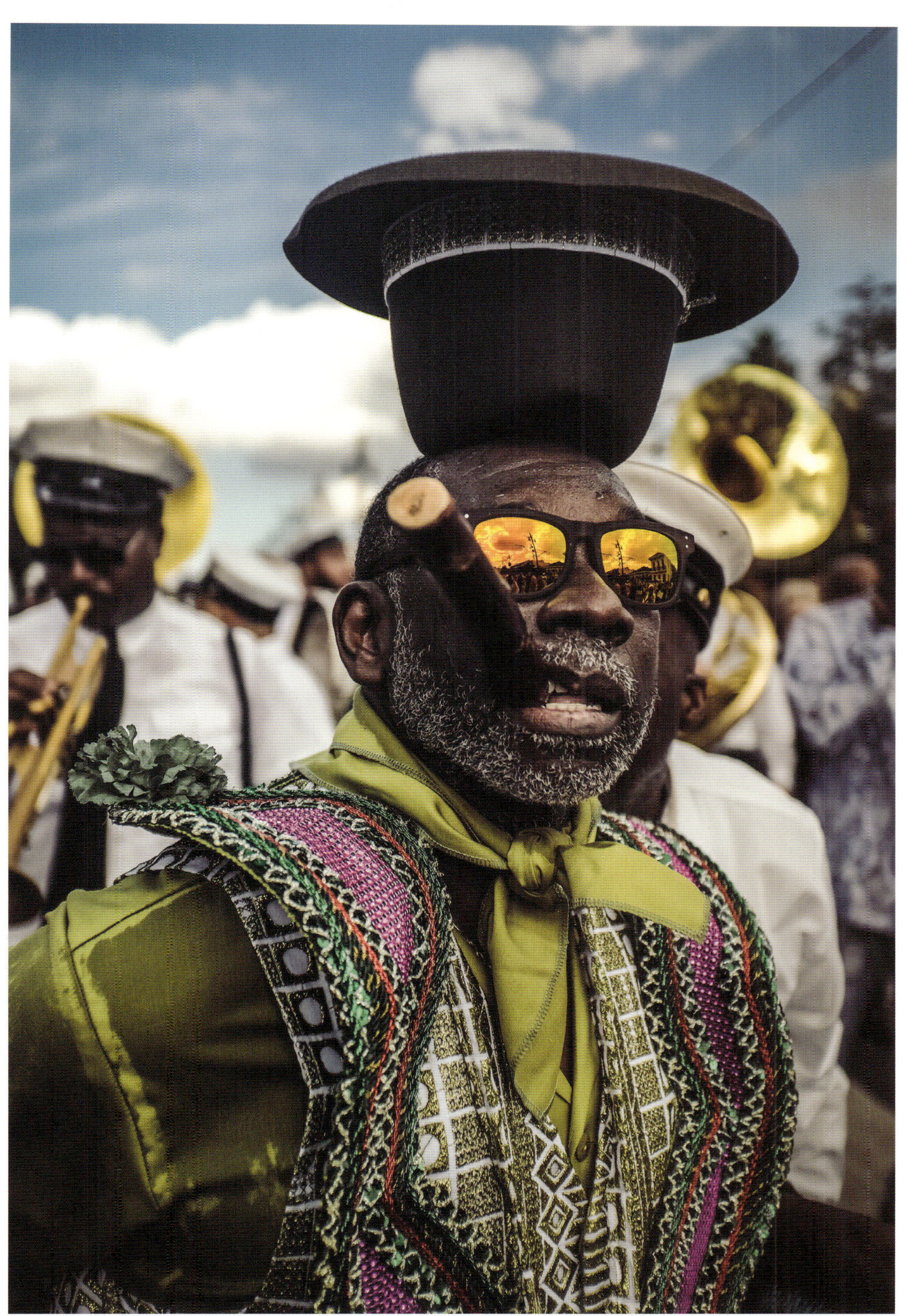

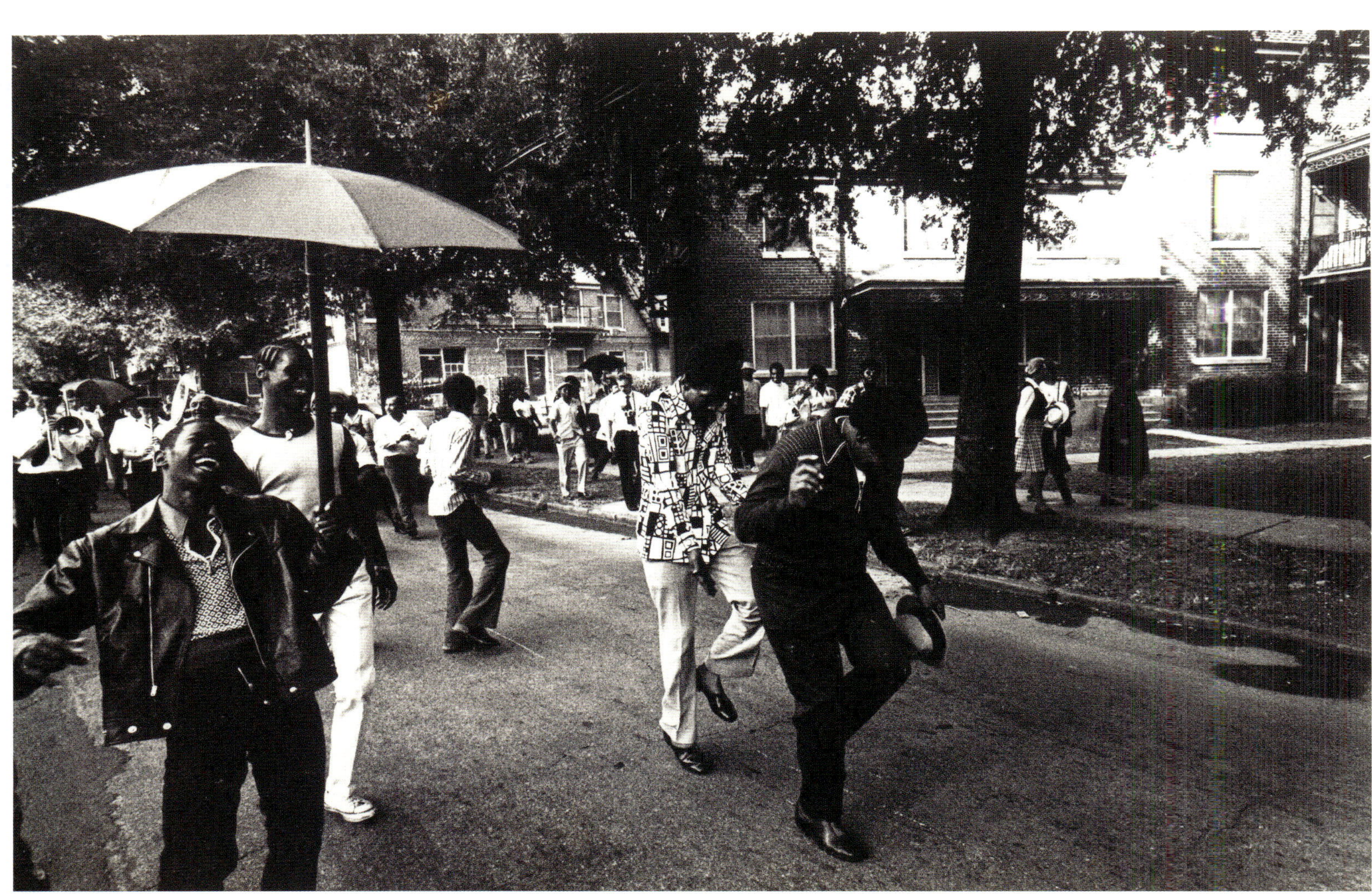

Larry Songy

Patio Royal
RESTAURANT
CREOLE SPECIALTIES
JAMBALYA
SHRIMP CREOLE
SEAFOOD GUMBO
RED BEANS & RICE
SANDWICHES • ICE CREAM
MIXED DRINKS
FINE BEERS

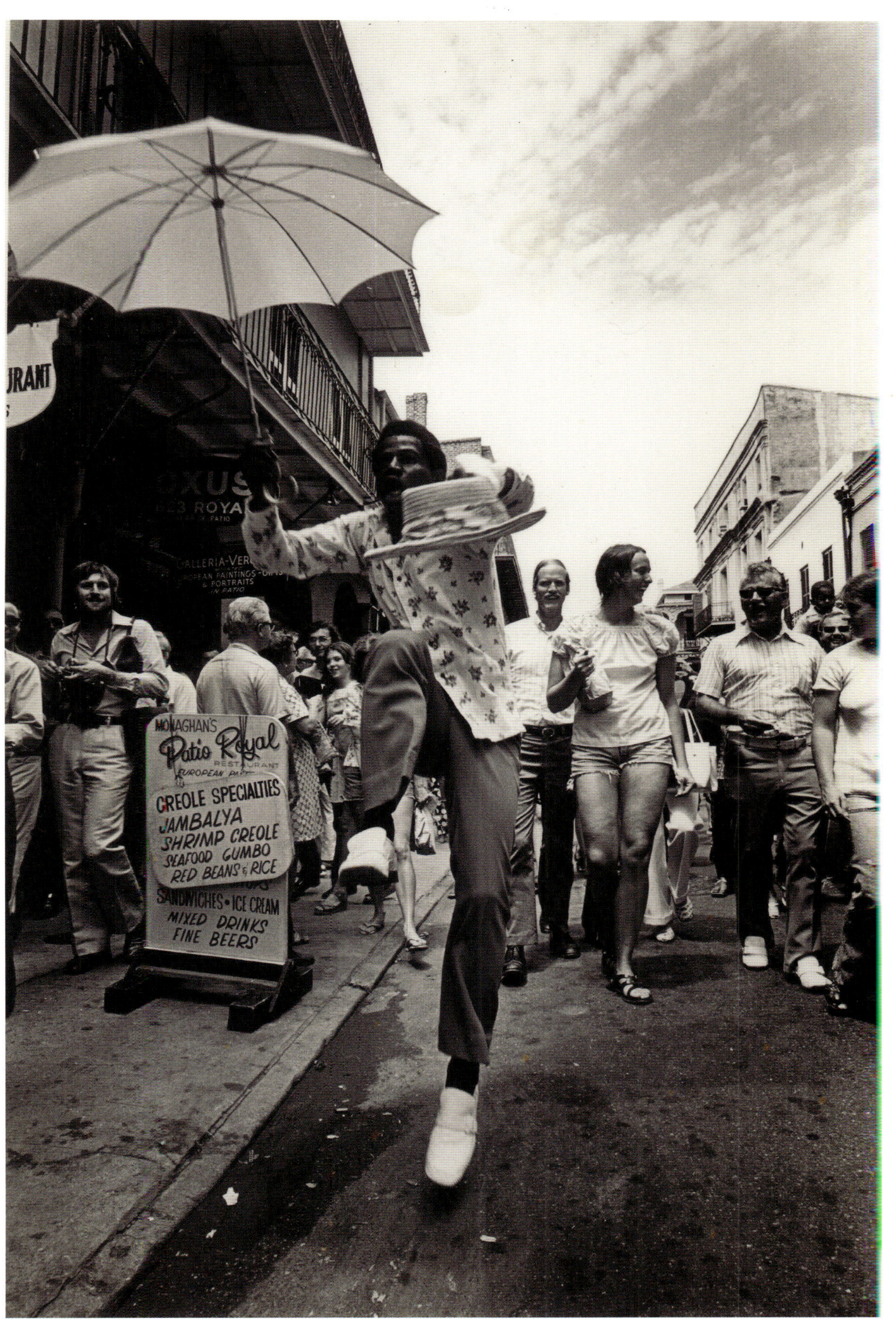

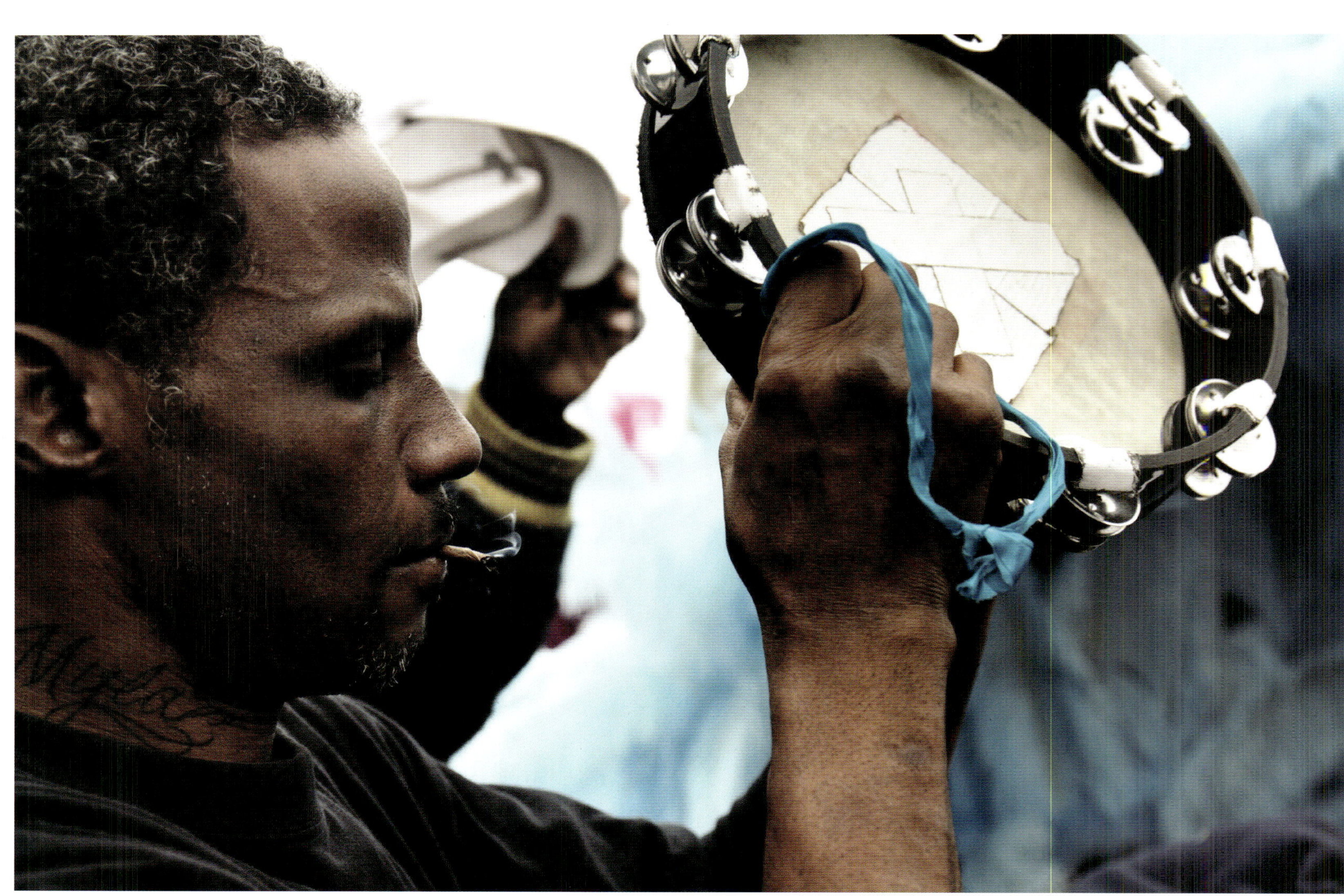

Leslie-Claire Spillman

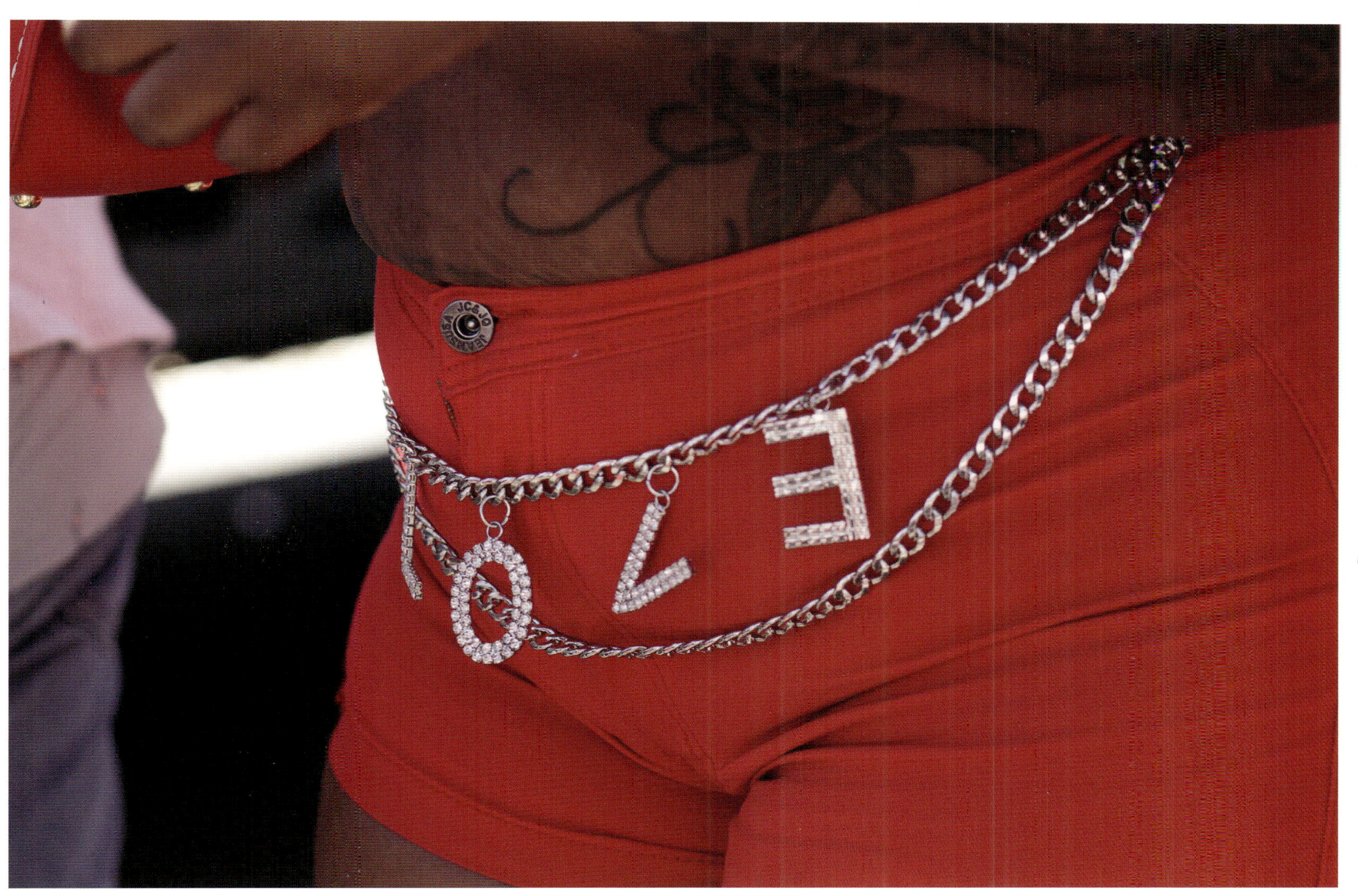

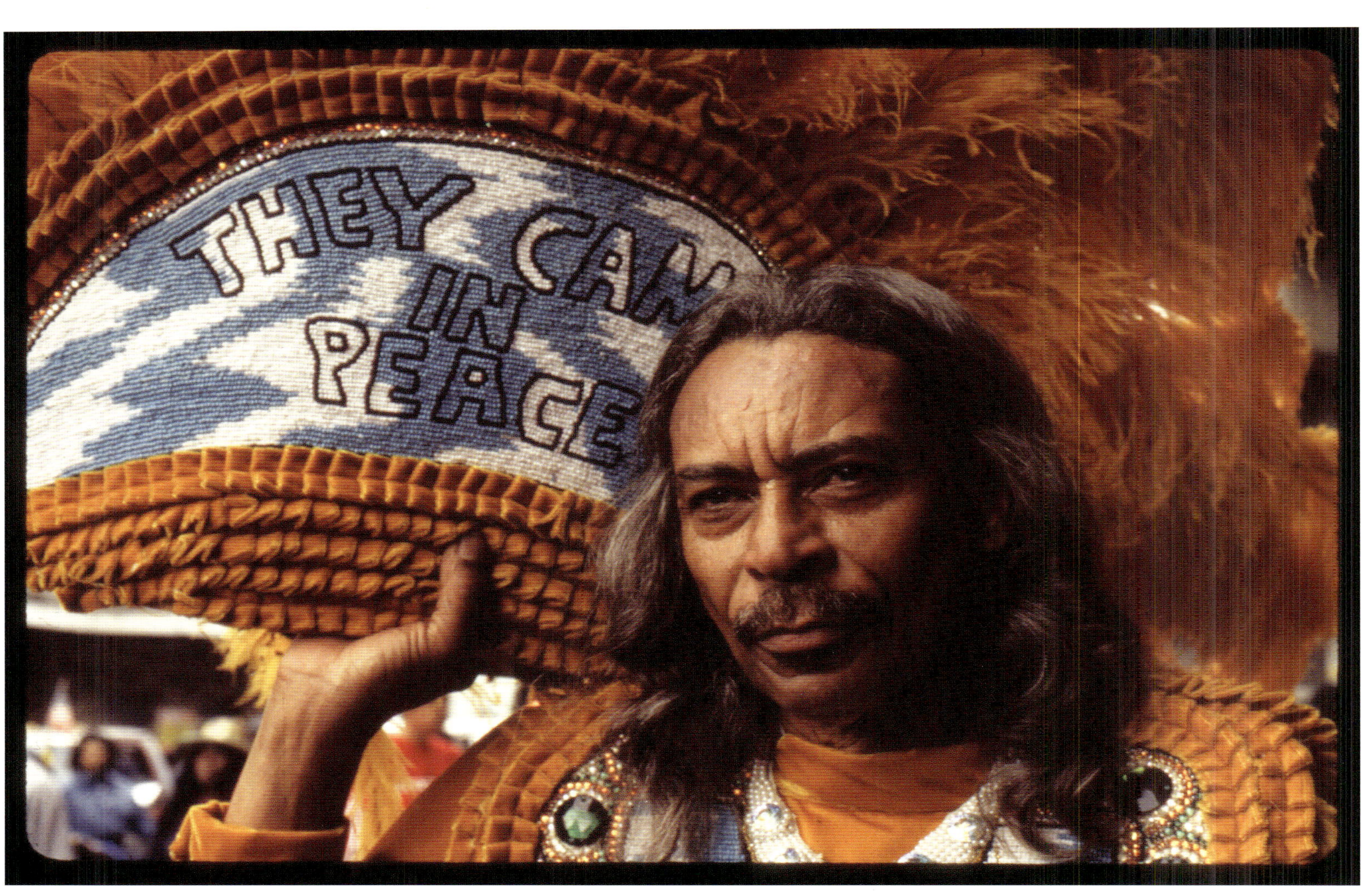
THEY CAM
IN
PEACE

Lidya Araya

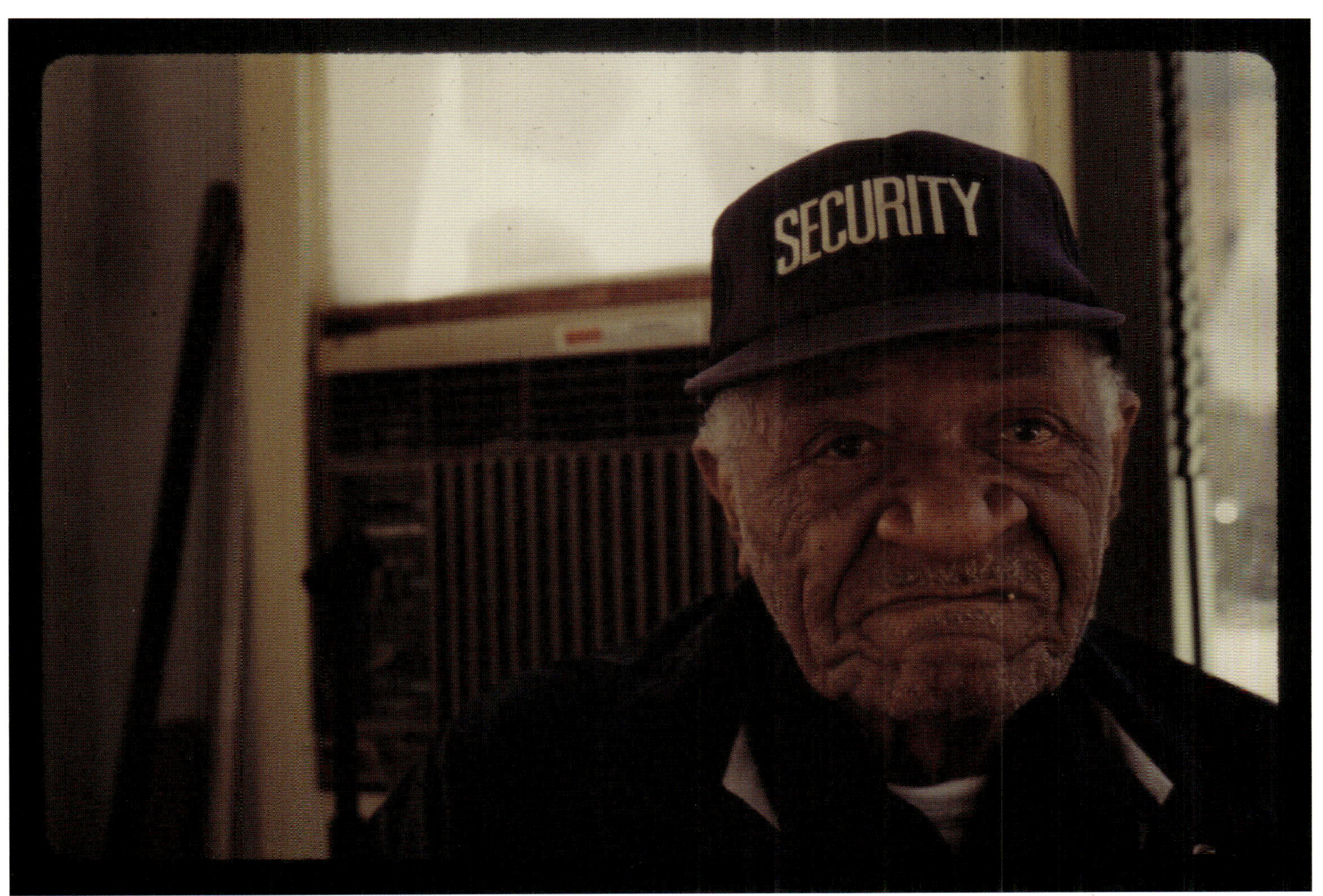

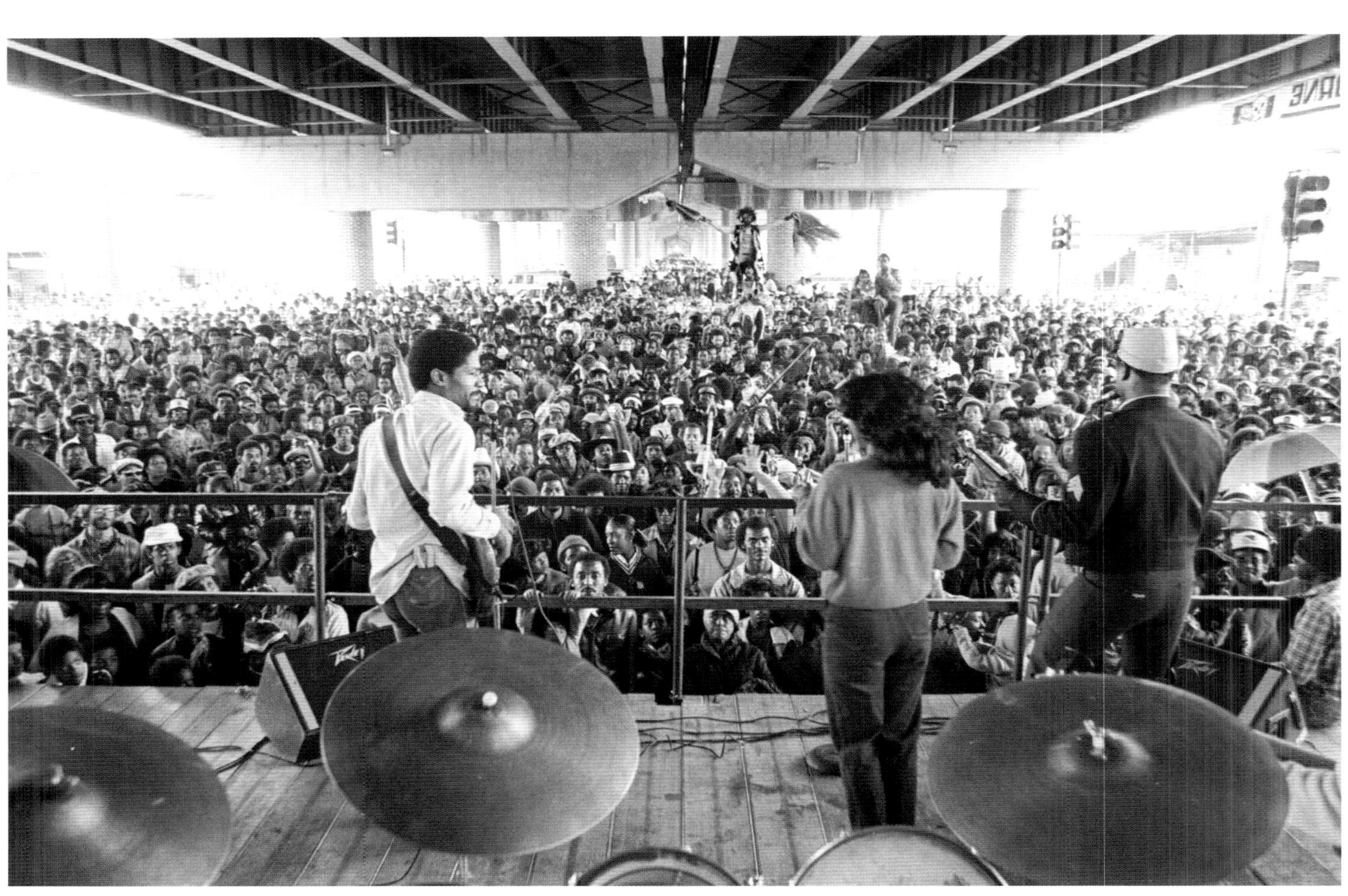

Lloyd Dennis

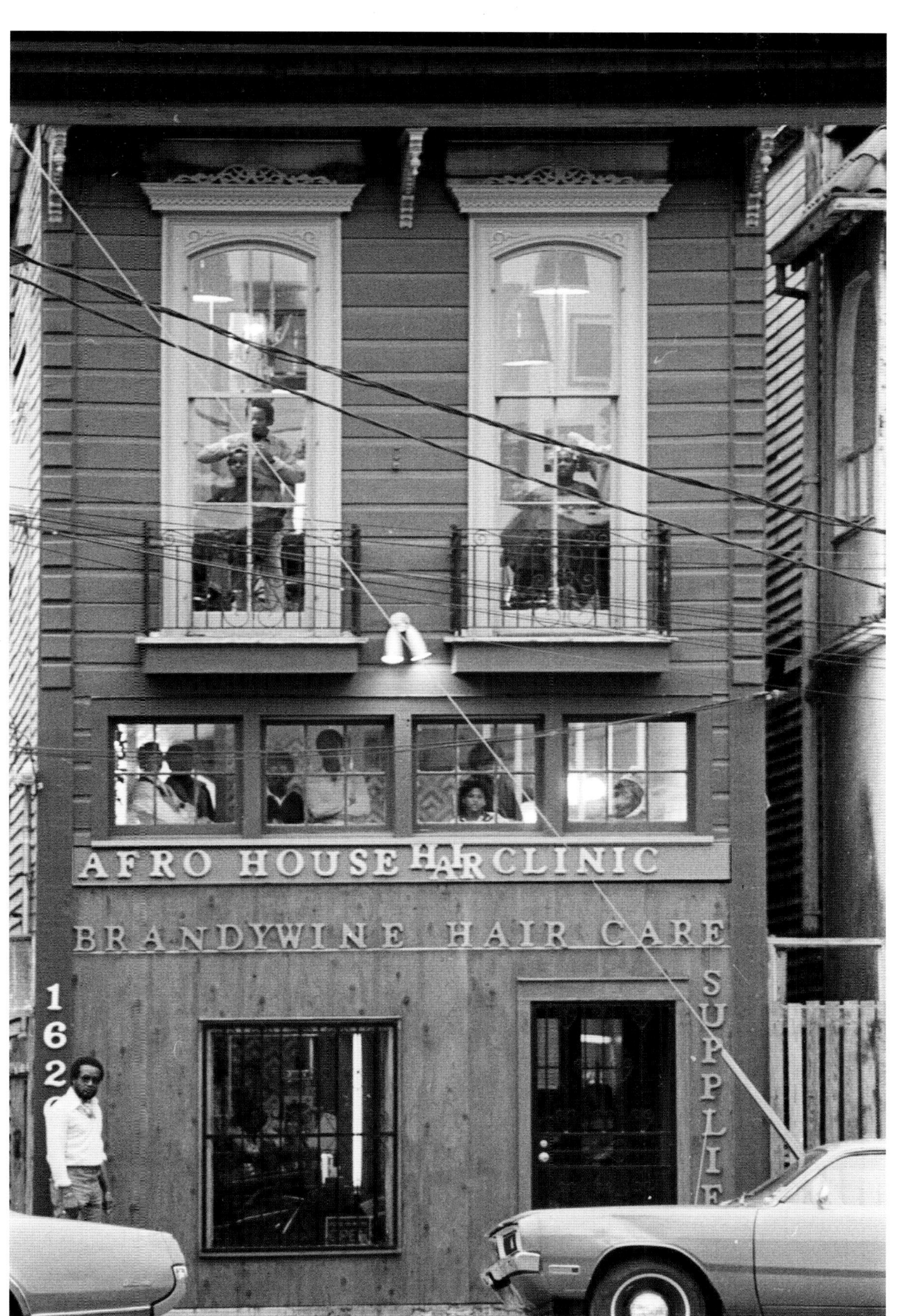

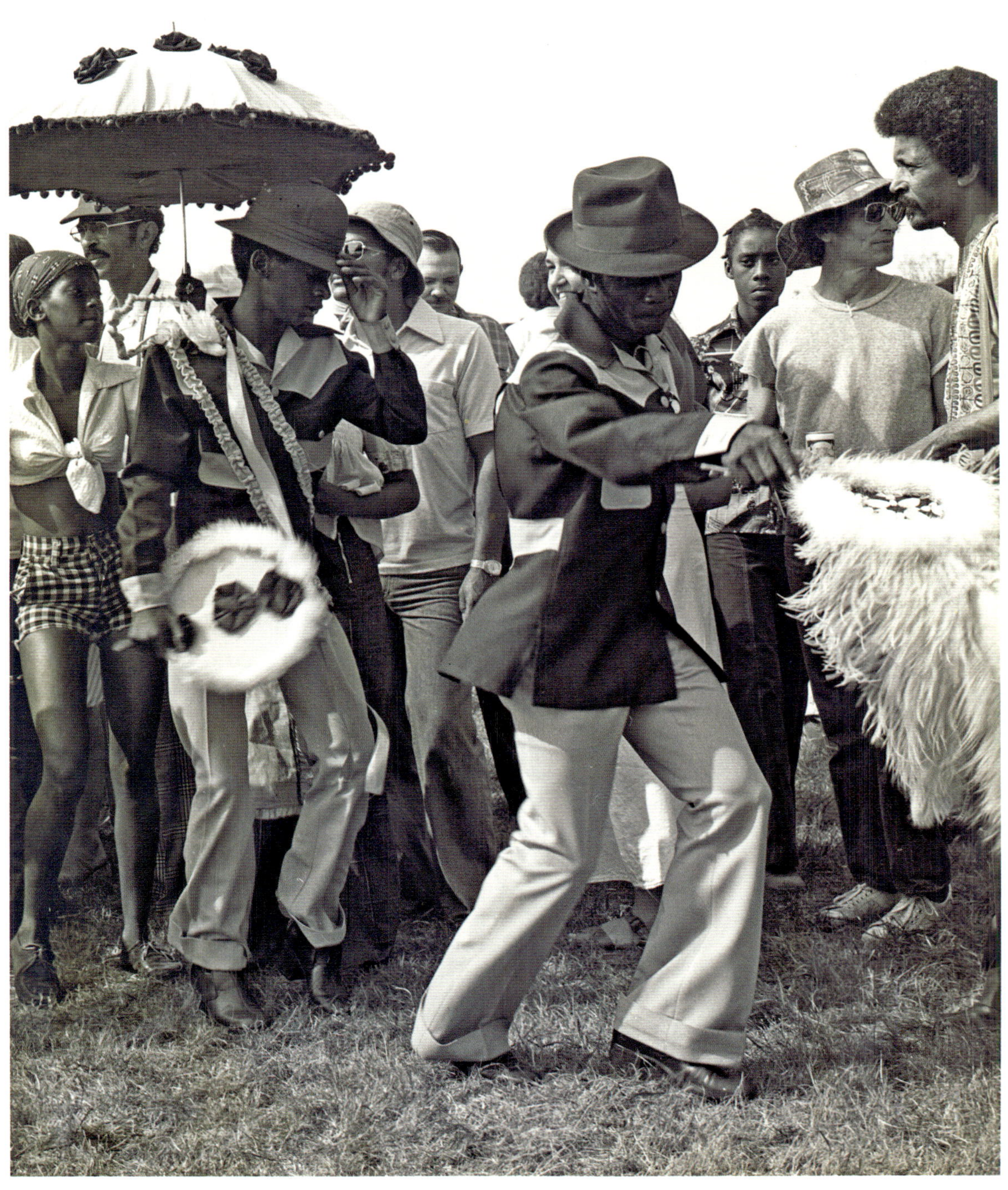

Lloyd J. Medley Jr.

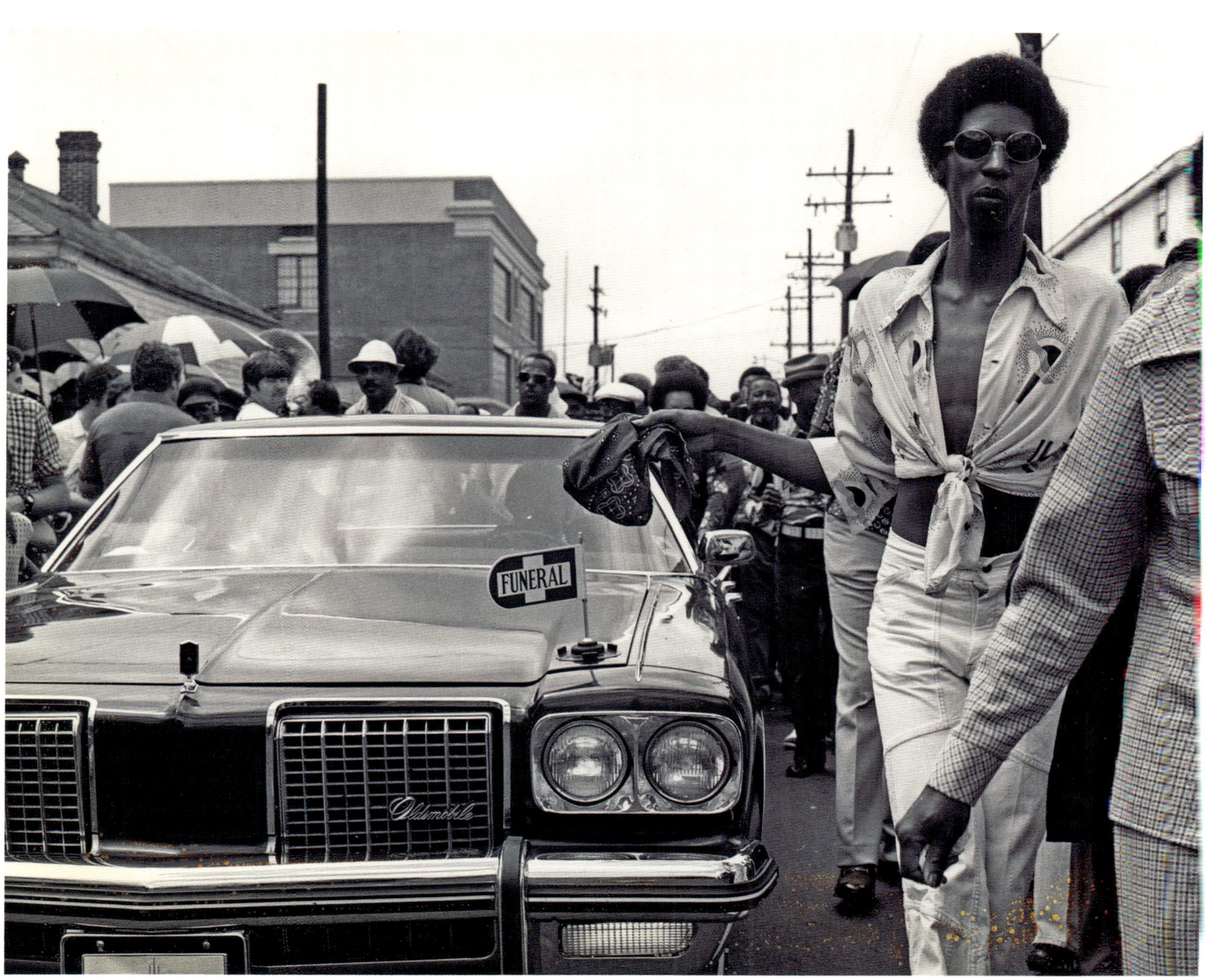

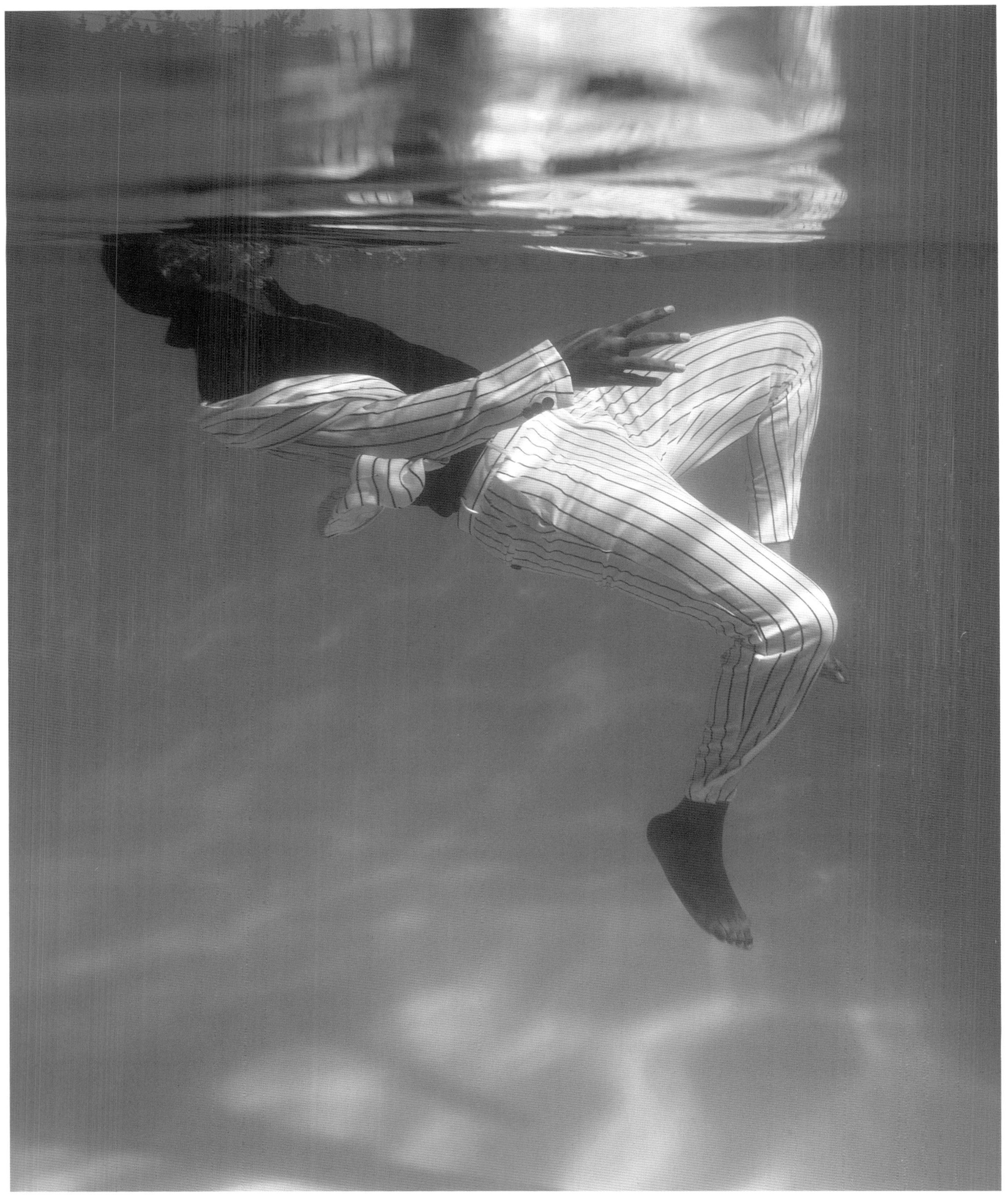

Malcolm Johnson Jr.

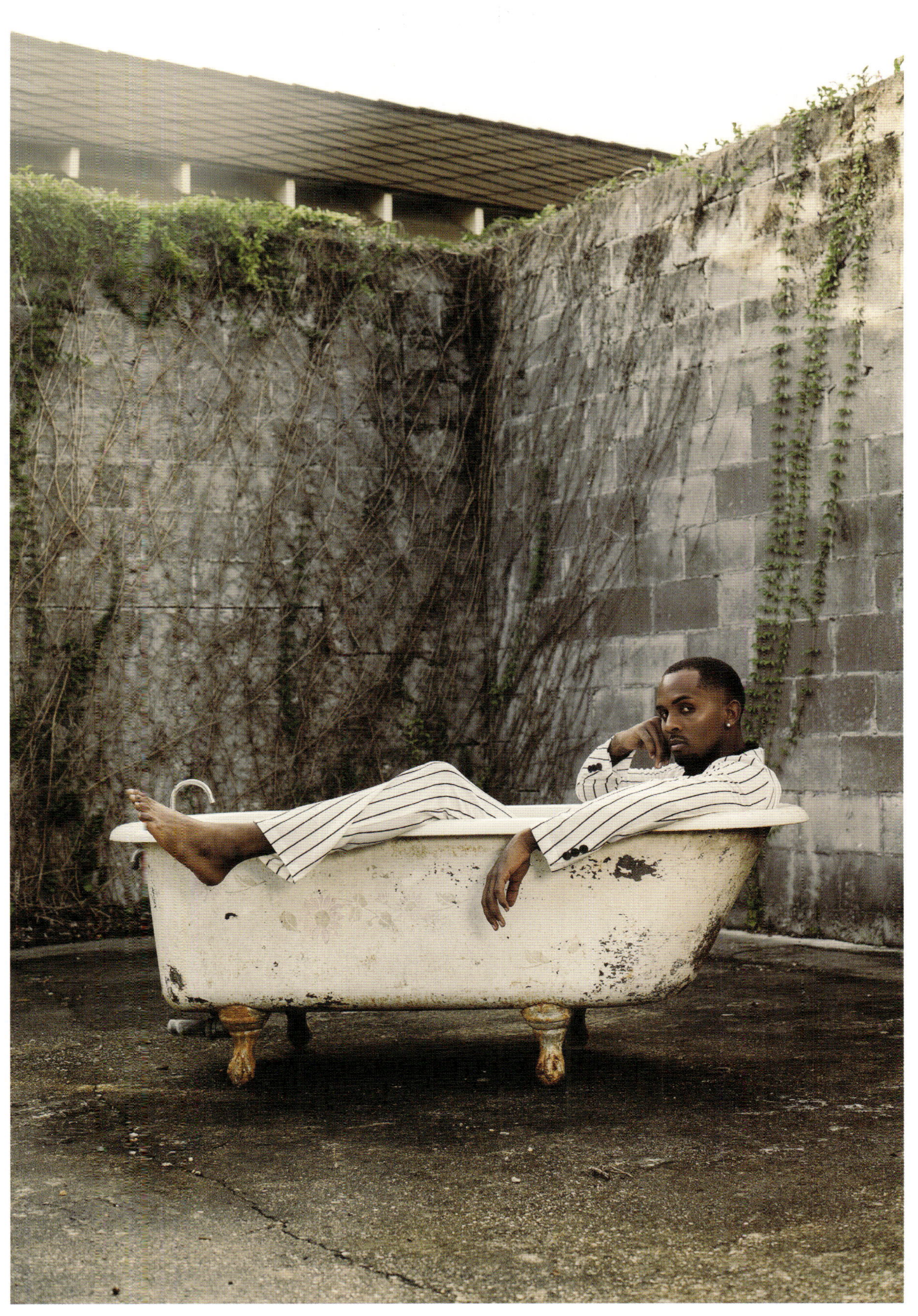

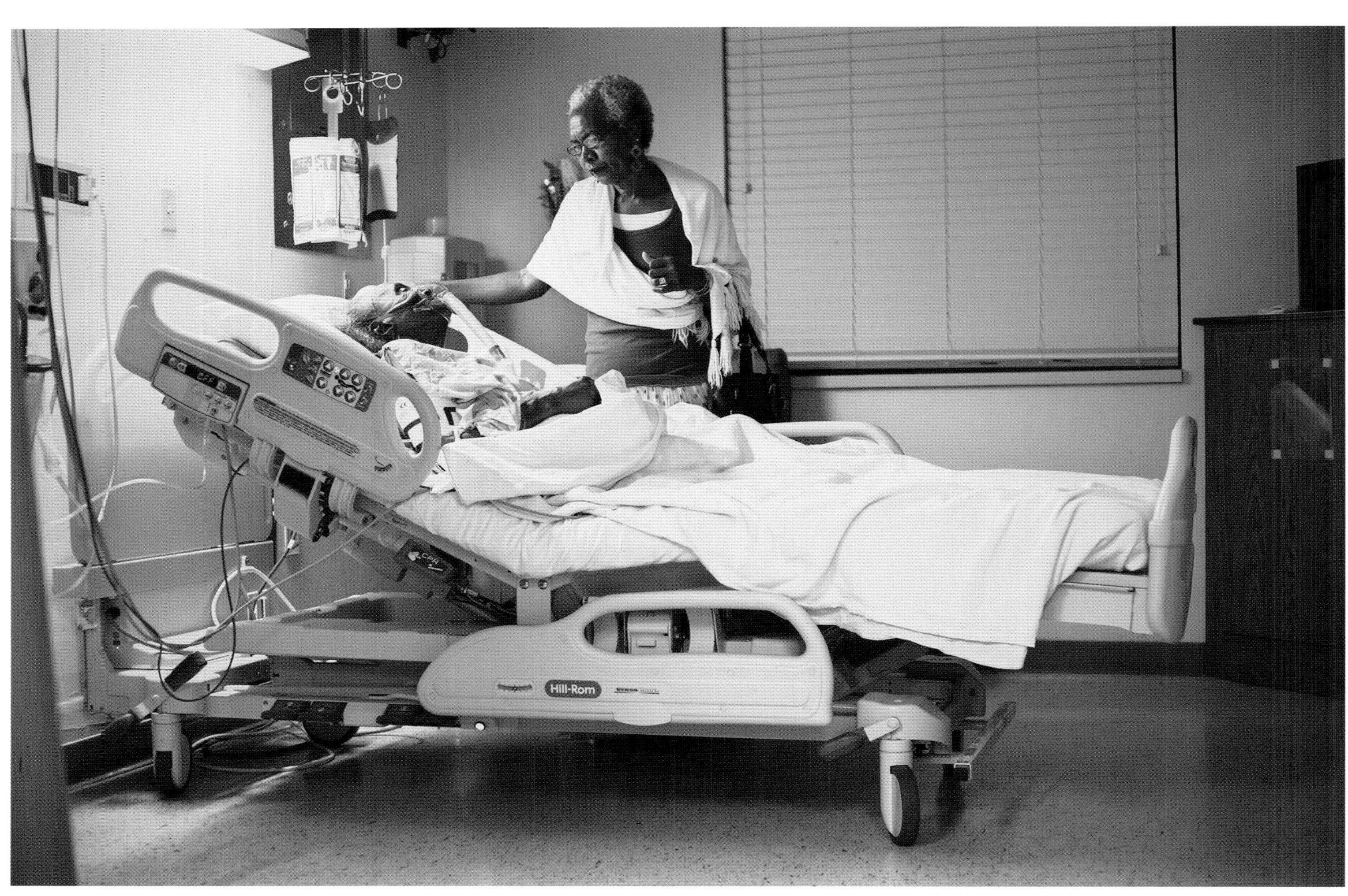
Hill-Rom

Malik Baloney

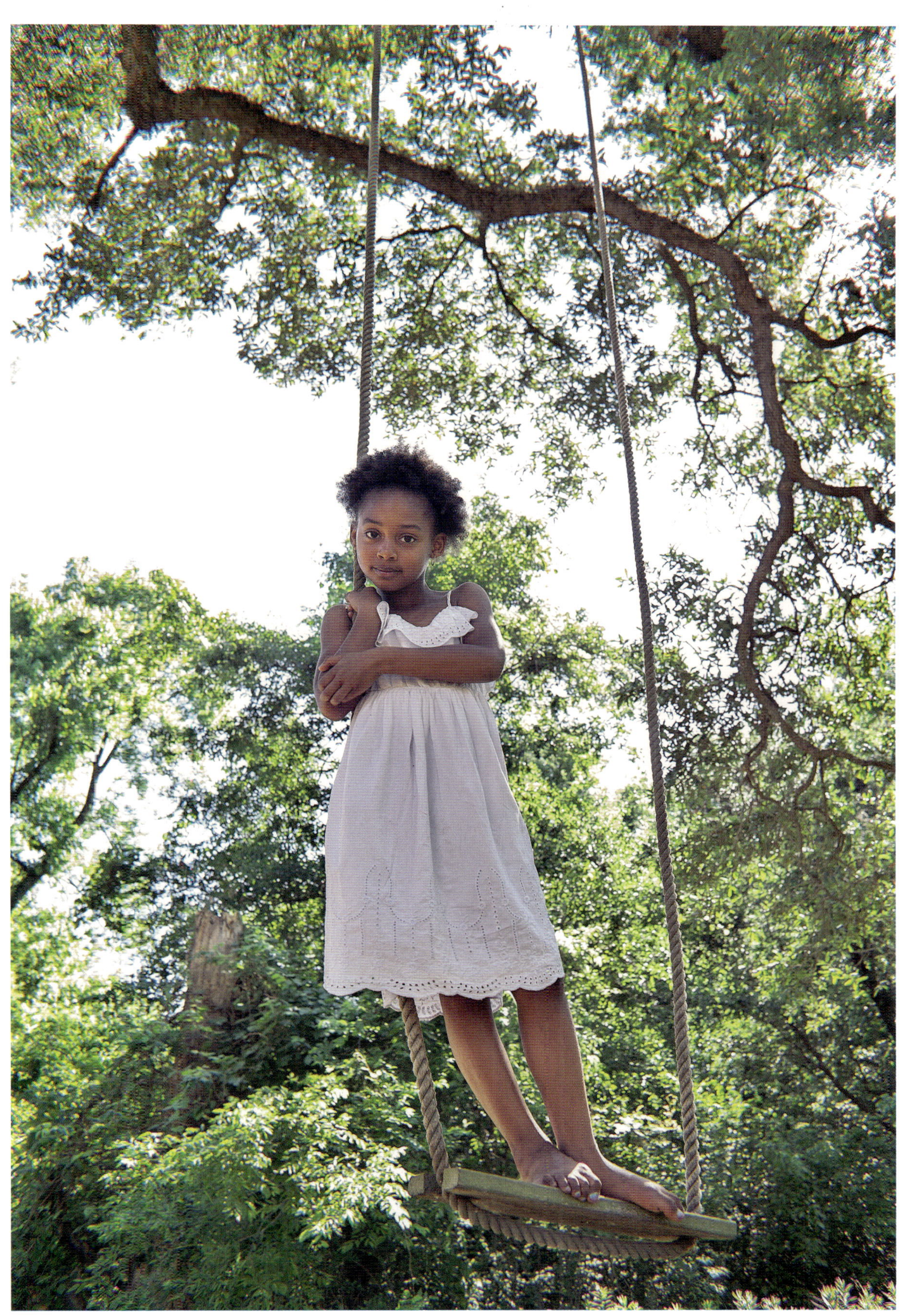

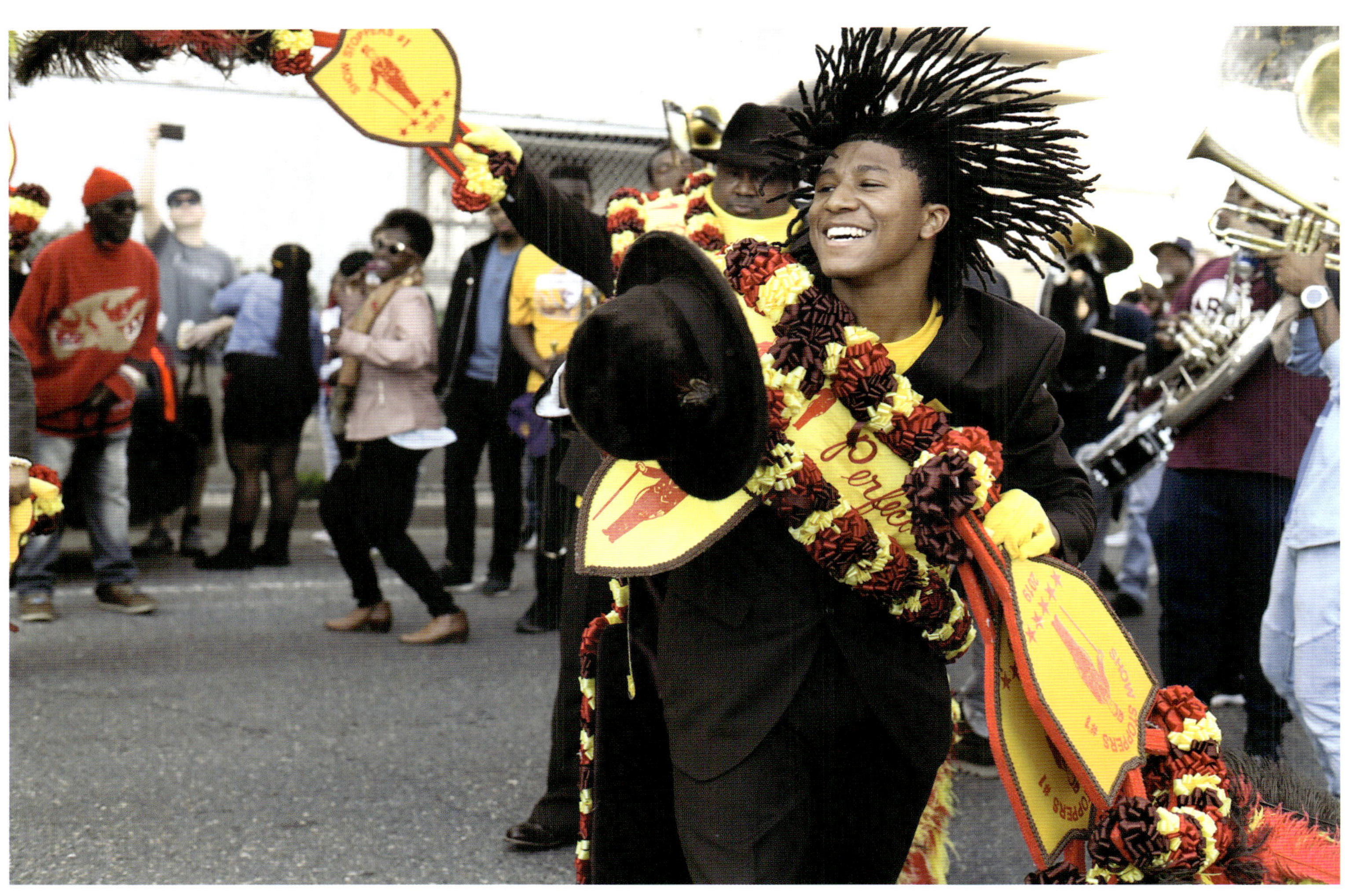

Malik Bartholomew

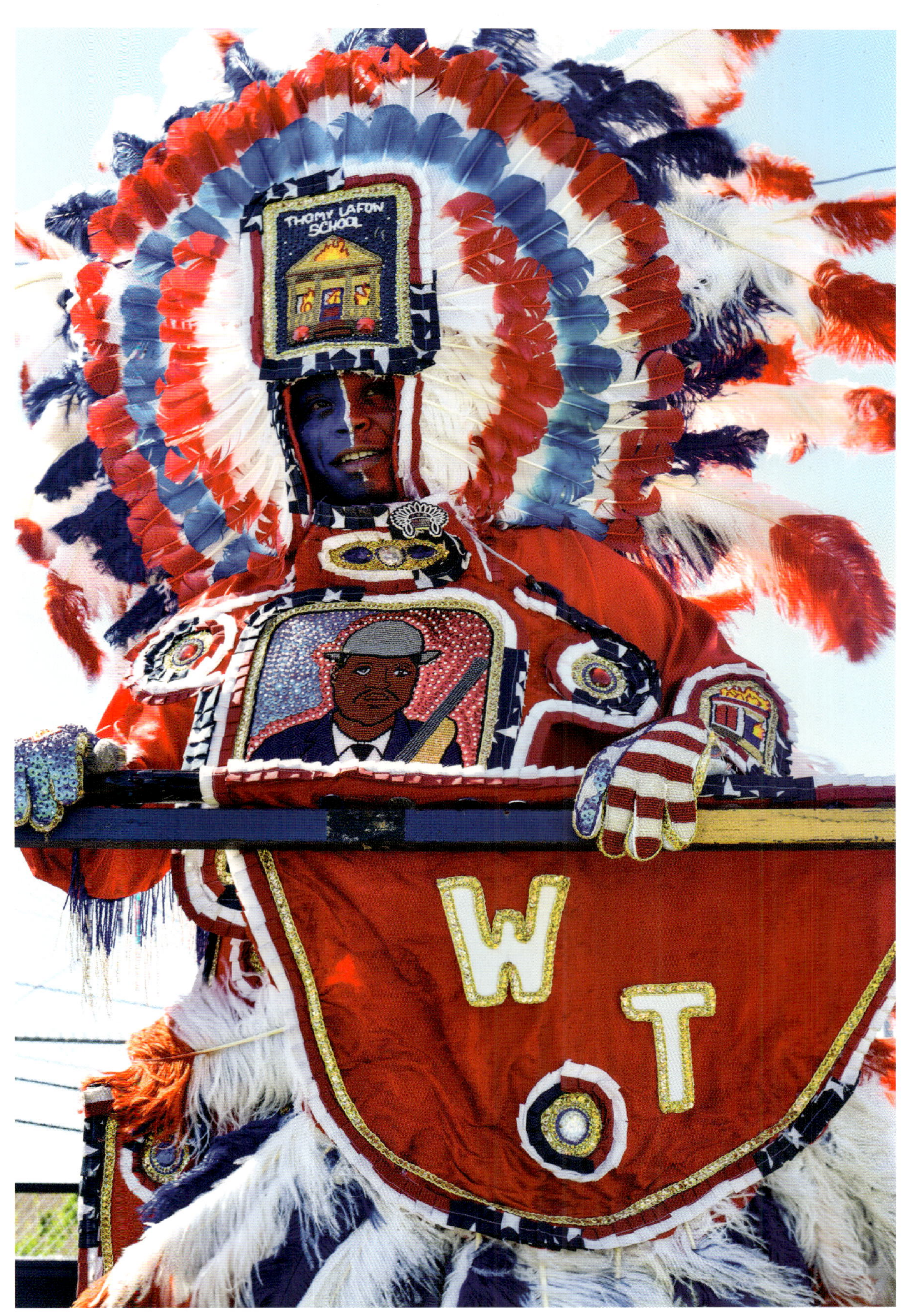

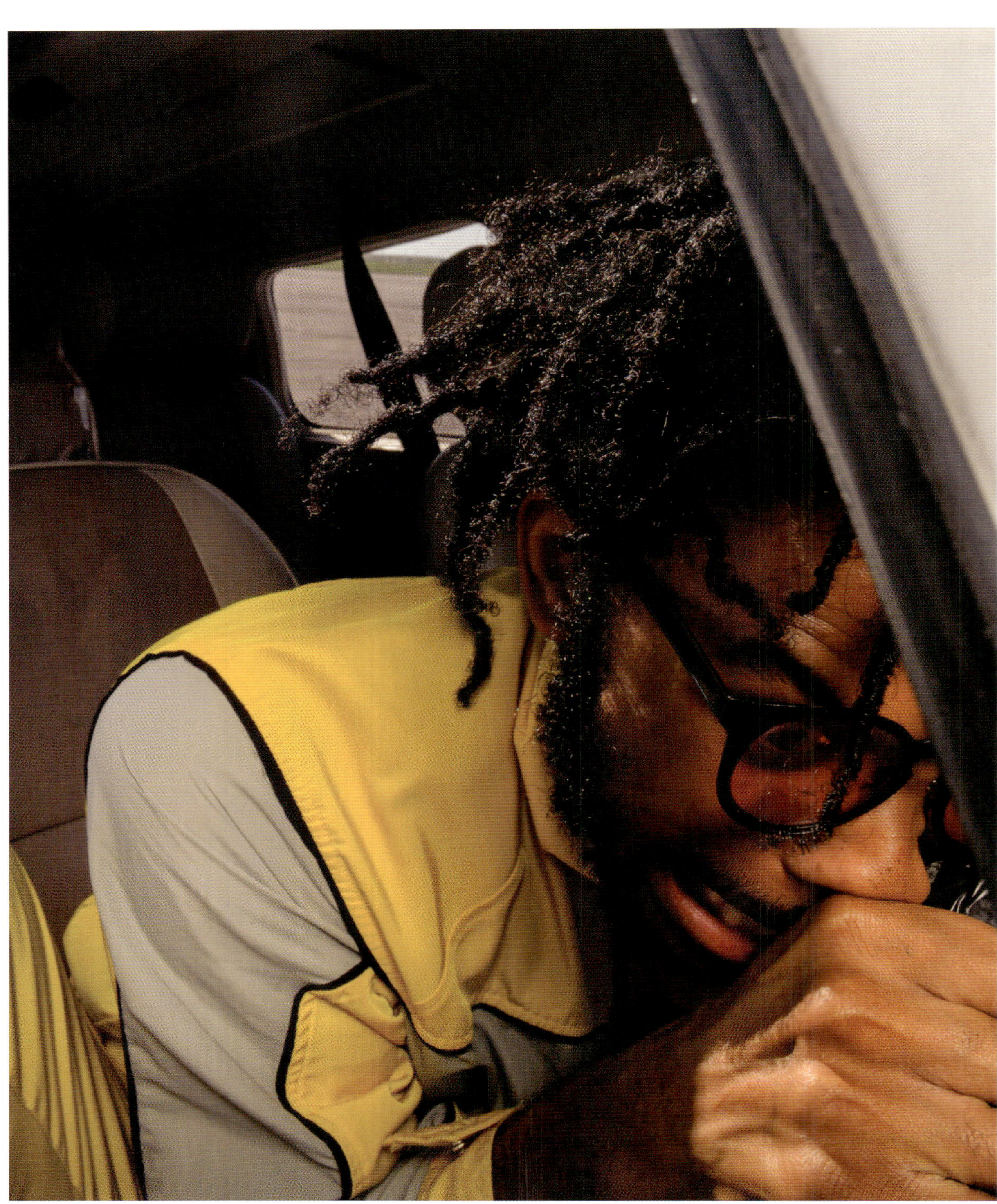

Malik Williams

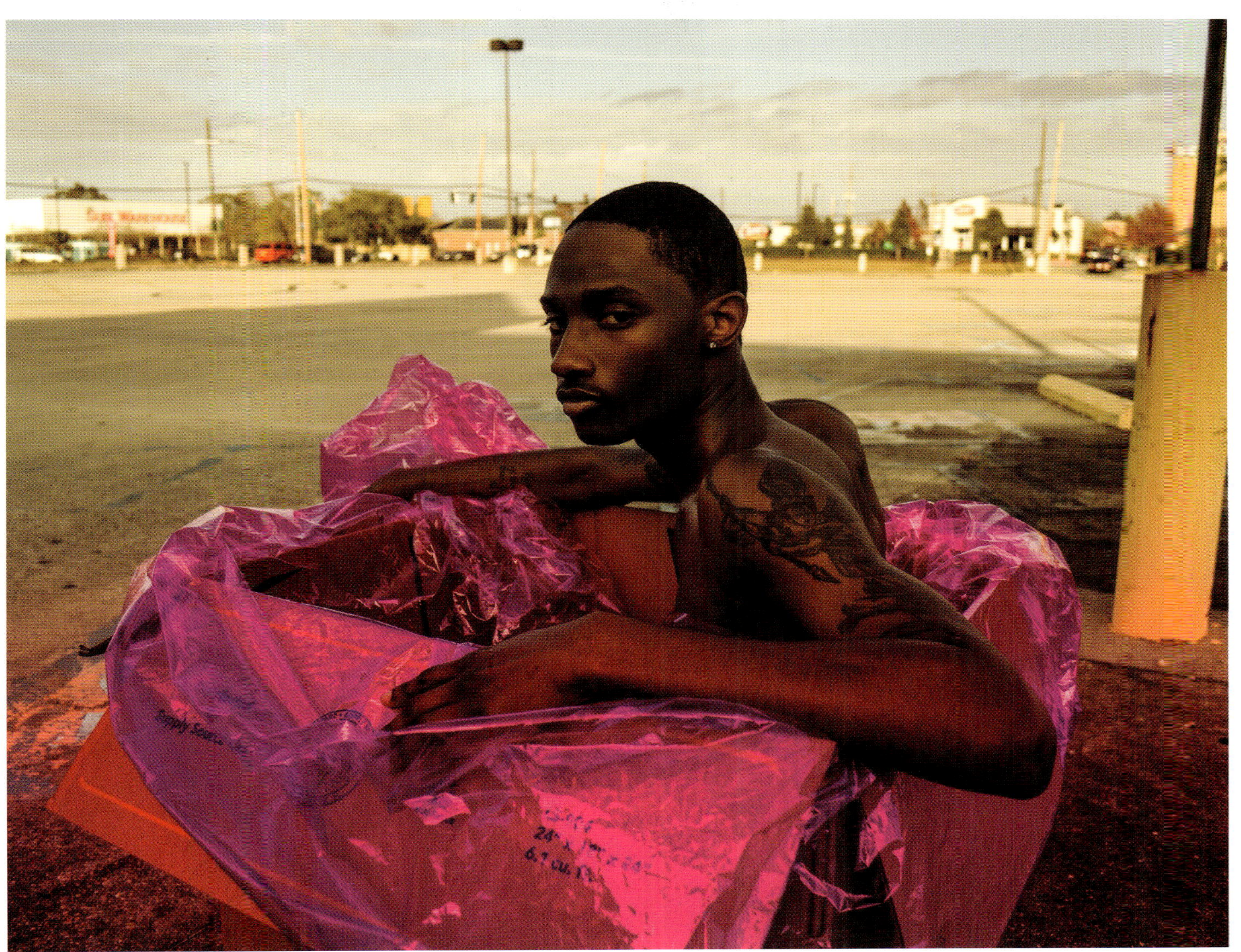

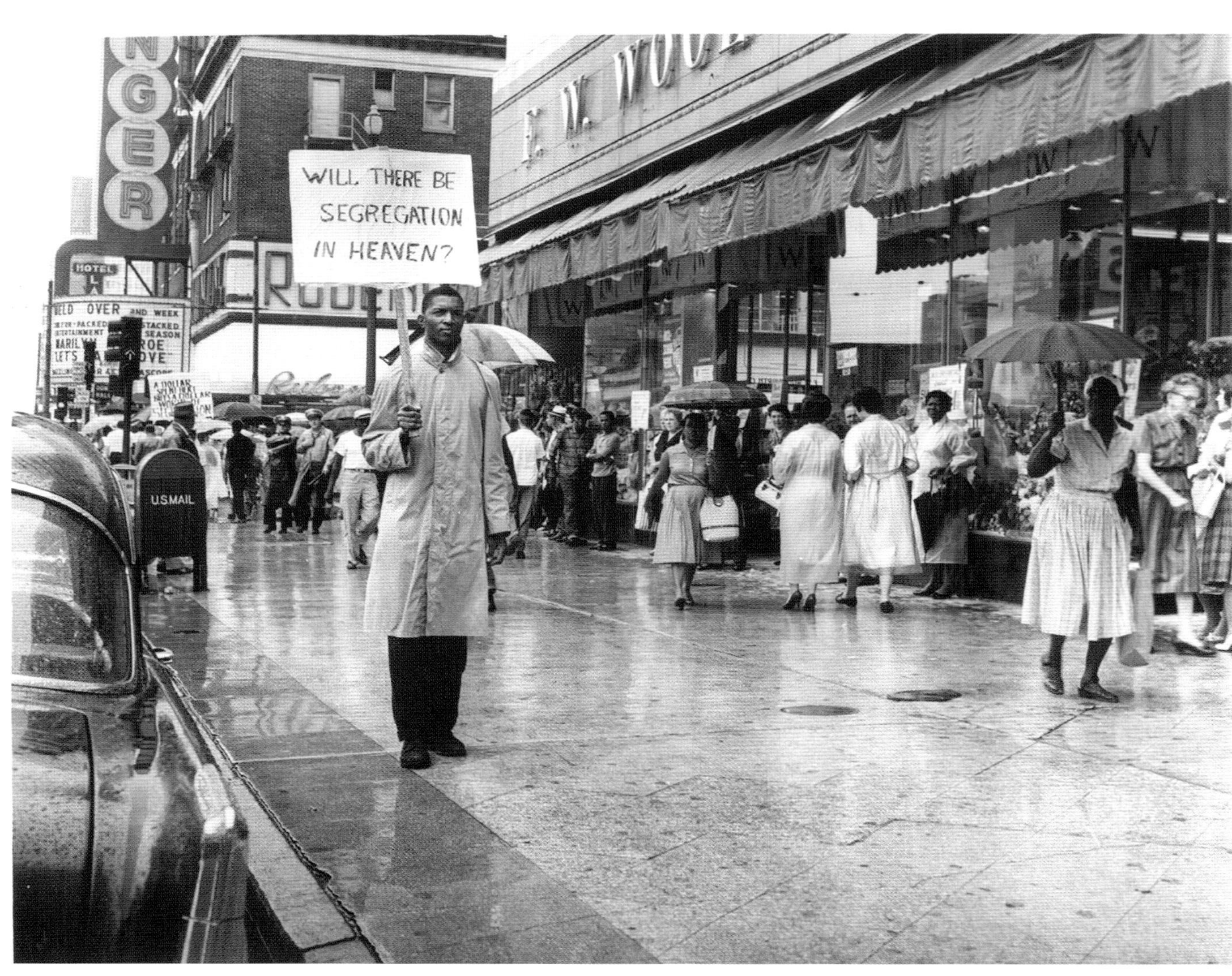
WILL THERE BE
SEGREGATION
IN HEAVEN?
U.S.MAIL
HELD OVER 2ND WEEK
HOTEL

Marion J. Porter

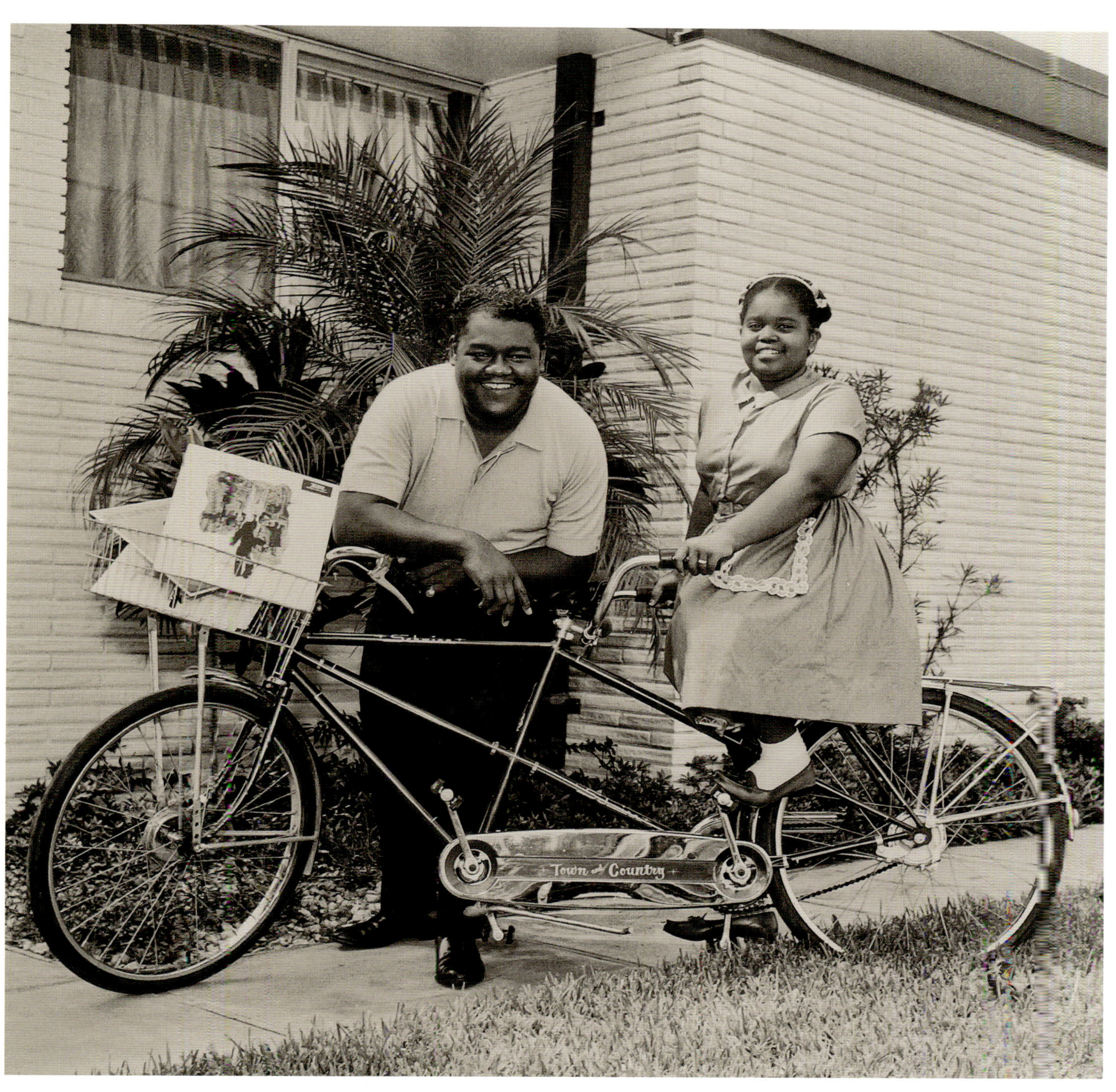

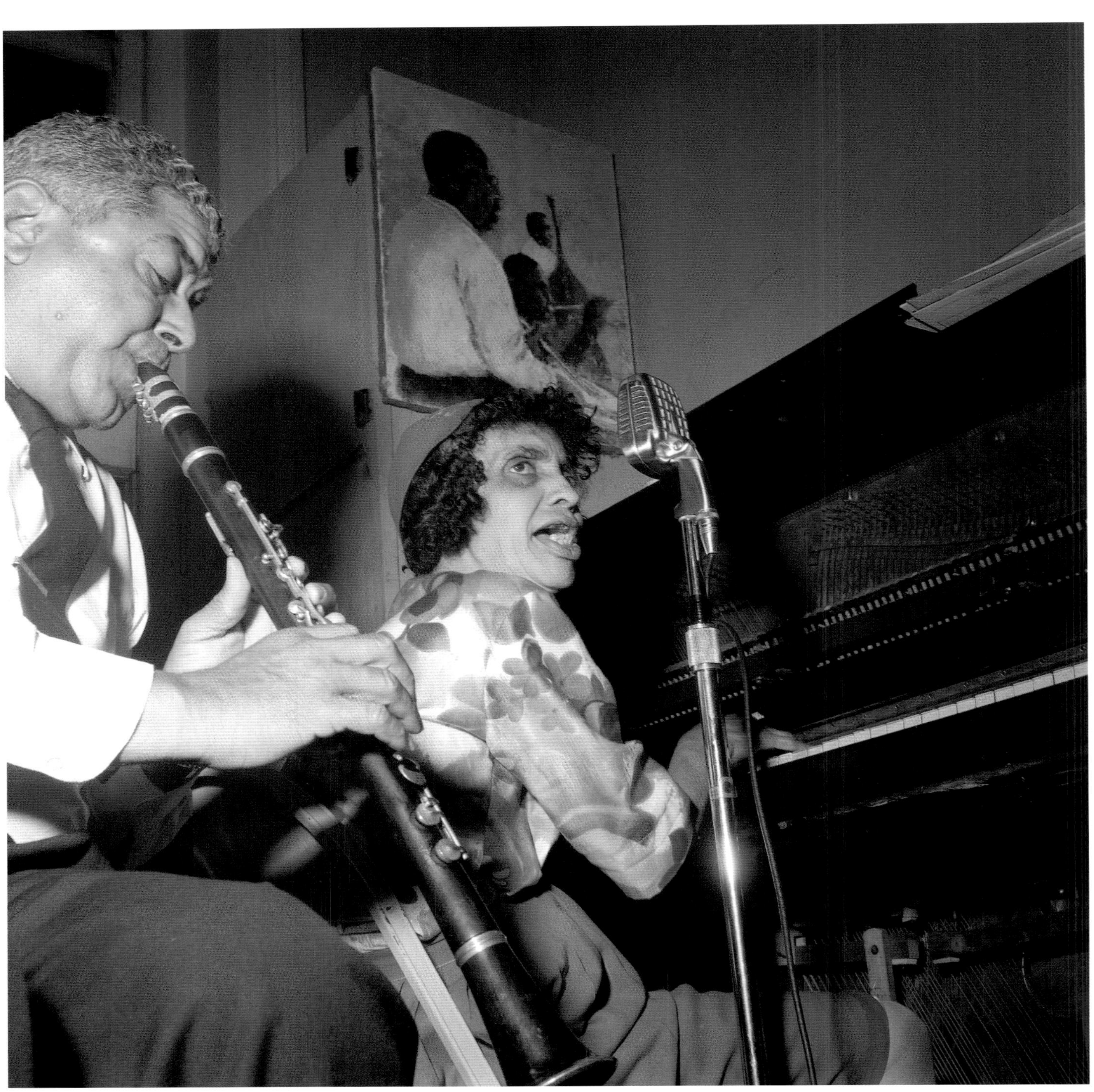

Maurice Martinez

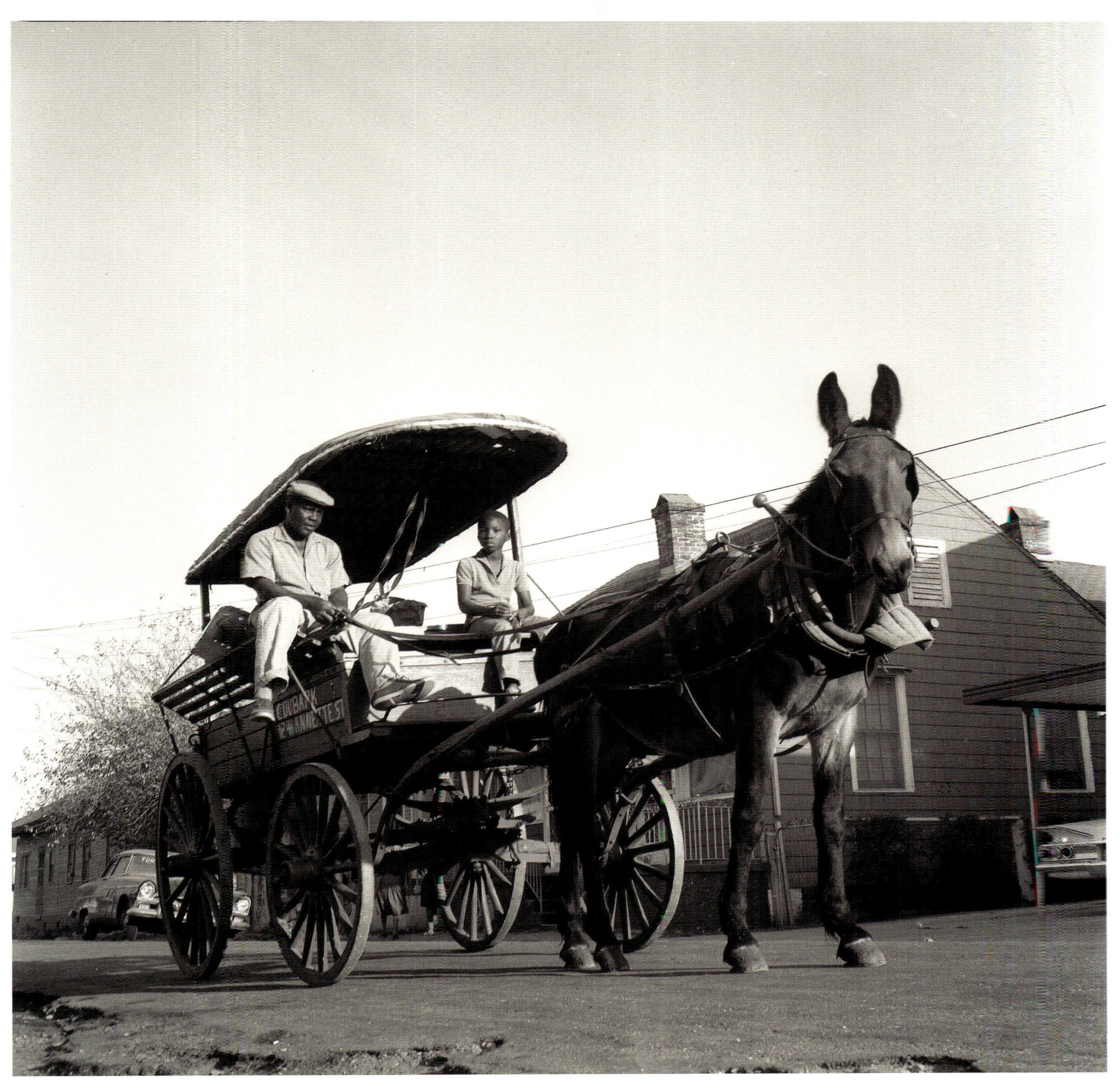

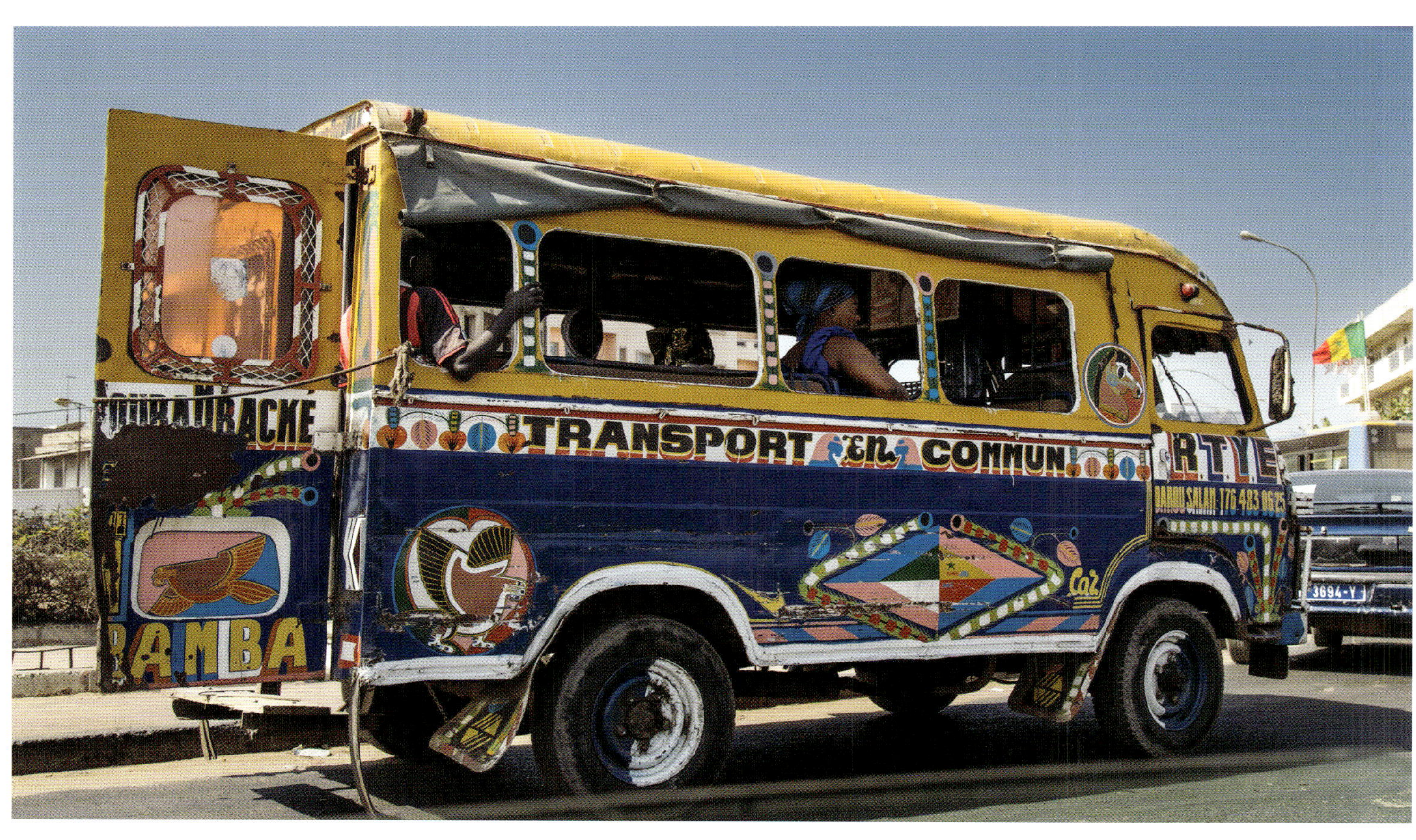
TRANSPORT en COMMUN
RTYE
3694-Y

Melissa Carrier

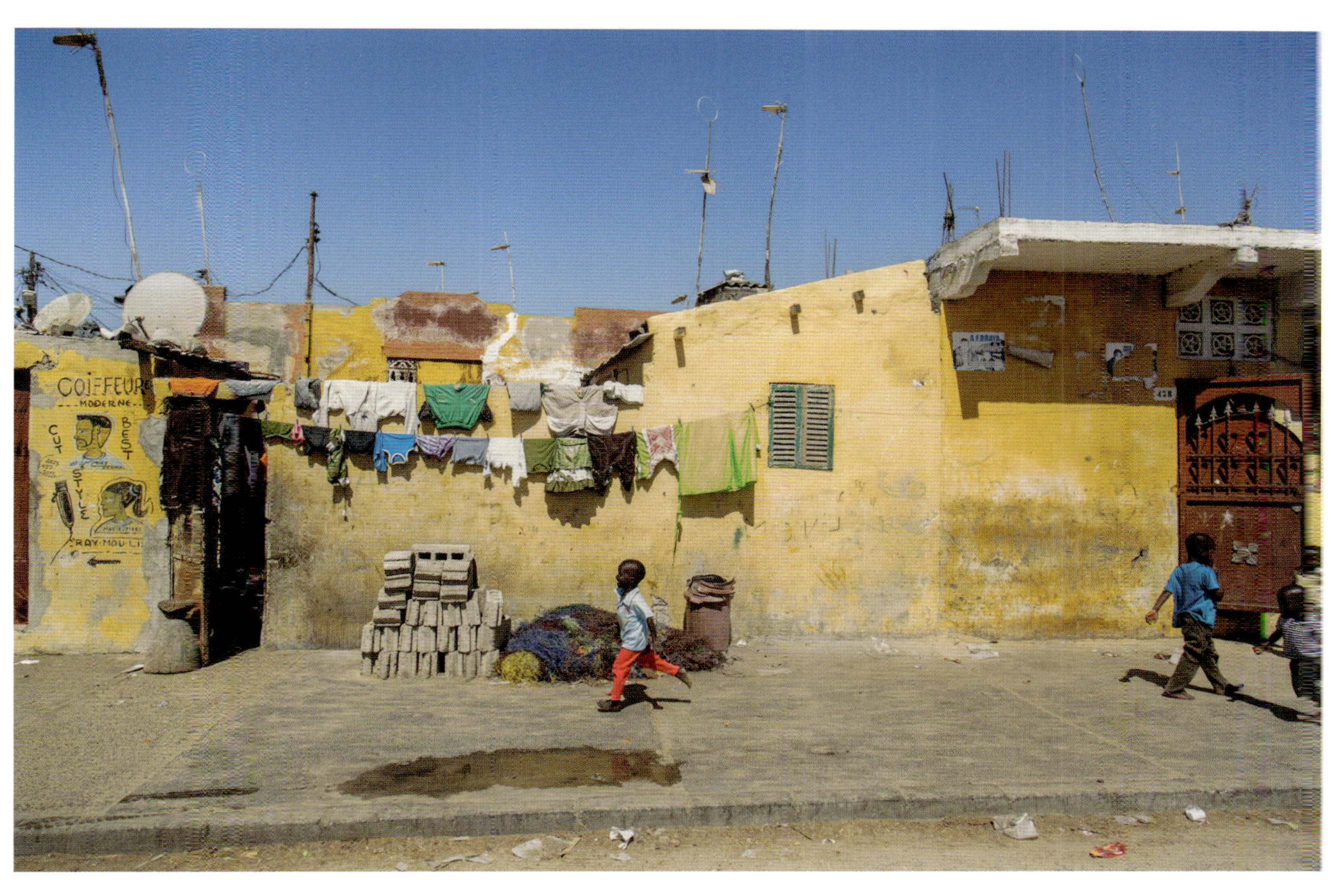

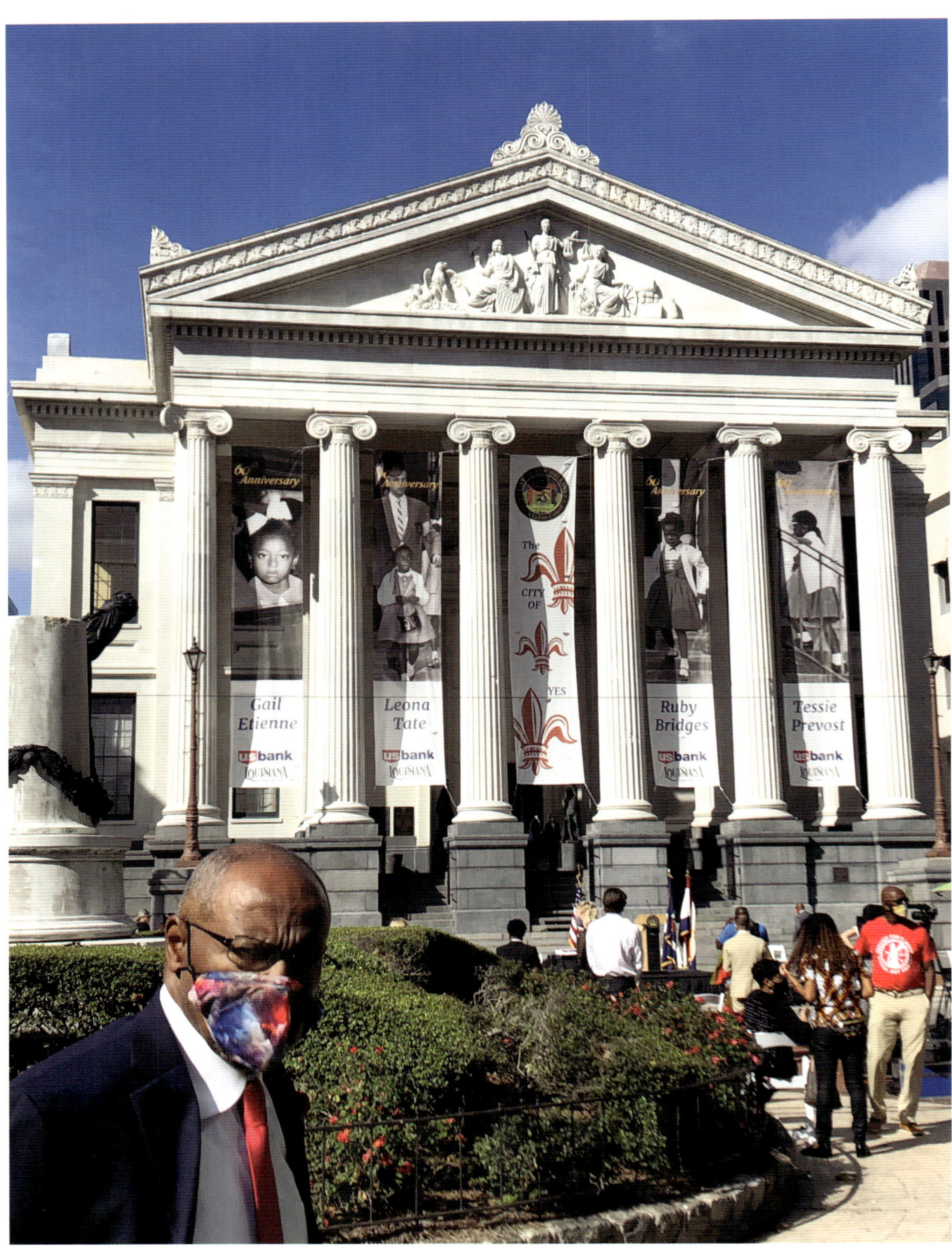

60 Anniversary
Gail Etienne
usbank
Leona Tate
usbank
The
CITY OF
YES
Ruby Bridges
usbank
Tessie Prevost
usbank

Monique Moss

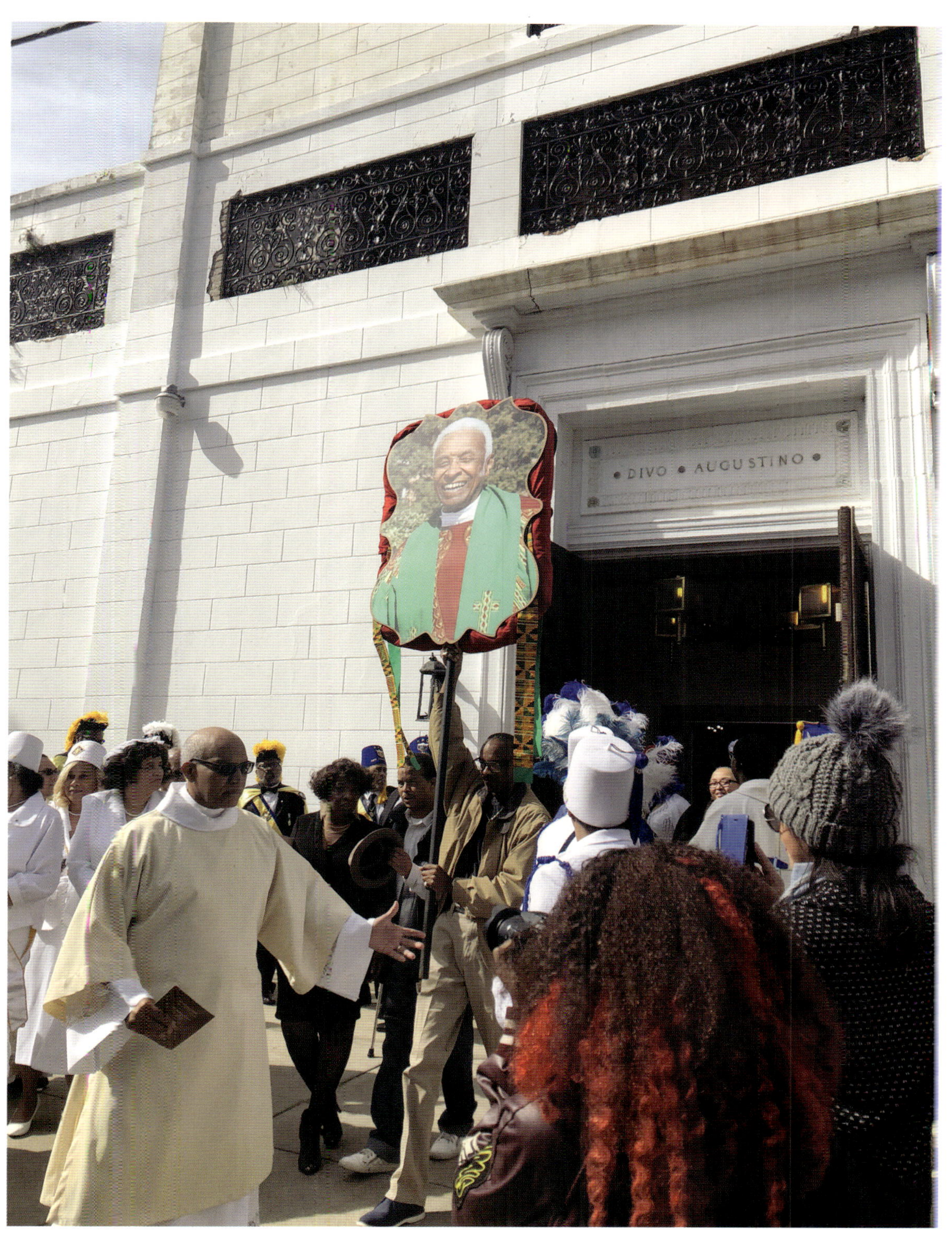

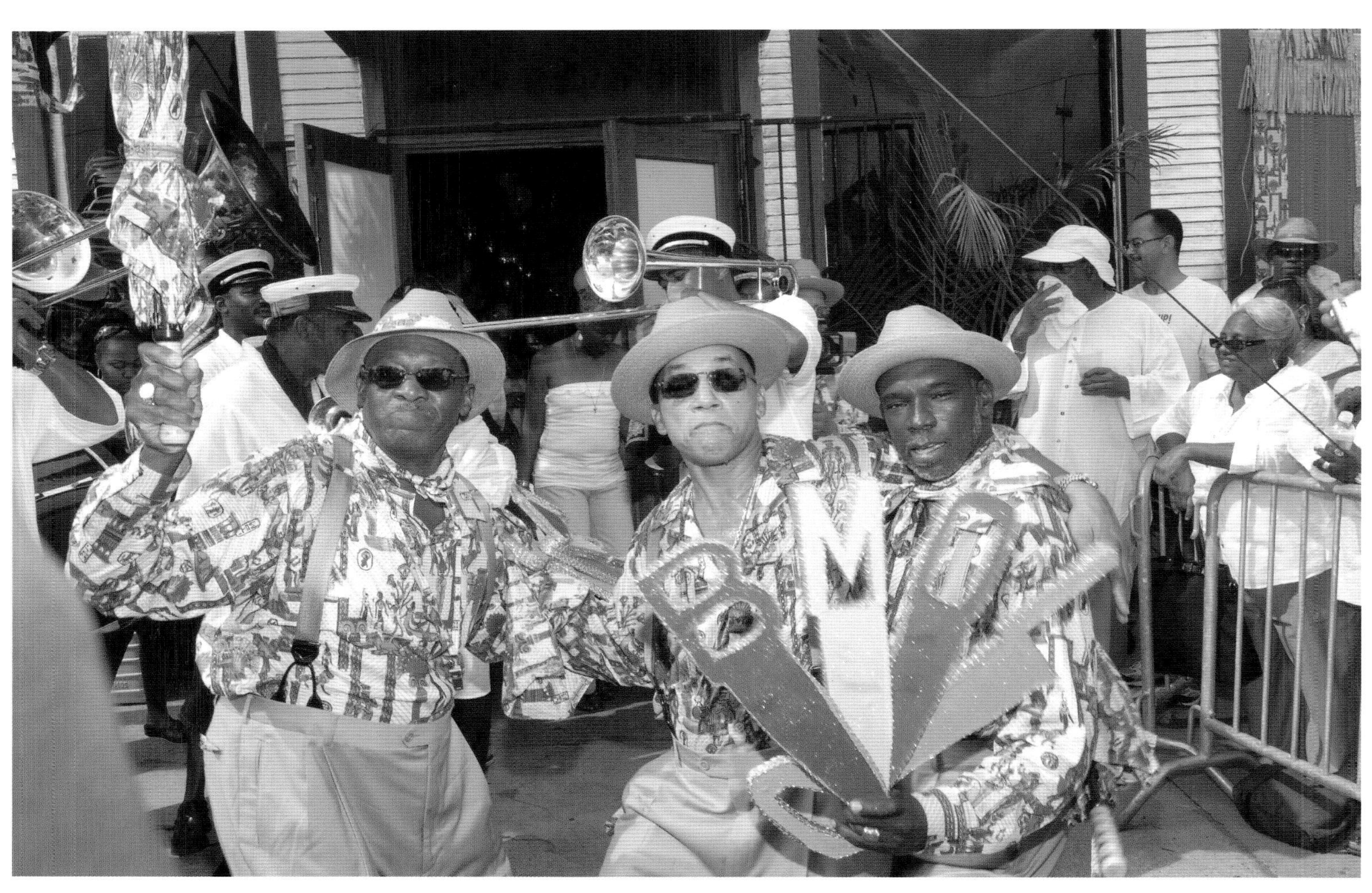

Morris Jones Jr.

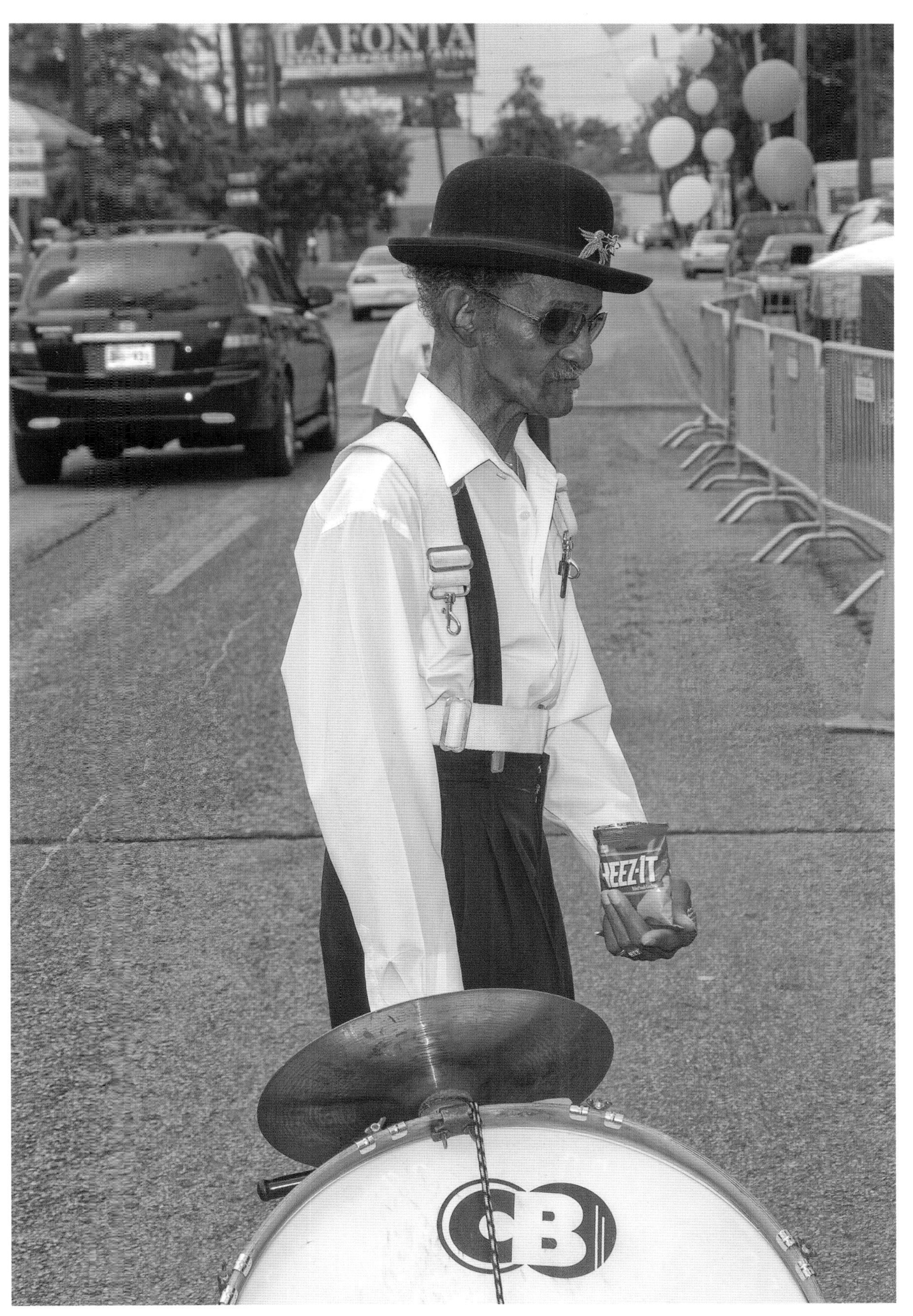

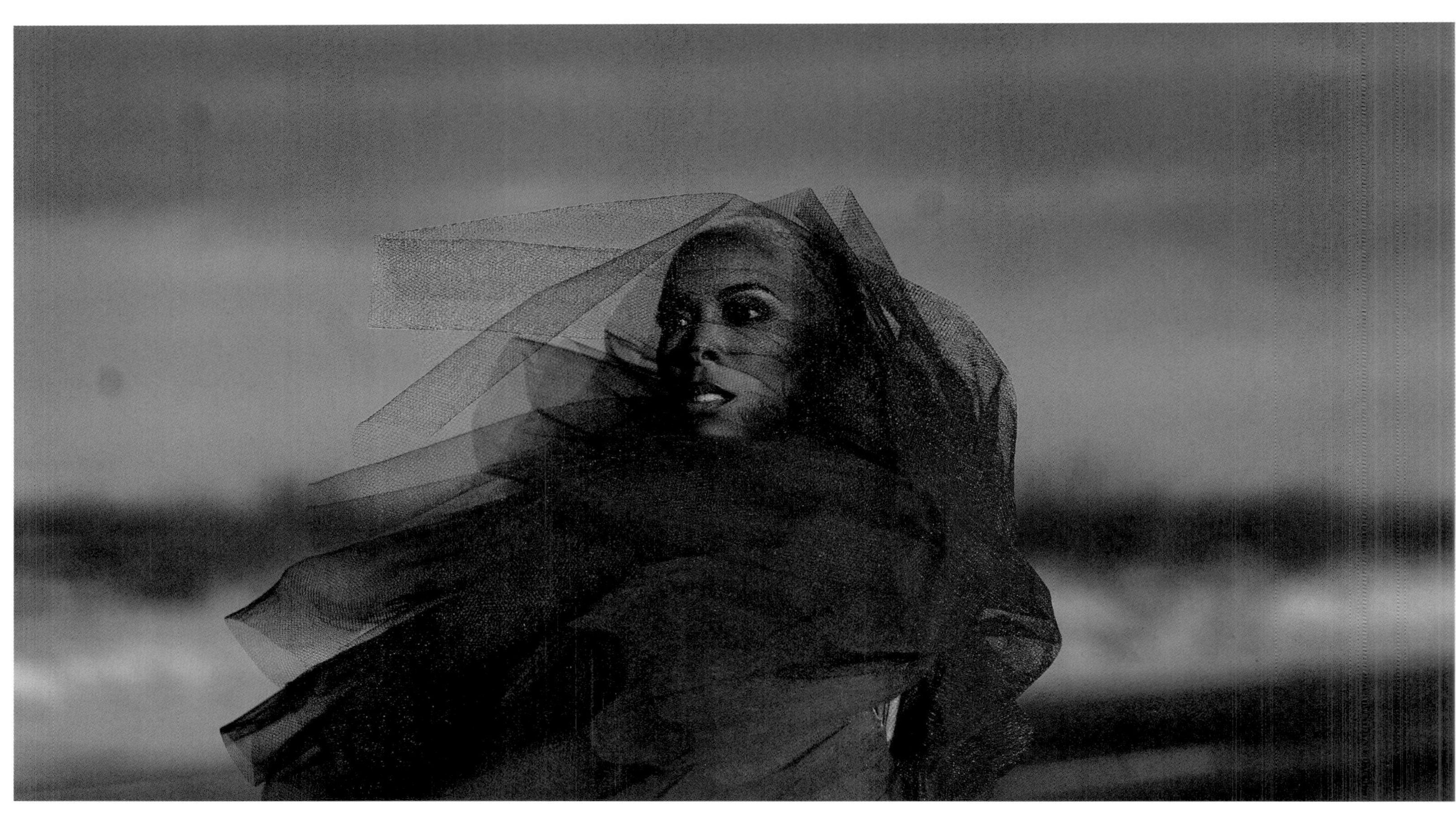

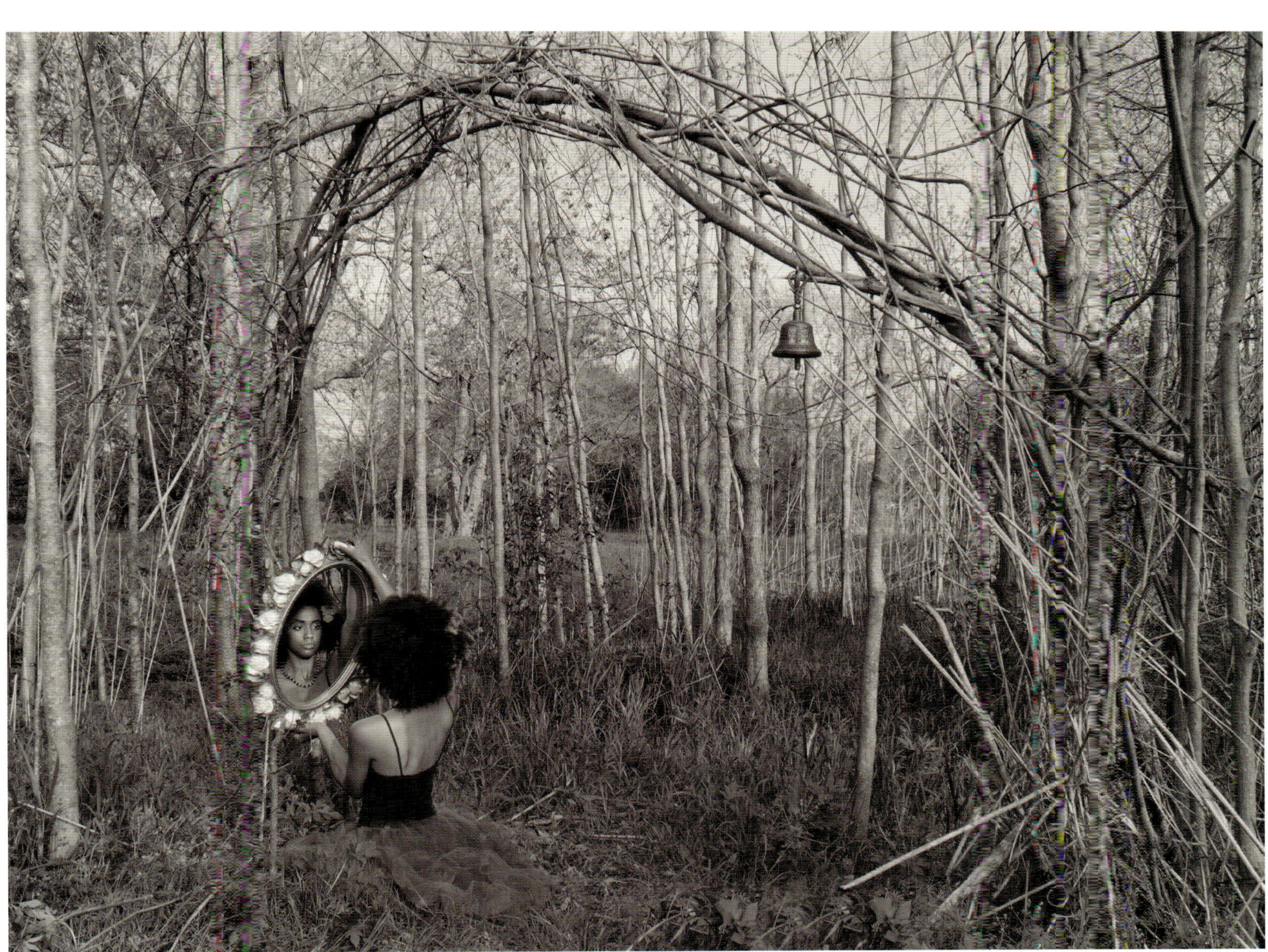

Shaquille Dunbar

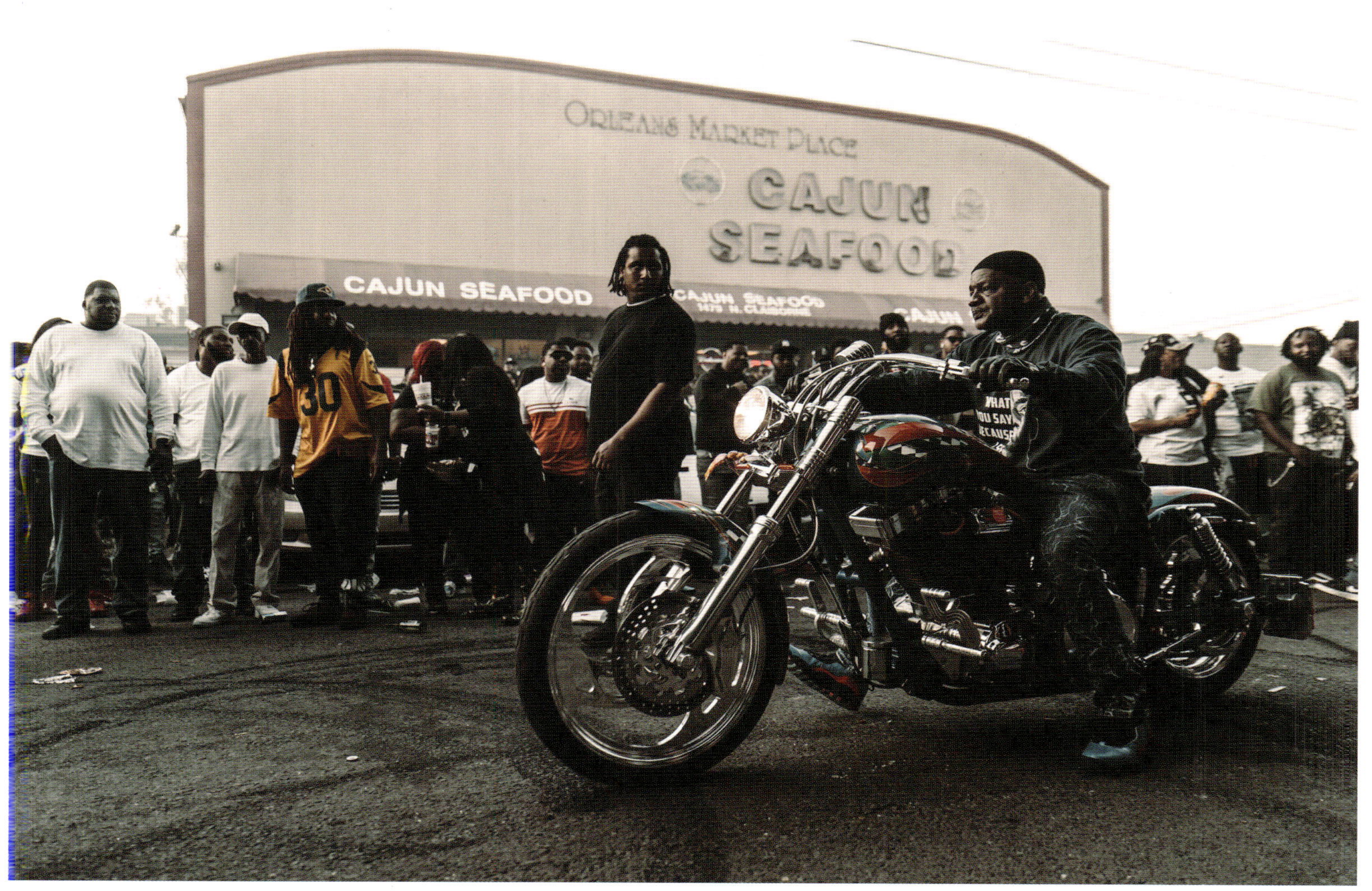

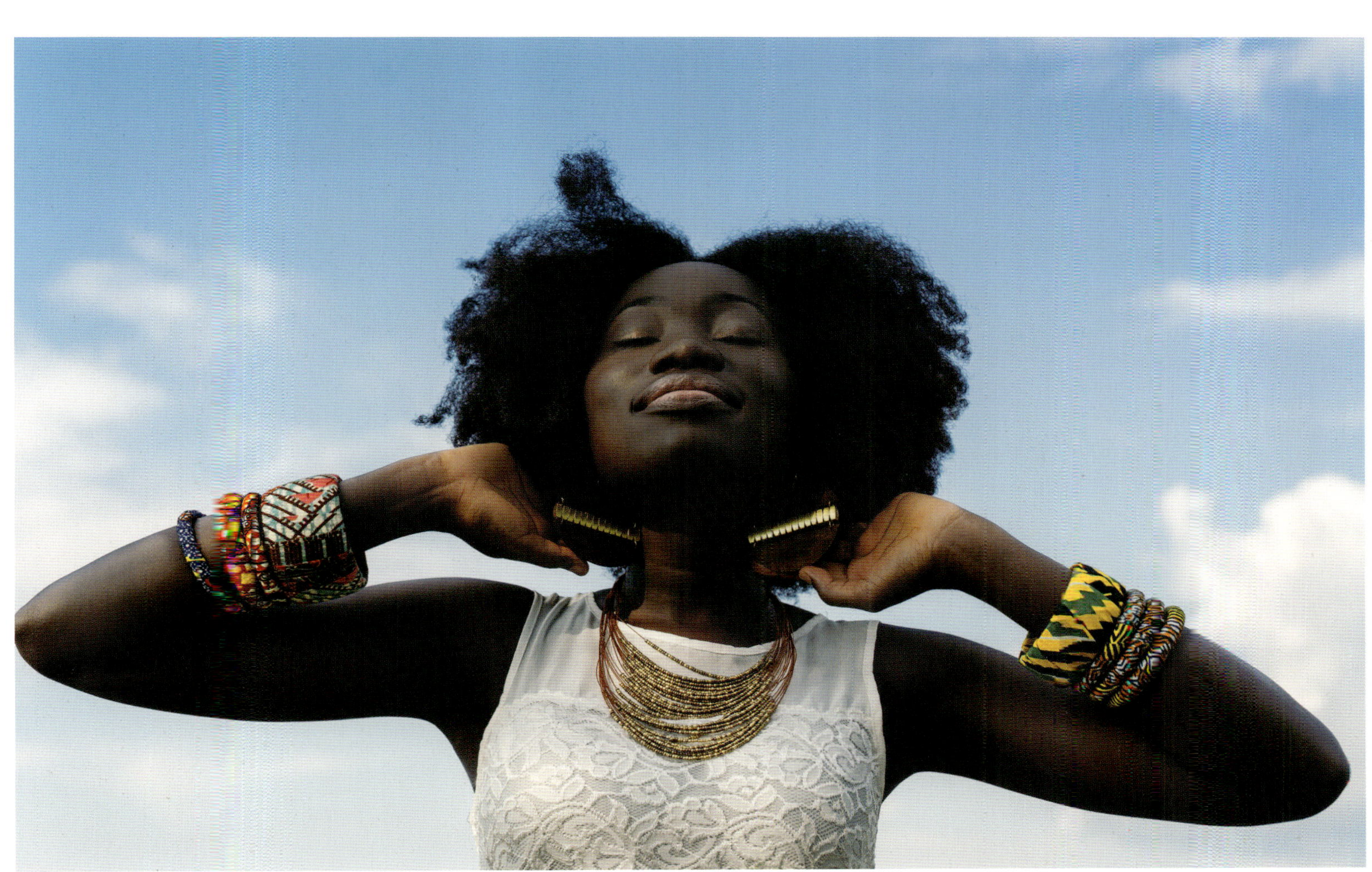

Shana M. griffin

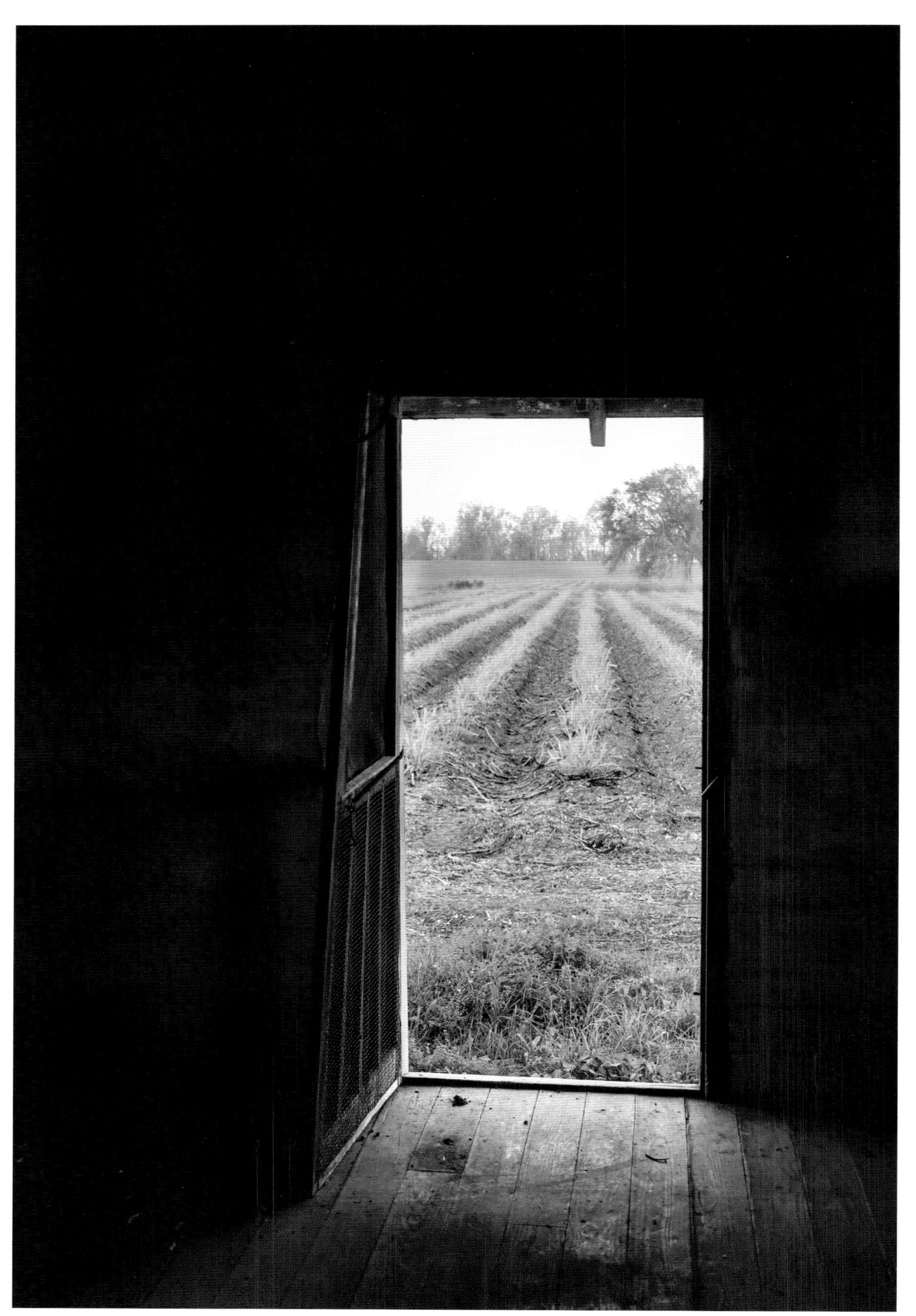

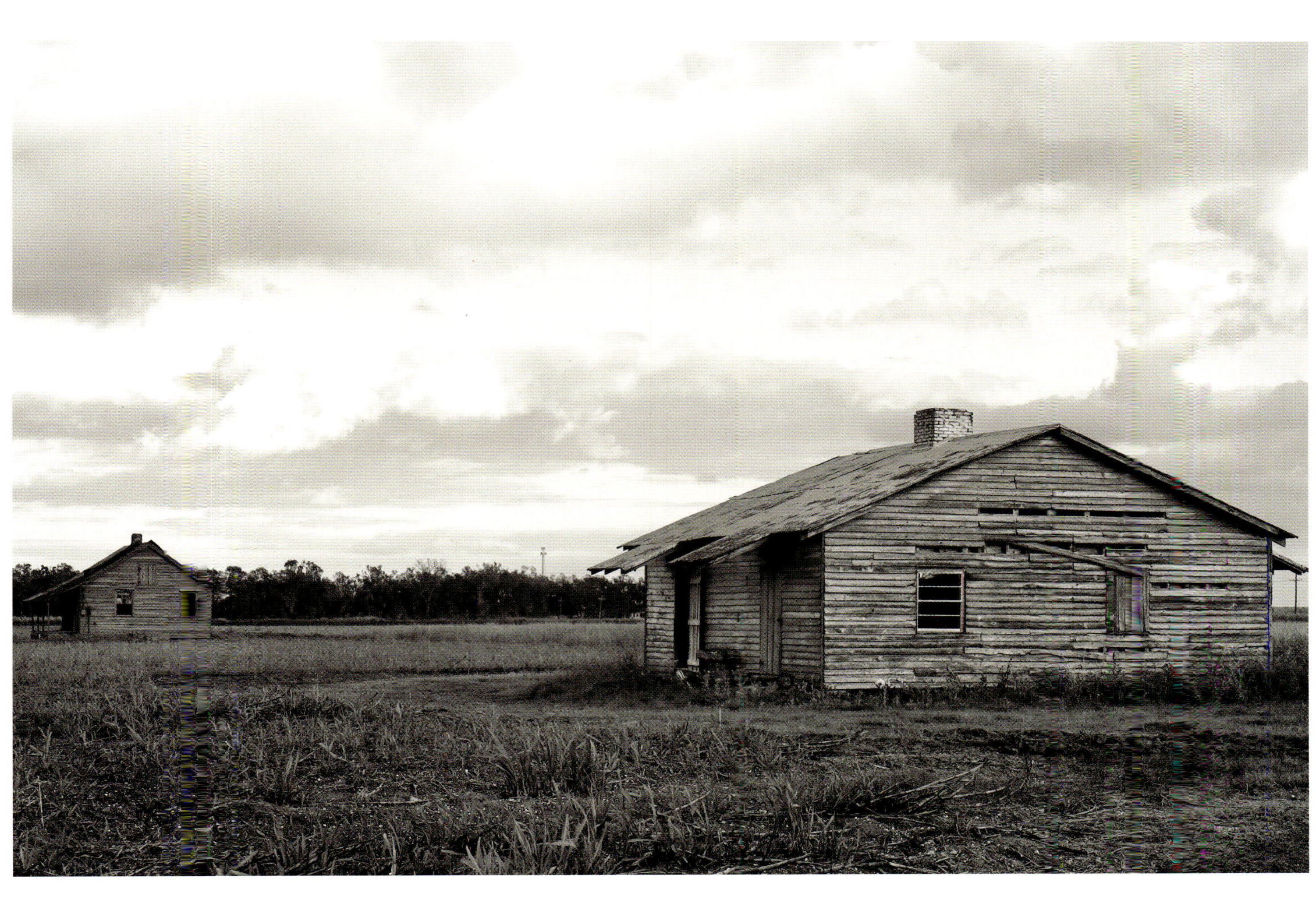

Shabez Jamal

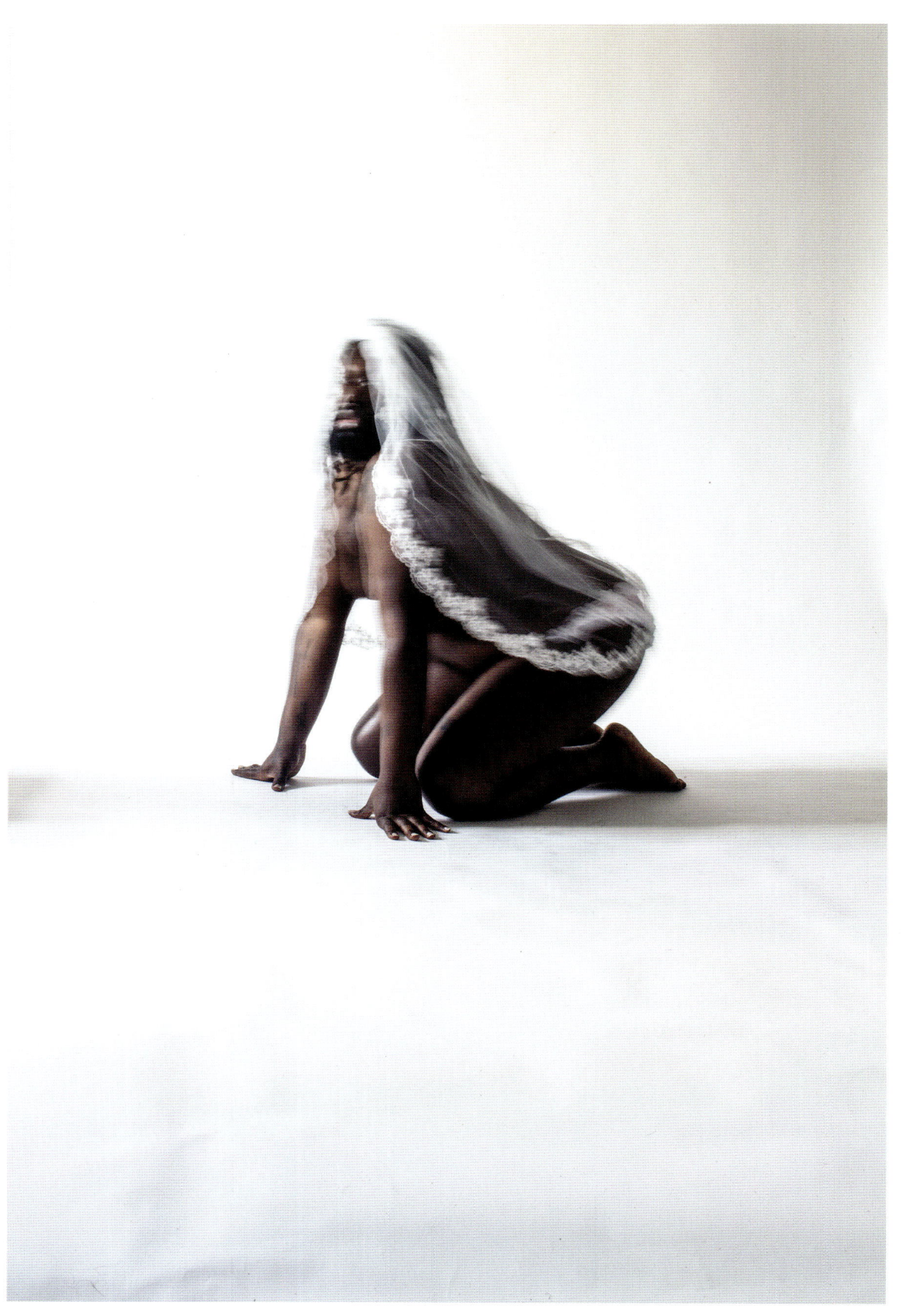

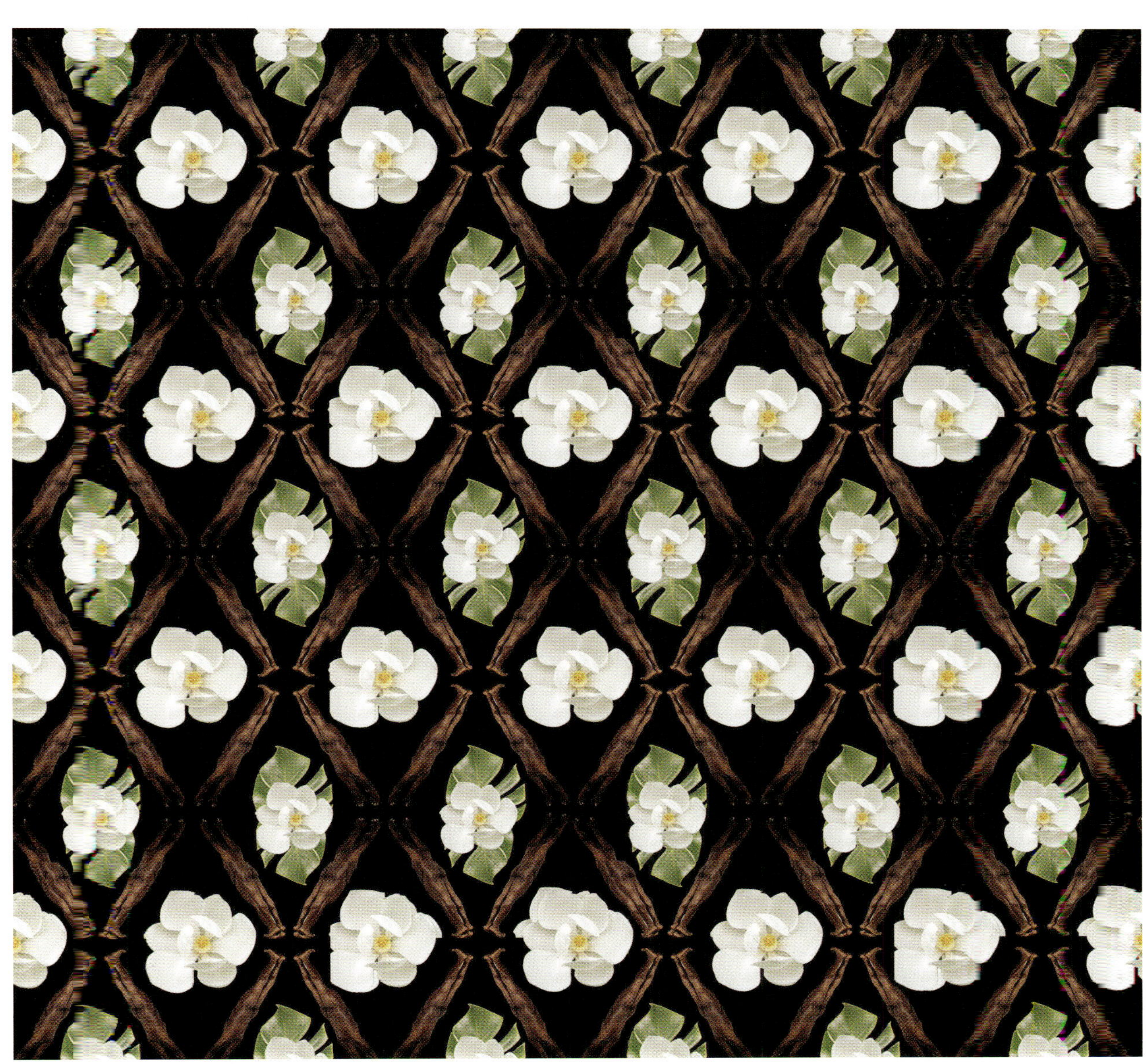

Selwhyn Sthaddeus “Polo Silk” Terrell

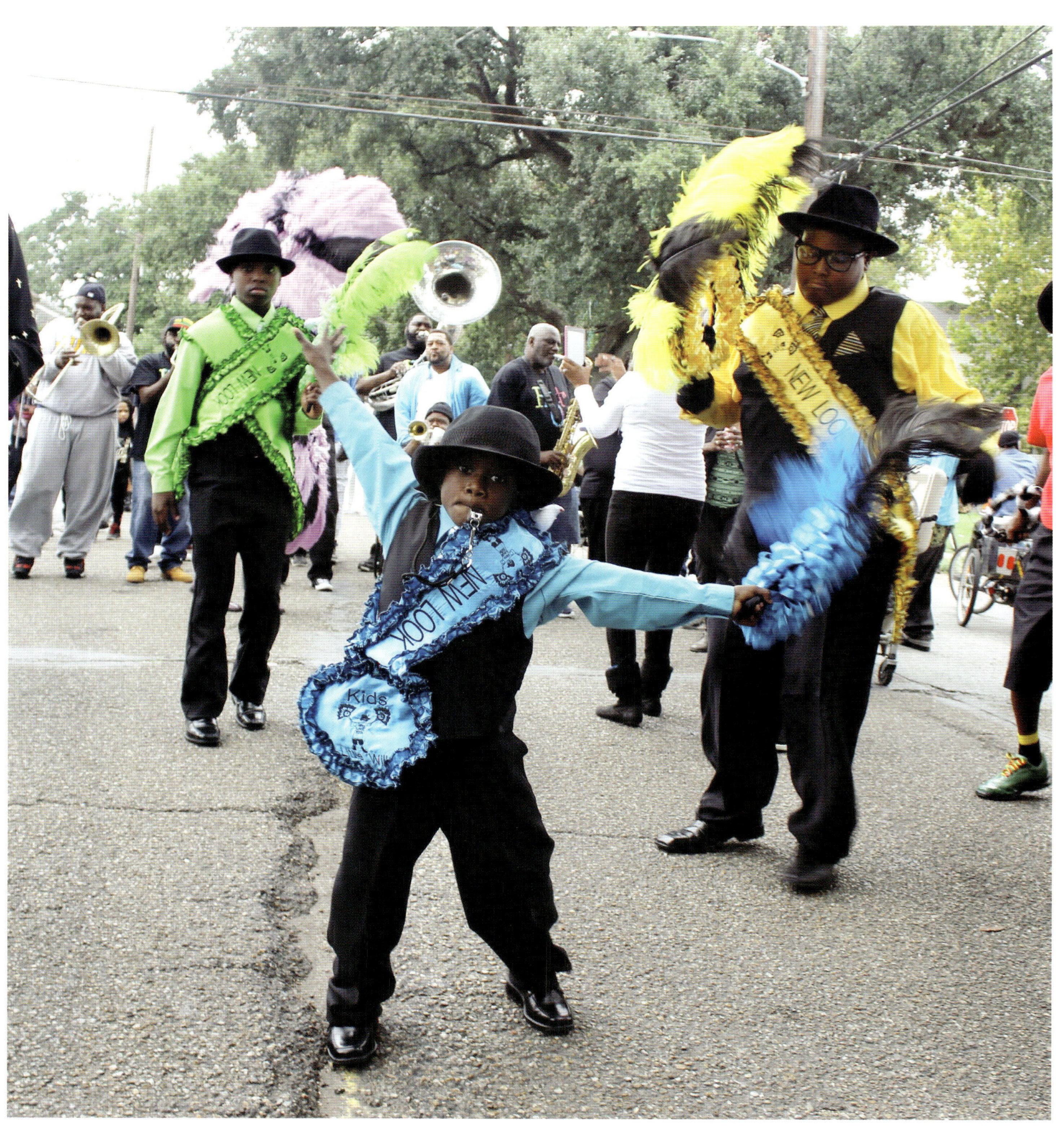

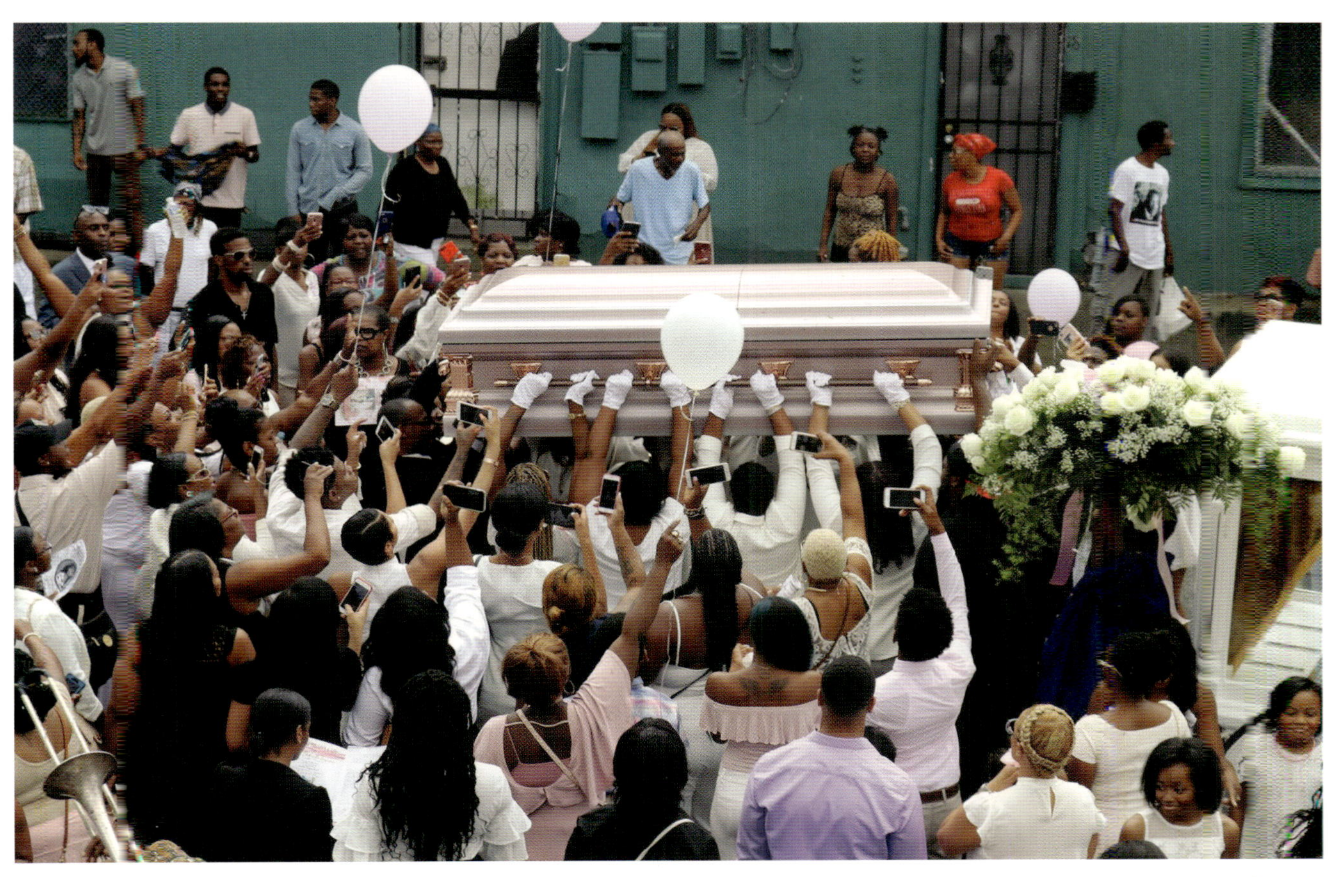

Sekou Fela

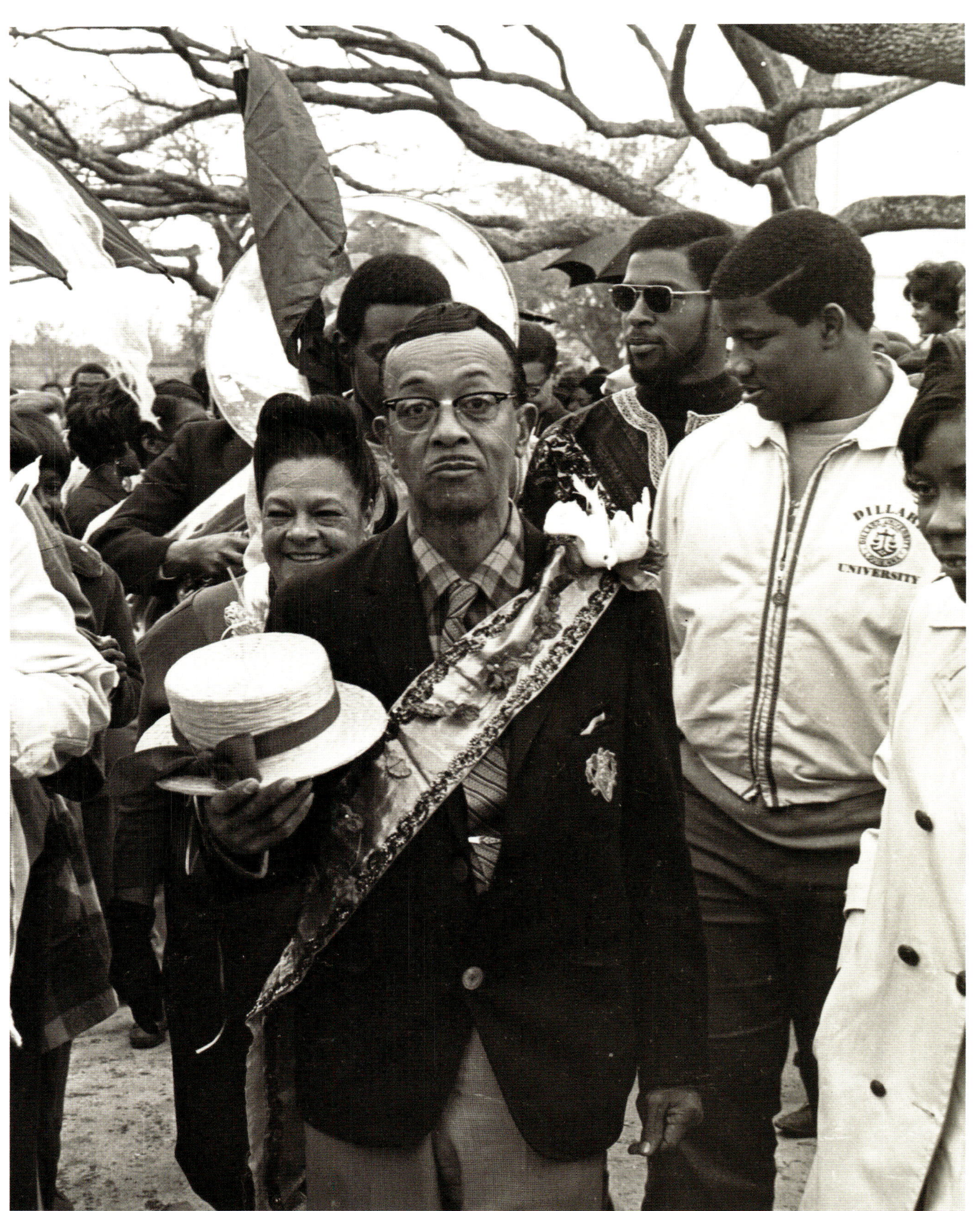

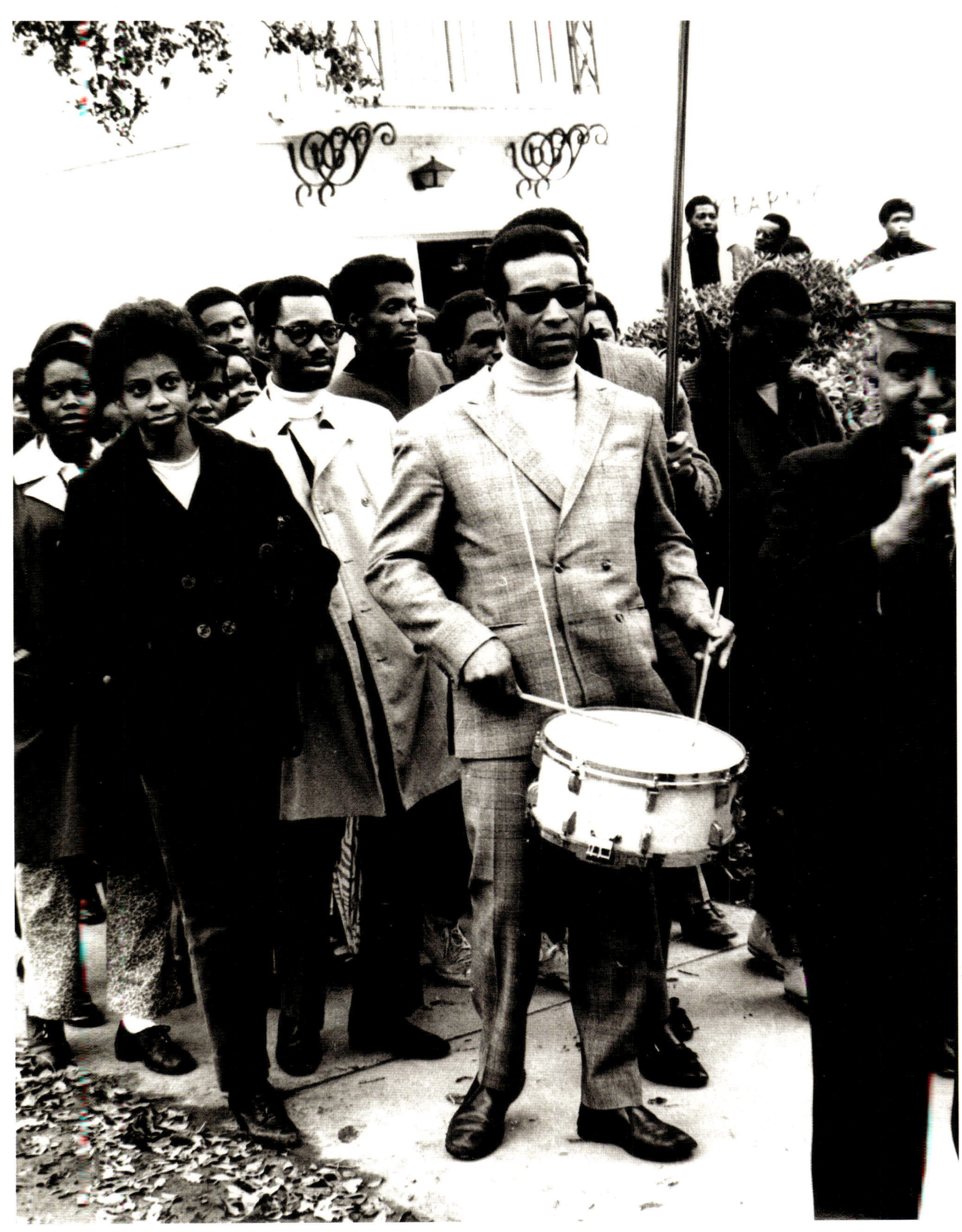

Saddi Khali

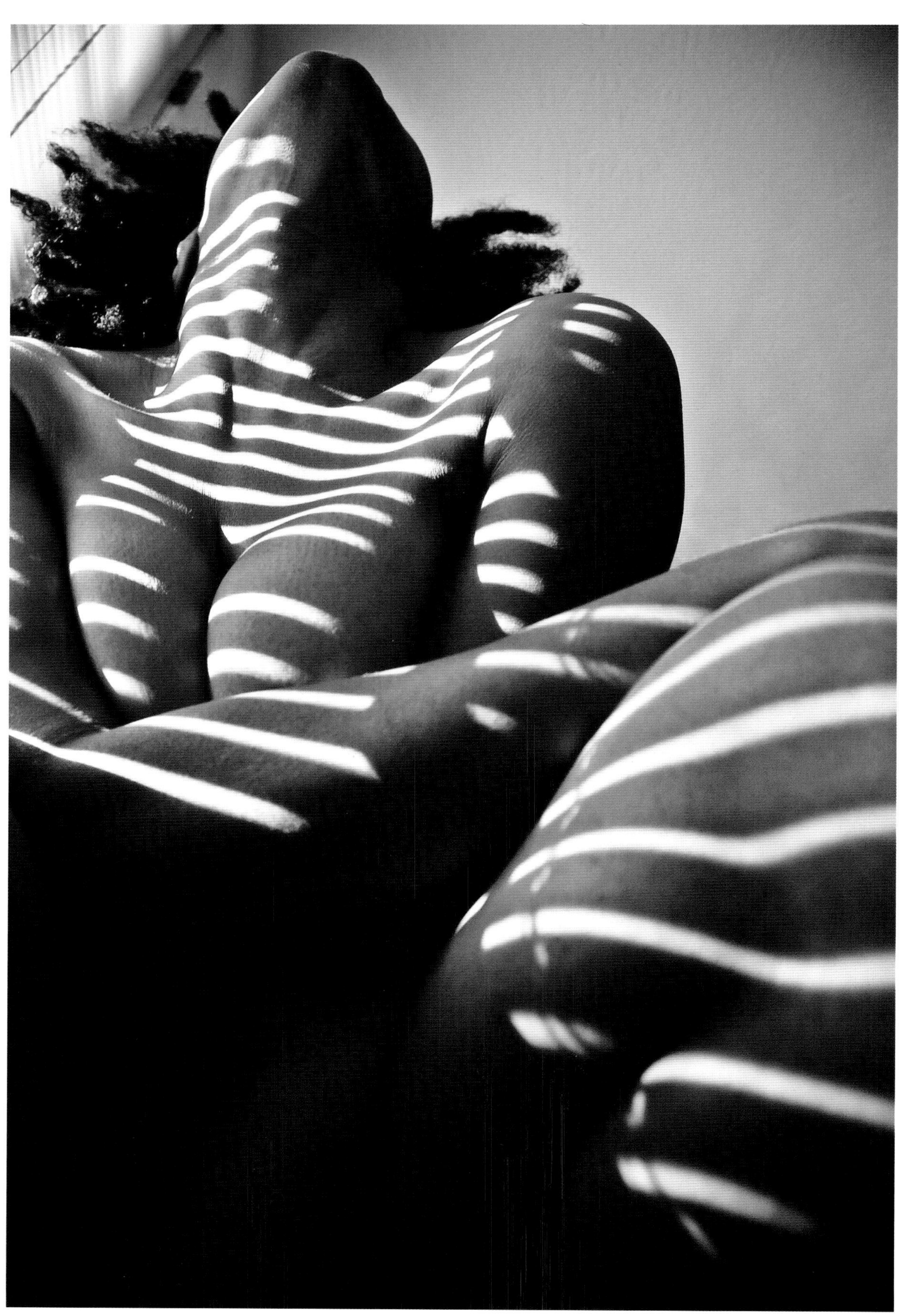

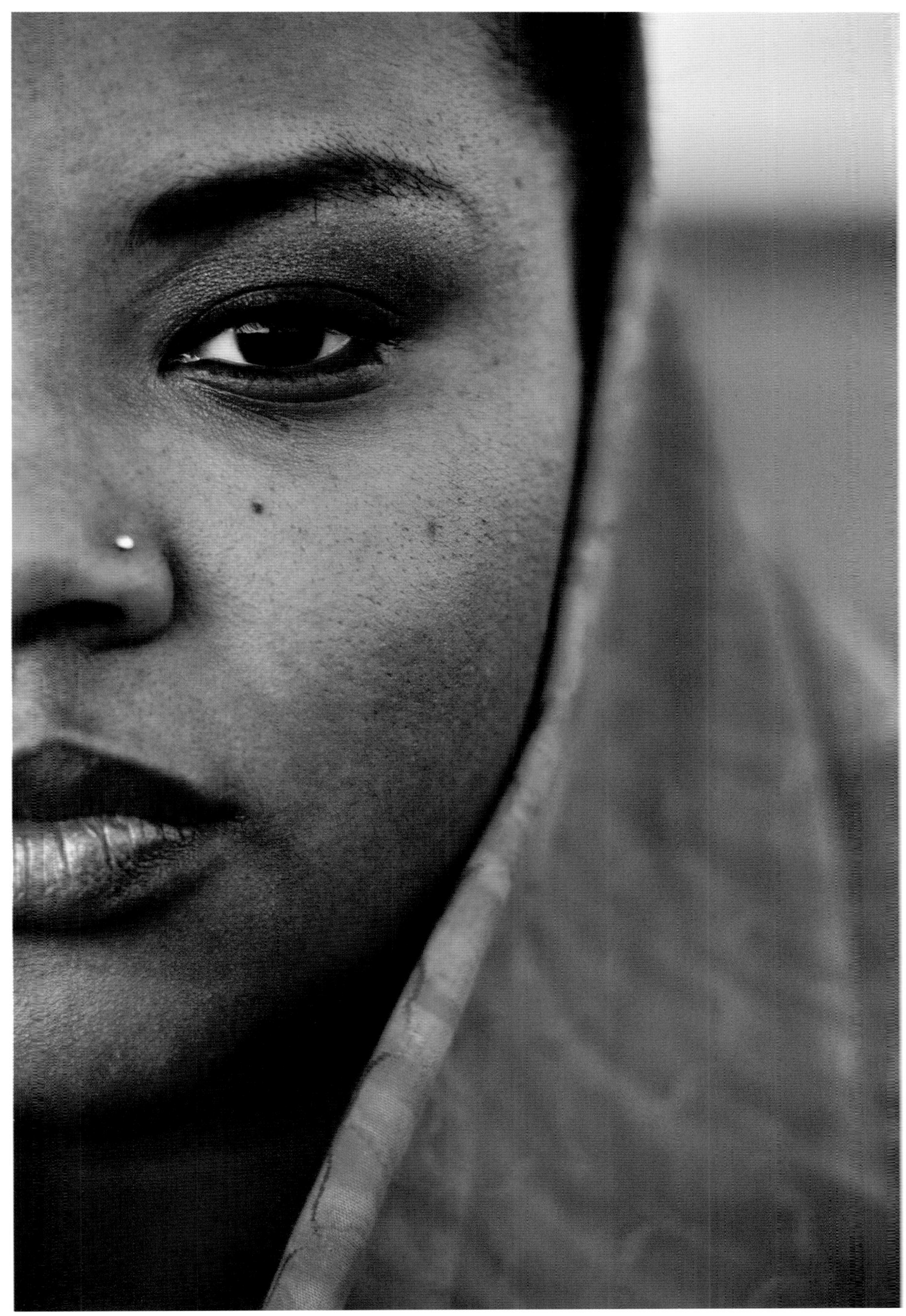

Roland Guerin

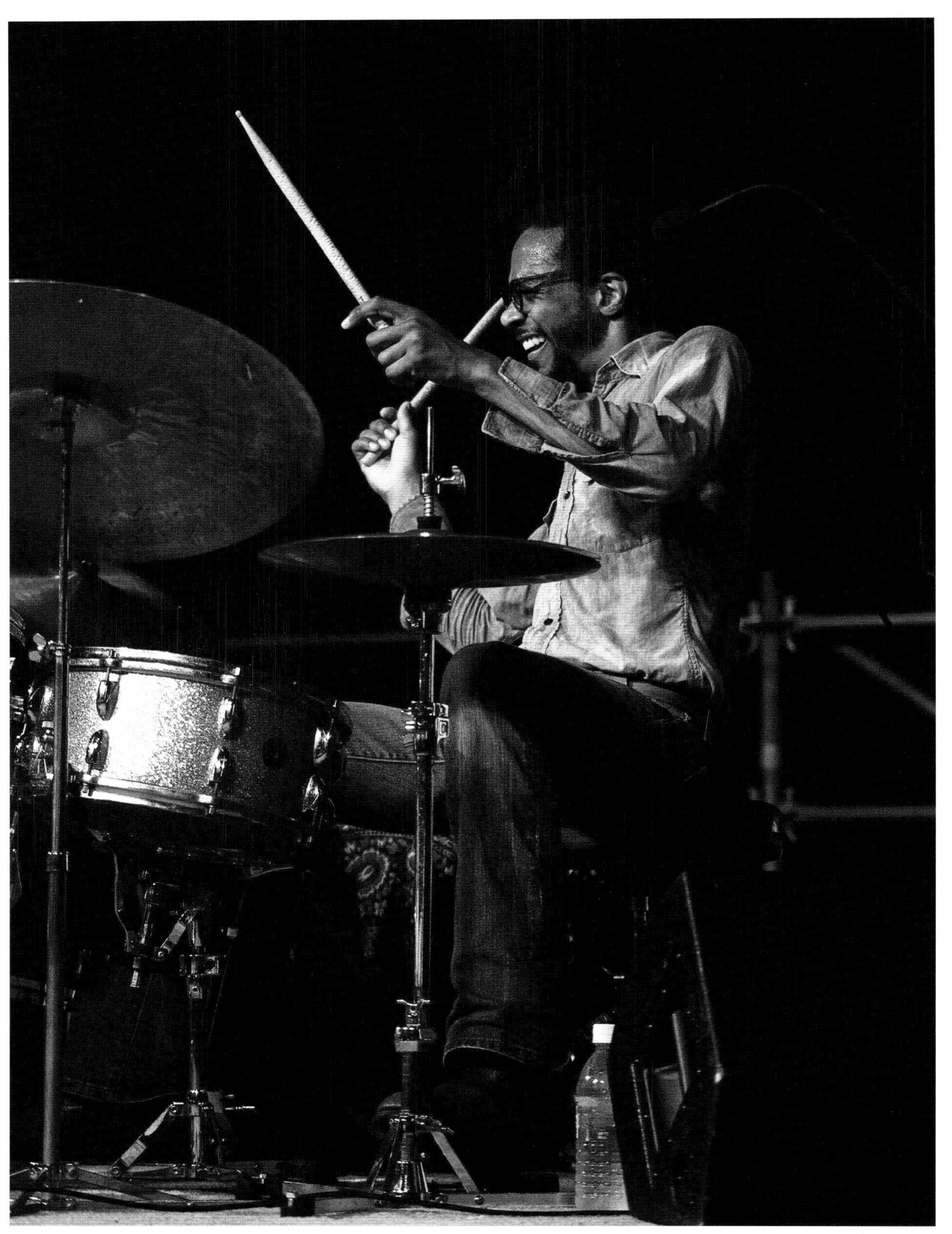

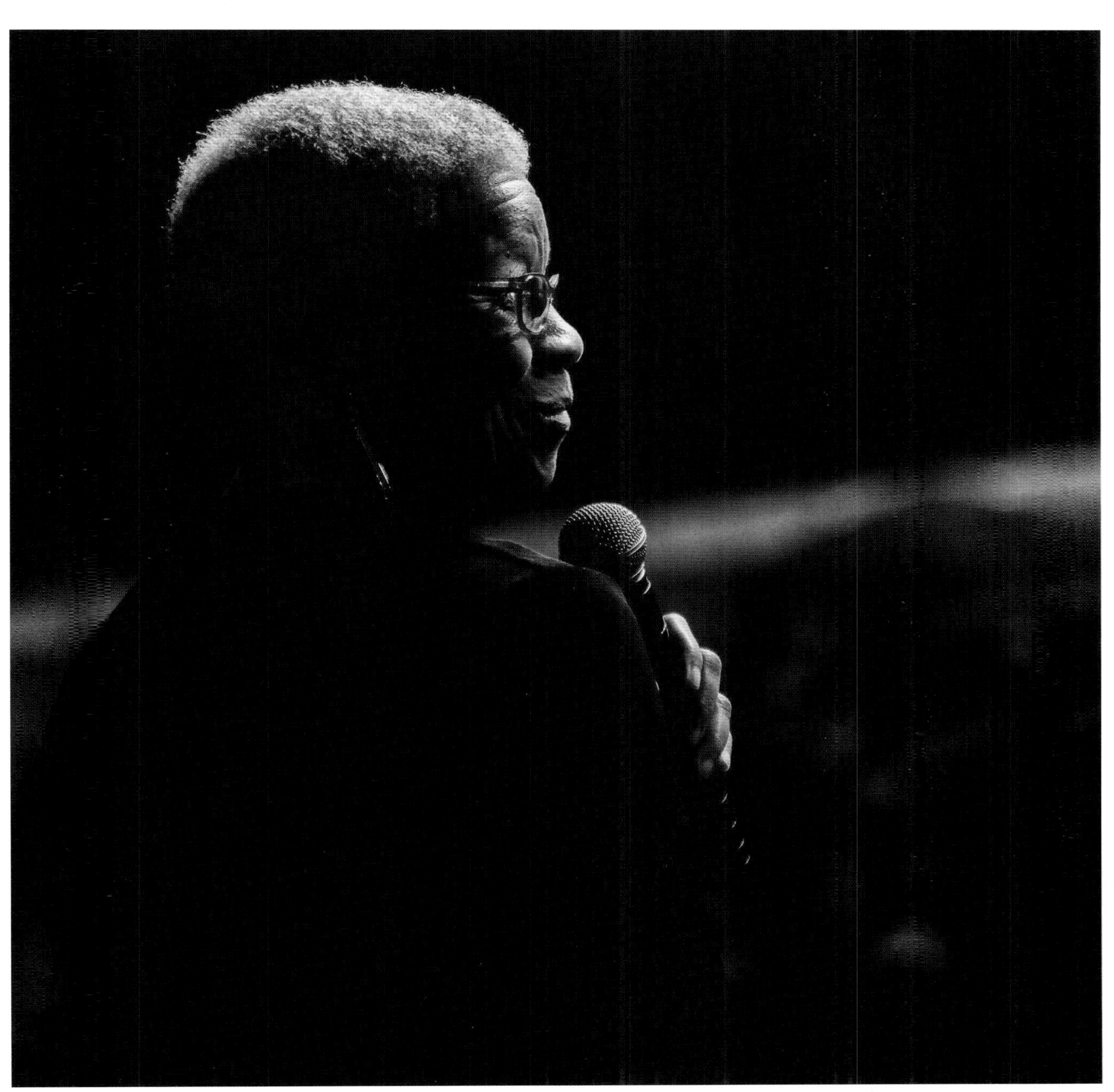

Rita Harper

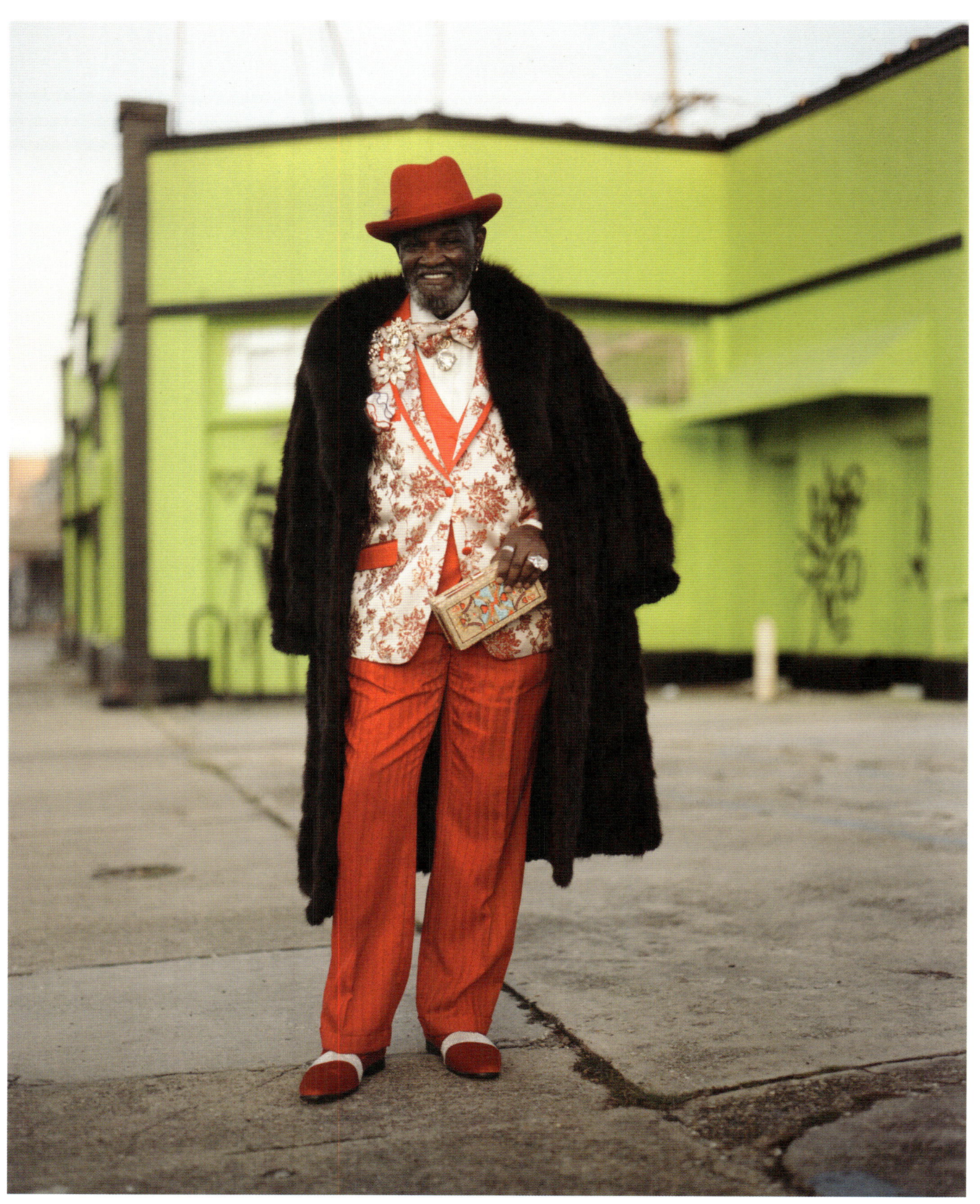

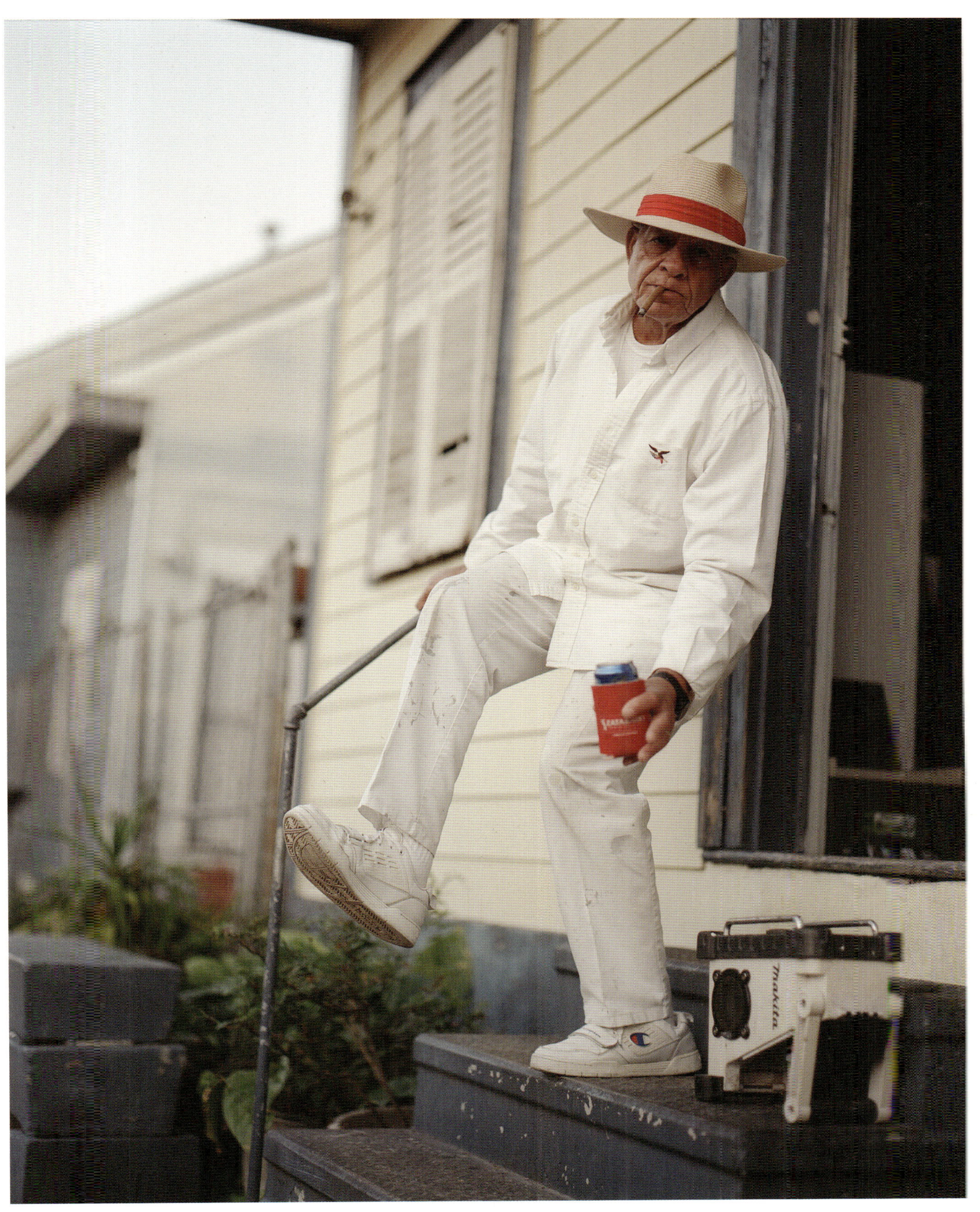
makita

Richard V. Keller Sr.

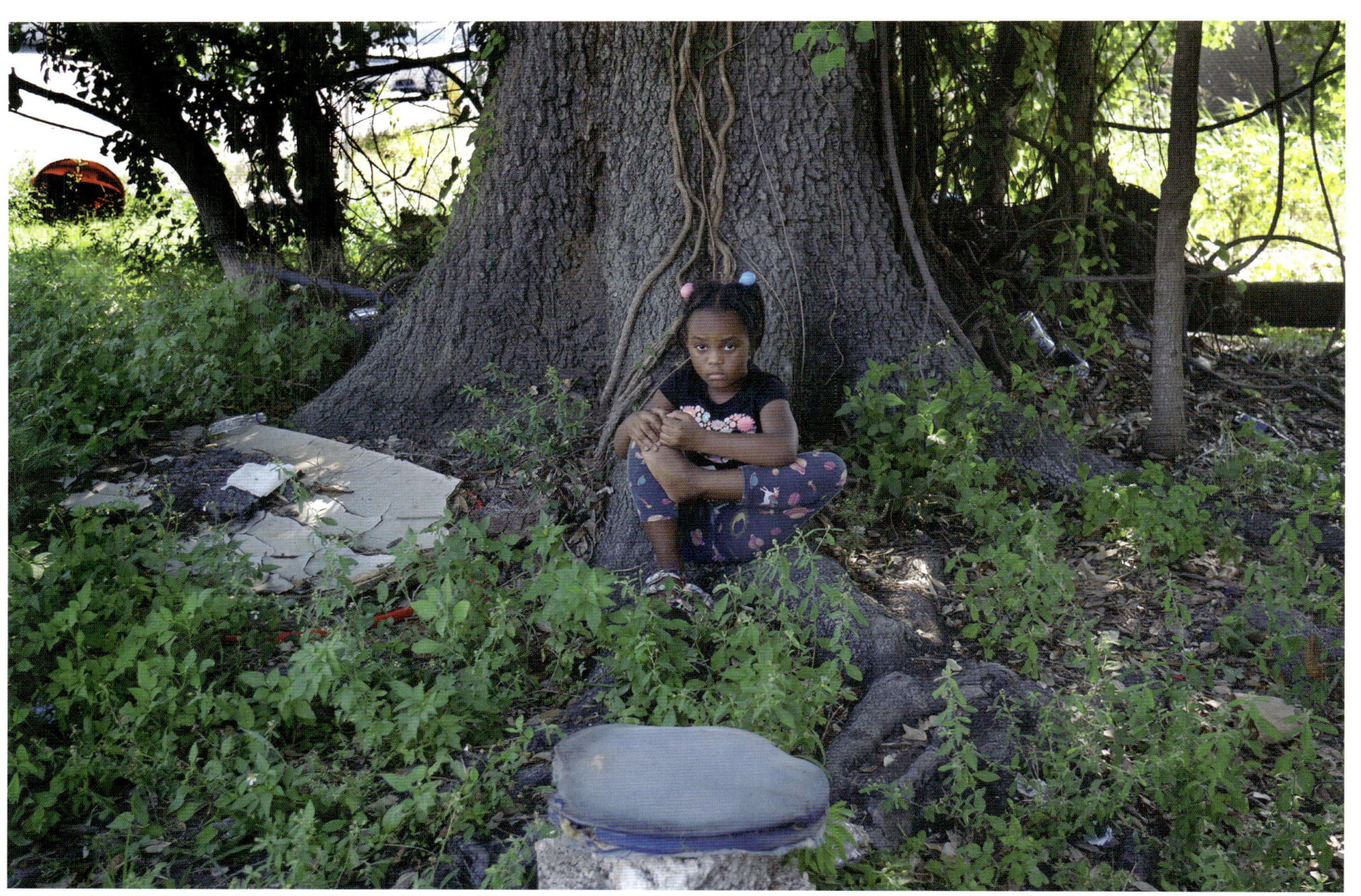

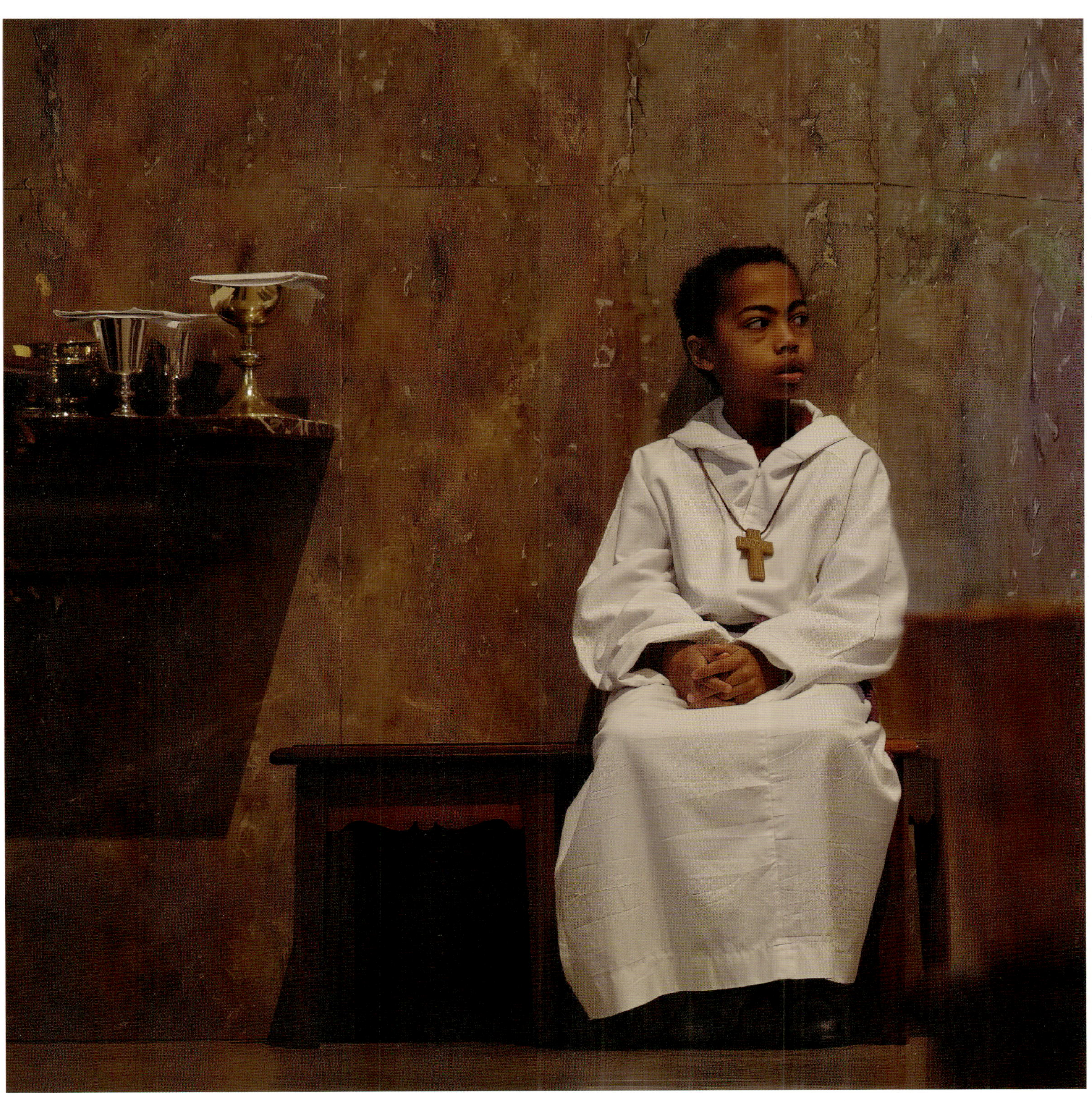

Ric Francis

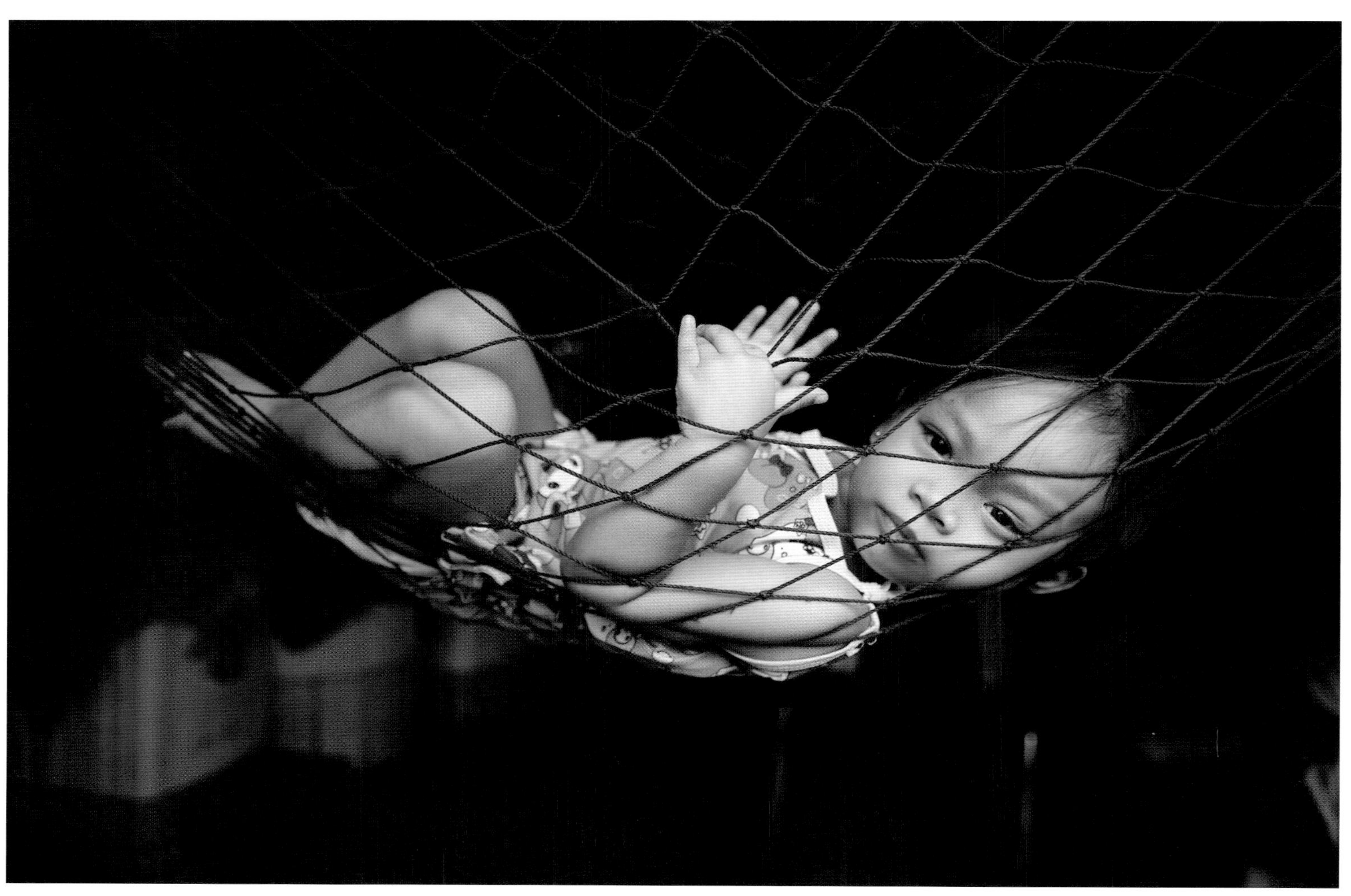

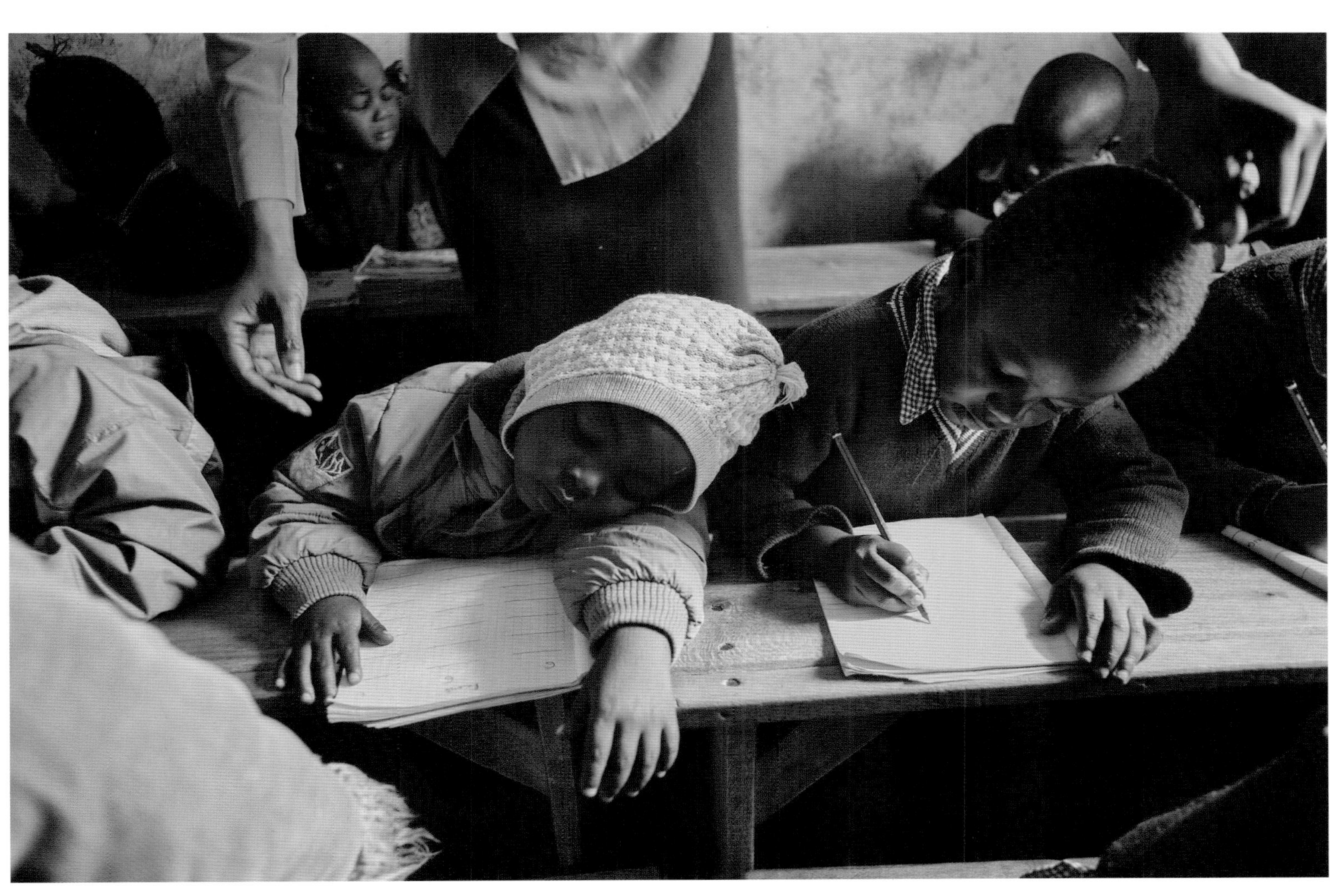

Renee Royale

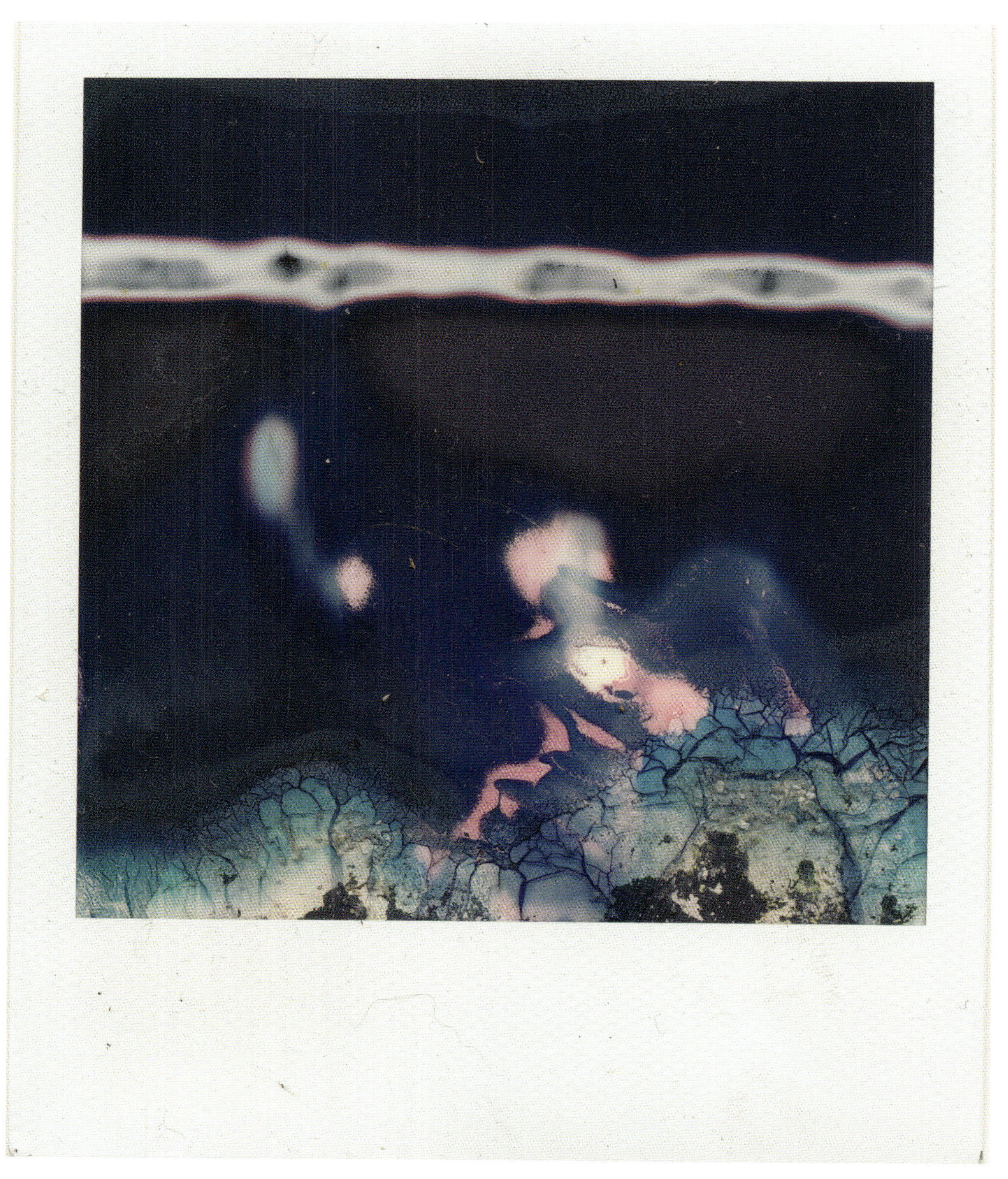

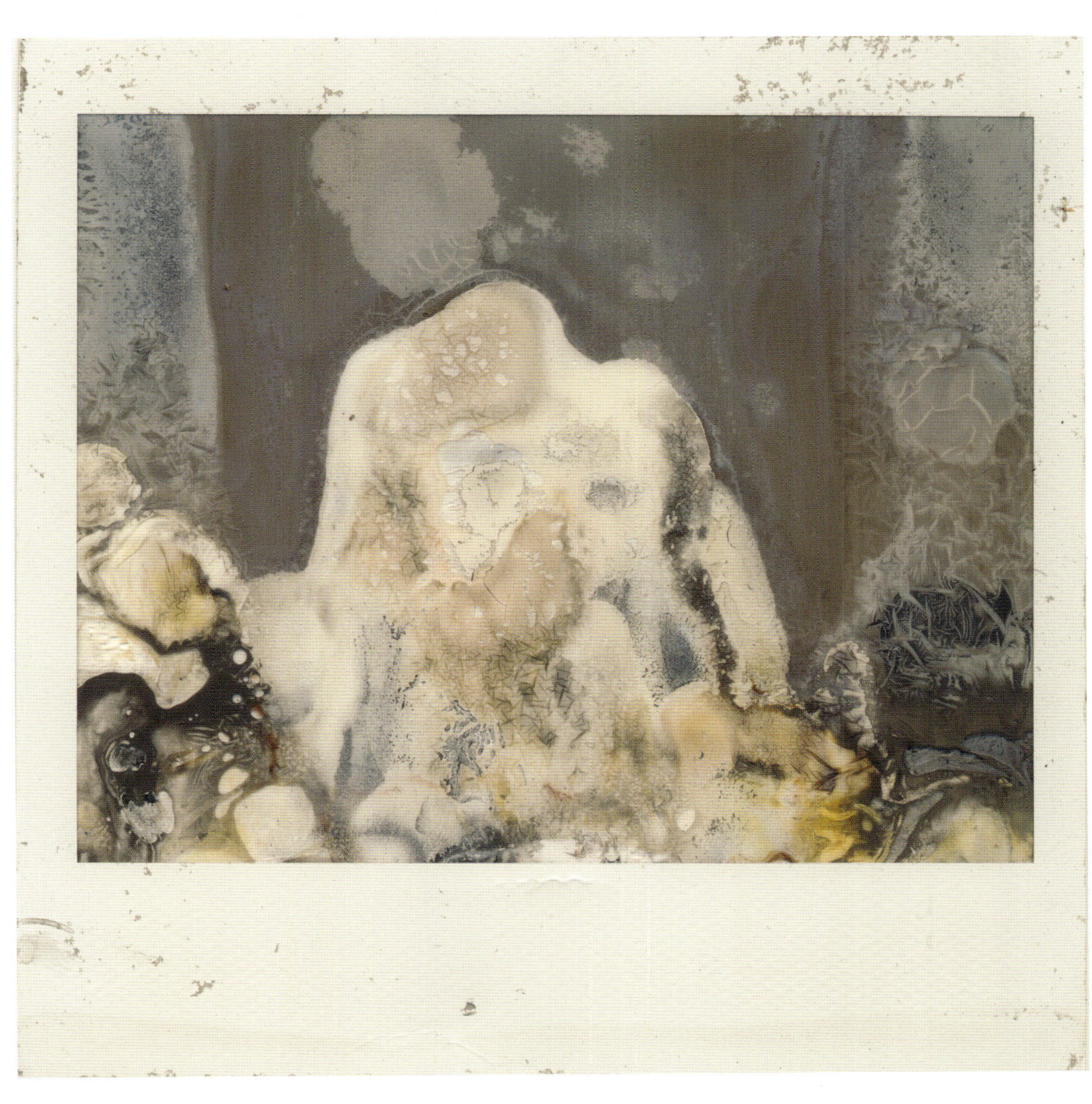

Remy "Bless the Freaks" Williams

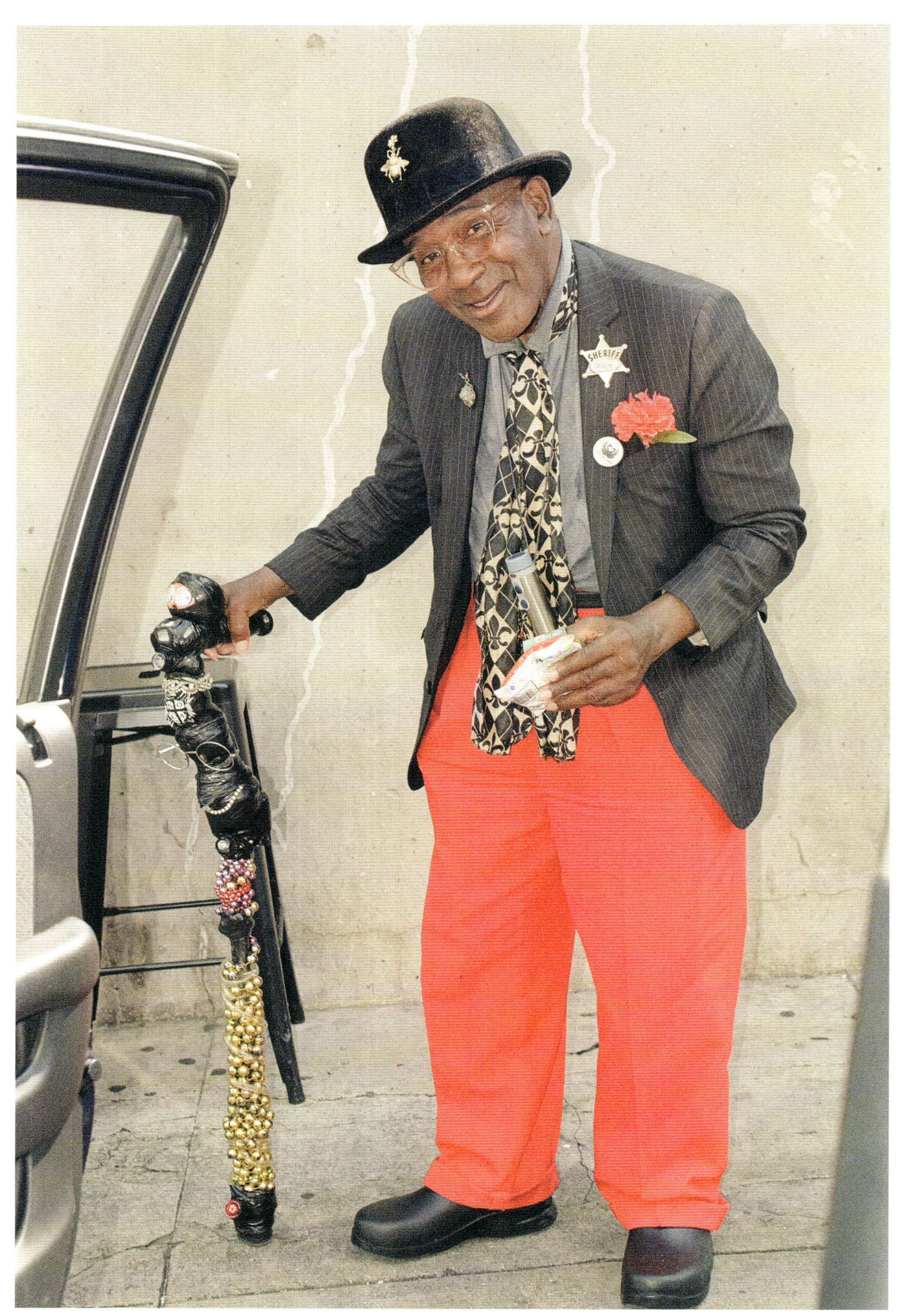

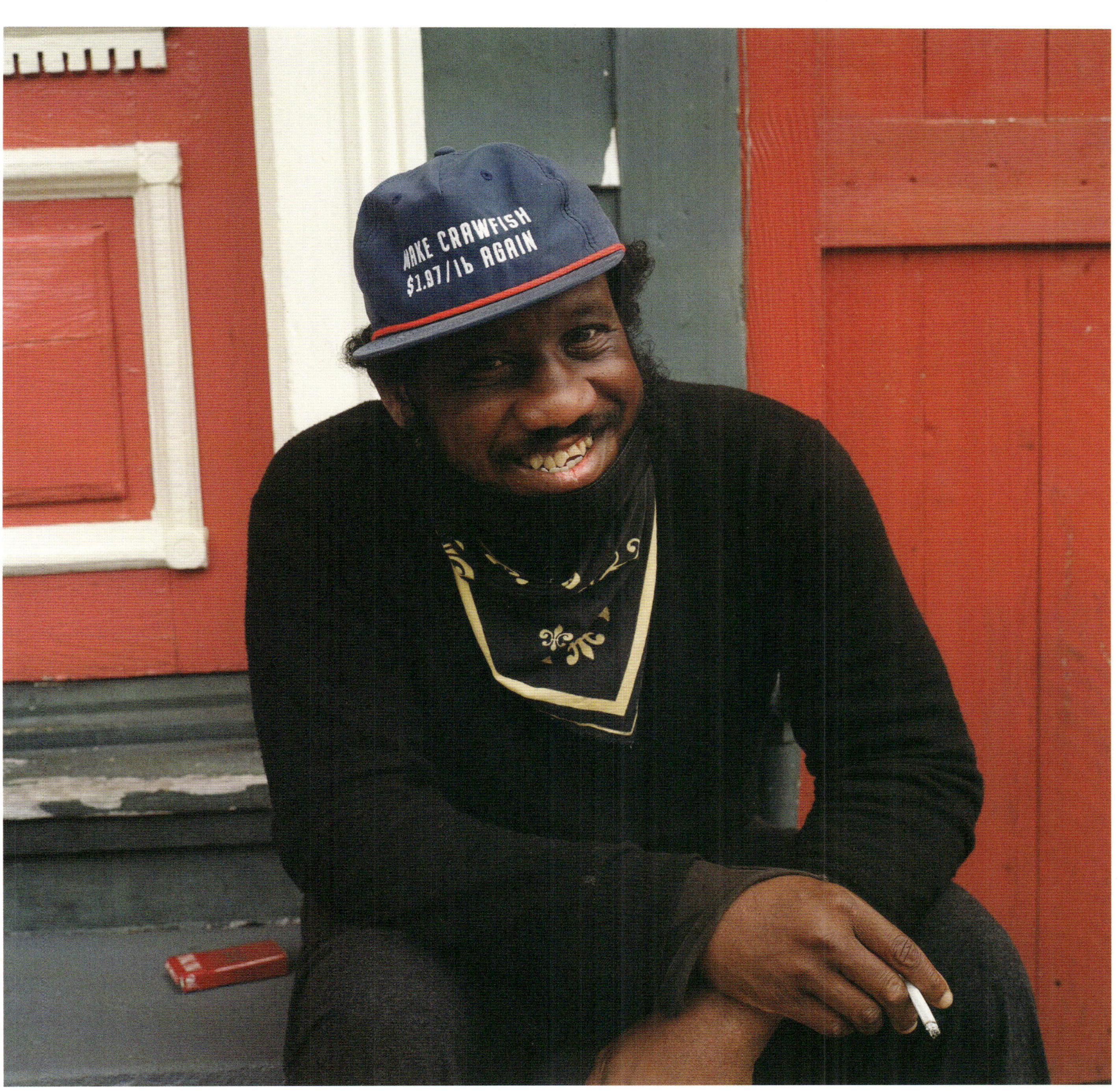
MAKE CRAWFISH
$1.97/lb AGAIN

Quinn Gordon

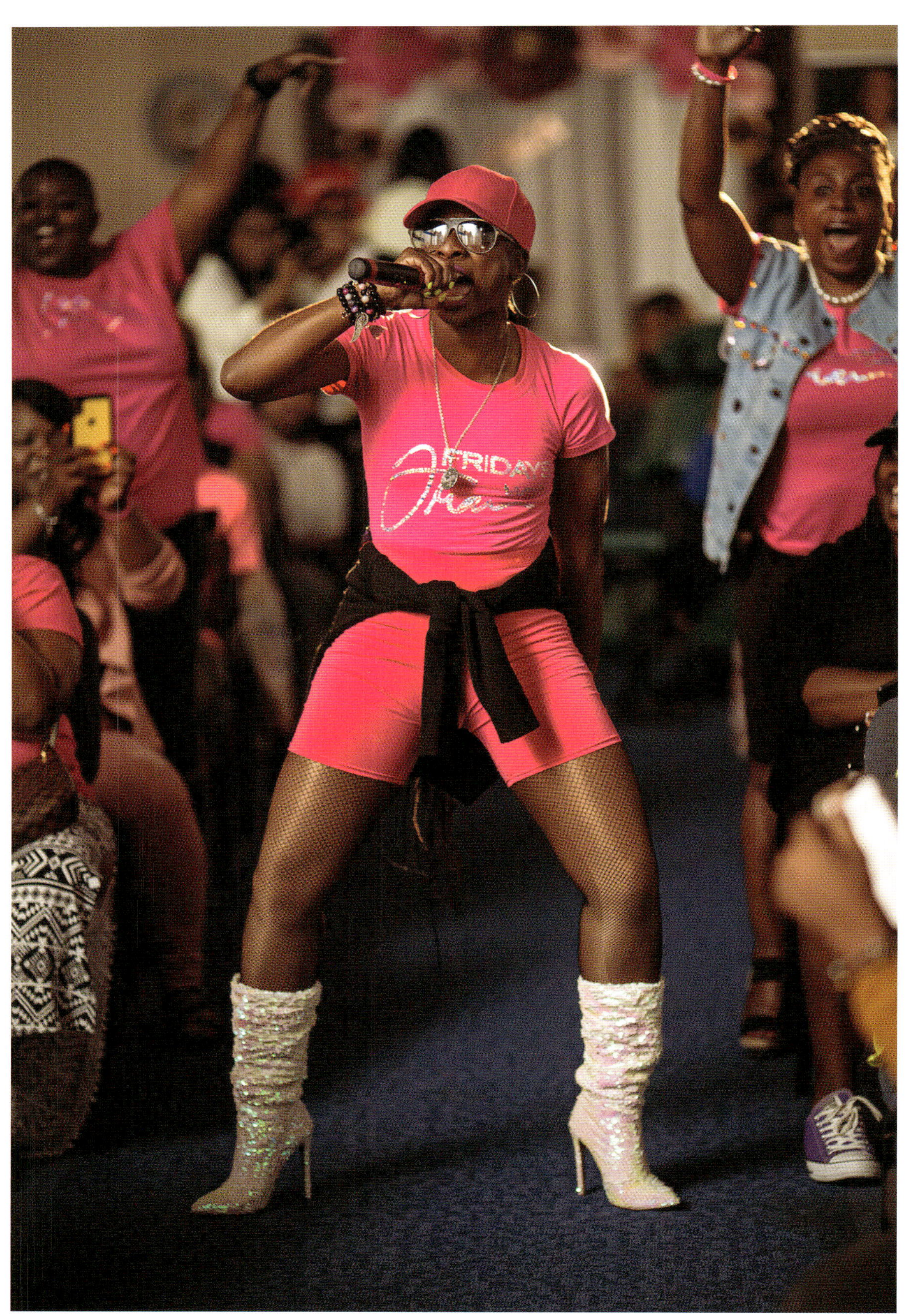

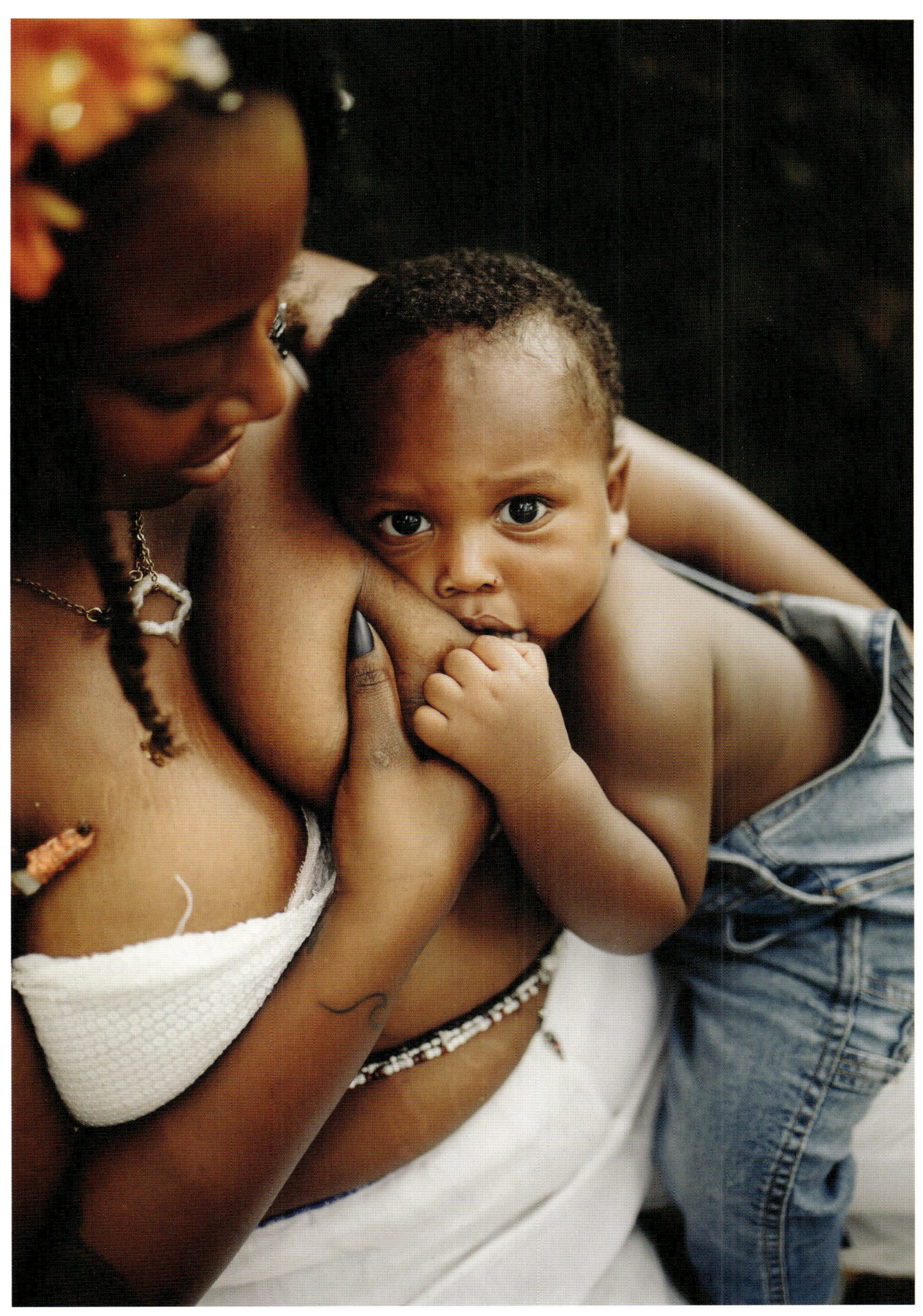

PRO$PER JONE$

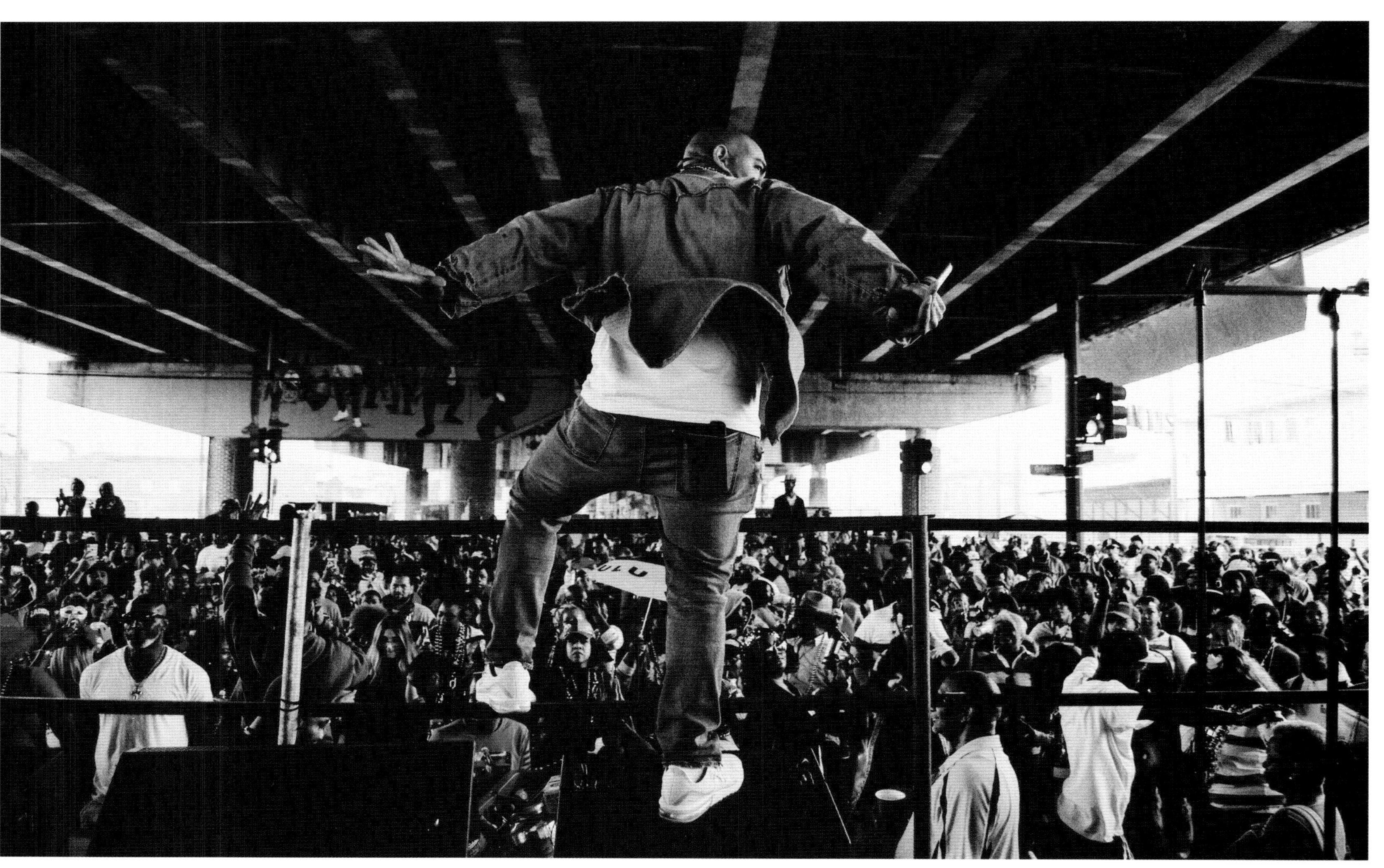

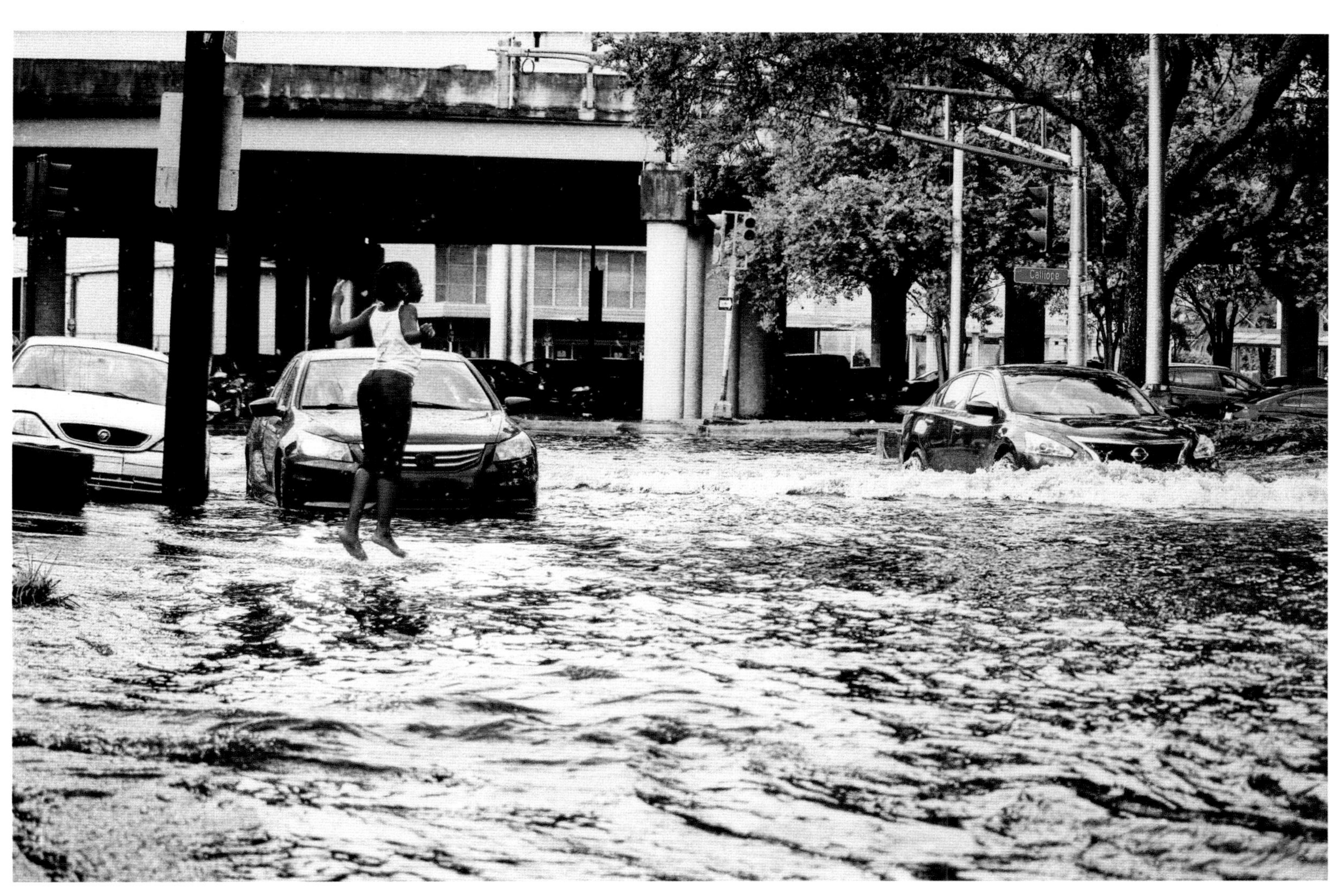
Calliope

Peter Nakhid

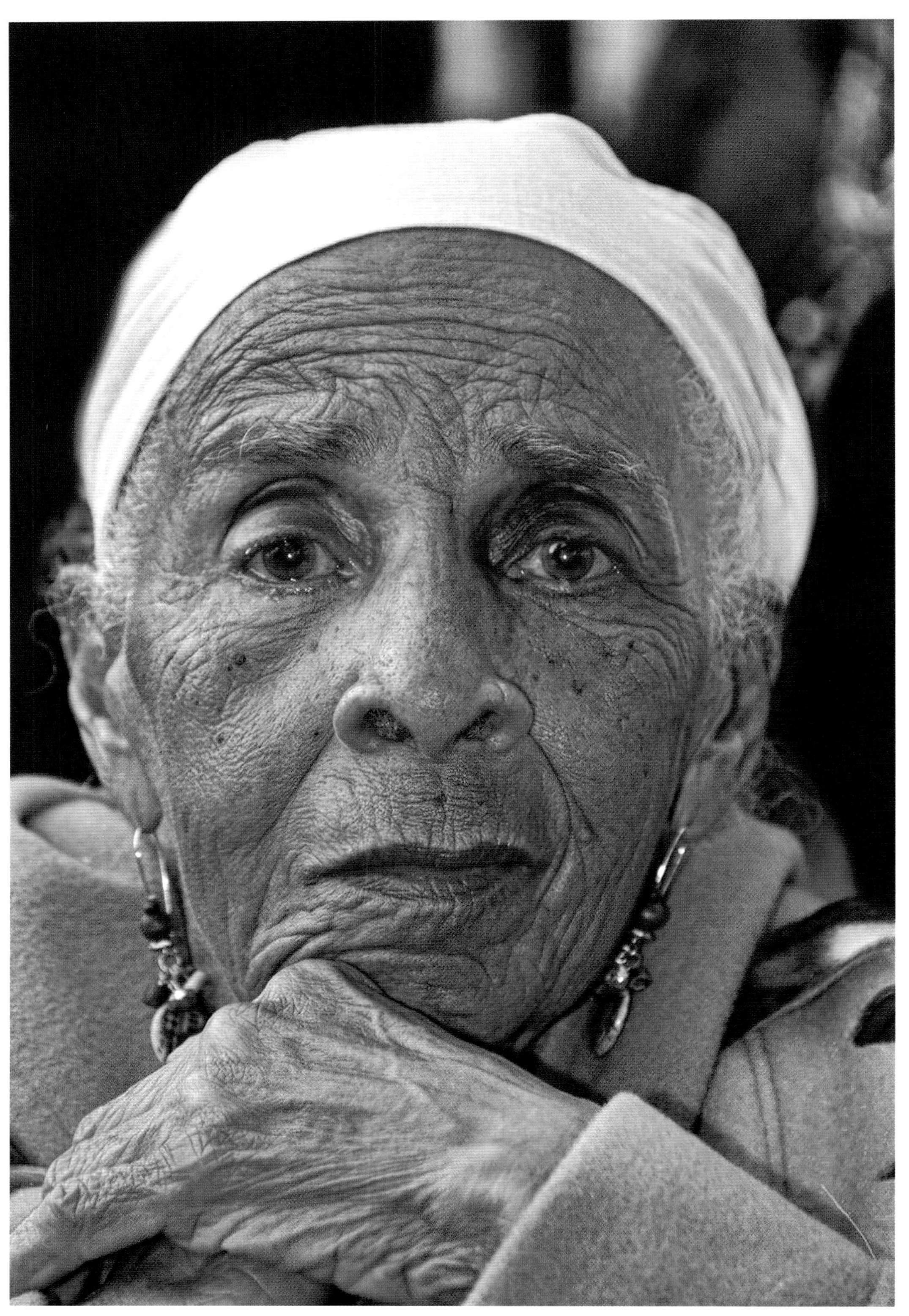

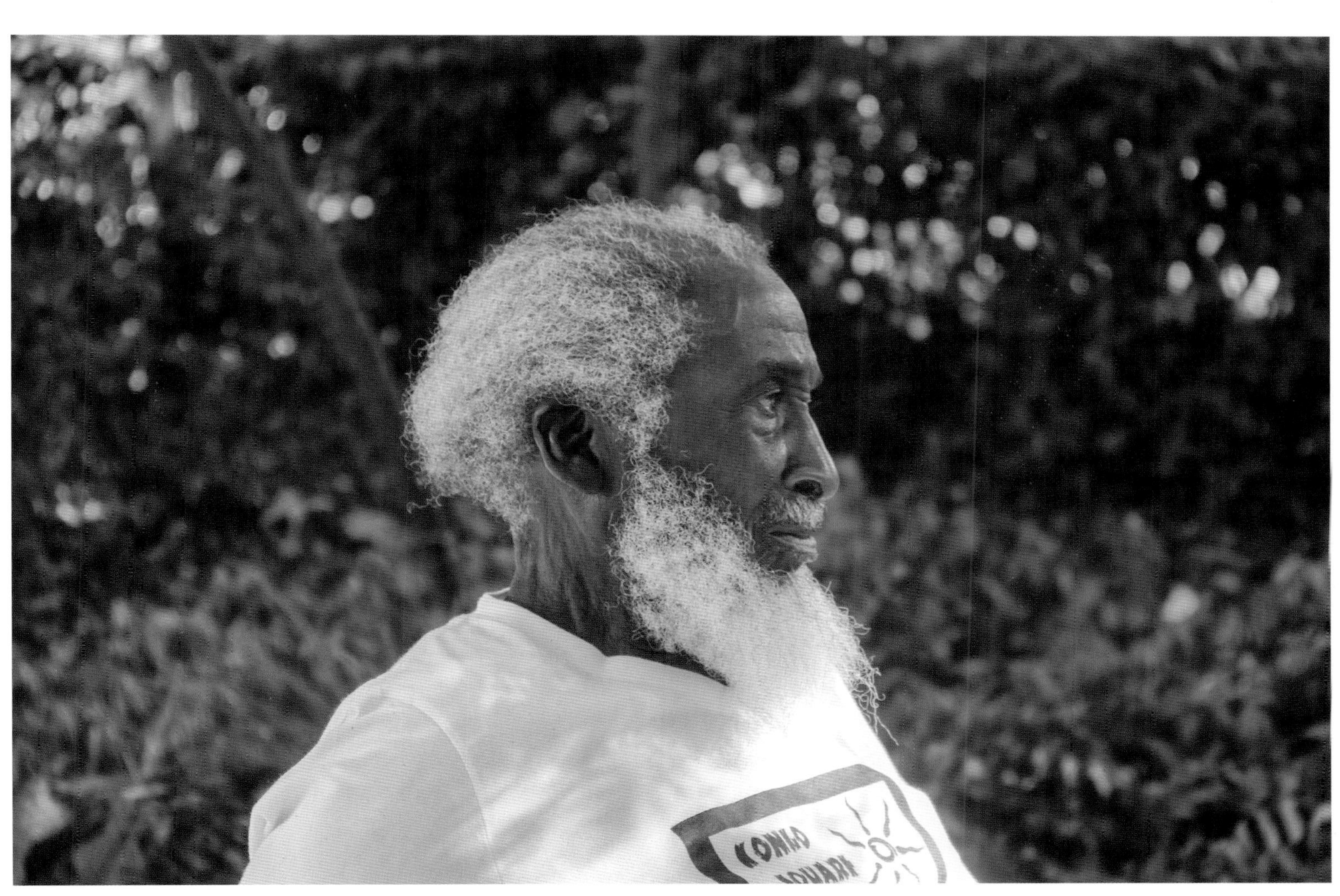

Peter G. Forest

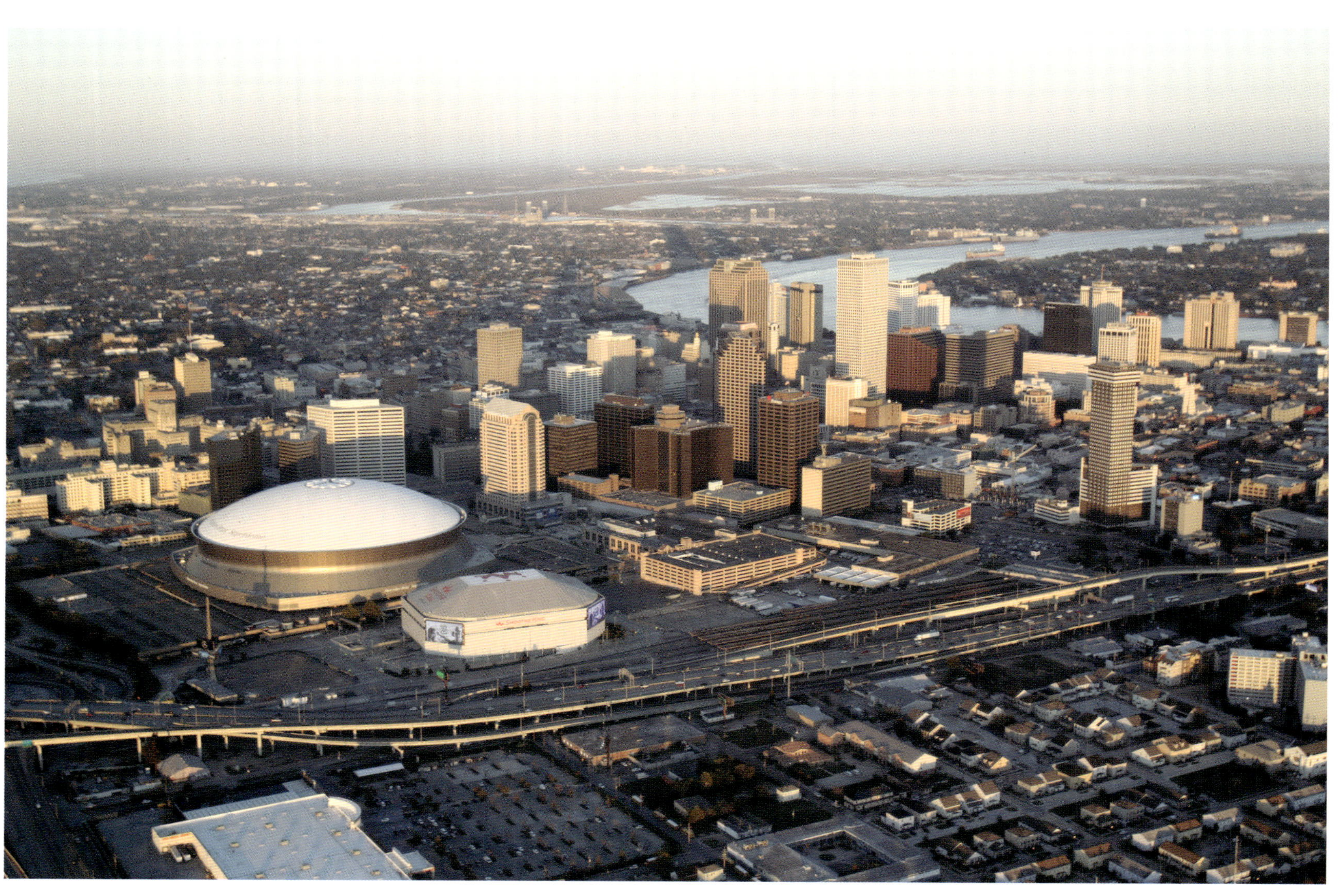

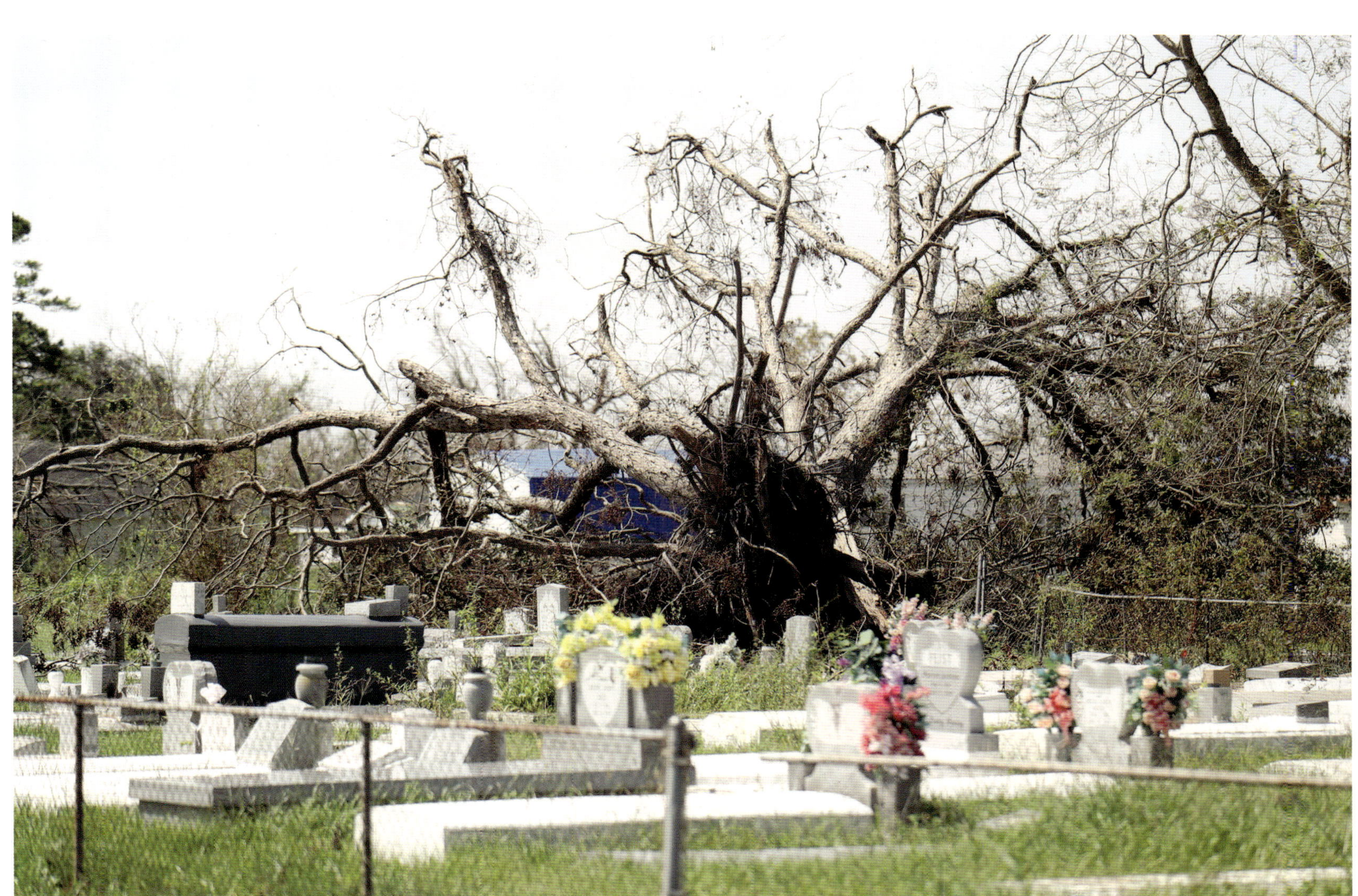

Othello Carter

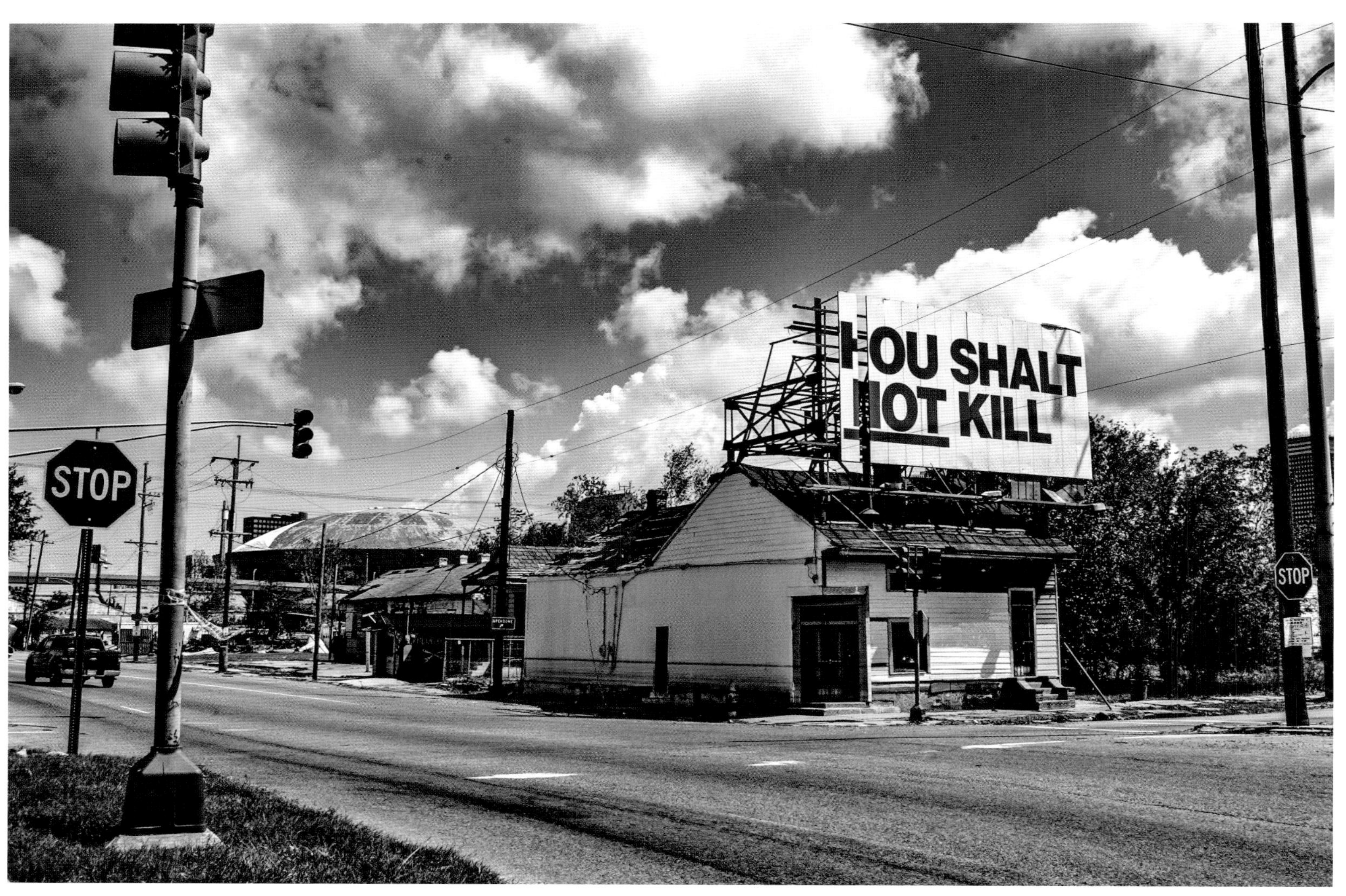

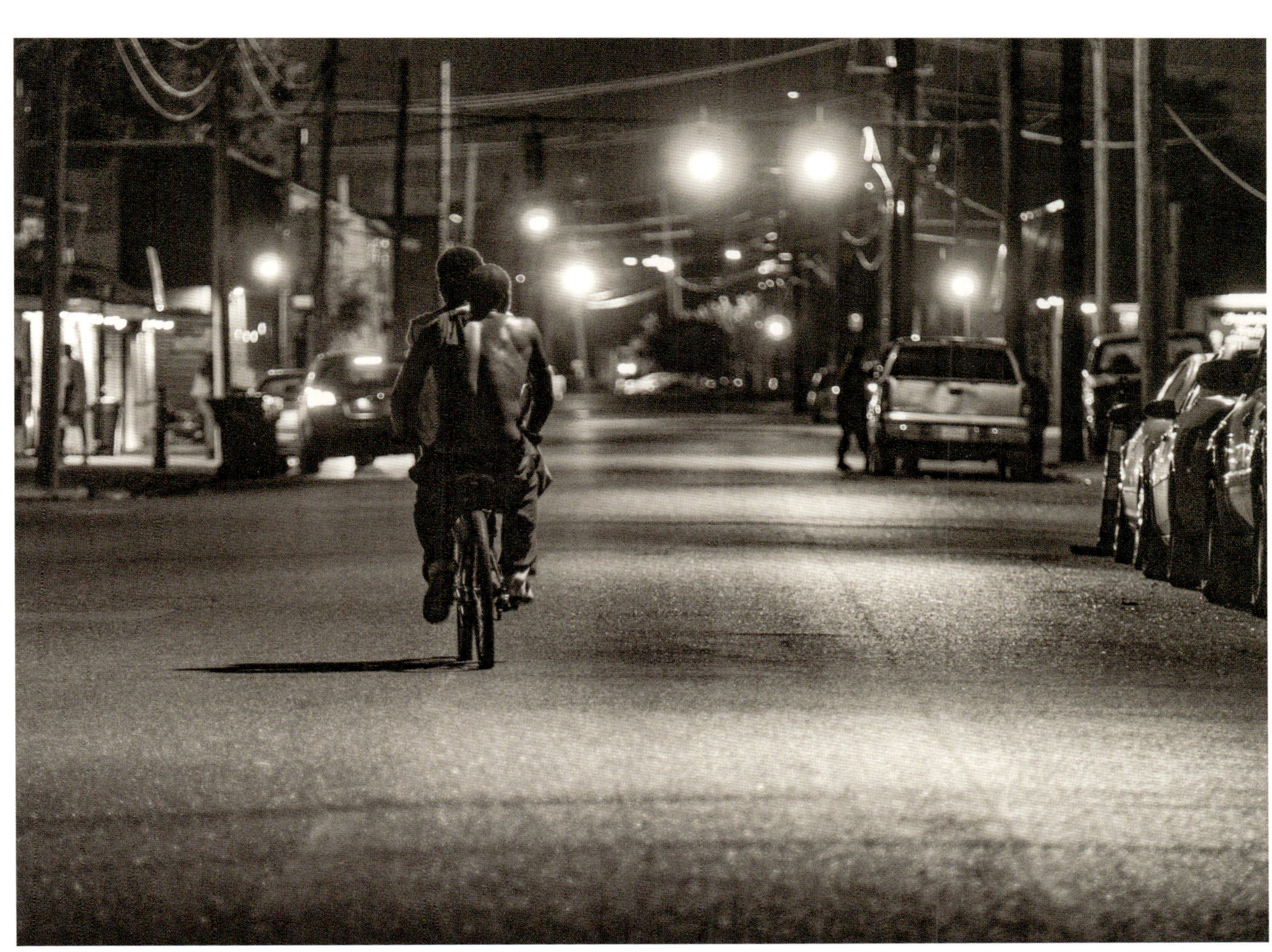

Nyejah Bolds

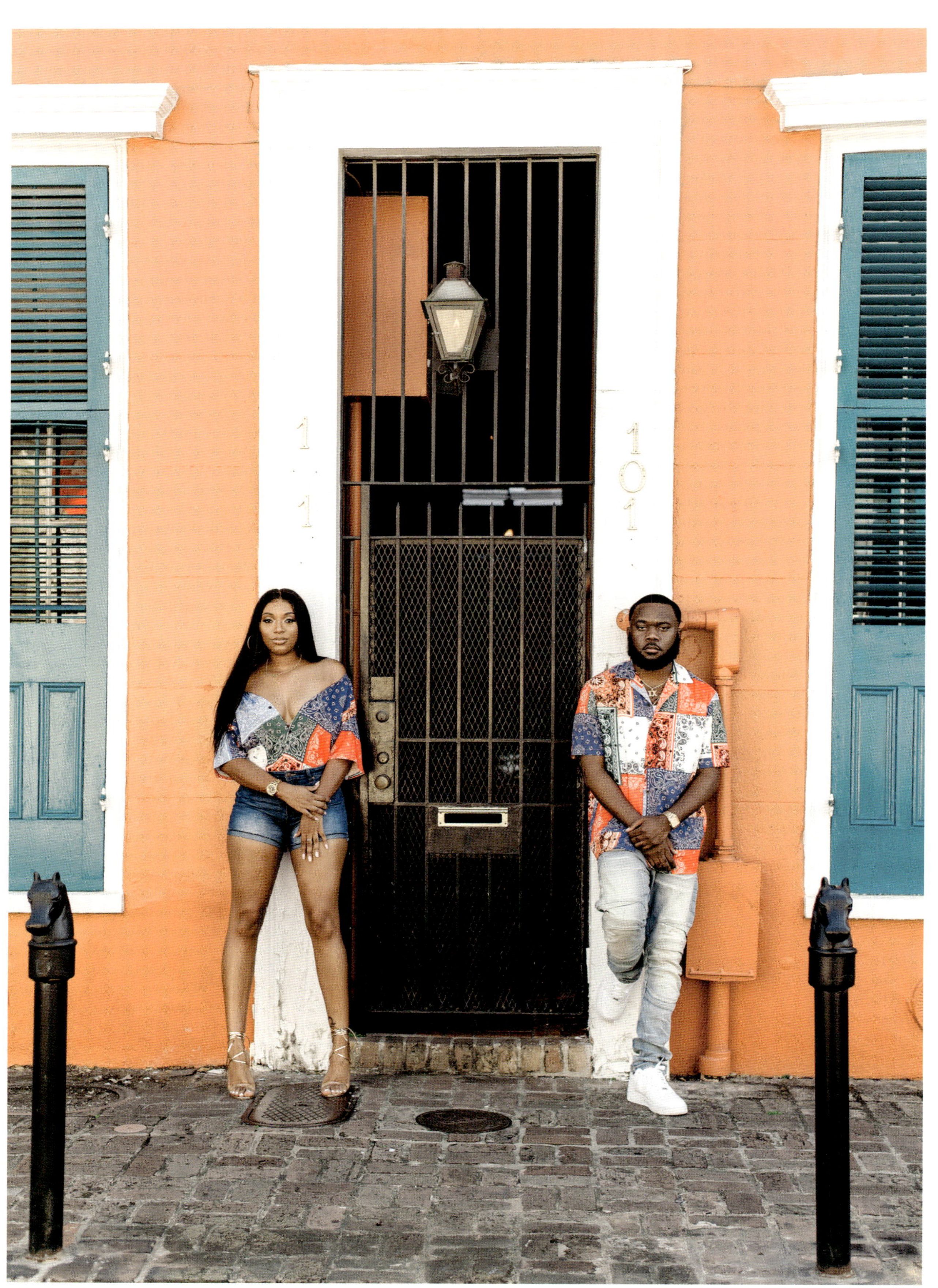

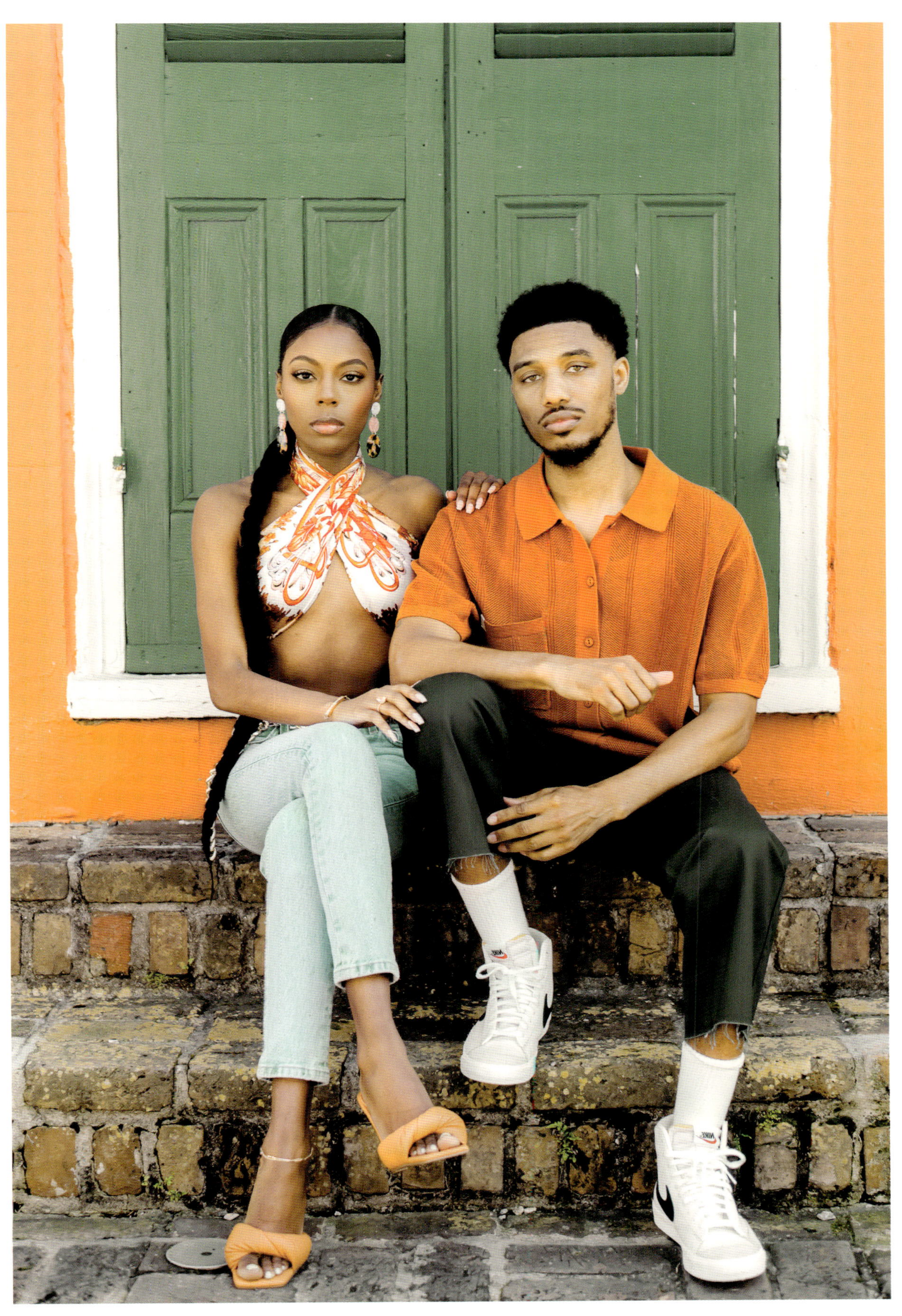

Norman R. Smith

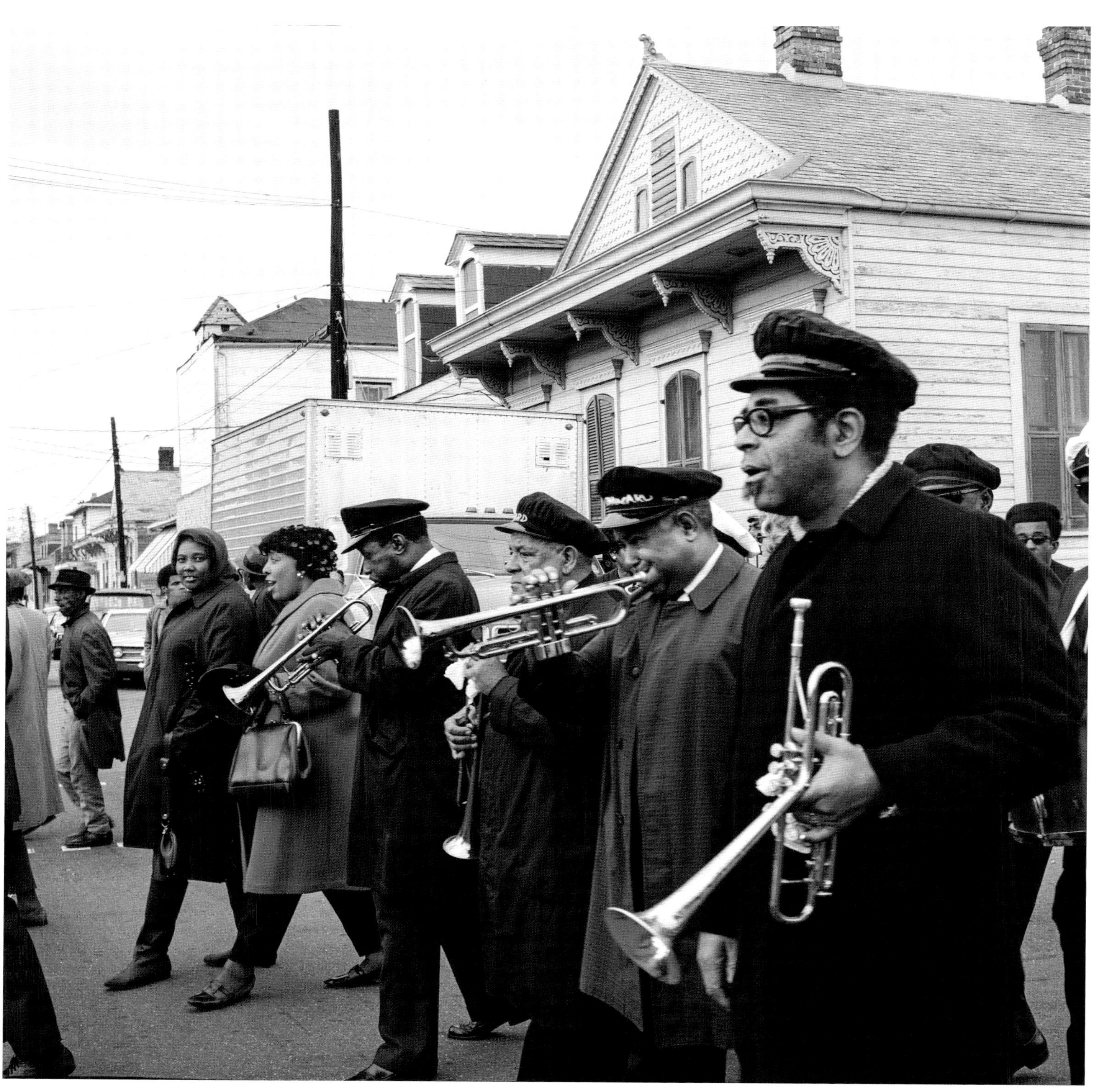

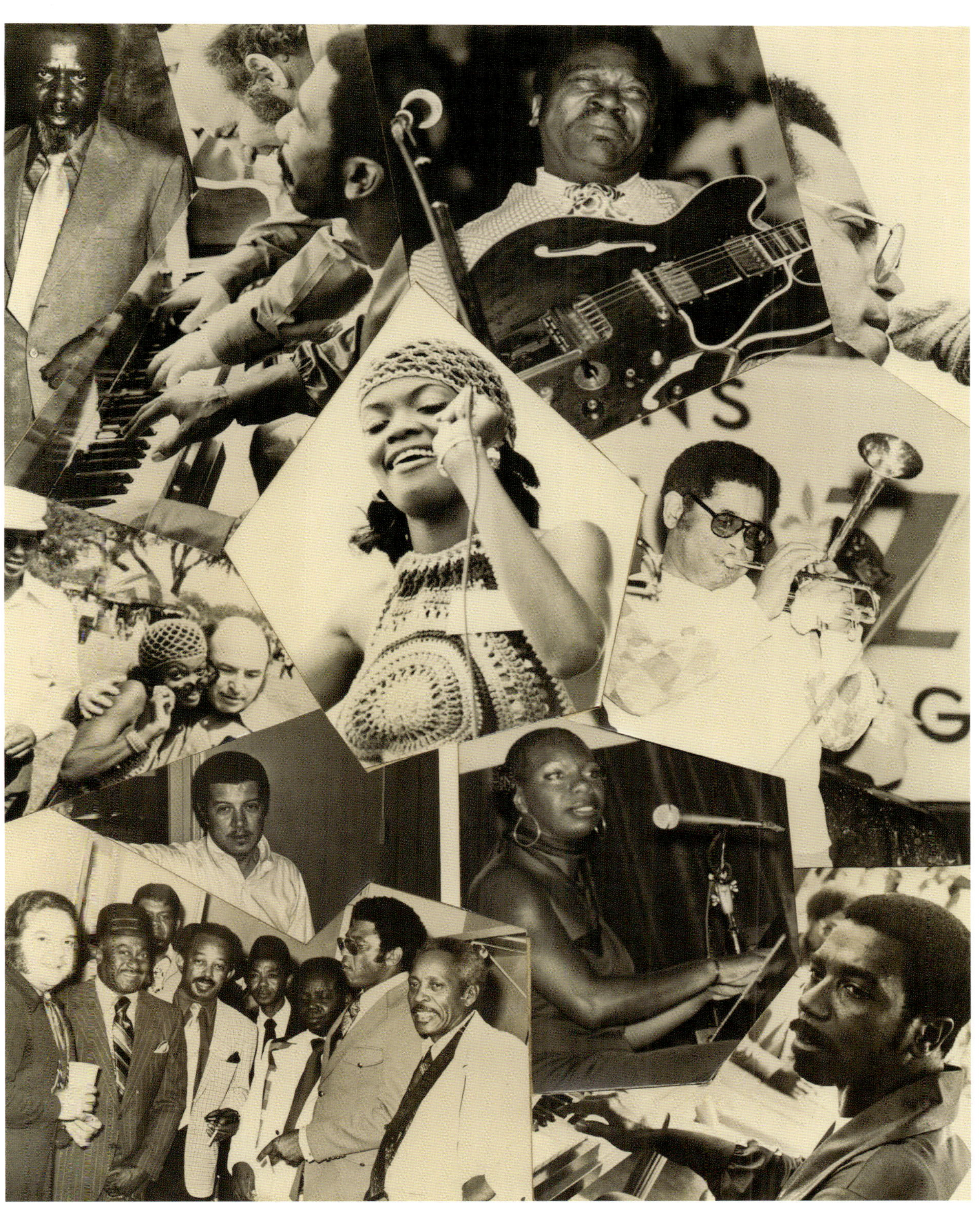

Nikki Brown

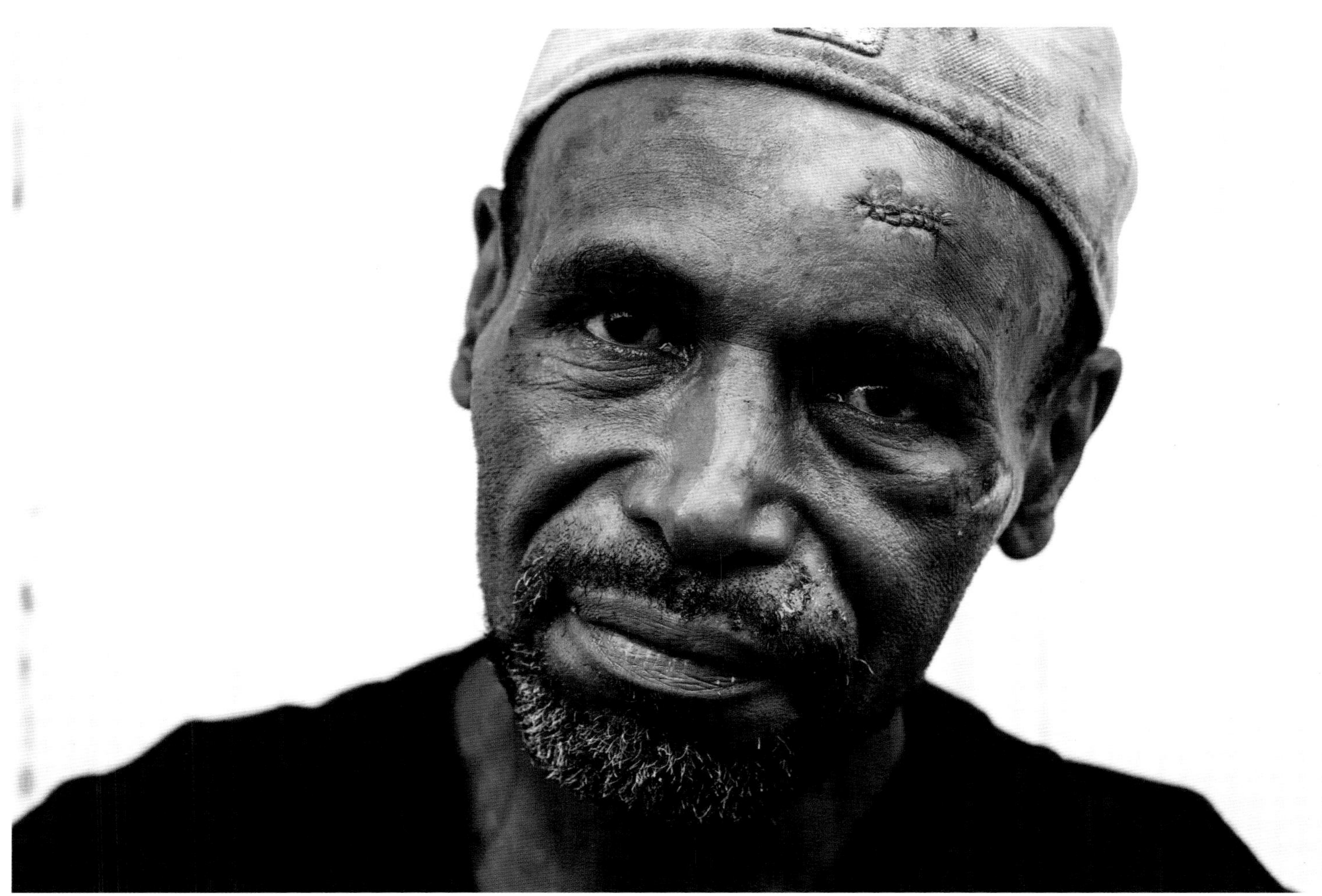

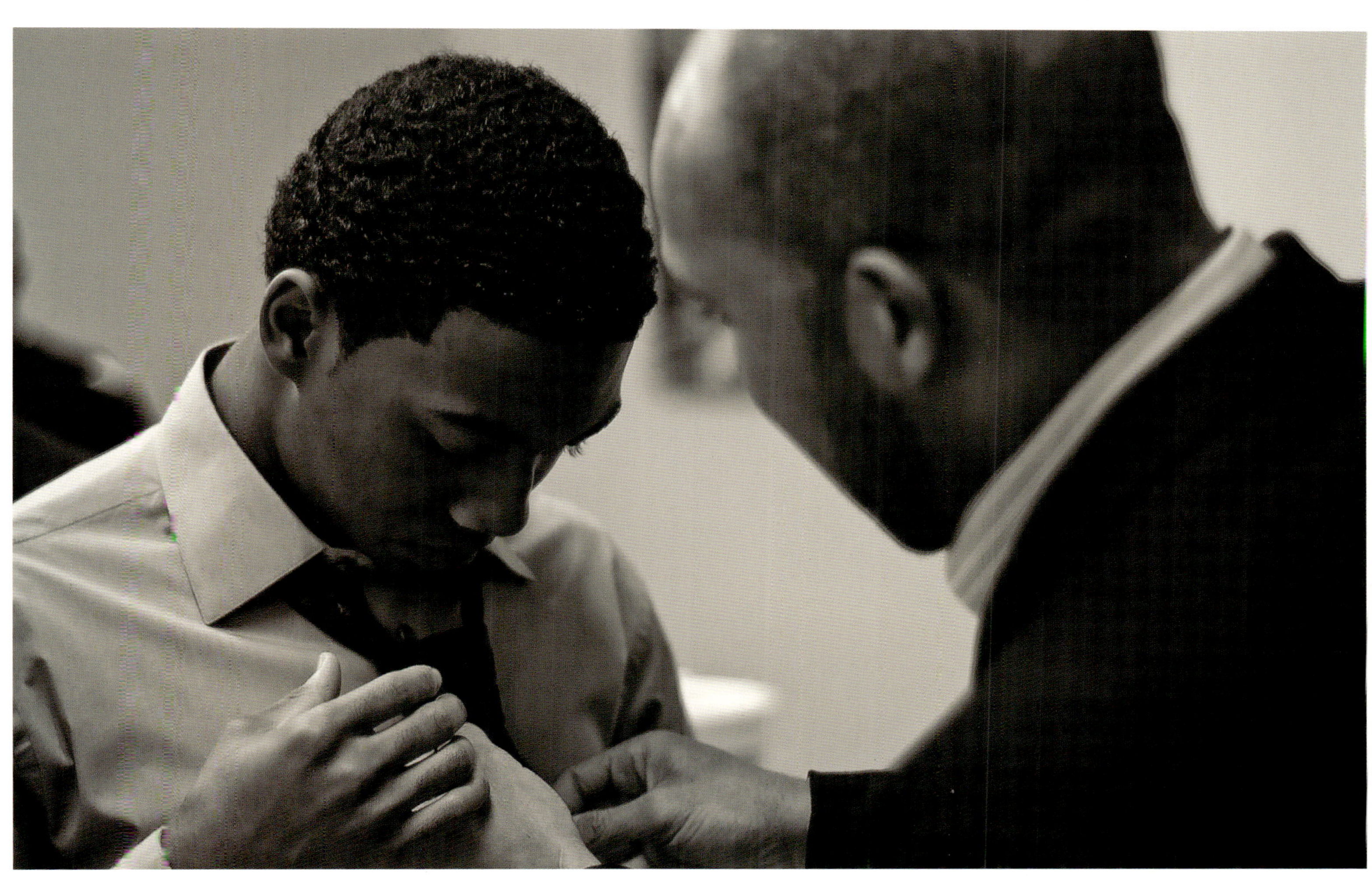

Nicholas Anderson Hall & Lindsey Smith

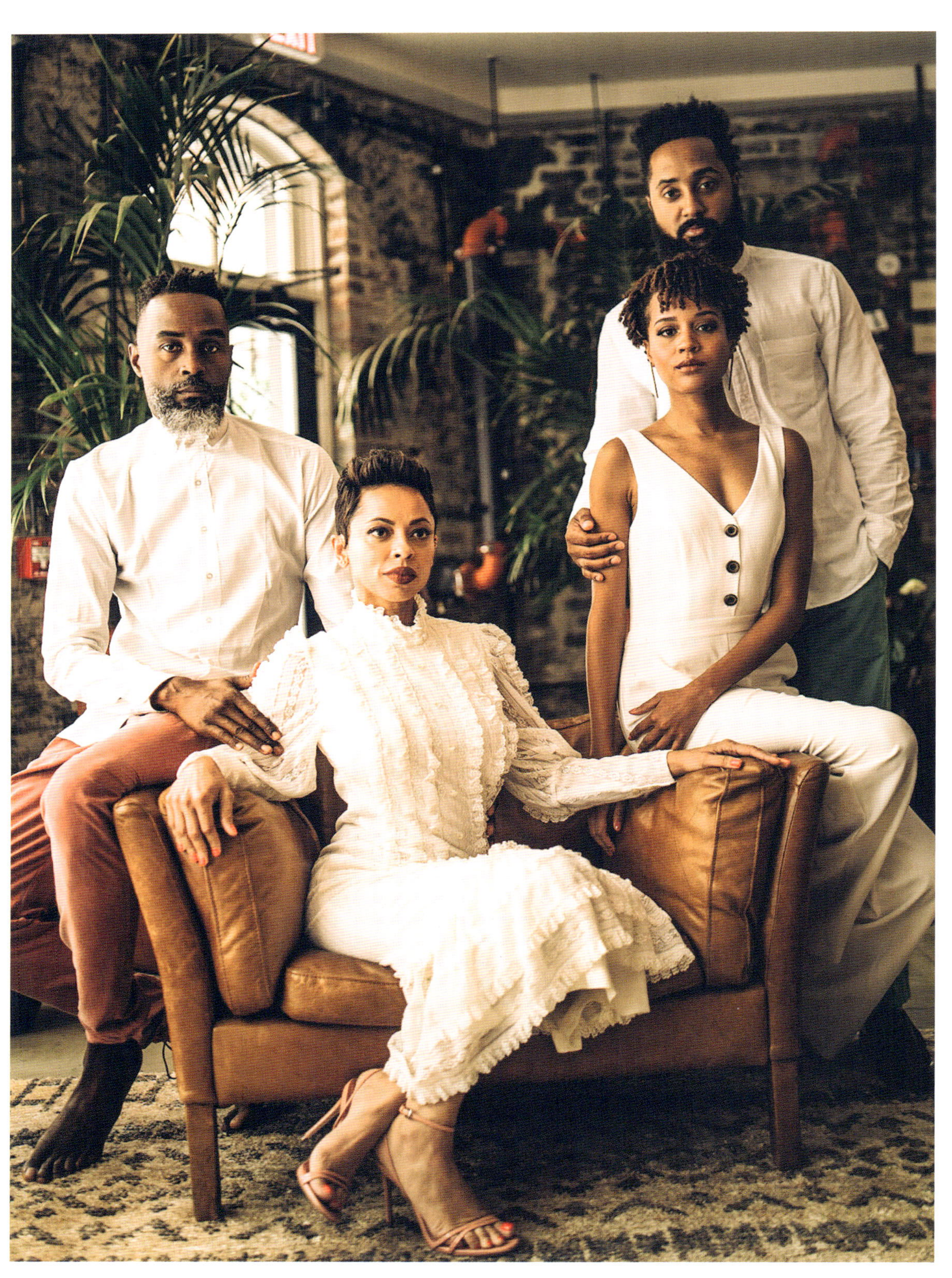

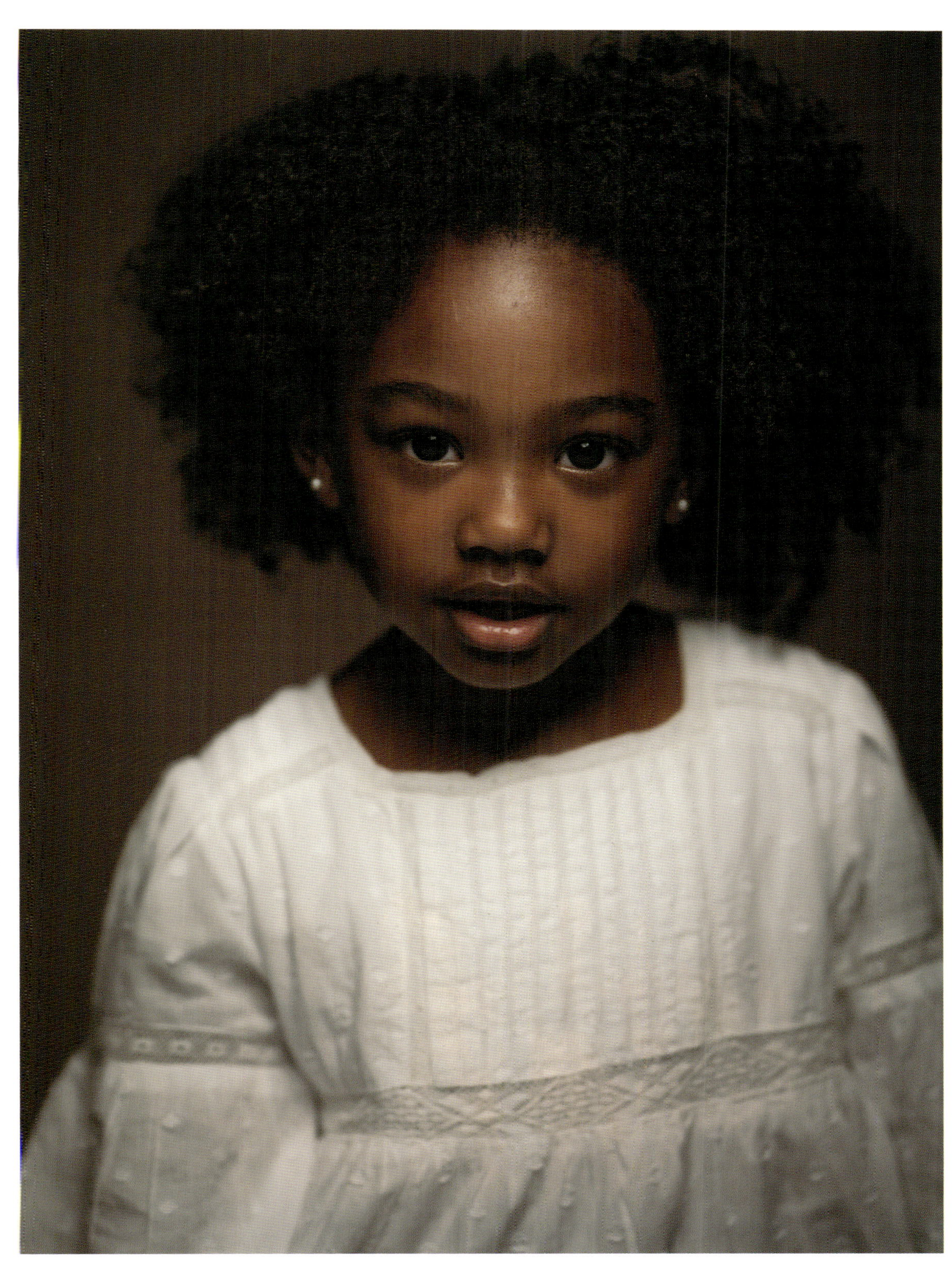

Najah Mushatt

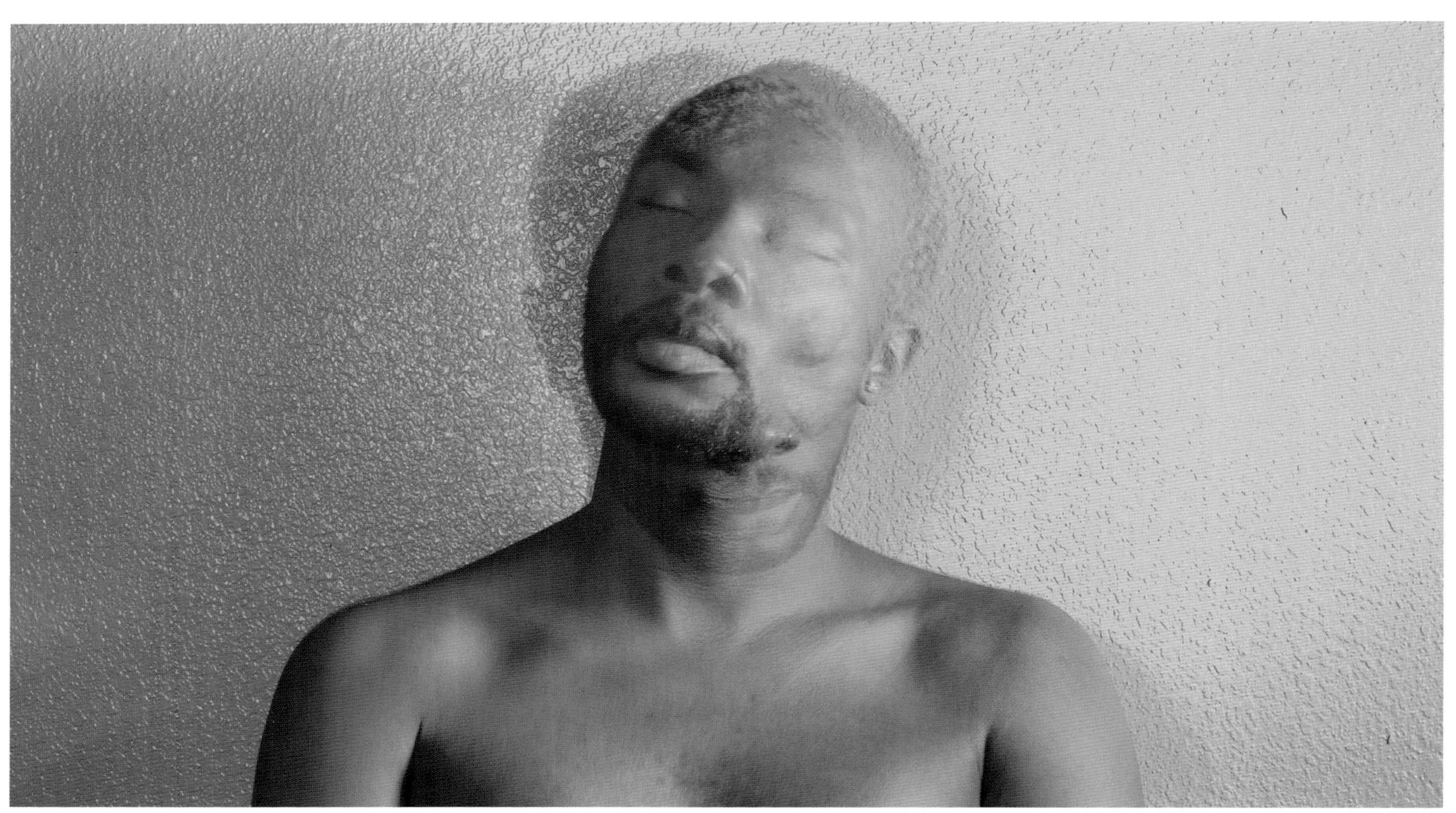

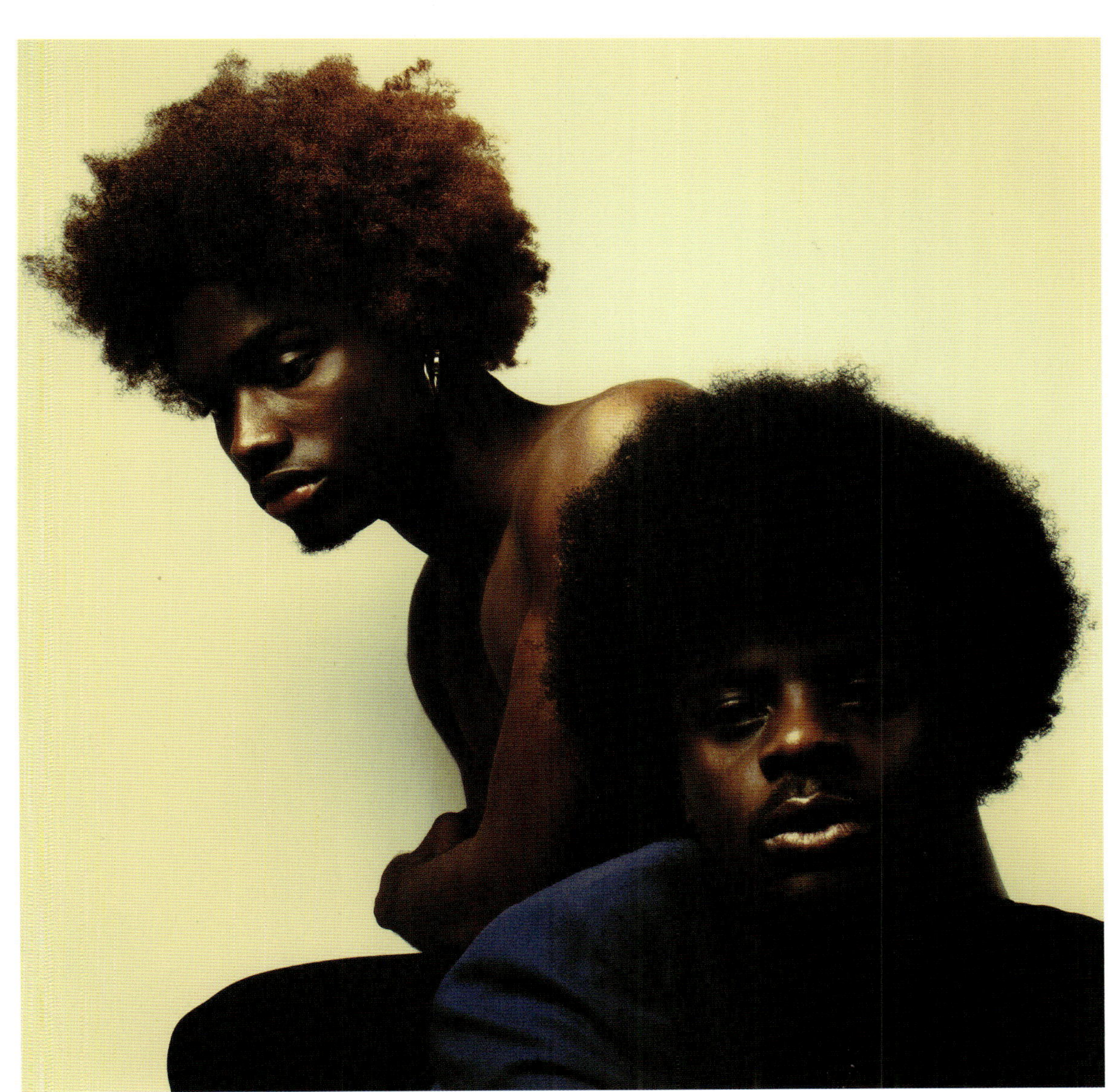

Tod Smith

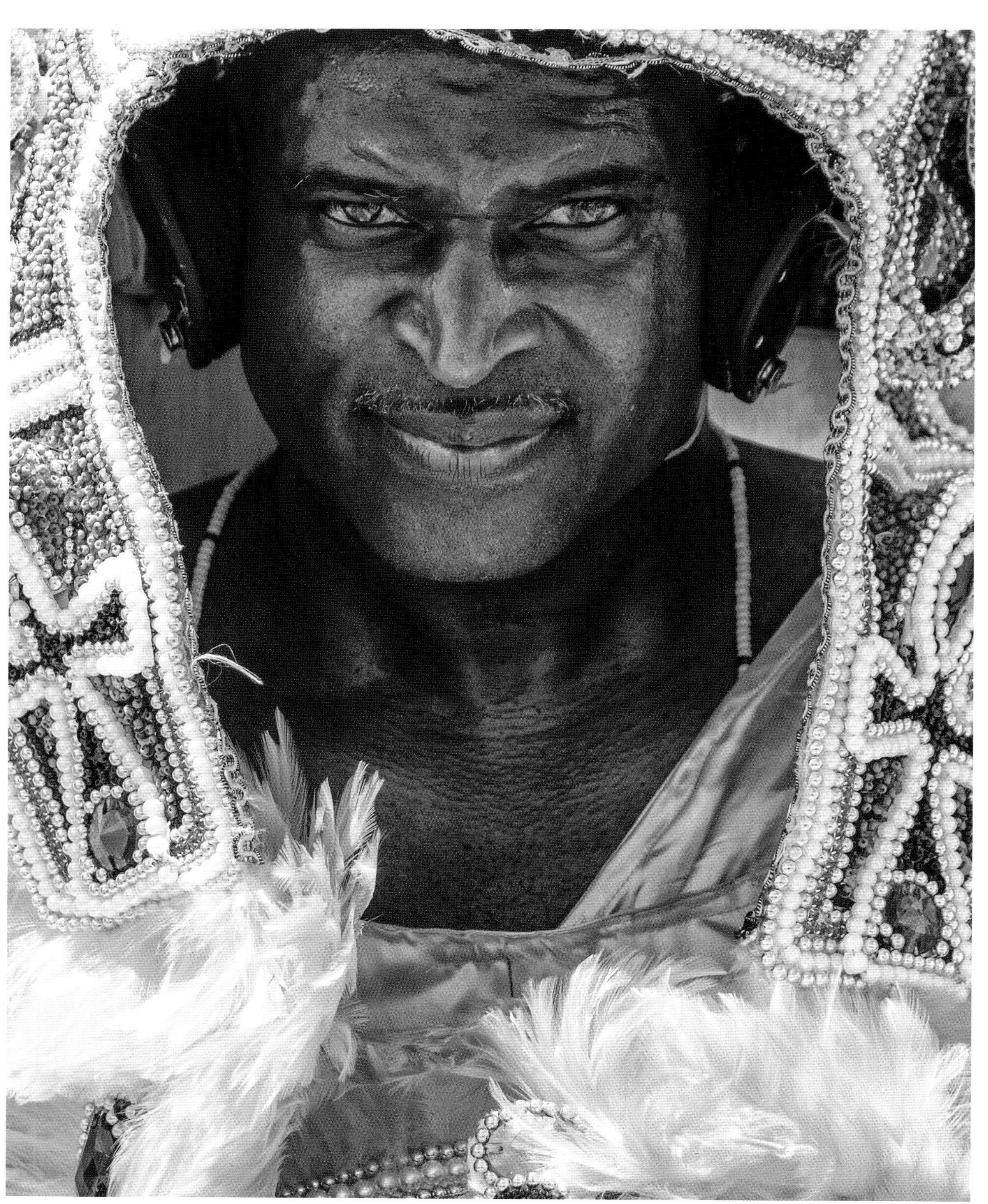

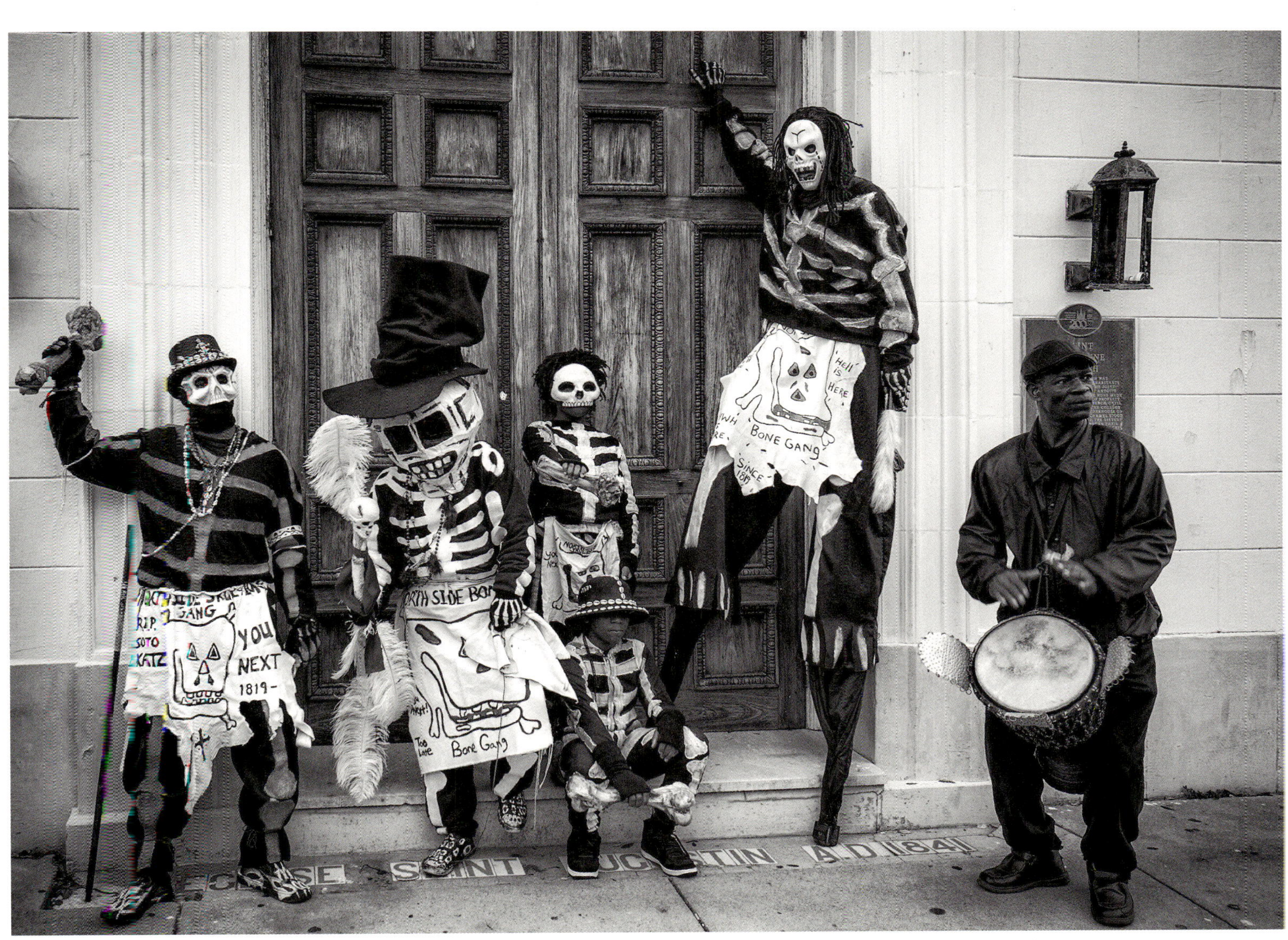
R.I.P.
SOTO
KATZ
YOU
NEXT
1819-
Bone Gang
HELL
IS
HERE
BONE GANG

Terri A. Mimms

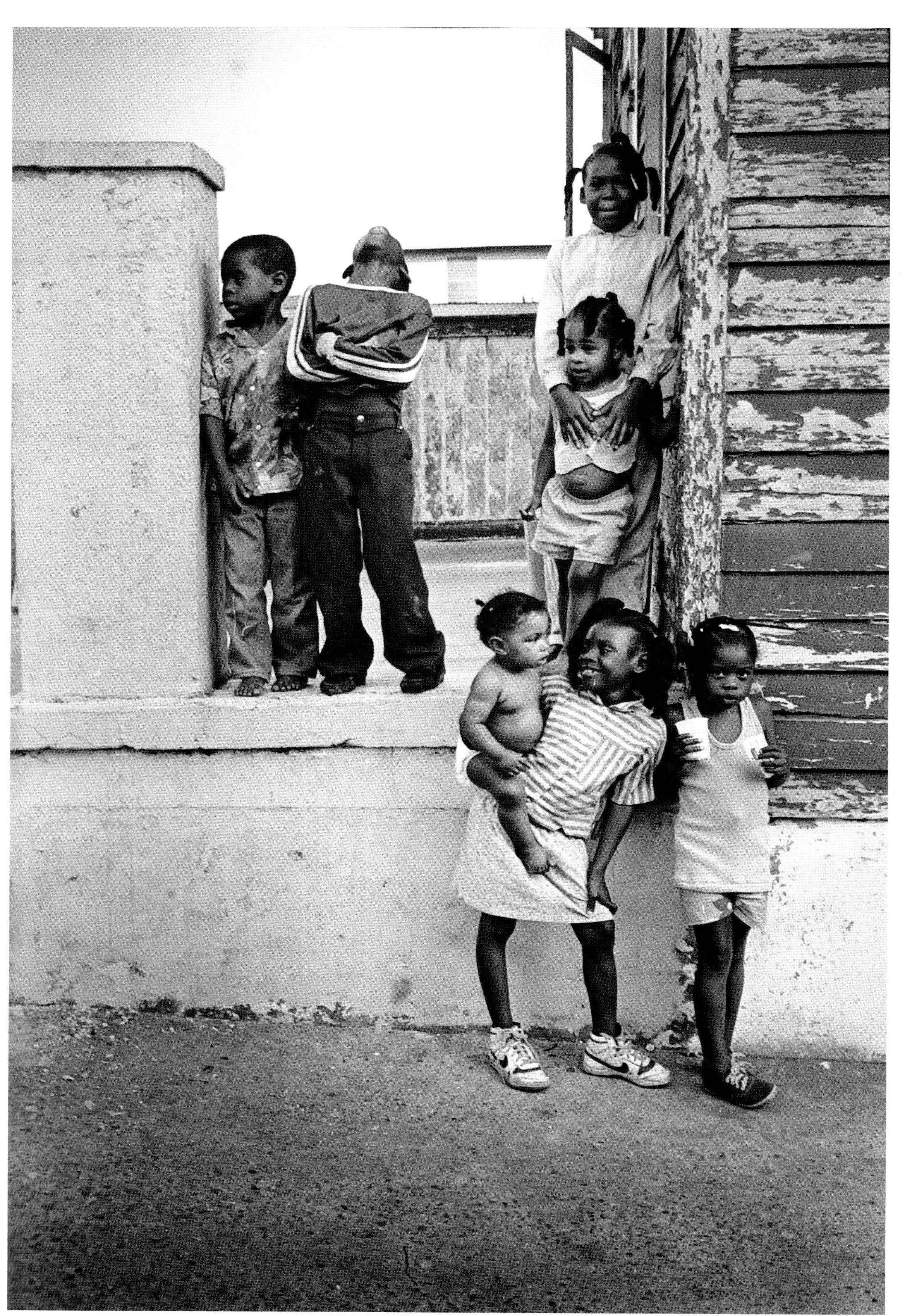

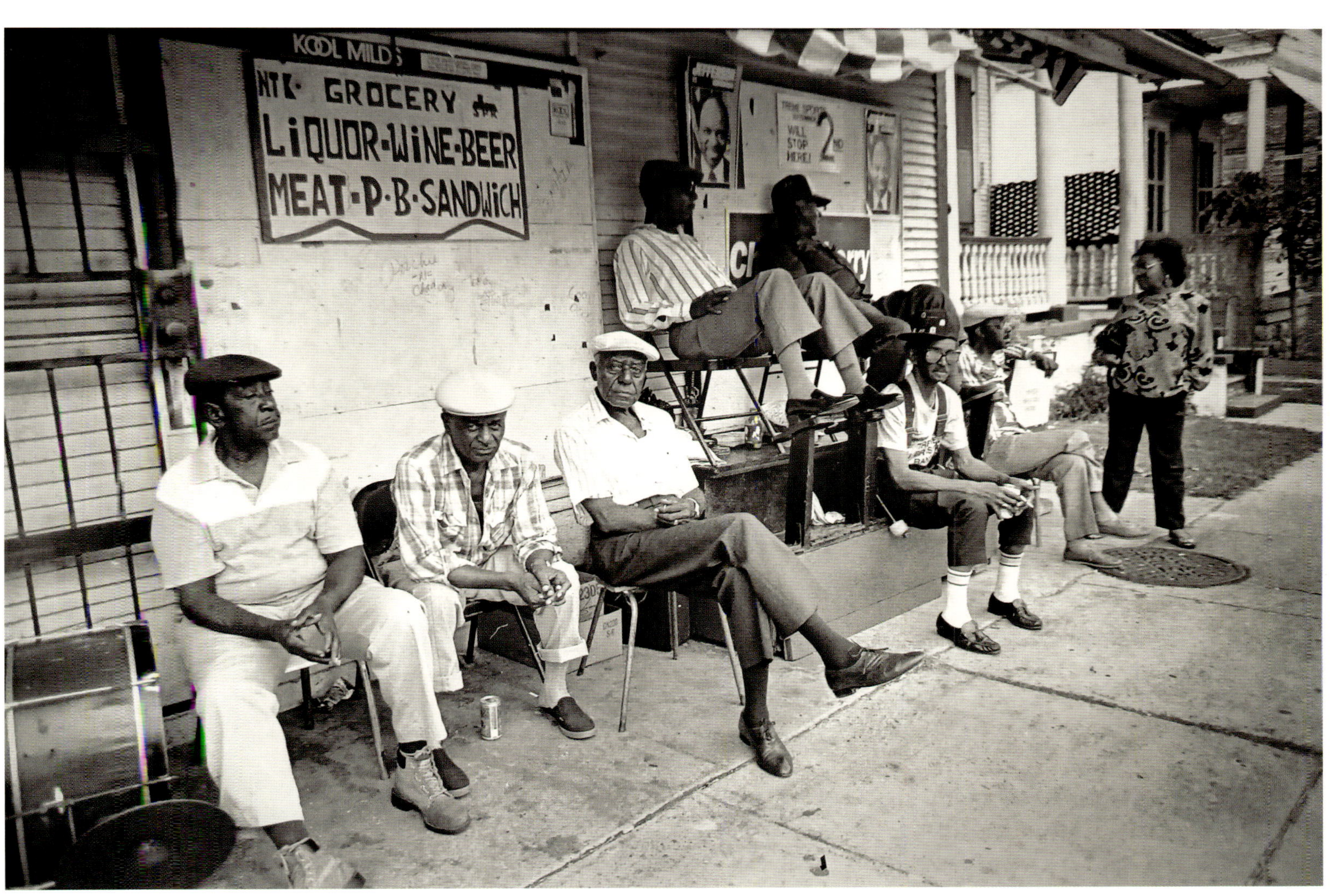

KOOL MILDS
GROCERY
LIQUOR-WINE-BEER
MEAT-P-B-SANDWICH
WILL STOP HERE!

Ted Quant

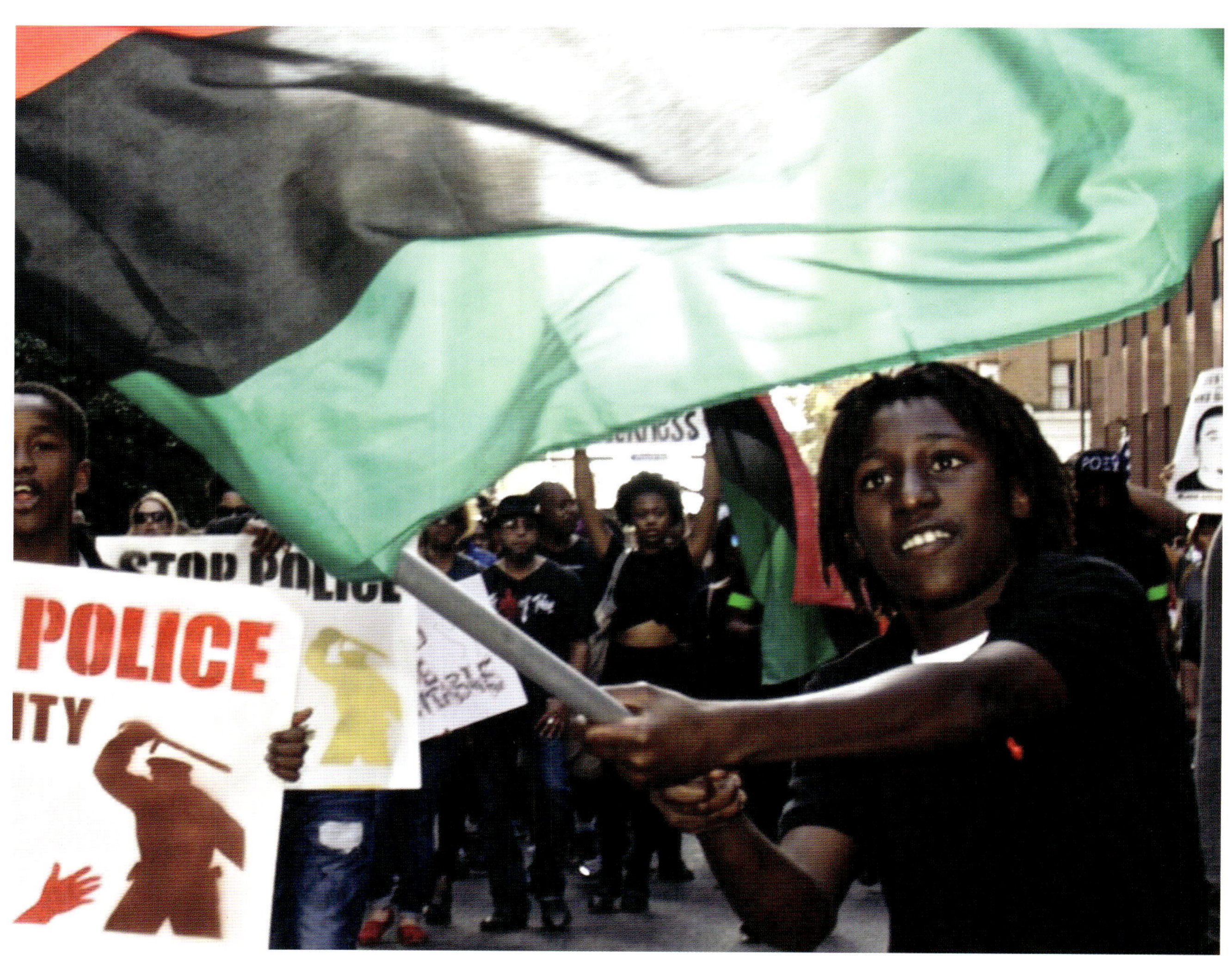

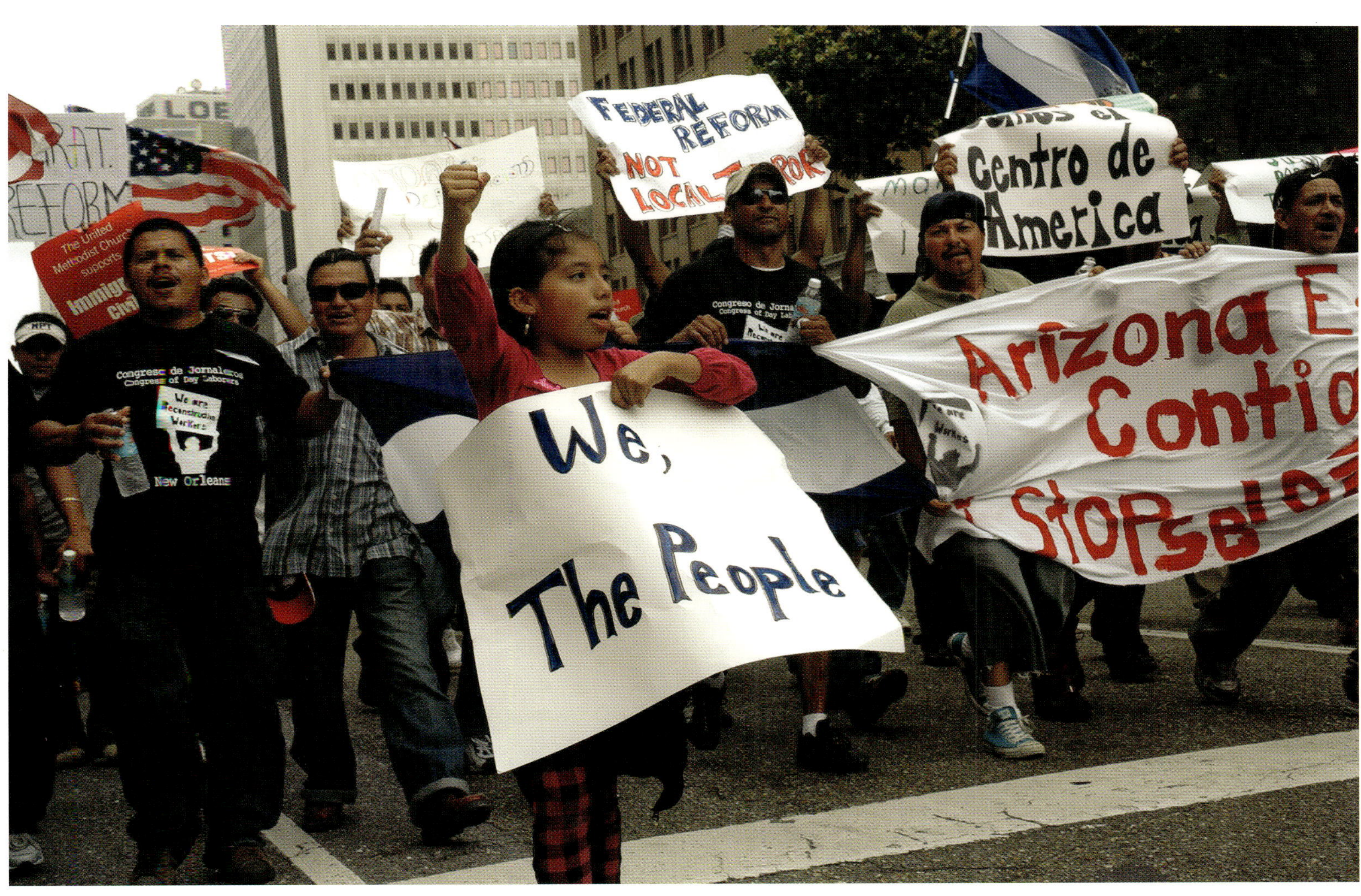

FEDERAL REFORM
NOT
LOCAL
Centro de
America
We,
The People
The United
Methodist Church
supports
Congreso de Jornaleros
Congress of Day Laborers
New Orleans

Taylor Simone

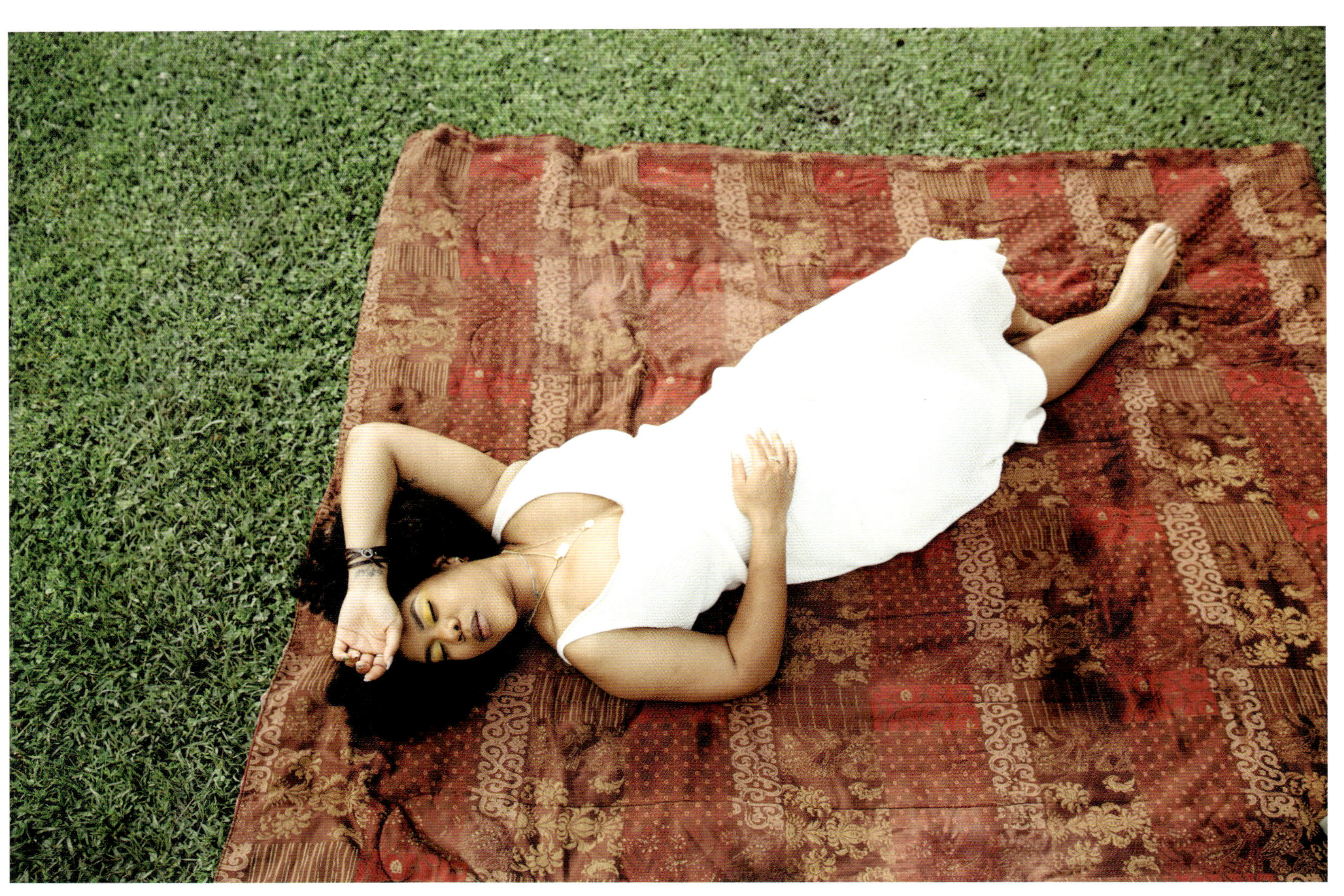

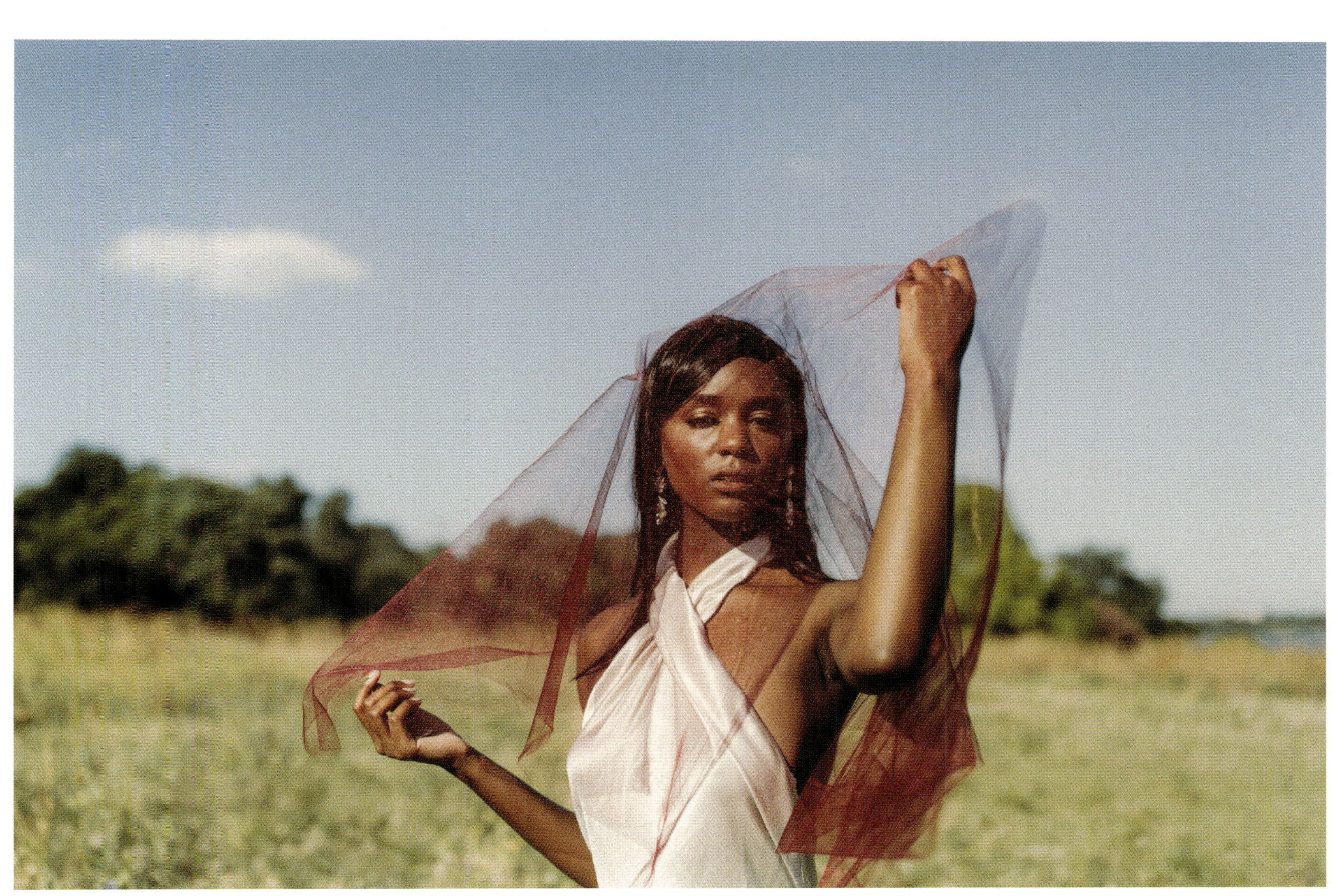

Sorena Briley

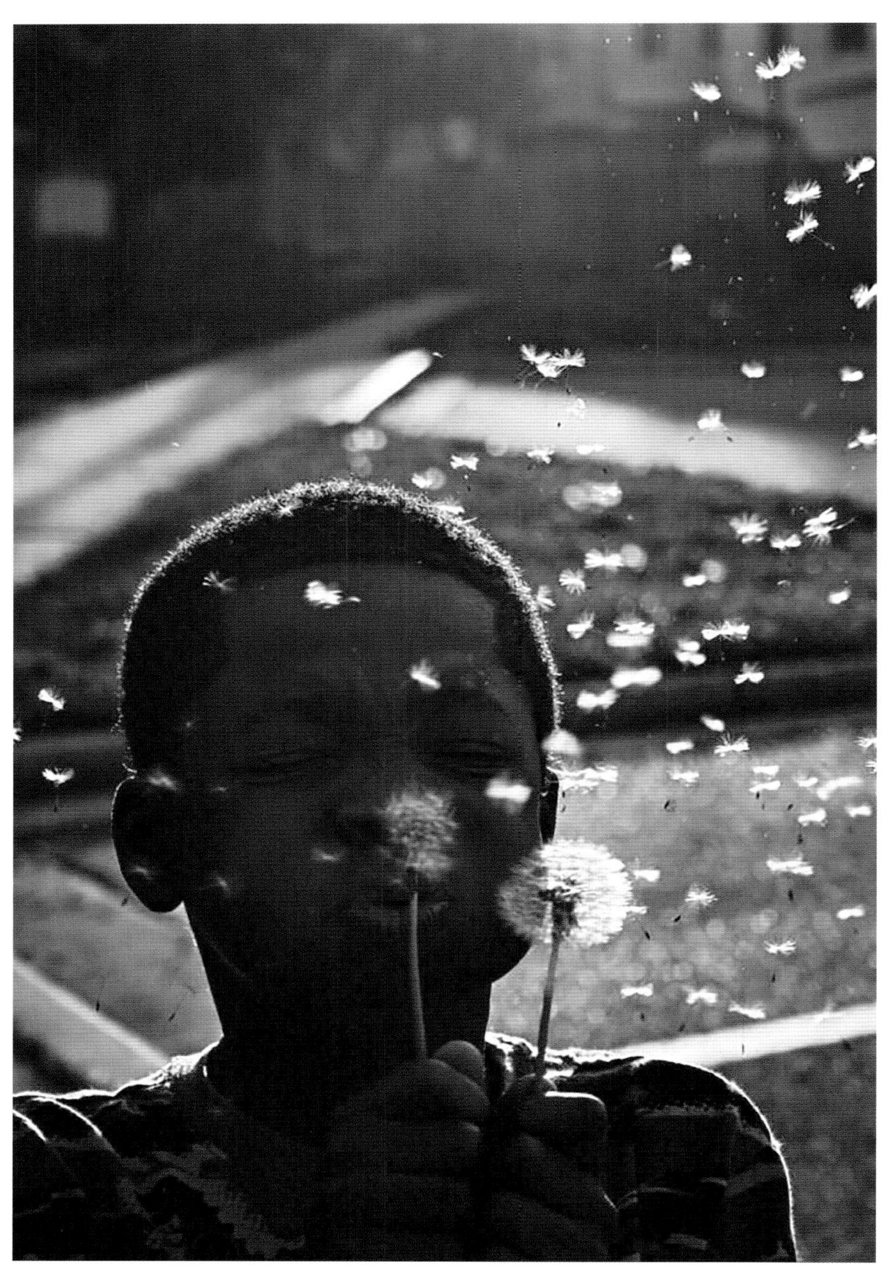

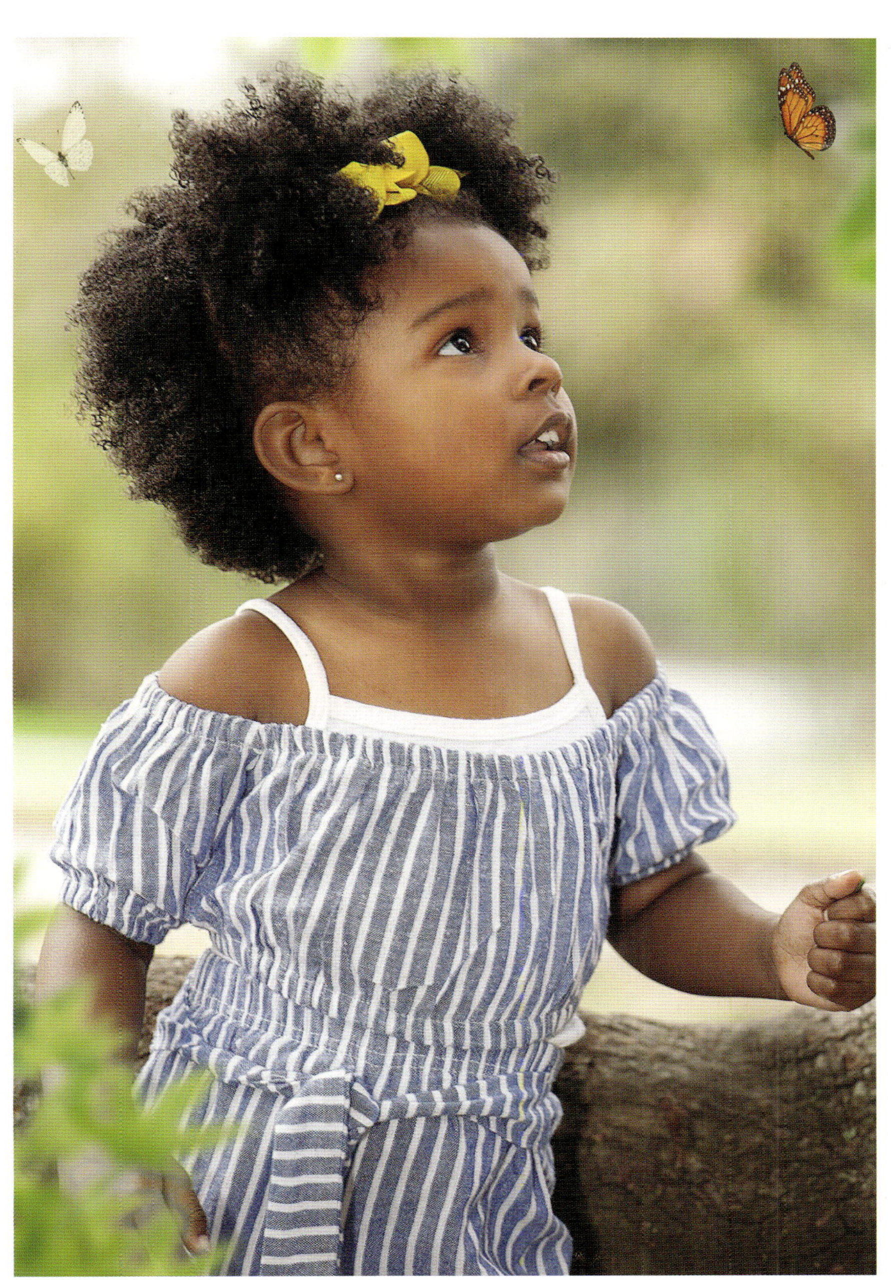

Sophia Little

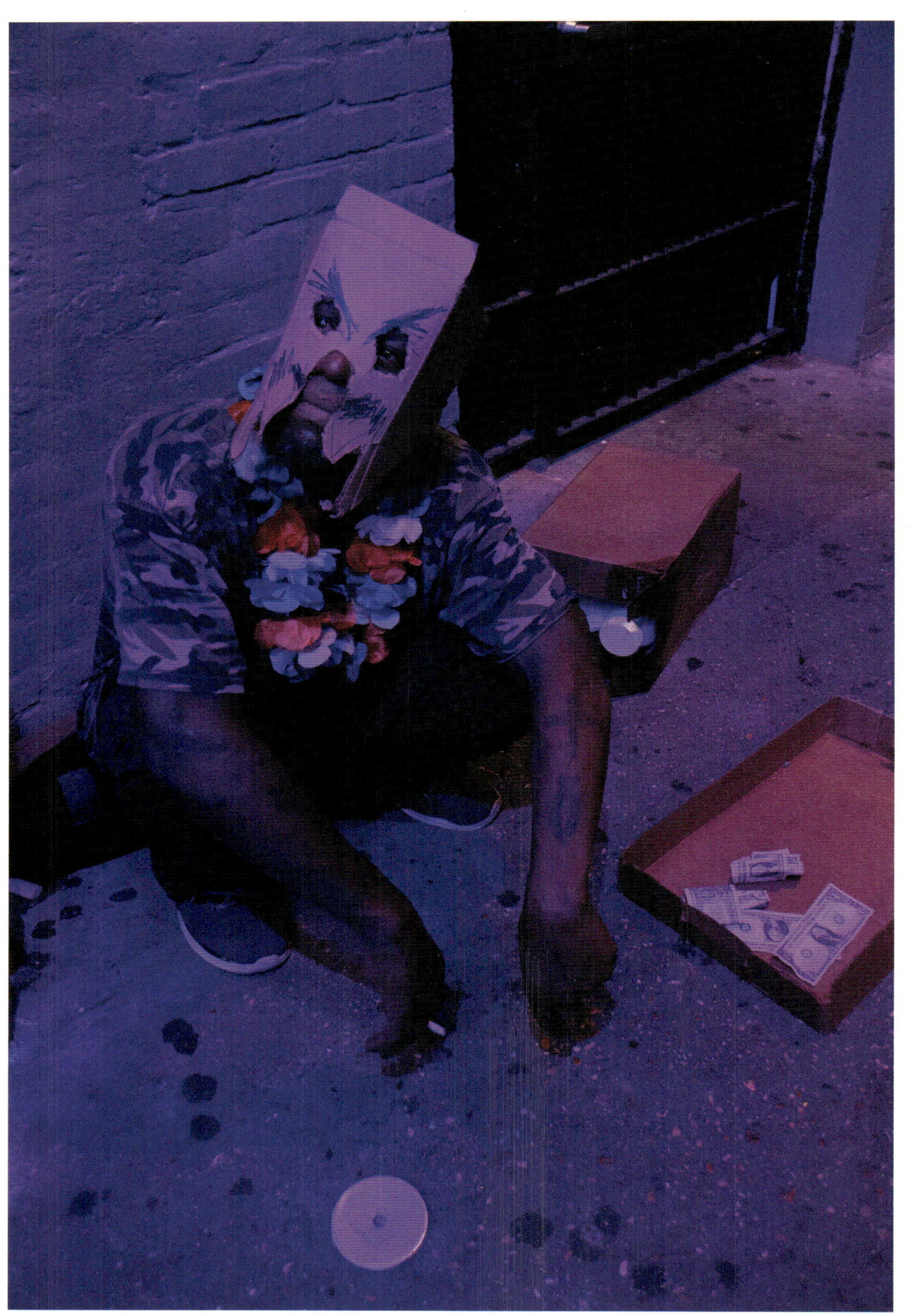

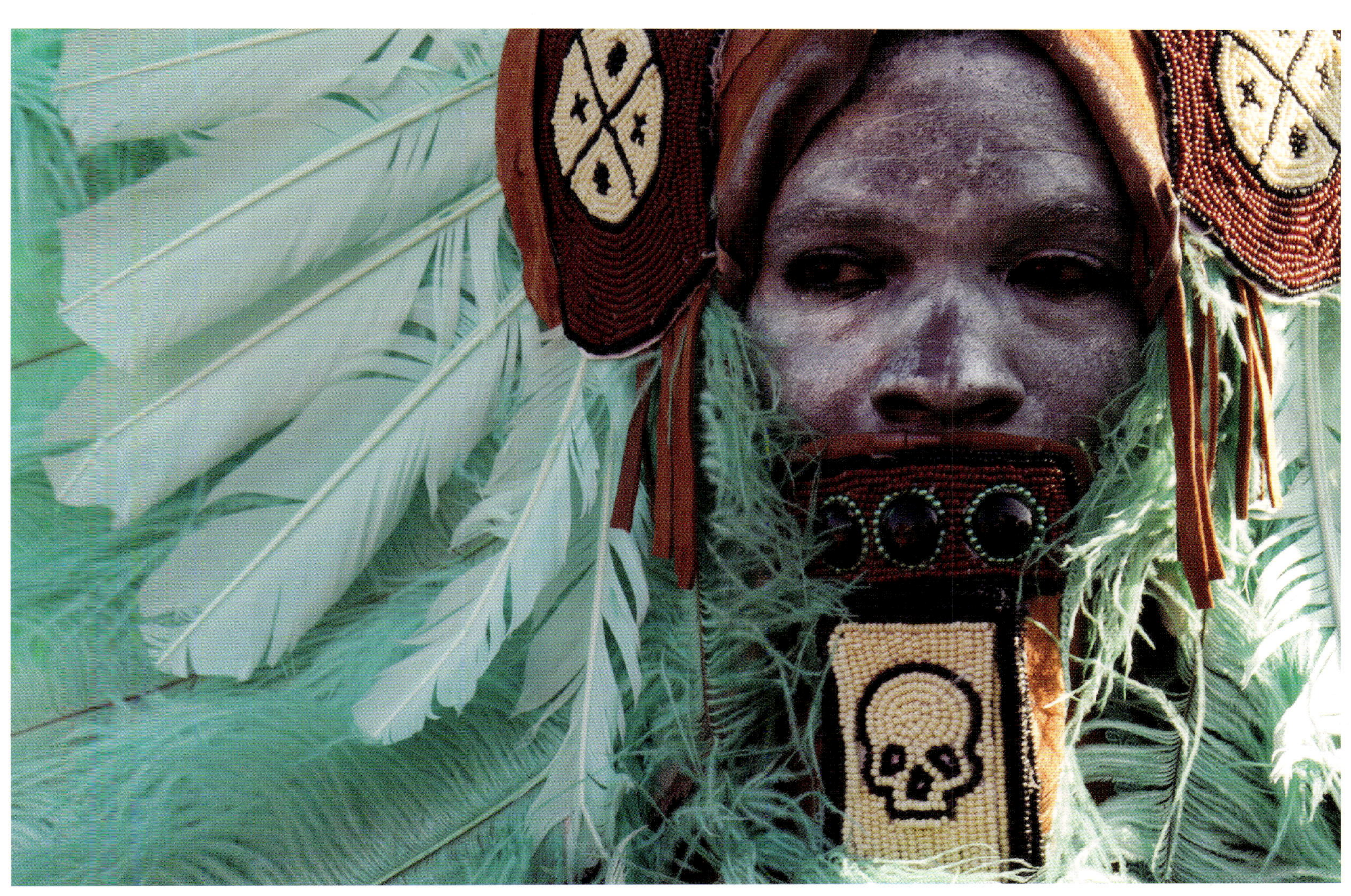

Sokari Ekine

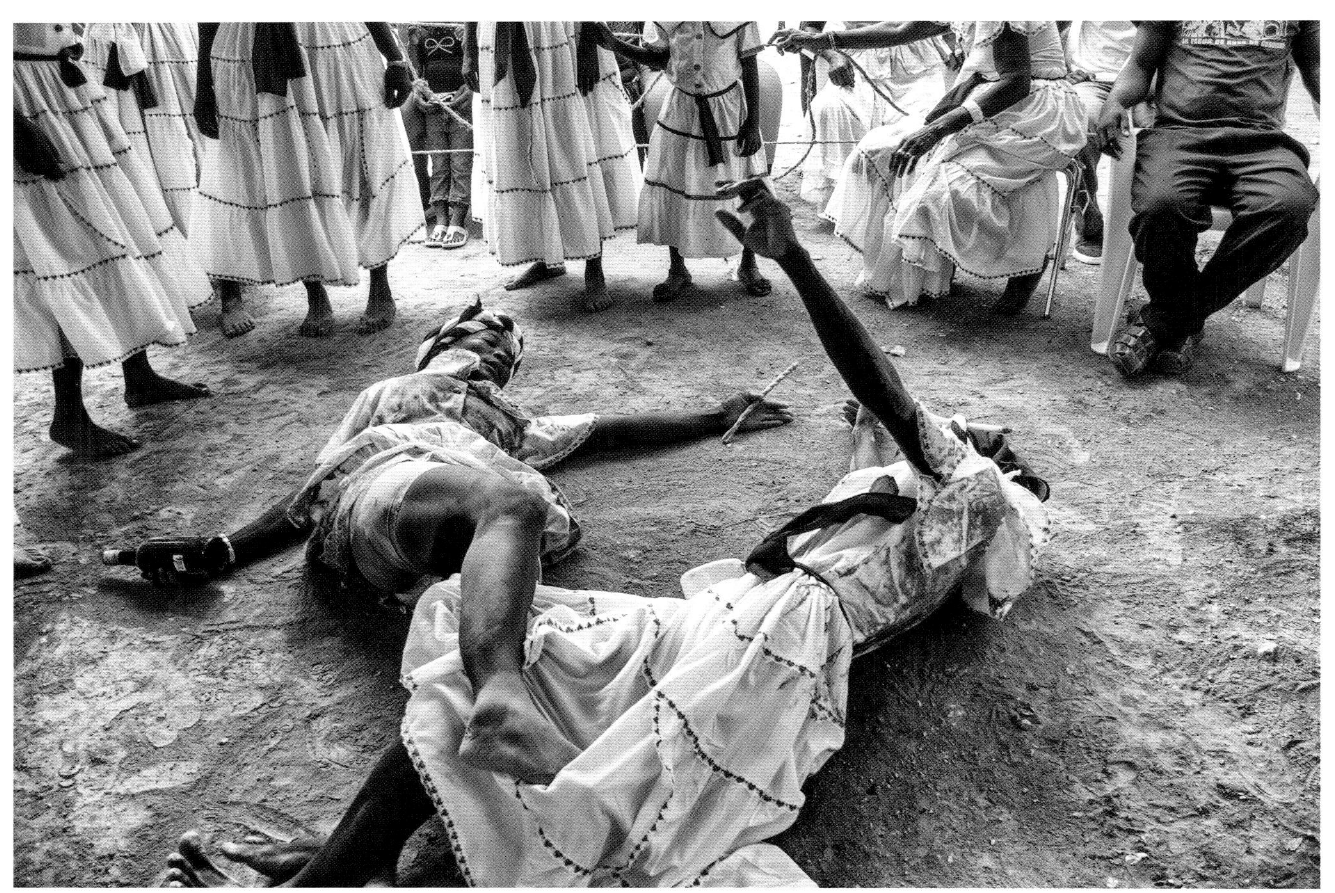

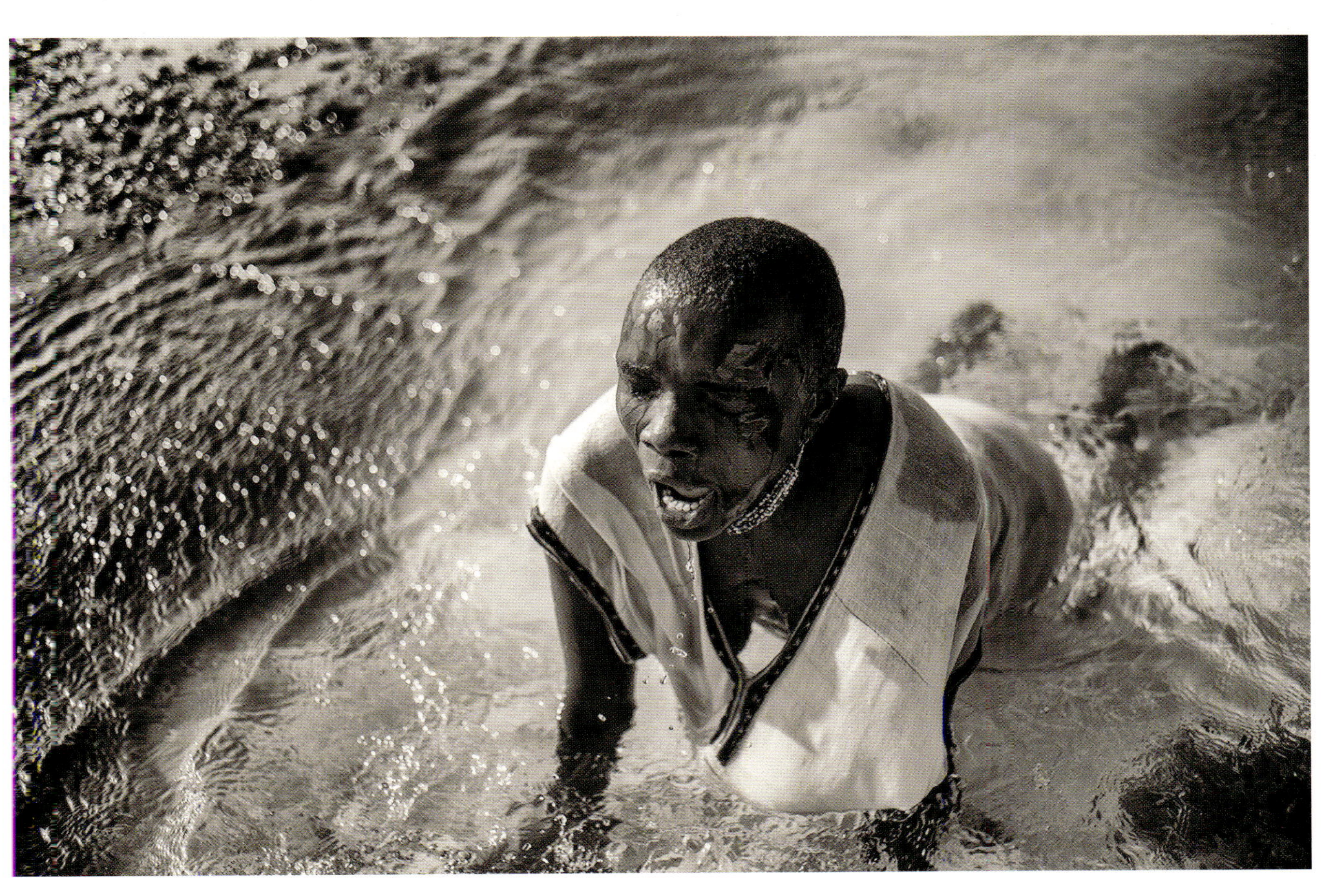

Sienna Pinderhughes

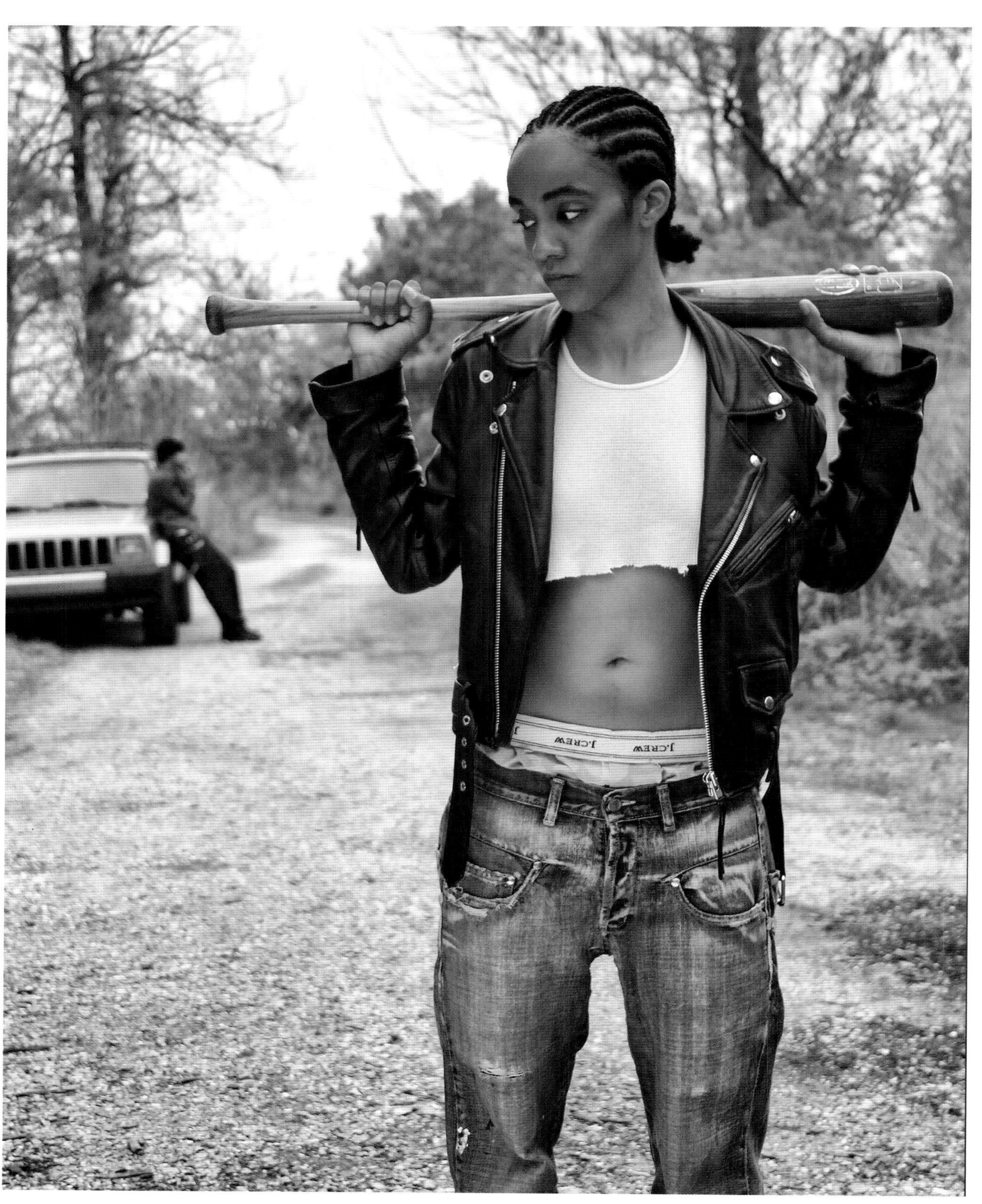

Trenity Thomas

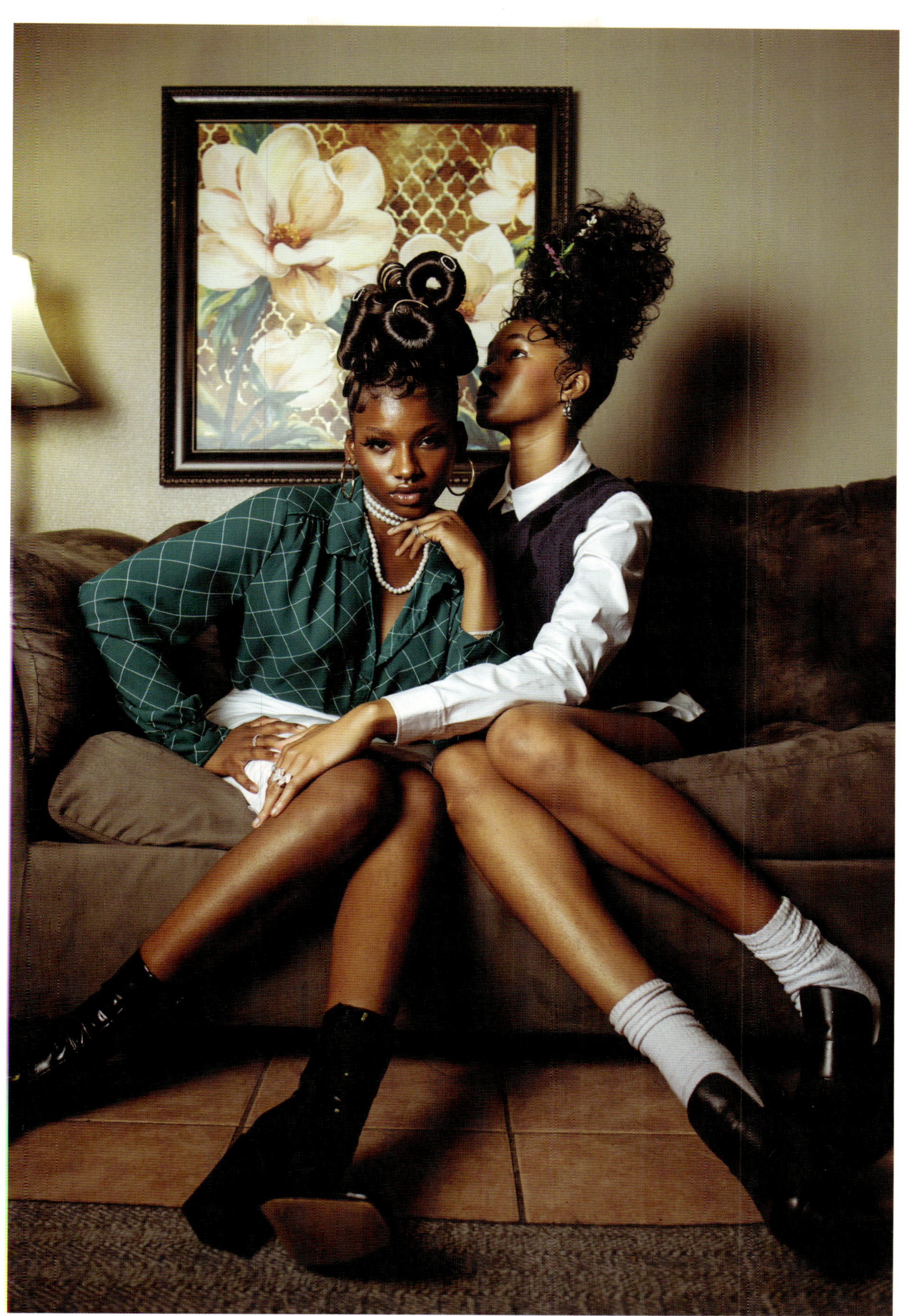

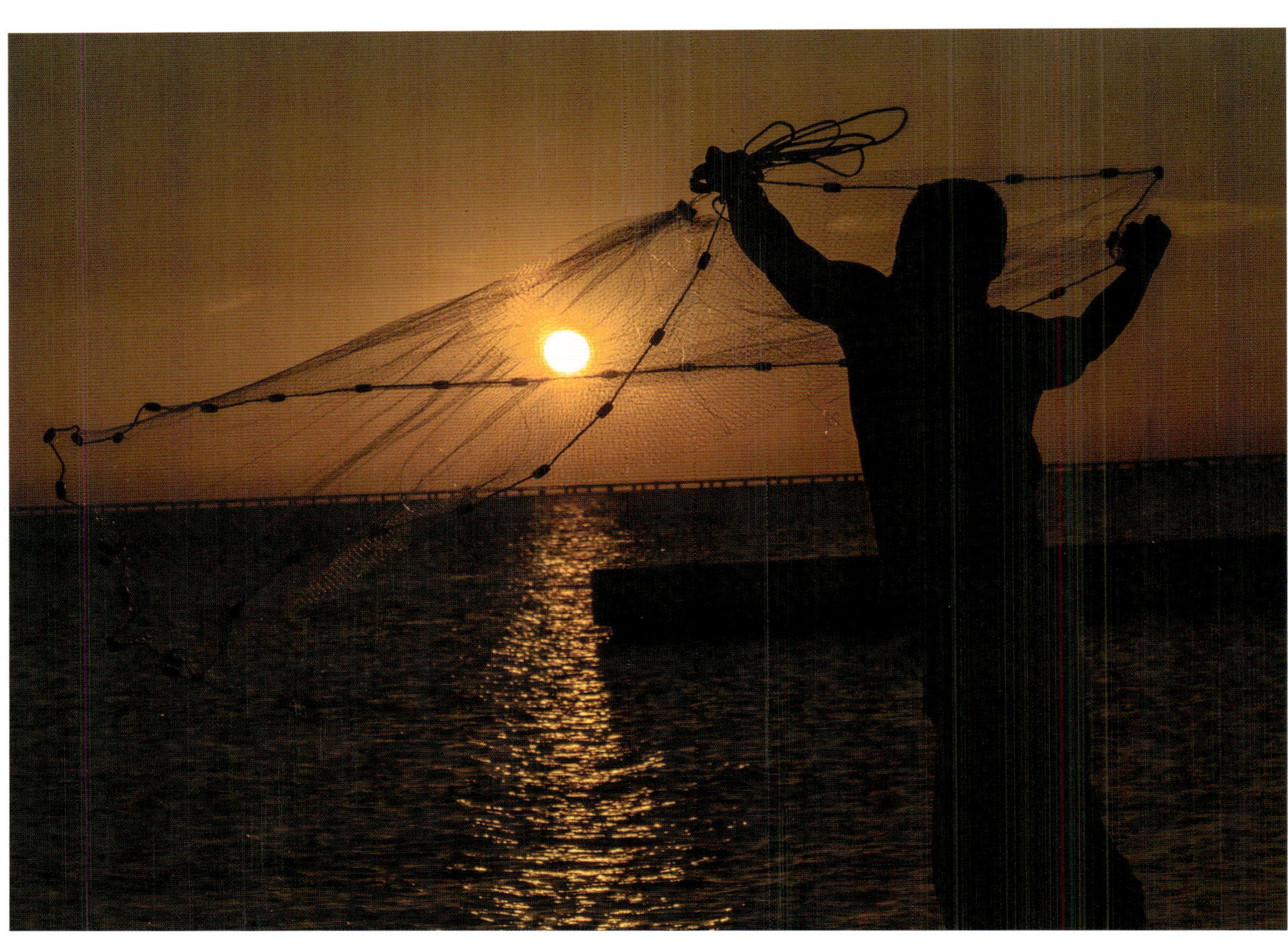

Vincent Simmons

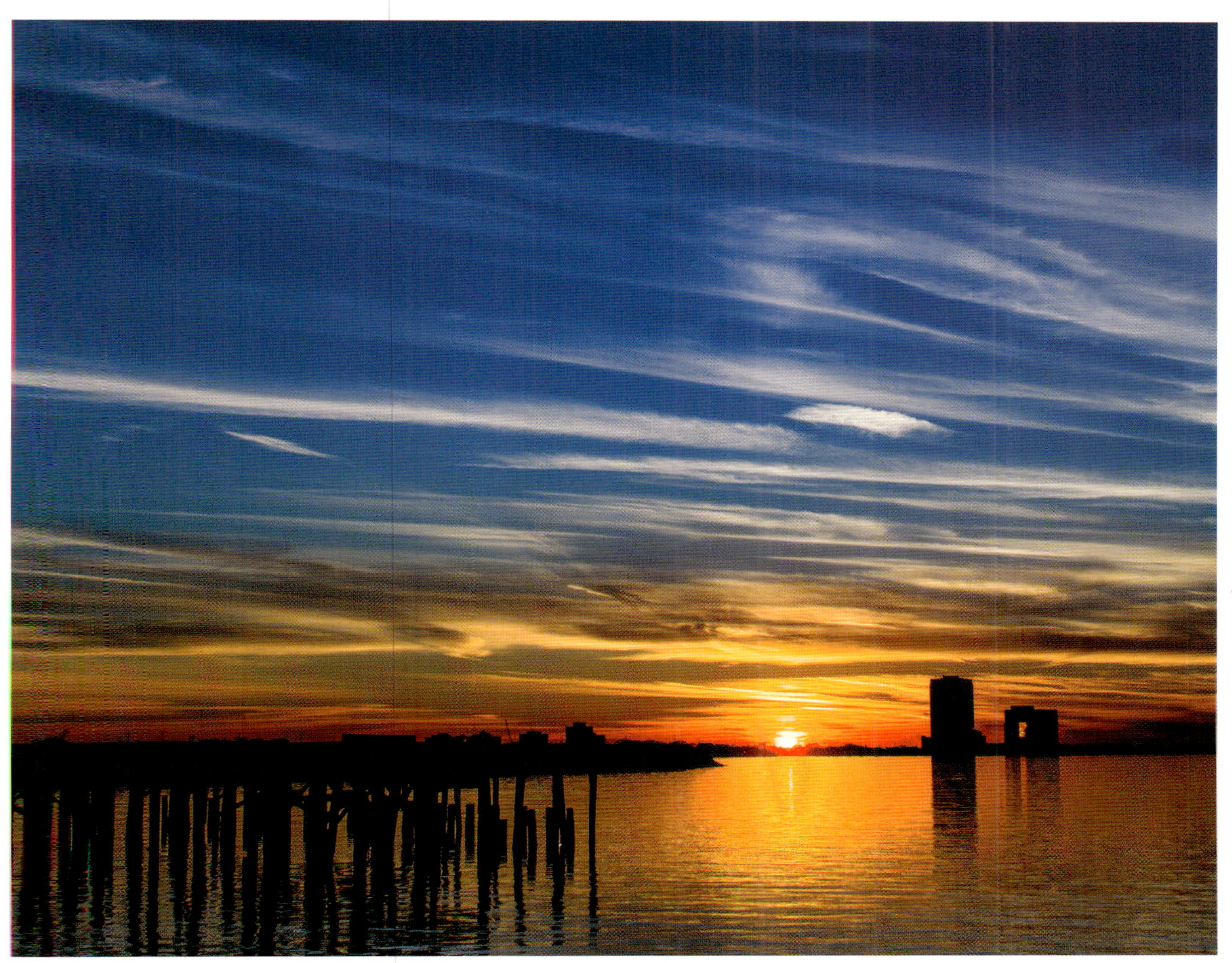

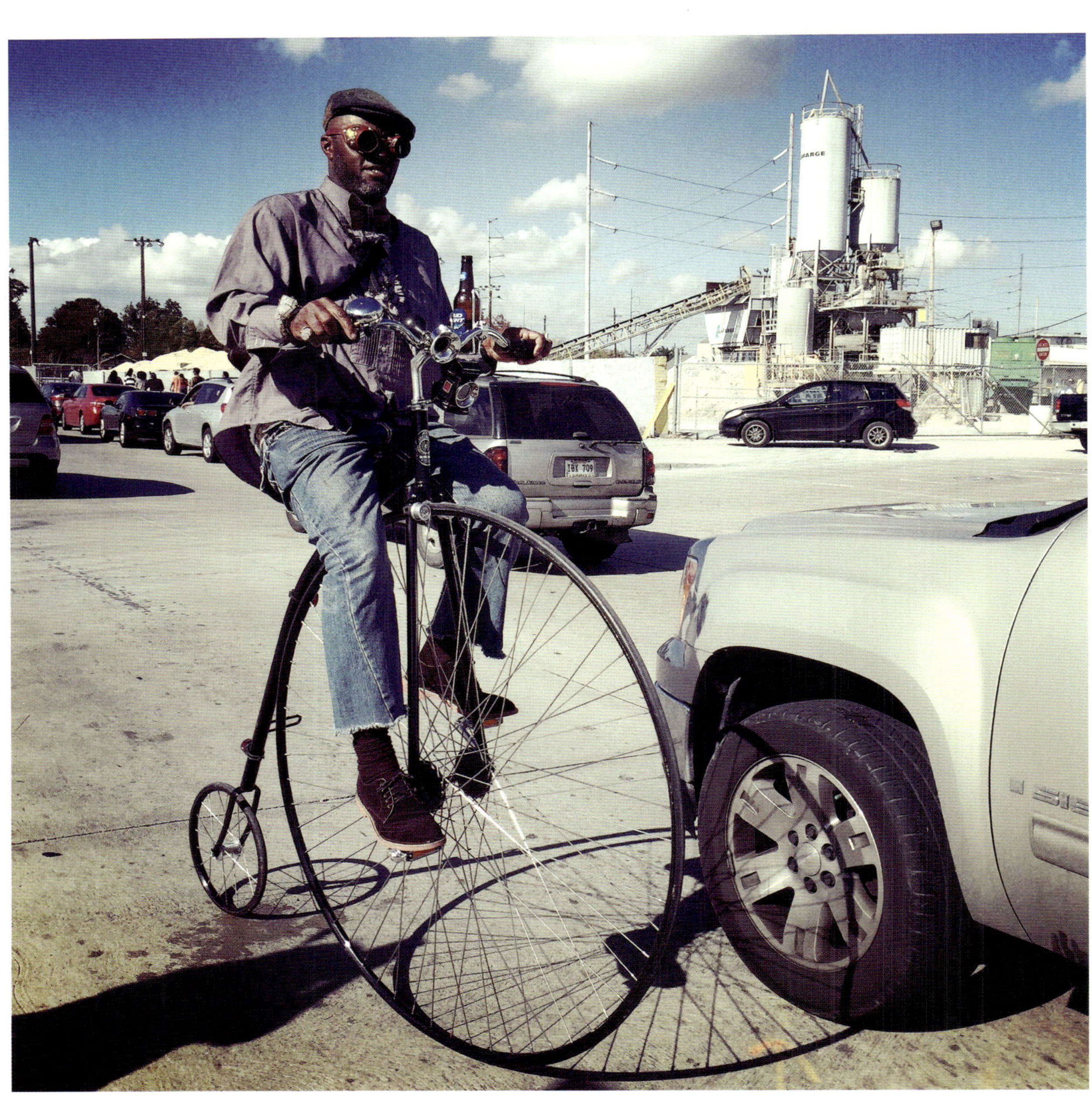

Will Horton

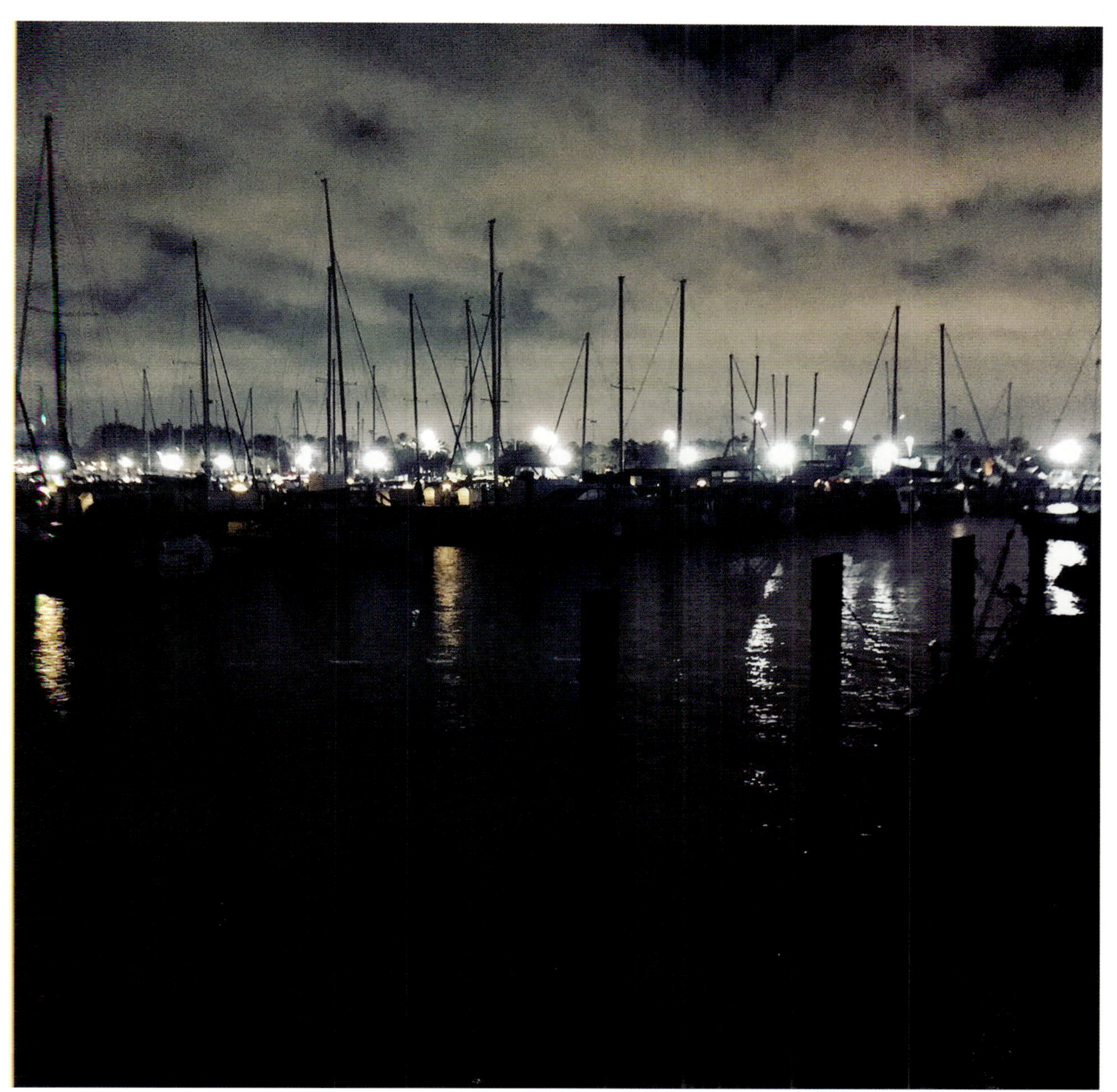

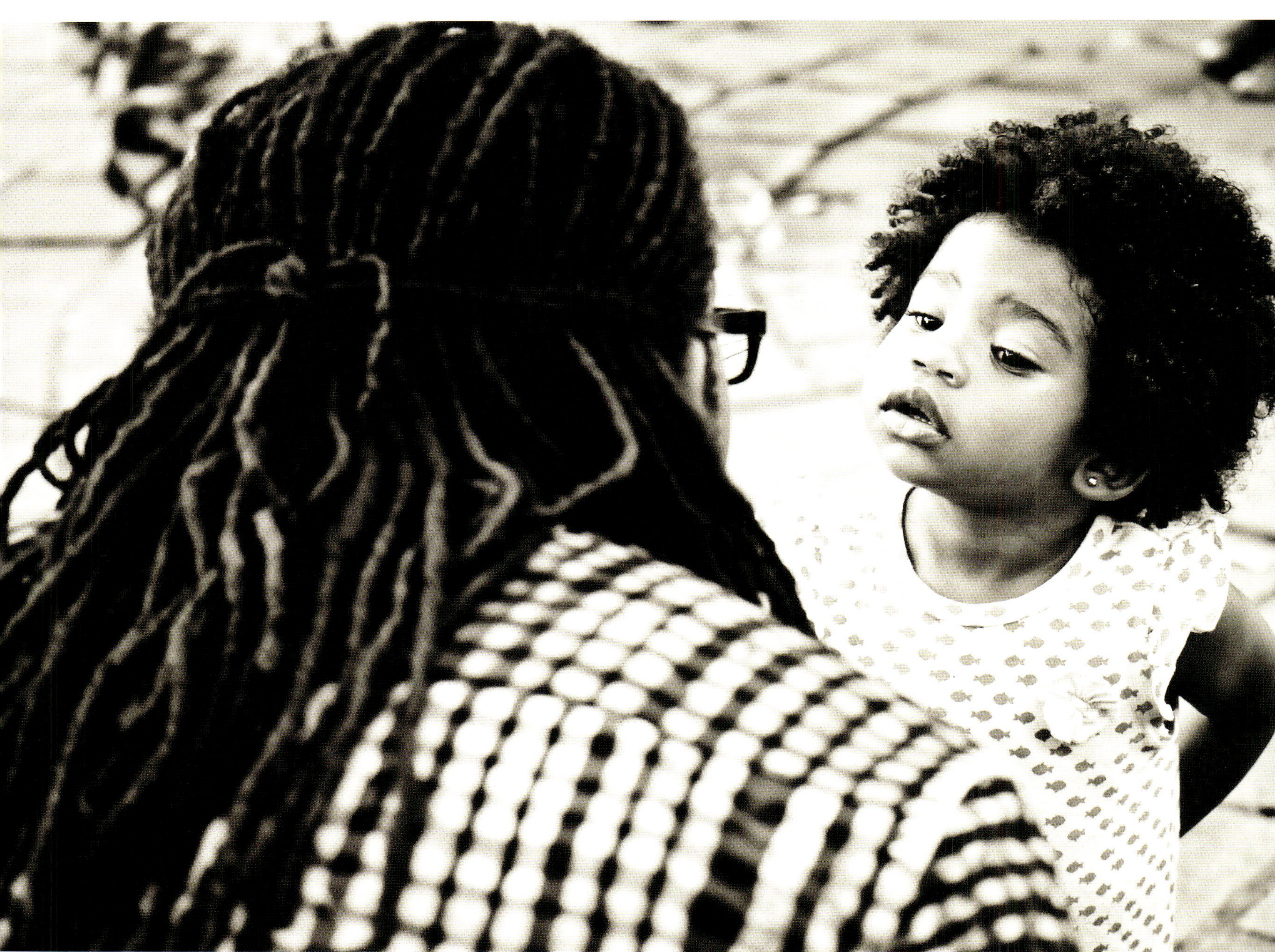

"Teaching the Teacher," 2014. Photo: Gason Ayisyin. Courtesy of the Artist.

essays

Girard Mouton, III | Eric Waters | Shana M. griffin | Kalamu ya Salaam

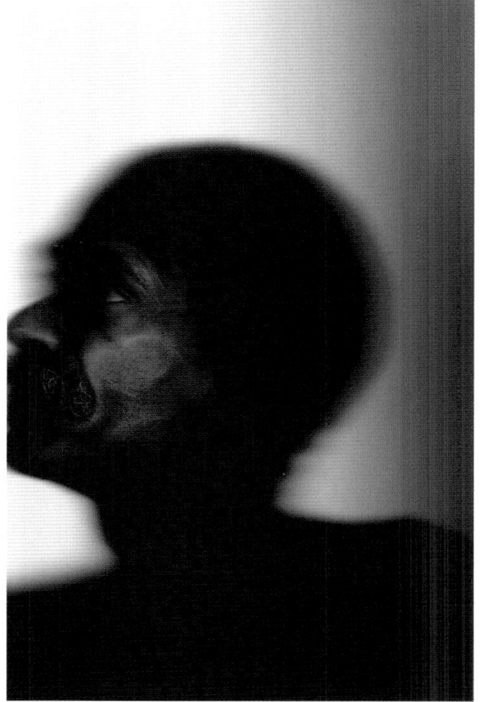

"Girard Mouton,III Obscura." Photo: Girard Mouton,III.

Girard Mouton, III

“It's impossible to look at a photograph and tell anything about the demographics of the photographer who took the picture.”

Girard Mouton,III

Opening remarks on a panel consisting of Norman R. Smith, Eric Waters, and Girard Mouton,III, moderated by Dr. Kara T. Olidge, director of the Amistad Research Center, on the closing night of *Full Circle*, an exhibition of the New Orleans Jazz & Heritage Festival photography of Norman R. Smith and of Eric Waters at the Ace Hotel New Orleans, curated by Sonali Fernando, director of cultural affairs, and co-curated by Mouton, made to a standing-room-only audience on Sunday, June 30, 2019.

PHOTOGRAPHERS OBSCURA

Girard Mouton, III

The word "photo" comes from the Greek word *phos*, meaning "light." The word "graph" also comes from Greek, meaning "to draw or write." The two come together as "photograph," meaning "to draw with light."

The word "obscure" comes from the Latin word *obscurus*, meaning dark. The word "camera" also comes from Latin, meaning "vault," or "vaulted room," and "chamber," or "box." "Camera obscura" describes a room or device used to project an image.

With a play on words, "photographers obscura" comes to mean "photographers who are dark, photographers who are hidden."

IN AND OUT OF THE PICTURE

Before the Frenchman Joseph Nicéphore Niépce produced the first known photograph in 1825—followed by the British inventor William Henry Fox Talbot in the mid-1830s and the French inventor Louis Daguerre in the late 1830s, with their respective eponymous processes—painting, drawing, etching, engravings, and lithography were employed to make representational images of objects, scenes, and people.

In Europe, where there has been an African presence for thousands of years, before photography or any of the reproduction processes evolving from photography, the images of African peoples have been ignored or depicted negatively. Paintings containing a Black person merely described them as a "negro," someone without a name. The ability to make and distribute multiple copies of a drawing or etching accompanied with words using a printing press enabled creators of negative descriptions of Black people to reach larger audiences than they could in person. Such wide distribution led to generally accepted stereotypes of African peoples. Blacks were hindered in responding with their own words and depictions due to lack of access to the means of production and dissemination.

In slave-era colonial America, and the later United States, stereotypes of Africans continued and flourished even post-emancipation. People of African descent were presented as lazy and indolent, rapists or jezebels. Caricatures of grinning, dancing, and perpetually happy Black plantation dwellers became popular in books and in songs. The purpose of these types of images was to comfort the white population in their superiority. Images of slaves being whipped were meant to instill in the Black population fear of punishment for not being "good."

Handbills, posters, and newspaper advertisements were used to describe slaves for sale and runaway slaves for capture. Physical descriptions of subjects were conveyed in words, rarely with an artist's rendition based on a photograph, as directly reproducing photographs in print did not occur until the early 1880s. The pictures of enslaved people usually showed them en masse at work on the fields of the plantation, rarely indoors engaged in domestic chores, and almost always without either their European or African names.

As valuable as slaves were to their owners, it seems the owners never embarked on identifying them individually photographically, as with a worker ID, in an album for the sake of trade or accounting, or for posterity, like a yearbook. From the owners' perspective, the enslaved had no identities, no individualities; they were all the same, interchangeable, and treated as such. When owners of slaves did have their human property photographed, the images often included the owners. Pictures of a master and his attendant, a white child with an enslaved child, or a female slave wet-nursing a white child were the usual images taken in the studio of a photographer. Subjects were well dressed, looked fit, healthy, and comfortable being in each other's company, perfect in the roles of their lives. Made for each other. For the camera, both sides seemed expressionless.

Singular portraits of slaves are rare. In 1850, J. T. Zealy took photographs of enslaved people in his Columbia, South Carolina, studio for Harvard University professor Louis Agassiz. The daguerreotypes are said to have been commissioned for scientific study. The humans were nude. In this instance, their given names were recorded. Zealy's photographs were not widely circulated at the time.[1]

The most widely circulated illustration based on a photograph of an enslaved person is that of the scarred "Whipped Peter," which appeared in *Harper's Weekly* in 1863. The former slave, named either Peter or Gordon, was photographed after his self-emancipation in a New Orleans studio. The illustration was effectively used on behalf of the movement for the abolition of slavery.

Lynchings predate the abolition of slavery and the invention of photography. It wasn't until after the end of slavery that America's first mass spectator sport came to be photographed for commercial purposes. Souvenir postcards of the events were sold and traded for profit and pleasure. Since such postcards were sent through the mail, the US federal government benefited financially from the executions. The limp bodies of those murdered were sometimes dressed in their US military uniform finest, sometimes partially nude, sometimes completely nude, sometimes covered with tar and feathers by their executioners for the occasion. Unlike the white people seen in portraits of slave owners with their slaves, members of white lynch parties exhibited glee on their countenances and joy in their gestures. The dead victims showed no emotion for the camera. As with the photos of slave owners with their slaves, there were women, children, and men, victims and victimizers,

1 *To Make Their Own Way in the World: The Enduring Legacy of the Zealy Daguerreotypes*, eds. Ilisa Barbash, Molly Rogers, and Deborah Willis (New York: Aperture, 2020): 108–111.

al comfortable in their roles. In the lynching photos, the descendants of slaves are almost always identified, while the descendants of slave owners are almost always unidentified.[2]

Even as early Western visual art and photography were bereft of people of color, photographs of people of African descent were used to exclude and oppress them. Louisiana State University in New Orleans, established in 1956 and later renamed the University of New Orleans, required that applicants to the school attach a photograph to their application for admission. This practice remained in place into the 1970s. Although never formally stated or admitted by the institution, the Black community knew that the reason for the photo was to eliminate or limit Black student enrollment. Decades later, the University of New Orleans Press is the publisher of *SEEING BLACK*.

IN LIVING COLORS

New Orleans is often described as the most colorful city in America. That comes from its yearly Carnival celebrations, when maskers attire themselves in costumes, and floats roll on the streets resplendent in colors that exceed those of the rainbow. The color of a person's skin in New Orleans has long been used as a determinant of their position in life. Other distinguishers, such as religion, country of origin, slave or free, were also used as stratifiers in the caste system. Color was the primary segmenter.

Color is not only seen; it is also perceived. The most precise scientific instrument used to measure color is the spectrophotometer. The human eye, not as precise, is also used to measure color. It is connected to the brain, where decisions are made about the color being seen. With the brain being a component in judging color, more than the visual appearance of color is used in its evaluation.

Scientists developed color systems in order to make identifying particular colors easy across applications. Munsell, RGB, CMYK, Adobe, and others have become universally accepted systems of measurement. Conversely, the brown paper bag test of the past, used to "measure" the color of a person's skin, was a non-standard and inaccurate test because there was no standard brown paper bag. The color of a person's skin is not only superficial; it is also internal.

In the 1970s, the Louisiana State Museum mounted an exhibition of the works of free people of color who were artists. Among them were painter Julien Hudson and lithographer Jules Lion. In 1982, Margaret Denton Smith and Mary Louise Tucker co-authored *Photography in New Orleans: The Early Years, 1840–1865*, in which they noted that the city's first photographer was a free man of color.[3] The publication of that book led to subsequent photo researchers and photo historians, including Mouton, accepting Smith and Tucker's findings and, further, asserting that Lion was the first Black photographer in America.

---

2 James Allen, *Without Sanctuary: Lynching Photography in America*, 15th ed. (Santa Fe: Twin Palm Publishers, 2021): 25–35.

3 Margaret Denton Smith and Mary Louise Tucker, *Photography in New Orleans: The Early Years, 1840–1865* (Baton Rouge: LSU Press, 1982): 17.

In 2017, Sara M. Picard published a paper on her Jules Lion research.[4] Picard's extensive research, going beyond New Orleans newspaper accounts, city directories, and legal documents, portrays the photographer as being of German-Jewish descent, not a person of color. Picard let it be known that many questions about Lion still remain unanswered and that there still is the possibility of him having Black ancestry. Smith, Tucker, and Picard all show that there is a paper trail on Lion showing his business activities, property acquisition and disposition, marriage, successors, and death. Picard, in reviewing those documents, never found a record in which Lion signified his race. When no indication of race was made, she points out, the person in question was presumably white. Due to Sara M. Picard's findings, Jules Lion must be reassessed and the history books rewritten.

In June 2022, Mouton and Picard had a telephone conversation.

Girard Mouton,III: Dr. Picard, what prompted you to do this research?

Dr. Sara M. Picard: I felt there was a lot of work that had to be done. There are so many questions.

GM: What were you studying at the time when your attention was drawn to Jules Lion?

SP: I was studying American art and African American Art. I spent six months doing research in New Orleans. For the portion on his family in France, I had the assistance of a genealogist in Paris. I did not travel to France. To me, Lion seemed to have been understudied.

GM: What did the Parisian genealogist find?

SP: She found that his parents were Bavarian and Alsatian Jews. Jews from those regions were not generally Sephardic Jews, who have a more Mediterranean and northern African connection. Since the publication of my paper, and articles on it, three Lions have contacted me. They have done DNA testing which showed no African ancestry.

GM: You know, Dr. Picard, there still are people by the name of Lion living in the city of New Orleans. I remember a person by that surname bringing in film to a one-hour photo lab I worked at in the 1990s. He worked for a law firm. Company policy prohibited employees from delving into non-photography matters of customers unless they volunteered it in a conversation. So, I never asked him if he was kin to Jules Lion.

SP: Yes, some are still in New Orleans.

GM: My research shows a Jules Lion in the city in the 1940s and Lions listed in the telephone book in 2012–2013.

SP: The work I have done is not a period at the end of a sentence.

GM: Let's talk about identity.

---

4 Sara M. Picard, "Racing Jules Lion," *Louisiana History: The Journal of the Louisiana Historical Association* 58, no. 1 (Winter 2017): 5–37.

SP: The definition of "Black" has changed over time.

GM: Those are the exact words of Kalamu ya Salaam, who is directing SEEING BLACK.

SP: Lion was thought to be a Black American. I don't think it's possible he hid any Black ancestry. The genealogy went only as far as his parents. There needs to be more genealogical research to round out his family history, on both ancestors and descendants.

GM: What about his Jewish identity? Was it downplayed by him in a state that was once part of the French empire, where the Code Noir banned Jews from settling in the New World, until the Louisiana Purchase?

SP: That's a great question on hiding his Jewish identity. In New Orleans, in its early history, there were Jews despite the Code Noir and other laws. Many became prosperous and prominent, including his brother Achille, who maintained a trans-ocean business relationship with Parisian Jewish merchants. It may be that Jules wanted to be an artist, and with that, he might not have cared as much to make choices taking into account his religion and heritage.

GM: In June 1988, while conducting research for the July issue of *The New Orleans Tribune*'s cover story, "The Way We Were: Our Family Album," I spoke to Mary Louise Tucker. She cowrote *Photography in New Orleans the Early Years, 1840–1865* with Margaret Denton Smith. We discussed an image in the 1983 book *A Century Of Black Photographers: 1840–1960*, by Valencia Hollins Coar. The book contains a reproduction of a tintype, said to have been done by Jules Lion, from an anonymous collector.[5] Smith told me the purchaser was Anthony Barboza, an African American photographer in New York City. She said the seller was antique dealer Eugene R. Groves. She also said that "Lion" is scratched on the back of the tintype. Smith told me she doubted that is an original Lion photograph. It should be noted that the tintype is not reproduced in her book. Dr. Picard, I also have doubts that the tintype is a Lion. As far as we know, Lion was a daguerreian, not a tintypist. By the time the tintype was invented, around the mid 1850s, Jules Lion had abandoned photography and continued his painting and lithography.[6] Also, Dr. Picard, his signature on his lithographs is rather distinguished. Why would he simply scratch "Lion" on the rear?[7]

SP: Mr. Mouton, that indicates you have a technical knowledge about photography from your education at R.I.T. that I don't have. That's an excellent observation.

---

5 *A Century of Black Photographers: 1840–1960*, ed. Valencia Hollins-Coar (Providence: Rhode Island School of Design Museum of Art, 1983): 13.

6 Smith and Tucker, *Photography in New Orleans*, 36.

7 Charles Gardner's *New Orleans Directory for 1861* lists a "Charles Lion, f.m.c., bricklayer." It also lists a "Joseph Lion, f.m.c., cigars." These listings give rise to the possibility that the person in the tintype may be one of these individuals. The name Jules Lion reappears in Polk's 1945–1946 City Directory. In the White Pages of the New Orleans Yellow Pages phone directory 2012–2013, five Lions are listed: A. Lion, D. Lion, E. Lion, Mark Lion, and Mark Lion.

GM: In the 1982 Smith and Tucker book is the reproduction of daguerreotype of an African American female attributed to Jules Lion from the collection of Eugene R. Groves. This image is not in the Hollins Coar book. In February 2021, Cowan's Auctions sold the daguerreotype to The Historic New Orleans Collection. The dealer's website states that the consignor had obtained the image from a Lion family member. It came from the Eugene R. Groves Collection. Some sources claim the female photographed is a Lion family member. Dr. Picard, if she is a relative of Lion, is she by blood or by marriage?

SP: If she has not been identified by name, she could be anybody. Again, a lot of research still needs to be done.

GM: When you did your research, Mary Louise Tucker was deceased. Since 2017, have any photography scholars contacted you?

SP: You are the only one.

GM: For anyone who reads your paper, "Racing Jules Lion," would you want them to draw their own conclusions about Jules Lion being Black or not?

SP: I don't want to be known as the person who made Jules Lion go from being Black to white. I have no problem in being wrong.

The *Photography in New Orleans* book and the "Racing" paper point out that there are many Jules Lion lithographs in existence, almost all with his distinguished signature. Both publications also say that there exists no photograph that can be absolutely attributed to Lion by a signature, imprint, folder, or case. A self-portrait in any of the mediums in which he was skilled has never been found. A portrait by another photographer or visual artist has never been found. A written description of his appearance has never been found. The lithograph by Lion of his dentist brother Achille may be an indication of the physical appearance of Jules. In many ways, Jules Lion remains a mystery man.

Not long after the enterprising Lion, hailing from the country that put the word "entrepreneur" into global parlance, introduced the daguerreotype process to New Orleans, competitors arose. Interestingly, few were native-born New Orleanians. Several were from abroad, like Lion. Soon after, Lion ended his photography practice and returned to drawing, painting, and lithography.

It may not have been competition alone that forced Lion from the photo trade. Photography, since its inception, has always been an expensive proposition for the sole proprietor. The professional equipment is not cheap, nor is the studio space, unless it is a home studio or the photographer works exclusively on location. With rent, property taxes, insurance, and utility overhead being necessary for a studio space that, unless the photographer elects to employ a large workforce to manufacture many items for sale, individual ownership of a studio is challenging. Artists have never been known as good businesspeople, as they must use their minds to concentrate on creativity.

Jules Lion was a 19th-century photographer who may have hidden his possible Black ancestry and also may have de-emphasized his being Jewish. In the early 20th century, Florestine Perrault made the decision that working as a domestic her entire Black life was not for her. Her great-niece, Dr. Arthé Anthony, culminated years of research with the 2012 publication of the book *Picturing Black New Orleans: A Creole Photographer's View of the Early Twentieth Century*. According to Dr. Anthony, "Florestine sought employment through classified ads in the daily newspaper. She saw an ad for a clerk in a photographer's studio. She was fourteen years of age at the time and never had any aspirations of being a photographer. The photographer assumed she was white." In her July 2022 conversation with Mouton, Dr. Anthony continued, "Some people have incorrectly stated she passed for white in order to get the job." Perrault simply did not reveal that she was Black.

However, outside of her inaugural employment opportunity in the photography field, Perrault never crossed the color line to live as white. She is photographically depicted in *The Crescent City Pictorial: A Souvenir Dedicated to the Progress of the COLORED CITIZENS of New Orleans, Louisiana, "America's Most Interesting City,"* a 1925 booklet designed to be a record of the accomplishments of Black New Orleanians. At that time, Perrault (later Perrault Collins) used her first married name of Bertrand. Although Dr. Anthony never notes it in her book, in every census during her lifetime, Perrault was always listed as Negro or Black, even in cases where she was the respondent. There is no doubt she always identified as Black.[8]

Anthony writes extensively of the intersectional matters of race and gender in the US as issues for all women, regardless of their ethnicities. She puts constructs of race and gender into the context of Perrault's time, and before. Mouton posed the following question to Dr. Anthony: "With knowledge of the history of white male aggression towards Black women during slavery and post-slavery, on and off the plantation, did your great aunt ever state or hint that the reason she never revealed her being Black to the white photographer was the fear of the possibility of unwelcome sexual advances towards her, especially because of her age?"

"No," Dr. Anthony replied. "Nor did I ask her that."

---

8 One of the fields of employment for author Kalamu ya Salaam was field census enumerator in 1970. He recalled to Mouton times when he and other census takers could not contact the assigned household for the survey. In those instances, they simply made a guess on the race of the household based on factors such as name and nearby neighbors. In his conversation with Dr. Picard, Mouton noted that the early US census enumerators were US Marshals and that, more than likely, all of them were white. Thus, judging a person's race was done through white eyes, which may not have been able to discern the subtle differences in Blackness and whiteness.

Mouton also pointed out to Dr. Picard that the publishers of city directories employed US Marshals to conduct their compilations. Mygatt's 1857 *New Orleans Business Directory* wrote on the frustration of compiling the information on individual households. The 1870 census was the last one employing US Marshals as enumerators. Around that same time period, New Orleans city directories no longer listed a Black person's race. The 2000 census was the first to allow a person to choose multiple racial designations.

"Passing" is not restricted to the human species. Many animals mimic the sounds of other animals or change their appearances; plants blend into their environments. As with humans, passing is about survival. What differs is that passing humans can internalize the changes they make with their identities and deceive other human beings. In the non-human animal kingdom, passing does not fool those of the same species, nor do these creatures have the mental ability to internalize their physical changes into their identities.

There were those who were Black, had the ability to pass as white due to their skin color, and chose to do so. Others who could have, did not. Some who chose to pass never went back to being publically Black and assimilated into the white world. Escaped slaves "dark as sin" also passed. Unable to pass as white with their dark complexions, these escapees passed by not answering to their given slave names, by a change of outward appearance with clothing, by adopting a different persona. There was no choice, after escaping, other to live in and blend into the Black community. The ability and desire to pass for white in America lasted long after slavery, into the late 20th century.

In early 1979, Mouton made one of his many social visits to Marion J. Porter at his studio, located in the International Longshoremen's Association (ILA) Building. A call had come in from a local hotel, where a convention was in need of a photographer. Porter's studio was busy completing other assignments and declined the job, but offered to reach out to another photographer who may have been able to pick up the work. That photographer was called in to come by and show Porter his work before being referred for the job. The photographer, a Black man, arrived with a stack of 8"x10" black-and-white prints mounted to 11"x14" matte boards. Most of the photographs were of African American New Orleanians. After having his portfolio reviewed by Porter, the photographer requested Mouton's help in bringing the work back to his car.

Mouton obliged and, noticing that the rather beat-up domestic luxury automobile had out-of-state plates, asked if the state was the photographer's home state. The photographer said yes. With Mouton saying no more as both put the prints in the trunk, the photographer expressed envisioning not "working in a factory making widgets" for his career. After the trunk was closed and before getting in the car, the photographer said to Mouton, "I'm not trying to pass for being Black. I'm trying to pass for being poor." Girard Mouton,III never revealed the conversation to Marion J. Porter.

Initially, the photographer was positively received by the Black New Orleans community. But after he began selling photographs at art fairs, festivals, and in galleries for "big money," as one Black Masking Indian chief described, members of the community ostracized the photographer and in some instances met him with physical violence.

On a different visit to Porter's studio in the early 1980s, Porter reached under the counter and pulled out a booklet, telling Mouton, "Here, take a look at this." Porter moistened his fingers, opened the booklet to a specific page, and raised his eyes to the woman who stood before him, who had naturally straight, reddish brown hair and a fair complexion. "OK, Charlene," he said, "everybody's gonna know you're not white."

She folded her arms and smiled with her mouth closed.

The booklet was a copy of *Blacks in City Government 1981*, issued by Mayor Ernest "Dutch" Morial. Charlene Legaux, Porter's second wife, is depicted in the booklet as the mayor's photographer.[9] Everybody who knew Porter knew Legaux. She had picked up his camera and eventually began shooting most of the studio's assignments, managing the business while Porter handled the projects of his choice.[10] She had never passed for white. In fact, Legaux's father was a member of the all-Black Local 1419 of the ILA union. Porter's humorous comment pointed out how people had mistakenly identified Legaux as being white. On contemporary social media, she calls herself a "Proud Creole Woman." Had anyone made the wrong moves towards Porter or Legaux, they would have become familiar with his constant companion besides his camera: his gun.

One fall day in the early 2000s, while driving up Freret St. in the University area on the way

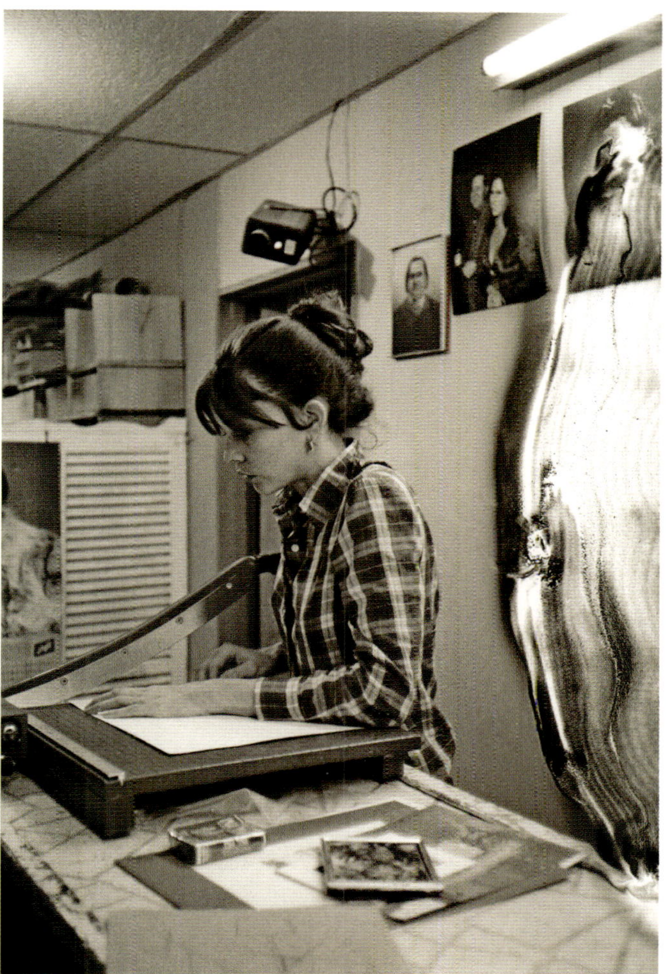

Charlene Legaux in Porter's Photo Studio, 1981.
Photo: Girard Mouton,III.

to Carrollton Cemetery, Mouton saw a familiar vehicle driving in the opposite direction. Mouton beeped his horn in recognition of the face. The other driver beeped back, and both drivers pulled over. The other driver gave his fellow photographer a hug only just looser than that of a straight jacket. They engaged in catching up with each other's goings ons and doings.

Then, with a face expressing anger, Mouton's friend—Harold Baquet—said, "_____'s going around town telling people, 'I'm not Black, I'm Italian.'" Baquet added, "He's a _____ ing lie!"

9 Mayor Ernest N. Morial, *Blacks in City Government 1981* (New Orleans: City of New Orleans, 1981): 14. Charlene Legaux was the first Black person to hold the position of Photographer to the Mayor of the City of New Orleans in the Office of Public Relations. She was succeeded by E. A. Kennedy, who was followed by Harold Baquet, who held the position into a portion of the Sidney Barthelemy administration.

10 Many of the photos with the credit line "Porter's Photo News" in *The Louisiana Weekly* were actually taken by Charlene Legaux.

Baquet, who never denied his Black identity, had expressed his disappointment in someone supposedly denying their own African heritage. What is resented in the Black community is the ambivalence of those who cross the color line back-and-forth, "being Black or white when it's convenient," and never staying Black and enduring the inequalities of anti-Blackness or actively engaging in the struggles against racism. Also resented are the descendants of passers who were innocently reared as white "all of a sudden wanting to become Black." For many who could pass, whiteness is seen as inferior as much as white people consider Blackness to be inferior; it is a means to an end.

Not having had neither professional interaction nor social contact with the photographer allegedly quoted, Mouton decided to check around with other Black photographers in New Orleans. One said he had never heard the statement nor heard of it, but that the person in question had siblings who attended one of the city's all-Black public high schools.

Mouton then decided to consult someone who knew a lot about photography and New Orleans photographers. He turned his attention to Reginald Fournier, who had worked as a wedding photographer with Roland James and had been a veteran salesperson at Katz & Besthoff Camera Center and later at Liberty Camera. Having sold photographic equipment and supplies to almost every professional in the New Orleans area for three decades beginning in the 1970s, Fournier said that he had never directly heard the statement but had heard of the photographer making it. Fournier also added that the photographer in question grew up in one of the city's all-Black public housing projects.

From the physical appearance of the "I'm not Black" photographer, most people, if asked to make a classification of the person by race or ethnicity, would identify the person as Black.

From Jules Lion in the mid-19th century to Florestine Perrault in the early 20th century, from the "not passing for Black" photographer in the late 20th century to the "I'm not a Black photographer" in the early 21st century, racial identity has long been a construct in the lives of New Orleans photographers. Each of these artists challenged the notions and definitions of Blackness or whiteness, which have changed many times over the decades: "pure Black," "half Black," "one-quarter," "one-eighth," "just a fraction," and now, thanks to the popularity of at-home DNA testing kits, "your precise DNA." White, conversely, has always been singular in its definition: "pure white."

Identity comes in two forms: self-identity and identification by others. Which is more powerful? The self-identity of each unique person in the world, or the identity of that person as seen by the billions of others on earth? Which is more important? Were the four making fools of themselves, or is the joke on everyone else?

For the self-identifying Black photographer in New Orleans, it's not just a matter of seeing Black. It is also a matter of being Black.

EYE AM NEW ORLEANS

If we accept the evidence presented by Dr. Picard that Jules Lion was not in fact a person of color, who *was* first Black photographer in New Orleans?

A ROBERTS, J. is listed in the 1867 city directory under the "photographers" profession as being colored and working for J. W. Petty at 181 1/2 Poydras St. Petty also had a location at 35 Poydras St.

ROBERTS, JOHN is listed in that same directory under residents as a photographer, also at 181 1/2 Poydras St.

JOHN ROBERTS is listed in the 1870 census as having been born in Louisiana in 1827, living in the 3rd Ward, mulatto, and a photographic artist. His wife was Leonora, listed as age twenty-four, born in Missouri, mulatto, and keeping house.

Going by these records, John Roberts seems to have been the first recorded Black photographer in New Orleans. It is stressed that Roberts *seems* to be the first Black New Orleans photographer because 1867 is a long twenty-seven years after Jules Lion first brought the daguerreotype process to the city, and four years after Lion's death.

One must keep in mind caveats for this possible conclusion. City directories did not list every inhabitant; primarily those who may have been of some value to the commerce of a city were surveyed.

During and after slavery, Black Americans, enslaved and free, found ingenious ways to evade restrictive laws and customs in order to survive. For those not familiar with the early photographic processes, the daguerreotype, the ambrotype, and the tintype all required expensive equipment and chemicals that had to be handled with care and precision. There were no photography schools. Photographers were trained in the European manner of apprenticeship to an established master. It was not a matter of picking up a camera and immediately shooting. There is a possibility someone Black used a camera of their own, or a camera of a white photographer for whom they worked, and took their own snaps. Were there other white photographers like J. W. Petty, who employed African Americans in their studios?

Within the photography field was the important role of the "finisher." Finishing happened after the camera work was done. It entailed the steps necessary for making a final product for the sitter to take home from the studio. When printing from negatives became more common than in-camera originals, finishers were replaced by darkroom technicians. Historically, city directories and other commercial directories seldom listed finisher as a distinct profession. A researcher would have to go through each name in a directory to look for a finisher. Sometimes the term finisher was applied to the construction trade, as well. So there may have been unrecorded or ambiguously recorded working Black finishers who took photographs before John Roberts.

Additionally, for most of those twenty-seven years between the dageurrotype's introduction to New Orleans and Roberts' appearance in the historical record, slavery was in effect. Did any white photographers own slaves who may have worked in their studios? Note that during the Civil War years, there were no New Orleans city directories, and those directories after 1867 did not note race after a person's profession. Regarding the Roberts themselves, were they born free or born enslaved?

There are many historical photographs of Black New Orleans taken by unknown photographers. But the Black subjects of those photographs do not mean that a Black photographer was behind the camera. For now, until further research is done taking into account the above parameters, John Roberts should be considered the first Black photographer in New Orleans.

The following historical names come from Mouton's research using newspapers, magazines, books, city directories, and censuses, and from asking contemporary photographers for names. The decade groupings indicate the earliest instance of the photographer being described as such. The racial designations listed match those recorded in public records.

1870

LOUIS FOUCHER: Born in 1848. Mulatto, lived in the 10th Ward, employed as a photographer's clerk.

1900

JESUS ALCANTARA: Born in Mexico in 1866. Immigrated to the United States in 1892, later became naturalized. Black, lived in the 7th Ward. Married Louisiana-born Isabella in 1894.

A. P. BEDOU (pronounced BAY-doo):[11] Born in New Orleans between 1880 and 1882.[12] It's not what can be said about Arthur Paul Bedou; it's what cannot be said about him. It wasn't until Mouton mentioned his name to Kalamu ya Salaam, that Salaam began to become familiar with Bedou and his photography. Eric Waters, who began his photography apprenticeship under Marion J. Porter, once mentioned the name of an internationally famous Black American photographer to Porter. In turn, Porter told Waters, "Bedou is the photographer you need to get to know." (When Waters started under Porter in the late 1960s, Bedou had been deceased as of 1966. By coincidence, Waters's mother's aunt was married to Bedou's brother.) Finally, in 2020, years after Mouton began urging Waters to go over to the Bedou archives of Xavier University, working on this book compelled Waters and Salaam to make the trip. Both were amazed by the quality and scope of Bedou's work. The trip would be better described as a pilgrimage.

---

11 Many records misspell Bedou's name and his family members' names; his wife Lilia Toledano becomes "Lilian" in some instances. Not being familiar with the variations can throw a researcher off track.

12 Bedou's date of birth is listed as 1880, 1881, and 1882 in various sources.

Given our book's breadth, there is a limit to the information that *SEEING BLACK* can include about each photographer involved in the project, including Bedou. But biographical information on him can be found in other writings, and his photographs can be seen in other books and on the website of Xavier University of Louisiana Archives & Special Collections. Of his parents, his father Armand was literate and mother Marie was illiterate. Bedou himself never went beyond seventh grade, which was not uncommon for the period.

As Booker T. Washington's personal traveling photographer, Bedou took pictures at Tuskegee Institute and at Hampton Institute without ever having a high school diploma in his back pocket. The Bedou family means were not modest, yet he went on to accumulate further wealth, which his widow shared with Saint Mary's Academy and with Xavier University by establishing academic scholarships in their names.

Bedou's methods of working soon became legend spread both by those fortunate enough to have been photographed by him and by those who witnessed him behind his camera. Photographers such as Baquet, Mouton, and Waters, who are two generations behind Bedou and were privy to first-hand accounts of him, and Irving Johnson III, who was the Xavier University photographer from the 1980s through the early 21st century, came to appreciate and admire Bedou by first hearing, then seeing, then believing. Those who measure a photographer's worth by their number of followers on social media, by the status of the media organizations employing them, or by the well-known figures the photographer shoots should follow the instructions Porter once gave to Eric Waters and familiarize themselves with A. P. Bedou.

ROBERT B. BROWN: Born in Louisiana in 1839. Black, lived in the 11th Ward, married Louise in 1872. Brown could neither read nor write.

JOSEPH DURAND: Born in 1870. Black, lived in the Tremé on Ursulines St. Married in 1898.

WILLIAM LONGMEYER: Born in 1871. Black, lived on N. Roman St. in the 7th Ward.

FERNAND MARTIN: Born in 1877. Black, worked as a photographer's clerk, lived in the Tremé on Hospital St. (now Gov. Nicholls St.). Married Julia in 1898.

DENIS PATTERSON: Born in Louisiana in 1852. Black, lived on Baudin St. in the 3rd Ward. Married Emma in 1879.

1910

H. CEVALLOS: Born in Louisiana in 1878. Black, lived on N. Derbigny St. in the 6th Ward.

ALBERT DOLHOUDE: Born in Louisiana in 1889. Black, worked as a photographer in a picture store, lived on Touro St. in the 7th Ward. Married.

GEORGE R. FLOYD: Born in Louisiana in 1885. Mulatto, lived on Foucher St. in the 12th Ward. Floyd had a studio on Dryades St. and photographed Black businesses.

ISIAH HATTON: Born in Maryland in 1873. Mulatto, single.

LEWIS PERRYINAN JR.: Born in Louisiana in 1895. Mulatto, worked as a porter for a photographer, lived in the 3rd Ward.

JOSEPH ROBERT: Born in Louisiana in 1884. Mulatto of Cuban ancestry, worked in the photography industry as a salesman, lived in the 8th Ward. Single.

CHARLES O. WILLIAMS: Born in New Jersey in 1880. Black, lived on Harmony St. in the 11th Ward, single. Williams had a studio on Dryades St.

ADOLPH ZERINQUE: Born in Louisiana in 1882. Mulatto, had a photo studio, lived on Columbus St. in the 7th Ward. Married Elvira Delay, whose mother was from Mexico.

1920

FLORESTINE PERRAULT: Born in Louisiana in 1895. Black, photographer, lived on Saint Peter St. First spouse was Eilert Bertrand, second spouse, Herbert W. Collins. Operated studios under the names of Bertrand, Claiborne, and Collins Studios. During the early years of World War II, her brother, Arthur J. Perrault, opened his studio on S. Rampart St.

JAMES BOYER: Born in Louisiana in 1901. Black, photographer, lived on Louisiana Ave. Spouse Corrine. Boyer was also the darkroom printer for Charles L. Franck's Baronne St. studio. Later had his own studio on Industry St.

BENNIE FOSTER: Born in Louisiana around 1881. Black, photographer, lived on Minion St. in the 3rd Ward. Single.

OSCAR GRIFFIN: Born around 1896. Mulatto, photographer, lived on Washington Ave. Spouse Viola. Griffin was also an artist and sign maker. He designed the 1925 publication *The Crescent City Pictorial*.

CHRISTOPHER HARRIS: Born in Mississippi in 1887. Black, photographer, lived on RR St. (now Franklin Ave.). Married.

MILTON C. HACKETT: Born in North Carolina in 1872. Black, photographer, lived on Eighth St. in the 11th Ward, had a studio on Harmony St. A widower.

AMY JACKSON: Born in Louisiana in 1891. Black, maid in the photography industry, lived on Allen St.

ALLIE KAHN: Born in Louisiana around 1890. Mulatto, photographer, lived on Conti St. Spouse Malvola.

I. M. MCCORMICK: Born in Mississippi around 1891. Mulatto, photographer, lived on Magazine St. Spouse Emie. McCormick was the person behind Magnolia Studio, located at 1610 Magnolia St. Magnolia

Studio photographed jazz groups in the 1940s inside nightclubs and the WPA Band during the 1930s.

CHARLES H. MICKENS: Born in Louisiana around 1883. Black, photographer, lived on Howard St. Spouse Alice.

JOHN W. MIDDLETON: Born in Florida around 1873. Black, photographer, lived on S. Franklin St. in the 12th Ward. Spouse Alice.

EMMETT TIGGE: Born in Alabama around 1882. Black, photographer, lived on Conti St. Spouse Mattie was Mulatto. Both Tigges could read but could not write.

ORYANA VALENTINE: Born in Louisiana in 1896. Mulatto, apprentice photographer, lived on Dumaine St. Single.[13]

1930

SIDNEY BONNOT: Born in Louisiana in 1877. Black, photographer, lived on Dauphine St. in the French Quarter. Single.

EMILE BOZONIER: Born in Louisiana in 1910. Black, photographer in a studio, lived on Lapeyrouse St. Single.

IRMA LANE: Born in Louisiana in 1909. Black, worked as a messenger in a photographer's studio, lived on Annunciation St. in the 12th Ward. Stepdaughter of Arthur Washington and Geneva Washington. Single.

IRMA LANE: Born in Louisiana in 1910. Black, worked as a helper for a photography company, lived on Magazine St. in the 13th Ward. Niece of Stella Johnson, who had a daughter, Eloise Johnson. Single.[14]

FELECIE MARCELIN: Born in 1876. Black, maid for a photographer, lived on N. Liberty St. in the 6th Ward. Widowed.

MANUEL THOMAS: Born in Louisiana in 1890. Black, photographer, lived on Simon Bolivar St. Spouse Silvia.

1940

MALCOLM BARROIS: Born in Louisiana in 1911. Negro, photographer, lived on Lapeyrouse St. Spouse Lenette. Both were college graduates.

WALTERINE CELESTINE: Born in Louisiana in 1917. Negro, photographer, lived on Valence St. Owned the studio Portraits Incorporated on Dryades St. into the 1980s. Like many others, she was influenced by A. P. Bedou. In the 1990s, while photographing at the New Orleans Jazz & Heritage Festival, Black Masking Indian Chief Donald Harrison Sr. (not in dress) and Mouton were discussing photography with photographer Terri A. Mimms. Chief

13 The 1920 Census lists Forestine [sic] Bertrand as a "Photographer" and Oryana Valentine as an "Apprentice Photographer." Both are among the city's first Black female photographers.

14 From the two listings in the 1930 census, it seems that these two Irma Lanes are the same person.

Harrison mentioned that studio portraits of the Monogram Hunters Tribe were once displayed in the window of Portraits Incorporated. In his 1976 documentary film *The Black Indians of New Orleans*, Dr. Maurice Martinez credits Portraits Incorporated for vintage still images of Black Masking Indians.

JOHN GARDINA: Born in Louisiana in 1917. Black, photographer, lived on Saint Bernard Ave. Spouse Mildred.

JAMES JENKINS: Born in Louisiana in 1917. Black, photographer, lived on Saint Peter St.

JOSEPH JONES JR.: Born in Louisiana. Negro, photographer, lived on Valence St. Married. Better known as "Scoop," a nickname acquired covering a fire in a Mississippi dancehall that resulted in two hundred fatalities, he photographed and wrote. For *The Louisiana Weekly*, Jones used photographs by his colleague Marion J. Porter, himself, and other Black photographers for his articles. When covering stories on the violence against Blacks in the South with John Rousseau for the *Weekly*, Jones often put his life in greater danger than when he was in the Pacific Theater during World War II, during which period he was a news correspondent. In 1966, he would establish a publication of his own, *New Orleans Data News Weekly*, which his son Terry continues to publish.

FREDERICK ALLEN MCLAIN: Born in Louisiana in 1902. Negro, photographer, lived on Bienville St. Spouse Cecile Smith.

IRENE MEYERS: Born in Louisiana in 1903. Black, photographer, lived on Saint Bernard Ave. Spouse Morris Meyers.

VILLARD PATIS (SIC) PADDIO: Born in Louisiana. Negro, photographer, lived on Kerlerec St. Spouse Hilda. Paddio was a World War I veteran from New Iberia, Louisiana, who learned photography from A. P. Bedou. This tutelage is apparent in the similarities in their photographic styles, and both men shot for the same clients. Paddio provided most of the photography seen in *The Crescent City Pictorial* of 1925. Dr. Arthé Anthony calls Bedou, Paddio, and her great aunt Florestine Perrault "the Trio." Indeed, they were the preeminent Black photographers of their era.

One distinct client of Paddio's was the Colored Waifs Home, administered by "Captain" Joseph Jones and Manuella Duplessis Jones. It was there that Paddio photographed the band that included a preteen Louis Armstrong. In his late teens, Armstrong brought his mother and sister to Paddio's studio for a portrait that has probably become the most reproduced photograph ever taken in New Orleans. Nearly every book or film documentary on Louis Armstrong, or on jazz, reproduces a version of that family portrait. In 1931, when Armstrong returned to New Orleans for the first time in a decade with international fame, Paddio was his preferred photographer. Photographically, just as Bedou is associated with Booker T. Washington, Paddio is associated with Armstrong. Unfortunately, Paddio never had the opportunity of photographing

Louis Armstrong's 1949 reign as King Zulu, for he committed suicide two years before.

OSCAR PAZON JR.: Born in Louisiana in 1914. Black, earned a wage or salary as a government worker with a usual occupation as a photographer. Lived on Pauger St. Married.

LEONARD SMITH SR.: Born in Alabama in 1895. Black, photographer, lived on Bienville St. Married.

NORMAN SMITH: Born in Michigan in 1909. Black, photographer, lived on Saint Ann St. Spouse Helen. (Norman R. Smith, the historian and photographer, is no relation to this Norman Smith.) Norman Smith established his popular studio on Dumaine St. near N. Claiborne Ave. in the 1940s. The popular French Quarter establishment Pat O'Brien's had "camera girls" who would circulate within the club taking pictures of patrons enjoying the casual atmosphere of food, drink, and entertainment. Before the advent of instant Polaroid film, the rolls of black-and-white film were brought into the club's darkroom for rapid processing and the making of prints to be sold to patrons before their departure. Norman Smith's son and daughter were two of those darkroom technicians making prints.

In 1988, while conducting research for the July issue of *The New Orleans Tribune*, featuring historic Black New Orleans photographers, Mouton spoke with Smith by telephone. At age eighty-eight, he was living on Tupelo St. in the Lower 9th Ward. He told Mouton to go to Saint Philip and N. Claiborne, where some guys had a shoe shine stand on the empty lot. They would give him Smith's old business card. Mouton followed Smith's instructions and obtained the card. Post-Hurricane Katrina flooding destroyed the keepsake. When Smith died, the two guys at the shoe shine stand erected a memorial in his honor.

FERNANDES WILTZ: Born in Louisiana in 1899. Black, photographer, lived on Saint Anthony St. Spouse Margarete.

HENDERSON WRIGHT: Born in Louisiana in 1905. Negro, photographer.[15]

EYES DON'T BOW DOWN

From the womb to the tomb and beyond, the lives of Black New Orleans photographers differ from the lives of photographers who are not Black. This has been the case throughout the city's history, regardless of whether the Black population was the majority or the minority. Their treatment by larger society has been without regard to whether a camera was strapped around their necks or whether it was resting in a case.

---

15 Marcus Christian wrote of a Works Progress Administration survey of S. Rampart St. conducted in 1941. On page four of chapter forty-three of his unpublished manuscript, *The History of The Negro in Louisiana*, he writes that "the former white and Negro street photographers have now dwindled down to one lone Negro who gives doubtful competition to established photographers." Further, on page eight, he notes that of the sixty-six Black-owned businesses, one is a photographer. Neither the street photographer nor the established (studio) photographer are named. Polk's 1940 *City Directory* lists Florestine Collins as a photographer at 170 S. Rampart St.

BEYOND EXPECTATIONS Photographer Nolan A. Marshall was one hardworking individual. Every dollar in his pocket, he earned through sheer hard work—an all-American success story. America, being the capitalist society that it is, touts and flaunts its wealth and encourages individuals to do the same. The symbols of achieving the "American Dream"—a nice house in a nice neighborhood, attending a nice school, owning a nice car—are known around the world. But Black people are not expected to possess any of those symbols. If they do acquire them, it's not because of their intelligence or because of their abilities; it's because of some criminal activity.

A World War II veteran, Nolan A. Marshall took a trip to New York City. He happened upon a utility post with a poem by an unknown street poet attached to it. He read the poem, titled "Then Some," removed it, and placed it in his wallet for the rest of his life. It inspired him to go beyond and give more.

Nolan A. Marshall recalled to Mouton an episode in his father's life. The elder Marshall had driven to northern Louisiana for a meeting with the principal of a school where he had an account. It was the 1960s, when desegregation was taking place throughout American life. He drove from New Orleans in his Cadillac, one of the symbols of having made it. Marshall had taken "Then Some" and expanded beyond merely taking pictures into being a dealer in class rings, caps and gowns, and more. His energy enabled him to have a staff of fifteen persons, probably the only photographer in New Orleans history to have such a large workforce, and over one hundred accounts in Louisiana. He was the number-two nationwide earner for the Herff Jones Corporation.

During Marshall Sr.'s meeting with the principal, a Black woman, a white male representative for a competitor to Herff Jones questioned her about hiring a photographer from the southern part of the state, who drove up in a Cadillac, to do work that a photographer up there could do. Nolan Marshall Sr. told the rep, "The reason I have a Cadillac is that it is big enough for me to stretch out my legs when I come up here because I can't stay in your hotels in this city." Marshall did not fume, rant-and-rave, pitch a fit. He professionally continued on with the proceedings, returned home, and told his family the story so that they would know what he went through in order to put their lives in a more comfortable condition than the one in which he grew up, and in many ways still experienced. The principal re-awarded him the account.

BACK AROUND In the spring of 2019, Director of Cultural Affairs of the Ace Hotel New Orleans, Sonali Fernando, curated an exhibition of the jazz photography of Norman R. Smith and Eric Waters. The hotel is located at 600 Carondelet St. The title of the exhibition, *Full Circle*, was selected by Mouton, as it was a homecoming for Smith. Prior to installation of the exhibition, Fernando gave Smith, Waters, and Mouton a tour of the exhibition space. Smith pointed out where the truck bays were located, where showrooms sat, the warehouse location, and where the elevators took personnel and customers. He was familiar with the structure in its past incarnation of Barnett's Furniture, where Smith had his first job out of high school in the 1940s.

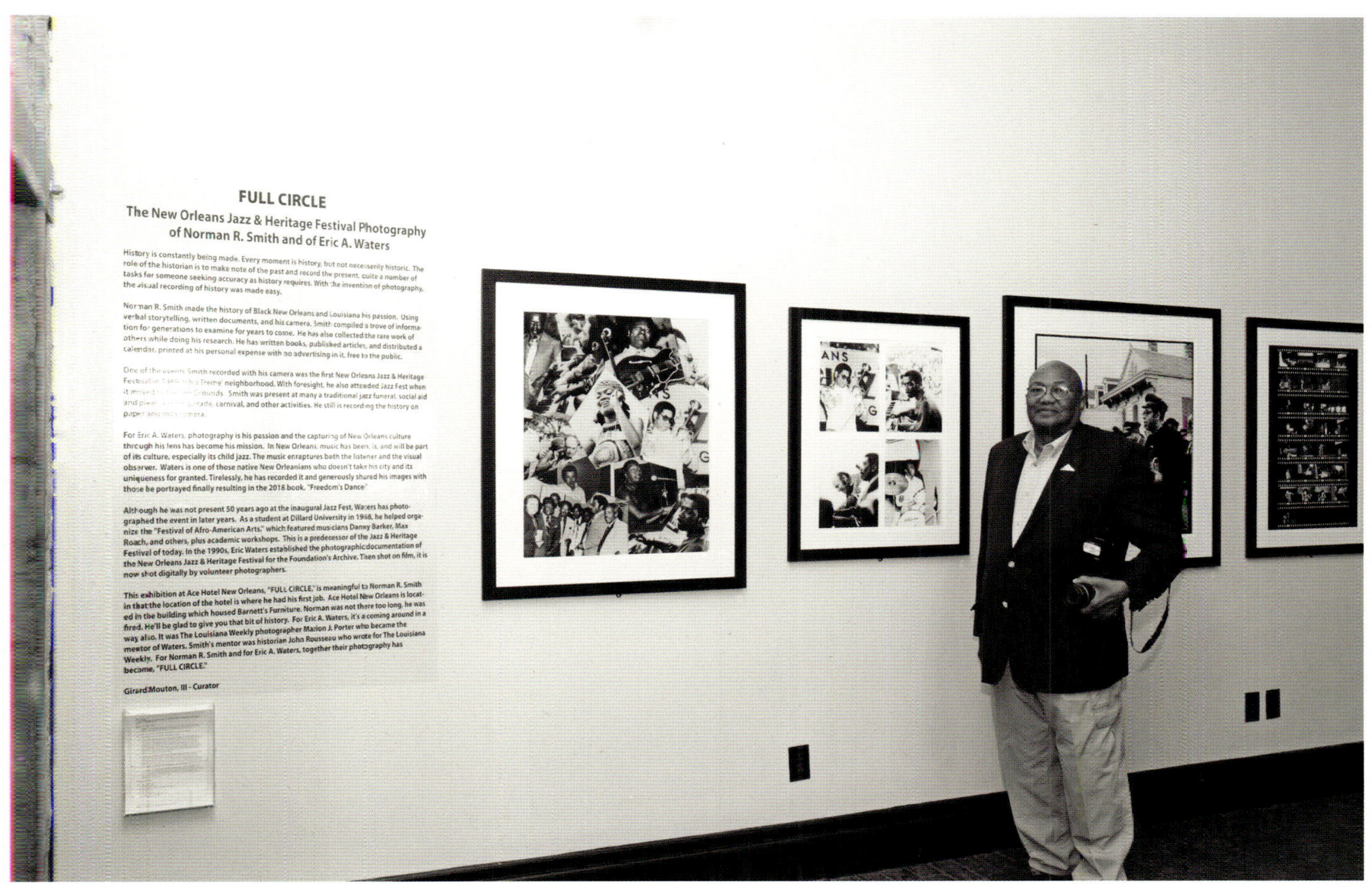

Norman R. Smith with his photographs at the opening of *Full Circle,* 2019. Photo: Girard Mouton,III.

On the closing Sunday night of the exhibition, Fernardo presented a panel of the photographers and show co-curator Mouton to a standing-room-only crowd. Smith recalled to the audience his experience on the first day of his job at Barnett's Furniture. A young white female office employee had spoken disrespectfully to a Black male employee "who was old enough to have been her father." The elderly Black man did not respond in kind. Young Smith stood up for the older Black worker, using "language that was not very French," and berated the young woman for the uncivil way in which she'd spoken. Smith was fired on his first day. If it had been 1840s instead of the 1940s, Norman R. Smith's fate would not have been being fired from his job.

Smith went on to become a historian with John Rousseau of *The Louisiana Weekly*, produce the annual "Sketches of Ebony" Black history calendar, and found Harmony House, an organization serving senior citizens, which he continues to administer today. Smith also served his country in Vietnam, where he worked in the mortuary unit.

COLLEGE TRY/ICE COLD Larry Songy was one of a group of Xavier University students who majored in art in the early 1960s. Others of "The Group," as it will be loosely referred to here, were Victor Labat, Warren Parker Jr., and John T. Scott. After graduation, Labat established an art gallery on Downman Rd. In the 1970s, Parker embarked upon a career in New York and in France, and Scott taught art at his alma mater, concentrating on sculpture, and received a MacArthur Foundation grant in 1992. Of The Group, Larry Songy was the one who also picked up the camera to express his artistic leanings.

The southpaw had equal ability and skill with an airbrush, pencil, paintbrush, and camera. In the 1970s, Songy could be seen capturing New Orleans culture on the city streets with his Leica. When a jazz funeral was held, usually led by Harold Dejan's Olympia Brass Band or by the Onward Brass Band, Songy was there capturing the scene in black and white, hopping into his Triumph convertible and heading to the gravesite in order to complete coverage of the ceremony.

Songy later decided to make a foray into the advertising, industrial, still commercial, and publicity photography market in New Orleans, which was white male-dominated. At the time, tourism was not the mainstay of the city's economy. But even in its nascent stage, it offered photographic income opportunities. The then booming oil industry, the ancillary services for it, and the flow of money into other areas of the economy provided an able cameraperson more possibilities than previous years. He shared studio space in the 100 block of Exchange Place at Canal St.—the same thoroughfare where the first photographer in New Orleans, Jules Lion, once established himself—with white male photographer David Richmond before "diversity in the workplace" became a phrase. He also employed a white assistant named Sue. Songy later set up shop independently at Elysian Fields Ave. and Royal St. with a full-fledged studio and darkroom. He also worked for a healthcare company located in the Claiborne Towers on the corner of Canal St. and Claiborne Ave. as the corporation's art director/photographer.

Songy was not as successful as white photographers, some of whom moved to his native city from other parts of the country, in the lucrative freelance market of New Orleans. On one of his many visits to the studio of photographer Marion J. Porter, he once said to Mouton, "You can't depend on Black folks alone in order to earn a living. Otherwise, you'd starve to death." In the mid-1970s, Songy told Mouton of a Black owner of a dance studio asking Songy about the possibility of his photographing her daughter's upcoming wedding. He gave her his proposed fee for the event, and didn't hear from her again after that. By coincidence, one day Songy was at a color photo lab conducting business when the dance studio owner came in to pick up the photos from her daughter's wedding, which she had hired a white photographer to cover. His fee was twice that of Songy's. There's the old expression, "The white man's ice is colder than the Black man's ice."

More than half a century after Larry Songy made pioneering efforts to crack the advertising and commercial New Orleans photography market, there's still no Black photographer who consistently garners a fair share of freelance jobs in the city. Eventually, in the 1980s, he returned to NASA's Michoud Assembly Facility for a more reliable and stable source of income, where he rounded out his working life in the art department. Larry Songy now resides in Atlanta, Georgia.

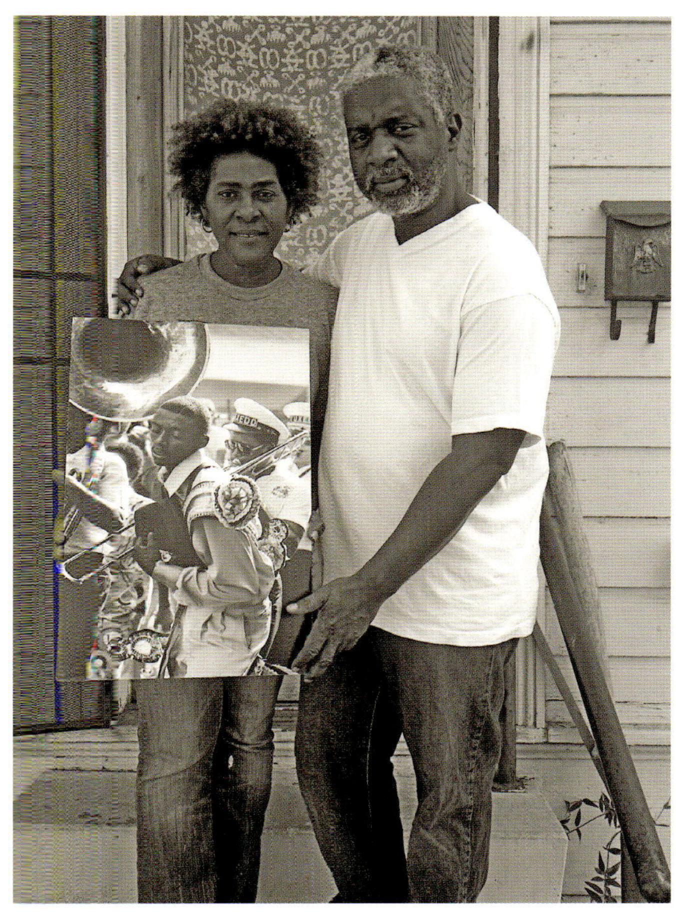

"Chandra McCormick and Keith Calhoun at L9," 2011.
Photo: Girard Mouton,III.

THE FINGER Black Masking Indian Chief of the Yellow Pocahontas Allison "Tootie" Montana chose the photography pair of Keith Calhoun and Chandra McCormick to work on a documentary film about him in conjunction with a show of Montana's suits at the New Orleans Museum of Art, planned for the early 1990s. The museum had other personnel in mind. A meeting between McCormick and a museum executive was scheduled to discuss the contract for the film. McCormick appeared at the office a few minutes before the 11:00 a.m. appointed time; the executive decided to leave for lunch, which would extend before and after the 11:00 a.m. appointed time. When he did finally show up, the executive used the phrase "You people"—which, to African Americans, is an insult—and invaded McCormick's personal space by putting his finger in her face, as if to teach her a lesson. Considering it an assault, McCormick pushed his hand away from her and, in the process, slapped him in the face. Black people, from the smallest child to the eldest adult, are expected to be obedient and docile without question. Chandra McCormick said of the encounter, "I gave him his finger back."

A BAD DAY Arts administrator Carol Bebelle and Louisiana State Museum curator Chuck Siler had an idea to get a lot of African Americans together at one time: Black New Orleans creatives would congregate for a single photograph of the entire group. The disciplines would encompass a broad range of the arts, including vocal and instrumental music, acting, painting, sculpture, photography, literature, the art and craft of Black masking traditions, and more. In the fall of 1998, their plans finally took place with a gathering in Congo Square. October 11, 1998 was Great Day New Orleans, A Historic Gathering of African-American Artists. It included photographers Harold Baquet, Gus Bennett, Keith Calhoun, Chandra McCormick, Dwight A. Harris, Irving Johnson, Morris Jones Jr., Girard Mouton,III, Bernadette "Bernie" Saul, Greg Simms, J. R. Thomason, Paul Sylvester Jr., and Eric Waters. All of the photographers were to be *in* the group shot, rather than taking it. Photographer Jim Cummins was flown in from New York City for the purpose of taking the group shot from a second-floor balcony of the Municipal Auditorium.

As the group stood in place for Cummins to take the picture, a white woman came around the Saint Ann St. side of the Municipal

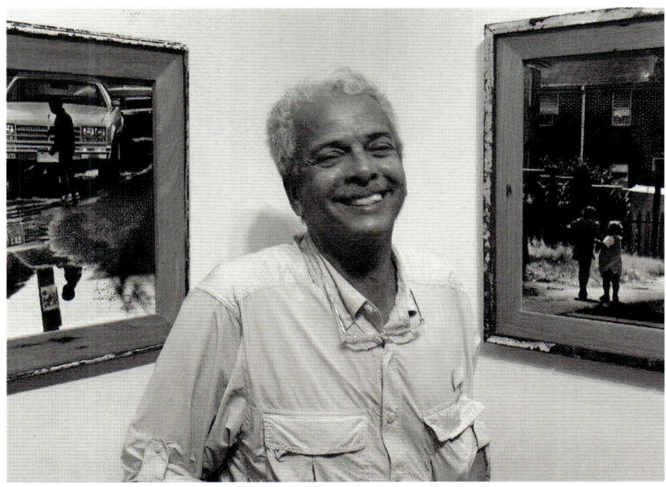

Harold Baquet with his Desire Project images at Stella Jones Gallery, 2012. Photo: Girard Mouton,III.

Auditorium with a camera bag on one shoulder and a small step stool in the other hand.[16] Carol Bebelle stepped out of the assembled group and halted the rogue photographer's advance. Out of ear range, they briefly talked. The photographer left the scene without getting the opportunity to capture a unique historical event. Bebelle returned to her position, Cummins took several exposures, and the whole gathering of Black creatives reassembled into several small groups for the New Orleans photographers to photograph inside the Municipal Auditorium and in Congo Square. For all but the white photographer, it was a great day.

AWARE Harold Baquet became the best known late 20th-century photographer in New Orleans due to his tenure as the Photographer to the Mayor of New Orleans, Division of Public Relations, first in the Ernest Morial administration and later in a portion of the Sidney Barthelemy administration. He was not the first Black photographer to hold that position. His immediate predecessor was E. A. Kennedy, who went on to establish a photojournalism career in Jackson, Mississippi; Palm Beach, Florida; and Philadelphia, Pennsylvania. Kennedy was one of the earliest photographers to adapt to the internet and create a website of his own for the distribution his pictures. The first Black person to ever be the mayor's photographer was Charlene Legaux of Porter's Photo News. She may have been the first woman in that position, as well.

Baquet also provided regional news coverage for Johnson Publishing Company, the publisher of *Ebony* and *Jet* magazines, and sold stock photography through the agency the Stock Market. For him, New Orleans was his subject, and the entire city was his backdrop. In 1989, after leaving city employment, he became the official photographer for Loyola University, where he utilized his photojournalism skills around the campus until his death in 2015.

Baquet was proud of his Creole heritage and never shied away from being Black. In 1986, crime in neighboring Jefferson Parish prompted Sheriff Harry Lee to order his deputies to stop Black drivers in predominantly white neighborhoods who were seen as being up to no good. Especially suspect were those driving "raggedy cars." Baquet's motor vehicle was a well-worn Japanese mini truck that could have used a good paint job and some body repairs. One night, he was driving in Old Metairie and was stopped. Baquet, very familiar to those in the local news media, was widely interviewed about the incident on the late night news,

16 The Saint Ann St. side of the Municipal Auditorium was the side of the city-owned structure that Black Orleanians had to enter for events held there that were open to the public. Once inside, their seating was restricted to the balcony, while whites only were allowed on the floor level.

where he wondered, "What would have happened if I were a darker-skinned brother?" Eventually, the New Orleans-born Chinese American sheriff rescinded the order.

Harold Baquet was not of a complexion that would have enabled him to pass for white, though there were ancestors of his that did, notably early 20th-century New Orleans jazz musician Achille Baquet. In one of his last lectures at Loyola University post-Katrina, Baquet pointed out this fact, one recorded in jazz history, to the audience. In that lecture he also reflected on the racial discrimination he experienced in the US Air Force Reserves, declaring to those in attendance, "I'm a Saint Aug. man." He was referring to his high school alma mater, Saint Augustine, where the students were taught that they were inferior to no one. In another appearance celebrating the Loyola University centennial in 2012, Baquet created a slideshow of his images and of historic images by past University staff photographers. One photograph showed a Loyola Jesuit at his desk. One side of the desk held a statue of the crucifixion; the other, the Confederate flag. This was Baquet's way of reminding the public that his Roman Catholic religion in New Orleans had a sinful past.

ONGOING BATTLE When the National D-Day Museum opened on June 6, 2000, celebrating the fifty-sixth anniversary of the invasion of Normandy during World War II, a highly publicized parade was held in New Orleans along Poydras St. The parade featured veterans of the invasion and of other conflicts in the war, including former Nazis who had been members of Hitler's armed forces. No Blacks who participated in the battle were included, nor any who had served in America's liberation of Europe from Hitler's reign. The Black community of New Orleans felt hurt, particularly its living veterans who had participated in the war.

Real estate appraiser and photographer Jim Thorns felt prompted to educate the public and the museum's founders on the fact that there were Black men who donned the uniforms of the United States armed services. His mission was to photograph them. The result was an exhibition in the Ernest N. Morial Convention Center. The National WWII Museum, renamed in 2004, has since been more inclusive in telling the stories of Black Americans, Asian Americans, Latino Americans, Native Americans, and American women of all races. But the fight was not over. In 2020, members of the museum's workforce accused it of being racist and sexist in its hiring, promotion, and pay. It sounded as if they were describing the United States military and society during World War II.

UNAVAILABLE The *Times-Picayune* newspaper traces its lineage back to the 1800s. It is the daily paper that has outlived all of its competitors. While there were no minority staff reporters or photographers in the early days of the publication, many of its news dealers and delivery boys were Black. Even if a person did not subscribe to it, the entire city knew of "The Paper." A person employed by it was considered to be reliable and trustworthy, a decent citizen.

Harlem-born Ric Francis moved to New Orleans in 1995 and began covering stories for the *Times-Picayune* with his camera. He lived in various locations in the Garden

District uptown while his lady friend lived in New Orleans East. In 1998, they decided to find a place for them both and found Faubourg Saint John to be a suitable environment. Ric and his companion Cassandra Lane, who worked at the *Picayune* as a reporter, answered a classified ad in their newspaper for an apartment available for rent. When they met with the white manager and his wife to tour the apartment, they were told it was now unavailable. Not mildly displeased with the situation, they pursued their case through a housing equality organization. Continuing their search, they eventually found living quarters nearby.[17] Francis left New Orleans prior to Katrina for Los Angeles, returning briefly to photograph the storm's aftermath, then went to South America, then to Africa, and currently lives in Norway, one of the whitest countries in the world.

THE WAY In 2018, L. Kasimu Harris was to have a talk and presentation of his work at the New Orleans Museum of Art—a rarity for a local Black photographer. NOMA had instituted a series of Friday night happy hour-type events with DJs, light refreshments, and mingling with the artists, and Harris was set to speak about his contribution to the museum's new exhibit, *Changing Course: Reflections on New Orleans Histories*. On the evening of his scheduled appearance, Harris made his way to the museum in his car. Not wanting to be the typical New Orleanian who is late for everything including their own funeral, as the natives say, he found a parking spot on Lelong Ave., which leads right up to the museum's entrance, and sought to ease his way into it. But close behind him was a car preventing his backing into the spot.

Harris exited his automobile to ask the driver, who he described as "an elderly white lady," to back up a bit so that he could park. Harris was not brandishing a weapon. His hair was not in braids, dreadlocks, or uncombed. He did not have a mouth full of gold teeth. There were no tattoos on his arms or face. He did not walk incumbered by trousers draped below his buttocks. His sartorial appearance was contemporary business casual. Loud rap music was not booming from the speakers of his car. He had graduated from the University of Mississippi. He grew up in a household with a mother and father present. He had no criminal background. His vehicle was not stolen. He addressed the driver in the Southern manner taught to him by his parents, which dictates that it is polite and proper to address people with "sir," "madam," "mister," or "miss" and that saying "please" and "thank you" is not servile. He did not address her with the word for a female dog. Fearing her life was in danger, the senior citizen called the police.

Harris found an alternative parking space, was not arrested, and made the show, albeit late with a valid reason rather than an excuse. In his anxiety to make his show on time that Friday summer evening, L. Kasimu Harris forgot that there's one thing the "elderly white lady" will always have: The White of Way.

THE SHOT In the English language, words and phrases in photography are identical or similar to those in weaponry. "Shot," "shoot,"

---

17 Cassandra Lane, "Discrimination Is More Subtle, but It Still Exists," *The Times-Picayune*, February 12, 1999.

"click," "fired off a series of shots," and "taking aim" are just a few examples. Like a projectile from a gun, a photograph can have an adverse outcome. From the Hollygrove section of New Orleans, Abdul Aziz has gone to Africa, Asia, the Middle East, and back to the United States to chronicle social injustice and conflict. In 2021, the Louisiana Endowment for the Humanities honored him as the Documentary Photographer of the Year for pointing his camera at topics in his home state revolving around long-standing social, racial, gender, economic, and civil injustice issues.

One of his local subjects was the effort to remove Jim Crow-era public monuments to white supremacy in New Orleans. At a protest over the monuments, Aziz photographed a supporter of keeping them in place. The person underscored his position by wearing regalia associated with Nazism. The subject was fired from his position as principal at a New Orleans charter school, whose student population was majority Black. After losing his job, the former educator sued Aziz in federal court for defamation. The American Civil Liberties Union of Louisiana defended Aziz. In 2020, the ACLU succeeded in having the case against Abdul Aziz dismissed.[18] Aziz never thought he would be in court over a photograph freely taken at a public event, nor did he imagine the impact and consequences it would have. Sometimes, with a camera or with a gun, all it takes is one shot.

18 ACLU of Louisiana, "ACLU of Louisiana Wins Victory in Dismissal of Defamation Case Against New Orleans Photographer," *American Civil Liberties Union*, last modified April 7, 2020, https://www.aclu.org/press-releases/aclu-louisiana-wins-victory-dismissal-defamation-case-against-new-orleans.

RIGHTS In the fall of 1984, Collins "Coach" Lewis, Director of Design, Spirit of Fi Yi Yi/ Mandingo Warriors Black Masking Indian Tribe, and Mouton made their way to the downtown location of Rhodes Funeral Home on N. Claiborne Ave. to visit Sylvester "Hawk" Francis. Francis, the Motor Vehicle Detail Specialist, was diligently keeping the signature Rhodes white limousines in showroom shape. He had begun the process of collecting funeral programs, fans, newspaper obituaries, route sheets, and other ephemera on Social Aid & Pleasure Clubs and their members. He expressed his dream of having a museum for his collection. He also had the desire to organize a parade in memory of the deceased who had contributed to the culture. Blessed he was to have been employed by the Rhodes family, for it was Joan Rhodes who became his chief backer and benefactor. After moving his growing collection around several places, Francis finally found a home for the Backstreet Cultural Museum in 1999 in a property owned by the Rhodes family. The former Blandin Funeral Parlor became its home.

The All Saints Day parade started from the Rhodes location where Francis worked. On that visit in 1984, Francis said, "I bring my films to Schwegmann for developing." He was referring to his still camera film and his 8mm color film. He never had the expensive equipment a professional photographer normally would, but his eye for the culture more than made up for the difference. Sometimes he would even shoot with a single-use camera, thus following one of the core dictums of photography: "Just take the picture." The content of his library of photos and movies is what mattered.

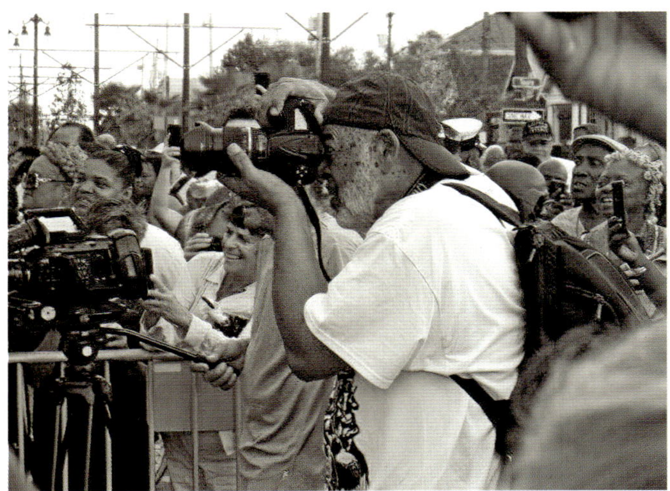

Eric Waters at the Black Men of Labor Social Aid & Pleasure Club parade, 2017. Photo: Girard Mouton,III.

Nevertheless, Francis was the same as his two visitors that day: just a Black man. On the top of recording his own culture, in his city, on his streets, in a voice of exasperation, Hawk said, "I gots rights!" The respect rendered to others was not accorded him. Being looked upon as a bothersome amateur, someone getting in the way of others, having his presence ignored, being pushed out of the way—in these and other ways, he was routinely scorned for even being on those streets with his camera. But Francis endured, and Backstreet Cultural Museum became a Tremé institution. He became an icon and an inspiration for others to showcase the culture. One evening in the kitchen of his mother's house while sewing a custom "Fire in the Eye" medallion for Mouton based on the Fi Yi Yi suit of the same name, Coach and Mouton discussed Mouton photographing white New Orleans culture. Coach chuckled and said, "There ain't none."

RESPECT/DISRESPECT "This white photographer comes and stands right in front of me. I told him I would kill him on the spot if he did not get out of my way."[19] The words of Eric Waters on a post-Katrina Mardi Gras morning in front of Saint Augustine Church while Rev. Jerome Ledoux, SVD, was blessing the suit of Donald Harrison Jr., Chief of the Guardians of the Flame Black Masking Indians, as Harrison emerged from the church. Being the cleric he was, Father Ledoux would have administered last rites to the white photographer, regardless of his religion, had Waters carried out his threat. But there was no mourning that Mardi Gras morning.

Why would one of the most respected photographers in New Orleans say such a thing? He was not present at Rhodes Funeral Home over two decades earlier, when Sylvester Francis had expressed the same feelings of not being respected. Still, Waters was echoing the words, "I gots rights!"

Waters has taken both the best second line photo and best jazz funeral photo ever. They have become iconic images that are frequently reproduced. The challenge to New Orleans photographers is to best those photographs. Meanwhile, participants on the parade scene still try to duplicate the actions he captured in those photographs. Waters's "Squirky Man Toe Touch Split" (1993) depicts Oliver Hunter Jr. in a Tambourine and Fan parade caught in midair, touching his toes with his legs perfectly spread apart, his derby suspended in the air over his head. "Coffin Dance" depicts Lois Nelson dancing in joyful grief atop her murdered son Darnell "D-Boy" Andrews' coffin

19 Karen Celestan and Eric Waters, *Freedom's Dance: Social, Aid and Pleasure Clubs in New Orleans* (Baton Rogue: Louisiana State University Press, 2018): 18.

as it is carried through a crowd of mourners. Due to his reputation, Eric Waters is the first photographer called by the culture to document a New Orleans cultural event, whether a jazz performance, a funeral, or a formal picture of a Black Masking Indian tribe. All of it he does gratis, with no thought of producing an image library for personal financial gain. Chief Allison "Tootie" Montana, who made 8mm films of his own, even once gave Waters a Metz photographic flash. Yet, like Francis, he still does not get respect on the street. Death threats are a rarity for the otherwise peaceful photographer, yet there have been times when his life was in danger due to the color of his skin.

The mother of Eric Waters and Ronald Waters was Marguerite Waters. Their father was George H. Waters Jr. Mother was a homemaker, and father was a delivery person for a dry cleaner, work with which his sons assisted him. And, from the 1950s through the 1990s, Mr. Waters was also an underground lineman for New Orleans Public Service, Inc., the corporation holding the exclusive contract with the City of New Orleans for utility services and public transportation.

The president of NOPSI was A. B. Paterson, who resided with his family on Audubon Place in the Garden District. Paterson also had a farm in rural Louisiana, which George Waters Jr. managed. If inside the private Paterson home or on the private Paterson farm, George H. Waters and his family could take a seat wherever they pleased. But there were two seats in the domain of New Orleans Public Service, Inc. that were off limits to all members of the Waters family: a seat in front of a Public Service bus's dividing screen for white passengers' "comfort," and the driver's seat of the city buses, trolleys, and streetcars. Segregation was the law for seating, and only whites were hired as drivers. Eric Waters humbly endured those indignities from his childhood through the mid-1960s, when segregation formally ended during his teenage years.

While Waters was a senior at Saint Augustine High School in 1964, Rev. Eugene McManus, SSJ, urged students to get involved in the efforts for people to register to vote, although the students themselves were not of voting age. McManus was part of the leadership of the National Urban League of New Orleans, an organization that taught students the non-violent tactics necessary for them to use for self-defense if and when they were attacked during their efforts. The sessions took place in the basement of of Mount Zion Baptist Church. When a group of trained advocates for voting rights picketed City Hall, District Attorney Jim Garrison had them arrested. Those under seventeen years of age were sent to the juvenile detention center, while those seventeen and older, including Eric Waters and Albert Miller, were sent to Orleans Parish Prison. Waters recalled, "While walking into the jail cell, there was a small American flag on a stick over a door. A Black cop was standing in the doorway laughing at me and Miller. The Black attorney for us forgot we were in jail. We stayed there until 11:00 p.m. It was a Friday. Our parents were upset." Today, Eric Waters does not participate in any ceremony honoring the American flag or in the singing of the National Anthem.

Waters has often told Mouton of a memorable off-court encounter he and other members of the Dillard University basketball team had in the mid-1960s. He recently told Mouton that Dean Irby and Walter Tillman were the guys to talk to for more on that encounter. In April 2022, Mouton spoke separately to each by telephone for their recollections.

Girard Mouton,III: When was it?

Walter Tillman: It was the 1965–1966 season. The members were Malbert Pradd, Dean Irby, John Thompson, Julius Green, and Thomas Gagnier. Eric was a freshman on the team. Jim Singleton was head coach. John Brown was assistant coach.

Dean Irby: Winston Lovett was on the team. I was a freshman. I had family members who went to Dillard before me. I was born in Jamestown, New York. At the time the city had maybe five hundred Black people out of a population of forty thousand. When I was a child, our family would drive to Alabama to spend time with other family. When we crossed the Mason-Dixon Line, you could feel the atmosphere change. One time, our father pulled into a gas station and was called "boy." He did not answer back.

GM: Recall for me what happened on that trip Eric has told me about.

WT: There were two station wagons of us headed to Little Rock, Arkansas, to play Philander Smith. We took Hwy. 61. We stopped in Junction City, Arkansas, to use a restroom. There were two Esso stations. One on our side of the road, another on the other side of the road, going in the opposite direction. The one on our side had gas, but no restrooms. We went to the one on the other side. It had restrooms. One of us went to the "colored" one, pulled on the door. It was locked.

WT: An attendant came out with a gun. He said, "You boys don't know how to ask for what you want?"

DI: The attendant said, "You boys can't go in there."

WT: Dean Irby said, "Who you calling boy?"

GM: Do you think the use of "boy" triggered the memory of your father not responding in protest when he was called "boy" at a gas station?

DI: You know, Mouton, I never thought about it that way.

DI: "Big" John Thompson intervenes between me and the guy with the gun. He picked me up, shoves me in the car, put his hand over my mouth and said, "Shut the ____ up! Don't you know you can get us killed here?"

WT: We left. Further up the way, we were stopped by the Arkansas State Police. They asked us if we had had any trouble. We said no. They didn't notice the "Colored" sign one of us had stolen sitting on the dashboard.

The Blue Devils met a devil of another color on their way to defeat Philander Smith. (In a subsequent in-person conversation with John Thompson, he revealed that he was the one who stole the "Colored" sign. No one knows its location today.)

THE LESSON Since the 1993 founding of the Black Men of Labor Social Aid & Pleasure Club, Eric Waters has been their official photographer. He photographs the annual banquet held the night before the parade, photographs the members prepping inside Sweet Lorraine's Jazz Club, takes the group shot outside the club, and covers the parade. Inside the club, the group shot of the previous year is displayed as a huge backdrop covering an entire wall. The series of photographs have become a visual history.

The organization of the shoot attracts other photographers trying to get their shots, too. Paul Sylvester Jr., proprietor of Sweet Lorraine's, makes efforts to prevent any interference with or disruption of Waters's concentration in getting the perfect exclusive photograph. In 2015, Mouton, who Waters has assist in the shoot and who has never taken a photo of the assembly, was standing in front of the police barricades, waiting for the members and Waters. Two members of the club walked up and saw a local university professor with his camera standing in front of the barricades.

One said, "Man, I don't want you taking my picture."

The white professor responded, "I put the pictures on a CD and give them to Fred [Johnson, co-founder of the Black Men of Labor]."

The Club member replied, "I don't care what you do! Take my picture, and I'll kick your mother________ ___! Mouton, you can stay, but he's gotta go!"

The white professor left. Mouton stayed and continued in his role as assistant to Waters.

Sylvester Francis was expressing the feelings of many Black people when he said, "I gots rights!" The Club member was voicing the feelings of pain from unhealed wounds of exploitation. Deposited in his memory bank were scenes of white people coming into his Black community for their benefit, visions of them coming to collect rent, insurance, take people to jail, solicit a sexual rendezvous, hook young people on drugs. The alphabet behind the name of the white professor meant nothing to him because as a child, he could not attend the school in the next block down from Sweet Lorraine's and learn his ABCs it was for white children only. His father could not even have had the dirtiest job of a City of New Orleans employee, a job where the trucks were the same color as the men who worked them: Garbage collectors. Whites only.

There was also within the Club member the specific experience of exploitation through a camera. By placing himself in front of the barricade, the white professor was saying he was privileged and special because of his relationship with Fred Johnson. He began his reply with the word "I," making himself and his actions of "niceness" more important than anyone with the Club. He did not say, "Fred gave me permission to be here." Saying such, if he did indeed have permission, may or may not garnered the same reaction from the club member. From being present at the kickoff of the Black Men of Labor parade many years before, the white professor knew of the restrictions imposed at the barricade. He felt he was an exception to the unwritten rules. If he was OK with the boss, he must be OK with everybody else. All Black people think the same, act the same—so it was assumed. Alvin Jackson, the Black Club member, asserted his individuality while being a member of the group.

As close as the professor and his white colleagues get to the culture of Black New Orleanians, there are some things they would never do to really be like them: reduce their net worth by 90%, reduce their salaries by 33%, leave no generational wealth to their successors, reduce their degrees to a high school diploma, live without healthcare, go for days malnourished, accept indecent housing, relentlessly and loudly demand that their country of origin pay its former colonies reparations, relentlessly and loudly demand that the United States of America pay reparations to its citizens who descend from slaves. As much as they listen with fascination and record stories of the culture in the past, before people like them re-colonized New Orleans and began lamenting its passing, they would never envision being enslaved, unpaid, brutalized, raped, and murdered. It's inconceivable. They may be experts on Black people, but they are experts without the experience of being Black and, thus, cannot see Black.

On that day in 2015, at the Black Men of Labor parade, a university professor was taught a lesson in the School of Hard Knocks on the streets of New Orleans.

THE NON-PHOTOGRAPHER Knowledgeable of the power of photography, Black leaders have embraced the medium and its practitioners. Frederick Douglass, who was alive when it was invented, not only sat for studio portraits numerous times, he also wrote about photography. Louisiana Governor P. B. S. Pinchback adorned a room in his house with photographs of Black leaders. New Orleans civil/human rights activist Jerome "Big Duck" Smith realized the impact a photograph can have after he was photographed by Marion J. Porter during demonstrations in New Orleans in the 1960s. Smith, a member of the New Orleans chapter of the Congress of Racial Equality, told Mouton, "Porter had a way of getting there before us." Not surprising, because Porter's business card read "Any Place, Anywhere, Anytime." He also advertised "Porter's Photos Make News."

In a 2011 evening talk presented by the African American Resource Center at the Main Library of the New Orleans Public Library, Smith told the intimate gathering that his mother, Leona Sampier, had had an amateur interest in photography. Those listening included his fellow CORE member Doratha Smith-Simmons, Mouton, musician Porgy Jones, who would occasionally call Mouton about technical matters on photography, and two others. Eric Waters revealed to Mouton that Smith's mother, Leona Sampier, once gave him a big manual on photography. Yet Smith never picked up the camera himself, despite it being present in his household and around him during the Civil Rights Movement. Smith preferred to coordinate shoots using the talents of Eric Waters, public school bus driver Al Peters, and Mouton.

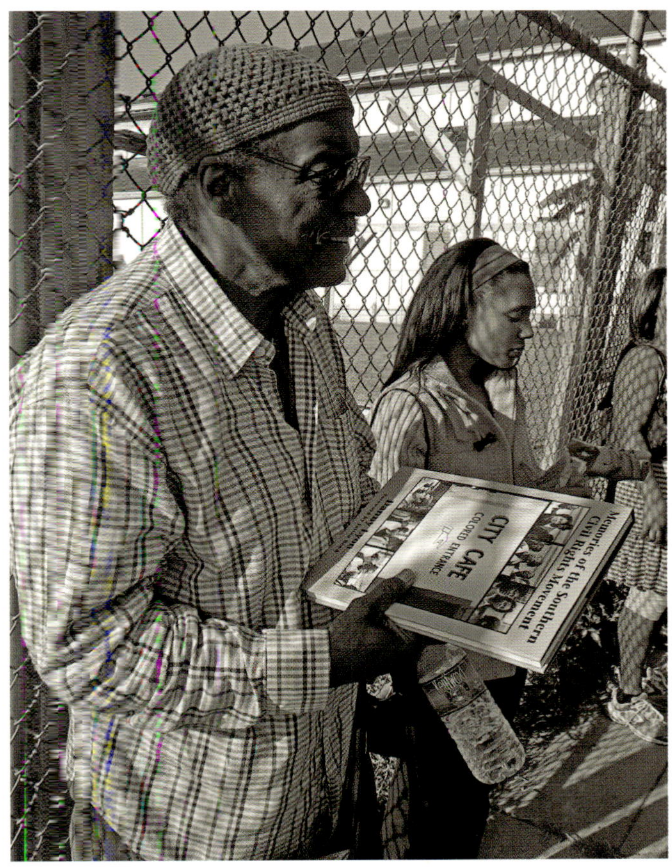

Jerome Smith with a signed dedicated copy of Danny Lyon's *Memories of the Southern Civil Rights Movement* gifted from Girard Mouton,III, 2011. Photo: Girard Mouton,III.

In 1984, while walking under the I-610 East overpass over N. Claiborne Ave. to one of those photo shoots, Jerome Smith began talking about photographers active during the 1960s, such as Richard Avedon. He said of another photographer, who had belonged to a prestigious photo co-operative, "____ ___ wouldn't even give us a Band-Aid during the Civil Rights Movement." He did praise Danny Lyon: "Danny Lyon was in that hole with us, too," Smith said.

Lyon was a white photographer from Brooklyn, New York. In his early twenties, Lyon became the first staff photographer of the Student Nonviolent Coordinating Committee. The "hole" Smith was referring to was jail. In his 1992 biography, *Memories of the Southern Civil Rights Movement*, Lyon recalls being held in the same segregated jail as Dr. Martin Luther King Jr. In his role as SNCC's official photographer, Lyon had unlimited access to its activities and, as a white person, was able to carry his camera into settings where no Black person could venture. However, there was still fear on his part, as anti-Semitism made him susceptible to violence.

It seems to some that Jerome Smith is hostile towards white photographers—the man who was photographed with Ike Reynolds in Avedon's studio for *Nothing Personal*, the book Avedon did with his high school classmate James Baldwin. The man who had no opposition to Danny Lyon pointing his lens at him during CORE's activities across the South. The man who was photographed on the streets of New Orleans by the white daily newspapers and television stations while peacefully protesting injustice. No, what Smith objects to is the camera being turned on Black New Orleans culture by those seeking to benefit from its existence without returning anything to the community.

Ask almost any Black Masking Indian in New Orleans how Super Sunday began, and most could not give the exact answer. Eric Waters, who has photographed many Super Sundays, never knew of its origin until he learned of it from Mouton. At Tootie Montana's funeral in 2005, held at Saint Augustine Church with Rev. Jerome Ledoux, SVD, officiating, Smith expressed how during the Civil Rights Movement, he would not have minded being in jail any day with the exception of Mardi Gras, for it was the defiant spirit of the Black

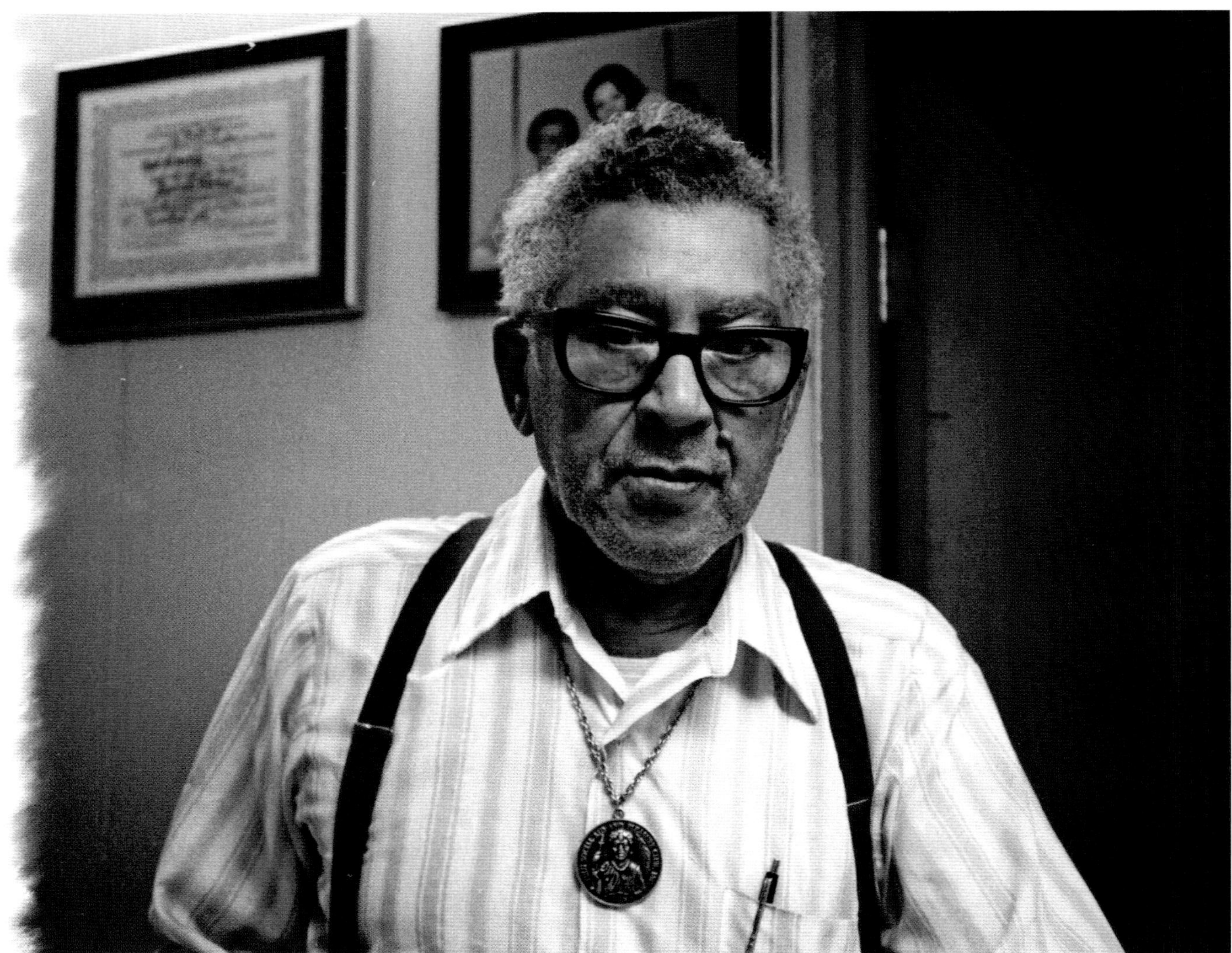

Marion J. Porter in Porter's Photo Studio, 1981. Photo: Girard Mouton,III.

Masking Indians that inspired him to join the fight for freedom. In the late 1960s, as he was able to spend more time in New Orleans than away from home, he turned to Porter for ideas on how to get those icons of culture more recognized. Knowing Smith's organizational skills, Porter suggested, "Jerome, why don't you start a parade?"

There was a parade of Black Masking Indians that began at the Jeunes Amis next to Charbonnet-Labat Funeral Home on Saint Philip St. and stayed in the general neighborhood. There was the traditional Saint Joseph's night reappearance of the Black Masking Indians post-Mardi Gras, where they stayed in their respective neighborhoods. In 1969, Porter's idea of a parade was born with "Super Sunday." It began downtown at Hunter's Field, went uptown to Shakespeare Park, and returned to Hunter's Field, thus allowing people to see gangs from all parts of town. At Hunter's Field, there were Black art vendors, food vendors, and a stage with entertainment. It alternated years of beginning at either park. As it became larger, banners by artist Doug Redd were hung from the Claiborne Ave. overpass publicizing "The Soireé."

Jerome Smith saw to it that Hunter's Field was a no man's land for white photographers seeking to exploit the culture. The first Super

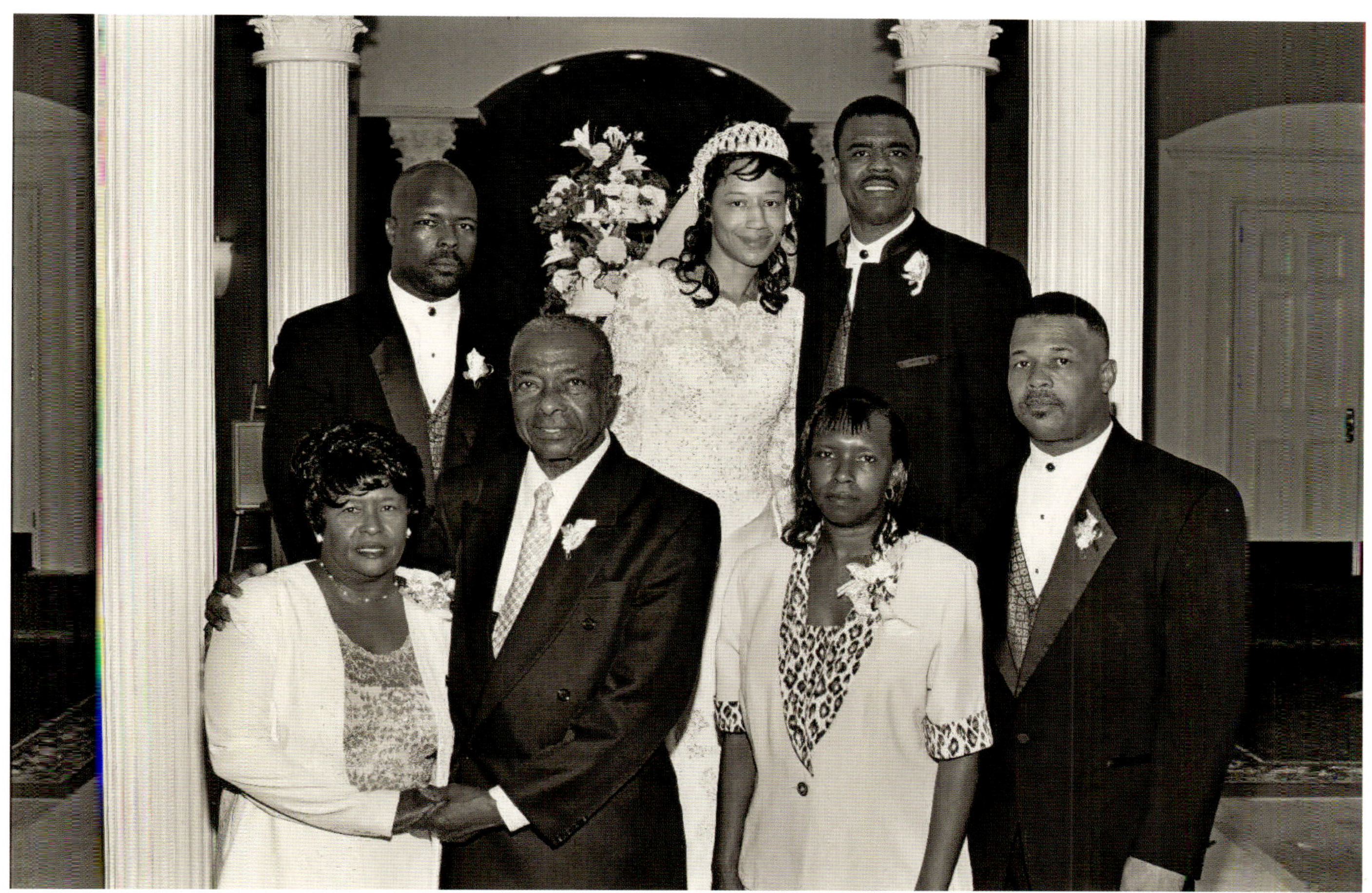

Cleary family at the wedding of Rick Cleary to Deborah Stephens, front row (left to right): Florence Cleary, Verrett Cleary, Gail Rivers Cleary, and Ronnie Cleary; rear row: Michael Cleary, Deborah Stephens Cleary, and Rick Cleary, 1999. Photo: Girard Mouton, III.

Sunday preceded the first New Orleans Jazz & Heritage Festival held in 1970, which presented performances by Black Masking Indians. The success of the original Super Sunday inspired the other Super Sundays, downtown in the 7th Ward and in Algiers on the Westbank. Marion J. Porter's greatest legacy is not one of his many well-known photographs, but his conception of a free showcase to the world of an important facet of Black New Orleans culture.

AT A TIME Rick Cleary is the audiovisual supervisor at Baylor College of Medicine in Houston, Texas, a position he has held since 1988, six years after he obtained a Bachelor of Fine Arts in Photography from Louisiana Tech. He is also the founder and pastor of the Apostolic Firehouse Pentecostal Church in Galveston, Texas. Prior to his career at Baylor, Cleary was the audiovisual technician at the National Aeronautic and Space Administration's Michoud Assembly Facility in New Orleans East from 1982 until 1988. Before working at Michoud, Cleary was employed as a camera salesperson in Lafayette, Louisiana. While traveling around the United States and abroad to Canada, Cuba, and Australia as a drummer in the United States Marine Drum and Bugle Corps, Cleary became interested in photography to record his travels. It was at Michoud that Cleary became a co-worker of Mouton.

Cleary was brought into the photo department at Michoud by his fellow 1982 photography graduate, Greg Simms of New Orleans. Michoud became known as a top facility for the manufacture of space exploration launch vehicles in the 1960s, when Saturn rockets were built there for the Apollo lunar program. The three were working at Michoud when the Space Shuttle became NASA's primary project. Under the prior Apollo program, the photo department at Michoud had nearly a dozen staff members. When Mouton, Simms, and Cleary were there, the department numbered four total. All four were African Americans with college degrees in photography. (Mouton's was a Bachelor of Science from the School of Photographic Arts and Sciences at Rochester Institute of Technology). There was one other African American who worked in the department with Mouton, who eventually returned to his hometown of Cincinnati, Ohio. It is not known if African Americans were working in the photo department during the Apollo program, but during the Space Shuttle Era, for the first time the photo department at Michoud was majority—indeed, exclusively—African American.

Mouton, Simms, and Cleary are Louisiana-born descendants of their state's enslaved African peoples. Mouton and Simms' families, being urban New Orleanians, were more removed from the plantation than Cleary's rural Franklin, Louisiana, family. He told Mouton of the experience of growing up in sugar cane country, outlining the structure of the system:

> "The families that owned the land during slavery still own the land today. During slavery, those families also owned the sugar mills that refined the sugar. After the end of slavery, they still did, but later, big corporations began to own the sugar mills. During slave days, the owners farmed the land. Today, they lease the land to farmers."

For generations, the Cleary family was at the bottom of this system. There was the typical corporate structure of workers, group head, boss, supervisor, and manager. Before the middle of the 20th century, before the birth of Rick Cleary and some of his siblings, and nearly a century after Emancipation, "The supervisor told my daddy, 'I can have your wife and you, too,'" Cleary recalled. "My daddy began getting his family off that plantation one by one." He succeeded, without either of Cleary's parents having to submit to the supervisor's advances. In the sharecropping system, there was always the possibility of an unwelcome entrance into either the working areas or the workers' living quarters. "You see, Mouton, the supervisor could fire you anytime. If you got fired, you had to be off the land in twenty-four hours. That was the law." Mr. Verrett Cleary and Mrs. Florence Cleary finally liberated themselves and their children, Michael, Ronnie, Gail, and Rick, in 1964. The family of Rick Cleary is only one of millions of those that endured physical and non-physical abuse during and after slavery.

The effects are still being felt today. On Old Gentilly Rd. in New Orleans East, in front of Michoud's Building 103 stands a sugar refining smokestack from the days when Antoine Michoud owned a sugar plantation on the land. Rick Cleary went from working on the land of one sugar plantation to another.

THE QUESTION Greg Simms works at a car dealership in Atlanta, Georgia. His friend and former coworker Mouton helped him and his family pack their belongings on their move from the Algiers section of New Orleans in 2003. Initially, Simms made an effort to support his family of four by freelancing as a photographer. Freelancing takes time to build a base of reliable, consistent clients. The going was tough, and immediate financial needs forced Simms in making the decision to forgo the profession for a commission job in sales. His daughter Lindsey says the only time her "dad takes pictures now is with his cell phone."

But Simms was once the lead photographer at Michoud, shooting black-and-white film, which he processed and printed, and color film, which Mouton, as color lab technician, processed and printed. In his role, he got around everywhere on the facility, and everybody knew his face. Simms' start in photography began with a rivalry between him and a teenage cousin who had a Polaroid camera. She said she could take better photos than he could. He acquired a Minolta 16 35mm camera. She got a better Polaroid. He then moved on to a Pentax K1000, which he says "was even better." Irving Anderson, his chemistry teacher at L. B. Landry High School, would develop and print pictures in the school chemistry lab. Fascinated by an image appearing in a tray of developer, Simms, who was failing science, was encouraged by Mr. Anderson to learn the process in order to improve his grades. Prior to those lessons from Anderson, Simms was sending his pictures off to a lab for developing and printing. Simms attended Louisiana Tech (where he was a classmate of Rick Cleary) in Ruston for two years, left to go back to New Orleans for two years, then completed his college education.

After earning his Bachelor of Fine Arts in Photography in 1982 from Louisiana Tech, Simms returned home to New Orleans and immediately found employment with the US Army Corps of Engineers' photography department. He described it as "an in-depth job. I made 10"x10" black-and-white reproductions from aerial image mapping, processed color slides, went up in a helicopter shooting 35mm slides of wetlands in southwest Louisiana and in Mississippi, a lot of different things." It was from his association with some of the top industrial and advertising photographers in New Orleans that Simms obtained the position at the Army Corps of Engineers and later at Michoud.

The photographers he had worked for included Don Scott, Joe Bergeron, and Paul Rico. Don Scott's Ace Photography, next to Immaculate Conception Jesuit Church on Baronne St., did executive portraits, weddings, and industrial photography in formats from 35mm to 8"x10". Joe Bergeron, on Union St., was an industrial photographer. Paul Rico, also on Union St. at the time, was becoming known for still life photography. Rico moved his studio from Union St. to a double house/commercial space on Prytania near Melpomene St. Simms continued to assist Paul Rico while being employed at Michoud. Rico moved out of the Prytania location into a building he had constructed from the foundation to the ceiling with the sole purpose of being a still photography studio. The 1,575 sq. ft. studio at 1533 Melpomene St. in the Lower Garden District had tracks in the ceiling for the precise positioning of lighting equipment, a spiral staircase in the rear to be used for observation during shoots or for a shooting position, a kitchen for food stylists to prep food for the food photography specialist, and a black-and-white darkroom for in-house processing and printing. A mid-sized parking area in front provided off-street parking for Rico and his clients. If Rico didn't drive his Jensen Healey convertible to work, he would borrow his wife's Mercedes and park it on the lot. Simms would sometimes accompany Rico to out-of-state shoots for national clients. In this period, Simms rented the previous Rico studio at 1504 Prytania. In the late 1980s he rented an old commercial space on Alix St. in Lower Algiers, near his residence.

After the Space Shuttle Challenger exploded in 1986, the entire space program came to a slowdown during an extensive investigation to find the cause of the tragedy. Though the external tank manufactured at Michoud was not the problem, there was uncertainty in the air about secure employment resulting from the slowdown. Mouton was the first to leave Michoud in 1986. Simms followed in that same year. Cleary stayed at Michoud until 1988.

Simms now had the time to put all of his efforts into his freelance photography career. He did jobs for a Royal St. antique and art dealer, shot portfolios at a modeling and acting school, became the staff photographer for *The New Orleans Tribune* monthly newspaper, continued to assist Paul Rico, and worked overnight at a large national retailer. He did what it took to provide for himself, his wife Toni, son Ruben, and daughter Lindsey. Whenever there was a project involving a group of Black photographers, whether it was gratis or minimally compensated, Greg Simms participated without question and delivered a photographic product of the same quality he would deliver to a paying commercial client. He took part in The Great Day, the documentation of the painting of the Claiborne Ave. overpass posts, and the *Ties That Bind* book and exhibition. A skilled black-and-white darkroom technician, Simms also custom-printed the black-and-white, homoerotic images of nude and seminude Black men taken by a white New Orleans male artist—"to a point," in Simms' words, that is, until his concerns about possible racialized sexual objectification in these photos made it impossible for him to continue developing them.

In the late 1990s digital photography was making its way as an affordable replacement for traditional still photography. The Paul Rico studio was not going to be left lagging behind. On a visit to the studio when Simms was setting up a children's clothing shoot for a Magazine St. retailer, Simms told Mouton what his young daughter had expressed to him one day when he brought her to the studio: "Daddy, how come you don't have something like this?" She was referring to Paul Rico's studio as compared to Simms' own studio around the corner.

"Mouton, what do you say to a child when they ask you a question like that?"

Every parent in the world expects a child to one day ask, "Where do babies come from?" and give a prepared answer of their choice. It may be assumed, but not expected, that a Black child would ask a Black parent about

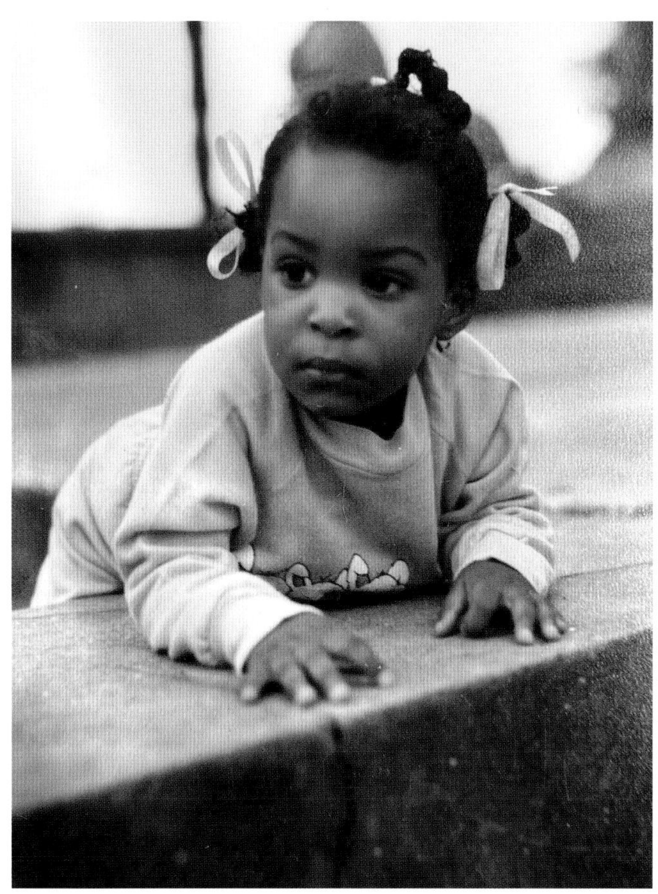

Lindsey Renee Simms, ca. 1984. Photo: Greg Simms. Courtesy of the Artist.

the difference in their lives compared to the lives of others. There is no prescriptive answer. Little Lindsey Simms was not the first child of her kind to ask that question. Millions of enslaved children asked their natural parents and their pseudo-parents, as African families were torn apart on the shores of Africa and in the slave markets of the New World, that same question. Ancestors of Lindsey Simms asked their parents the same question. After the end of slavery, millions more Black children asked their parents the same thing.

However, Lindsey was not questioning her daddy. She was not questioning a Black man who has been working since the age of nine, in a bakery alongside other members of his family. A Black man who has never had a year of not working in over fifty years. A Black man who grew up in the Algiers Fischer Housing Development and raised dogs as a hustle. A Black man who, as a teen, was on the wrong side of the law. A Black man who put himself through college. A Black man who went from no class in the projects to middle-class homeowner. Lindsey was not questioning him. She was questioning America, America in its entirety.

This was not a moment for Greg Simms to break out with an inspirational gospel song of his Baptist church dating back to the plantation days, or to borrow from the more reflective African American Methodist hymnal book. This was not a moment for him to recite the lyrics of a mournful blues song, or jump up with joy to a jazz rhythm born, like him, in New Orleans. A supercomputer with the artificial intelligence to consistently defeat the world's grand masters of chess could not answer her question. A supercomputer with the artificial intelligence to consistently beat the winningest *Jeopardy!* contestants could not answer her question. Lindsey wanted a different kind of AI to give her the answer: a human being with Actual Intelligence, that being her daddy.

Greg Simms, with a smile not on his lips but one in his eyes, looked at Mouton and gave him the answer to The Question. "Mouton, I just keep on going. I just keep on going."

Girard Mouton, III is a 1974 honors graduate of the School of Photographic Arts and Sciences at the Rochester Institute of Technology. In 1968, while a student at Saint Augustine High School, he took art classes on weekends from Xavier University art graduate Warren Parker Jr. Sessions were held at the school or at a

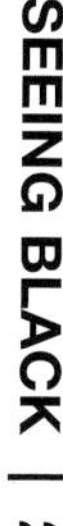

studio Parker shared with Victor Labat and John T. Scott on Burgundy St. near Dumaine St. in the French Quarter. In the summer of 1969, Mouton continued taking classes from Mr. Parker at the Free Southern Theater in a building it shared with a dry cleaner on the corner of Louisa St. and Law St. in the 9th Ward. In 1966, prior to becoming Mouton's art instructor, Warren Parker Jr. co-produced Aaron Neville's first solo hit recording, "Tell It Like It Is." Girard Mouton,III tells it like it is—whether you like it or not.

EXPOSURES

Black New Orleans photographers may not have received significant attention from the general media. They have given attention to themselves in many forms. This is an abbreviated list of events.

APRIL 1944: Dillard University exhibited the photography of A. P. Bedou. Curated by Vernon Winslow.

1948: The Louisiana School of Photography established on Dryades St. for World War II veterans, and others, to enter the profession. The instructors were Jack Berquist, George F. Hall, and Vincent P. McCormick. Berquist and Hall were white. The racial identity of McCormick is unknown. African Americans were among its students.

1949: Southern University hosted an exhibition of the work of students in the photography program.

1969: Lloyd Edwards became the first Black television news cameraperson at ABC affiliate WVUE-TV Channel 12. He gained his skills behind the camera as a photographer for Nolan Marshall.

1971: Arnold Bourgeois became the first Black television news cameraperson at NBC affiliate WDSU-TV Channel 6. Bourgeois learned the craft while in the United States Air Force.

1973: Wille Wilson Jr. became the first Black television cameraperson at CBS affiliate WWL-TV Channel 4. Wilson began working at the station in maintenance in 1968.

CIRCA 1980S: An exhibition of the photos by Marion J. Porter, documenting the Civil Rights Movement in New Orleans, in a building, possibly housing Total Community Action, on the lakeside of Chef Menteur Hwy., near the Danziger Bridge. Tom Dent hosted the opening.

1980S: The Backstreet Cultural Museum, the idea of Sylvester Francis, found a permanent home in 1999 in the former Blandin Funeral Parlor. The museum housed still photos, 8mm films, and videotapes by Francis of Black New Orleans Carnival culture and music traditions.

1980: *Dock Workers* by Keith Calhoun, exhibited at the Earl K. Long Library at the University of New Orleans.

1983: *Etches of Ebony Louisiana*, Black history calendar on noteable Louisianians, places, and events, began being published by Norman R. Smith.

1983–1985: *Summer Fun Photo Tips* by Lloyd Dennis, broadcast between June and August on WYLD-AM and WYLD-FM. One-minute broadcasts on weekdays ". . . without intruding on the 'groove' of urban contemporary radio."

MAY 1991: *The Eyes of Jazz* by A. P. Bedou, Magnolia Studio, Villard Paddio, and William Ranson, at the Hogan Jazz Archive at Tulane University. Curated by Girard Mouton,III and Alma Williams.

CIRCA 1992: *Crescent Eyes* at Perseverance Hall No. 4 in Armstrong Park. Organized by Harold Baquet, Girard Mouton,III, and Eric

Waters. Self-curated works by Harold Baquet, Bryan Berteaux, Keith Calhoun, Veronica James, Chandra McCormick, J. R. Thomason, and Eric Waters. Nearly twenty years earlier, Berteaux had become the first Black staff photographer for *The Times-Picayune*. His brother, Norman, followed him. This was Berteaux's first photo exhibition.

1992: Photography of the New Orleans Jazz & Heritage Festival for the New Orleans Jazz & Heritage Festival Foundation archives. Prior to the 1990s, Eric Waters rarely attended the annual Jazz Fest, although he lived two blocks from the Fair Grounds where it is held. Upon attending, he noticed the dearth of Black photographers covering an event where the majority of the talent is Black. (Girard Mouton,III, a colleague of Waters's, is on a roster of photographers who shoot the Festival for the company producing the Jazz Fest, Festival Productions, not for the Foundation itself. Their mission is to promote, not to document, the Jazz Fest.) Eric Waters and Wali Abdel Ra'oof, Executive Director of the Foundation, conceived of Waters photographing the Jazz Fest for himself and for the Foundation's permanent records. Previously, the Foundation had neither a permanent photographic record of the Festival nor an organized archive.

Initially, Waters covered the entire Jazz Fest singlehandly. He later had Ron Green and Morris Jones Jr. join him. Ra'oof suggested Texan non-African American photographer Brenda Ladd become part of the process. This team was able to more fully photograph the event. Eventually, circa 2004, the Foundation began the formal process of soliciting photographers for its Volunteer Photographer Program, where the photographers are selected by a blind jury based solely on the quality of their work.

MARCH 1992: *"It's Carnival Time," A Photographic Exhibit of New Orleans Mardi Gras Indians* by Dwight A. Harris at the Neighborhood Gallery.

CIRCA 1994: *The Mookie Square Show* shown on Cox Cable Community Access. Broadcasts of Social Aid & Pleasure Clubs parades videotaped by Randolph "Mookie" Square, along with information on upcoming parades.

APRIL 1994: *Capturing the Flash: African-American Photographers' View of the Black Indians of New Orleans* at the Louisiana State Museum at the Presbytère. Organized by Louisiana State Museum curator Chuck Siler. Siler, and many Black New Orleans photographers, observed how white photographers received many accolades for photographing Black Carnival and for being considered experts on the subject. He used his position to bring to light some of the Black photographers who had been photographing their own culture. Photographers: Harold Baquet, Bryan Berteaux, Keith Calhoun, Roland Charles, Dwight A. Harris, Veronica James, Chandra McCormick, J Nash Porter, Paul Sylvester Jr., and Eric Waters. Videographers: Arnold Bourgeois and Lloyd Edwards. Screening and discussion of *Black Indians of New Orleans* documentary led by Dr. Maurice Martinez on opening night, April 26, 1994.

1996: Ebon Images, Inc. created by Eric Waters to preserve the photographic legacy of Marion J. Porter. Girard Mouton,III assisted in archiving original negatives and prints.

SEPTEMBER 1997: *Tribute to Gordon Parks* at the Southern University at New Orleans Center for African and African American Studies. Organized by SUNO photographer Gus Bennett for the visit by Gordon Parks on a lecture and audio/visual presentation of his work. Photographers: Gus Bennett Jr., Keith Calhoun, Dwight A. Harris, Veronica James, Chandra McCormick, Girard Mouton,III, and Eric Waters.

OCTOBER 11, 1998: Great Day in New Orleans: A Historic Gathering of African-American Artists in Congo Square. Organized by Carol Bebelle and Chuck Siler. Photo shoot of two hundred Black New Orleans creatives by Jim Cummins of New York. Photographers included in shoot and participating in post-shoot portraiture of subjects: Harold Baquet, Gus Bennett, Bryan Berteaux, Stanley Chatman, Lloyd Dennis, Dwight A. Harris, Irving Johnson III, Morris Jones Jr., Saddi Khali, Chandra McCormick, Girard Mouton,III, Peter Nakhid, Jafar M. Pierre, J Nash Porter, Bernadette "Bernie" Saul, Greg Simms, Paul Sylvester Jr., J. R. Thomason, and Eric Waters. Video of portrait sessions by J. R. Thomason.

DECEMBER 1998: *Marion J. Porter* by Marion J. Porter at Ashé Cultural Arts Center. Mural-sized prints hung from ceiling during ceremony announcing the conversion of Venus Gardens market into the Ashé Cultural Arts Center. Curated by Eric Waters.

1999: *Marion J. Porter* by Marion J. Porter at the Coker Room of the Municipal Auditorium. Curated by Lynn LeBeaud. Opening remarks by George "Tex" Stevens.

FEBRUARY 2000: *The Ties That Bind: Making Family New Orleans Style* at Ashé Cultural Arts Center, coinciding with release of the same titled book. Photographers: Lidya Araya, Harold Baquet, Keith Calhoun, Veronica James, Morris Jones Jr., Girard Mouton,III, Marion J. Porter, Greg Simms, and Eric Waters.

CIRCA 2001: Photographs of Black World War II Veterans by Jim Thorns, shown at the Ernest N. Morial New Orleans Convention Center, in response to the absence of Black veterans participating in the opening day ceremonies of The National D-Day Museum (renamed The National WWII Museum in 2004).

2003: Opening of The House of Dance and Feathers by Ronald W. Lewis, founder. Black New Orleans cultural museum with emphasis on that in the 9th Ward. Collection of photographs by Eric Waters and others.

MAY 2003: Gallery Claiborne LLC grand opening exhibition of art by Natalie Keller and photography by Gus Bennett, Morris Jones Jr., Girard Mouton,III, Greg Simms, Paul Sylvester, J. R. Thomason, Jim Thorns, Eric Waters, and Nat Williams. Guest photographer: Lou Jones of Boston, Massachusetts.

2003–2020: Unnamed informal group meeting at Café Rose Nicaud to discuss photographic and non-photographic topics. Participants: Ron Green, Cedric Ellsworth, danielle c. miles,

Girard Mouton,III, Selwhyn Sthaddeus "Polo Silk" Terrell, Eric Waters, and Conrad Wyre. Out-of-town guests: John Glenn, Louis Mendes, and John Pinderhughes.

2003–2020: Café Rose Nicaud hosted various photographers exhibitions and talks. Photographers included Gus Bennett and Eric Waters.

2003–PRESENT: Capturing the Flash Awards, conceived by Chuck Siler, presented by Cherice Harrison-Nelson as part of the Mardi Gras Indian Hall of Fame annual ceremony recognizing photographers who respectfully photographed Black Masking Indians. Recipients: Harold Baquet, Gus Bennett, Kichea Burt, Sylvester Francis, Dwight A. Harris, Dr. Freddye Hill, Morris Jones Jr., danielle c. miles, Girard Mouton,III, Paul Sylvester Jr., J. R. Thomason, and Eric Waters.

2005: Launch of the Gulf South Photography Project, to teach children in New Orleans and the greater Gulf South photography, founded by Harlem, New York, native Jim Belfon after his relocation to New Orleans following Hurricane Katrina.

CIRCA 2007: Exhibition of various young Black photographers at the McKenna Museum of African American Art. Primarily the works of non-New Orleans photographers. Curated by Shantrelle P. Lewis.

AUGUST 2007: *Medley of Melodies: Portraits of Their Souls* by Jim Thorns at the Darkroom.

APRIL 2008: *A Celebration of Faith: Henriette DeLille and the Sisters of the Holy Family*, A. P. Bedou, Villard Paddio, Jim Thorns, other photographers. Tremé Villa of the New Orleans African American Museum of Art, History, and Culture. Executive Producer: Jim Thorns, Curated by Mora J. Beauchamp-Byrd.

2009: "Cfreedom Photography presents: The Essence of N.O.W. (New Orleans Women)," still and video on Facebook.

DECEMBER 2009: *Wine, Women & Song* by Brian Perkins and Eric Waters at Studio 1318.

DECEMBER 2009: *Winter Wonders* by Brian Perkins and *Solemn Hues of Silence* by Eric Waters at Studio 1318.

FEBRUARY 2010: *Harold Baquet: A Retrospective* by Harold Baquet at Miller Hall, Loyola University New Orleans. Curated by Harold Baquet.

DECEMBER 2011: *Wine & Women* by Brian Perkins at Objets Trouvés.

FEBRUARY 2011: *In the Blink of an Eye* by Harold Baquet, at the Collins C. Diboll Art Gallery, Loyola University New Orleans. he exhibit was inspired by *In the Blink of an Eye: Photographic Memories of New Orleans No More*, a book co-written by Baquet and Cheron Brylski.

DECEMBER 2014: *Talk That Music Talk* by Bruce "Sunpie" Barnes at the New Orleans Jazz Museum, with book of same name co-written by Barnes and Rachel Breunlin.

MARCH 2015: *The Legend Behind the Lens* by Harold Baquet at Loyola University New Orleans. Curated by Harold Baquet.

MAY 2015: *Polo Slim*, pop-up exhibition inside 3711 Saint Claude Ave., by Cashew Company Journal of Atlanta, Georgia.

DECEMBER 2015: *Noirlinians: danielle c. miles, Asia-Vinae Palmer, LaToya 'Blaze Like Fyre' Edwards, and Patrick Melon* at the McKenna Museum of African American Art. *Noirlinians* is an AfroFashion blog founded in 2015 by Denisio Truitt and Mwende "FreeQuency" Katwiwa.

JANUARY 2016: *Blak Code Series* by Gus Bennett, at the Isaac Delgado Fine Arts Gallery, Delgado Community College. Curated by Myesha Francis.

APRIL 2017: *Kusherehekea: The Photographs of Sekou Fela: A Fifty-Year Retrospective* by Sekou Fela at Café Istanbul. Curated by Monique Moss.

JUNE 2017: *Live on the Streets of New Orleans* by Randolph "Mookie" Square Jr. at the New Orleans Jazz & Heritage Festival Foundation Gallery with Joan Rhodes. Curated by Randolph "Mookie" Square.

AUGUST 2017: *Pop That Thang!!!* by Selwhyn Sthaddeus "Polo Silk" Terrell at Antenna Gallery. Exhibition and book release.

OCTOBER 2017: *Through His Lens* by Harold Baquet at Le Musée de f.p.c. Curated by Cheron Brylski.

NOVEMBER 2017: *Jazz Funeral Secondlines and Protest: TAKING OVER THE STREETS* by Sekou Fela at the New Orleans Jazz Museum. Curated by Monique Moss.

APRIL 2018: *New Orleans People Project* by Gus Bennett at the Cultural Exchange Pavilion at the New Orleans Jazz & Heritage Festival.

MAY 2018: *Jazz Funeral Secondlines + Protest: TAKING OVER THE STREETS* by Sekou Fela at the Millie M. Charles School of Social Work, Southern University at New Orleans. Curated by Monique Moss.

JUNE 2018: *Changing Course: Reflections on New Orleans Histories* by L. Kasimu Harris and six other artists at the New Orleans Museum of Art. Curated by Brian Piper.

JULY 2018: *Rivertown Artist Talk Series* by Eric Waters at Fleur de Lily Bakery & Cafe, Kenner, LA. Organized by Dwight A. Harris of the Rivertown Arts Council.

APRIL 2019: *Full Circle: The New Orleans Jazz & Heritage Festival Photography of Norman R. Smith, and of Eric Waters* by Norman R. Smith and Eric Waters at the Ace Hotel New Orleans. Sonali Fernando, director of cultural affairs, Ace Hotel New Orleans was the chief curator with Girard Mouton,III serving as co-curator.

APRIL 2019: *Purpose and Passion: A Colorful Quilt* by Eric Waters at the New Orleans Jazz Museum.

JUNE 2019: *We the Culture* at the Axxiom Gallery. Photography and videography by House of the Young, Edward X Buckles, Monique Constance, E'Jaaz Ammaad Mason, Stacey Muhammed, and Selwhyn Sthaddeus "Polo Silk" Terrell.

DECEMBER 2019: *Lion's Shadow: In Tribute to Jules Lion* at the Stella Jones Gallery. Photography by Lorenzo Baker, Durado Brooks, Cedric A. Ellsworth, Delaney George, PRO$PER JONE$, Juliana Kasuma, Benicia King, Mariana Shepard, Leslie Claire-Spillman, Bruce Williams, and Olivia Vega. A project of PhotoNOLA 2019 curated by Brent Irving of Diversify Photo.

JUNE 2020: *No justice, no peace, photographs of resistance* at The Front Gallery. Photography by Abdul Aziz, PRO$PER JONE$, and Ashley Lorraine. Curated by Leslie Claire-Spillman.

APRIL 2022: *NOLA Hip-Hop & Bounce Party* by Selwhyn Sthaddeus "Polo Silk" Terrell at the New Orleans Jazz Museum.

JULY 2022: *Picture Man: Portraits by Polo Silk* by Selwhyn Sthaddeus "Polo Silk" Terrell, with backdrops by Otis Spears and outdoor installation for visitor self-portraits with Spears' backdrops. Curated by Brian Piper.

SEPTEMBER 2022: *Called to the Camera: Black American Studio Photographers* at the New Orleans Museum of Art. Photography by A. P. Bedou, Florestine Perrault Collins, Nolan A. Marshall, Villard Paddio, Arthur J. Perrault, Selwhyn Sthaddeus "Polo Silk" Terrell, Eric Waters, and others. Curated by Brian Piper.

OCTOBER 2022: *First Frame: The Prelude of SEEING BLACK, Black Photography in New Orleans 1840 & Beyond* at the New Orleans African American Museum. Photography by A. P. Bedou, Florestine Perrault Collins, and Villard Paddio, with installations simulating an early 20th-century portrait studio and the first studio of Florestine Perrault Collins, housed in her living room parlor. Curated by Shana M. griffin, Kalamu ya Salaam, Eric Waters, and Girard Mouton,III.

ADDENDUM

MARCH 2023: *In the Spirit of Black* at Ashé Cultural Arts Center and Ashé Powerhouse Theater, in partnership with SEEING BLACK, featuring the works of seventy-five contemporary Black photographers. Curated by Shana M. griffin.

JANUARY 2024: *Gestures of Refusal: Black Photography and Visual Culture* at the Contemporary Arts Center, New Orleans, in partnership with SEEING BLACK, featuring over a hundred Black photographers, five installations, and over 250 photographs and art objects. Curated by Shana M. griffin.

JUNE 2024: *Frames of Black Portraiture: From the Early 1900s to the Present* at Xavier University of Louisiana, in partnership with SEEING BLACK, featuring contemporary and historical photography and installations. Curated by Shana M. griffin and Anne Collins Smith with Kalamu ya Salaam, Eric Waters, and Girard Mouton,III.

COMMENDATIONS

Bruce "Sunpie" Barnes elected Executive Director of the New Orleans Photo Alliance for term 2022–2024.

Joan Mitchell Foundation in New Orleans residencies: 2017, Clifton J. Faust; 2018, Cecelia Fernandes; 2019, Gus Bennett; 2019, Eric Waters; 2020, Jourdan Barnes; and 2022, L. Kasimu Harris.

Louisiana Endowment for the Humanities Documentary Photographer of the Year: 2017, Eric Waters; 2021, Abdul Aziz; and 2022, L. Kasimu Harris.

Photographers Obscura Bibliography

Allen, James. *Without Sanctuary: Lynching Photography in America*, 15th ed. Santa Fe: Twin Palm Publishers, 2021.

ACLU of Louisiana. "ACLU of Louisiana Wins Victory in Dismissal of Defamation Case Against New Orleans Photographer." *American Civil Liberties Union*. Last modified April 7, 2020. https://www.aclu.org/press-releases/aclu-louisiana-wins-victory-dismissal-defamation-case-against-new-orleans.

Anthony, Arthé A. *Picturing Black New Orleans: A Creole Photographer's View of the Early Twentieth Century*. Florida: University Press of Florida, 2012.

Barbash, Ilisa, Molly Rogers, and Deborah Willis, eds. *To Make Their Own Way in the World: The Enduring Legacy of the Zealy Daguerreotypes*. New York: Aperture, 2022.

Bertrand's Studio. "Why Not a Picture of the Child." Advertisement. *The New Orleans Herald/The Louisiana Weekly*, October 3, 1925.

Blassingame, John W. *Black New Orleans, 1860–1880*. Chicago: University of Chicago Press, 1973.

Brierly, Dean. "2009 Portfolio Contest Selection: Eric Paul Julien." *B&W Magazine* 68, August 2009. 92–95.

Celestan, Karen and Eric Waters, photographer. *Freedom's Dance: Social, Aid and Pleasure Clubs in New Orleans*. Baton Rouge: Louisiana State University Press, 2018.

Celeste, photographer. "Gayiety [sic] And Masking Rules Cool Mardi Gras Day." *The Louisiana Weekly*. March 5, 1949.

"A Child's Eye View." *The Times-Picayune/New Orleans Picayune*. May 8, 2008.

Christian, Marcus. Unpublished manuscript, *The Negro in Louisiana*, 1942. MSS 011. Earl K. Long Library, University of New Orleans, New Orleans.

Clark, Peter Wellington. *Delta Shadows: A Pageant of Negro Progress in New Orleans*. New Orleans: Graphic Arts Studio, 1942.

Cohen, H. and A. Cohen. Cohen's *New Orleans and Lafayette Directory, for 1849*. New Orleans: H. and A. Cohen, 1848.

—. *Cohen's New Orleans and Lafayette Directory, for 1850*. New Orleans: H. and A. Cohen, 1849.

—. *Cohen's New Orleans and Lafayette Directory, for 1851*. New Orleans: H. and A. Cohen, 1850.

—. *Cohen's New Orleans and Lafayette Directory, for 1852*. New Orleans: H. and A. Cohen, 1851.

—. *Cohen's New Orleans Directory, for 1853*. New Orleans: H. and A. Cohen, 1852.

—. *Cohen's New Orleans Directory, for 1854*. New Orleans: H. and A. Cohen, 1853.

Cowan's Auctions. "[DAGUERREOTYPE - PORTRAITURE]. LION, Jules, photographer (attributed). Ninth plate daguerreotype of young African American woman. [New Orleans, ca late 1840s]." *Cowan's*. Last modified February 26, 2021. https://www.cowanauctions.com/lot/daguerreotype-portraiture-lion-jules-photographer-attributed-ninth-plate-daguerreotype-of-young-african-american-woman-new-orleans-ca-late-1840s-4073456.

The Crescent City Pictorial. "The Crescet [sic] City Pictorial." Advertisement. *The New Orleans Herald/The Louisiana Weekly*, October 3, 1925.

Desdunes, Rodolphe Lucien. *Our People and Our History*. Translated and edited by Sister Dorothea Olga McCants. Baton Rouge: Louisiana State University Press, 1973.

Diversify Photo. "Louisiana, United States (13)." *Diversify Photo*. Accessed April 23, 2023. https://diversify.photo/where/united-states/louisiana/.

—. "Louisiana, United States (2)." *Diversify Photo*. Accessed April 23, 2023. https://diversify.photo/upnext/united-states/louisiana/.

Ebon Images, Inc. *The Ties That Bind: Making Family New Orleans Style*. New Orleans: Ashé Cultural Arts Center, Ebon Images, Inc., 2000.

Edney, Hazel Trice. "Data News Founder Joseph M. Scoop Jones Honored as Distinguished Black Publisher." *Data News Weekly*. March 27–April 2, 2010.

Edwards, Richard. *Edwards' Annual Director, City of New Orleans and Suburbs for 1870*. New Orleans: Edwards & Co., Southern Publishing Co., 1869.

—. *Edwards' Annual Director, City of New Orleans, for 1871*. New Orleans: Edwards & Co., Southern Publishing Co., 1870.

—. *Edwards' Annual Director, City of New Orleans, for 1873*. New Orleans: Edwards & Co., Southern Publishing Co., 1873.

"464 Wedding Photographers in New Orleans." *The Knot*. Accessed April 26, 2023. https://www.theknot.com/marketplace/wedding-photographers-new-orleans-la.

Gardner, Charles. *Gardner's New Orleans Directory, for 1859*. New Orleans: Charles Gardner, 1858.

—. *Gardner's New Orleans Directory, for 1861*. New Orleans: Charles Gardner, 1861.

—. *Gardner's New Orleans Directory for 1866*. New Orleans: Charles Gardner, 1866.

—. *Gardner's New Orleans Directory for 1867*. New Orleans: Charles Gardner, 1867.

—. *Gardner's New Orleans Directory, for 1868*. New Orleans: Charles Gardner, 1868.

—. *Gardner's New Orleans Directory for 1869*. New Orleans: Charles Gardner, 1868.

Gibson, John. *Gibson's Guide and Directory of the State of Louisiana, and the Cities of New Orleans & Lafayette*. New Orleans: John Gibson, 1838.

Hollins Coar, Valencia. *A Century of Black Photographers: 1840–1960*. Providence: Rhode Island School of Design, 1983.

Honora, Jari C. "The Photographer—Arthur Paul Bedou (1880–1966)." *CreoleGen*. Last modified July 1, 2013. https://www.creolegen.org/2013/07/01/the-photographer-arthur-paul-bedou-1880-1966/.

Hunter, Beryl F. "Black Photographers: Documentarians of Social History." Master's Thesis, Southern University at New Orleans, 2011.

Joan Mitchell Foundation. "Cecelia Fernades." *Joan Mitchell Foundation*. Accessed April 23, 2023. https://www.joanmitchellfoundation.org/cecelia-fernandes.

—. "Clifton J. Faust." *Joan Mitchell Foundation*. Accessed April 23, 2023. https://www.joanmitchellfoundation.org/clifton-j-faust.

—. "Eric Waters." *Joan Mitchell Foundation*. Accessed April 23, 2023. https://www.joanmitchellfoundation.org/eric-waters.

—. "Gus Bennett." *Joan Mitchell Foundation*. Accessed April 23, 2023. https://www.joanmitchellfoundation.org/gus-bennett.

—. "Jose Cotto." *Joan Mitchell Foundation*. Accessed April 23, 2023. https://www.joanmitchellfoundation.org/jose-cotto

—. "Jourdan Barnes." *Joan Mitchell Foundation*. Accessed April 23, 2023. https://www.joanmitchellfoundation.org/jourdan-barnes.

—. "L. Kasimu Harris" *Joan Mitchell Foundation*. Accessed April 23, 2023. https://www.joanmitchellfoundation.org/l-kasimu-harris.

King, Nathan J. *King's Tan Mardi Gras New Orleans 1968: A Pictorial of Carnival Season And Social Clubs*. New Orleans: Nathan J. King, 1968.

Ksiazkiewicz, Noah and Diwang Valdez, photographer. "Sthaddeus 'Polo Silk' Terrell." *Cashew Journal* 1, no. 2 (2014): 84–101.

Lane, Cassandra. "Discrimination is More Subtle, but It Still Exists." *The Times-Picayune*. February 12, 1999.

Learson, Berweida E. "Broadway Show: A Tribute to Photographer Celeste Broadway." *Arthur Hardy's Mardi Gras Guide*, 2010. 46–47.

Lyon, Danny. *Memories of the Southern Civil Rights Movement*. Chapel Hill: University of North Carolina Press, 1992.

McKenna, Beverly S. *The New Orleans Blackbook: Rebuilding A City, Empowering a Community*. New Orleans: McKenna Publishing Company, 2011.

Mygatt, A. and Co. *A. Mygatt & Co.'s New Orleans Business Directory 1857*. New Orleans: A. Mygatt and Co., 1857.

—. *A. Mygatt & Co.'s New Orleans Business Directory 1858*. New Orleans: A. Mygatt and Co., 1858.

Michel, E. A. *New-Orleans Directory for 1841*. New Orleans: E.A. Michel & Co., 1840.

Michel and Co. *New-Orleans Annual and Commercial Directory for 1843*. New Orleans: Michel & Co., 1842.

Minor, John L., ed. *The Weekly Pelican*. 1886–1889.

Morial, Mayor Ernest N. *Blacks in City Government 1981*. New Orleans: City of New Orleans, 1981.

Mouton, Girard,III. "Behind the Lens: Arthur Paul Bedou—African American Photographer Extraordinaire." *Arthur Hardy's Mardi Gras Guide*, 2018. 62–63.

—. Collection of photographers' business cards. New Orleans, 1972–2022.

—. "Greg Sim

ms' Positive Approach." *The Rangefinder Magazine* 38, no. 9, September 1989. 30–34.

—. "A look at 'our history': The lady and the lens." *The Louisiana Weekly*. February 22–February 28, 2010.

Mouton, Girard,III and Alma D. Williams. "The Eyes of Jazz." *The Jazz Archivist: A Newsletter of the William Ranson Hogan Jazz Archive*. May 1991.

Mouton, Girard,III, and Tribune Staff. "The Way We Were: Our Family Album." *The New Orleans Tribune*. July 1988.

Moutoussamy-Ashe, Jeanne. *Viewfinders: Black Women Photographers*. New York: Writers and Readers Publishing, 1993.

OffBeat Staff. "Photo Op: Nightdares, Street Skating the City by Brad McCormick." *Offbeat*, December 1, 2013. https://www.offbeat.com/articles/photo-op-nightdares-street-skating-city-brad-mccormick/.

The Peoples Ind. Life Ins. Co., of La. "Peoples' Perfect Protection Policy Pays Promptly." Advertisement. *The New Orleans Herald/The Louisiana Weekly*, October 3, 1925.

Perkins, Archie E. *Who's Who in Colored Louisiana*. Baton Rouge: Douglas Loan Company, 1930.

"Photography Exhibit At SU April 1–3." *The Louisiana Weekly*, March 12, 1949. 3.

Picard, Sara M. "Racing Jules Lion," *Louisiana History: The Journal of the Louisiana Historical Association* 58, no. 1 (Winter 2017): 5–37.

Pitts, and Clarke. *New-Orleans Directory for 1842*. New Orleans: Pitts & Clarke, 1842.

Polk, R. L. *Polk's New Orleans City Directory 1940*. R. L. Polk & Co. New Orleans: 1940.

—. *Polk's New Orleans City Directory 1945–1946*. R. L. Polk & Co. New Orleans: 1945.

Porter, Marion J. *Crescent City Sepia Host: 1956–1957 Issue*. New Orleans: Gateway Publishing Company, 1956.

Price-Current. *Crescent City Business Directory, for 1858–1859*. New Orleans: Price-Current, 1858.

Reed, Glynn Johns. *Black Pages New Orleans: A Guide to African American Businesses in New Orleans* 1, no. 1 (April/May/June 2011).

Rousséve, Charles Barthelemy. *The Negro In Louisiana: Aspects of His History and Culture*. New Orleans: Xavier University Press, 1937.

Smith, Mary Denton, and Mary Louise Tucker. *Photography in New Orleans the Early Years, 1840–1865*. Baton Rouge: Louisiana State University Press, 1982.

Soards Directory Co., Ltd. *Soards' New Orleans City Directory, for 1902*. New Orleans: Soards Directory Co., Ltd., 1902.

—. *Soards' New Orleans City Directory for 1907*. New Orleans: Soards Directory Co., Ltd., 1907.

—. *Soards' New Orleans City Directory for 1913*. New Orleans: Soards Directory Co., Ltd., 1913.

—. *Soards' New Orleans City Directory for 1919*. New Orleans: Soards Directory Co., Ltd., 1919.

—. *Soards' New Orleans City Directory for 1920*. New Orleans: Soards Directory Co., Ltd., 1920.

—. *Soards' New Orleans City Directory 1928*. New Orleans: Soards Directory Co., Ltd., 1928.

Soards, L. *Soards' New Orleans City Directory, for 1881*. New Orleans: L. Soards & Co., 1881.

—. *Soards' New Orleans City Directory, for 1889*. New Orleans: L. Soards, 1889.

Taylor, Kathy. "A Fascinating Career, Among Giants: The Amazing Story of Lloyd Edwards." *Diversity Employers*. December 2015. 17–19.

Taylor, O. C. W. *The Crescent City Pictorial: A Souvenir Dedicated to the Progress of the Colored Citizens of New Orleans, Louisiana*. New Orleans: O. C. W. Taylor, 1926.

Terrell, Selwhyn Sthaddeus "Polo Silk." *Polo Silk presents Pop That Thang!!!* New Orleans: Antenna, 2017.

US Census Bureau. "1860 United States Federal Census." Generated by Ancestry.com; using NARA microfilm publication M653, 1,438 rolls; National Archives and Records Administration <ancestry.com> (accessed April 25, 2023).

—. "1870 United States Federal Census." Generated by Ancestry.com; using NARA microfilm publication M593, 1,761 rolls, National Archives and Records Administration <ancestry.com> (accessed April 25, 2023).

—. "1880 United States Federal Census." Generated by Ancestry.com; using NARA microfilm publication T9, 1,454 rolls, Bureau of the Census, Record Group 29; National Archives <ancestry.com> (accessed April 25, 2023).

—. "1890 United States Federal Census." Generated by Ancestry.com; using Microfilm Publication M407, 3 rolls; NAID: 2353580; Records of the Bureau of the Census, Record Group 29; National Archives <ancestry.com> (accessed April 25, 2023).

—. "1900 United States Federal Census." Generated by Ancestry.com; using T623, 1854 rolls; National Archives and Records Administration <ancestry.com> (accessed April 25, 2023).

—. "1910 United States Federal Census." Generated by Ancestry.com; using NARA microfilm publication T624, 1,178 rolls; Records of the Bureau of the Census, Record Group 29; National Archives <ancestry.com> (accessed April 25, 2023).

—. "1920 United States Federal Census." Generated by Ancestry.com; using NARA microfilm publication T625, 2076 rolls; Records of the Bureau of the Census, Record Group 29; National Archives <ancestry.com> (accessed April 25, 2023).

—. "1930 United States Federal Census." Generated by Ancestry.com; using T626, 2,667 rolls; National Archives and Records Administration <ancestry.com> (accessed April 25, 2023).

—. "1940 United States Federal Census." Generated by Ancestry.com; using T627, 4,643 rolls; National Archives and Records Administration <ancestry.com> (accessed April 25, 2023).

V. Paddio, Photographer. "Not Merely Pictures—But Good Pictures." Advertisement. *The New Orleans Herald/The Louisiana Weekly*, October 3, 1925.

"Veterans Learn Fine Points of Photography." *The Louisiana Weekly*. December 18, 1948.

Willis, Deborah. *Reflections in Black*. New York: W. W. Norton & Company, 2000.

Willis-Thomas, Deborah. *Black Photographers, 1840–1940: A Bio-Bibliography*. New York: Garland, 1985.

Woods, Allen T. *Woods Directory*. New Orleans: Allen T. Woods, 1911.

—. *Woods Directory.* New Orleans: Allen T. Woods, 1912.

—. *Woods Directory.* New Orleans: Allen T. Woods, 1913.

—. *Woods Directory.* New Orleans: Allen T. Woods, 1914.

YP Intellectual Property LLC. *Greater New Orleans: The Real Yellow Pages, September 2012–2013.* Tucker, GA: YP Intellectual Property, LLC, 2012.

Photographers Obscura Acknowledgments

Lidya Araya, for her aesthetic design.

Dr. Arthé A. Anthony, for retrieving her research, additional insights, and support.

Vincent Barraza, of the Xavier University of Louisiana Archives & Special Collections, for access to images.

Arnold Bourgeois, for the fond memories.

Cheron Brylski, for images by Harold Baquet.

Christina Bryant, Amanda Fallis, Andrew Mullins III, Greg Osborne, and Brittany Silva, of the Louisiana Division/City Archives & Special Collections of the New Orleans Public Library, for their knowledge of source material.

Rick Cleary, Sylvester Francis, and Greg Simms, for telling without being asked.

Phillip R. Cunningham, formerly of the Amistad Research Center, for retrieving folders.

Kenneth and Melba Ferdinand, of Café Rose Nicaud, for tables and wall space.

Sonali Fernando, for her enthusiasm.

Reginald Fourier, for the names of photographers.

Ric Francis, for immediately responding from the other side of the globe.

Shana M. griffin, for viewpoints, energy, and hospitality.

Arthur Hardy, for the articles on Carnival photographers.

Dwight A. Harris, for the names of photographers, lists of shows, and sponsoring photographers talks.

Cherice Harrison-Nelson, for awards of recognition.

Christopher S. Harter, formerly of the Amistad Research Center, for guides to collections.

Jari C. Honora and Rebecca Smith, of The Historic New Orleans Collection, for retrieving original material and reference to online sources.

Dean Irby and Walter Tillman, for their vivid recollections, and John Thompson, for his restraint.

Nolan A. Marshall, for a seldom told story on his father.

Dr. Maurice Martinez, for his knowledge of Portraits Incorporated.

Monique Moss, for curating the work of Sekou Fela.

Dr. Kara T. Olidge, formerly of the Amistad Research Center, for moderating a panel and for support beyond the book.

Wayne Phillips, of The Louisiana State Museum at The Presbytère, for researching its holdings.

Dr. Sara M. Picard, for the conversation.

Marion J. Porter, for just talking, and giving.

Wali Abdel Ra'oof, for the names behind Magnolia Studio and the vision of the importance of documenting Jazz Fest.

Kalamu ya Salaam, for the idea.

Chuck Siler, for capturing more than a flash.

Jerome Smith, for his love of photography and photographers.

Mary Louise Tucker, for the details.

Norman R. Smith, for the history.

Jim Thorns, for turning an insult into a tribute.

Eric Waters, for the phone call.

Conrad Wyre, for being a protégé and for obtaining information.

Chief Donald Harrison Sr. of the Guardians of the Flame, for the details in photographs and the studio.

Chelsey K. Shannon, for the editing.

And all who have made Black photographers in New Orleans possible.

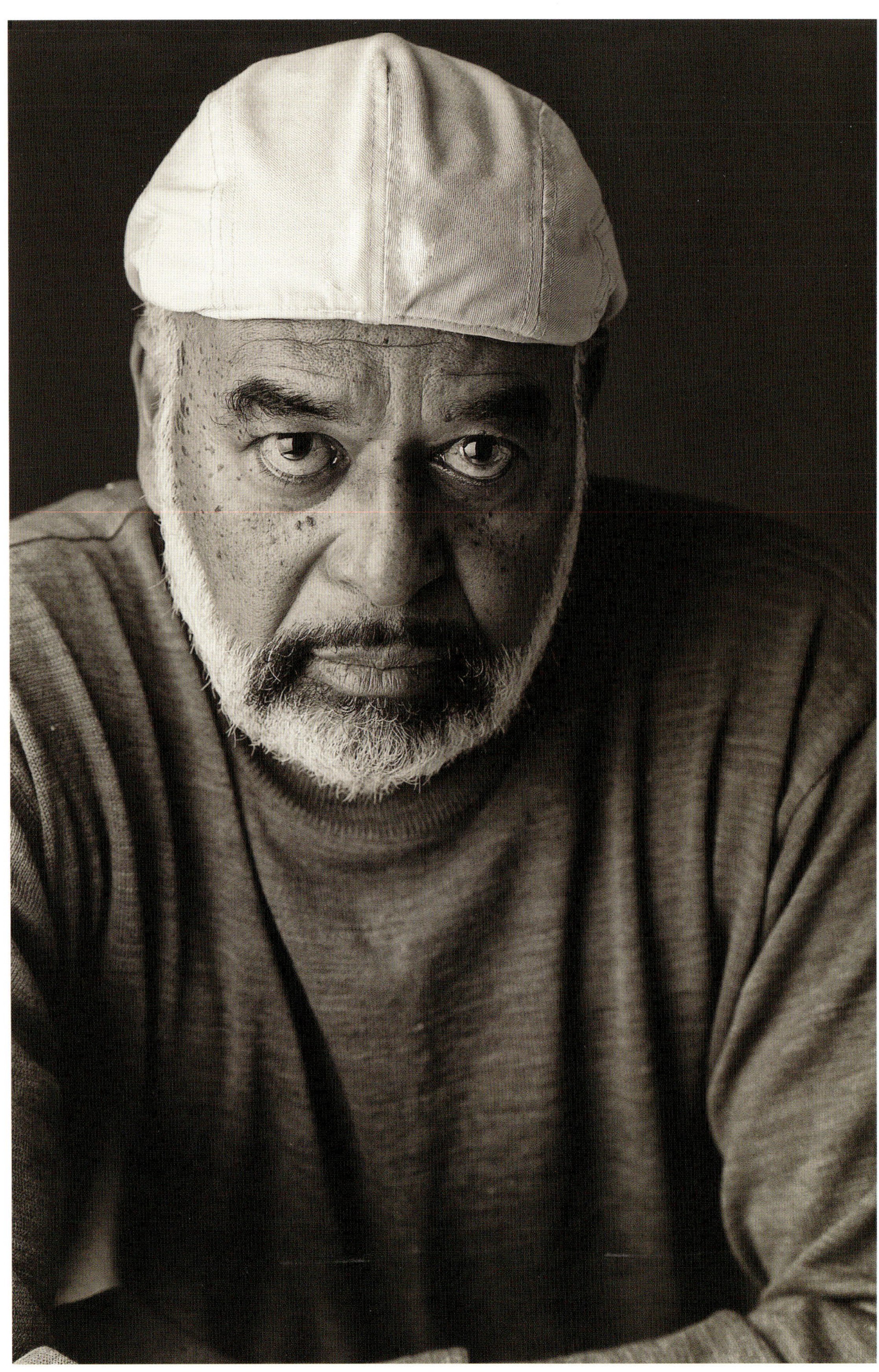

Photo: Julie Yarbrough. Courtesy of the Artist.

Eric Waters

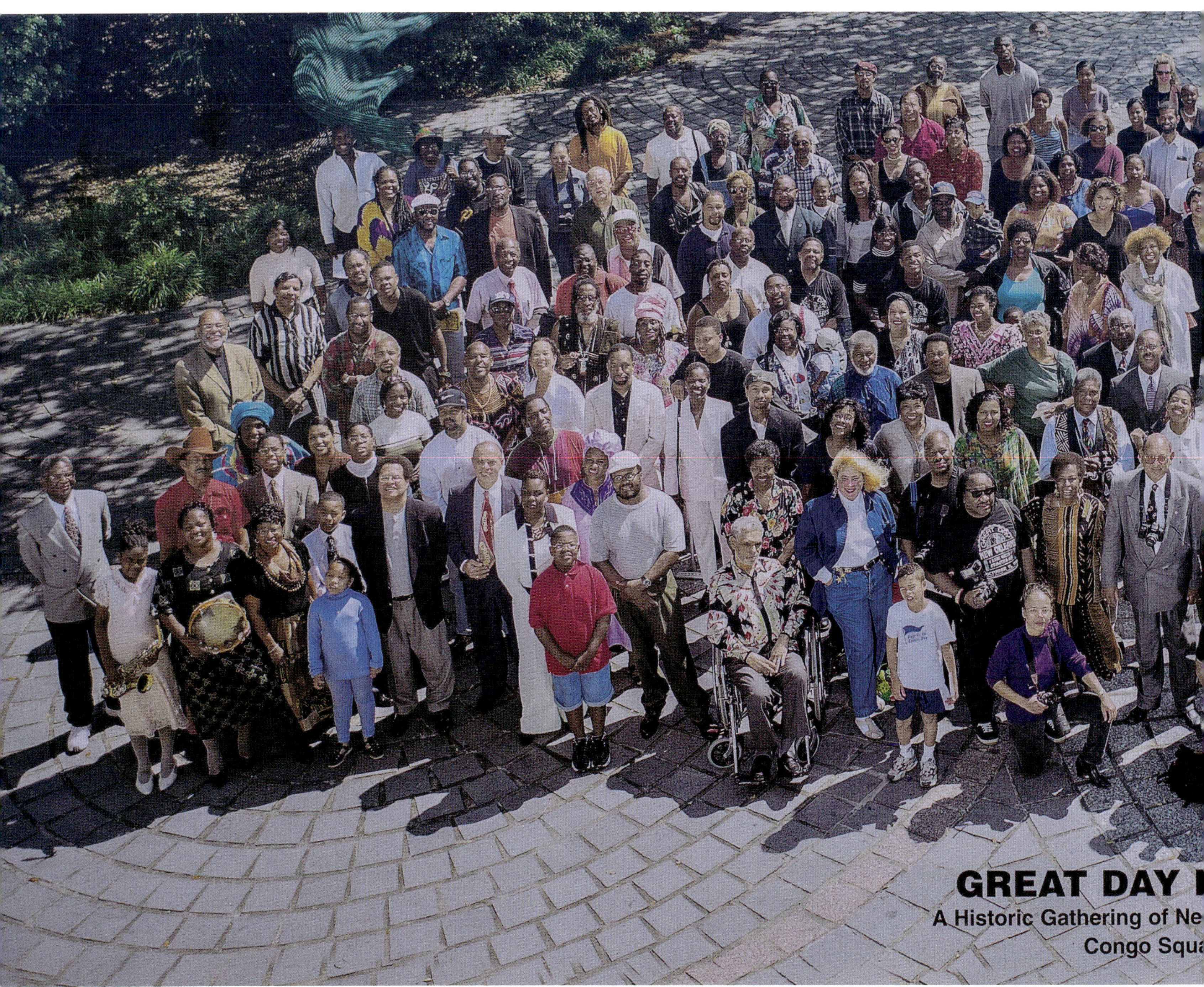

Photo: Jim Cummins. Courtesy of the Artist.

Eric Waters

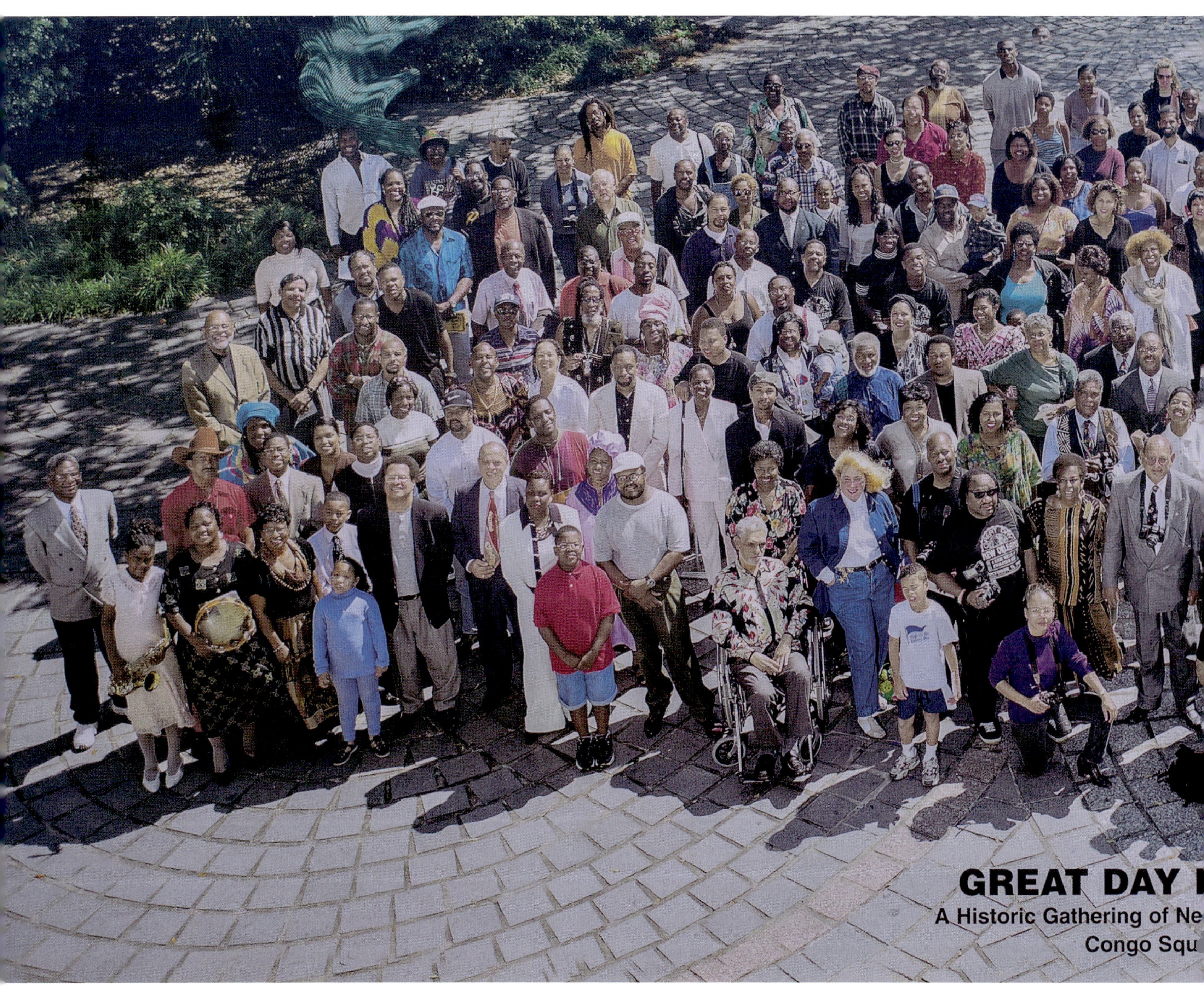

Photo: Jim Cummins. Courtesy of the Artist.

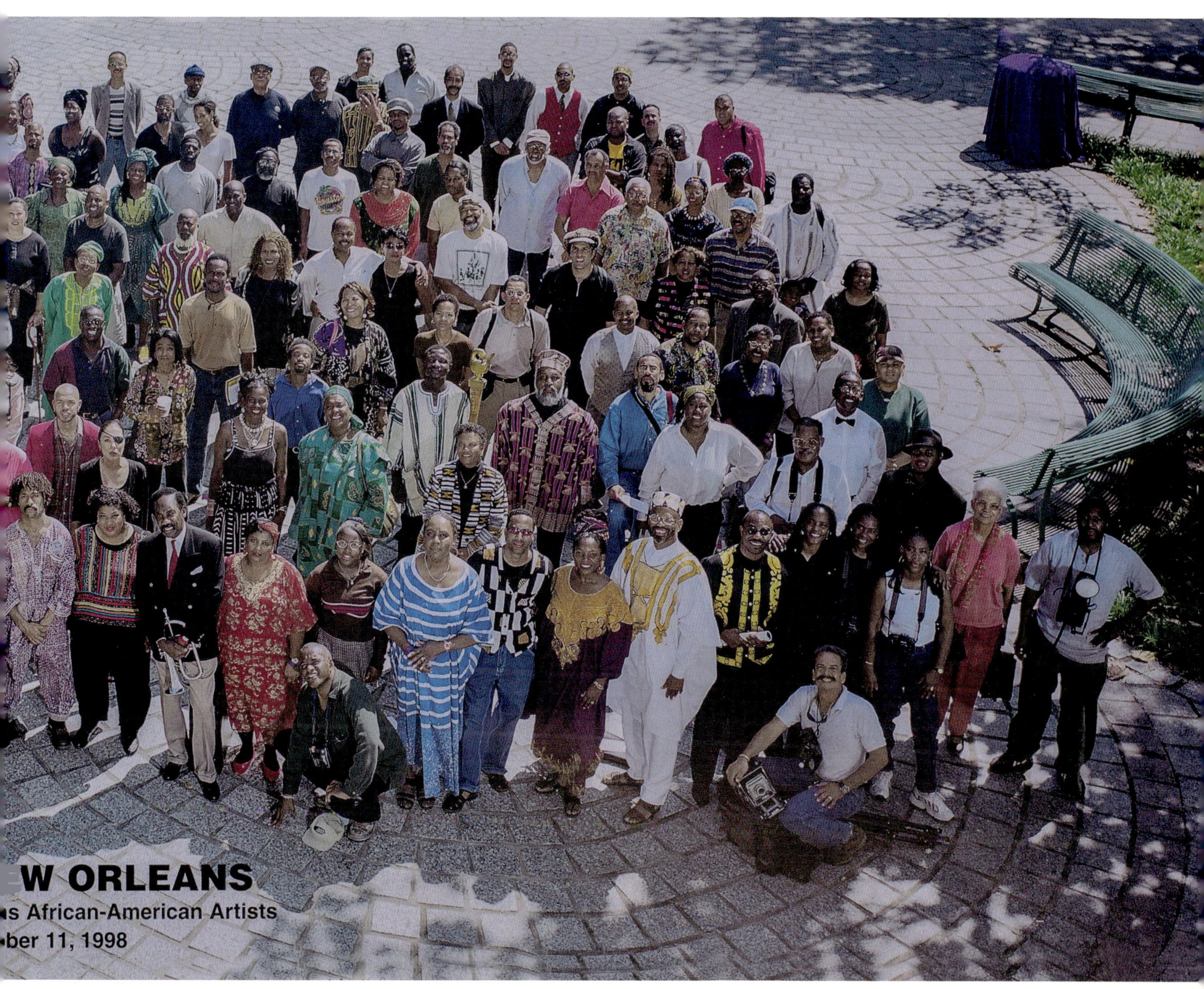

W ORLEANS
s African-American Artists
ber 11, 1998

WE ARE WHO WE SAY WE ARE

Eric Waters

Throughout Amerikkka's history, people of the diaspora, i.e., of African descent, have been stereotyped, erased, marginalized, and fictionalized by a false narrative perpetrated by white European colonizers and a culture that exalts them.

This pathological myth has been combatted by the images of Black photographers past and present. Racism is the foundation of Amerikkka's history, a pompous sense of privilege and entitlement. Understanding how Amerikkka has tried to dehumanize and erase Black people, Black photographers have long been cataloging our existence and value. Their narrative intervention continues to be essential to our existence. Black photographers will continue to expose the cancer of Amerikkka's white privilege and entitlement which threatens our right to exist. As Maya Angelou wrote, ". . . and still we rise."

We are self-defining people. Out of Amerikkka's dark history, we have emerged by strength of Spirit. "Life, Liberty and the Pursuit of Happiness" rings hollow and empty in our struggle to just live. Yet the story is ours to tell. This generation of contemporary photographers are today's memory keepers, our visual griots. In the words of Roy DeCarava: "There were no black images of dignity, no images of beautiful black people. There was this big hole. I tried to fill it." This hole being an enduring condition of anti-Blackness, we must always work toward this kind of corrective imagery.

As a collective, Black photography and photographers are relevant in each of the following senses:

Historical Important because old and interesting or impressive; recorded in history and recording of history; employing and so preserving historical conditions and technologies.

Contemporary Marked by characteristics of the present period; commenting on current events and discourse; employing modern and emerging technologies.

Legacy Important to the identity of the African diaspora across generations and place; something that helps Black people understand our full, collective dimensionality. Something handed down or created in response to something handed down; in conversation with an ancestor or predecessor; something corrective of the anti-Black images imposed on Black people in the past and still today.

AFFIRMATION THROUGH CORRECTIVE IMAGERY

New Orleans is a city known widely for its food and music, as the place where jazz was born, an epicurean's delight. In the immortal words of Ellis Marsalis, "In New Orleans, culture doesn't come down from on high, it bubbles up from the streets." But less widely know is the history of photography in New Orleans from 1840 to present–and how Black New Orleans photographers have long created counternarratives to Black existence as portrayed by whites.[1]

Black contemporary photographers have a duty to correct historical misrepresentations of Black people. Two examples of corrective imagery of which I personally have been an integral part are "The Great Day in New Orleans" group photo and *The Ties that Bind*. These two events exemplify our celebration of life, majesty and beauty.

THE "GREAT DAY" PHOTO

In 1997, Carol Bebelle and Charles "Chuck" Siler wanted to pay homage to the artistic wealth of Black people in New Orleans. Their prescient idea was a group photo celebrating and recognizing local Black artists. Their idea reached fruition on October 11, 1998. At that time, Carol Bebelle (founder and director of Ashé Cultural Center) and Chuck Siler (curator of public programs, Louisiana State Museum) made a declarative statement of the existence of the brilliance and beauty of our artistic community.

The title "Great Day in New Orleans" was a takeoff of "A Great Day in Harlem" photo, celebrating a collection of some of the greatest jazz artists at that time. But that is where the similarity ends. The Great Day in New Orleans was a gathering of Black artists of all genres. Just as Harlem was a significant place in Black American cultural history, Congo Square in today's Armstrong Park is a most spiritual place in the US for Blacks.[2] Congo Square is located in that part of New Orleans called Tremé, one of the oldest historically Black communities in the US. This photo is proof of our existence and excellence.

In this sacred space, more than two hundred artists gathered for a full group portrait as well as individual and sub-group portraits by artistic discipline. The spirits of our ancestors were present as evidenced by the weather conditions, which were near perfect. To encourage artists' awareness of the opportunity to participate, Carol Bebelle asked the iconic Ellis Marsalis to appear on WWOZ, New Orleans' Community Radio station, to promote the event and speak on its importance. Mr. Marsalis stated ". . . we will not be a rumor, we will have proof of our existence." It was an auspicious, once in a generation event.

> "America has prepared many lies for the general and specific population. Ours has been the myth of our ugliness. All wrong

---

1 See "Black Images Matter: How Cameras Helped—and Sometimes Harmed—Black People" by Ainissa G. Ramirez, *Scientific American*, July 8, 2020.

2 See *Congo Square: African Roots in America* by Freddie Williams Evans.

were our skin tones, ranging, as they do, from mahogany to cream. Misshapen have our features been in spreading the broad nose and large lips across the mag of faces descended from Africa's coastal tribes and inland royalty by way of this nation's southern parts of entry, slave markets dotting America's recent historical landscape.

Challenging these things, doing urgent battle with them, is a task, a difficult act of special defiance, but so worthy, so deeply significant, we must note and acknowledge and revere all those responsible, all those involved. The artist, for example. The creator, the visionary, moving, doing, seeing things to be shared finally with a public too long taught to respect limitation and narrow perspectives."

– Clayton Riley,
The Black Photographers Annual, 1973

Although I was given the opportunity to conduct the photography specifics, much of the success can also be attributed to the photographers who helped to document "The Day." Other local photographers documenting activities that Day include:

Girard Mouton,III

J. R. Thomason	Bryan S. Berteaux Sr.
Lloyd Dennis	Irving Johnson III
Morris Jones Jr.	Bernie Saul
Greg Simms	Paul Sylvester
Gus Bennett	Peter Nahkid

THE TIES THAT BIND: MAKING FAMILY NEW ORLEANS STYLE

The second corrective imagery endeavor of which I've been a part is *The Ties That Bind* photography exhibit and corresponding book, which included essays, poems, and photos. This project was powered by Carol Bebelle's relationship with the Casey Foundation.

The Foundation was looking for a way to connect community families and to recognize the unique culture of New Orleans and its varied family dynamics, which encompass ties of many kinds. The Casey Foundation's communications officer, Joy Thomas Moore, understood the thread connecting spiritual, cultural and biological types of Central City families. This event validated a people ". . . in where we find ourselves," to quote James Baldwin. The exhibit's corresponding book is a comprehensive compilation of memory and historical musings of who we were, who we are, and who we continue to be.

CONTINUING A LEGACY

What a cultural inheritance New Orleans photographers have access to. But it's the responsibility of Black photographers to tell our cultural story as it continues to emerge and evolve. We, of the diaspora, document the essence of us, whereas non-Black photographers shoot the spectacle of Black culture.

When I use the word "culture" as it pertains to New Orleans, I define it as occupying a span four hundred years or more. The foundation has been sturdily set by those who came

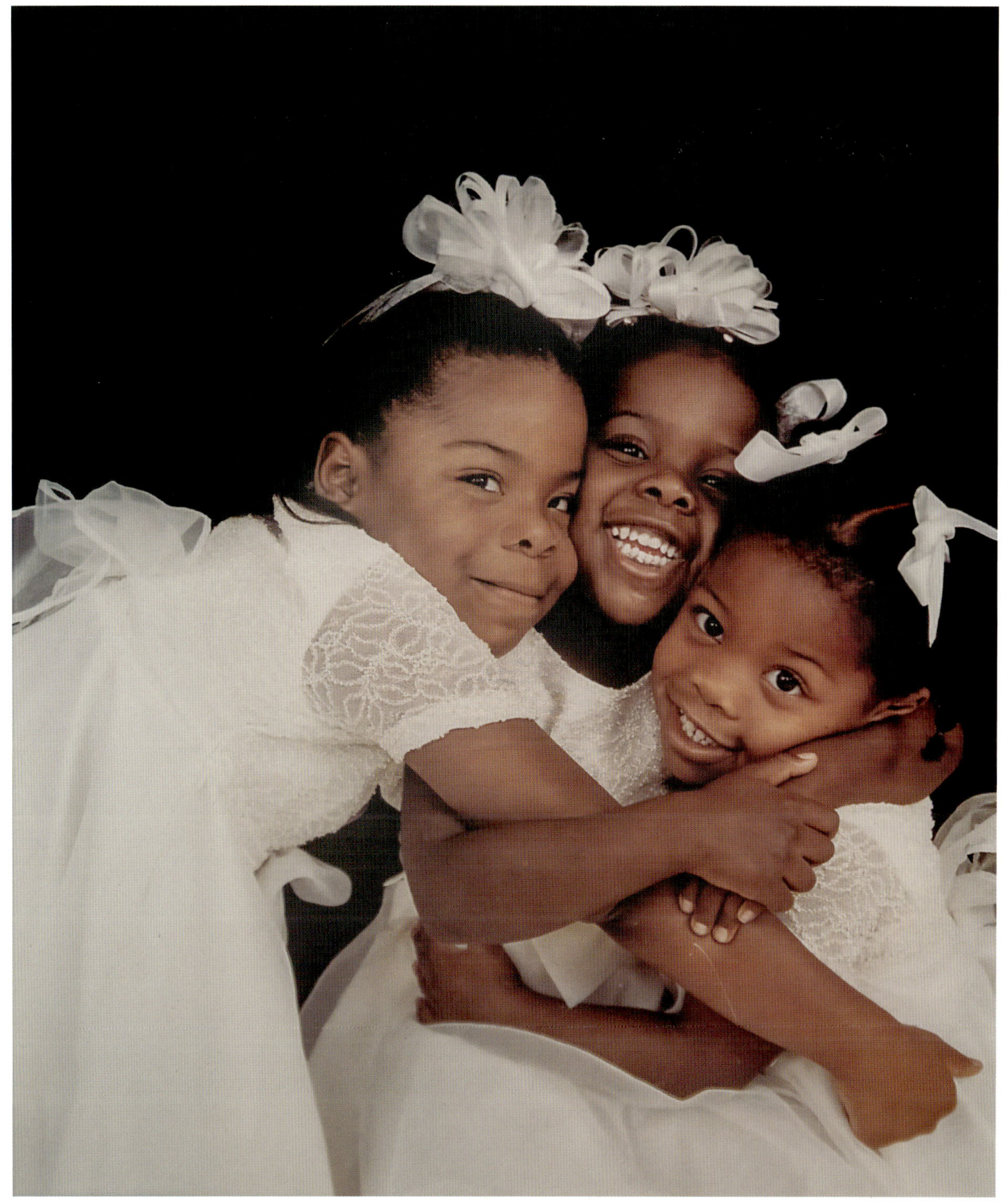

"Three Sisters," 2000. Photo: Morris Jones Jr. Courtesy of the Artist.

before us. Now, what will *we* contribute? My queries to the Black photography community today: What will be your legacy? What visual stories will you tell? How are you going to capture our humanity for others to witness decades into the future?

Today's technology affords a panoply of tools for photographers to choose, broadening and diversifying the legacy of Black photography to come. From the advent of daguerreotype photography to digital capture, we—Black photographers from the beginning of the art to today—have a large toolbox. Remember when cameras had mechanical moving parts with an attached lens? Today, we have a lens with an entire computer attached. We've gone from a chemical darkroom to a digital room, a virtual photography studios consisting of a computer, monitor, and seemingly unlimited selection of software and apps. To take a quote from John Scott, "Our only limitation is our imagination."

The advancements have been incredible. But still, the fundamentals apply. The trilogy of aperture, shutter speed, and ISO plus composition are still practiced—all basic tenets of capturing a specific moment in time, that instance's realization of reality.

INSPIRATIONAL QUOTES

In closing, I offer two quotes that often come to my mind when I'm thinking of photography:

"A photograph is a photograph, a picture, an image, an illusion, complete within itself, depending neither on words reproductive processes or anything else. For it's life, its reason for being."

— Roy DeCarava

"You try to develop the sensitivity and the 'eye' to see that very special mood of the moment. You develop the discipline to block out everything but you. The camera and the subject and you develop the tenacity to stick with it. To have patience. The picture will happen—that very special picture will happen."

— Moneta Sleet

ϴ

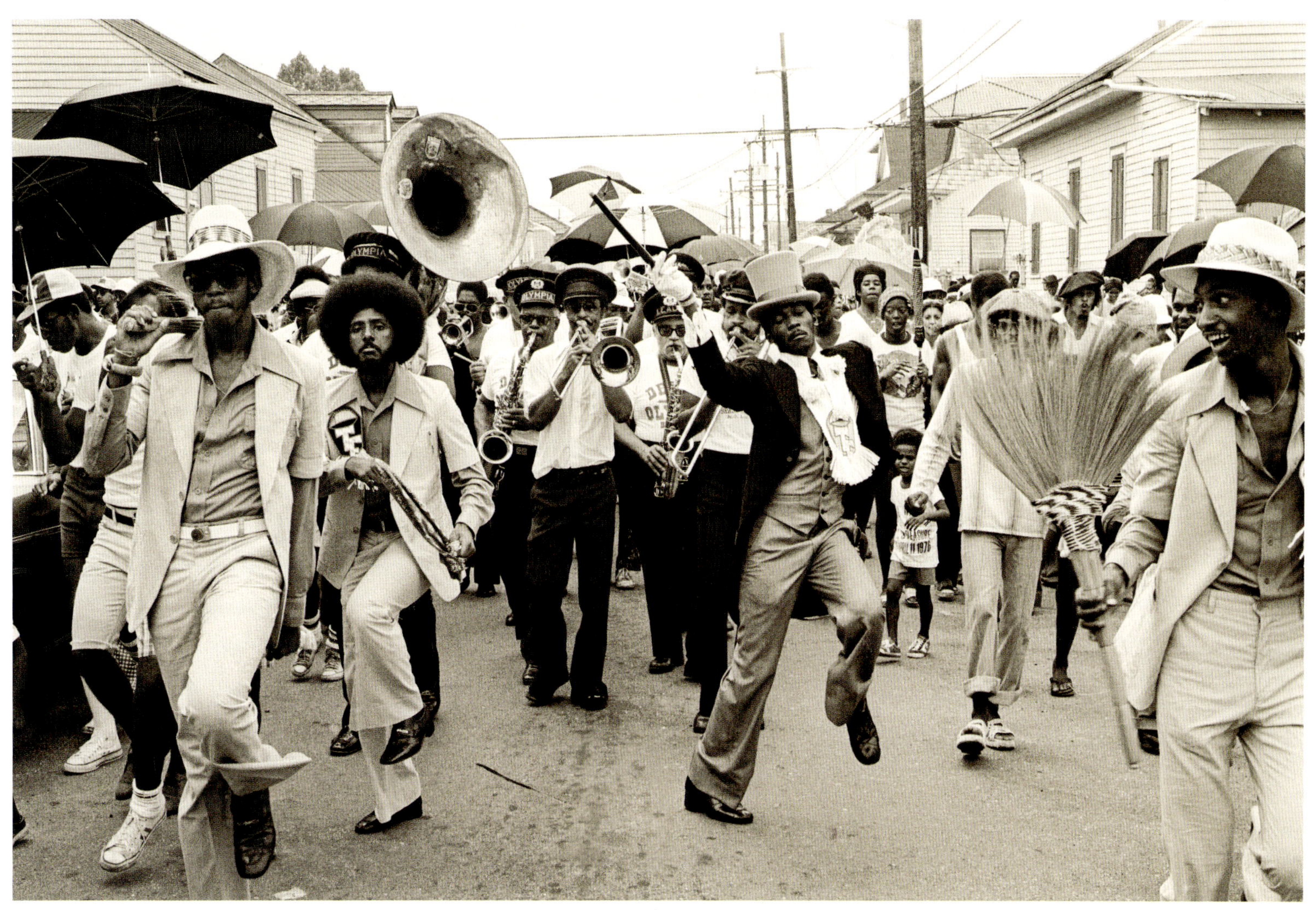

"Franklin 'Wingie' Davis Grand Marshal," ca. 1970s. Photo: Eric Waters.

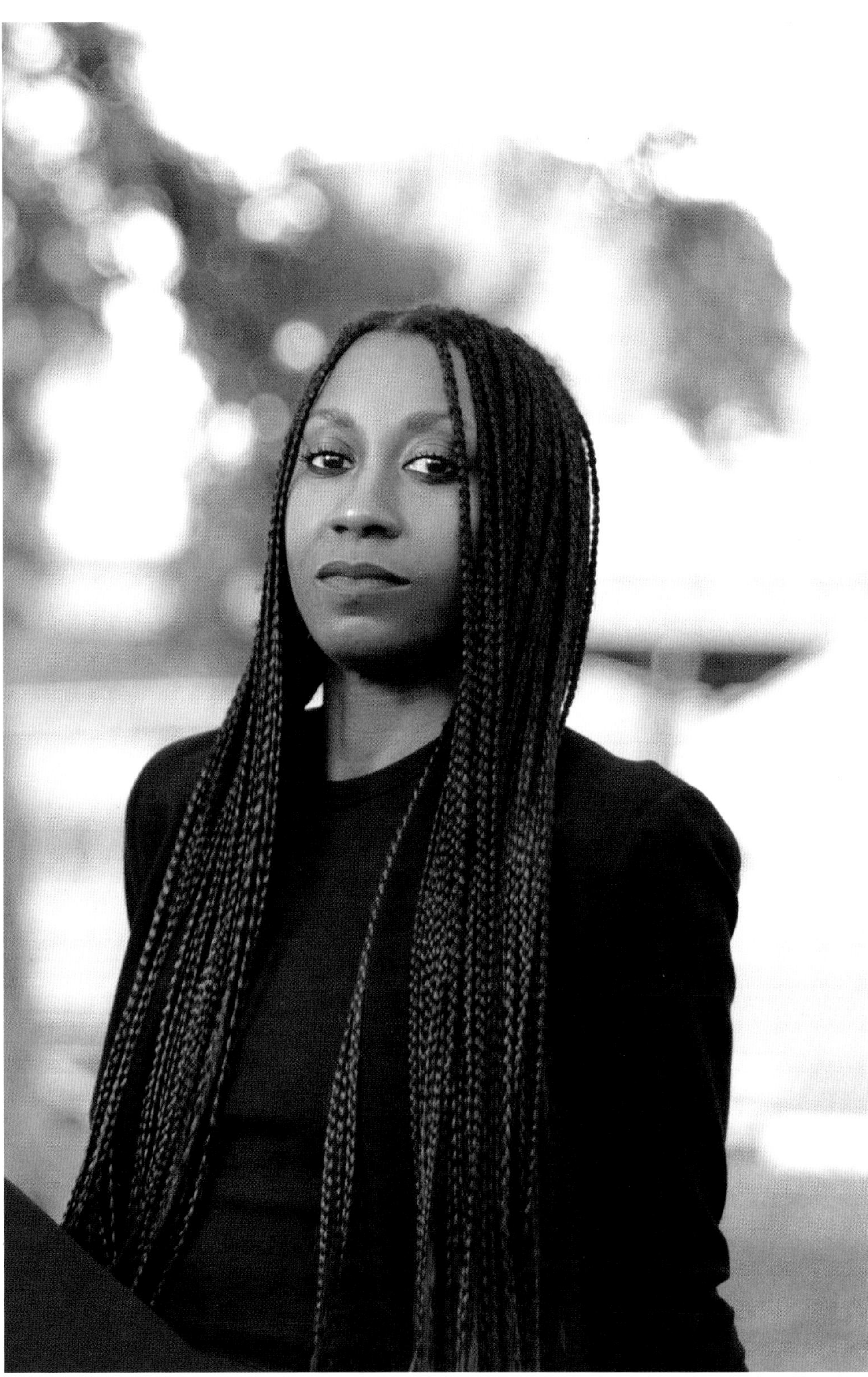

Photo: Jeremy Tauriac. Courtesy of the Artist.

Shana M. griffin

"Let's face it. I am a marked woman, but not everyone knows my name. . . . My country needs me, and if I were not here, I would have to be invented."

— Hortense Spillers

"Mama's Baby, Papa's Maybe: An American Grammar Book," 1987

"What does it mean for a black feminist to think about, consider, or concede the concept of futurity?"

— Tina M. Campt

"Quiet Soundings: The Grammar of Black Futurity" in *Listening to Images*, 2007

"Concede nothing, You alone own the reckoning. The world is a reflection of what YOU see, I beg of you namesake, look AGAIN."

— Jeri Hilt

"There Are No Survivors Without Scars," *Bitch Media*, 2015

PHOTOGRAPHIC GESTURES OF FUTURITY

Shana M. griffin

In the introduction of *Listening to Images*, Black feminist theorist and scholar of visual culture and contemporary art Tina M. Campt states: "For blacks in the diaspora, both quiet and quotidian are mobilized as everyday practices of refusal."[1] Such gestures of refusal, which are neither passive nor restrained, are regularly exercised and creatively engaged by Black photographers and visual artists challenging everyday forms of violence, subjectivity, and dispossession through the lens of their cameras and creative practices.

1
INSURGENT APPROACHES

A shrewd understanding of visual politics and its potential to perpetuate harm became ingrained in the practices of many Black photographers in the United States and throughout the diaspora. From photography's inception in Paris in 1839 with the daguerreotype, the first photographic process, to its immediate arrival in New York City and New Orleans in 1840 during the antebellum period, Black photographers and our communities' engagement with the medium often centered the importance of making ourselves visible among controlling images and discourses that held *and* still hold us "captive" to racist and sexist constructs. In *Art on My Mind: Visual Politics*, feminist theorist, writer, and social critic bell hooks notes, "Though rarely articulated as such, the camera became in Black life a political instrument, a way to resist misrepresentation as well as a means by which alternative images could be produced."[2]

Such discourses of captivity and control, like the "American grammar" described and interrogated by Black feminist scholar and literary critic Hortense Spillers in her groundbreaking 1987 article, "Mama's Baby, Papa's Maybe: An American Grammar Book," speaks to this dynamic.

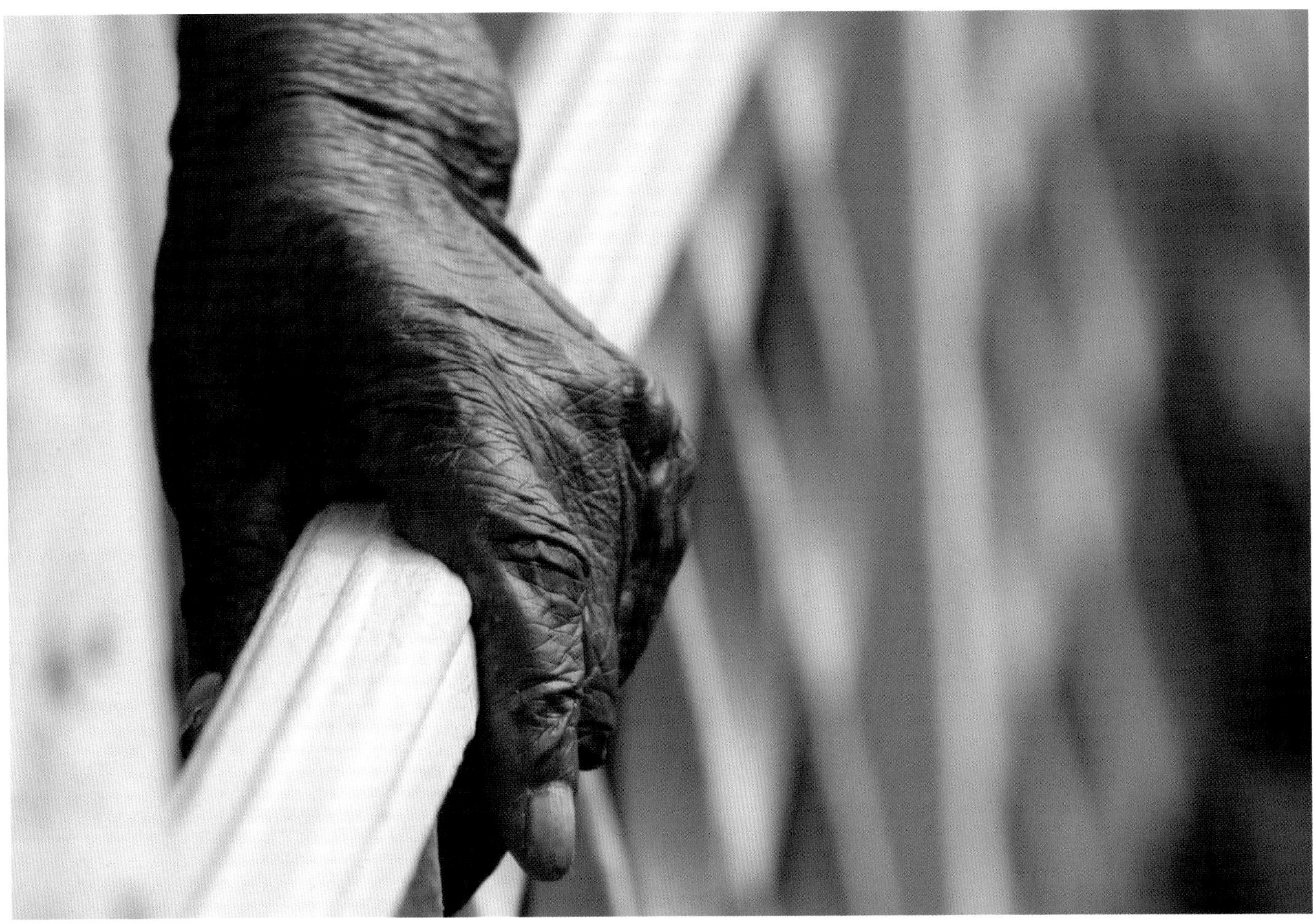

"Ageless," 2016. Dularge, LA. Photo: Danette M. Vincent. Courtesy of the Artist.

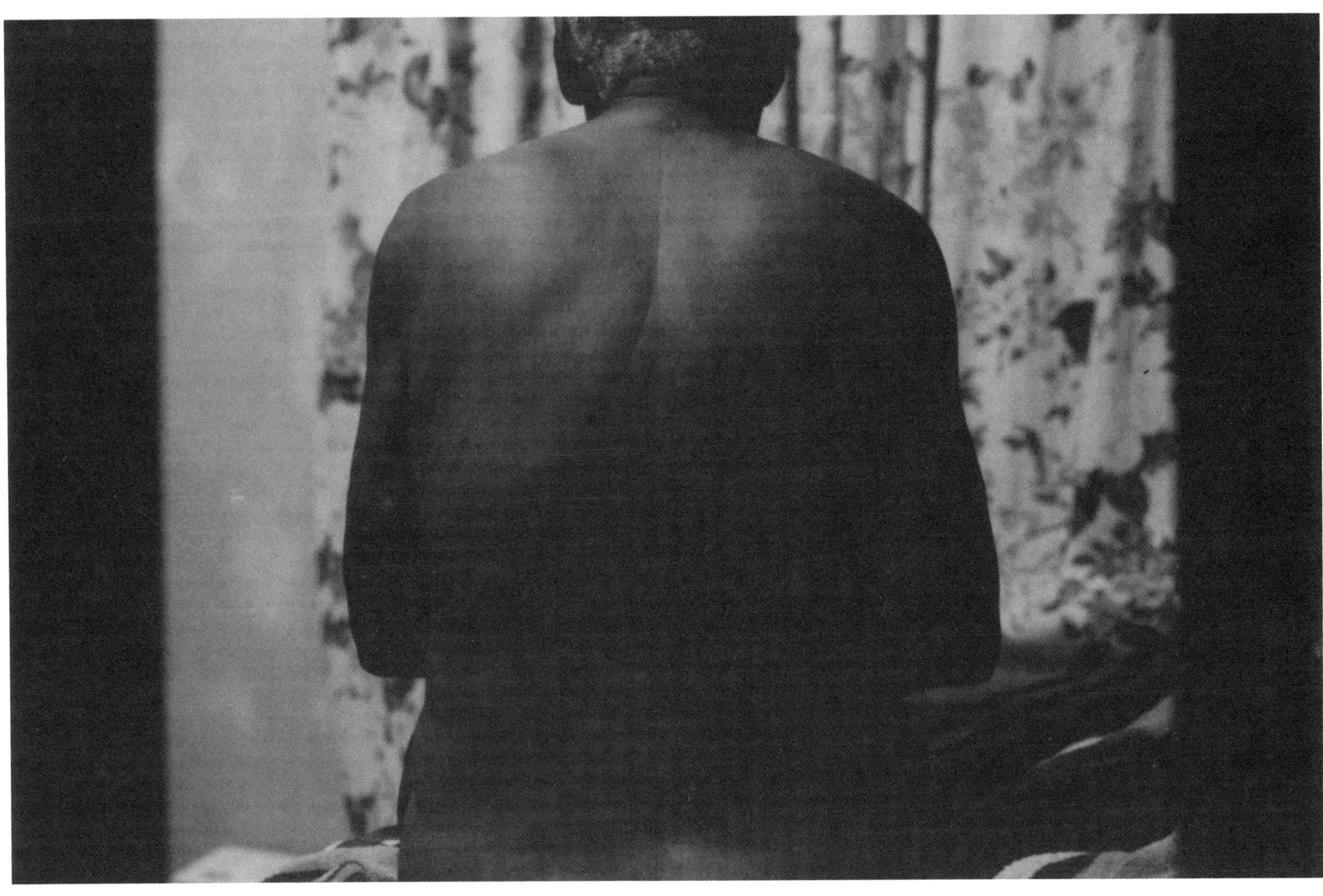

"Millicent Eudora Gittens (Babygirl, the Matriarch)," 2013. Photo: Renee Royale. Courtesy of the Artist.

Spillers makes a theoretical intervention in situating the complex and violent ways that the "Black female flesh" is marked, rendered invisible, dispossessed, entangled, and imagined within the American grammar of captivity, conquest, confinement, and control. Her intervention illuminates the degree to which white supremacist distortions and restrictions of blackness are historically and hegemonically embedded, thus necessitating an insurgent position of "monstrosity" in order to reimagine "a radically different text" that centers the "Black female flesh."[4]

The visual implications of Spillers' analysis of gestures of refusal and new grammars of engagement are evident in the photographic approaches employed by Black photographers, past *and* present, and in the cultural and political messages conveyed in our image-making.

2
GESTURES OF REFUSAL AND NEW GRAMMARS OF ENGAGEMENT

Gestures and grammars of Black "monstrosity" that challenge dominant racial and gender frames are often embraced by Black photographers, scholars, activists, and social critics—particularly among women, non-binary, trans, and queer photographers who daily navigate a patriarchal and white-dominated industry that often invisibilizes or trivializes our practices and contributions to the field. Despite the marginalization and obscuration of Black women and queer artists who engage the photographic lens, the insurgent position of "monstrosity" that Spillers speaks of—and the opening clarion call by Black Native feminist scholar, artist, and contributing photographer to this volume Jeri Hilt—encourages us to counter the persistent flattening and violent erasure of Black subjectivity, in all its forms, and to embody counter-narratives and ways of being, hearing, writing, advocating, imagining, photographing, performing, and seeing Black. "Concede nothing," writes Hilt. "You alone own the reckoning."[5] Take, for example:

- **Sall**,[6] **Jenne**,[7] **Kitty**,[8] **Harriet**,[9] **Marry**,[10] **Sabina**,[11] **Hannah**,[12] **Celia**,[13] **Elizabeth**,[14] **Judy**,[15] **Nancy**,[16] **Cassey**,[17] **Queen**,[18] **Mima**,[19] **Susan**,[20] **Mary Ann**,[21] **Edey**,[22] **Jane**,[23] **Hana**,[24] **Polly**,[25] **Eliza**,[26] **Eugenia**,[27] **Sophy**,[28] **Christine**,[29] **Mahala**,[30] **Fanny**,[31] **Maria**,[32] **Corine**,[33] **Sarah**,[34] and **Adeline**[35]—thirty Black women and girls whose gestures of refusal and defiance in the form of self-emancipation in New Orleans between the years of 1820 and 1854 are limited by violent archival fragments of their existence. The carceral visuality of newspaper runaway advertisements and jailed announcements restricts our understanding of their lives even while allowing us to imagine their rebellious longing for freedom and the impossible circumstances they navigated to achieve it.

$20 REWARD.—Ran away on Thursday night, the 17th inst., a Mulatto Woman named POLLY, goes sometimes by the name of MARY CRISSWELL. She is small in person, hair straight and gray, aged about 55 yrs. She carried with her a large bundle of clothing. The above reward will be paid to any person who will deliver her to the subscriber and give evidence sufficient to convict the person or persons suspected of harboring her; or $10 for the delivery of the slave alone.
ELIZABETH PRICE, 162 Gravier street,
s23—3t* between Carondelet and Baronne sts.

Runaway ad posted by enslaver Elizabeth Price in *The Daily Picayune*, 1846. Courtesy of Freedom on the Move Project.[3]

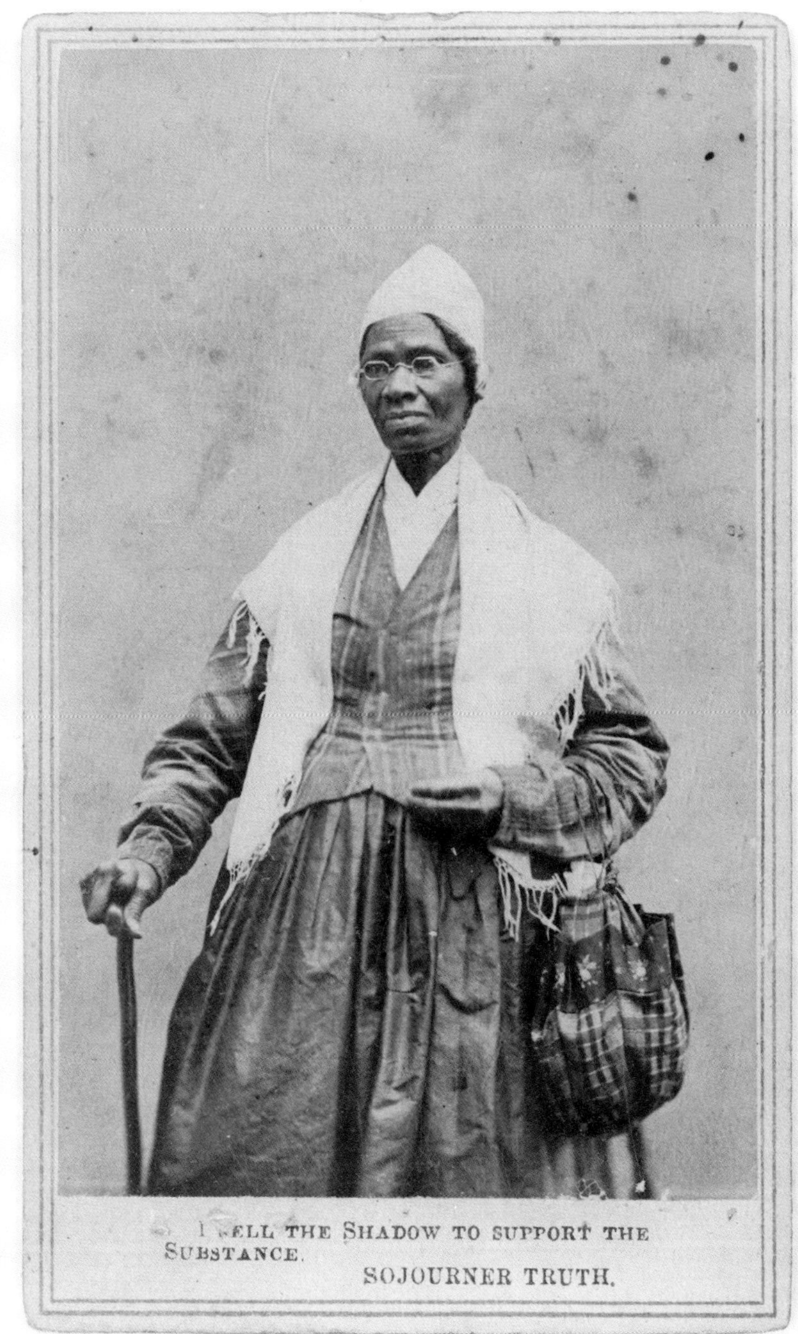

Sojourner Truth, ca. 1864. Photographer unknown.
Courtesy of the Library of Congress.[36]

- **Sojourner Truth**'s embracement of photography in the 1850s, when she copyrighted her photographic *cartes de visite* portraits (photographs mounted on cardboard) with the caption "I Sell the Shadow to Support the Substance" to call attention to the violence of slavery and to finance her abolitionist and feminist activism.
- **Harriet Tubman**'s fugitive cartographies, abolitionist geographic practices, and imaginative possibilities of freedom through her social activism, racial and gender rights advocacy, caretaking, and engagement with the visual politics of photography from the 1860s to 1910s, often commanding the attention of the viewer in her shape-shifting portraits.

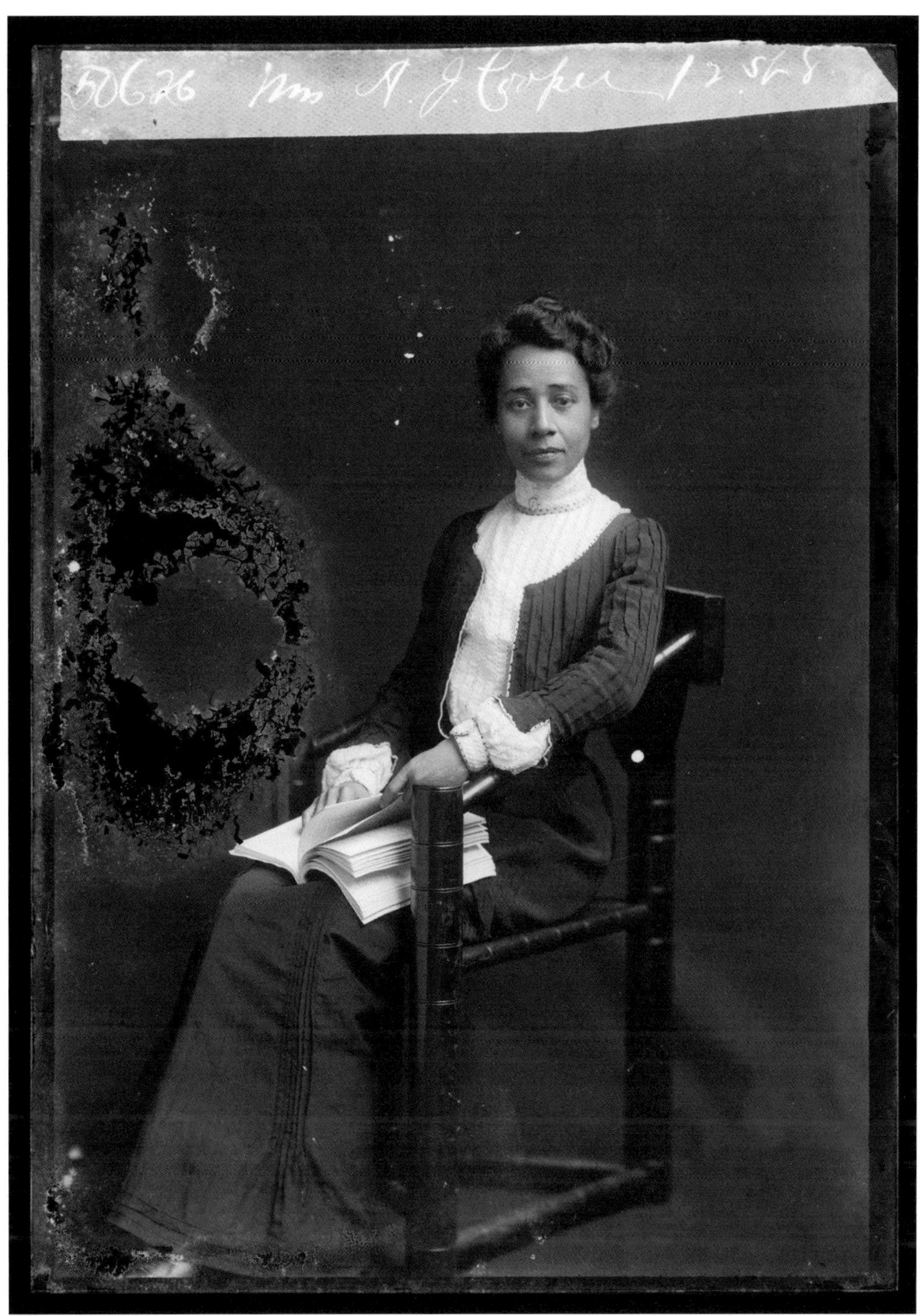

Mrs. A. J. Cooper, 1901. Photo: C. M. Bell. Courtesy of the Library of Congress.[37]

• The descriptive visuality of **Harriet Jacob**'s enslavement, confinement, and fugitivity to escape sexual violence, protect her children, and avoid re-enslavement as recorded in *Incidents in the Life of a Slave Girl, Written by Herself*, and the physical disfigurement she experienced while hidden in the "crawl-space" of a garret she designated as a "loop-hole of retreat"—a cramped enclosure in her grandmother's house from which she performed, planned, and reimagined freedom.[38]

• **Anna Julia Cooper**'s forceful and polemical text *A Voice From the South: By a Black Woman of the South* (1892), which is widely credited as one of the first book-length formulations of Black feminist theory and calls for the education of Black women and girls,

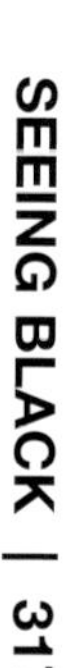

descriptively centering the experiences and standpoints of Black women as the answers to questions of freedom and liberation. Through her teaching, scholarship, writing, and activism, Cooper challenged white supremacist and patriarchal ideas that perpetually confined Black women to the sphere of domesticity and of being "seen" in the home while routinely being rendered muted and voiceless, famously stating: "Only the Black woman can say 'when and where I enter, in the quiet, undisputed dignity of my womanhood, without violence and without suing and special patronage, then and there the whole Negro race enters with me.'"[39]

- **Ida B. Wells-Barnett**'s capacity to engage the visual politics of photography and its negation of blackness in the 1890s through her frequent encounters with the violent effects of lynching and convict leasing photographs in newspapers and postcards amid her investigative journalism, lectures, and writings on lynching and prison in *Southern Horrors: Lynch Law in all its Phases* (1892), *The Reason Why the Colored American Is Not in the World's Columbian Exposition* (1893), *The Red Record* (1895), and *Mob Rule in New Orleans* (1900)—*and* through her subversive awareness of the politics of representation that challenged early 20th-century racist and sexist logics that dehumanized images of Black womanhood. Wells-Barnett's participation in family and solo portraits constituted a practice of refusal as self-representation in photographic form.

- **Frances Joseph-Gaudet**, **Victoria Earle Matthews**, **Mary Church Terrell**, and other **Black club women's** tenacious and unconventional prison reform activism to abolish convict leasing, prison abuse of Black women and young people, and institutional failure to protect Black mothers, as outlined by scholar and contributing photographer, **Nikki Brown** in "Keeping Black Motherhood Out of Prison: Prison Reform and Women Saving in the Progressive Era."[40] Through their collective activism, Joseph-Gaudet, Matthews, Terrell, and others used written accounts to evoke vivid pictures of the horrors of carceral confinement and control while engaging their photographic images of respectability to secure the legitimacy of their work and advocate for change.

- The **Phyllis Wheatley Club of New Orleans**, an affiliate member of the National Association of Colored Women's Clubs (NACWC), founded by prominent local Black women activists, including **Sylvanie Francoz Williams** and **Alice Dunbar-Nelson,** in the early 1890s. Williams, an educator, women's rights advocate, suffragist, and civil rights leader, served as its president, establishing a training hospital for Black nurses and physicians in 1896 within a building of the New Orleans University Medical College, at a time when hospitals frequently denied services to Black people.[41] Originally called the Phyllis Wheatley Sanitarium and Training Hospital for Nurses and later renamed the Flint-Goodridge Hospital, the Club's commitment to expanding educational opportunities for Black women and reimagining infrastructures of possibilities included the founding of a kindergarten and daycare for working women, a free clinic, suffragist activism, prison reform organizing, and public playgrounds for Black residents. The photographic documentation of Flint-Goodridge Hospital and its recorded history often erases the contributions of its founders.

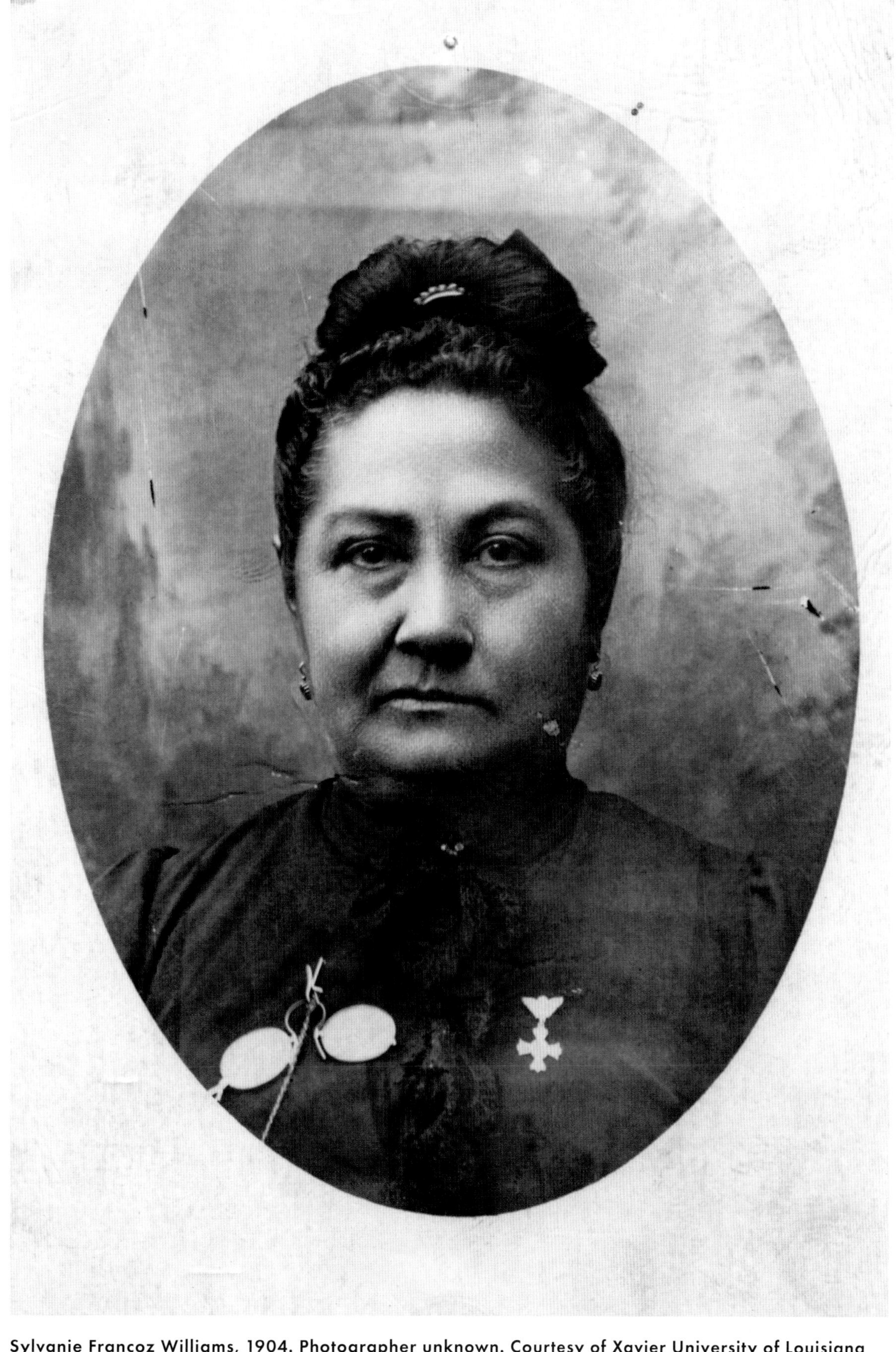

Sylvanie Francoz Williams, 1904. Photographer unknown. Courtesy of Xavier University of Louisiana Library, Digital Archives and Collections.

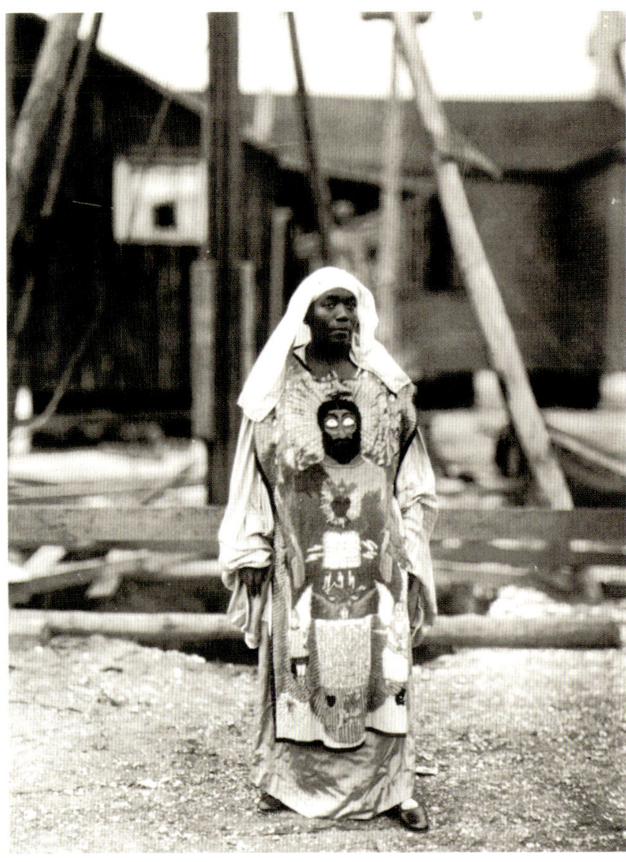

Mother Catherine Seals, ca. 1920s. Photo: Photographer unknown, but some suspect Zora Neale Hurston took this photo. Courtesy of Xavier University of Louisiana Library, Digital Archives and Collections.

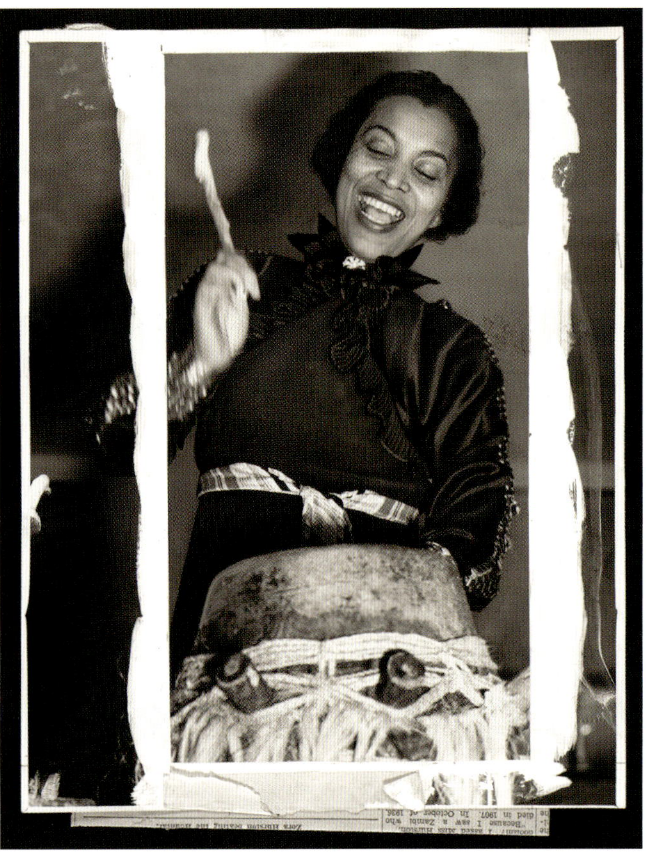

Zora Neale Hurston, 1937. Photo: Unnamed *New York World-Telegram* & *The Sun* staff photographer. Courtesy of the Library of Congress.[46]

- **Zora Neale Hurston**'s bold, nonconventional, and unabashed engagement with Black and Caribbean folklore, vernacular, cultural practices, and ways of living as documented in her writing, anthropology, filmmaking, photography, ethnography, research, and recorded sounds.[42] Hurston's refusal to conform to racist and sexist expectations of what her practice should be or how it should be publicly presented are evident in her accounts chronicling her travels collecting folklore in Eatonville, Florida; her writings, participation in, and documentation of (photography and filming) Voodoo, Hoodoo, and spiritualists culture and practices among its leaders in New Orleans, Louisiana, including Mother Catherine Seals[43]; and her study of Vodou culture in Port-au-Prince all during the 1920s–1930s, circumventing traditional methodologies. Hurston's unstinting approach in her filmmaking in *Children's Games* (1928), *Logging* (1928), and *Baptism* (1929)[44]; her productions of *A Great Day* (1932) and *Singing Steel* (1934); her groundbreaking publication of *Mules and Men* (1935); and her photography of a Haitian "zombie," published in *Life* magazine (1937)[45], is an abbreviated reflection of the thematic scope of her complex anthropological, folklore, and artistic work.

- **Jeanne Moutoussamy-Ashe**'s groundbreaking publication, *Viewfinders: Black Women Photographers* (1986). In the introduction, Moutoussamy-Ashe states:

> One of the most inspiring things in writing this book was discovering not only the number of black women who have devoted

themselves to photography but, more important, how these women dealt with forces that were much more oppressive and severe than those that women face today. . . . [T]he purpose of compiling a record of the black women who ventured into photography, both professionally and artistically, was to integrate the accomplishments and contributions they made with the history of photography, which to date ignored their participation.[47]

- **bell hooks**' *Art on My Mind: Visual Politics* (1995), a critical response to Michele Wallace's call for "revolution in vision"—a challenge to Black intellectuals and social critics to write about Black visuality, art, and aesthetics as part of revolutionary movement work. hooks' assessment of the ways Black "female" critics risk "having our ideas appropriated or go unacknowledged" and how "works by men receive more attention and are given greater authority of voice than works by women"[48] and among artists existing outside the gender binary continue to shape the field today. Her attention to the importance of Black vernacular images in the chapter "In Our Glory: Photography and Black Life" speaks to the depths of Black refusals both in front of and behind the camera. She notes:

  The walls of images in Southern black homes were sites of resistance. They constituted private, black-owned and operated gallery spaces where images could be displayed, shown to friends and strangers. These walls were a space where in the midst of segregation, the hardship of apartheid, dehumanization could be countered.[49]

- **Deborah Willis**' multidisciplinary practice, monumental scholarship, photography, exhibitions, and publications on Black photography and image-making, which have transformed the study of photography, starting in the 1980s with the publication of *Black Photographers 1840–1940: An Illustrated Bio-Bibliography* (1985), while she served as head of the photography at the Schomburg Center for Research in Black Culture. Willis' trailblazing publications, including *Reflections in Black: A History of Black Photographers, 1840 to the Present* (2000), *Posing Beauty: African American Images from the 1890s to the Present* (2009), and *The Black Civil War Soldier: A Visual History of Conflict and Citizenship* (2021), continue to shape the field and how we engage photography and its historical and contemporary visual lexicons.

- Multidisciplinary artist **Lorna Simpson**'s engagement with a Black feminist conceptual lens of juxtaposing image-making and the written word in her much-acclaimed works "The Waterbearer" (1986), "Five Day Forecast" (1988), "Stereo Styles" (1988), and "Wigs" (1994–2006), where she expressively challenges photography's assumption of objectivity through a visuality that centers the figurative experiences of Black women. Often devoid of direct engagement with the viewer, Simpson's work critically examines the ways race, gender, and cultural references are used to regulate, stereotype, silence, and police Black women's everyday experiences and expressions of sexuality.

- **Carla Williams**' contributions and writings on Black photography, its aesthetics, and the politics of the body in image-making through her co-authorship of *The Black Female Body: A*

Photographic History (2002) with Deborah Willis, as editor of *Exposure*, the journal of the Society for Photographic Education, and her publication *Tender* (2023), which won the 2023 Paris Photo-Aperture First PhotoBook Award. Whether on the page, in the photograph, or behind the camera, Williams' work invites the possible.

- **Carrie Mae Weems**' poetic interrogation and unsettling visual meditation on the violent and enshrined social hierarchies of race, gender, geography, and power in *The Louisiana Project* (2003), a series of choreographed photographs, prints, video, and publication in response the 2003 bicentennial of the Louisiana Purchase. Centering the experiences of Black women, Weems interrupts time by juxtaposing the past with the present, bearing witness to relics of slavery and its ongoing policies and infrastructures of violence and control.

- **Hélène Amouzo**'s *Autoportrait* series (2007–2011) of haunting self-portraits that ontologically drift in and out of the frames through long exposure techniques, speaking to the precarity of her unseen existence situated in an attic with a suitcase symbolically ready for immediate escape should she need to vanish. Amouzo's palimpsest-style documentation of her experiences as a Togolese immigrant woman without papers in an abandoned attic in Belgium is reminiscent of Harriet Jacob's crawlspace, but hers is a loophole of insecurity and invisibility, necessitated by a society that does not see her.

- **Beryl F. Hunter**'s 2011 monograph, *Black Photographers In Late Twentieth Century New Orleans: Documentarians of Social History*, which examines the role of five New Orleans-based photographers, all of whom are featured in this collection, in documenting the social history of New Orleans and the unrecognized impact of their work on politics, cultural traditions, and social life in the city.

- **Arthé A. Anthony**'s critical research on Florestine Perrault Collins, the first documented Black woman photographer in New Orleans, and her practice that defied racial and gender norms and expectations in the early twentieth in her article "Florestine Perrault Collins and the Gendered Politics of Black Portraiture in 1920s New Orleans" (2002) and her spellbinding book *Picturing Black New Orleans: A Creole's Photographer's View of the Early Twentieth Century* (2012), bringing attention to the visual history and pioneering photography of Collins.

- **Brenda Marie Osbey**'s prose, narrative poetry, and scholarship in *All Souls: Essential Poems* (2015), *History and Other Poems* (2013), and *All Saints: New and Selected Poems* (1997), which weave history, memory, and cartographies of slavery and conquest, traversing the violent formation of the Americas, waterways, people, places, and time. Her work evokes visual portraits of the past alive in the present, with new grammars and glossaries of engagement that move across the page, creating new frames for seeing Black.

- **Christina Sharpe**'s *In the Wake: On Blackness and Being* (2016), where she piercingly examines the visual, literary, and quotidian representations of Black life within the "orthography of the wake"—the ongoing, repetitive, catastrophic, yet in/visible, registers of everyday violence and terror marked by slavery and its afterlife in "the wake," "the

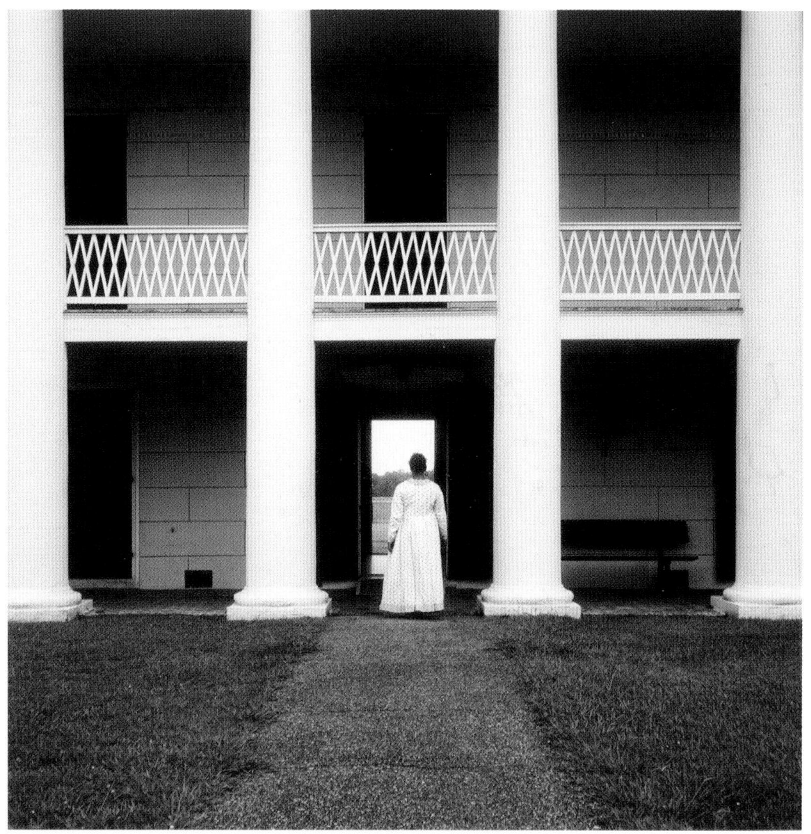

"Approaching Time," 2003. Photo: Carrie Mae Weems. Courtesy of Newcomb Art Museum.

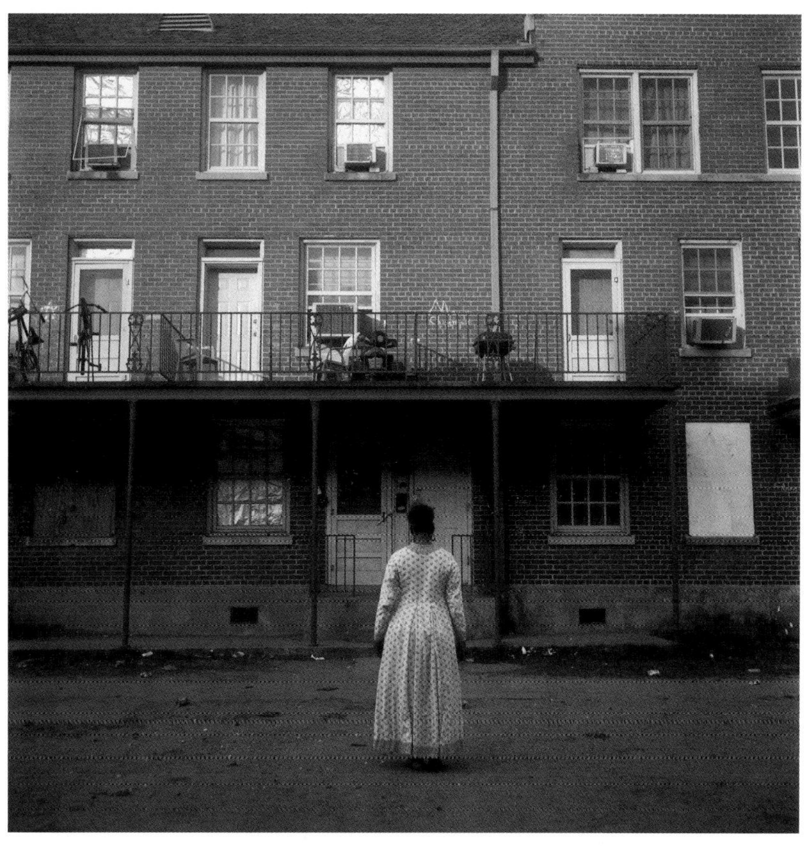

"In The Abyss," 2003. Photo: Carrie Mae Weems. Courtesy of Newcomb Art Museum.

ship," "the hold," and "the weather," constructing conditions of anti-Black containment, regulation, punishment, and disappearance. Within this framework, Sharpe states her interests *and* invites us to attend to the "ways of seeing and imagining responses to terror in the varied and various ways that our Black lives are lived under occupation; ways that attest to the modalities of Black life lived in, as, under, and despite Black death."

- **Tina M. Campt**'s essay "Black Visuality and the Practice of Refusal" (2019), which movingly asks, "How do we write, think, perform, practice, visualize, engage, theorize, story, or enact a practice of refusal?"[50] Campt outlines how the practice of refusal is one of "black visuality" that moves with sound, contemplation, and beyond abstraction.

- **kai lumumba barrow**'s abolitionist project—"[b]REACH: adventures in heterotopia," that challenges the politics *and* material consequences of carcerality in visual culture and how it shapes and constructs what we see and do in upholding the violence of policing, prisons, punishment, and confinement in and outside prison walls. barrow's art provocatively invites us to engage in abolitionist artmaking, including photography, "as an act of resistance" to capitalist, racist, and heterosexist systems of exploitation and extraction.[51]

Photography is inherently colonial, patriarchal, and racially biased in its technology *and* representations. Yet the Black women highlighted above, and the scholarship, literary works, and social criticism by Audre Lorde, Toni Morrison, Michelle Wallace, Kimberly Juanita Brown, Rizvana Bradley, Nicole R. Fleetwood, Saidiya Hartman, Marisa J. Fuentes, Renée Mussai, Tiffany King, Dionne Brand, Katherine McKittrick, Tia-Simone Gardner, Mona Lisa Saloy, Anne Collins Smith, others, and generations past, who embraced the photographic frame, reflect a multiplicity of practices of refusal and grammars of Black feminist possibilities within living histories of the past and future presents of the now.

Beginning in the early to mid-19th century with Florestine Perrault Collins, Oryana Valentine, Walterine Celestine, Irene Meyers, and Celeste T. Broadway, and later in the 1970s throughout 1990s with contemporary artists like Charlene Legaux Richard, Chandra McCormick, Terri A. Mimms, Veronica James, Bernie Saul, and Arana Sonier, Black women photographers in New Orleans have navigated hostile terrains that often marginalized their practice and contributions. Yet their work inspires thousands, including many of the artists in this collection. Spanning a range of subject matters, genres, and expressions beyond Black pain and suffering, the Black photographers featured here expand these gestures and grammars of resistance through various tenses, tones, punctuations, and frequencies, creating new visual vocabularies for futurity.[52]

3
GESTURING A HISTORICAL INTERVENTION, MAPPING BLACK PHOTOGRAPHY IN NEW ORLEANS

Historical archival practices and notarized transactions are known to violently erase the histories, narrative experiences, and contributions of Black people. The documentation of photography's arrival in the city of New Orleans in 1840 is uncontested. Still, the names and work of many historical Black photographers—*enslaved* and *free*—have been erased, unrecorded, or lost in historical archives. Through Girard Mouton,III's independent research on Black women and men who worked in the photography industry, as reported in census records and city directories from the 1860s to the 1940s, the fragments of what has been recorded and the images we have access to reveal a rich and burgeoning community of Black photographers, artists, and technicians who worked in the photography industry.

4
A GESTURE OF CREATIVE DEFIANCE: FLORESTINE PERRAULT COLLINS

The photography career of Florestine Perrault Collins began in 1909 when she was fourteen years old.[53] Assumed white by a prospective employer, Collins gained access to opportunities unavailable to most Black women during this time, who were often relegated to agricultural, nursing, textile, and domestic service occupations.

After working as a photography clerk, finisher, portraitist, stationery embosser, and developer,[54] Collins opened her first studio,

"Self-Portrait," ca. early 1920s. Photo: Florestine Perrault Collins. Courtesy of Dr. Arthé A. Anthony.

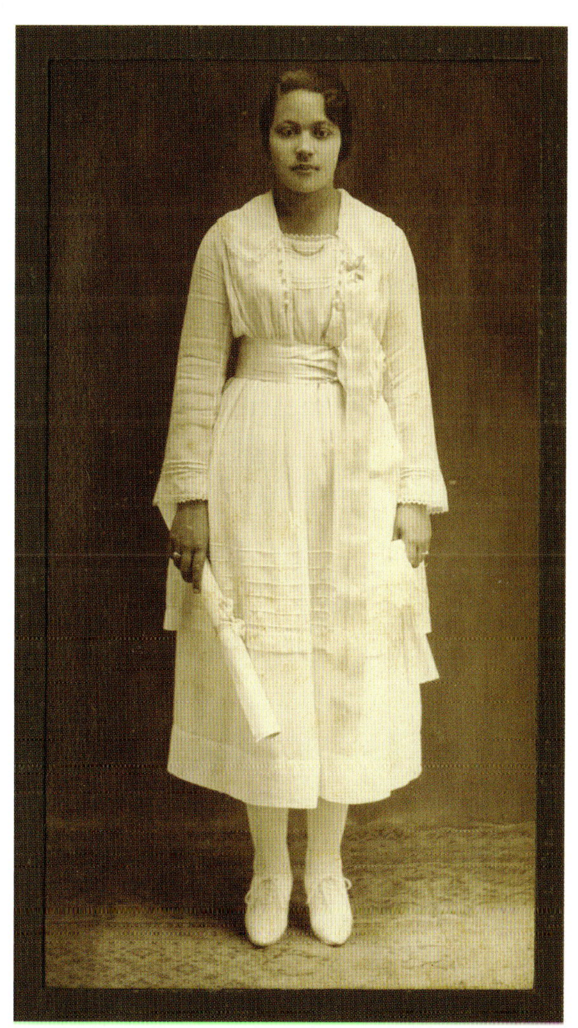

Portrait of a young woman dressed in white, ca. 1920–1923. Photo: Florestine Perrault Collins, F. Bertrand Studio. Courtesy of The Historic New Orleans Collection.

F. Bertrand Studio, in her living room parlor located at 2328 Saint Peter St. (presently part of the Faubourg Lafitte Public Housing Development footprint) in 1920 while married to her first husband, Eilert W. Bertrand, who did believe women should work outside the home.[55]

Unintimidated by a field dominated by men and by racist depictions of blackness in the early 20th century, Collins navigated various forms of racial and gendered subjectivities, transforming the confines of imposed patriarchal domesticity into a site of creative defiance and feminist possibilities. Collins took photos of family, friends, and new clients in her parlor room studio.

With a growing clientele, Collins moved into a new studio at 610 N. Claiborne Ave. under the name Bertrand's Studio in 1923. Conscious of photography's growing importance in Black life, she specifically advertised her business to women and children in local Black news publications.[56]

In 1925, working with Black photographer Villard Paddio, she contributed photographs to *The Crescent City Pictorial: A Souvenir Dedicated to the Progress of the COLORED CITIZENS of New Orleans, Louisiana, "America's Most Interesting City."* This booklet, published by O. C. W. Taylor and designed by O. T. Griffin, highlights various local Black businesses, schools, civic organizations, churches, and related establishments in New Orleans.

Despite actively working during the New Negro and New Woman movements, Collins was not exempt from the era's prevailing white supremacist and patriarchal views and

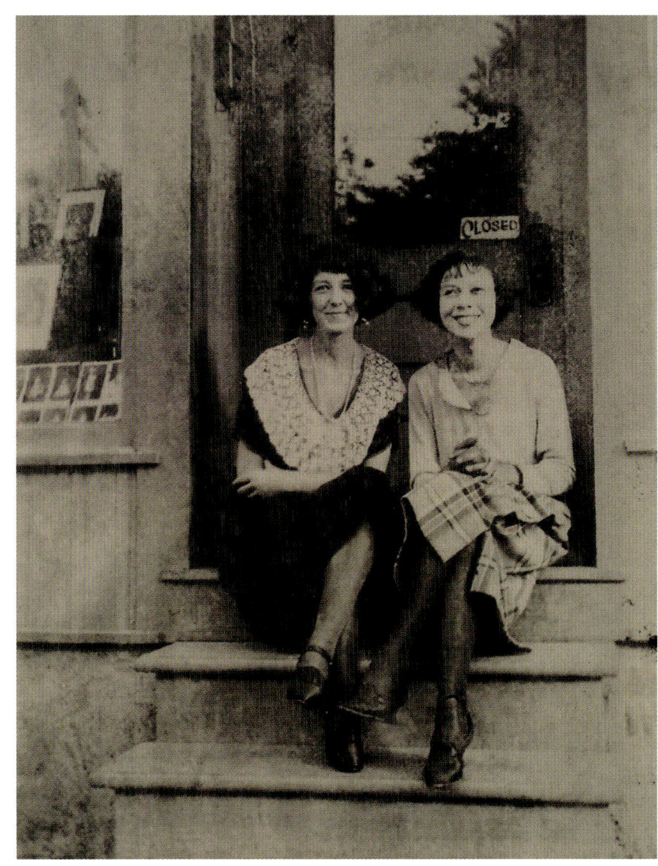

Jeannette Warburg and Daisy Fuller modeling in front of Bertrand's Studio, mid-1920s. Photo: Florestine Perrault Collins. Courtesy of Dr. Arthé A. Anthony.

expectations of Black womanhood, which sought to restrict and control women's place in society, professionally, politically, and personally, and the visual representation of blackness.

After ten years of a restrictive marriage, Collins divorced Bertrand in 1927 and took time away from her business. The following year, she married Herbert W. Collins and reopened her studio, rebranding it under Claiborne Studio. She remained at the Claiborne site until 1934.[57]

As part of a pioneering generation of Black photographers who used their studios and cameras to push back against racist depictions of blackness and redefine the practice of taking and processing photographs, Collins created portraits of her clients that spoke to the essence of who they were and how they

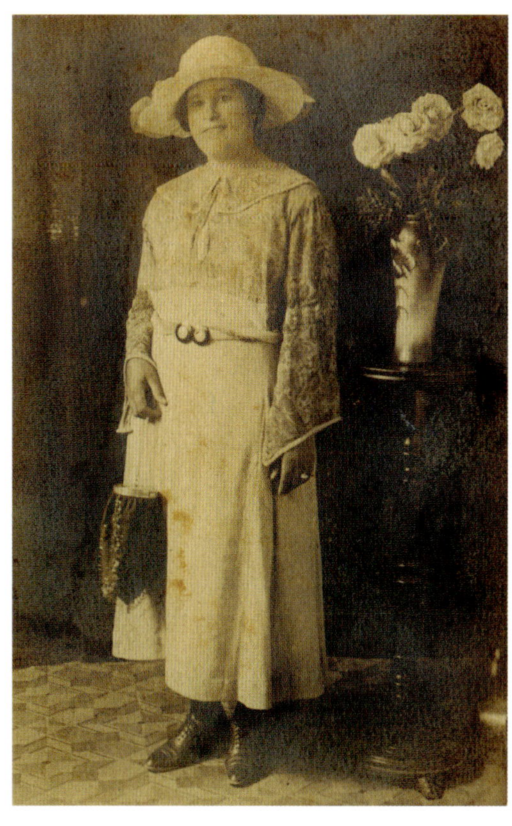

Portrait of Marie Louise St. Leger Wilcox, ca. 1922–1926. Photo: Florestine Perrault Collins, Bertrand Studio's. Courtesy of The Historic New Orleans Collection.

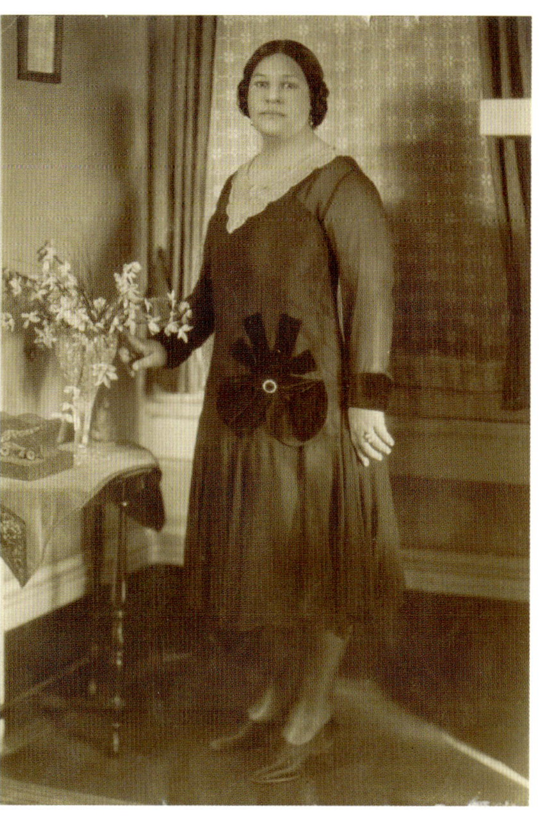

Portrait of Marie Louise St. Leger Wilcox, ca. 1924–1927. Photo: Florestine Perrault Collins, Bertrand's Studio. Courtesy of The Historic New Orleans Collection.

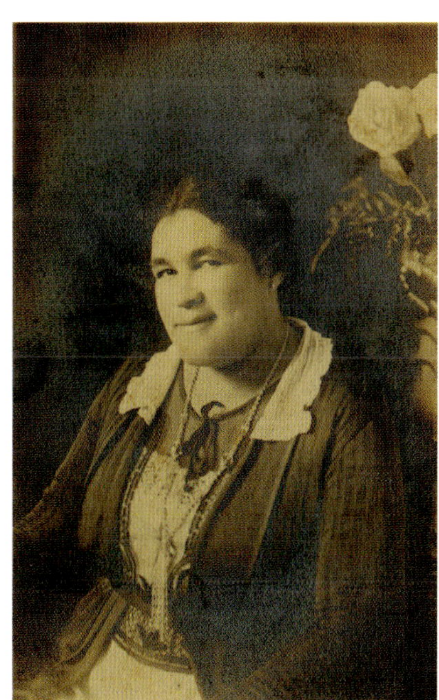

Portrait of Marie Louise St. Leger Wilcox, ca. 1922–1927. Photo: Florestine Perrault Collins, Bertrand Studio's. Courtesy of The Historic New Orleans Collection.

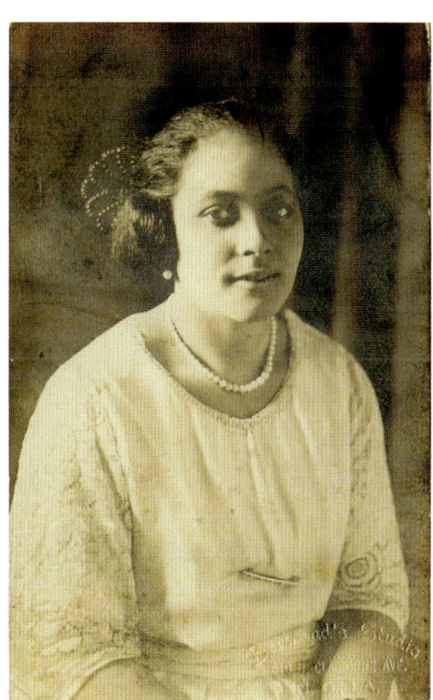

Portrait of an unidentified woman in pearls, ca. 1925–1927. Photo: Florestine Perrault Collins, Bertrand Studio's. Courtesy of The Historic New Orleans Collection.

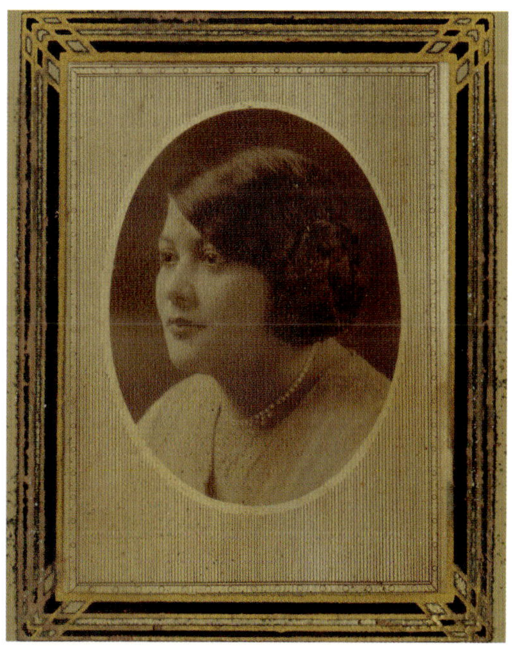

Studio portrait of woman, possibly Marie Theresa Collins, ca. 1928. Photo: Florestine Perrault Collins, Bertrand Studio's. Courtesy of The Historic New Orleans Collection.

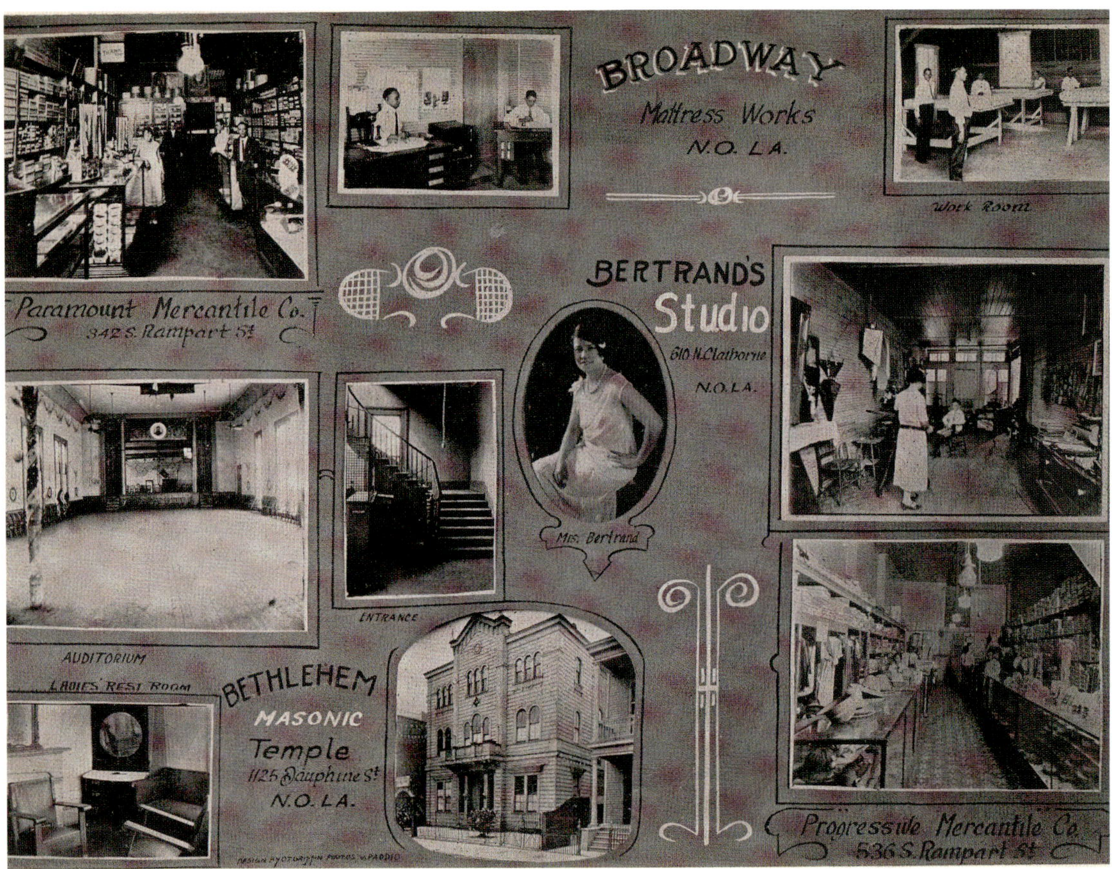

From *The Crescent City Pictorial*, featuring Bertrand's Studio, 1925. Photo: Villard Paddio. Courtesy of Amistad Research Center.

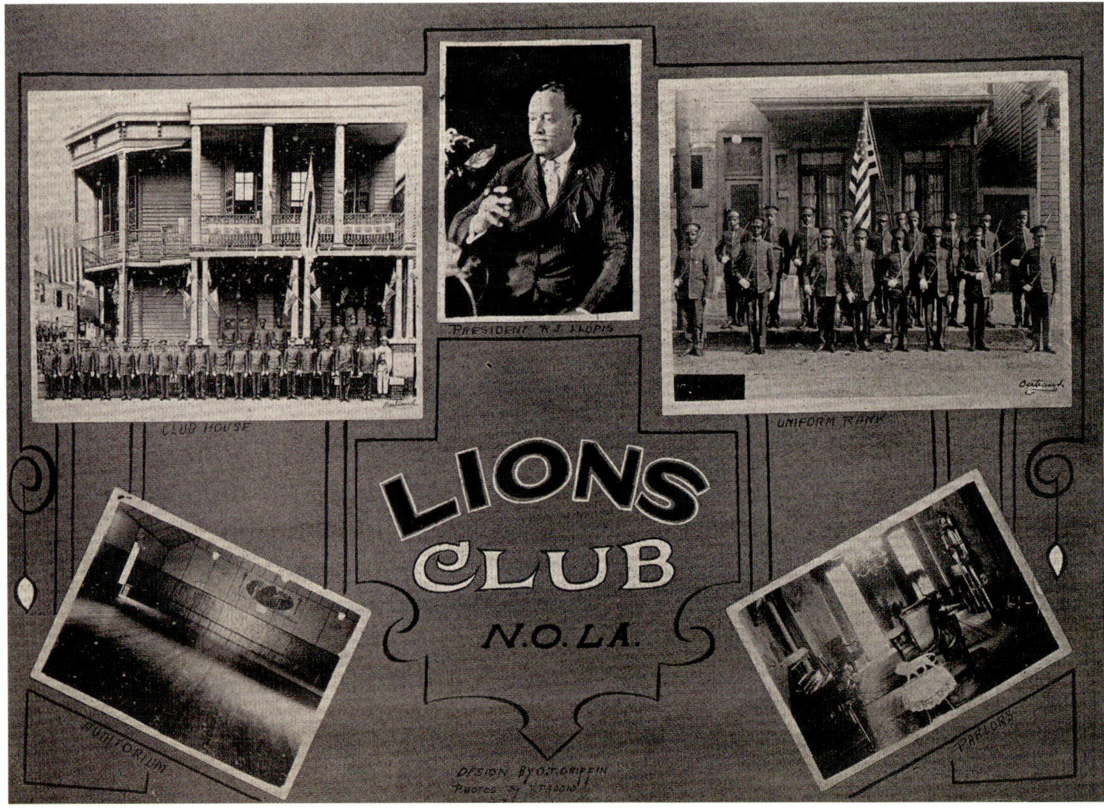

From *The Crescent City Pictorial*, featuring the Lions Club, 1925. Photo: Florestine Bertrand. Courtesy of Amistad Research Center.

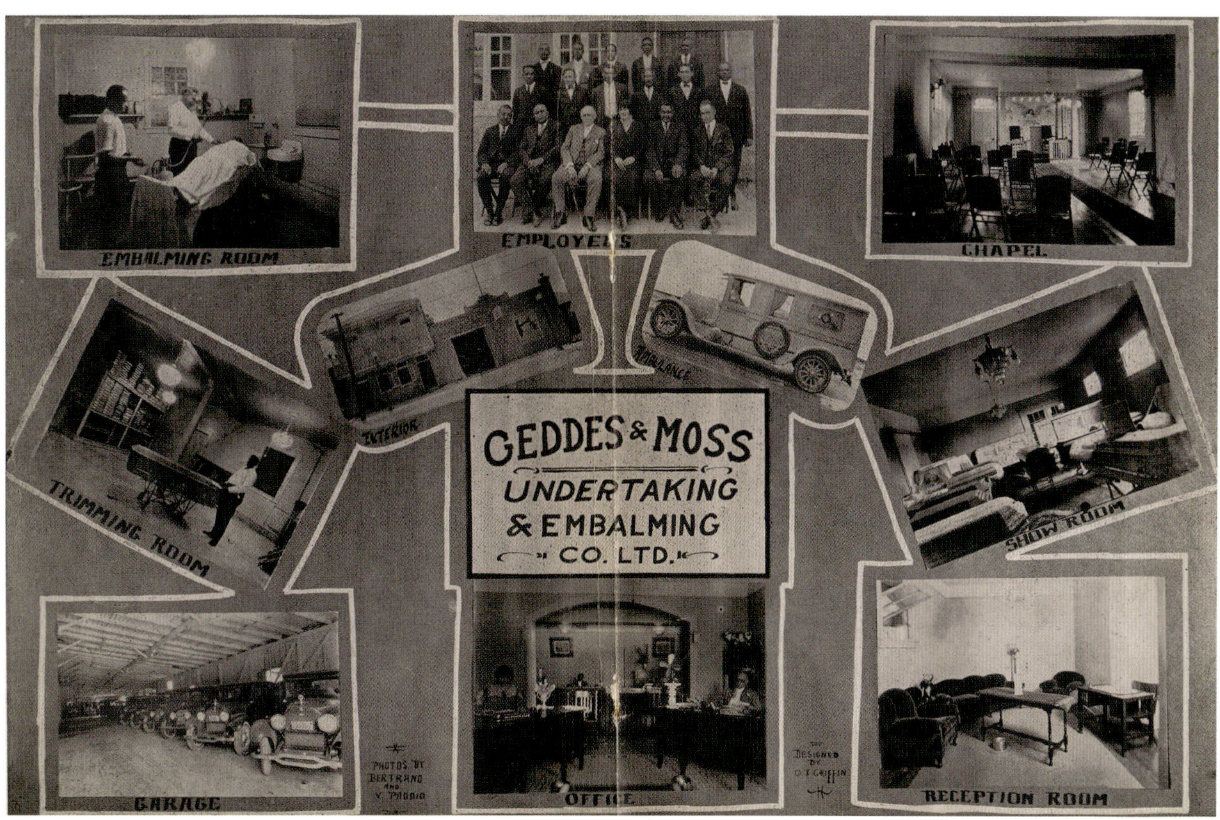

From *The Crescent City Pictorial*, featuring Bertrand's Studio, 1925. Photo: Florestine (Bertrand) Collins, working with Villard Paddio. Courtesy of Amistad Research Center.

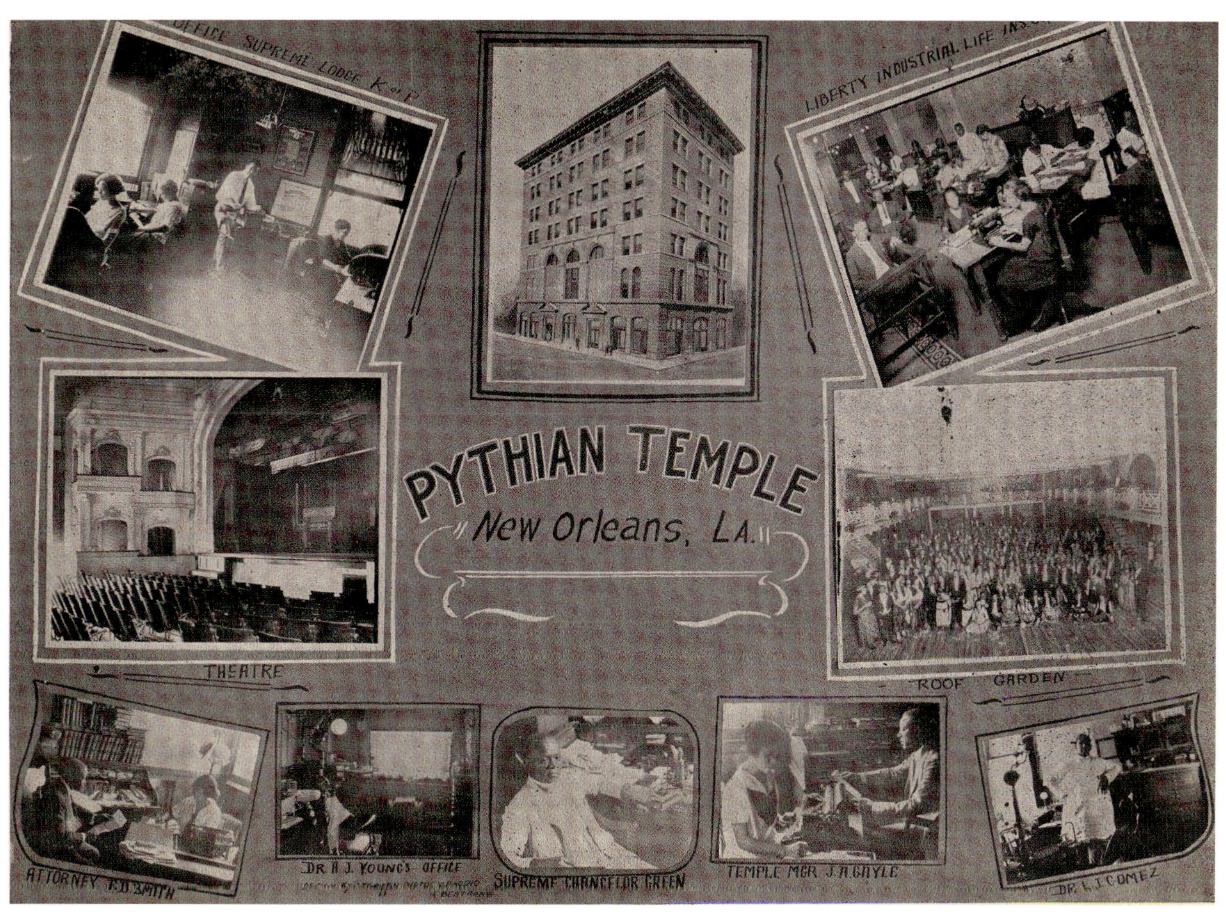

From *The Crescent City Pictorial*, featuring Bertrand's Studio, 1925. Photo: Florestine (Bertrand) Collins, working with Villard Paddio. Courtesy of Amistad Research Center.

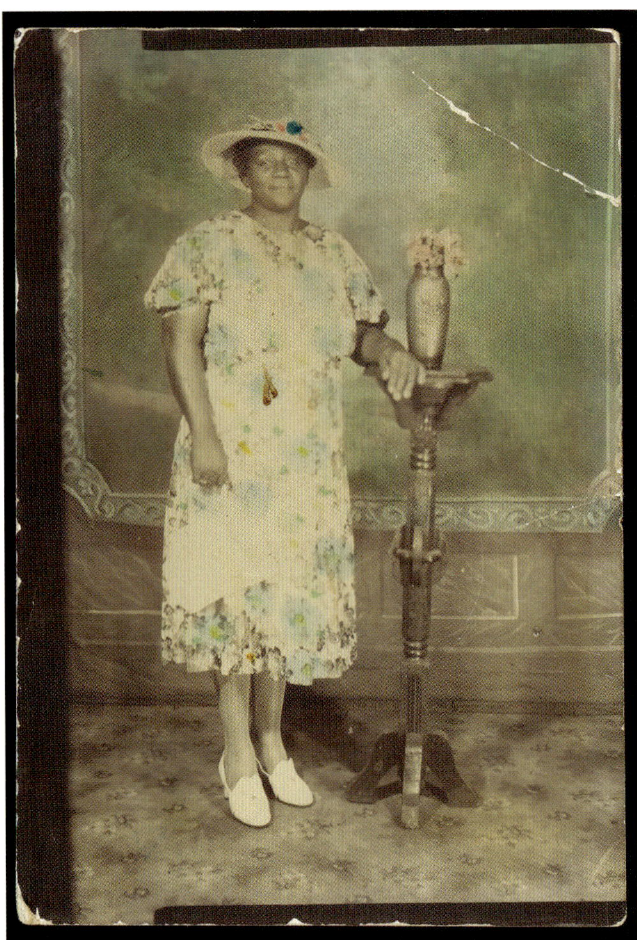

Hand-colored studio portrait of an older woman, ca. 1930–1940s. Photo: Florestine Perrault Collins. Courtesy of The Historic New Orleans Collection.

wanted to be seen in and by society.

With the continued success of her business, Collins relocated her studio to 170 S. Rampart St., in a flourishing Black and multiethnic neighborhood steeped with iconic jazz establishments, Black businesses, and educational institutions.[58] At the newly renamed Collins Studio, she produced a large body of work for clients from 1934 to 1947, employing predominately women photographers and finishers.

In 1947, Collins relocated her studio again to 157 S. Rampart St. She retired in 1949 and moved to Los Angeles, California, engaging in other artistic practices while keeping her camera nearby to take photos of family and friends. In 1975, at eighty years old, Collins returned to New Orleans, where she remained for the next thirteen years until her death in 1988, at ninety-three years old.[59]

Her aesthetic practice of producing images of self-possession and dignity that challenged stereotypes and controlling images of the Black body spanned a forty-year career in photography, including three decades of owning and operating several photography studios from 1920–1949. Like many of her contemporaries, Collins engaged the visual power of the camera, *"seeing Black,"* and embodied a distinctive approach to documenting Black accomplishments and everyday life experiences while also creating new futures and expanding Black potentiality through the photographic image.

5
THE PRELUDIAL GESTURE—*FIRST FRAME*

First Frame, the preludial exhibition for SEEING BLACK: Black Photography in New Orleans 1840 & Beyond, was mounted at the New Orleans African American Museum from October 2022 to June 2023 as an immersive installation engaging the photography of Florestine Perrault Collins and other early Black photographers' documentations of Black life, self-expression, political struggle, and social achievement through the camera.

Inspired by the location of Collins' first studio in the historic Tremé neighborhood and early 20th-century Black photographic practices, *First Frame* featured over 150 objects across two installations: a reimagination of Collins'

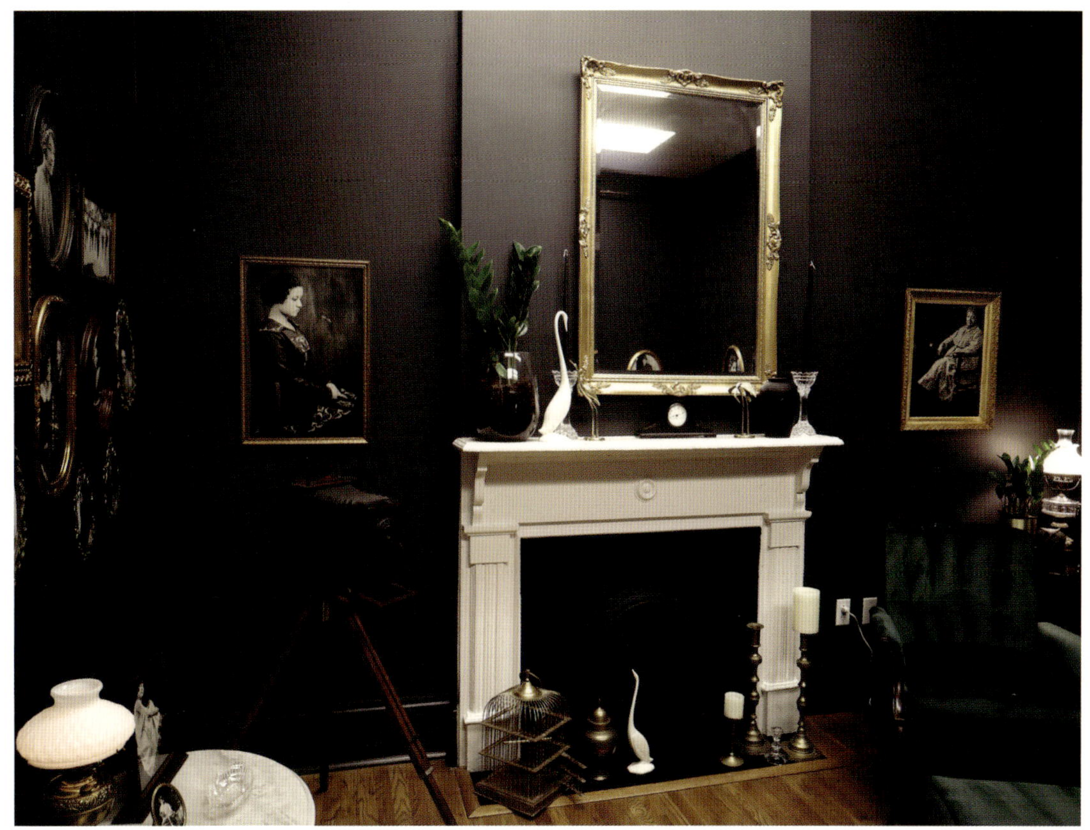

Living room parlor studio, *First Frame* exhibition, 2022. New Orleans African American Museum. Photo: Shana M. griffin.

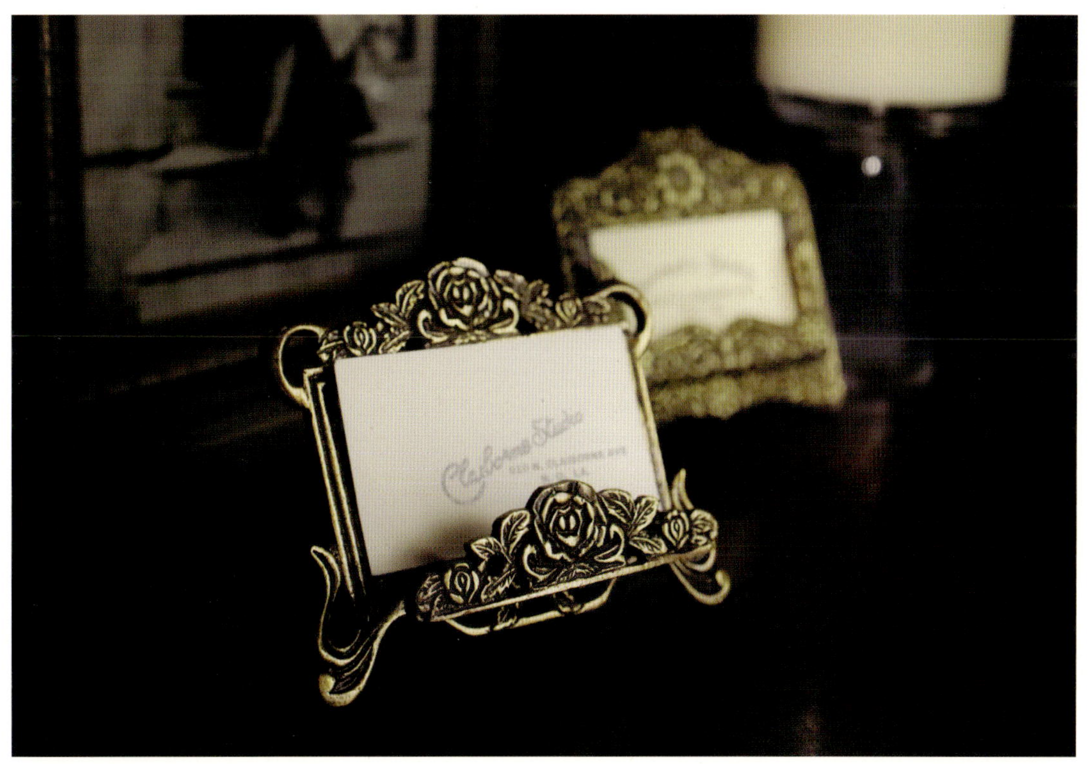

Parlor room office studio, *First Frame* exhibition, 2022. New Orleans African American Museum. Photo: Shana M. griffin.

parlor room studio and a Black portrait studio of the 1920s. The intentionally dark galleries that housed the installations served as symbolic gestures of refusal, circulating and signifying blackness as a counternarrative for imagining how New Orleans-based Black photographers like Collins, A. P. Bedou, Villard Paddio, and others used studio portraiture to "trouble the vision of the Western discourse," as theorized by Nicole R. Fleetwood, filling "in [the] space . . . between looking and being looked upon."[60]

The Collins parlor room introduced the thematic focus of the exhibition, displaying nearly forty reproduced portraits and photos taken by Collins between the early 1920s and the mid-1940s, including a series of cabinet card prints and a gallery wall, amid period-specific furnishings, Eastman Kodak cameras, reimagined business ephemera, and the sounds of jazz and blues by Piron's New Orleans Orchestra, Ma Rainey, Kid Ory & His Creole Jazz Band, King Oliver's Creole Jazz Band, Bessie Smith, Louis Armstrong, and others, situating the historical retelling of the past through a new photographic grammar in the present.

The portrait studio included a late-1920s Century Master Studio camera and stand by Folmer Graflex, Victorian and Edwardian chairs and related studio props, and a display of photo cabinet cards and advertising ephemera featuring the photographs by A. P. Bedou, copies of *The Crescent City Pictorial*, and the 1911, 1912, and 1913 *Woods Directories* produced and published by Allen Woods.

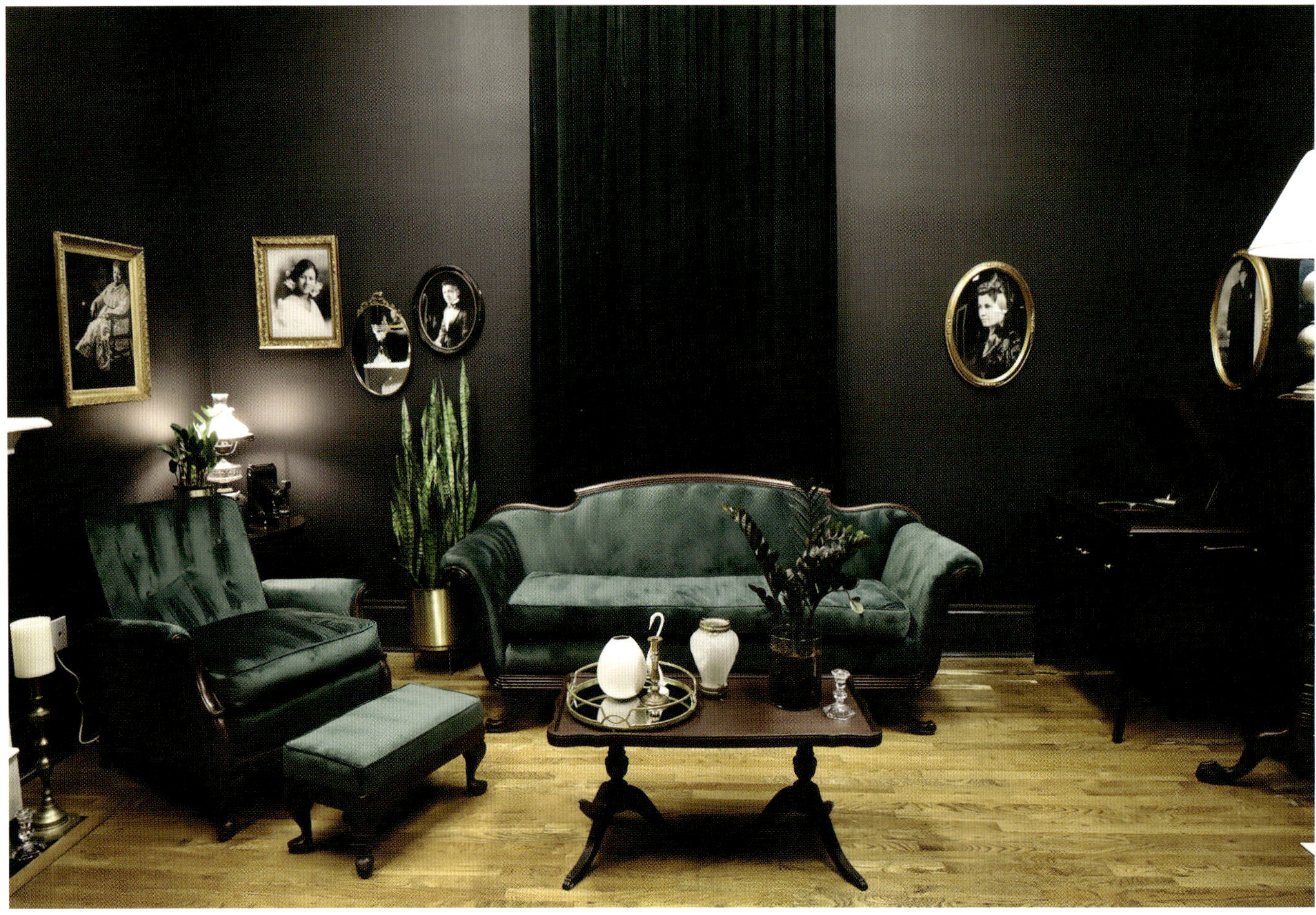

Living room parlor studio, *First Frame* exhibition, 2022. New Orleans African American Museum. Photo: Shana M. griffin.

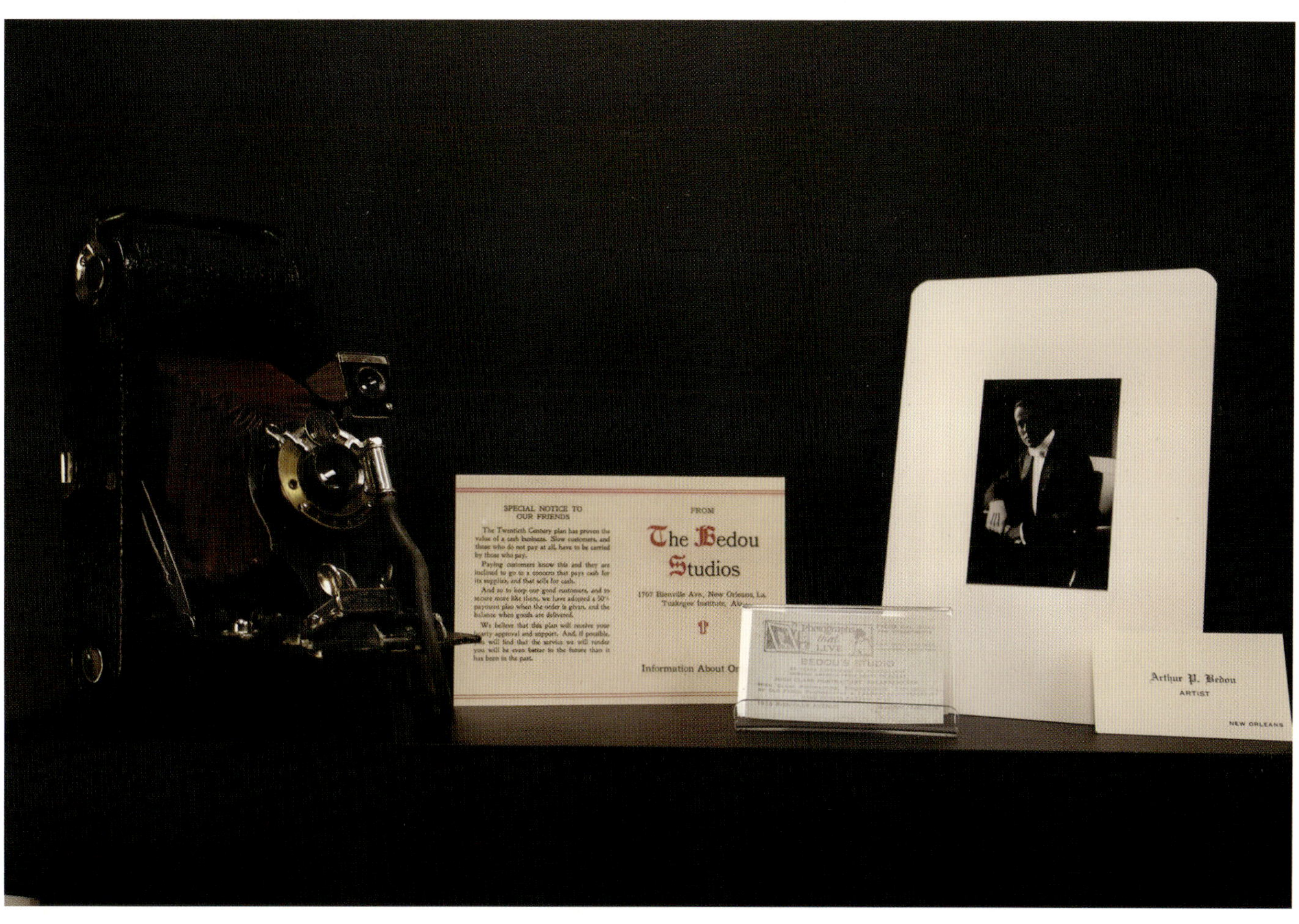

Portrait studio, *First Frame* exhibition, 2022. New Orleans African American Museum. Photo: Shana M. griffin.

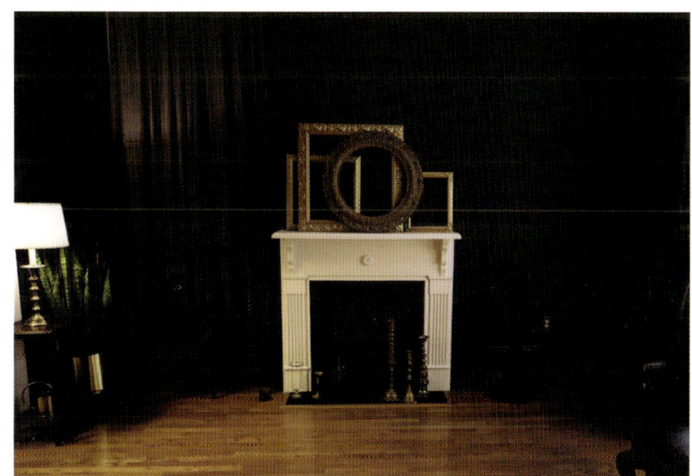

Portrait studio, *First Frame* exhibition, 2022. New Orleans African American Museum. Photo: Shana M. griffin.

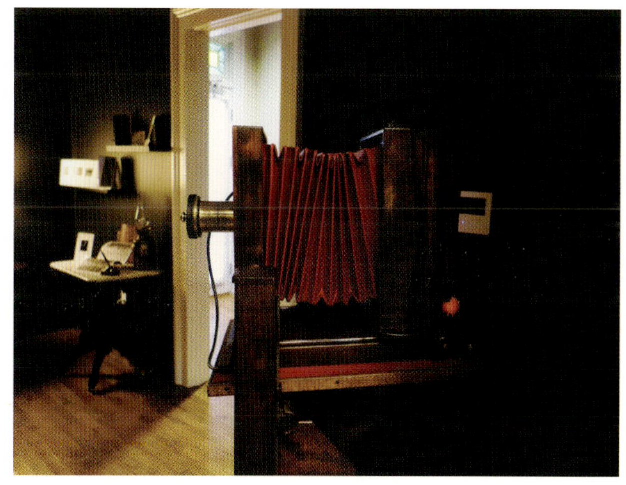

Portrait studio, *First Frame* exhibition, 2022. New Orleans African American Museum. Photo: Shana M. griffin.

6
A VISUAL GRAMMAR OF THE UNCONVENTIONAL—SEEING BLACK

Situating historical inquiry alongside contemporary practices of Black image-making in New Orleans, *SEEING BLACK: Black Photography in New Orleans 1840 and Beyond* is no ordinary investigation of how we experience, render visible, and see blackness in its complexity and possibilities for new frames of engagement. Initially conceptualized by Kalamu ya Salaam as a book on photography's pre-Civil War beginnings to its 21st-century practices, SEEING BLACK evolved to include a series of exhibitions spanning multiple sites, a digital platform, and public programming that challenged traditional exhibition didactics, conventional object presentations, and historical assumptions of Black representation and visuality.

From *First Frame* at the New Orleans African American Museum (2022–2023) and *In the Spirit of Black* at Ashé Culture Arts Center (2023) to *Gestures of Refusal: Black Photography and Visual Culture* at the Contemporary Arts Museum, New Orleans (2024) and its final exhibition at Xavier University Art Gallery of Louisiana (2024), *Frames of Black Portraiture: From the Early 1900s to the Present*, the photographs featured in *SEEING BLACK* reflect a Black visuality of "monstrosity," possibilities, and fullness as defined by the photographers and the social conditions that shape our practices.

Featuring more than 250 photographs by over one hundred Black photographers whose work embraces the camera's visual power of discerning, beholding, and documenting people, places, events, collective memories, encounters, and ever-present moments of blackness, *SEEING BLACK* is an exercise in the unconventional and the splendid. From the invisible to the obvious, the mundane to the spectacular, the overlooked to the seen, the erased, and the remembered, the artists explore a range of photographic frequencies, styles, tenses, punctuation, and rhythmic scores through portrait, self-narrative, street, landscape, experimental, conceptual, and documentary photography, engaging a broad spectrum of subject matter.

SEEING BLACK invites us to explore historical and contemporary archives of Black life while challenging dominant viewing practices, asking who is taking the picture, who is in or missing from the frame, and how to shift our default interactions with the visual image through an intentionally embodied Black gaze.

7
GESTURES OF FUTURITY

As reflected in this volume and elsewhere, Black photography is an exercise of refusal. An aesthetic practice with a visual sound. An artistic expression that rejects erasure. It is a movement of engagement—a protest *and* a fine art. A living memory, a future present. A vernacular language commanding recognition. Reflections of hope, redactions of violence. A Black visuality of expansive possibilities. A collective-self narrative gesturing to futurity.

θ

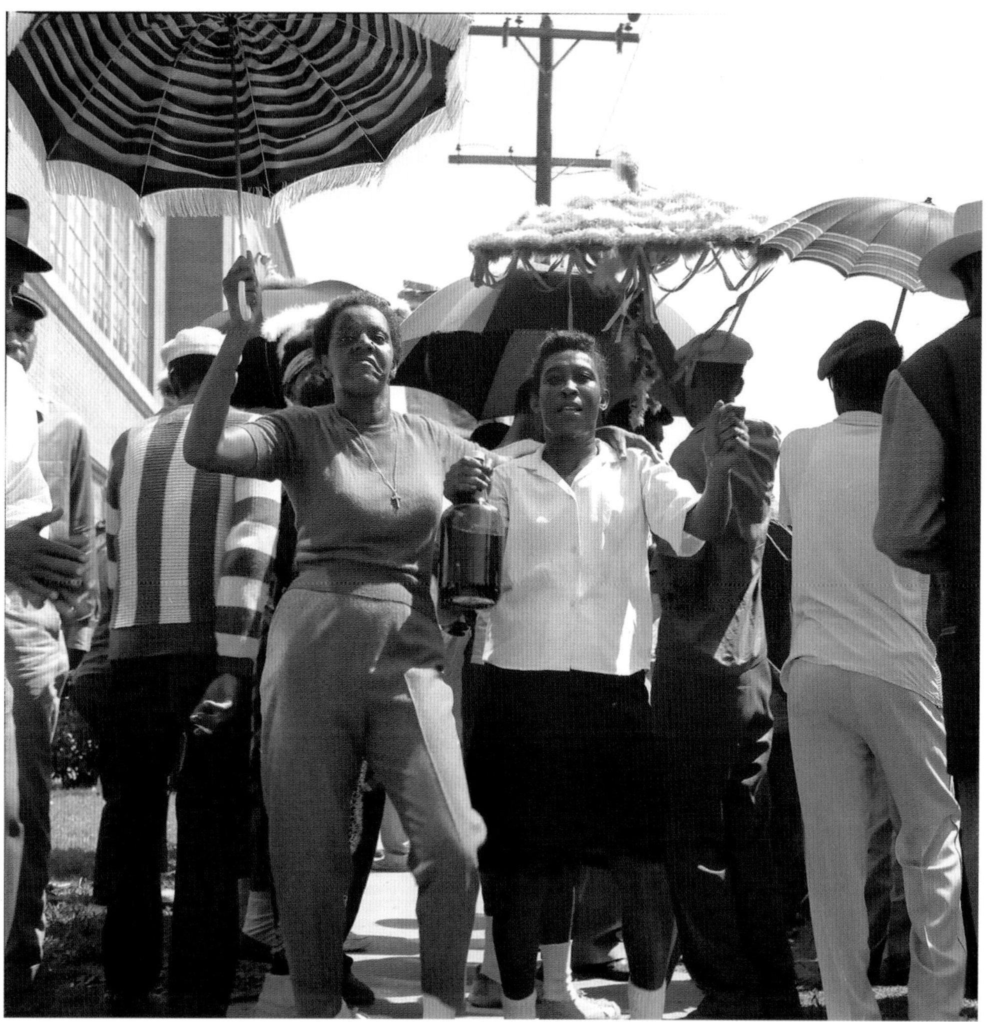

"Women in Tremé," ca. 1960s. New Orleans, LA. Photo: Maurice Martinez. Courtesy of the Artist.

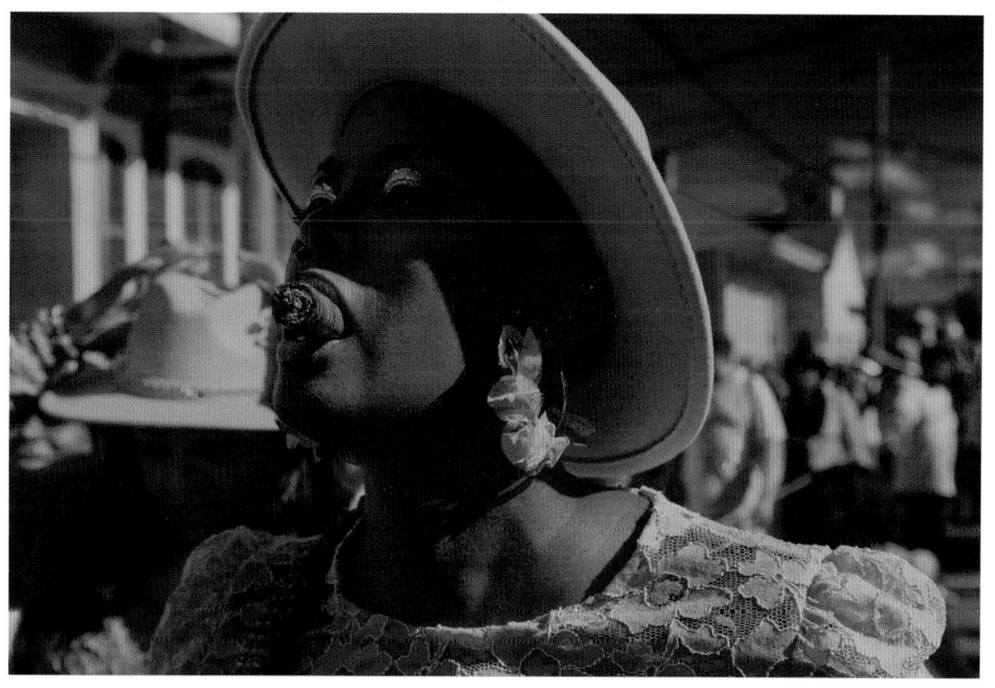

"Woman with Cigar," 2013. New Orleans, LA. Photo: Eric Waters. Courtesy of the Artist.

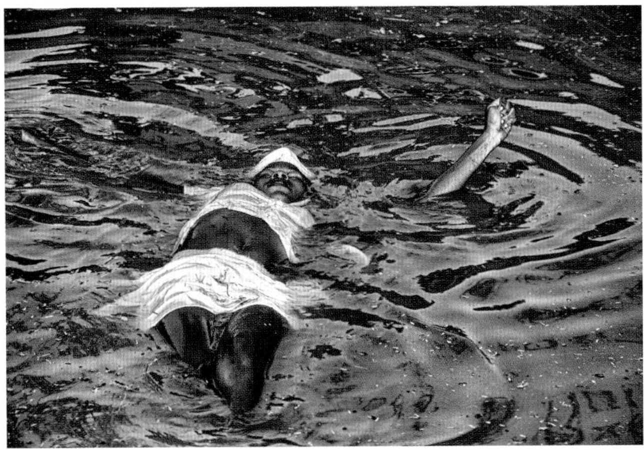

"The body as archive of our collective ancestors. In the beginning," ca. 2010. Haiti, Vodou Series. Photo: Sokari Ekine. Courtesy of the Artist.

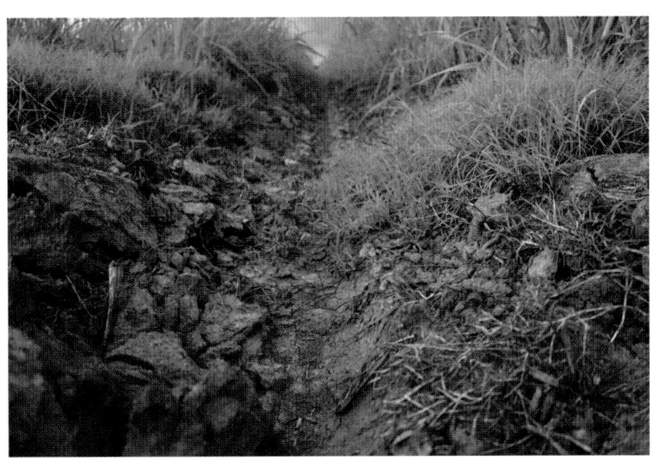

"Violent grounds," 2022. Felicity Plantation, Slave Quarters, Vacherie, LA, SOIL Series. Photo: Shana M. griffin.

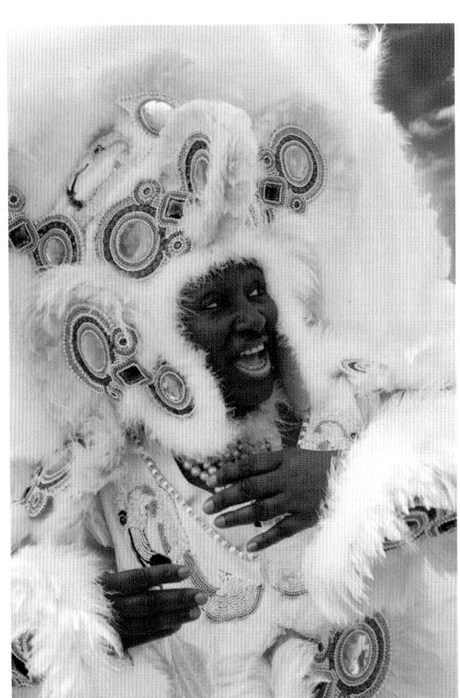

Ausettua AmorAmenkum, Big Queen Washitaw. Photo: Eric Waters. Courtesy of the Artist.

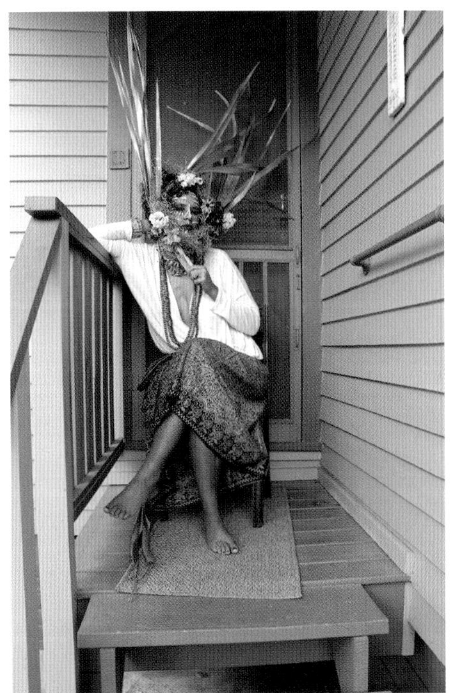

"Neighborhood Watch," 2016. Photo: Jeri Hilt. Courtesy of the Artist.

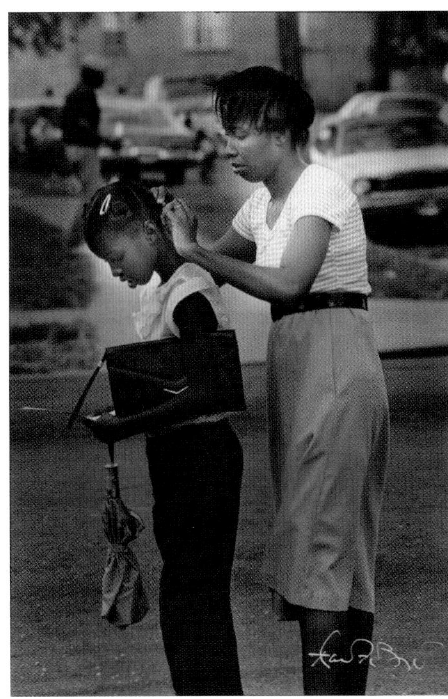

School girl, 1984–89. Photo: Harold Baquet. Courtesy of The Historic New Orleans Collection.

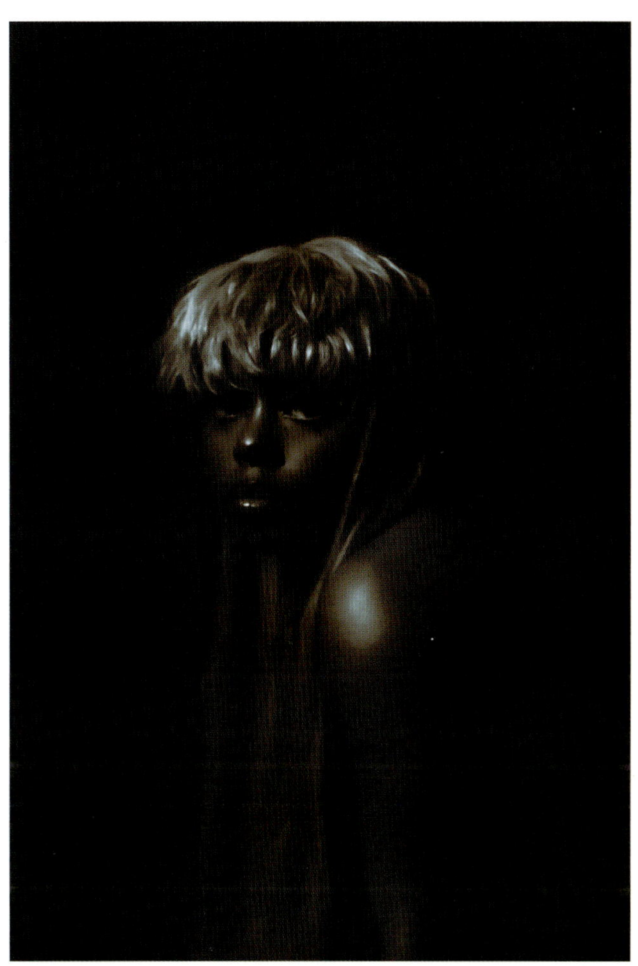

"Dark Fairy," 2020. Photo: Trenity Thomas. Courtesy of the Artist.

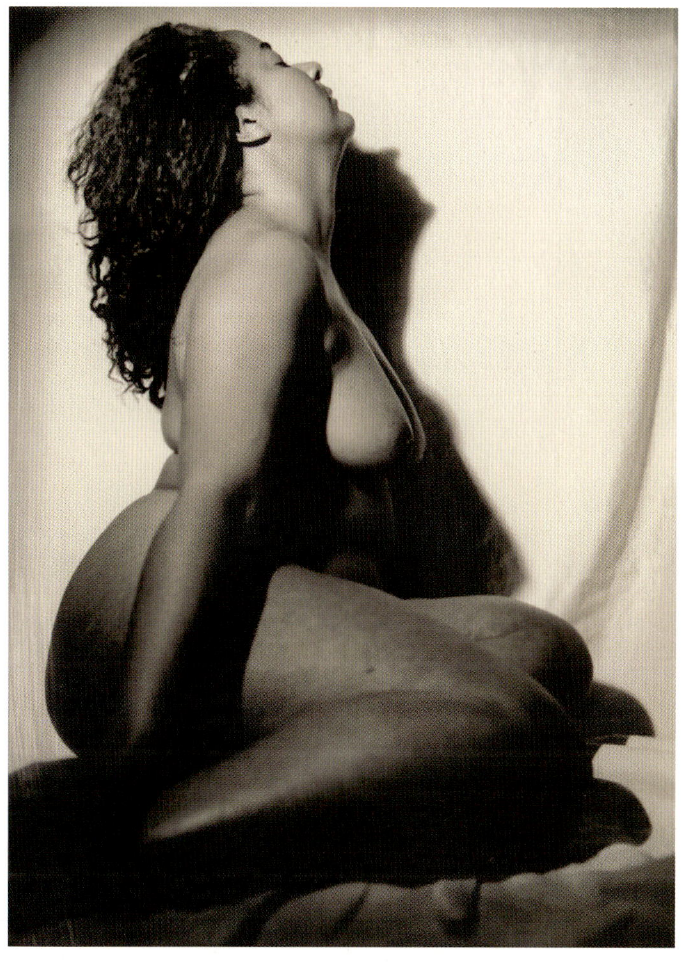

"Venus," Polaroid Type 55 positive print, 1994–1995. Los Angeles, CA. Photo: Carla Williams. Courtesy of the Artist.

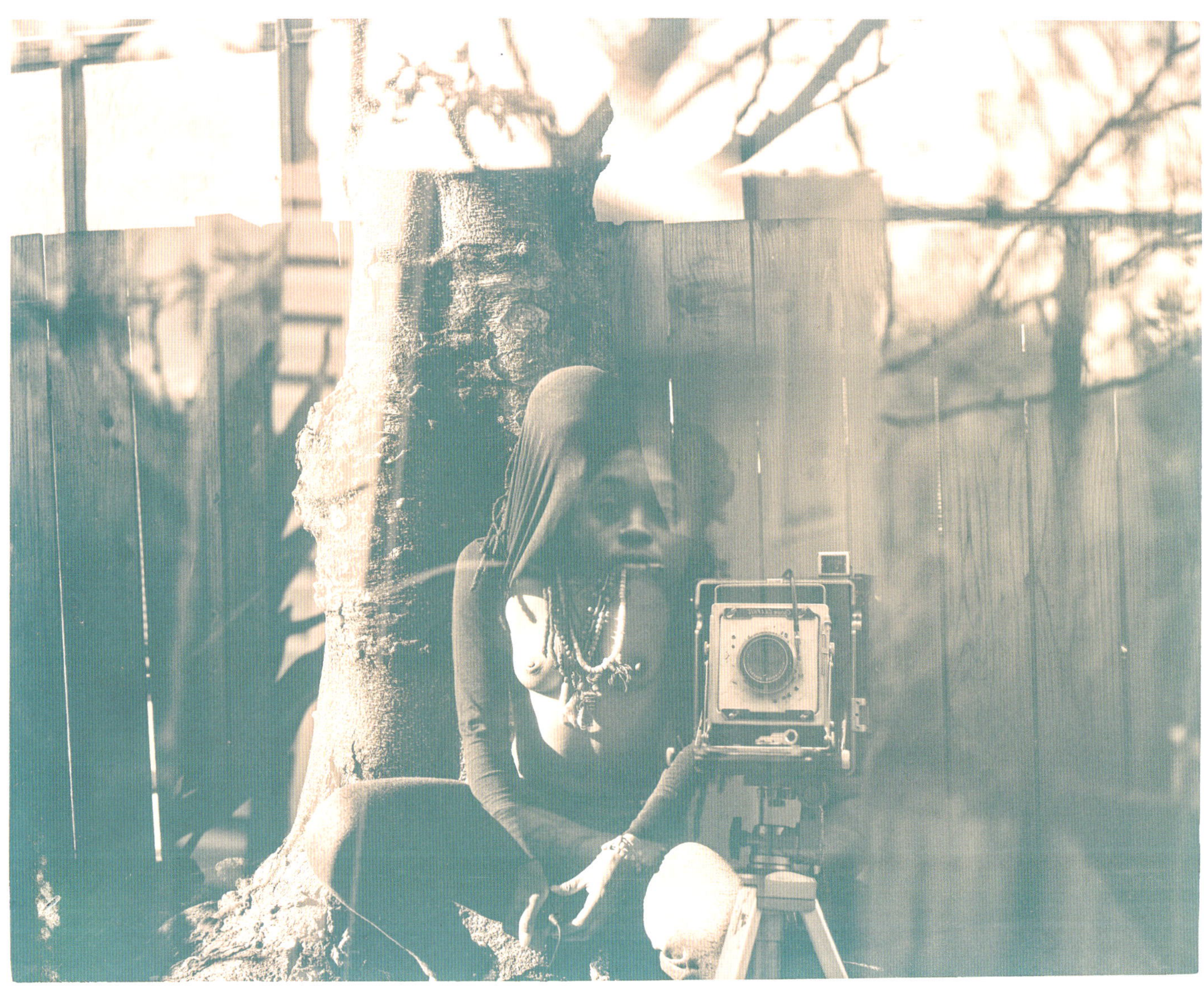

"Untitled (Imagining the Womb)," 2019. Photo: Felicita Felli Maynard. Courtesy of the Artist.

Endnotes

1 Tina M. Campt, *Listening to Images* (Durham and London, Duke University Press, 2007), 4.

2 bell hooks, *Art on My Mind: Visual Politics* (New York: The New Press, 1995), 60.

3 "The Daily Picayune, 1854," *Freedom on the Move Project*, accessed March 7, 2024, https://database.freedomonthemove.org/advertisements/563f7810-e086-4b2c-8fa1-7a253f-097bad.

4 Hortense Spillers, "Mama's Baby, Papa's Maybe: An American Grammar Book," *Diacritics* 17, no. 2 (1987): 65–81.

5 Jeri Hilt, "There Are No Survivors Without Scars," *Bitch Media*, August 26, 2015, https://www.bitchmedia.org/article/there-are-no-survivors-without-scars.

6 "Louisiana Advertiser, 1820," *Freedom on the Move Project*, accessed March 7, 2024, https://database.freedomonthemove.org/advertisements/47a5c73e-ceff-40b6-87bb-511ad51fb888.

7 "New-Orleans Argus, 1828," *Freedom on the Move Project*, accessed March 7, 2024, https://database.freedomonthemove.org/advertisements/68c30866-ed7a-447f-9873-dd1cf971057a.

8 "New-Orleans Argus, 1828," *Freedom on the Move Project*, accessed March 7, 2024, https://database.freedomonthemove.org/advertisements/6e82f65b-6def-4b46-a928-e3d3e0627dc7.

9 "New-Orleans Argus, 1828," *Freedom on the Move Project*, accessed March 7, 2024, https://database.freedomonthemove.org/advertisements/bd909116-a564-4714-80e3-eeb77d846c0e.

10 "New-Orleans Argus, 1828," *Freedom on the Move Project*, accessed March 7, 2024, https://database.freedomonthemove.org/advertisements/5e1ac4a7-d705-482e-8bca-75e438d812e5.

11 "The Daily Picayune, 1837," *Freedom on the Move Project*, accessed March 7, 2024, https://database.freedomonthemove.org/advertisements/3e1523b5-082c-4842-8324-796b2fe53fcb.

12 "The Daily Picayune, 1837," *Freedom on the Move Project*, accessed March 7, 2024, https://database.freedomonthemove.org/advertisements/2ae3832b-ace7-4bd0-bd63-b891f6478b9a.

13 "The Daily Picayune, 1837," *Freedom on the Move Project*, accessed March 7, 2024, https://database.freedomonthemove.org/advertisements/2dcc95b5-cb7d-4b5a-b116-20e67dff6e8b.

14 "The Daily Picayune, 1838," *Freedom on the Move Project*, accessed March 7, 2024, https://database.freedomonthemove.org/advertisements/81857493-88e3-4bbd-878d-ba1350b321cc.

15 "The Daily Picayune, 1840" *Freedom on the Move Project*, accessed March 7, 2024, https://database.freedomonthemove.org/advertisements/4027bc90-e552-49d9-a38d-bc1ef0c00bb6.

16 "The Daily Picayune, 1840," *Freedom on the Move Project*, accessed March 7, 2024, https://database.freedomonthemove.org/advertisements/162cef00-a715-4003-ba70-6c52bda234b4.

17 "The Daily Picayune, 1844," *Freedom on the Move Project*, accessed March 7, 2024, https://database.freedomonthemove.org/advertisements/b6b8c34a-945d-4a5b-9b98-d8355062c200.

18 "The Daily Picayune, 1844," *Freedom on the Move Project*, accessed March 7, 2024, https://database.freedomonthemove.org/advertisements/3ef26332-60b5-4f78-a9f1-f6ec27f34f13.

19 "The Daily Picayune, 1844," *Freedom on the Move Project*, accessed March 7, 2024, https://database.freedomonthemove.org/advertisements/599bb875-f89b-4f70-be78-1e991564dd2c.

20 "The Daily Picayune, 1845," *Freedom on the Move Project*, accessed March 7, 2024, https://database.freedomonthemove.org/advertisements/0572ede4-34b8-4cfc-bd79-7fe584fd4e10.

21 "The Daily Picayune, 1846," *Freedom on the Move Project*, accessed March 7, 2024, https://database.freedomonthemove.org/advertisements/1f49bb28-e7b8-4ddb-a16e-9b701542484b.

22 "The Daily Picayune, 1846," *Freedom on the Move Project*, accessed March 7, 2024, https://database.freedomonthemove.org/advertisements/c2225ea8-b296-4c26-9a6a-1cdbb8932b65.

23 "The Daily Picayune, 1846," *Freedom on the Move Project*, accessed March 7, 2024, https://database.freedomonthemove.org/advertisements/a06acb48-4c65-4a15-b89b-e7abd15e6fd3.

24 "The Daily Picayune, 1846," *Freedom on the Move Project*, accessed March 7, 2024, https://database.freedomonthemove.org/advertisements/3e1337df-fab3-42b9-8b23-320fa5631638.

25 "The Daily Picayune, 1846," *Freedom on the Move Project*, accessed March 7, 2024, https://database.freedomonthemove.org/advertisements/491f698c-997f-4899-803b-3802d6f8ebdd.

26 "The Daily Picayune, 1847," *Freedom on the Move Project*, accessed March 7, 2024, https://database.freedomonthemove.org/advertisements/170d4cd8-bfd7-45d2-86d7-9dd707c324c7.

27 "The Daily Picayune, 1847," *Freedom on the Move Project*, accessed March 7, 2024, https://database.freedomonthemove.org/advertisements/e749d6f3-b73d-40ea-8944-3e714493f931.

28 "The Daily Picayune, 1847," *Freedom on the Move Project*, accessed March 7, 2024, https://database.freedomonthemove.org/advertisements/fbdd58fe-e634-409c-ab7f-5f6662b62fd5.freedomonthemove.org/advertisements/fbdd58fe-e634-409c-ab7f-5f6662b62fd5.

29 "The Daily Picayune, 1847," *Freedom on the Move Project*, accessed March 7, 2024, https://database.freedomonthemove.org/advertisements/fdc412de-c64b-4601-8fef-dbb0b433227b.

30 "The Daily Picayune, 1849," *Freedom on the Move Project*, accessed March 7, 2024, https://database.freedomonthemove.org/advertisements/4ccd3a41-47b9-4d3d-ad87-76c67a5d9f0d.

31 "The Daily Picayune, 1851," *Freedom on the Move Project*, accessed March 7, 2024, https://database.freedomonthemove.org/advertisements/021d-caf6-8075-4de5-8f95-2b5b14cb106b.

32 "The Daily Picayune, 1851," *Freedom on the Move Project*, accessed March 7, 2024, https://database.freedomonthemove.org/advertisements/bf465996-548c-4972-ae96-79a4359a3766.

33 "The Daily Picayune, 1854," *Freedom on the Move Project*, accessed March 7, 2024, https://database.freedomonthemove.org/advertisements/4ff75b21-dc7f-4e89-bdca-10d6aa5178fc.

34 "The Daily Picayune, 1854," *Freedom on the Move Project*, accessed March 7, 2024, https://database.freedomonthemove.org/advertisements/ffb3e188-bede-4b33-a3e2-f89cea00596b.

35 "The Daily Picayune, 1854," *Freedom on the Move Project*, accessed March 7, 2024, https://database.freedomonthemove.org/advertisements/563f7810-e086-4b2c-8fa1-7a253f097bad.

36 C. M. Bell, *Mrs. A. J. Cooper, 1901*, 1903, photograph, Library of Congress, https://www.loc.gov/item/2016702852/.

37 *Sojourner Truth, three-quarter length portrait, standing, wearing spectacles, shawl, and peaked cap, right hand resting on cane*, 1864, photograph, Library of Congress, Detroit, https://www.loc.gov/item/97513239/.

38 Harriet A. Jacobs, *Incidents in the Life of a Slave Girl: Written by Herself*, ed. L. Maria Child (Boston: Thayer & Eldridge, 1861), 173–178.

39 Shirley Moody-Turner and Anna J. Cooper, "'Dear Doctor Du Bois': Anna Julia Cooper, W. E. B. Du Bois, and the Gender Politics of Black Publishing," *MELUS* 40, no. 3 (2015): 47–68.

40 Nikki Brown, "Keeping Black Motherhood Out of Prison: Prison Reform and Women Saving in the Progressive Era," *The Journal of African American History* 104, no. 1 (2019): 6–30.

41 Jari Honora, "Flint-Goodridge Hospital," *64 Parishes*, April 5, 2023, https://64parishes.org/entry/flint-goodridge-hospital.

42 Alice Walker, "On Refusing to Be Humbled by Second Place in a Contest You Did Not Design: A Tradition by Now," in *I Love Myself When I'm Laughing . . . And Then Again When I'm Looking Mean and Impressive: A Zora Neale Hurston Reader*, ed. Alice Walker (Old Westbury, New York: The Feminist Press, 1979): 1–5; Mary Helen Washington, "Zora Neale Hurston: A Woman Half in Shadow," in *I Love Myself When I'm Laughing . . . And Then Again When I'm Looking Mean and Impressive: A Zora Neale Hurston Reader*, ed. Alice Walker (Old Westbury, New York: The Feminist Press, 1979): 7–25.

43 Mona Lisa Saloy, "Zora Neale Hurston on River Road: Portrait of Algiers, New Orleans, and Her Fieldwork," *Louisiana Folklore Miscellany* 21 (2011): 43–61; Susan Edwards Meisenhelder, *Hitting A Straight Lick with a Crooked Stick: Race and Gender in the Work of Zora Neale Hurston* (Tuscaloosa, Alabama: University of Alabama Press, 1999): 1–13; Zora Neale Hurston, *The Sanctified Church* (Berkeley: Turtle Island, 1981), 24.

44 Pearl Bowser, Jane Gaines, and Charles Musser, *Oscar Micheaux and His Circle: African-American Filmmaking and Race Cinema of the Silent Era* (Bloomington, Indiana: Indiana UP, 2016).

45 "Black Haiti: Where Old Africa and The New World Meet," *Life* 3, no. 24 (December 13, 1937): 26–31.

46 *Zora Hurston, half-length portrait, standing, facing slightly left, beating the hountar, or mama drum*, 1937, photograph, Library of Congress, https://www.loc.gov/item/93513271/.

47 Jeanne Moutoussamy-Ashe, *Viewfinders: Black Women Photographers* (New York: Dodd, Mead & Company, 1986), xvi.

48 hooks, *Art on My Mind*, xiii.

49 hooks, *Art on My Mind*, 59.

50 Tina Marie Campt, "Black visuality and the practice of refusal," *Women & Performance: a journal of feminist theory* 29, no. 1 (2019): 79–87.

51 kai lumumba barrow, "Radical Imaginations Beyond Carceral Borders," *Undoing Time* (exhibition lecture, Contemporary Arts Center, New Orleans, July 2, 2023).

52 Rizvana Bradley, "Picturing Catastrophe: The visual politics of racial reckoning," *The Yale Review*, May 25, 2021, https://yalereview.org/article/picturing-catastrophe-rizvana-bradley.

53 Arthé A. Anthony, *Picturing Black New Orleans: A Creole's Photographer's View of the Early Twentieth Century* (Tallahassee: University Press of Florida, 2012), 2.

54 Arthé A. Anthony, "Florestine Perrault Collins and the Gendered Politics of Black Portraiture in 1920s New Orleans," *Louisiana History: The Journal of the Louisiana Historical Association* 43, no. 2 (2002): 167–88, http://www.jstor.org/stable/4233837.

55 Anthony, *Picturing Black New Orleans*, 2.

56 Anthony, "Florestine Perrault Collins," http://www.jstor.org/stable/4233837.

57 Anthony, *Picturing Black New Orleans*, 76–78.

58 Anthony, *Picturing Black New Orleans*, 76–78

59 Anthony, *Picturing Black New Orleans*, 108.

60 Nicole R. Fleetwood, introduction to *Troubling Vision: Performance, Visuality, and Blackness* (Chicago and London: The University of Chicago Press, 2011), 6.

Institutional Image Credits

"Portrait of a young woman dressed in white" by Florestine Perrault Collins, The Historic New Orleans Collection, 2001.78.

"Portrait of a woman with flowers" by Florestine Perrault Collins, The Historic New Orleans Collection, 2001.79.41.

"Marie Collins' daughter" by Florestine Perrault Collins, The Historic New Orleans Collection, 2001.79.2.

"Portrait of woman" by Florestine Perrault Collins, The Historic New Orleans Collection, 2001.79.40.

"Woman in pearls" by Florestine Perrault Collins, The Historic New Orleans Collection, 2001.79.9.

"Portrait of an African-American woman, possibly Marie Collins" by Florestine Perrault Collin, The Historic New Orleans Collection, 2001.79.3.

Page from *The Crescent City Pictorial*, featuring Bertrand's Studio by Villard Paddio, 1925. Joseph A. Hardin papers. Amistad Research Center, New Orleans, LA.

Page from *The Crescent City Pictorial*, featuring the Lions Club by Florestine Bertrand, 1925. Joseph A. Hardin papers. Amistad Research Center, New Orleans, LA.

Page from *The Crescent City Pictorial*, featuring Bertrand's Studio by Florestine (Bertrand) Collins and Villard Paddio, 1925. Joseph A. Hardin papers. Amistad Research Center, New Orleans, LA.

Page from *The Crescent City Pictorial*, featuring Bertrand's Studio by Florestine (Bertrand) Collins and Villard Paddio, 1925. Joseph A. Hardin papers. Amistad Research Center, New Orleans, LA.

"Studio portrait of an unidentified woman" by Florestine Perrault Collins, The Historic New Orleans Collection, MSS 782.2.2.3.

"School girl" by Harold Baquet, The Historic New Orleans Collection, Gift of Harold F. Baquet and Cheron Brylski, 2016.0172.2.45.

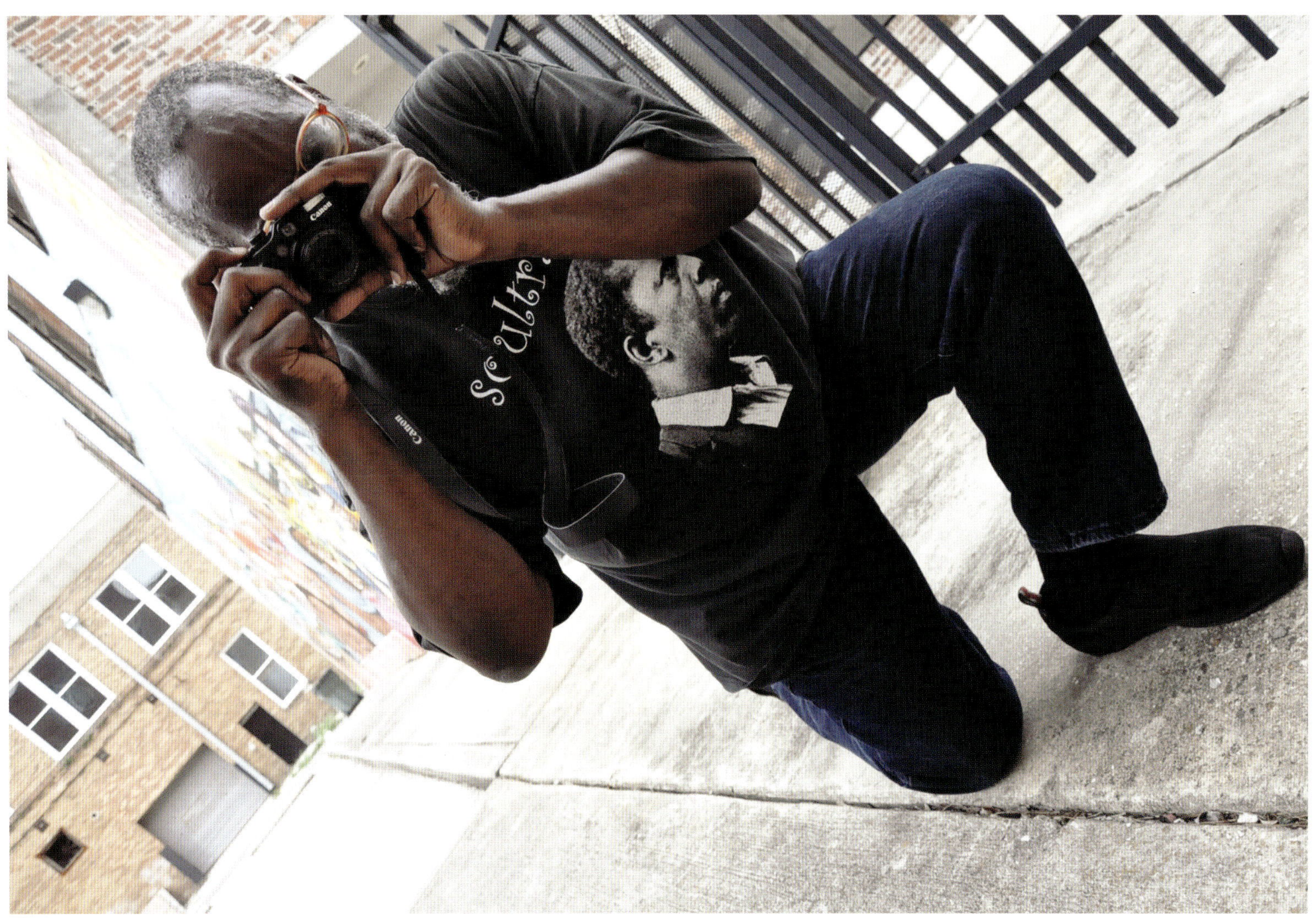

Photo by Alexandra Lear. Courtesy of the Artist.

Kalamu ya Salaam

"Tree on a Foggy River," 2020. Photo by Tod Smith. Courtesy of the Artist.

THE ART AND SCIENCE OF PHOTOGRAPHY

Kalamu ya Salaam

THE PHILOSOPHY OF PHOTOGRAPHY

1.

Photography is a relatively new human art.

Photography is now practiced worldwide.

The photographic image can be either facile or fantastic, just a jejune reflection of the obvious or a deep look into the soul of a situation.

Insightful photography enables us to see the essence of our reality rather than only view the surface of what is in front of us.

2.

In human history, photography is the youngest of the cultural arts. Music, dance, painting and literature have been with us for centuries. Photography was developed in 1839, less than two hundred years ago.

How can it be that something so young, in human terms, is now so dominant? More over, consider that movies and video–the leading forms of contemporary art work–are simply photography in motion, enhanced with sound.

Why?

How?

3.

The folk wisdom of "seeing is believing" says it all. Given our five senses—touching, tasting, smelling, hearing and seeing—sight is the one we most rely upon in the 21st century. In today's world of computers, cell phones, and the internet, of TikToks and other image-rich social media, the technology that most of us use daily heavily emphasizes the ability to see.

We look at the world from the comfort of our own caves, staring at our individual fires, which we now carry with us wherever we go. Wherever we live. Call them what you will. The structures the majority of Americans live and sleep in, whether apartments, houses, mansions, whatever—they are retreats that separate us from the surrounding environment.

Nevertheless, images of the outside flood our daily doings, particularly through the use of cable television, live stream channels, and cell phones with cameras. People simultaneously want to be private while simultaneously retaining public access. Or, in the commercial parlance of advertising, we want to have it our way: we want both to be alone and to be in touch.

Think about how we live. Think about the last movie you watched. Think about what we reach for to call a loved one, to check up on a friend, to find out what is happening in the world around us—a world that could be anywhere on the globe.

The surface of our verdant third-rock-from-the-sun may be majority water blue, yet most of us survive on the one-third that is the red/brown, dark of soil. The land is where we live.

4.

The truth is, we often clamor to see an image before we can or will fully accept reality as real. Implicitly we require proof. We want to have reality revealed to us. Moreover, in far too many cases, we are only willing to believe what we see.

Of course, sight has boundaries, beyond which we are blind. The spectrum of light in which our unaided eyes are able to see is limited. We routinely use microscopes, telescopes, infrared and satellite photography, and other optical devices to observe what the naked eye cannot.

We have more daily devices to aid our vision than we do for any of our other senses. Hearing comes in a distant second. In our world, we rarely use our senses of taste and smell. This is especially true in the United States, where ordinary foods are drenched in salt and sugar, thereby blunting our ability to taste.

Usually, as we communicate with and comprehend the surrounding world, most of us rarely touch anything, not even—or should we say, "especially not"—each other.

Technology, rather than simply improving life, actually also encases, restricts, and sometimes even prohibits the use of our bodies to interact with the world. Literally, our humanity suffers as we develop a dependence on objects and machines to actually sense the world around us and beyond us.

5.

In photography, two people could shoot the same subject, and one view would be silly while the other vision might be profound. Worse yet, one could mislead us while the other takes us right to the heart of the subject.

In the age of cell phones, there are now so many pictures and yet so few insightful photographers. So few people who can show us the essence of what we see.

Why? We are so used to judging the covers, we rarely read the insides of anything. Without exaggeration, we often look without seeing. One important task of serious photography is to help us understand, and even value, what we see.

6.

Of course, it is possible to feel, and even to understand, the presence of the unseen by the sound it makes. Sound is emotional. What we hear has an emotional affect and effect, i.e., we are reflexively changed by and respond to what we hear, but also, and importantly, the sounds we make alter our environment, which includes everyone and everything with whom and with which we interact.

On the other hand, we respond to sight both intellectually and emotionally, and often intellectually and *then* emotionally—as, for example, when we respond to writing, if and when we can read (i.e., decode the writing).

Nevertheless, although "reading" is very important, we can interpret language even if we are not literate. For instance, even if we cannot read or write a specific language, we may still be able to understand its meaning when we hear it in context. Listening to a book as an audiobook still "counts" as reading it, even though that doesn't involve sight-based language.

This is why so many of us respond to the spoken word even though we don't, or can't, actually read the words that are spoken. In one sense, regardless of how important literacy is in the modern era (in America, modern means the post-Civil War era), literacy is not necessary to live a full life, a life in which we respond to, interact with, and in some cases also shape our environment.

I argue for developing a sense of *visual* literacy, which can help us parse the impact of photography, images being a language all their own.

An important reality is that emotion often trumps intellectual truth; indeed, emotionally we can be convinced that falsehoods are facts. The deep beauty of photography is that an image can be both emotional and intellectual, which is why expert photography is deeper than mere words alone—deeper, even, than images alone.

Or, as the famous French painter said when referring to the image of a pipe: This is not a pipe. Meaning, the image is not the thing, even though we may think the image (a mere reference) is actually the thing itself. "Things" are three-dimensional in the real world. An image is a two-dimensional projection or approximation of the real, three-dimensional thing.

7.

Photography has gone through three major eras.

First there was the daguerreotype, a one of a kind physical representation of an image and/or a social reality. This process was developed in France by Louis-Jacques-Mandé Daguerre (1787–1851) and soon after became the first widely used form of photography.

The next major era of photography was the negative and print era, during which a specific image could mechanically be reproduced numerous times whereas the daguerreotype was a one-off image.

In the 21st century, photography is now in the digital era, which is able to reproduce images without the need for or expertise in using darkrooms and chemicals that were previously required. Moreover, images can be easily reproduced, as well as easily altered, via computers and on the internet.

On a basic level, photography started out as a means to reflect a given reality, initially a portrait of a person (or people) and/or the surrounding environment. Today, photography is no longer limited to the real, even when real elements are manipulated with Photoshop and other image-altering tools.

We can now be shown seemingly realistic images that did not actually exist in the real world. We may believe an image, but that does not mean the image is real, i.e., that the image is an actual reproduction of reality.

Now more than ever, an image can be far more imaginative. Rather than simply a reflection, photography can also be a projection of our imaginations.

8.

The collection of images in *SEEING BLACK* generally represents reality but also often creates and/or reinterprets the reality that is presented. Seeing may be believing, but what we are led to believe may not be real.

Regardless of where an image lands in the realm of the real, we can ask: Does an image help us interact with others? Can an image help us understand the world we live in? Rather than explore how photography works, what we chose to do with *SEEING BLACK* is offer images for enjoyment and interpretation by any and all who have eyes to see. The implications and understandings of the shared images are up to those who view this work.

I will end this section by asking two simple questions of those who encounter the images and the book itself: 1) Do the images move you, and 2) Is there anything to be learned from or enjoyed by regarding these images?

CONTENT & CONTEXT

Every image has both content (what it shows) and context (what it means in relation to its environment). The relevance of both content and context is open to interpretation and to criticism.

Content has two aspects: the aesthetics it implicitly espouses and also the impressions it engenders, i.e., how the image looks and what the image projects. Of course, different eyes see the same image and deduce different information, sometimes radically different, even contradictory meanings—making social exchange essential for a fuller interpretation of a given image.

Thus, photography is one of, if not indeed the most, socially significant art form. *SEEING BLACK* is no mere glance at the art, nor just an example of racial chauvinism. This book contextualizes photography in New Orleans to suggest the history, present, and future of Black people and Black culture(s) as documented and/or imagined by photographers of color, who, to various degrees, represent or reflect the lives, experiences, and dreams of their people.

Thus, we have photographers such as A. P. Bedou, who captured Black life of the early 20th century. Here, he documents an order of nuns who were a major educational force among African Americans at and immediately after the turn of the 20th century in New Orleans.

On the other hand, he also photographed the popular music ensembles of his era. Bedou's promotional shots pictured the wide range of brass, percussion and woodwind instruments,

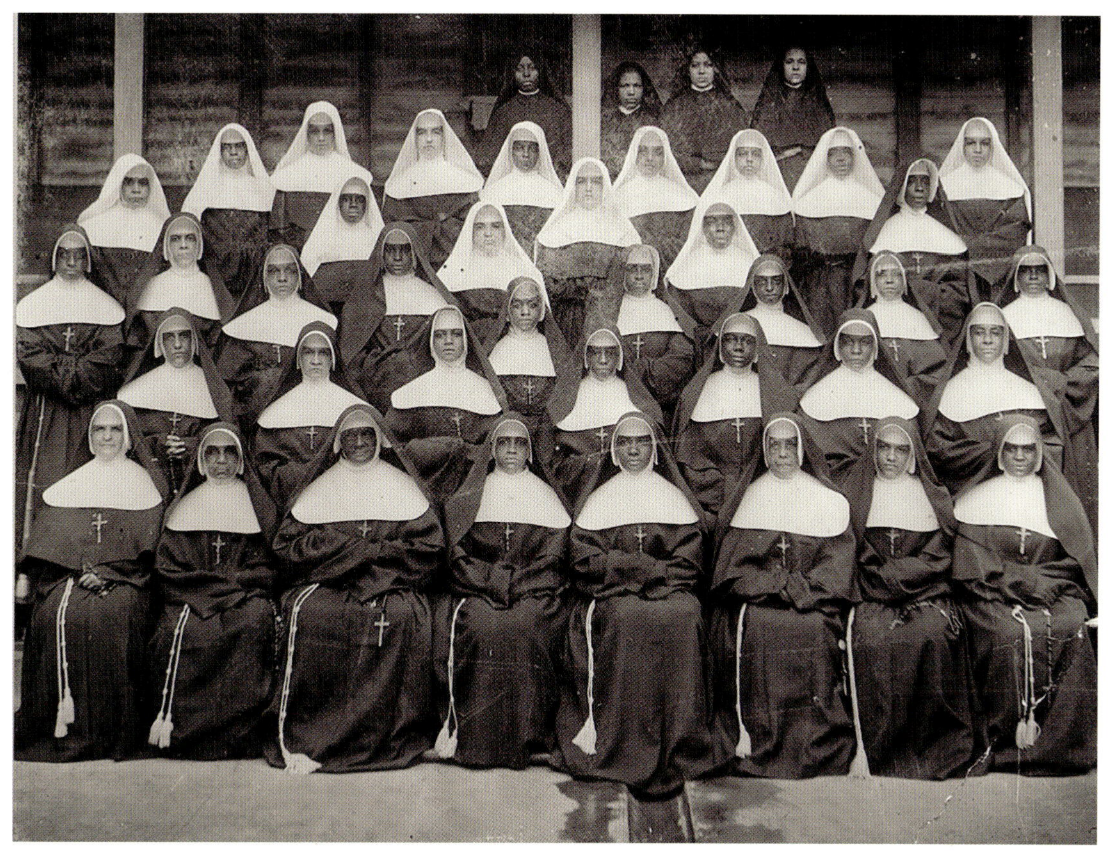

Nuns in a row, ca. 1899. Photo: A. P. Bedou. Courtesy of the Library of Congress.[1]

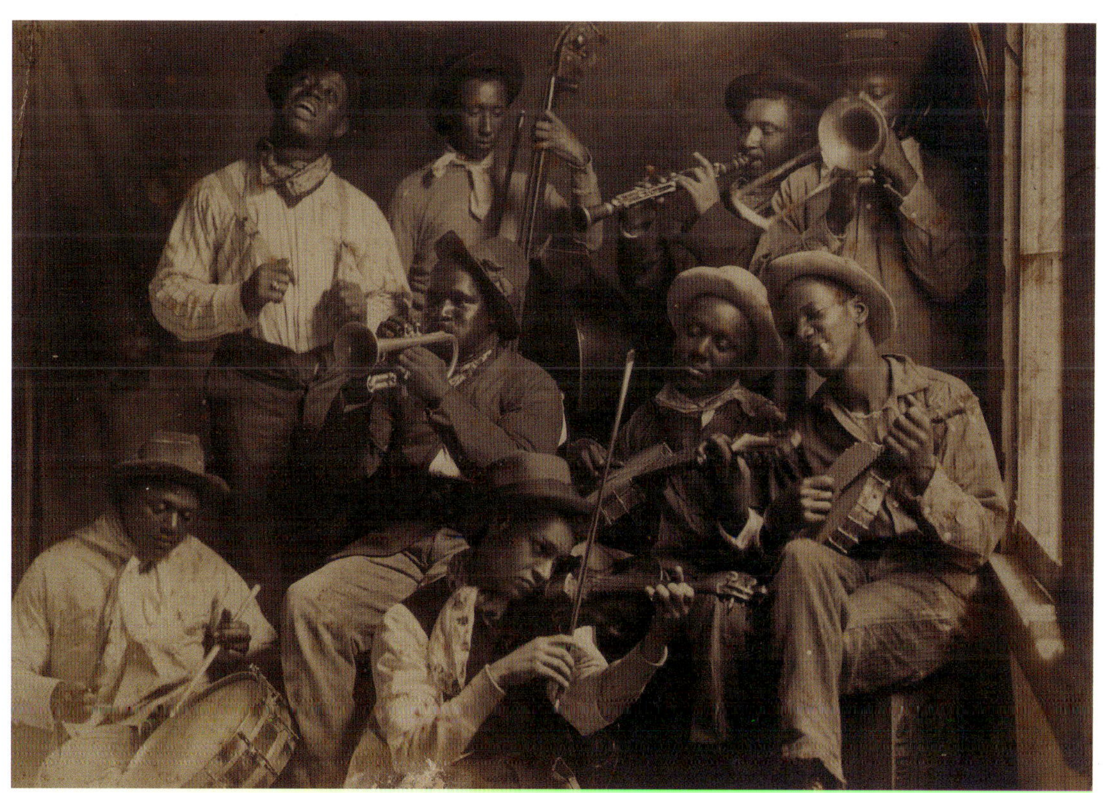

"Clarence Williams—Piron Band," 1916. Photo by A. P. Bedou.
Courtesy of the Historic New Orleans Collection.

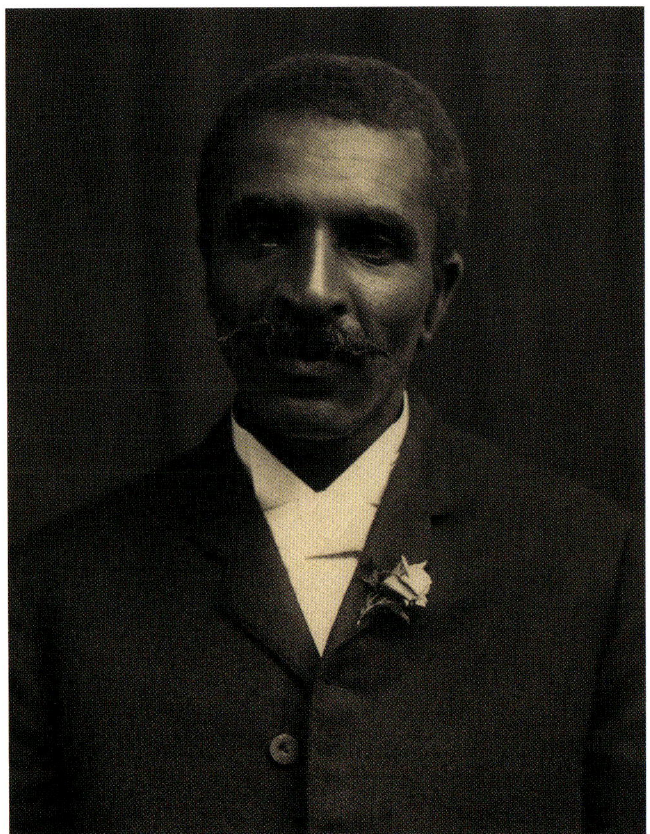

George Washington Carver, ca. 1910. Photographer unknown, but possibly A. P. Bedou, who is known to have photographed Carver. Courtesy of the Library of Congress.[2]

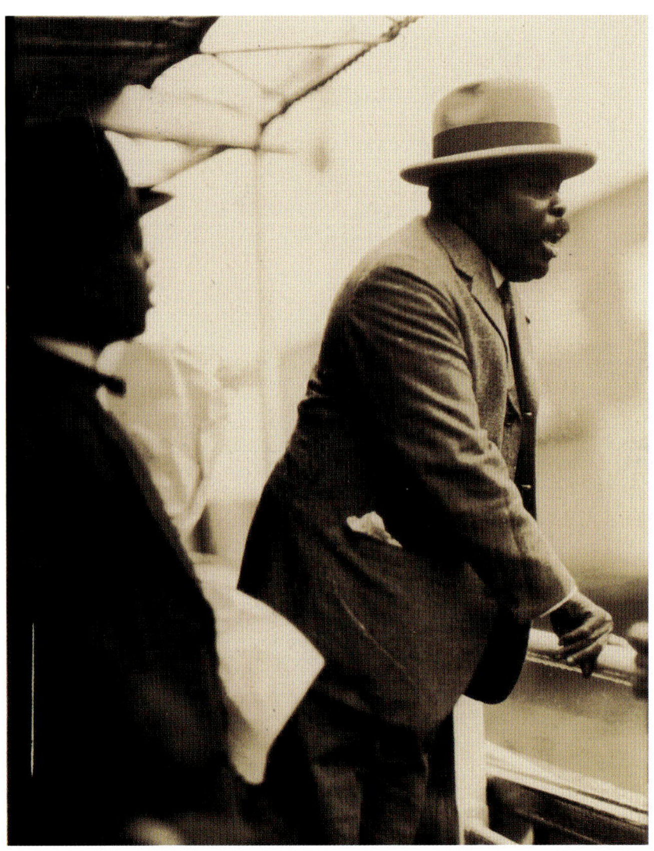

Marcus Garvey, 1927. Photo: A. P. Bedou. Courtesy of Xavier University of Louisiana, Archives & Special Collections.

which replaced string orchestras in the then emerging jazz context.

Rather than being relegated to a diminished role in the music, as is the case with classical music, drums were foundational to African American musical expressions, and hence the prominence of percussion instruments (often including "trap sets" and bass drums), which sometimes were used to advertise band names or specialties.

Bedou was also aware of the historical importance of his work. Thus, included is a beautiful portrait of George Washington Carver as a mature man whose pride and self-confidence is apparent.

Another interesting Bedou photograph is of Marcus Garvey, on the dock of a ship in Algiers (on the East Bank of the New Orleans riverfront), taken when Garvey was deported from the United States.

Bedou also served as Booker T. Washington's official photographer of the last half-decade of Mr. Washington's life, when he traveled throughout the South speaking and organizing.

That all of these photographs and many others exist is because Bedou had the foresight to understand that photography could make a major contribution to documenting Black life and culture of his time period. Bedou's skillful use of photographic technology stretched far beyond the formality of documenting individuals and groups.

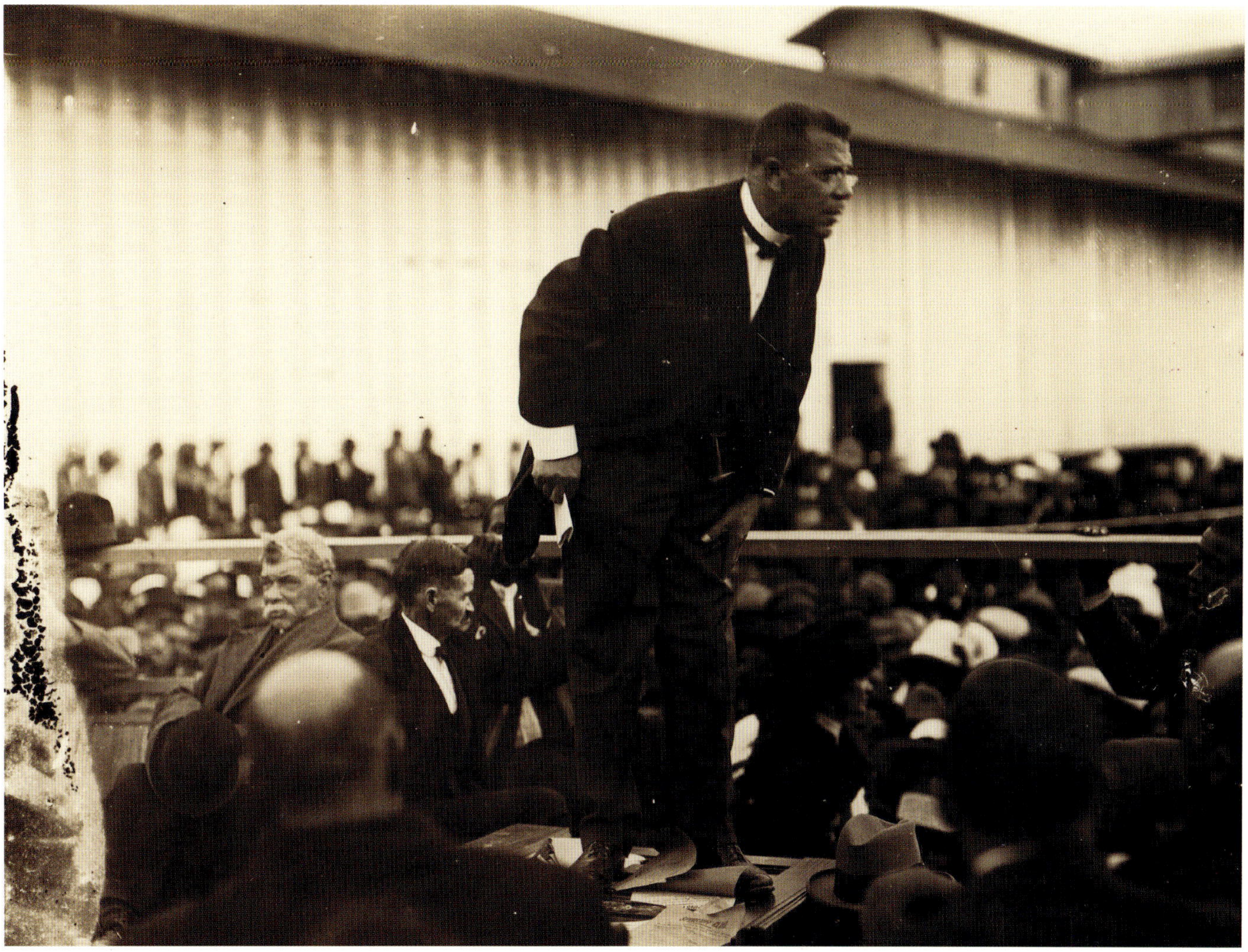

Booker T. Washington, 1915. Photo: A. P. Bedou. Courtesy of Xavier University of Louisiana, Archives & Special Collections.

In the first part of the 20th century, many Blacks made their mark in photography. Especially noteworthy is the Kamoinge Workshop collective of photographers, who since 1963 have banded together to do workshops and publish their work.

Where Kamoinge is New York-based, SEEING BLACK specifically focuses on New Orleans as a locus of photographic creativity and expertise.

Although recognized worldwide for food, music and, to a lesser extent, architecture, an often overlooked reality is that New Orleans was also a major home base of photography. Without the specific cultural, geographic, and economic contexts of New Orleans, the early development of the art itself would be profoundly changed.

As this volume shows, photographic content is never divorced from social and cultural context. In this new millennium, cameras on cell phones are not only used to capture snapshots of whatever a person finds memorable or significant in private life; these cameras are instrumental in documenting police brutality, creating documentation that is sometimes used as part of court-admissible evidence. This was an extremely socially significant use of photography, especially given the near universal availability and ease of use of mobile phones.

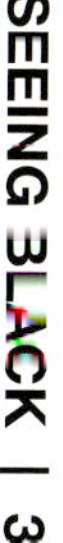

Most US citizens have a camera in their pocket and take both the science and art of photography for granted. One no longer has to know and have facility with the technology of photography either in terms of taking photographs and in terms of processing the image. Using a camera used to require a facility with aperture, shutter speed, lighting, lens size and quality, plus other technicalities. However, point and shoot has now become the standard. The photo album is in our pocket, and specific images can be shared with an immediacy that now feels normal.

The ubiquity and ease of taking and sharing images and video in the internet age enables nearly everyone to become a photographer. Many of us are not aware of how momentous were technical developments during the 20th century, especially in photography. Nevertheless, aware or not, we all benefit from and use technical advancements in photography in our everyday life.

This newly broadened access to photographic technology has also sparked a steady increase in the public displays of what were formerly private and hidden aspects of life, especially concerning gender issues and nudity. To cite just one example, Saddi Khali made his mark as a photographer whose work focused on the beauty of Black bodies. His images often portrayed intimacy and nudity, and not exclusively for the heterosexual gaze.

In the majority of their work, photographers such as Khali and many others focus on nudity. Yes, there is often an obvious emphasis

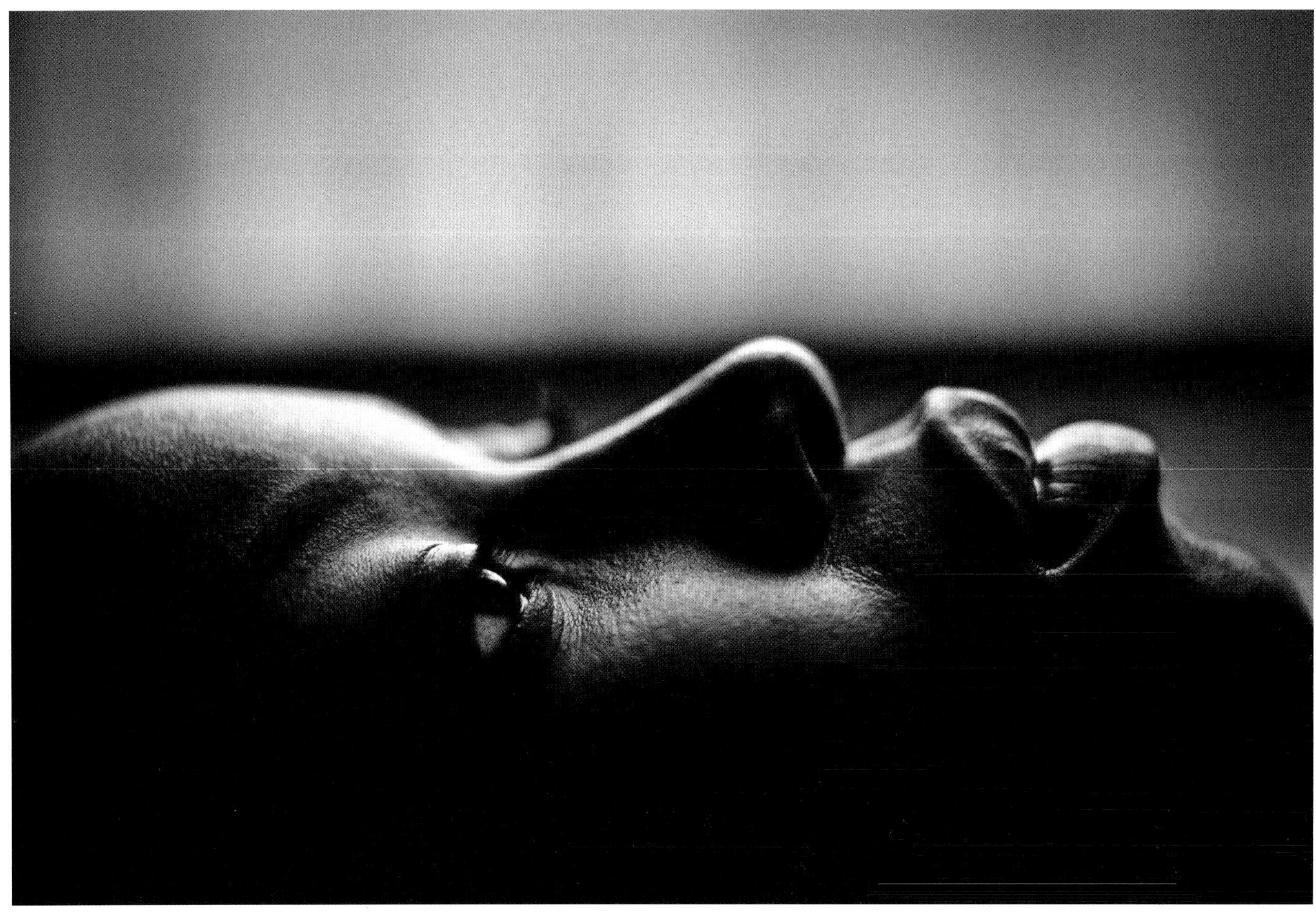

"Things Are Looking Up," 2011. Photo: Saddi Khali. Courtesy of the Artist.

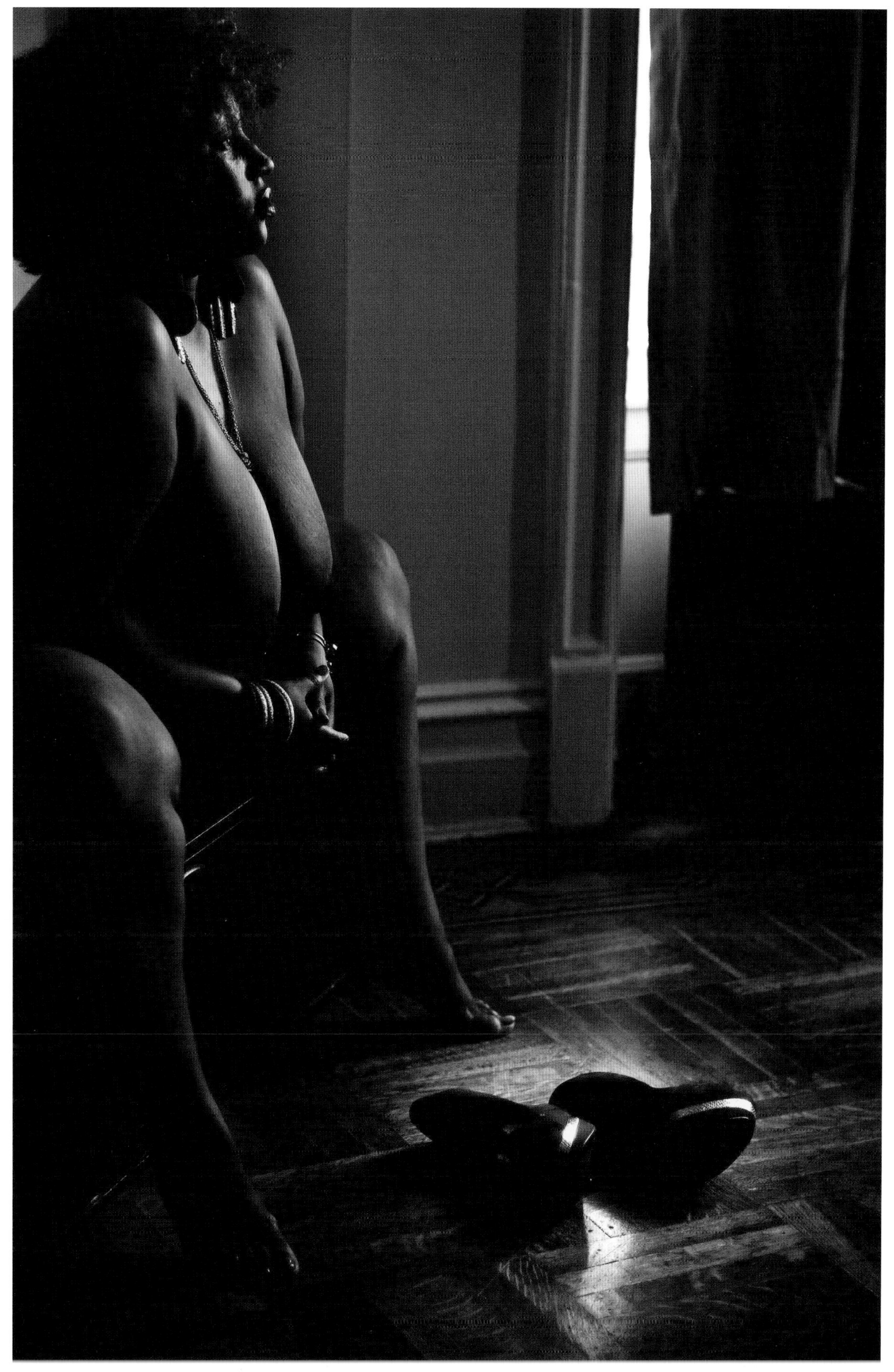

"I Don't Wanna Wait in Vain," 2011. Photo: Saddi Khali. Courtesy of the Artist.

on popularity and commerciality in their work. However, there is also a sense of commitment to creating alternatives to the status quo. The majority of commercial imaging of intimacy, especially for film and television, focuses on women of child-bearing age and a physicality that advances established beauty standards: slim and physically attractive based on Eurocentric norms, which, counterintuitively, is not how the majority of human beings in the world look. In creating beautiful images of people whose bodies do not fall into these exclusive constraints, Khali and others open other possibilities for the ways that we see and understand human intimacy.

The battle to promote or, conversely, to counter the dominance of white supremacy happens with every click of the camera—with each image created, an idea of what the average person looks like or wants to look like is asserted. In America today, the standard of beauty, especially physical norms, are political and not just aesthetic. The real battle is between diversity, i.e., multiple "looks," as opposed to monoculture or one dominant look. In this context, photography is critical to promoting diversity, especially because the physical image of women, men, and children is central to evaluations of one's own social environment as well as one's own self-evaluation.

"Black is beautiful" is much more than a marketing slogan. Moreover, being Black is an embrace of diversity rather than solely a monochromatic movement: being Black ranges from the lightest bright to the darkest face. Thus, *SEEING BLACK* is multicolored. This book offers a wide range of human expressions in the visual form of photography.

Standards of beauty are significant in terms of hair, particularly on the heads of women, and increasingly on the faces of men. Braids and beards, dreadlocks and goatees: there is more to that battle than simply a personal choice—for example, what is deemed "professional" for the workplace remains a battlefront.

The first great Black male model in photography, Frederick Douglass in the Civil War period, both established and embodied the presentation of hair in popular photography. Significantly, Douglass was the most photographed person of his generation, more often photographed even than Abraham Lincoln.

Douglass was the first great promoter of the art. During the 1860s, Douglass lectured on photography. Indeed, he was the first American of note to be a cultural critic focusing on the social and political uses of photography.

Three of Douglass' important lectures are contained in the major book *Picturing Frederick Douglass*. In addition to the lectures, the book also contains over 150 portraits of Douglass taken over his lifetime. At the beginning of the age of photography, Douglass not only understood the importance of this technical development; he also understood how photography contributed to the cause of abolition, thus recognizing photography's cogent contribution to both aesthetics and politics.

From historic Bedou images to contemporary Khali images, photography offers the opportunity for us to interpret and to project our social realities which are diverse, and sometimes even

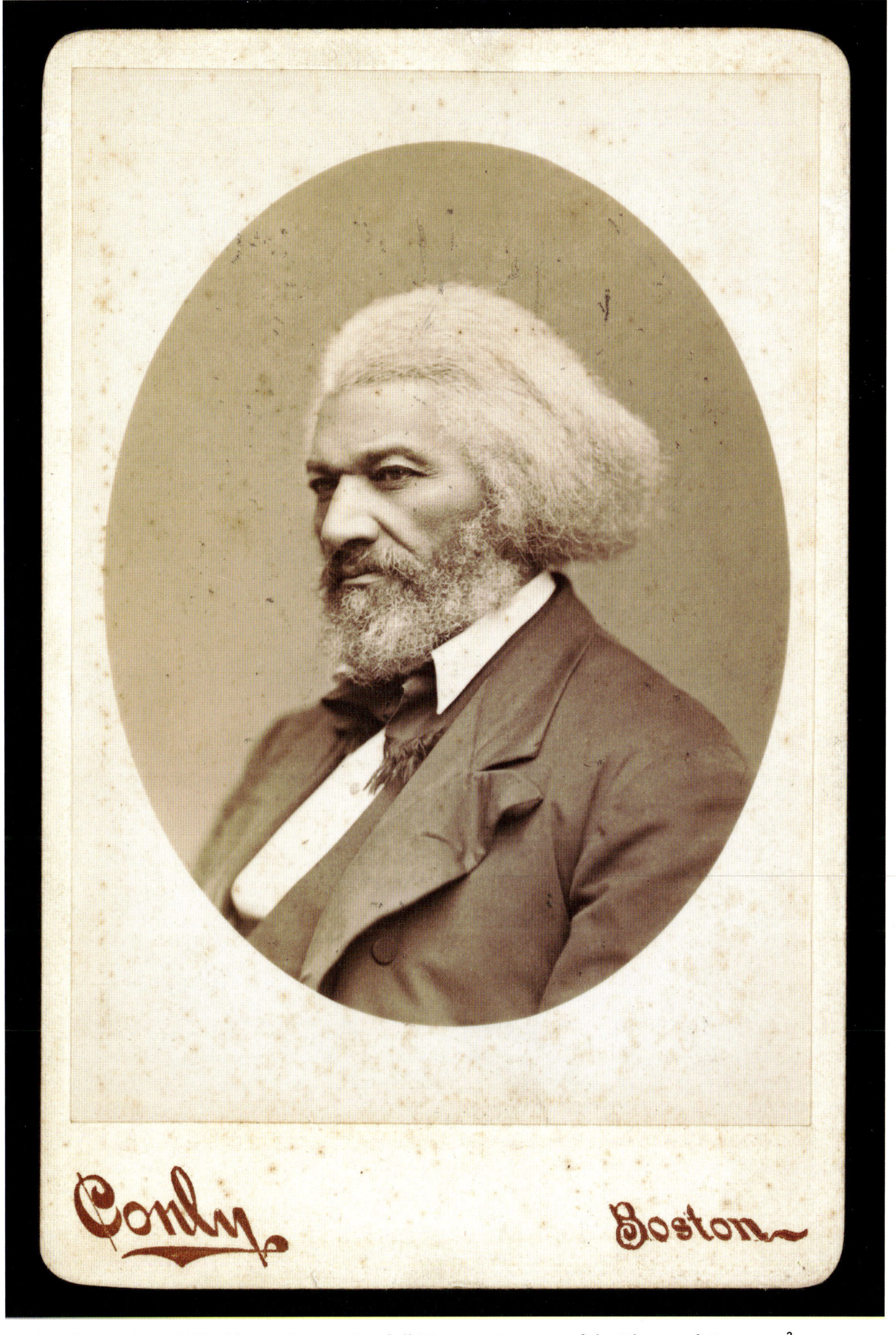

Frederick Douglass, 1876. Photo: George Kendall Warren. Courtesy of the Library of Congress.[3]

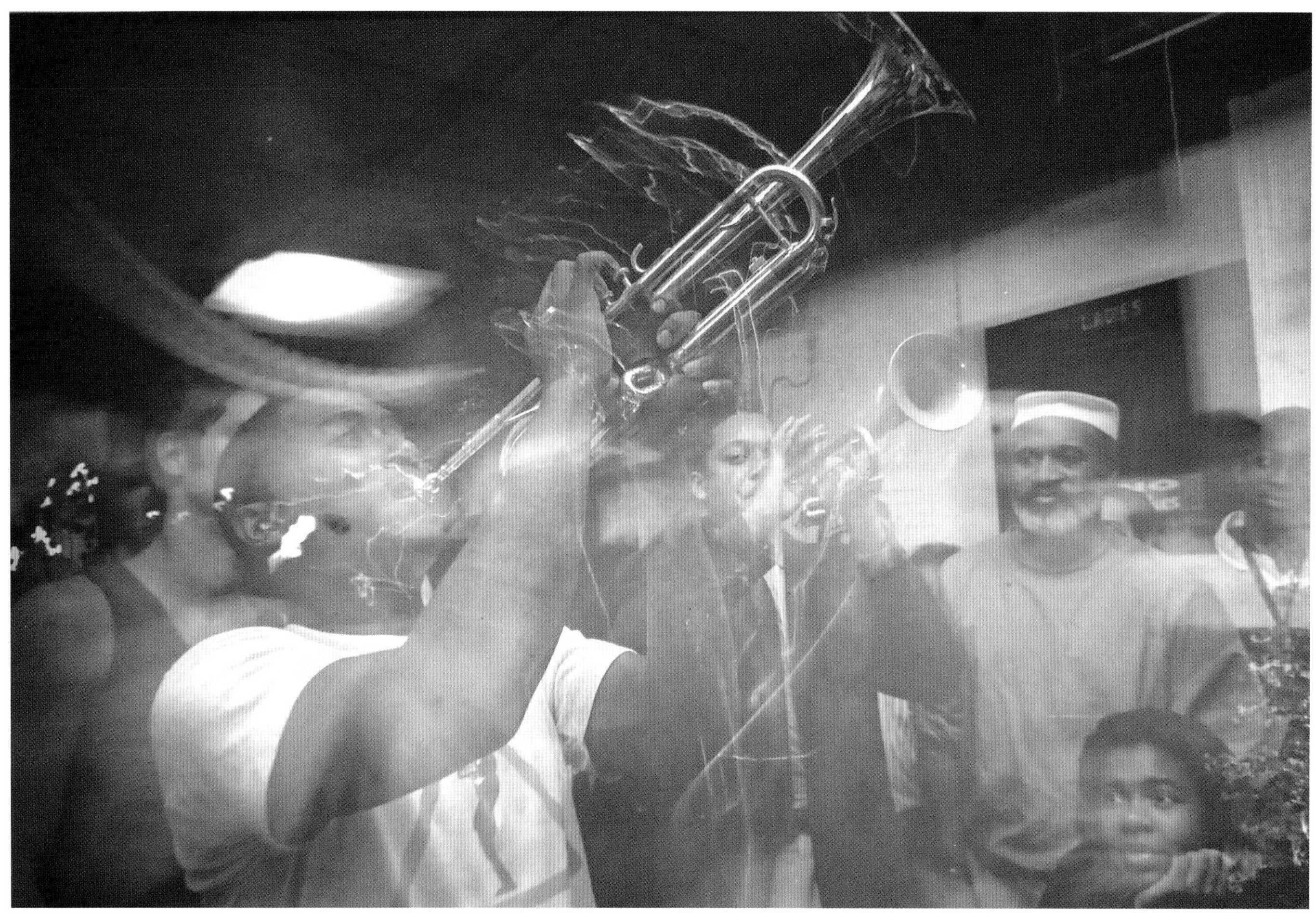

"When Wynton Met Kermit / Ruffins' Monday Night Jam at Little People's Place," 1991. Photo: Terri A. Mimms. Courtesy of the Artist.

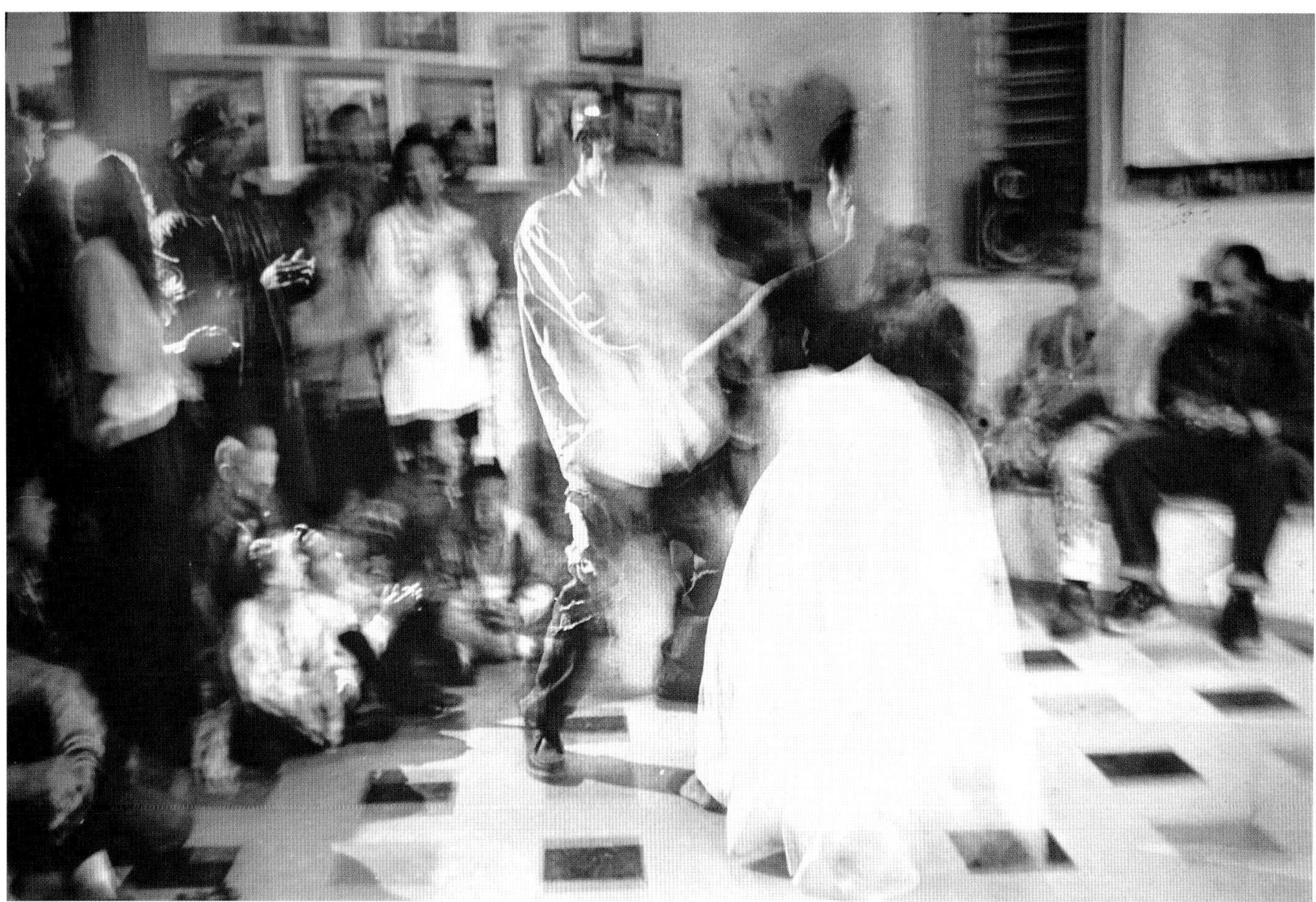

"The Dance / A Cultural Exchange at the Neighborhood Gallery," 1992. Liverpool, England. Photo: Terri A. Mimms. Courtesy of the Artist.

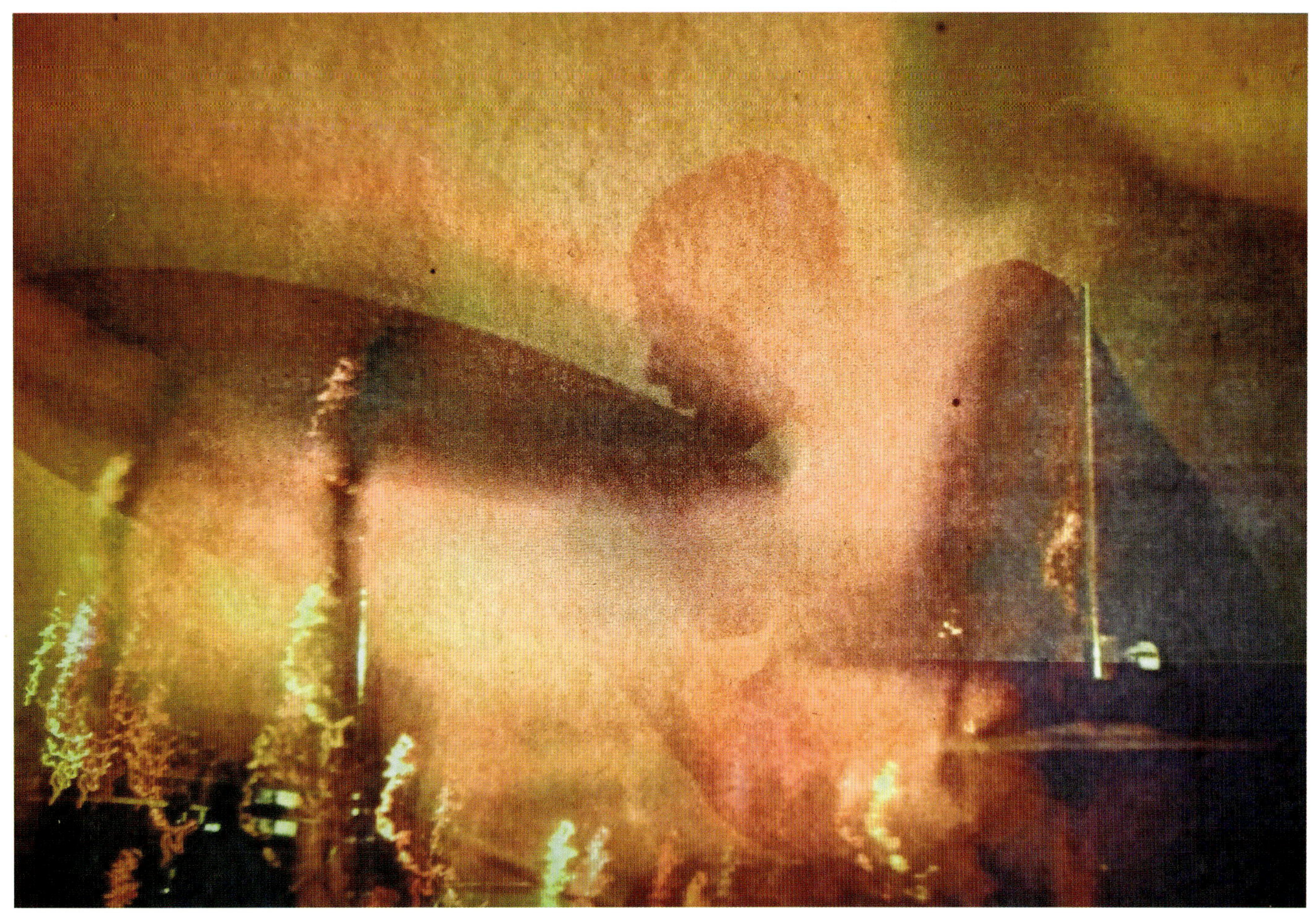

"Brian Blade / The Beat of a Different Drummer," 1990. Photo: Terri A. Mimms. Courtesy of the Artist.

controversial and/or contradictory. Indeed, photographers tactically employ aesthetics in order to convey social, cultural, and political realities. New Orleans photographers such as Terri A. Mimms advance straight documentary—images that reflect life as is—but Mimms also proffers innovative images in motion. One might even call some of her shots, in the word of New Orleans musician Kermit Ruffin, "blurry."

One blurry photo could be a mistake—accidental, or the result of some special serendipity. Moreover, in the digital age, shooting a blurry shot is damn near impossible because, with contemporary cameras, focus is automatic. Nevertheless, Terri A. Mimms is the expert of blurry photographs. Sometimes, the whole photograph is in motion, other times, only the subject is. Whichever way she decides to do it, her shots are no accident. She uses blurs the way most photographers aim for sharpness. Oh, what a marvel Mimms is.

For example, check this (and be sure to see the woman admiring the trumpet player). The blurring is subtle, mainly capturing Kermit Ruffins' horn movement. If you think this is easy, try it. Just try to do it.

And to prove that she seriously knows what she is doing with her picture machine, check Terri giving us a saxophone player in motion.

And, to take it to another level, check out what Mimms does in offering us a dancing couple. Check: You can see the audience looking on at the same time she presents the dancers in motion. Man, you had to be there. In order to capture a picture like this, you'd have to be an image-taking savant.

Additionally, Mimms also works in color—and clearly she loves dealing with music. Mimms might even be viewed as an avant-garde artist who combines representational and abstract in one image. Oh, what a joy.

Here is Mimms from way back in the day, capturing drummer Brian Blade in motion. Notice that this is a double image: sitting up and leaning into the music. Somehow sister lady captures the cymbals when they are static even as the stands are pictured in motion—i.e., blurry. This is ghost photography at its best.

A second and significant example is offered by my colleague Eric Waters, who is a respected New Orleans photographer. The bulk of his work pictures Black culture, but he also makes artistic statements that go far beyond what is typically thought of as "Black photography." He has created astounding still life images: an orchid in a cast iron skillet, found plants artfully arranged, and water-drenched clarinets post-Katrina.

Eric Waters is both a sensitive portrait photographer and an expert at street documentation. His portrait work is often unorthodox and yet effective.

As he moved through the streets, Waters not only captured specifics of a particular moment; he also was able to catch the same subject year after year.

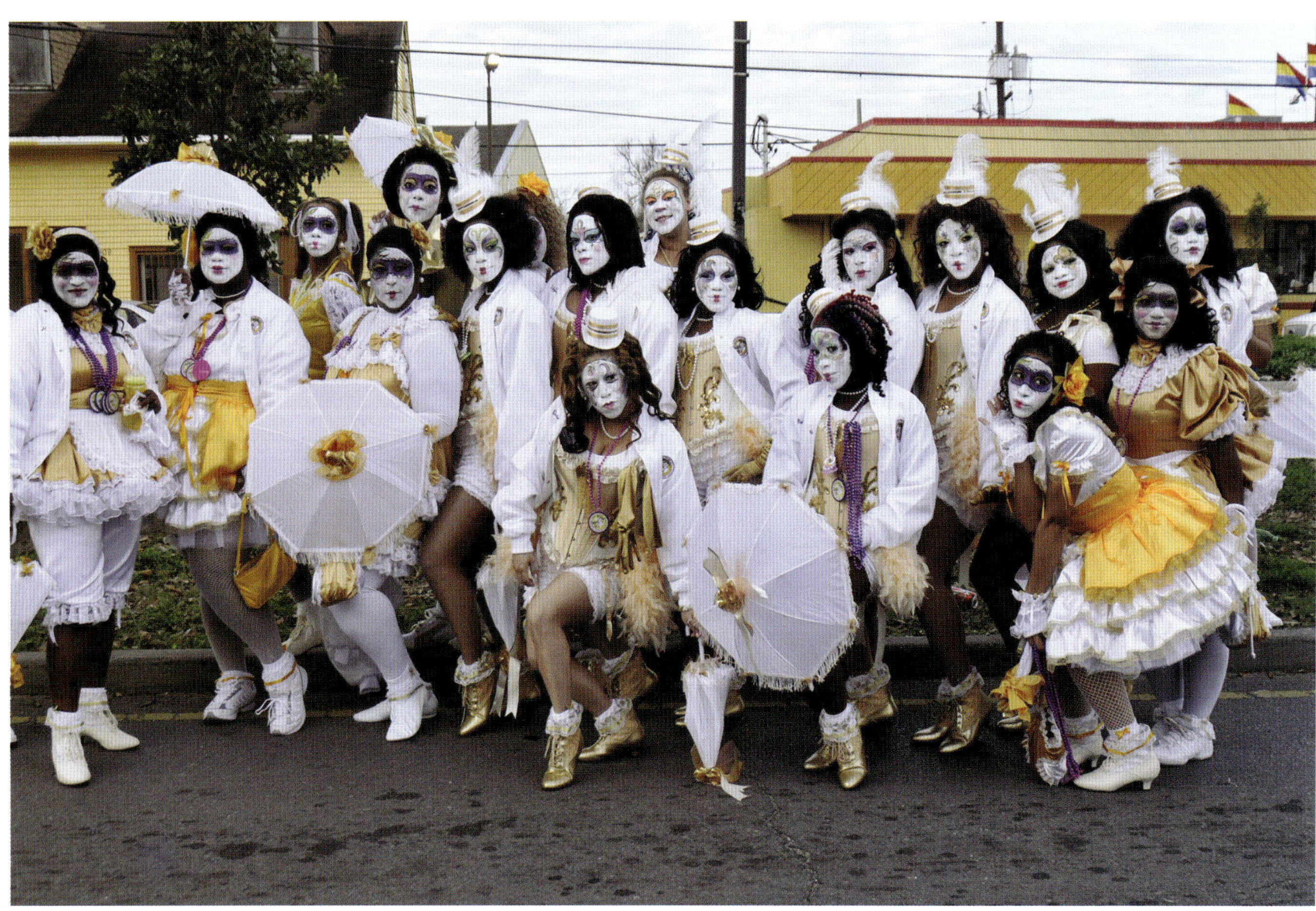

"Baby Dolls," 2012. Photo: Eric Waters. Courtesy of the Artist.

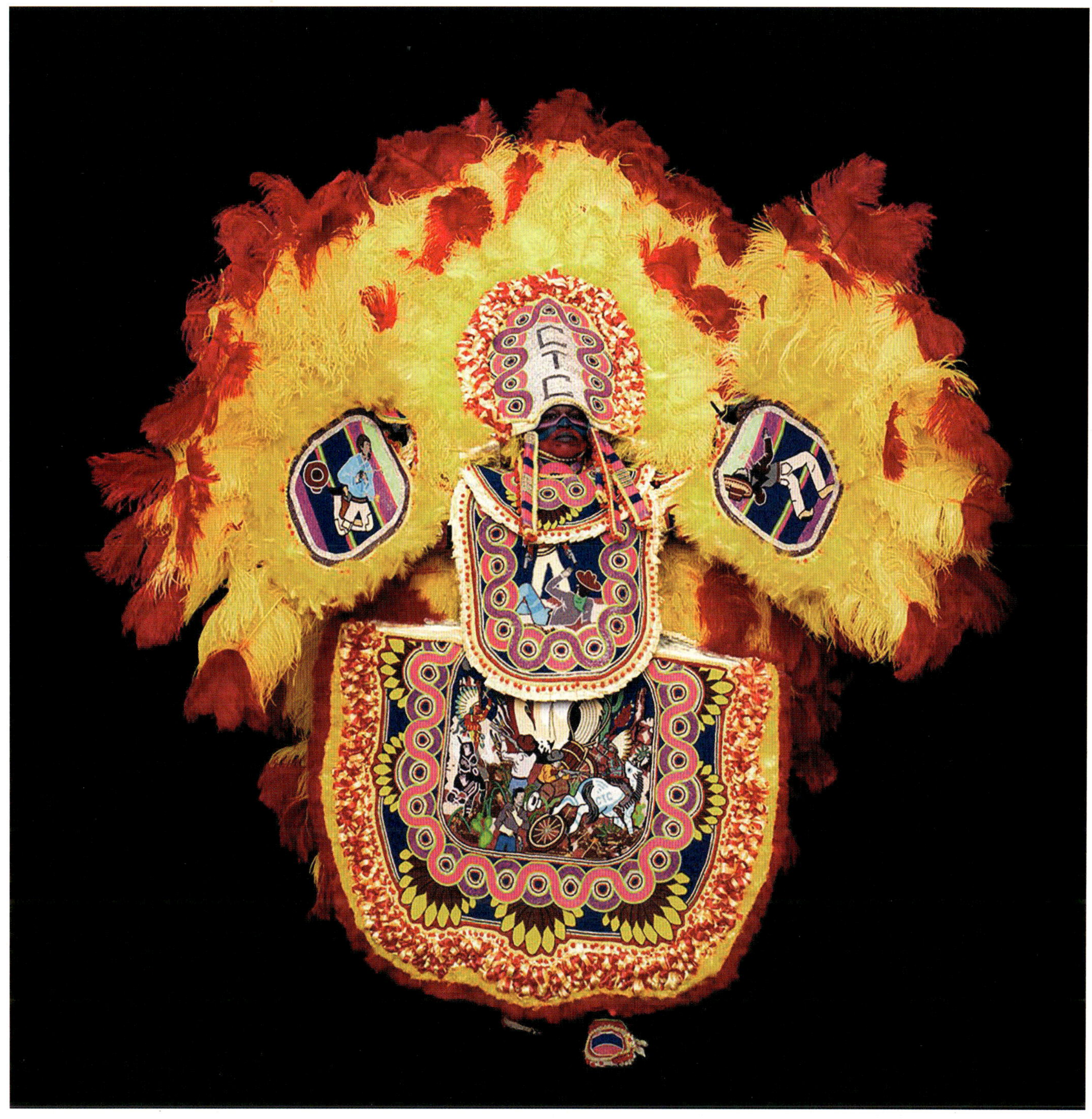

Alphonse "Dowee" Robair, Chief of Black Hatchet Tribe, 2019. Photo: Eric Waters. Courtesy of the Artist.

New Orleans is famous worldwide for its vibrant street culture, particularly the Black Masking Indians and the lesser known but equally distinctive "bones characters."

Waters is particularly good at capturing the play and apprenticeship of Black youth growing into proponents of Black street culture in New Orleans. Rather than staging set pieces, Waters is adept at capturing significant moments that illustrate cultural continuums.

Saddi Khali, Terri A. Mimms, and Eric Waters are three very different photographers, yet taken together they illustrate the wide range of New Orleans photography. There is no one viewpoint that illustrates how either amateurs or professionals literally picture life and culture in New Orleans and elsewhere.

There is a dynamic culture in New Orleans that bubbles up from the street level. Yes, the established and even standardized art forms, such as symphony, opera, and ballet, exist in New Orleans. However, there is also a profound respect for street culture in a metropolitan environment that is able to function outside year round. This dynamic Black culture is counterintuitively captured in still photography.

Yes, the technical aspects of photography are important. From the quality of lens to the questions of exposure, perspective, printing and so forth, all contribute to making an impactful photograph whether in black and white or in color. However, capturing what is there, even what is sometimes overlooked, unseen, or misunderstood, is the hallmark of a good photograph made in the moment. How an image is created is an important question, but not as important as what the image illustrates—"what," not "how," is the essence of great photography.

Photography is no longer limited to professionals who spend years studying and practicing their craft. Although millions can now take pictures, a truly insightful photograph remains a one in a million image. *SEEING BLACK* celebrates New Orleans photographers both native-born and domiciled, living and deceased, who have artfully used a camera as a means of exploration and cultural expression, who illuminate both their subject's content as well as its context.

Endnotes

1. *Sisters of the Holy Family*, New Orleans, La., ca. 1899, photograph, Library of Congress, https://www.loc.gov/pictures/item/2001705864/.
2. "Visual materials from the Booker T. Washington papers," Library of Congress, accessed March 13, 2024, https://www.loc.gov/pictures/item/99472031/; *George Washington Carver c1910 - Restoration.jpg, c. 1910*, photograph, Wikimedia Commons, https://en.wikipedia.org/wiki/.File:George_Washington_Carver_c1910_-_Restoration.jpg#filelinks.
3. *[Frederick Douglass] / C. F. Conly, Photographer, 465 Washington St., Boston*, print created between 1884 and 1890, from negative taken in 1876, photograph, Library of Congress, https://www.loc.gov/item/2018651422/.

Institutional Image Credit

"Clarence Williams—Piron Band" by A. P. Bedou, The Historic New Orleans Collection, MSS 520.2574.

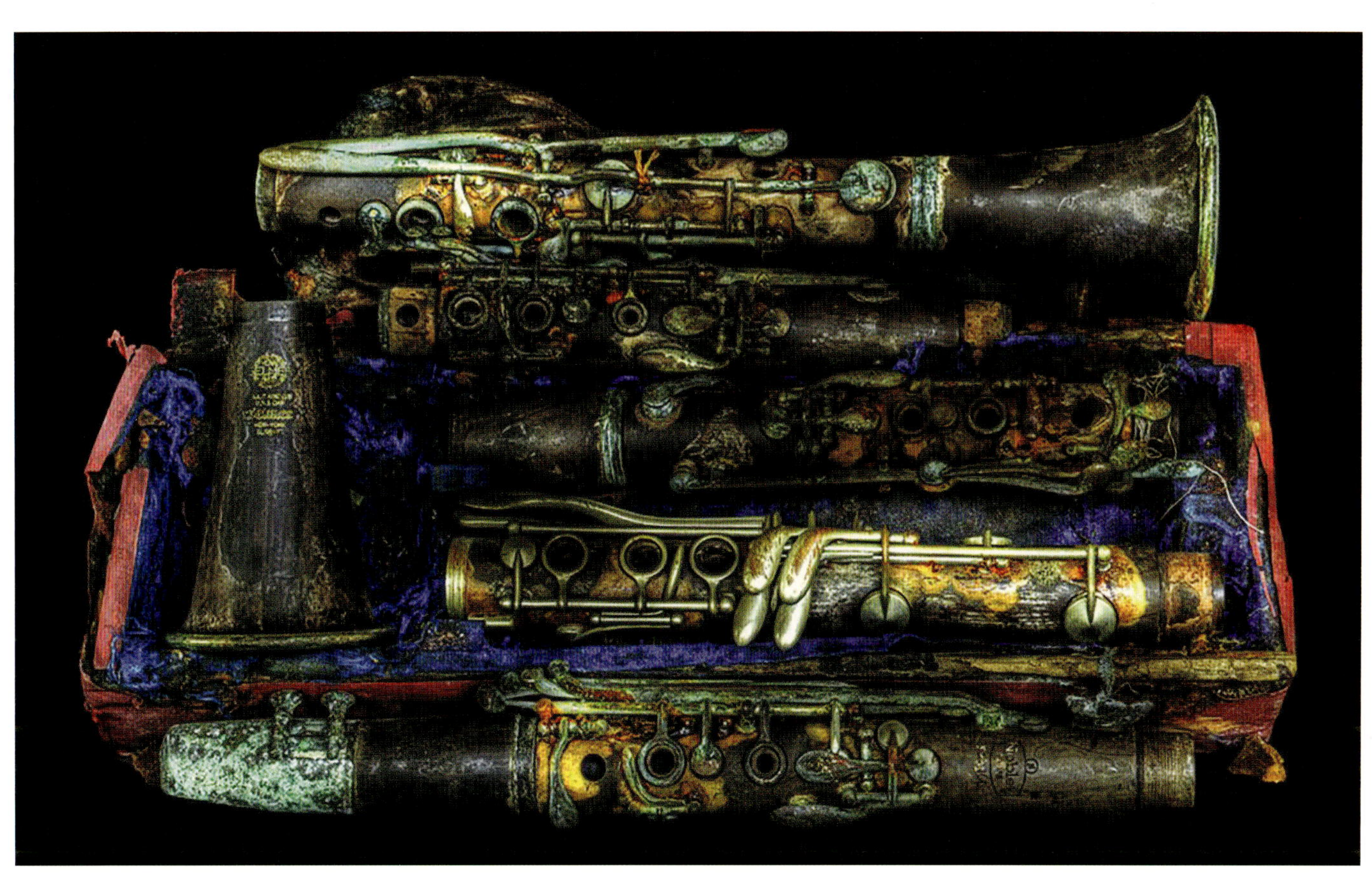

"Keloid Scars (clarinets)," 2019. Photo: Eric Waters. Courtesy of the Artist.

The publication of this volume owes its existence to the invaluable vision, scholarship, expertise, research, generosity, contributions, and support of multiple individuals, projects, institutions, and partners. Their roles were instrumental in assisting SEEING BLACK engage a diverse range of Black photographers featured within these pages.

SEEING BLACK is indebted to the families, archival stewards, and contributing photographers who shared and permitted us to use their photos to present to the public. Specifically, we wish to thank Dr. Arthé A. Anthony, great-niece of Florestine Perrault Collins; Jacques J. Detiege, grandson of Rene Jacques Roussève; Cheron Brylski, widow of Harold Baquet; Charlene Legaux Richard; Ebon Images, LLC; and the George "Tex" Stevens Collection for access to and use of photographs taken by Marion J. Porter; Marjorie Martinez, widow of Dr. Maurice Martinez; Dr. Joyce Jackson, widow of J Nash Porter; and Eric Waters for access to photographs by taken Morris Jones Jr.

SEEING BLACK appreciates the unwavering support of directors, archivists, curators, historians, and researchers of several institutions, collections, and independent projects who filled archival questions, assisted with research inquiries, approved licensing requests, and shared photographs in support of this publication and exhibitions presented by SEEING BLACK and its collaborating partners. We would like to expressly thank Kathe Hambrick, Lisa Moore, and former staff members Phillip Cunningham and Christopher S. Harter at the Amistad Research Center; Kevin Williams at the Hogan Archive of New Orleans Music and New Orleans Jazz at Tulane University Special Collection; Wayne Phillips, Kira Kikla, and Michael Leathem at the Louisiana State Museum; the Library of Congress; Eric Seiferth, Rebecca Smith, Heather Green, Jari Honora, Dhani Adomaitis, Amanda McFillen, Jason Wises, and John H. Lawrence at The Historic New Orleans Collection; Christina Byrant, Amanda Fallis, Andrew Mullins III, Greg Osborne, and Brittany Silva at the New Orleans Public Library; Judy Jumonville at *The Times-Picayune/The New Orleans Advocate* archives; James Hodges and Connie Phelps at the University of New Orleans Earl K. Long Library's Louisiana and Special Collections; Vincent Barraza at Xavier University of Louisiana Library Digital Archives & Collections; and Sierra Polisar of the Newcomb Art Museum. Additionally, we would like to acknowledge the scholarship and historical research of Debra Willis, Beryl Hunter, Brenda Marie Osbey, Dr. Joyce Jackson, and Carla Williams.

Partnerships deepened the scope and scale of this publication and the exhibitions presented. SEEING BLACK wishes to thank Gia Hamilton, the board of directors, and former curatorial fellows Amaya Cooper and Cammy White at the New Orleans African American Museum;

Acknowledgements

Asali Devan Ecclesiastes, Frederick Delahoussaye, Constance Thompson, and the board of directors at Ashé Cultural Arts Center; Anne Collins Smith and Daniele Gair at Xavier University of Louisiana; Ron Bechet at the Xavier University of Louisiana Department of Art and Performance Studies; Schuyler Williams, Jaclyn Majewski Woollam, Gina Monette, DiQuan Forcell, Josh Casimier, Alissa Pivaral, Mia Bailey, Jas Rogers, Dale Gunnoe, and the board of directors at the Contemporary Arts Center, New Orleans; Carole Frances Lung, Mónica Mejía, Leslie Moore, former staff members Jessica Peterson and Amelia Broussard, and the board of directors at Antenna; and Leslie Bourgeois and Matt Tessier at the Louisiana Public Broadcasting. SEEING BLACK thanks Ruben Rodriguez, Cameron Wood, Brice White, Jennifer Ward, Art Conscious, Porter Art Services, and the organizational and project support of PUNCTUATE, Paper Machine, Southern Letter Press, Support Black Art, PATOIS, Junebug Productions, Gallery of the Streets, Louisiana Public Broadcasting for PBS Digital Studios, and Houston Public Media.

The immense time, goodwill, patience, care, and partnership of the University of New Orleans Press made this project possible. SEEING BLACK thanks editor-in-chief Abram Himelstein for his skillful guidance and flexibility as the project evolved and shifted. Sincere gratitude is due to the editor Chelsey K. Shannon, who edited all of the contributions with integrity, patience, and tact for clarity, soundness, and coherence. Much appreciation to Laura DeFazio for her patience and punctilious review of the text, agreements, missing materials, and editorial assistance. Alex Dimeff's design assistance and care in upholding the project's design aesthetic have contributed to a beautiful book. Together with managing editor G. K. Darby, they helped shape the creation of an engaging and monumental publication, securing critically important funding for this undertaking through a grant from the National Endowment for the Humanities.

Additional support for SEEING BLACK was provided by the New Orleans Jazz & Heritage Foundation, New Orleans Tourism and Cultural Fund, New Orleans Center for the Gulf South's Monroe Fellowship, Platforms Fund, and the Rosenberg Foundation.

The publication of *SEEING BLACK: Black Photography in New Orleans 1840 & Beyond* was exceedingly enriched by the vision and poetic approach of Kalamu ya Salaam; the independent research of Girard Mouton,III; the scholarship and curatorial guidance of Shana M. griffin; the written contribution of Eric Waters; the design approach and visual aesthetics developed by Lidya Araya and Vizual; the curatorial assistance of Renee Royale; and the editorial care of Chelsey K. Shannon.

Captions Index

HISTORICAL PHOTOGRAPHERS

Lending credits are italicized.

34: A. P. Bedou, "Scene in Flint-Goodridge Hospital." Circa 1930, New Orleans, LA. *Dr. Rivers Frederick performing surgery by A. P. Bedou. Vining Family scrapbook, 1925–1946. Amistad Research Center, New Orleans, LA.*

35: A. R. Dela Houssaye, [Untitled]. Undated, New Orleans, LA. *8"x10" wedding photo in home by A. R. Dela Houssaye. Sellers Family papers. Amistad Research Center, New Orleans, LA.*

36: Arthur J. Perrault, [Untitled], Martinez Kindergarten class photo. 1959–1960, New Orleans, LA. *Martinez Kindergarten class photo by Arthur Joseph Perrault, The Historic New Orleans Collection, Gift of George Dansker, 2016.0335.1.*

37: Celeste T. Broadway, [Untitled], Ina Claire Watts, Queen of Young Men Illinois Club. 1955, New Orleans, LA. *Courtesy of the Louisiana State Museum.*

38: Florestine Collins, [Untitled]. 1919–1927, New Orleans, LA. *Portrait of a young woman and boy dressed in white by Florestine Collins, The Historic New Orleans Collection, 2001.79.7.*

39: George R. Floyd, "Orleans Ice Cream Works," advertisement in an annual city directory of Black commerce, 1912, New Orleans, LA. Woods directory, *1912, advertisement, Library of Congress, https://www.loc.gov/resource/lcrbmrp.t8074/?sp=82&r=-0.444,-0.02,1.966,1.666,0.*

40: Joseph "Scoop" Jones, [Untitled], King Delmas Davis and Queen Juanita Chambers with members of their court at the Beaux Art Ball held at Xavier University of Louisiana. Undated, New Orleans, LA. *Courtesy of Xavier University of Louisiana, Archives & Special Collections.*

41: Magnolia Studio (Isom M. McCormick & Walter Abadie Sr.), [Untitled]. Circa 1938, New Orleans, LA. *New Orleans Rhythm Boys by Magnolia Studio, Hogan Jazz Archive, PH002938, Tulane University Special Collections, Tulane University, New Orleans, LA.*

42: Nolan A. Marshall, [Untitled], group of sophomore students at Xavier University of Louisiana. Circa 1953, New Orleans, LA. *Courtesy of Xavier University of Louisiana, Archives & Special Collections.*

43: Rene Jacques Roussève, "Mother and Son," Valentine Mansion Roussève with son, Rev. Maurice L. Roussève, SVD, one of the first Black people in the United States to be ordained a Roman Catholic Priest by the Society of the Divine Word. 1934, New Orleans, LA. *Courtesy of Jacques J. Detiege.*

44–45: Villard Paddio, [Untitled], a group portrait at Dillard University taken on August 13, 1935 during a joint convention of the National Medical Association, National Hospital Association, and National Association of Colored Graduate Nurses. 1935, New Orleans, LA. *Medical Convention at Dillard University by Villard Paddio, The Historic New Orleans Collection, 1979.325.6715.*

CONTEMPORARY PHOTOGRAPHERS

Where applicable, lending credits are italicized; all other images are courtesy of the artists.

48: Abdul Aziz, "Hail Caesar." 2020.

49: Abdul Aziz, "Not Fuckin Around." 2020.

50: Adrien Broussard III, [Untitled], Mayah Huges pictured. Circa 2010–2020, New Orleans, LA.

51: Adrien Broussard III, "Love Transcended." Undated, Metairie, LA.

52: Ashley Lorraine, "Joy, Lady Buck Jumpers." 2022, New Orleans, LA.

53: Ashley Lorraine, "Secondline Sunday." 2020, New Orleans, LA.

54: Benicia King, [Untitled], from the Black Nationalism as a Commodity series. 2018.

55: Benicia King, "Pastor Calvin Tinson," from the Church Attire series. 2016.

56: Bruce Q. Williams, "Cityscape Silhouette Shadows and Purple Sky." 2021, New Orleans, LA.

57: Bruce Q. Williams, "Flambeaux lighting the parade for Knights of Babylon." 2022, Uptown, New Orleans, LA.

58: Bruce "Sunpie" Barnes, "Papa Sunpie in the woods, self-portrait." 2020, Crown Point, LA.

59: Bruce “Sunpie” Barnes, “Bringing him on down: Pallbearers exiting Charbonnet Funeral Home with the casket of Lionel Batiste Sr.” 2012, New Orleans, LA.

60: Bryan Hithe, “Past and Future.” Undated, New Orleans, LA.

61: Bryan Hithe, “Dejan’s Olympia MC.” Undated, New Orleans, LA.

62: Bryan S. Berteaux Sr., “Muhammad Ali addresses a crowd.” New Orleans, LA. The Times-Picayune/The New Orleans Advocate, *April 20, 2020, Capital City Press/Georges Media Group, and Baton Rouge, LA.*

63: Bryan S. Berteaux Sr., “B. B. King performs at Alcee Fortier High School.” New Orleans, LA. The Times-Picayune/The New Orleans Advocate, *April 20, 2020, Capital City Press/Georges Media Group, and Baton Rouge, LA.*

64: Carla Williams, “Untitled (standing nude #1).” 1987–1990.

65: Carla Williams, “Untitled (drawing studio).” 1983–1995.

66–67: Cecelia Fernandes, “Fugida.” 2019.

68: Cedric A. Ellsworth, [Untitled], Big Chief Monk Boudreaux pictured. Undated, New Orleans, LA.

69: Cedric A. Ellsworth, [Untitled], Travis “Trumpet Black” Hill’s funeral. 2015, New Orleans, LA.

70: Chandra McCormick, “Big Chief Robbie.” 2018 (circa 1990s), New Orleans, LA.

71: Chandra McCormick, “Mark Gale,” from the Sugar Cane series. 2010 (circa 1985), Saint John the Baptist Parish, LA.

72: Chanelle Harris, “Love on the Carousel.” 2021, New Orleans, LA.

73: Chanelle Harris, “Nouvelle-Orléans Belle Dame.” 2015, New Orleans, LA.

74–75: Charlene Legaux Richard, “Mayor Ernest N. Morial and Allison ‘Tootie’ Montana, Chief of the Yellow Pocahontas.” 1980, New Orleans, LA.

76: Christine “Cfreedom” Brown, “Bubble Bath 2nd Liners.” 2017, New Orleans, LA.

77: Christine “Cfreedom” Brown, “Candles for Charleston.” 2015, New Orleans, LA.

78: Clifton J. Faust, “Ellis Marsalis.” 2014, Mackinac Island, MI.

79: Clifton J. Faust, “Delfeayo Marsalis.” 2014, Mackinac Island, MI.

80: Corey Anthony, “‘When you speak of Home, where do you go?’” Undated, New Orleans, LA.

81: Corey Anthony, “‘. . . I remember the first time I heard Jazz.’” Undated, New Orleans, LA.

82: Danette M. Vincent, “‘Thinking’ (unsymbolized).” 2016, Tremé, New Orleans, LA.

83: Danette M. Vincent, “Sharing the Burden.” 2015, Tremé, New Orleans, LA.

84: danielle c. miles, [Untitled], Spyboy Walt and Big Chief Beautiful of the Beautiful Creole Apache pictured. Super Sunday 2013, New Orleans, LA.

85: danielle c. miles, “Ọṣun Festival in New Orleans.” 2018, Old Algiers, New Orleans, LA.

86: Dawnie Marie, “Strictly Business.” 2020, New Orleans, LA.

87: Dawnie Marie, “Rocket (Wo)man.” 2017, New Orleans, LA.

88: Dean Gagé, “Masked Griot.” 2022, New Orleans, LA.

89: Dean Gagé, “War Council Advisor.” 2022, New Orleans, LA.

90: Delaney George, “The King Is Dead.” 2022.

91: Delaney George, “Chipo.” 2019, New Orleans, LA.

92: Durado Brooks, [Untitled], excerpted from artist’s *Something in the Water* graphic novel photo shoot. Circa 2019–2022, New Orleans, LA.

93: Durado Brooks, [Untitled], excerpted from artist’s *Something in the Water* graphic novel photo shoot. Circa 2019–2022, New Orleans, LA.

94: Dwight A. Harris, [Untitled]. Undated, Kenner, LA.

95: Dwight A. Harris, [Untitled]. Undated, Kenner, LA.

96: Ellis Marsalis III, “Summer Respite.” 2001, Baltimore, MD.

97: Ellis Marsalis III, “First Born.” 2004, Baltimore, MD.

98: Epaul Julien, [Untitled]. Undated.

99: Epaul Julien, [Untitled]. Undated.

100–101: Eric Waters, “Squirky Man, Diptych.” 1993 (left), 2012 (right), New Orleans, LA.

102: Felicita Felli Maynard, “Loren.” 2020.

103: Felicita Felli Maynard, “Untitled (Vermont).” 2020.

104: Freddye Hill, “In Praise of All The Saints.” 2018, New Orleans, LA.

105: Freddye Hill, “Big Queen Kim: ‘Who Dey Talk About?’” Mardi Gras Day 2019, Claiborne Ave. and Columbus St., New Orleans, LA.

106: Gason Ayisyin, “Greater Than the Link.” 2015, New Orleans, LA.

107: Gason Ayisyin, “Look Out.” 2018, Galveston, TX.

108: Giani M. Jones, [Untitled]. 2023, Ghana.

109: Giani M. Jones, “Mama’s babies.” 2023, Cape Coast, Ghana.

110: Gillian Maris Jones, “The Power of Creation.” 2013, Salvador, Bahia, Brazil.

111: Gillian Maris Jones, “O Pensador.” 2013, Salvador, Bahia, Brazil.

112: Girard Mouton,III, “Boys With Skatemobiles.” 1984, New Orleans, LA.

113: Girard Mouton,III, “Coon Meat.” 2000, New Orleans, LA.

114: Gus Bennett, [Untitled], from the New Orleans Second Line Season series. 2023–2024, New Orleans, LA.

115: Gus Bennett, [Untitled], from the New Orleans Second Line Season series. 2023–2024, New Orleans, LA.

116: Harold Baquet, “Trampoline.” 2016, Desire Housing Project, New Orleans, LA. *“Trampoline,” The Historic New Orleans Collection, gift of Harold F. Baquet and Cheron Brylski, 2016.0172.2.1.*

117: Harold Baquet, “Baton Pass.” Undated. *Courtesy of Cheron Brylski.*

118: Heidi Hickman, “Black Boy Joy.” 2019, New Orleans, LA.

119: Heidi Hickman, “Glad-ney.” 2017, New Orleans, LA.

120: Irving Johnson III, “The Eagle Has Landed.” 2020.

121: Irving Johnson III, “Alligator.” 2021, Avery Island, LA.

122: J Nash Porter, [Untitled]. Undated. *Courtesy of Dr. Joyce Jackson.*

123: J Nash Porter, [Untitled]. Undated. *Courtesy of Dr. Joyce Jackson.*

124: J. R. Thomason, “Overture Gate.” Undated, 7th Ward, New Orleans, LA.

125: J. R. Thomason, “Happy Songbirds.” Undated, Dillard University Chapel, New Orleans, LA.

126: Jacques Detiege, “. . . in the faith of the Church.” 2012, Saint Raymond & Saint Leo the Great Catholic Church, New Orleans, LA.

127: Jacques Detiege, “. . . acceptable in thy sight.” All Saints Day, 2010, Saint Vincent de Paul Cemetery No. 1, New Orleans, LA.

128: Jamal Denzel Barnes, “You See Me.” 2020, New Orleans, LA.

129: Jamal Denzel Barnes, “Needle and Thread.” 2023, New Orleans, LA.

130: Jason R. A. Foster, [Untitled]. Undated, New Orleans, LA.

131: Jason R. A. Foster, “Mr. Henry’s Domain.” 2021, New Orleans, LA.

132: Jeremy Tauriac, “Hard Head Hunters.” Undated, New Orleans, LA.

133: Jeremy Tauriac, “Gerald and Geriah Davis.” Undated, New Orleans, LA.

134: Jeri Hilt, “Native Resurrection.” 2014, New Orleans, LA.

135: Jeri Hilt, “Blood Work.” 2017, New Orleans, LA.

136: Jose Cotto, “I Come From Warriors.” Super Sunday 2019, LaSalle Ave., New Orleans, LA.

137: Jose Cotto, “Poets, 2018: Cubs The Poet and 1985Poet.” 2018, Royal St. and Saint Phillip St., New Orleans, LA.

138: Jourdan Barnes, “Growth.” 2019, New Orleans, LA.

139: Jourdan Barnes, “Be.” 2019, New Orleans, LA.

140: Keith Calhoun, “Our Resurrection Is Stronger Than the Silence of Our Death.” 2018 (circa 1990), New Orleans, LA.

141: Keith Calhoun, “Portrait of Chandra McCormick.” 2018 (circa 1987), New Orleans, LA.

142: Kevin Jones, “Cycle of Rhythm.” 2016, French Quarter, New Orleans, LA.

143: Kevin Jones, “Iconic Accordion Maestro.” 2013, French Quarter, New Orleans, LA.

144: Kewon Hunter, “Dell in the Sky.” 2018, New Orleans, LA.

145: Kewon Hunter, “The Kids Turned Out Fine.” 2019, New Orleans, LA.

146: L. Kasimu Harris, “The Struggle Begins Before School (War on the Benighted).” 2018, New Orleans, LA.

147: L. Kasimu Harris, “Liquid Filled Repass, Part I,” from the Vanishing Black Bars & Lounges series. 2019, Sandpiper Lounge, New Orleans, LA.

148: Larry Everage, “The Culture Lives On.” 2019, New Orleans, LA.

149: Larry Everage, “Sunday in the 9.” 2022, New Orleans, LA.

150: Larry Songy, “Secondlining by public housing.” 1975, New Orleans, LA. *“Secondlining by public housing.” Tom Dent papers. Amistad Research Center, New Orleans, LA.*

151: Larry Songy, "Secondlining on Royal Street." 1975, New Orleans, LA. *"Secondlining on Royal Street." Tom Dent papers. Amistad Research Center, New Orleans, LA.*

152: Leslie-Claire Spillman, "Multitask." 2013, New Orleans, LA.

153: Leslie-Claire Spillman, "Love." 2022, New Orleans, LA.

154: Lidya Araya, "They Came In Peace," Big Chief Alfred Doucette pictured. 2000, New Orleans, LA.

155: Lidya Araya, [Untitled]. Undated, New Orleans, LA.

156: Lloyd Dennis, "Under The Bridge." Undated, New Orleans, LA.

157: Lloyd Dennis, "Afro House." Undated, New Orleans, LA.

158: Lloyd J. Medley Jr., "Secondline." Undated. *"Secondline." Tom Dent papers. Amistad Research Center, New Orleans, LA.*

159: Lloyd J. Medley Jr., "Funeral Procession." Undated. *"Funeral Procession." Tom Dent papers. Amistad Research Center, New Orleans, LA.*

160: Malcolm Johnson Jr., "Stay A Float: Underwater." 2020, Uptown, New Orleans, LA.

161: Malcolm Johnson Jr., "Stay A Float: Hard Times." 2020, Uptown, New Orleans, LA.

162: Malik Baloney, "The Day before she died." October 9, 2011, LaPlace, LA.

163: Malik Baloney, "Girl on Swing." 2014, Mount Airy, LA.

164: Malik Bartholomew, "Dancing Locks at the Second Line." 2019, Central City, New Orleans, LA.

165: Malik Bartholomew, "Flagboy Giz's Rebellion." Downtown Super Sunday 2022, New Orleans, LA.

166: Malik Williams, "Flight Prep," Sly Watts pictured. 2021, New Orleans, LA.

167: Malik Williams, "Hot Commodity," Torry Holmes pictured. 2020, New Orleans, LA.

168: Marion J. Porter, [Untitled], protest against F. W. Woolworth. Circa 1960–1964, Canal St., New Orleans, LA. *Courtesy of The City Archives & Special Collections, New Orleans Public Library.*

169: Marion J. Porter, [Untitled], Fats Domino and his daughter. Circa 1960s. *Courtesy of the George "Tex" Stevens Collection.*

170: Maurice Martinez, "Willie Humphrey (clarinet) and Sweet Emma (the Bell Gal), Preservation Hall." Undated, New Orleans, LA.

171: Maurice Martinez, "The Vegetable Man." Undated, New Orleans, LA.

172: Melissa Carrier, "Taxi." 2014, Dakar, Senegal. *Courtesy of The Historic New Orleans Collection and of the Artist.*

173: Melissa Carrier, [Untitled]. 2014, Saint Louis, Senegal. *Courtesy of The Historic New Orleans Collection and of the Artist.*

174: Monique Moss, "Five Pillars and a Toppled Confederate," Leon A. Waters, Gail Etienne, Leona Tate, Ruby Bridges, Tessie Prevost, and John McDonogh Bust on the sixtieth anniversary of desegregation of New Orleans Public Schools at Gallier Hall, formerly City Hall. 2020, New Orleans, LA.

175: Monique Moss, "Royalty of Tremé," funeral of Father Jerome LeDoux at Saint Augustine Catholic Church. 2019, Tremé, New Orleans, LA.

176: Morris Jones Jr., "Black Men of Labor." 2007, New Orleans, LA.

177: Morris Jones Jr., "Uncle Lionel." 2007, New Orleans, LA.

178: Najah Mushatt, "Melanie Smith." 2023, Marfa, TX.

179: Najah Mushatt, "Self Portrait." 2022, Atlanta, GA.

180: Nicholas Alexander Hall and Lindsey Smith, "CMH." 2020, New Orleans, LA.

181: Nicholas Alexander Hall and Lindsey Smith, "Love and Family." 2018, New Orleans, LA.

182: Nikki Brown, "Mentoring and the art of tie tying at Mr. Chill's Barbershop." 2011, New Orleans, LA.

183: Nikki Brown, "William on Bourbon St., Migrant worker." 2012, New Orleans, LA.

184: Norman R. Smith, photo collage of jazz greats at the New Orleans Jazz & Heritage Festival. Circa 1970, New Orleans, LA.

185: Norman R. Smith, trumpeter Dizzy Gillespie in a traditional New Orleans jazz funeral. Circa 1970, New Orleans, LA.

186: Nyejah Bolds, "NOLA French Quarter Date." 2021, French Quarter, New Orleans, LA.

187: Nyejah Bolds, "Paisley." 2019, French Quarter, New Orleans, LA.

188: Othello Carter, "The Block is Hot." 2016, Felicity St., Central City, New Orleans, LA.

189: Othello Carter, "I'm Still Standing." September 5, 2005 (two weeks after Hurricane Katrina), Central City, New Orleans, LA.

190: Peter G. Forest, "A large tree is overturned inside of a cemetery during the aftermath of Hurricane Ida . . ." 2021, Edgard, LA.

191: Peter G. Forest, “Aerial photo of the downtown area in the City of New Orleans . . .” 2016, New Orleans, LA.

192: Peter Nakhid, “Congo Square.” Undated, New Orleans, LA.

193: Peter Nakhid, “Honoring Mama Suma.” Undated, New Orleans, LA.

194: PRO$PER JONE$, “Nu Atlantis.” 2019, New Orleans, LA.

195: PRO$PER JONE$, ”Hollywood.” Mardi Gras Day, 2020, New Orleans, LA.

196: Quinn Gordon, “Black Breastfeeding Week.” 2020.

197: Quinn Gordon, “Friday’s With Fran: I’m A Boss Event.” 2019, New Orleans, LA.

198: Remy “Bless the Freaks” Williams, [Untitled]. Undated, New Orleans, LA.

199: Remy “Bless the Freaks” Williams, [Untitled]. Undated, New Orleans, LA.

200: Renee Royale, “Shade from the Heat,” expired Polaroid Spectra Film, shot in ninety-five-degree weather, submerged in water for twenty-four hours. 2021, Houston, TX.

201: Renee Royale, “Miami Miami,” Polaroid 600 Film, submerged in saltwater for three days. 2021, Miami Beach, FL.

202: Ric Francis, “Early Childhood Development.” 2012, Nairobi, Kenya.

203: Ric Francis, “Observing the Street.” 2022, Cubao, Quezon City, Philippines.

204: Richard V. Keller Sr., [Untitled], young child in a church sanctuary. Undated, New Orleans, LA.

205: Richard V. Keller Sr., [Untitled], young child sitting at a tree. Undated, New Orleans, LA.

206: Rita Harper, “Spider.” 2022, New Orleans, LA.

207: Rita Harper, “M.J on St. Claude.” 2022, New Orleans, LA.

208: Roland Guerin, “Story Time,” 2014, Germaine Bazzle pictured.

209: Roland Guerin, “Brian Blade: Playing The Song, Living The Moment.” 2010, New Orleans Jazz & Heritage Festival, New Orleans, LA.

210: Saddi Khali, “The Half of It.” 2009, Katy, TX.

211: Saddi Khali, “Blinds on Bliss.” 2007, Decatur, GA.

212: Sekou Fela, “Max Roach at Dillard University.” 1968, New Orleans, LA.

213: Sekou Fela, “Danny Barker.” 1968, New Orleans, LA.

214: Selwhyn Sthaddeus “Polo Silk” Terrell, “Celebration Of Life.” Undated, New Orleans, LA.

215: Selwhyn Sthaddeus “Polo Silk” Terrell, “Prince William Sunday.” Undated, New Orleans, LA.

216: Shabez Jamal, “Les Fleurs.” Undated.

217: Shabez Jamal, “Untitled (Sissy Bride).” Undated.

218: Shana M. griffin, [Untitled], from the OIL series. 2022, Felicity Plantation, Slave Quarters, Vacherie, LA.

219: Shana M. griffin, “Door of Servitude,” from the SOIL series. 2022, Felicity Plantation, Slave Quarters, Vacherie, LA.

220: Shaquille Dunbar, “Queen Yeboah.” Undated, New Orleans, LA.

221: Shaquille Dunbar, “Cajun Drive.” Undated, New Orleans, LA.

222: Sienna Pinderhughes, “They Are A Reflection Of You.” 2014, New Orleans, LA.

223: Sienna Pinderhughes, “Wearing Masculinity.” 2014, New Orleans, LA.

224: Sokari Ekine, “Lespri a rele timoun yo (Ceremony for the children).” 2014, Gonaives, Haiti.

225: Sokari Ekine, “Wudu Takasa.” 2017, Kipini, Kenya.

226: Sophia Little, “Silver and Black,” led by Spirit. 2017, New Orleans, LA.

227: Sophia Little, “Untitled III,” led by Spirit. 2017, New Orleans, LA.

228: Sorena Briley, “Butterfly Girl.” 2018, New Orleans, LA.

229: Sorena Briley, “A Kid’s Wish.” 2009, Manassas, VA.

230: Taylor Simone, “UNVEILED.” 2019.

231: Taylor Simone, “REST IS SACRED.” 2021.

232: Ted Quant, “We the People: May Day demonstration led by members of New Orleans Workers Center for Racial Justice.” 2010, New Orleans, LA.

233: Ted Quant, “Boy waving Black Liberation flag at Black Lives Matter demonstration.” 2014.

234: Terri A. Mimms, “The Sit Down (After the Secondline).” Undated, New Orleans, LA.

235: Terri A. Mimms, “A Branch from the Family.” Undated, New Orleans, LA.

236: Tod Smith, “Bone Gang.” Mardi Gras morning, 2014, Saint Augustine Church, Tremé, New Orleans, LA.

237: Tod Smith, “Big Chief Shaka Zulu.” 2022, Bayou Saint John, New Orleans, LA.

238: Trenity Thomas, “Amicable.” 2021, New Orleans, LA.

239: Trenity Thomas, “Home Girls.” 2020, New Orleans, LA.

240: Vincent Simmons, “Sunset Cast.” 2015.

241: Vincent Simmons, “West End Sunset.” 2015.

242: Will Horton, “Time Traveler.” 2019, New Orleans, LA.

243: Will Horton, “Electric Moon.” 2019, New Orleans, LA.

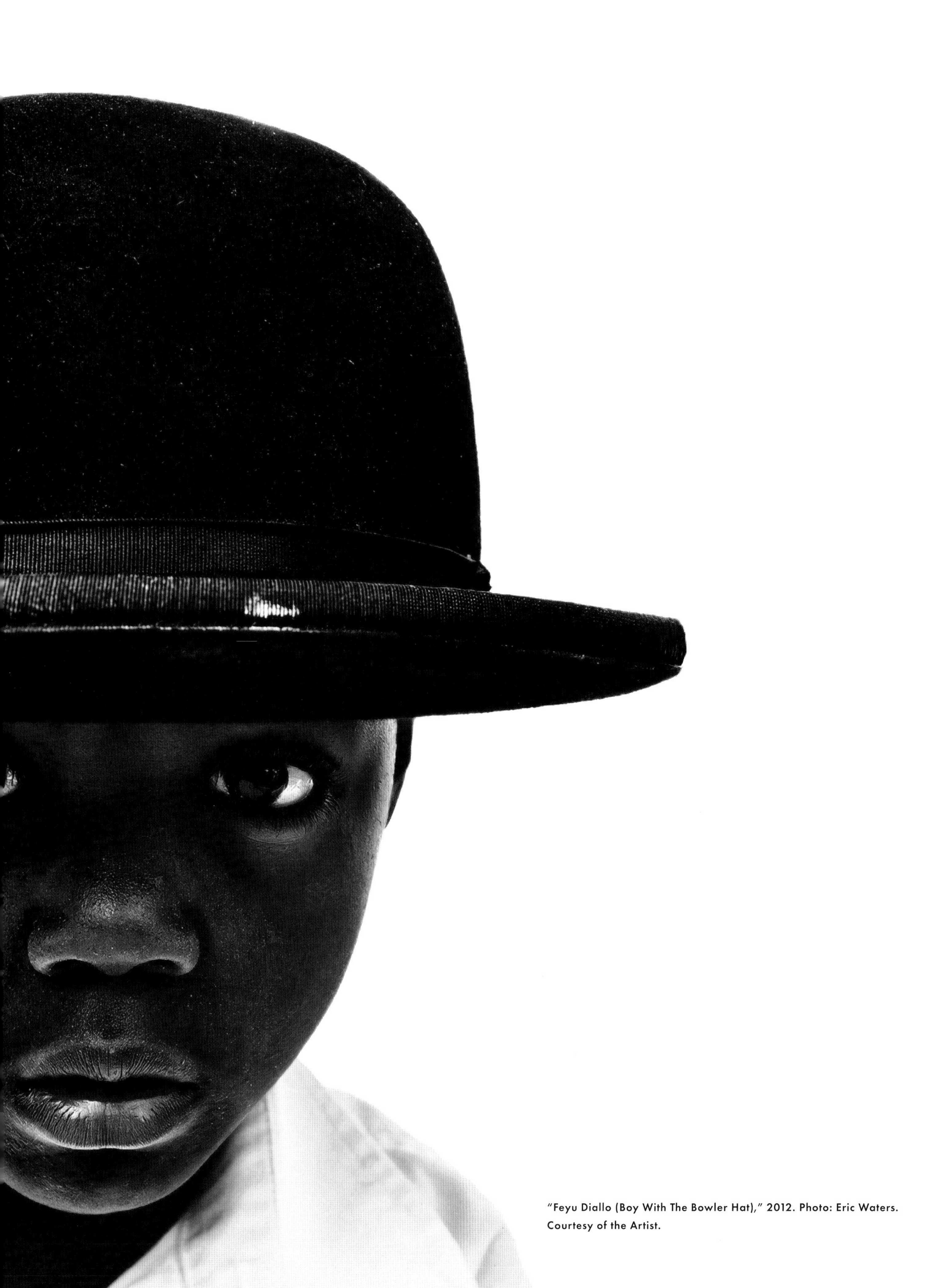

"Feyu Diallo (Boy With The Bowler Hat)," 2012. Photo: Eric Waters. Courtesy of the Artist.

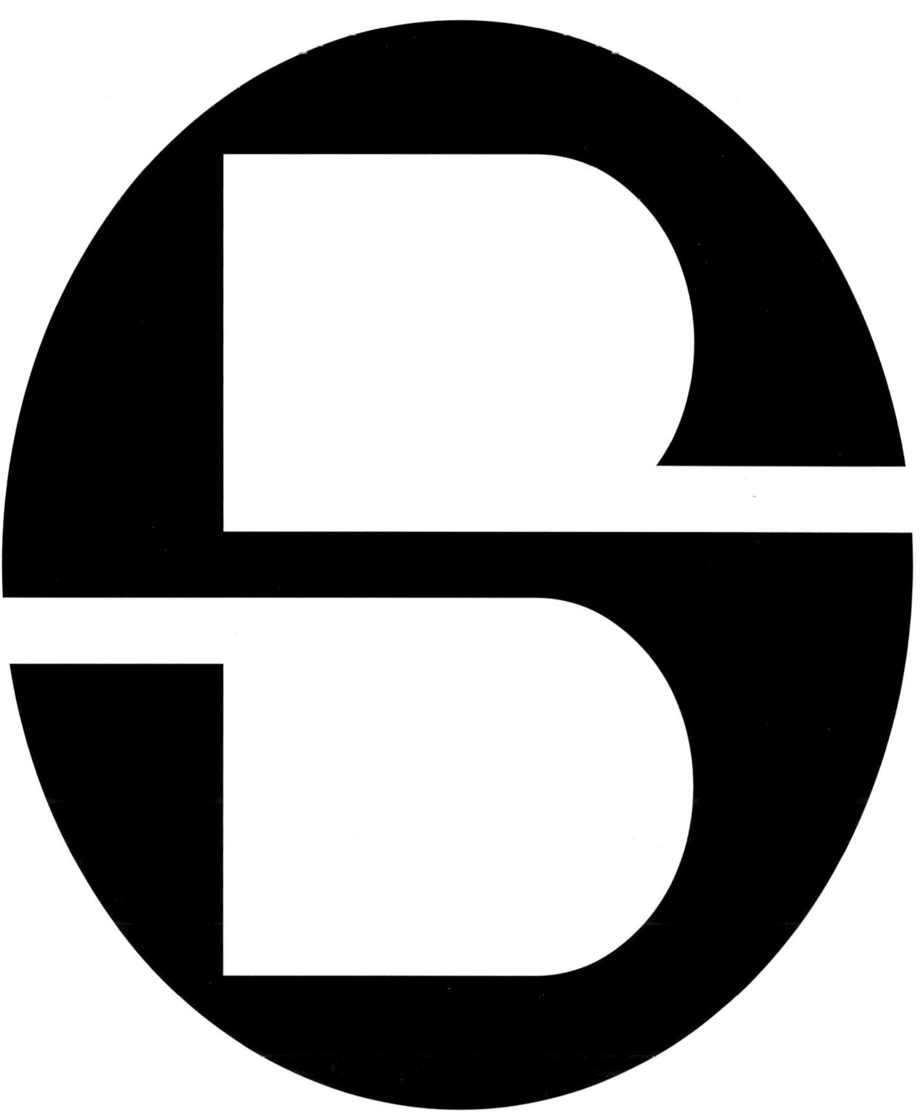